American
Jewish
Year Book

American

Jewish

Year Book 1993

VOLUME 93

Prepared by THE AMERICAN JEWISH COMMITTEE

Editor

DAVID SINGER

Executive Editor

RUTH R. SELDIN

THE AMERICAN JEWISH COMMITTEE
NEW YORK
THE JEWISH PUBLICATION SOCIETY
PHILADELPHIA

ISBN 0-8276-0447-5

Library of Congress Catalogue Number: 99-4040

PRINTED IN THE UNITED STATES OF AMERICA
BY THE HADDON CRAFTSMEN, INC., SCRANTON, PA.

Preface

The special articles in this year's volume focus attention on the Jews of Europe. In "Anti-Semitism in Europe Since the Holocaust," Robert Wistrich traces the threads leading from the genocidal savagery of the war years to the recent revival of a more populist anti-Semitism. In "Jews in the European Community: Sociodemographic Trends and Challenges," Sergio DellaPergola provides fascinating data on the Jews in the 12 EC countries, analyzing developments since World War II and weighing prospects for the future.

The volume also includes an update on "Israeli Culture," by Rochelle Furstenberg and Micha Odenheimer, and obituary articles on Louis Finkelstein, by Abraham J. Karp, and I.B. Singer, by Hillel Halkin.

Regular articles on Jewish life in the United States are "Intergroup Relations," by Jerome A. Chanes; "The United States, Israel, and the Middle East," by Kenneth Jacobson; and "Jewish Communal Affairs," by Lawrence Grossman.

Menachem Shalev provides extensive coverage of the year's events in Israel. Reports on Jewish communities around the world this year include Canada, Great Britain, France, the Netherlands, Italy, Germany, the former Soviet Union, Eastern Europe, Australia, and South Africa.

Updated estimates of Jewish population are provided: for the United States, by Barry Kosmin and Jeffrey Scheckner, of the North American Jewish Data Bank; and for the world, by U.O. Schmelz and Sergio DellaPergola, of the Hebrew University of Jerusalem.

Carefully compiled directories of national Jewish organizations, periodicals, and federations and welfare funds, as well as religious calendars and obituaries, round out the 1993 AMERICAN JEWISH YEAR BOOK.

We gratefully acknowledge the assistance of Terry Smith and of many colleagues at the American Jewish Committee, especially Cyma M. Horowitz and Michele Anish of the Blaustein Library.

THE EDITORS

Contributors

HENRIETTE BOAS: Dutch correspondent, Jewish Telegraphic Agency and Israeli newspapers; Amsterdam, Holland.

Y. MICHAL BODEMANN: associate professor, sociology, University of Toronto, Canada; visiting professor, Humboldt University, Berlin, Germany.

JEROME A. CHANES: co-director for domestic concerns, National Jewish Community Relations Advisory Council.

M.M. CONSONNI: research fellow, Diaspora Research Institute, Tel Aviv University, Israel.

SERGIO DELLAPERGOLA: associate professor and head, Division of Jewish Demography and Statistics, A. Harman Institute of Contemporary Jewry, Hebrew University of Jerusalem, Israel.

ALLIE A. DUBB: Mendel Kaplan Professor of Jewish Civilization, and director, Kaplan Centre for Jewish Studies and Research, University of Cape Town, South Africa.

ROCHELLE FURSTENBERG: journalist, critic; Jerusalem, Israel.

ZVI GITELMAN: professor, political science, and Preston R. Tisch Professor of Judaic Studies, University of Michigan.

ANNICK GOULET: free-lance reporter; Paris, France.

LAWRENCE GROSSMAN: director of publications, American Jewish Committee.

HILLEL HALKIN: writer, translator, critic; Zikhron Yaakov, Israel.

KENNETH JACOBSON: director, international affairs, Anti-Defamation League of B'nai B'rith.

ABRAHAM J. KARP: Philip S. Bernstein Professor Emeritus of Jewish Studies, University of Rochester; Joseph and Rebecca Mitchell Adjunct Research Professor of American Jewish History and Bibliography, Jewish Theological Seminary of America.

LIONEL E. KOCHAN: Wolfson College, Oxford; Oxford Centre for Post-Graduate Hebrew Studies, England.

MIRIAM L. KOCHAN: writer, translator; Oxford, England.

BARRY A. KOSMIN: director, North American Jewish Data Bank, City University of New York Graduate Center; director of research, Council of Jewish Federations.

MICHA Z. ODENHEIMER: journalist, critic; Jerusalem, Israel.

ROBIN OSTOW: Canada Research Fellow, sociology, McMaster University, Hamilton, Ontario, Canada.

HILARY RUBINSTEIN: research fellow, history, University of Melbourne, Australia.

JEFFREY SCHECKNER: administrator, North American Jewish Data Bank, City University of New York Graduate Center; research consultant, Council of Jewish Federations.

U.O. SCHMELZ: professor emeritus, Jewish demography, A. Harman Institute of Contemporary Jewry, Hebrew University of Jerusalem, Israel.

MILTON SHAIN: senior lecturer, Hebrew and Jewish studies, University of Cape Town, South Africa.

MENACHEM SHALEV: diplomatic correspondent, *Davar*, Tel Aviv; Israel correspondent, *Forward*, New York.

HAROLD M. WALLER: associate dean (academic), Faculty of Arts, McGill University, Montreal, Canada; director, Canadian Center for Jewish Community Studies.

ROBERT S. WISTRICH: Jewish Chronicle Professor of Jewish Studies, University of London, England; Neuberger Chair, Hebrew University of Jerusalem, Israel.

MICHAEL M. ZLOTOWSKI: European bureau chief, Jewish Telegraphic Agency, Paris, France.

Contents

DIRECTORIES, LISTS, AND OBITUARIES

Special
Articles

Anti-Semitism in Europe Since the Holocaust

by ROBERT S. WISTRICH

THE COLLAPSE OF COMMUNISM IN THE Soviet Union and Eastern Europe and the end of the Cold War are events of such magnitude that they must undoubtedly affect one's perspective on the last 45 years of European history. This applies to the Jewish experience as well, most especially the phenomenon of anti-Semitism. As Europe enters a new phase of its development, the time seems ripe to reexamine the course of European anti-Semitism in the period 1945–1990, to trace the threads leading from the genocidal savagery of the war years to the recent revival of a more populist form of anti-Semitism. While an essay of brief compass cannot hope to touch upon all aspects of the subject, the major contours, at least, may emerge.

The Immediate Postwar Period

In Germany, despite Allied efforts at de-Nazification, many Germans in the immediate postwar era maintained strong prejudice against Jews, even as they denied all knowledge of Hitler's crimes. Thus, according to polls taken in 1947, three-quarters of all Germans considered Jews to belong to a different race, more than one-third felt that it was better for there to be no Jews in Germany, while one-third argued that anti-Semitism was caused by Jewish behavior.[1]

In the Soviet Union, where many Jews had been saved during World War II and which strongly supported the creation of Israel, the authorities began in 1948 to systematically implement—for the first time in Soviet history—explicitly anti-Jewish policies. A vicious campaign against "rootless cosmopolitans" and Jewish bourgeois nationalism was launched, which led to the murder of Soviet Jewry's leading figure, Solomon Mikhoels, by the secret police. Other leading Jewish cultural figures were also arrested, with many being executed in 1952. All the main Jewish cultural institutions in the country were closed down, while Jews began to be removed systematically from top positions in academic life as well as state, party, and bureaucratic apparatuses. The "Black Years of Soviet Jewry" culminated in Stalin's

---

[1]See Elizabeth Noelle and Erich Peter Neumann, eds., *The German Public Opinion Polls 1947–1966* (Westport, Conn., 1981), pp. 185–92, 202, 206, 219, 311–16, 333.

attempted Soviet-style "Final Solution" to the Jewish problem—the notorious Doctors' Plot, in which a group of prominent Soviet Jewish physicians were accused of seeking to poison several top Soviet leaders.[2] According to this wholly fabricated scenario, the Jewish doctors had received their criminal instructions from the American Jewish Joint Distribution Committee and had also collaborated with Western and Zionist intelligence agencies. All this was meant as a prelude to Stalin's planned deportation of virtually all Soviet Jews to Siberia, which was halted only by his unexpected death in March 1953.

Elsewhere in the Soviet bloc, the influence of Stalin's anti-Semitic campaign was also felt, particularly in Czechoslovakia, which had fewer than 20,000 Jews in 1950. There, in 1950, the most notoriously anti-Jewish Stalinist show trial of postwar Eastern Europe was held. The general secretary of the Czech Communist party, Rudolf Slansky, a veteran Communist of Jewish origin, was tried and sentenced to hanging in 1952, along with 11 other leading "Jewish" Communists accused of treasonous collaboration with Western imperialism, Zionism, Titoism, and Trotskyism. The proceedings, orchestrated by Soviet advisers from Moscow, inspired an ugly burst of anti-Semitic incitement in the Czech Communist media.[3] The fictitious charges against Jews as subversive intriguers, "petty-bourgeois" Zionist spies, "fifth columnists," and counterrevolutionary agents were to be repeated after August 1968, when Soviet tanks crushed Alexander Dubcek's Prague Spring, and with it the hopes of socialism "with a human face." Thus was anti-Semitism as a neo-Stalinist and "anti-Zionist" masquerade successfully grafted onto a country which before 1939 had a better record than its neighbors in East-Central Europe with regard to the treatment of Jews.

In Poland and Hungary, the ghastly slaughter of Jews during the war years did not prevent the revival of popular anti-Semitism after 1945. Before 1939, Poland had the largest Jewish community in Europe—over 3 million Jews, representing more than 10 percent of the total population. Throughout the 1930s Jews had suffered from an increasingly violent, xenophobic anti-Semitism, which was reflected in economic boycotts, government discrimination, the hostility of the Catholic Church, and allegations that Jews were agents of Soviet Communism.[4] After World War II the last charge was

---

[2]See Yehoshua A. Gilboa, *The Black Years of Soviet Jewry* (Boston, 1971), and more recently Louis Rapoport, *Stalin's War Against the Jews* (New York/Toronto, 1990).

[3]See Artur London, *L'Aveu* (Paris, 1969); Euegen Loebl, *Sentenced and Tried: The Stalinist Purges in Czechoslovakia* (London, 1969); and Robert S. Wistrich, ed., *The Left Against Zion: Communism, Israel and the Middle East* (London, 1979), pp. 57–64, 72–85, 156–60.

[4]See Celia S. Heller, *On the Edge of Destruction: Jews of Poland Between the Two World Wars* (New York, 1977); Pawel Korzec, *Juifs en Pologne: La Question Juive pendant l'entre deux guerres* (Paris, 1980); and Yisrael Gutman, Ezra Mendelsohn, Jehuda Reinharz, and Chone

revived in the form of claims that Jews in eastern Poland had welcomed the invading Red Army with open arms in September 1939, and that Jewish Communists who had spent the war years in the USSR had returned to Poland in 1945 to dance on the country's grave together with the new Soviet conquerors.[5]

After the Polish Communist seizure of power in 1948 there were, indeed, a number of Jews, like Jakob Berman, Hilary Minc, and Roman Zambrowski, who played key roles in the party and the security services and in economic planning. They were seen by Moscow as less susceptible to Polish nationalist feelings, though in the eyes of many Poles they were little better than agents of a foreign, semicolonial power. This was one important reason for the intensification of Polish anti-Semitism after the Holocaust, especially since the anti-Communist underground was convinced that Jews were deliberately betraying Poland. But Jews returning from the Soviet Union were also killed simply for trying to reclaim their property or when they sought to open stores.[6] There were several pogroms, the worst one at Kielce in July 1946, in the wake of a local blood libel, which resulted in 41 Jewish deaths and more than 75 wounded.[7] About 100,000 surviving Jews left Poland in 1947, and a further 50,000 emigrated between 1948 and 1950.

In Hungary, where over half a million Hungarian Jews had been killed by the Germans in collaboration with the local police during the final year of hostilities, there were also anti-Semitic pogroms immediately after the war.[8] The pogroms reflected the general brutalization engendered by the Nazi occupation, fear of a Communist coup, and protest against the payment of reparations to Jews who had suffered losses during the war. Anti-Semitism in postwar Hungary, which had the largest surviving Jewish community in Eastern Europe, was also influenced by the central role which Communists of Jewish origin like Mátyás Rákosi, general secretary of the Hungarian Communist party and a faithful ally of Stalin, played in the Sovietization of the country. Many of Rakosi's leading lieutenants were Jews; they were particularly prominent in the political police and security

Shmeruk, eds., *The Jews of Poland Between Two World Wars* (University of New England Press, 1989), pp. 97–140.

[5]See Michal Borwicz, "Polish-Jewish Relations, 1944–1947," in *The Jews in Poland*, ed. C. Abramsky, Maciej Jachimczyk, and Antony Polonsky (Oxford, 1986), pp. 190–98. See also the controversy sparked by Norman Davies' assertions, "Poles and Jews: An Exchange," *New York Review of Books*, Apr. 9, 1987, pp. 40–44.

[6]Lucjan Dobroszycki, "Restoring Jewish Life in Post-War Poland," *Soviet Jewish Affairs*, 3 (1972), p. 66.

[7]See Borwicz, "Polish-Jewish Relations," pp. 195–96, and S. E. Schneiderman, *Between Fear and Hope* (New York, 1947).

[8]See Randolph L. Braham, *The Politics of Genocide: The Holocaust in Hungary*, I (New York, 1981).

services, a fact that strengthened the popular identification of Jews with Communism. Still, the revolution against Stalinist rule in October 1956 did not lead to virulent anti-Semitism, perhaps because Jews were also well represented among the reform Communists.[9]

In neighboring Austria, the number of Jews had been drastically reduced from its prewar level. Between the Anschluss of March 1938 and November 1939, 126,445 Jews were driven out of the country, and a further 65,000 were killed as a result of wartime deportations to the death camps.[10] A mere 5,700 Jews survived in Vienna in 1945, compared to the 250,000 Hungarian Jews still in Budapest when the Red Army entered that city. Official Austrian government policy toward the survivors or Jewish refugees wishing to return was far from friendly, reflecting strong congruence with popular attitudes.[11] Any affirmative action on behalf of Jews was ruled out, and there were various maneuvers and delays by government officials to avoid paying financial compensation to Jewish victims of Nazism.[12]

De-Nazification was even more superficial in Austria than in the Federal Republic of Germany. By 1949 many lower-level ex-Nazis had been given the vote, and by 1955 even prominent National Socialists like Anton Reinthaller, who became leader of Austria's postwar Freedom party, were fully integrated into the political process.[13] The dominant political parties—the Socialists and the Conservatives—were interested in attracting the former Nazi vote and in making political deals, when expedient, with the Freedom party. As a result, anti-Nazi traditions within Austria were played down, those who had fallen while serving in the wartime German Wehrmacht were honored, and even cases against proven mass murderers of Jews were thrown out by Austrian courts with noticeably less hesitation than in neighboring West Germany. Collective amnesia about Austria's role during the Third Reich was further encouraged by the support of the Western Allies for the myth that Austria had been the first "victim" of the Nazis, and by the obvious need to develop a separate and distinctive Austrian national identity that had nothing further to do with Germany. Still, anti-Semitism

[9]See Paul Lendvai, *Anti-Semitism Without Jews: Communist Eastern Europe* (New York, 1971).

[10]See Gerhard Botz, *Wien vom "Anschluss" zum Krieg* (Vienna/Munich, 1978), for the immediate prewar period.

[11]George E. Berkley, *Vienna and Its Jews: The Tragedy of Success, 1880–1980's* (Boston, 1988), pp. 352ff.

[12]This has been extensively documented from Austrian government sources by Robert Knight, ed., *"Ich bin dafür, die Sache in die Lange zu ziehen": Die Wortprotokolle der österreichischen Bundesregierung von 1945 bis 1952 über die Entschadigung der Juden* (Frankfurt a.M, 1988).

[13]Anton Pelinka, "The Great Austrian Taboo: The Repression of the Civil War," *New German Critique* 43 (Winter 1988), pp. 69–82.

did not play a major role in public life in Austria during the early postwar years.[14]

In postwar France, popular hostility to the Jews was still in evidence, with one opinion poll indicating that over one-third of the French population felt that Jews could never become loyal French citizens.[15] In 1946, the philosopher Jean-Paul Sartre published his *Réflexions sur la Question Juive*, which condemned the silence of his compatriots about the suffering of the Jews, the deportations and the gas chambers, and the Jewish role in the resistance and the liberation of France. "For four years French society has lived without them," Sartre ironically observed, "it is just as well not to emphasize too vigorously the fact that they have reappeared."[16] Indeed, silence about the complicity and collaboration of Vichy France in the German "Final Solution" was the norm in postwar French society. Many French continued to pretend that Marshal Philippe Pétain's Vichy regime sought to protect the Jews, despite the strict racial laws, institutional anti-Semitism, and daily vilification in the French wartime media, not to mention the role of the French police and judicial system in the deportation of Jews to the death camps.[17]

Political anti-Semitism, particularly on the nationalist and Catholic Right, also remained a continuing feature of French society in the first decade after World War II, especially after the appointment of a Jewish prime minister, Pierre Mendès-France, in 1954. Some of the anti-Semitic invective that greeted Mendès-France's decolonization policy was reminiscent of the campaign led by the Action Française against the Popular Front government of 1936 and its Jewish Socialist leader, Léon Blum, though without reaching quite the same pitch of ferocity.[18] In the mid-1950s, hostile criticism of the Jewish role in the French state and in financial capitalism was also advanced by the populist, lower-middle-class Poujadist movement.[19]

---

[14]See John Bunzl and Bernard Marin, eds., *Antisemitismus in Österreich* (Innsbruck, 1983), for facts and figures about anti-Semitic attitudes in postwar Austria. See also Marin's article in *Jews, Anti-Semitism and Culture in Vienna*, ed. Ivar Oxaal, Michael Pollak, and Gerhard Botz (London/New York, 1987), pp. 216–33.

[15]For postwar opinion polls in France concerning attitudes to Jews, see Doris Bensimon and Jeannine Verdès-Léroux, "Les Français et le problème juif: Analyse secondaire d'un sondage de l'Institut Français d'Opinion Publique (IFPO)," *Archives de Sociologie des religions* 19 (1970), pp. 53–91.

[16]Jean-Paul Sartre, *Anti-Semite and Jew* (New York, 1948), p. 71.

[17]See the standard work by Michael A. Marrus and Robert O. Paxton, *Vichy France and the Jews* (New York, 1981). For an apologia of Vichy, see Alfred Fabre-Luce, *Pour en finir avec l'antisémitisme* (Paris, 1979).

[18]See Pierre Birnbaum, *Un mythe politique. La "République juive" de Léon Blum à Pierre Mendès-France* (Paris, 1988), pp. 382–92.

[19]Ibid., pp. 334–39.

At the same time, in France, unlike Austria and Poland, there was a vigorous tradition of antiracism and anti-anti-Semitism, which retained its vitality in the postwar period. This, together with a campaign of patient education by the churches, the schools, and the media, led to anti-Semitism becoming rather marginalized in the immediate postwar years.[20]

In postwar Britain, popular prejudice against Jews had by no means disappeared after 1945. Indeed, despite the tenacious British war for survival against Nazi Germany, anti-Semitism may have actually increased during this period as a result of the strains provoked in British society by the external threat.[21] While Oswald Mosley's prewar fascist movement had been banned by the British government in 1940 (it never regained its strength after 1945), the Jewish underground war against British colonial rule in Palestine gave a new impetus to anti-Semitism. In 1947 there were anti-Jewish riots in several British cities following the execution of two British army sergeants in Palestine by the Irgun. In the occupying British army during this period anti-Semitic sentiments were fairly rampant. Nor were they altogether absent in the higher echelons of the Arabophile British Foreign Office, where the creation of Israel and the behavior of Israeli Jews were often regarded with profound distaste, down to and beyond the Suez War of 1956.

At the same time, anti-Semitism had little significance in British domestic politics, where the representation of Jews as members of Parliament, especially in the Labor party from 1945 until the mid-1970s, was striking.[22] Moreover, Anglo-Jewry, while still suffering from the ingrained social snobbery of the British class system, began to enjoy a new affluence and acceptance by the late 1950s. As in the Scandinavian countries and in Holland during this period, Jews benefited from a mixture of compassion, guilt, and shame over the Nazi atrocities and the goodwill of most liberal and socialist opinion toward the newly created State of Israel.[23]

---

[20]See E. Roditi, "Anti-Semitism in France," *Midstream*, Nov. 1980, pp. 9–14; Shmuel Trigano, *La République et les Juifs* (Paris, 1982); and Michael R. Marrus, "Are the French Anti-Semitic? Evidence in the 1980's," in *The Jews in Modern France*, ed. Frances Malino and Bernard Wasserstein (Univ. of New England Press, 1985), pp. 224–41, for opposing views on this issue.

[21]Tony Kushner, *The Persistence of Prejudice: Anti-Semitism in British Society During the Second World War* (Manchester, 1989).

[22]See W.D. Rubinstein, *The Left, the Right and the Jews* (London/Canberra, 1982), pp. 17–18, 156–60.

[23]This began to change in the 1970s and 1980s as a result of left-wing and liberal attacks on Israel's legitimacy and on Diaspora Jewry's support for it. See Geoffrey Alderman, *London Jewry and London Politics 1889–1986* (London, 1989), pp. 111–42. See also the chapter on British anti-Semitism today in Stephen Brook's popular survey *The Club: The Jews of Modern Britain* (London, 1989), pp. 382–98; the comments by Angela Lambert, "In the Shadow of the Swastika," *The Independent*, Mar. 25, 1989; and the recent symposium in *Jewish Quarterly*, no. 141 (Spring 1991), pp. 33–43.

Anti-Semitism in Retreat: 1956–1967

The period between 1956 and 1967 was one of the most philo-Semitic in European and Western history, much more so than the immediate postwar era. Jews, especially in America, but also in Western and Central Europe, achieved unprecedented wealth and enjoyed a level of comfort, personal security, and self-esteem unknown to their parents or grandparents. Traditional religious hostility, particularly in Catholic countries, began to be attenuated by the Second Vatican Council's document *Nostra Aetate* (1965), lifting the blame for the crucifixion from the Jewish people as a whole and in particular from contemporary Jewry. The sense of guilt among Gentiles over the Holocaust, stimulated by the Eichmann trial in Jerusalem in 1961 and similar trials in Germany, was more palpable than in the previous decade. Moreover, prior to the Six Day War, Israel was still regarded with considerable sympathy throughout the continent, west of the Iron Curtain.[24]

Even in the Communist Bloc, where Zionism was routinely attacked as a "bridgehead" of Western imperialism, diplomatic relations with Israel were maintained until the Six Day War. Anti-Semitism, too, was relatively mild in the USSR during the immediate post-Stalin years, despite atheistic campaigns against the Jewish religion and the implication of Jews in economic crimes under Nikita Khrushchev. When an openly anti-Semitic book by the Ukrainian academician Trofim Kychko, *Judaism Without Embellishment*, published in 1963, aroused international protest and provoked intervention by Western Communist parties, it was criticized by Soviet party authorities and silently withdrawn from circulation, though the author was not accused of violating any articles in the Soviet legal code. (A few years later such publications not only became widespread, but were officially encouraged in the USSR.) Another sign of a more positive attitude was the speech of Soviet prime minister Aleksey Kosygin in July 1965 at a large rally in Riga, where he denounced manifestations of nationalism, chauvinism, racism, and anti-Semitism as "absolutely alien to and in contradiction to our world view."[25]

In Hungary, too, under the regime of János Kádár, anti-Semitism was set aside as a means of establishing popular legitimacy. But as in the USSR, the prevailing tendency was to deny the existence of a "Jewish question" and to suppress discussion of other embarrassing issues, such as Hungarian collaboration during the Holocaust.[26]

---

[24]See the articles in Robert S. Wistrich, ed., *Anti-Zionism and Antisemitism in the Contemporary World* (London, 1990) by J. Gould, Shlomo Avineri, and the present author, pp. 46–52, 171–77, 181–94.

[25]Lionel Kochan, ed., *The Jews in Soviet Russia Since 1917* (Oxford, 1970).

[26]See Ferenc Feher's notes on the "Jewish Question" in Hungary in A. Rabinbach and J. Zipes, eds., *Germans and Jews Since the Holocaust* (New York, 1986), pp. 333–36.

Sweeping the Jewish issue under the carpet was less easily achieved in Poland, where so-called Jewish Stalinists were targeted as a convenient scapegoat for popular wrath during the crisis of October 1956. During the next ten years, under Wladyslaw Gomulka's rule, anti-Semitism was relatively quiescent on the surface, but behind the scenes it was a political factor in an internal Communist party factional struggle. From the early 1960s on, Jews were weeded out of party, state, and security organs. A full card index for Polish Jewry was in preparation as a step toward the complete purge of all Jews planned by General Mieczyslaw Moczar as a lever in his struggle to overthrow Gomulka and institute an even more nationalist form of Polish Communism.[27]

In Austria, the case of Taras Borodajkewicz, an anti-Semite and former Nazi who held a chair at the Vienna College of Economics but was forced to resign in 1965 as a result of anti-Nazi demonstrations, was seen as a positive sign.[28] The election of a Jewish-born Marxist, Bruno Kreisky, to head the Austrian Socialist party in 1967 was viewed by some as another signal that Austria wished to liberate itself from the Nazi legacy, though this hope proved to be illusory.[29]

In West Germany, where Konrad Adenauer served as chancellor from 1949 to 1963 and quickly inaugurated a reparations policy toward Israel and Jewish Holocaust survivors, philo-Semitism at an official level became almost obligatory, though it by no means reflected popular attitudes. There was a flurry of support for the neo-Nazi NPD party in the mid-1960s, but this soon ebbed, and it was another 20 years before radical-right extremism revived in a significant way.[30]

In the Aftermath of the Six Day War

The Six Day War of June 1967, which expanded Israel's boundaries and changed the Jewish state's image to that of a conquering, occupying power, brought in its wake a strong revival of anti-Semitism.

In France, the key event was President Charles de Gaulle's press conference of November 1967. De Gaulle not only criticized Israel's "arrogance" and aggressiveness, but referred to Jews in general as an "elite people, sure of itself and domineering." This was the first time that a Western head of

---

[27]Michael Chechinski, *Poland: Communism, Nationalism, Anti-Semitism* (New York, 1982).
[28]Heinz Fischer, ed., *Einer in Vordergrund: Taras Borodajkewycz: Eine Dokumentation* (Vienna, 1966).
[29]Robert S. Wistrich, *Between Redemption and Perdition: Modern Antisemitism and Jewish Identity* (London/New York, 1990), pp. 121–32.
[30]Eva Kolinsky, "Nazi Shadows Are Lengthening Over Germany," *Patterns of Prejudice*, vol. 12, no. 6 (Nov.-Dec. 1978), pp. 25–31. Also M. Ellerin and S. Rabinove, "Does Neo-Nazism Have a Future?" *Midstream*, Oct. 1983, pp. 1–6.

state had publicly conjured up such a stereotype since the end of the Second World War.[31] De Gaulle's utterances undoubtedly gave a new respectability to both right- and left-wing traditions of anti-Semitism in France, especially when expressed under the mask of anti-Zionism. If the Gaullist Right tended to focus on alleged Jewish "dual loyalties," the anti-Zionist Left denounced Jews for acting as accomplices of so-called Israeli racism, colonialism, and repression of the Palestinians. Similar malicious attempts to morally delegitimate Israel could be found in Holland, the Scandinavian countries, and Britain.[32] In its obsessive quality, use of double standards, and hate-ridden language, anti-Zionism was often indistinguishable from classical anti-Semitism.[33]

It was in the Soviet Union and its satellites that the anti-Zionist campaign achieved full blossoming. An almost cosmic omnipotence was attributed to "world Zionism," which was depicted as a perfidious, reactionary monster locked in a death struggle with the Soviet state, the forces of peace and progress, and national liberation movements throughout the world. The theory of the world Jewish conspiracy as laid out in the *Protocols of the Elders of Zion*—itself a Russian secret-police fabrication from the turn of the century—was revived in a suitably Sovietized version to suggest that Zionist Jews were seeking global domination; that they regarded the *"goyim"* as subhumans to be exploited and manipulated; and that, together with Freemasons, Jews were working to subvert and overthrow the Socialist system.[34]

The anti-Zionist campaign, whose seeds had been sown in Stalin's Doctors' Plot of 1953 (though officially repudiated after Stalin's death as an aberration), continued unabated for at least two decades after the Six Day War, beamed at the Arab and Third Worlds no less so than at Russian or European public opinion. It was used in Czechoslovakia from the summer of 1968 on as a means of undermining the short-lived experiment to humanize and liberalize Communism, by depicting the Prague Spring as a counter-revolutionary, "Zionist," and capitalist conspiracy against the socialist camp. In Poland, the anti-Zionist campaign led to an extraordinary witch-hunt in 1968, which forced two-thirds of the country's remaining Jews into emigration. "International Zionism" was blamed for inciting Polish students to antigovernment protests in March 1968; the ringleaders were denounced as being of "Jewish origin" or "Jewish nationality," and their

[31]Raymond Aron, *De Gaulle, Israël et les Juifs* (Paris, 1968), p. 18. Also Henry H. Weinberg, *The Myth of the Jew in France 1967–1982* (New York/London, 1987), pp. 31–40.

[32]See Wistrich, ed., *Anti-Zionism and Antisemitism*, pp. 46–62, 155–70, 178–94.

[33]Robert S. Wistrich, *Anti-Zionism as an Expression of Antisemitism in Recent Years* (Study Circle on World Jewry in the Home of the President of Israel, Jerusalem 1985).

[34]Wistrich, *The Left Against Zion*, pp. 272–300.

"real" Jewish names were put in brackets after their Polish-sounding names. Polish Communist party leader Gomulka vied with his rival General Moczar in exploiting anti-Semitism for political advantage.[35]

At the beginning of the 1970s, Soviet propagandists like Yuri Ivanov and Vladimir Bolshakov advanced the theory that Zionism was a prime enemy of the Soviet people, rooted in bellicose chauvinism, anti-Communism, and a long history of collaboration with counterrevolutionary forces.[36] Vicious anti-Semitic novels, like those of Ivan Shevtsov, published in huge editions and sponsored by state publishing houses, further elaborated on the sinister, covert role of "Zionism" in undermining Soviet power. For Shevtsov and writers of a similar ilk, "Judas Trotsky (Bronshtein)" was a "typical agent of Zionism" and of the international Jewish conspiracy. A vast industry of Judeophobic and anti-Zionist literature was created; according to one expert, the number of books of this type officially sponsored during the late 1960s and 1970s reached a total of 112.[37]

Anti-Zionism was given international legitimacy by Soviet sponsorship of the 1975 United Nations resolution defining Zionism as "a form of racism and racial discrimination," which encouraged a further escalation of this propaganda line. By the late 1970s and early 1980s, Zionism was being widely equated in the Soviet Union with Nazism, and Zionist leaders were being accused of collaborating with the Germans in the mass murder of European Jewry—a Goebbels-style lie that found a ready echo not only in the Arab world but also in some Western quarters.[38]

A number of publicists, like Valery Emelyanov, Yevgeny Yevseev, Lev Korneyev, Vladimir Begun, and Aleksandr Romanenko (some of whom would become closely involved with Pamyat in the 1980s), developed a particularly poisonous form of "anti-Zionism" under Communist party auspices at this time. As early as 1974 Emelyanov was telling Moscow audiences that Zionism aimed at "world mastery toward the year 2000." In his book *De-Zionisation*, published in 1980, he traced in classic Protocols fashion the origins of the Zionist-Masonic conspiracy back to King Solomon 3,000 years ago. Emelyanov and others saw the roots of the Zionist danger in the Torah itself, depicting the Pentateuch as the most criminal

---

[35]L. Hirszowicz, "The Jewish Issue in Post-war Communist Politics," in *The Jews in Poland*, ed. Abramsky et al., pp. 199–208; Josef Banas, *The Scapegoats* (London, 1979).

[36]Y. Ivanov, *Ostrozhno! Sionizm!* (Moscow, 1969); V. Bolshakov, "Antisovietizm—professiya sionistov," *Pravda*, Feb. 18–19, 1971, and ibid., Jan. 17, 1984. See also Robert S. Wistrich, *Hitler's Apocalypse* (London, 1985), for an analysis of the "Protocols of Zion" in their Sovietized version.

[37]William Korey, *Glasnost and Soviet Anti-Semitism* (American Jewish Committee, New York, 1991).

[38]Wistrich, *Hitler's Apocalypse*, pp. 205–25.

book in history, legitimizing a "chosen people" ideology of racial superiority. This was a favorite theme of Yevseev's *Fascism Under the Blue Star* (1972), which attributed to Judaism the "genocidal" policies implemented by Zionist Israel against the Arabs.[39] Such works had support in the highest Communist party circles and the cachet of "academic" approval by prestigious scholarly institutions like the Soviet Academy of Sciences.

The mushrooming of anti-Zionist literature in the Soviet Union coincided with a policy of consistent discrimination against Jews in higher education, not to mention the near-total exclusion of Jews from military, political, and diplomatic careers. Without doubt, the official anti-Zionist campaign of the Leonid Brezhnev years also paved the way for the even more vicious populist anti-Semitism that, ironically enough, began to blossom after Mikhail Gorbachev's more liberal policy of *glasnost* was instituted after 1985.[40]

In West Germany in the 1970s and 1980s, the radical Left also contributed to the intensification of anti-Semitism. An important development in this regard was the play *Garbage, the City and Death*, written by the radical filmmaker Rainer Werner Fassbinder in 1975 and banned from public performance in 1985 after vehement Jewish protests. Fassbinder stereotypically linked Jews to wealth and power, insisted that Jews could not be immune from criticism, and reduced the problem of anti-Semitism to a matter of popular anticapitalism.[41] Others on the radical Left focused on the Jewish state, depicting Israelis as worse than the Nazis in working toward the "extermination" of the Palestinians. This was a favorite theme of the Baader-Meinhof "Red Army Faction" in the early 1970s; a decade later it found wide acceptance among the pacifist Green party, on the one hand, and the neo-Nazi Right, on the other.[42] If the Greens felt a "special responsibility" to the Palestinian victims of Israeli occupation, this was because, in the words of one Green party Euro MP in 1984: "The genocide of the Jews created the psychological prerequisites for setting up Israel as an

---

[39]Y. Yevseev, *Fashizm pod goluboy zvezdoy* (Moscow, 1972); V. Skurlatov, *Sionizm i aparteid* (Kiev, 1975); V. Begun, *Polzuchaya Kontrrevolutsiya* (Minsk, 1974); L. Korneyev, "Sami sionistkii byzness," *Ogonyok*, July 8, 1978. See also William Korey, *The Soviet Cage: Anti-Semitism in Russia* (New York, 1973), p. 303, and Robert S. Wistrich, *Antisemitism: The Longest Hatred* (New York, 1992), pp. 180–82.

[40]L. Dymerskaya-Tsigelman, "Anti-Semitism and Opposition to It at the Present Stage of the Ideological Struggle in the USSR," *Jews and Jewish Topics in the Soviet Union and Eastern Europe* (Hebrew University of Jerusalem, Summer 1988), pp. 3–27. Also personal interviews conducted in the USSR with Oleg Kalugin, Sergei Lezov, Mikhail Chlenov, and a number of other Jewish activists at the end of 1990.

[41]Heiner Lichtenstein, ed., *Die Fassbinder-Kontroverse oder Das Ende der Schonzeit* (Konigstein, Ts. 1986); Johann N. Schmidt, *These Unfortunate Years: Nazism in the Public Debate of Post-War Germany*, Public Lecture Series, Indiana University, 1987.

[42]Rabinbach and Zipes, *Germans and Jews*, pp. 12ff.

internationally recognized state. The expulsion of the Palestinians is therefore indirectly the result of the Nazi persecution of the Jews."[43] The neo-
Nazis, by contrast, cynically juxtaposed the "real" Holocaust inflicted on
the Palestinians by Israel with the purely "fictive" Holocaust, which they
denied that Germans had ever perpetrated against Jews.

In Austria in the mid-1970s, at a time when Jewish-born Socialist chancellor Kreisky was at the peak of his popularity, polls indicated that one-
third of Austrians were either strongly or moderately anti-Semitic.[44]
Kreisky's attacks on Nazi-hunter Simon Wiesenthal, whom he branded as
a "Jewish fascist," as well as Kreisky's courting of Freedom party leader
Friedrich Peter and his unrestrained vituperation against "Zionist racism,"
no doubt gave a new legitimacy to anti-Semitic feelings in the Austrian
population—the more so since they came from an Austrian Jew who had
lost most of his family in the Holocaust.[45]

The election campaign of Kurt Waldheim, the former UN secretary-
general, who in 1986 was the successful Conservative party candidate for
the Austrian presidency, broke down whatever taboo remained about expressions of anti-Semitism in postwar Austrian society. The investigations
by the World Jewish Congress into Waldheim's Nazi past (he had served
as a Wehrmacht staff officer in the Balkans, with a unit that supervised mass
deportations of partisans and Jews) provoked a strong reaction from members of Waldheim's own party. Conservative party Secretary-General Michael Graff declared that unless Waldheim could be personally shown to
have strangled five or six Jews with his own hands, he must be considered
blameless. He denounced the "mafia of slanderers" who would stop at
nothing to blacken Austria's good name. Many Austrians appeared to agree
that Waldheim had only done his "duty" as an Austrian patriot and was
being unjustly persecuted by all-powerful Jewish interests that allegedly
dominated the world media.[46] The former vice-mayor of Linz even com-

[43]Quoted by Micha Brumlik, "Fear of the Father Figure: Judeophobic Tendencies in the
New Social Movements in West Germany," *Patterns of Prejudice*, vol. 21, no. 4 (1987), p. 34.

[44]For the empirical survey material, see Bunzl and Marin, *Antisemitismus in Österreich*, and
Hilde Weiss, "Antisemitische Vorurteile in Österreich nach 1945. Ergebnisse empirischer
Forschungen," in *Antisemitismus nach dem Holocaust*, ed. J. H. Schoeps and A. Silbermann
(Köln, 1986), pp. 53–70.

[45]Robert Wistrich, "The Strange Case of Bruno Kreisky," *Encounter*, May 1979, pp. 78–86.
Also my reassessment in Robert S. Wistrich, ed., *Austrians and Jews in the Twentieth Century:
From Franz Joseph to Waldheim* (London, 1992), pp. 234–51.

[46]"*Wir sind alle Unschuldige Täter!*" *Studien zum antisemitischen Diskurs im Nachkriegs-
österreich* (Vienna, 1989), 2 vols., documents the Waldheim presidential campaign, media
responses, and the anti-Semitic discourse that developed in Austria. See also the essay by
Richard Mitten on the Waldheim Affair in Wistrich, ed., *Austrians and Jews*, pp. 252–73, and
Richard H. Mitten, *The Waldheim Phenomenon in Austria: The Politics of Antisemitic Prejudice* (Boulder, Colo., 1992).

pared the "persecution" of Waldheim with the crucifixion of Jesus, in a letter to the World Jewish Congress.

In France, anti-Semitism remained an active force into the 1970s, though it had to confront more militant opposition from groups committed to republican ideals. In the 1980s, beginning with the terrorist attack on the Rue Copernic synagogue (October 1980), followed by the assault on a Jewish restaurant in the Rue des Rosiers (August 1982), and culminating in the desecration of the Carpentras cemetery (1990), the situation became considerably more alarming to many French Jews.[47] Jews became prominent in French politics, both under Valéry Giscard d'Estaing (Simone Veil, Lionel Stoleru, Jacques Wahl) and even more so under François Mitterrand after 1981 (Laurent Fabius, Robert Badinter, Jacques Attali, Jacques Lang, and others), but the development inevitably attracted much adverse comment on the radical Right. Admittedly, such negative sentiment seemed to be waning in the French population as a whole, and was far weaker than the rampant prejudice against North African Arabs who were flocking to France. But the danger for Jews in a situation of generalized racism and xenophobia was evident as France became home to Europe's largest, postwar radical Right movement, the National Front, led by Jean-Marie Le Pen.[48]

Le Pen was a politician who built his career on vocal opposition to Arab and Muslim immigration, while being more quietly and insidiously anti-Jewish. His movement, which by 1990 was supported by about 15 percent of the electorate, thrived on the cynical exploitation of real social problems provoked by immigration, unemployment, and urban neglect, as well as anxiety about the religious and national identity of France. Increasingly in National Front literature, the classical imagery of anti-Semitism found a populist voice.[49] Jews were identified by their wealth, prominence in the Socialist government, and "cosmopolitanism," while the "Jewish International" or the "Judeo-cosmopolitan *médiocratie*" were depicted as controlling the mass media and high finance. These classical themes of French anti-Semitism were reinforced by the cult of a monolithic Catholic civilization, intolerant of liberalism, pluralism, or dissent. The traditional Catholic

---

[47]Trigano, *La République et les Juifs*, p. 37, claimed in 1982 that the Rue Copernic bomb revealed the "terrible precariousness" of the Jewish situation in France. For a sharp rejection of this view, see Dominique Schnapper, "Perceptions of Antisemitism in France," in *Antisemitism in the Contemporary World*, ed. M. Curtis, 1986, pp. 261–71.

[48]E. Plenel and A. Rollat, "The Revival of the Far Right in France," *Patterns of Prejudice*, vol. 18, no. 2, 1984, pp. 26ff. For a more recent survey, see James G. Shields, "The Front National and the Politics of Discrimination in France," *Analysis*, no. 2 (June 1992), a research report published by the Institute of Jewish Affairs in London.

[49]"L'Extrême Droite," *Passages*, Dec. 1987, pp. 8–18; "L'antisémitisme en France," *L'Événement du Jeudi*, Oct. 15–21, 1987, pp. 58–86.

theology of the Jews as a God-rejected people could be seen as once again fusing with the xenophobic racism of the radical Right, as it often did before the Holocaust.[50]

The only truly novel element in radical Right anti-Semitism in France was its espousal of so-called revisionism, i.e., the denial that the Holocaust took place. This trend was not confined solely to the Right nor, indeed, to France, but it gained more pseudo-academic currency in France and had a longer pedigree there than in any other European country. Already in the early 1950s it was being propagated by a former French socialist, Paul Rassinier, and it gained notoriety when it was espoused by Prof. Robert Faurisson at the end of the 1970s in the French media. According to Faurisson, "The claims of the existence of gas chambers and the genocide of the Jews constitute one and the same historical lie, which opened the way to a gigantic political fraud of which the principal beneficiaries are the state of Israel and international Zionism."[51] In 1985 Henri Rocques, at the University of Nantes, successfully defended a "revisionist" doctoral dissertation, whose main thrust was to deny the existence of the Nazi gas chambers.[52] Le Pen, while initially equivocal over the Rocques affair, later went on record as saying that the Holocaust was "just a detail in the history of World War II."[53]

Denial or trivialization of the Holocaust was at one and the same time a way of undermining Jewish legitimacy, reinforcing fantasies about Jewish conspiracies, and rehabilitating fascism from the taint of mass murder. It also forged a link with pro-Palestinian militants and Arab governments— Libya and Saudi Arabia were known to have financed Holocaust denial literature in the West—who claimed that Jews invented the Holocaust to legitimate Israel and to neutralize the injustice done to the Palestinians.[54]

The Gorbachev Years and Beyond

The changes that came about during the Gorbachev years (1985–1991) held out the promise of a new dawn in the former Soviet Union and former Soviet empire in Eastern and Central Europe. It quickly became apparent, however, that anti-Semitism was hardly a spent force on the European scene, that indeed it could be greatly energized under the new conditions of freedom.

[50]David Selbourne, "French Jews Begin to Feel Alien All Over Again," *Sunday Times* (London), June 3, 1990.
[51]See *Le Monde*, Dec. 29, 1978, for Faurisson's article on the "problem of the gas chambers," and Weinberg, *Myth of the Jew in France*, pp. 64–65.
[52]Henry Weinberg, "Revisionism: The Rocques Affair," *Midstream*, Apr. 1987, pp. 11–13.
[53]"Les fourriers de l'antisémitisme," *L'Express*, May 25, 1990.
[54]For the attraction of Holocaust "revisionism" to the extreme Left, see in particular Alain Finkielkraut, *L'Avenir d'une Négation. Réflexions sur la Question du génocide* (Paris, 1982).

In Russia, Pamyat and other Russian nationalist organizations that came into being in the Gorbachev period were open and direct in their use of anti-Semitic propaganda—claiming that the satanic Zionist-Masonic conspiracy was responsible for Chernobyl, for alcoholism, crime, drugs, pornography, and the infiltration of Western-style rock music into the country.[55] The "Zionists" were also blamed for the disintegration of Russia as a great power, its military and economic failures, and its loss of internal cohesion. Above all, Jews were seen as responsible for the catastrophe brought about by the Russian Revolution of 1917, the Gulag system, and the "genocide" of the Russian people during the years of Soviet terror.

The new anti-Semitism, especially in the Russian Republic, was by no means a marginal protest phenomenon. The leader of Pamyat, Dmitri Vasiliev, claimed in 1989 that his organization had 20,000 members in Moscow alone and many more in other major Russian cities. Pamyat meetings were well attended and attracted people from a wide spectrum of Soviet society. From 1987 on, Pamyat and the anti-Semitic nationalists controlled the Moscow section of the All-Russian Society for the Restoration of Historical and Cultural Monuments, the Russian Republic Culture Fund, and a number of environmental movements. The organization had many sympathizers in the Russian Writers' Union, including one of its presidents, Yuri Bondarev, and a number of popular novelists like Valentin Rasputin, Victor Astafiev, and Vasily Belov, whose widely read books disseminated ugly anti-Jewish stereotypes.[56]

In addition, several prominent conservative publications—*Nash Sovremennik*, *Molodaya Gvardiya*, *Moskva*, *Sovietskaya Rossiya*, and *Nedelya*—promoted anti-Semitism as part of their nationalist ideology. Additional credibility was given to anti-Semitism by the writings of the renowned academician Igor Shafarevich, whose *Russophobia*, published in 1989, epitomized the intellectual paranoia of the new anti-Western, anti-Socialist, and anti-Semitic gospel, obsessed with finding scapegoats for the spiritual crisis of Soviet society.[57]

There were undoubtedly powerful conservative forces in the Communist party hierarchy and the KGB that were interested in using anti-Semitism as a weapon in the battle against liberalization and *perestroika*. Soviet authorities appear to have understood this belatedly, insofar as some major Soviet journals started publishing articles sharply critical of Black Hundred

[55]Yitzhak M. Brodny, "The Heralds of Opposition to Perestroyka," *Soviet Economy* 5, 1989, pp. 162–200; Walter Laqueur, "From Russia with Hate," *New Republic*, Feb. 5, 1990, pp. 21–25.

[56]"Anti-Semitism in the USSR and the Reactions to It," *Jews and Jewish Topics*, Spring 1989, pp. 5–44.

[57]Andrei Sinyavsky, "Russophobia," *Partisan Review* 3, 1990, pp. 339–44.

and Nazi-style anti-Semitism in the USSR.[58] But matters were not helped by occasional statements from President Gorbachev linking Zionism and anti-Semitism as equivalent nationalist aberrations which had no place in civilized society. Nor did conciliatory steps like those of Boris Yeltsin, when he was still Communist party head in Moscow and spent two hours with Pamyat leaders, signal strong opposition or even understanding of the threat that anti-Semitism represented to Russian society.

In Poland in the 1980s, with the rise of the powerful trade-union movement Solidarity, the beginnings of a Catholic-Jewish dialogue involving liberal Catholic Polish intellectuals, and a general movement toward democratization, it seemed that the ghosts of anti-Semitism from the past might at last be laid to rest.[59] True, in the early 1980s the Communist regime tried to discredit Solidarity by charging that it was manipulated by "Jewish" advisers and dissident intellectuals like Adam Michnik, Bronislaw Gieremek, and Karol Modzelewski;[60] even labor activists like Jacek Kuron and Jan Josef Lipski, who had no Jewish ancestry at all, were tarred with fictitious "Zionist" links. But despite the efforts of the Communist government and the anti-Jewish Grunwald Patriotic Association, there was no sign that public opinion would swallow a rerun of the 1968 "anti-Zionist" crusade.

Paradoxically, it was the fall of Communism in 1989 that revived the language of anti-Semitism and the search for "hidden" Jews in Poland in an electorate embittered by economic mismanagement, poverty, and the soured promises of democracy.[61] Against this background, prewar slogans like "Judeo-Communism" once again came to the fore, along with attempts to revive the National Democrat tradition of Poland as a purely Catholic and Polish nation. The controversy over the Carmelite monastery in Auschwitz sparked an anti-Semitic homily from the primate of Poland, Jozef Cardinal Glemp, delivered in Czestochowa on August 26, 1989, in which he warned Jews not to "talk to us from the position of a people raised above all others." Deploring the attacks of "world Jewry" on the nuns at Auschwitz, he admonished Jewish leaders: "Your power lies in the mass media that are easily at your disposal in many countries. Let them not serve to spread anti-Polish feeling."[62]

In the Polish elections of 1990, anti-Semitic sentiments took a new turn

---

[58]For documents relating to Pamyat and criticism of it, see the Summer 1988 issue of *Jews and Jewish Topics*, pp. 30–88.

[59]Henryk Grynberg, "Is Polish Anti-Semitism Special?" *Midstream*, Aug./Sept. 1983, pp. 19–23.

[60]"Blaming the Jews Again," *Newsweek*, Feb. 15, 1982.

[61]Abraham Brumberg, "The Problem That Won't Go Away: Anti-Semitism in Poland (Again)," *Tikkun*, Jan./Feb. 1990, pp. 31–34.

[62]D. Warszawski (Konstanty Gebert), "The Convent and Solidarity," *Tikkun*, Nov./Dec. 1989, pp. 30ff; *New York Times*, Aug. 30, 1989; *The Guardian*, Aug. 31, 1989.

when Lech Walesa's supporters (half-encouraged by their leader) began to smear his opponent, the liberal Catholic prime minister, Tadeusz Mazowiecki, as a crypto-Jew who was soft on Communism.[63] The Walesa camp played on the theme that Mazowiecki's government was allegedly controlled by Jews and that the time had come for "real Poles" like Walesa to govern. Walesa himself was highly equivocal in this situation, suggesting that he admired Jews who were open about their ancestry, but did not understand why his former advisers hid behind Gentile names. It was such behavior, he argued, that created anti-Semitism in Poland. The campaign was successful and seemed to demonstrate that anti-Semitism was alive and well in a Poland that was virtually *judenrein*.[64]

In Hungary, too, prewar anti-Semitic tendencies that had been frozen for more than 40 years under Communist rule came to the surface after Hungary's "quiet revolution" of 1989. While the overthrow of Communism was beneficial in terms of human rights and the rule of law, it also brought with it greater political instability, inflation, and growing unemployment. Those searching for scapegoats and simplistic answers were, as in the past, tempted to blame the Jews. During the elections of March 1990, the victorious populist Democratic Forum called on the public to vote for "true Hungarians," and stars of David were daubed on some posters of the Social Democratic party, in which Jewish intellectuals were known to play an important role.[65] Still, anti-Semitism in Hungary remained relatively contained.[66]

Anti-Semitism also showed itself in Romania, the only East European Communist state not to have broken off diplomatic relations with Israel after the 1967 war. Paradoxically, under the hard-line Stalinist dictatorship of Nicolae Ceausescu, Romanian Jews had enjoyed greater autonomy and freedom to emigrate than any other Jewish community in the Eastern bloc. Though Ceausescu was scarcely philo-Semitic, he found it financially and politically advantageous to trade his Jews for a "most favored nation" status in the United States.[67]

The fall of the Ceausescu regime in 1989 brought with it a revival of the

---

[63]"Bez maski," *Gazeta Wyborcza* (Warsaw), Sept. 22, 1990; B. Lecomte, "Walesa après Walesa," *L'Express*, Sept. 28, 1990. Also Wistrich, *Antisemitism*, pp. 164–65.

[64]Z. Ben-Shlomo, "Boiling Cauldron," *Jewish Chronicle*, Feb. 15, 1991. See also Murray Gordon, *The Jewish Community of Poland* (American Jewish Committee, New York, 1991).

[65]"Alarm in Hungary," *Jewish Chronicle*, Apr. 20, 1990. See also Murray Gordon, *The Hungarian Election: Implications for the Jewish Community* (American Jewish Committee, New York, 1990) and Renae Cohen and Jennifer L. Golub, *Attitudes Toward Jews in Poland, Hungary, and Czechoslovakia: A Comparative Survey* (American Jewish Committee, New York, 1991).

[66]Neal Ascherson, *The Independent on Sunday*, Nov. 11, 1990, pp. 3–5.

[67]Glen Frankel, "Saving Jews: Ceausescu's High Price," *International Herald Tribune*, Feb. 22, 1990.

visceral anti-Semitism that was endemic to prewar Romania. Articles appeared in the Romanian press depicting the Jews as the Antichrist, and blaming them for imposing the Communist scourge on Romania.[68] The "diabolical" role of the postwar "Jewish" Stalinist foreign minister of Romania, Ana Pauker, was commonly recalled. At the same time, Hitler's ally, the wartime dictator Marshal Ion Antonescu, who was responsible for the mass murder of Jews in Bessarabia and northern Bukovina, was honored by Parliament in silent tribute. In addition, a cult was growing around the prewar fascist Iron Guard leader Corneliu Zelea Codreanu, a notorious anti-Semite. Publications like *Romania Mare*, with a mass circulation, disseminated the myth of Judeo-Bolshevism.

In post-Communist Slovakia, anti-Semitism was also inextricably linked to an inward-looking chauvinism and a return to the wartime fascist past as a source of inspiration. There were strong efforts to rehabilitate the Roman Catholic priest Josef Tiso, who as head of the clerico-fascist Slovak state during World War II was implicated in the genocide of Slovak Jewry. Anti-Semitism was further encouraged by the unreconstructed anti-Communism brought back to Slovakia by returning exiles.[69]

Even powerful, prosperous, newly reunited Germany was not free of a resurgence of anti-Semitism. According to figures published at the beginning of 1992, the number of neo-Nazi activists in the whole of Germany had doubled in two years, due mainly to their successes in the east.[70] The radical right-wing Republikaner party, led by a former Waffen-SS soldier, Franz Schönhuber, was also making political gains. Most certainly, the spectacle of rampaging mobs of skinheads running amok in the summer of 1992 in nightly attacks on asylum-seekers and foreigners in Rostock and other East German cities was a grim reminder of the fascist potential among the youth of Germany. While Gypsies and Third World immigrants were the first targets of attacks, there were also desecrations of Jewish cemeteries and Holocaust memorials and threats against individual Jews. All this was deeply troubling in the context of a unified Germany in which the memory of the Holocaust was fading into the background and

[68]"Nasty Writing on the Wall for Jews," *Observer*, Feb. 11, 1990; *Newsweek*, May 7, 1990, pp. 22–23. See also Murray Gordon, *The New Face of Anti-Semitism in Romania* (American Jewish Committee, New York, 1991).

[69]See Zora Bútorová and Martin Bútora, *Wariness Toward Jews and "Postcommunist Panic" in Slovakia* (American Jewish Committee, New York, 1992) and Cohen and Golub, *Attitudes Toward Jews*.

[70]*Searchlight*, Jan. 1991, "Fascists Consolidate in Western Europe." For more recent incidents and the strain on consensus politics posed by the refugee influx and neo-Nazi activity, see Peter Millar, "Still Proud to Be German?" *The Times*, Nov. 24, 1992, p. 15, and the report by Christine Toomey, "Fear and Loathing Show Deep Cracks," *The Sunday Times*, Nov. 29, 1992.

in which one-third of the population expressed some anti-Semitic senti-ments.[71]

Conclusion

What has been happening in Europe in recent years does seem to repre-sent a definite loosening of the taboos that temporarily held anti-Semitism in check during a part of the postwar period. As a result, there has been a resurgence of many classical anti-Jewish themes from before 1939. This is particularly obvious in the former Soviet Union, Poland, Hungary, Ro-mania, and East Germany, where a state-controlled Communist anti-Semi-tism from above has given way to a popular Jew-hatred from below. Ancient prejudices embedded in the popular psyche have come to the fore in these societies, even where there are scarcely any Jews left, intensified in some cases by the very abstractness of the anti-Jewish stereotypes and their protean nature, which can be readily transformed and adapted to new situations.

Nor have the older, more traditional forms of stereotyping disappeared from the democratic societies of Central and Western Europe. In Germany and Austria one still finds Christian Judeophobia alongside mounting rac-ism and xenophobia, not to mention more modern forms of "anti-Zionist" anti-Semitism, though the specifically religious component has somewhat declined in importance. The unresolved problems of national identity in these countries, as well as their difficulties in living with the burdens of the Nazi past, suggest that there is still a living potential for anti-Semitism, which adverse economic conditions and political instability can easily acti-vate.

In France, as in the former Soviet Union, the revival of a "Jewish ques-tion" is more directly related to the physical presence of a large Jewish community. To be sure, one might argue that, despite the very worrying growth of the National Front, French Jews have never enjoyed such accept-ance, security, and success, even if they frequently do not perceive their situation in these terms. But even in France, anti-Semitism has hardly disappeared as a popular prejudice, a semirespectable sentiment, or even occasionally as a political weapon in domestic or foreign affairs. It may appear as relatively benign when compared with the pathologies of hatred unleashed in ex-Communist societies like Poland, Romania, or Russia, but

---

[71]David A. Jodice, *United Germany and Jewish Concerns: Attitudes Toward Jews, Israel, and the Holocaust* (American Jewish Committee, New York, 1991), pp. 5–6, 15–16, 23–25. See also Jennifer L. Golub, *German Attitudes Toward Jews: What Recent Survey Data Reveal* (American Jewish Committee, New York, 1991).

it stems from similar religious roots, cultural stereotypes, socioeconomic resentments, and political manipulation.

The new Europe of the 1990s, while providing great potential opportunities for Jews to consolidate their postwar achievements, prosperity, and revived culture after the devastation of the Holocaust, also contains within itself all the dangers of a resurgent, inward-looking nationalism leading to fragmentation, ethnic unrest, and growing anti-Semitism. As indicated above, anti-Semitism never went away after 1945, even though it was no longer openly espoused as an ideological worldview by serious politicians. Since the early 1970s it has slowly gained ground, as the Holocaust receded into memory, as anti-Zionism began to provide a new political framework, and as new challenges to liberal democracy from the Right and the Left emerged in the West. Throughout this period, anti-Semitism was also deliberately exploited for political ends throughout the Soviet-controlled part of Europe, preparing the ground for the explosion of popular resentment we have seen more recently.

The decade of the 1980s also saw an upsurge of violent acts against Jews and Jewish institutions in Europe, whose origin came not from within Western countries or indigenous anti-Semitic traditions, but from the Middle East. This anti-Jewish terrorism was an offshoot of the Arab-Israeli conflict and served as a reminder that what happens in the Middle East can directly affect the security and well-being of Jewish communities in Europe. While technically extraneous to the phenomena we have been discussing, the reverberations of Israel's existence, wars, policies, and impact on Diaspora Jewry cannot be divorced from the future prospects of anti-Semitism.

But in the last analysis, the future of Jews in the new Europe will depend on whether the continent succeeds in moving forward to a harmonious, prosperous, and more tolerant society, open toward minorities in general. For the present, there are worrying indications that contrary trends are developing that are likely to ensure the persistence and even an increase in levels of European anti-Semitism through the 1990s. Neither Central nor Western Europe is immune to the combination of economic chaos, political instability, and the ideological vacuum in which both fascism and violent anti-Semitism can flourish.[72] True, the countries of the region are not exposed (except for the present-day eastern part of Germany) to the specific kind of postrevolutionary panic that has overtaken Eastern Europe and Russia and that expresses itself in fear of rapid change and anxieties about privatization and the growing influence of foreign capital. It is no accident that in lands where capitalism was always regarded with suspicion and hostility—from Russia to Slovakia—nostalgia for Communist regimes can

---

[72]Wistrich, *Antisemitism*.

merge with fantasies of blood purity and ethnic homogeneity.[73] Nor is it coincidental that in Western and Central Europe it is those who fear the loss of national identity and culture in a united Europe, who most distrust the capitalist free market and American influence, who are protectionist and intolerant of multiculturalism or religious pluralism who seem more prone to racism and anti-Semitism.

The virus of anti-Semitism is embedded, as it were, in the heart and in the very bloodstream of European society and culture, ready to be activated at the first major crisis—whether it be war, revolution, the fall of empire, economic depression, or the unleashing of ethnic conflict. With the end of the Communist era, many of these conditions are now in place—a not very encouraging prospect.

---

[73]Robert S. Wistrich, "Ghosts from the Past in Czechoslovakia," *The Times Literary Supplement*, July 3, 1992.

Jews in the European Community: Sociodemographic Trends and Challenges

by SERGIO DELLAPERGOLA

AT MIDNIGHT OF DECEMBER 31, 1992, the European Community moved one important step ahead in bringing about the economic integration of 12 Western European countries (EC-12): Belgium, Denmark, France, Germany, Greece, Ireland, Italy, Luxembourg, the Netherlands, Portugal, Spain, and the United Kingdom.[1] Implementation of the Single Market, following the 1987 Single European Act, opened the borders of EC member states to free, mutual circulation of people, goods, and services and advanced the EC one step forward toward what could become, in due course, fuller political integration. At the same stroke of midnight on December 31, Czechoslovakia, a country having common borders with the European Community, was in the process of splitting into two new sovereign states, the Czech and Slovak Republics, putting an end to a union that had lasted since the end of World War I. Even more dramatically, a devastating civil war accompanied by episodes of atrocity and "ethnic cleansing" was ravaging what was once Yugoslavia, another of the EC's close neighbors.

Thus, at the start of 1993, the European continent was emitting ambivalent and troubling political signals. Even as some areas were advancing toward the dream of peace and harmony envisioned by the fathers of European federalism after World War II, their neighbors were burying the thousands killed in the merciless destruction of Sarajevo and many more places in Bosnia. At the same time, the ramifications of major geopolitical changes, such as the crisis and dismemberment of the Soviet Union, the fall of the Berlin wall, and the unification of Germany, were not yet fully

Note: Research on Jewish demographic trends in Western Europe reported in this article was supported by a grant from the Vigevani Fund of the Hebrew University of Jerusalem. Research on Jewish educational statistics was supported by the L.A. Pincus Jewish Education Fund for the Diaspora.

[1]For an introduction to the concept, legal framework, and main socioeconomic aspects of the European Community, see L. Gladwyn, *The European Idea* (London, 1967); Jacques Delors, *Le nouveau concert européen* (Paris, 1992); Dennis Swann, *The Economics of the Common Market* (Harmondsworth, 7th ed., 1992); G.N. Minshull, *The New Europe into the 1990s* (London, 1990); The Economist, *Pocket Europe* (London, 1992).

absorbed or understood. These political transformations, among other factors, unleashed an impressive wave of international migrations, adding a serious economic burden to nations already experiencing economic woes. These developments account for growing social turmoil and outbursts of xenophobia, primarily in Germany but in nearly every other EC member state as well. With European society as a whole still lacking a definitive and stable political order, and perhaps more significantly, a clear vision of what might be expected in the future, hopes for a more prosperous, stable, and powerful Europe in the aftermath of the cold war go hand in hand with fears of large-scale sociopolitical destabilization, increasing outbursts of ethnic violence, and the menace of resurgent Nazi and fascist ideologies.

When one tries to assess the current status of Jewish communities within the framework of the EC, these developments obviously arouse some anxiety. The primary concern is for the political and economic stability of Europe in general, and in the EC in particular. Amidst a growing mood of disillusionment with national political leadership and institutions, the centrifugal forces aiming to break up countries such as Belgium or Italy seem at times more powerful than the centripetal strivings toward European unity. The ambivalence shown by the Europeans over the Maastricht agreement, which by establishing monetary union provides a basis for constitutional harmonization among the EC member states, demonstrates that the process of European union cannot yet be considered unquestionably irreversible. Clearly, the Jews will experience the effects of the more general trends that may emerge, for better or worse—along with other sectors of European society.

The question of cultural identification is increasingly complex, too. Basically there is little tolerance for pluralism and diversity in the individual historical backgrounds of EC member states. Rather, each European nation has tended to emphasize both the superiority of its own culture over others and the sacred territorial base of its own political sovereignty. Can a new, more pluralistic and tolerant order be created within a unified EC framework, in which the various component national cultures are recognized as equals, and which grants minority cultures not defined by a specific territory the same recognition and legitimacy? And can such nonterritorial cultures and communities hold their own against the stronger EC national cultures and maintain their own viable existence in a united Europe? How will the Jews fare, caught as they seem to be between these two opposing forces: latent—and sometimes very real—hostility on the part of the surrounding society, and the benign acceptance by that society that encourages assimilation?[2]

---

[2]For a historical overview of anti-Semitism in Europe, see Robert S. Wistrich, "Anti-Semitism in Europe Since the Holocaust," elsewhere in this volume.

Clearly, these are difficult questions of a general nature and with broad implications. A survey of much larger scope than the present one would be needed to do justice to the complexity of the issues at stake for the Jewish presence in the EC. This article reviews the major sociodemographic processes that currently characterize the Jewish population within the EC. Some basic historical background to the current trends is provided, and brief attention is paid to a few issues of broader significance for the present and future of Western European Jewry, such as the organizational structure of Jewish communities and the process of socialization of the new generation through formal Jewish education. In our concluding remarks, we will try to draw some broader conclusions about the issues that now confront the Jews in the European Community.[3]

Conceptual Problems and Sources

The study of Western European Jewish communities can draw from mature historical and, to a lesser extent, sociological traditions, at the country and local levels;[4] however there has been little attempt to study

---

[3]With regard to some of the topics not dealt with in the present article, the reader may be interested in the following. On the current status of the teaching of Jewish civilization in European universities: Doris Bensimon, *L'enseignement des disciplines juives dans les universités européennes* (Jerusalem, 1988); Sharman Kadish, *The Teaching of Jewish Civilization at British and Irish Universities and Other Institutions of Higher Learning* (Jerusalem, 1990). On recent anti-Semitism and other forms of prejudice: Tony Lerman, ed., *Antisemitism World Report 1992* (London, 1992); David A. Jodice, *United Germany and Jewish Concerns: Attitudes Toward Jews, Israel and the Holocaust* (New York, American Jewish Committee, 1991); *L'immagine dell'ebreo nell'Italia degli anni '80, La Rassegna Mensile di Israel* 56, no. 3, 1990. On the representation of Israel in the European press: Hanna Pout, *European Perspectives on Israel with Special Reference to Eight British and French Weeklies* (Ramat Gan, 1991). On European Community-Israel relations: Ilan Greilsammer and Joseph H. Weiler, eds., *Europe and Israel: Troubled Neighbours* (Berlin, 1988). Data on Jewish emigration from EC countries to Israel are analyzed in Sergio DellaPergola, "Mass *Aliyah*—A Thing of the Past?" *Jerusalem Quarterly*, 51, 1989, pp. 96–114.

[4]Since the literature on Jews in individual European countries is too extensive to be even tentatively summarized here, a selection of relevant works is offered, most of which stress a social perspective. On Belgium: Jacques Gutwirth, *Vie juive traditionnelle: ethnologie d'une communauté hassidique* (Paris, 1970); Willy Bok, "Vie juive et communauté; une esquisse de leur histoire au vingtième siècle," in *La grande Synagogue de Bruxelles; contributions à l'histoire des juifs de Bruxelles* (Brussels, 1978), pp. 151–68; Willy Bok, "L'entrelacs du religieux et du laïc dans les milieux juifs en Belgique," in *Eglises, mouvements religieux et laïques*, ed. L. Voye, K. Dobbelaere, J. Remy, and J. Billiet (Louvain-la-Neuve, 1985), pp. 333–46; on Denmark: Jacques Blum, *Danske og/eller Jode?* (Copenhagen, 1972); Adina Weiss Liberles, "The Jewish Community of Denmark," in D.J. Elazar et al., *The Jewish Communities of Scandinavia* (Lanham, Md.-Jerusalem, 1984), pp. 57–102; on France: Otto Klineberg, Georges Levitte, and Georges Benguigui, *Aspects of French Jewry* (London, 1969); Dominique Schnapper, *Jewish Identities in France: An Analysis of Contemporary French Jewry* (Chicago, 1983); Doris Bensimon, *Les juifs de France et leur relations avec Israel (1945–1988)* (Paris,

the Jewish scene in a coherent and integrated regional context.[5] This lag reflects several general problems hindering contemporary Jewish demographic, socioeconomic, and sociocultural research. For one thing, there barely exists a meaningful sociological-historical framework for the study of general society within the European Community, let alone for the

---

1989); on Germany: Leo Katcher, *Post Mortem: The Jews in Germany Today* (New York, 1968); Monika Richarz, "Jews in Today's Germanies," *Leo Baeck Institute Year Book* 30, 1985, pp. 265–74; Frank Stern, "From Overt Filosemitism to Discreet Antisemitism and Beyond: Anti-Jewish Developments in the Political Culture of the Federal Republic of Germany," in *Antisemitism Through the Ages*, ed. S. Almog (Oxford, 1988), pp. 385–404; on Greece, Adina Weiss Liberles, "The Jews of Greece," in D.J. Elazar et al., *The Balkan Jewish Communities* (Lanham, Md.-Jerusalem, 1984), pp. 102–26; on Italy: Sergio DellaPergola, *Anatomia dell'ebraismo italiano: caratteristiche demografiche, economiche, sociali, religiose e politiche di una minoranza* (Roma-Assisi, 1976); Sergio DellaPergola and Eitan F. Sabatello, "The Italian Jewish Population Study," in *Studies in Jewish Demography: Survey for 1969–1971*, ed. U.O. Schmelz, P. Glikson, and S.J. Gould (Jerusalem-London, 1975), pp. 53–152; H. Stuart Hughes, *Prisoners of Hope: The Silver Age of the Italian Jews, 1924–1974* (Cambridge, Mass., 1983); on the Netherlands: S.J. Wijnberg, *De Joden in Amsterdam* (Assen, 1967); Ph. van Praag, *Demography of the Jews in the Netherlands* (Jerusalem, 1976); on Spain: Haim Avni, *Spain, the Jews and Franco* (Philadelphia, 1982); Samuel Toledano, "La situation actuelle de la communauté juive d'Espagne," in *European Jewry: A Handbook*, ed. E. Stock (Ramat Gan, 1983), pp. 84–90; on the United Kingdom: Maurice Freedman, ed., *A Minority in Britain* (London, 1955); Shaul Esh and S.J. Gould, eds., *Jewish Life in Modern Britain* (London, 1964); S.L. Lipman and V.D. Lipman, eds., *Jewish Life in Britain 1962–1977* (New York, 1981). The AMERICAN JEWISH YEAR BOOK regularly publishes surveys of Jewish affairs in a number of EC countries. See also the respective country entries in the *Encyclopedia Judaica* (Jerusalem, 1971) and subsequent *Encyclopedia Judaica Yearbooks*.

[5]Two seminal symposia held in Brussels in the 1960s introduced the need for an integrated research perspective on European Jewry. The proceedings were published in Centre National des Hautes Etudes Juives, Brussels, and Institute of Contemporary Jewry, Hebrew University, Jerusalem, *Jewish Life in Contemporary Europe* (Brussels, 1965); Willy Bok and U.O. Schmelz, eds., *Démographie et identité juives dans l'Europe contemporaine* (Brussels, 1972). Two more recent conferences were held, respectively, at the Oxford Centre for Postgraduate Hebrew Studies, on "Jewish Identities in the New Europe" (July 1992); and, organized by the Fonds Social Juif Unifié, on the premises of the French Senate-Palais du Luxembourg in Paris, on "1992—Les juifs dans l'Europe d'aujourd'hui et de demain" (Nov. 1992). The proceedings are due to appear in the near future. Selected portions of the present article were presented on these occasions. Among other writings introducing a comprehensive Western European Jewish perspective, see Cecil Roth, "The Jews of Western Europe," in *The Jews: Their History, Culture and Religion*, ed. L. Finkelstein (New York, 1960, 3rd ed.), pp. 250–86; Morris Ginsberg, "A Review of the European Jewish Communities Today and Some Questions for Tomorrow," *Jewish Journal of Sociology* 6, no. 1, 1964, pp. 118–31; Arnold Mandel, "The Jews in Western Europe Today," AJYB 1967, vol. 68, pp. 3–28; Zachariah Shuster, "Western Europe," in *World Politics and the Jewish Condition*, ed. Louis Henkin (New York, 1972), pp. 181–206; Doris Bensimon, Sergio DellaPergola, Joel S. Fishman, and Fritz Hollander, "Western Europe," in *Zionism in Transition*, ed. M. Davis (New York, 1980), pp. 141–77. Two very useful and comprehensive works are Ernest Stock, ed., *European Jewry: A Handbook* (Ramat Gan, 1983); and Daniel J. Elazar, *People and Polity: The Organizational Dynamics of World Jewry* (Detroit, 1989).

Jewish segment.[6] For another, the very nature of European Jewry—geographically dispersed and with extremely varied forms of communal organization—makes it difficult to collect, organize, and meaningfully analyze information.

Viewed broadly, the size, corporate profile, and cultural content of Jewish communities in Europe are the products of the deepening integration and assimilation of Jews in the surrounding social and cultural environment that has proceeded since emancipation. These processes have affected individuals' perceptions of themselves as Jews and the ways in which they express their Jewishness. As the boundaries of the Jewish collective have tended to become increasingly complex, sometimes blurred, or even inconsistent, new concepts have become part of the research vocabulary, such as the "core" versus the "enlarged" Jewish population. The former definition applies to the aggregate of those who consider themselves, or are willing to be considered, Jewish by any identificational criterion, and do not possess an incompatible alternative identification; the latter includes the larger aggregate of all current Jews, former Jews, other persons of recent Jewish descent, and any other related non-Jewish persons who share household ties with Jews.[7] Different definitions of the Jewish collective obviously result in different population counts, assessments of ongoing social trends, and evaluations of the future prospects of Jewish communities.

Another complicating factor is immigration. Since the end of 1989, the volume of Jewish international migration, especially from the former Soviet Union, has again reached historic peak levels—an unmistakable sign of the ongoing European continental crisis. This additional factor overlaps with the question of how significant the EC-12's geographical boundaries actually are. Is it really relevant, from the point of view of assessing contemporary and future trends, to address a Jewish collective that is limited to the EC member countries? Or is a broader geographical definition preferable, one that includes other Central and Eastern European countries? The broader framework is surely relevant, since the bonds and commonalities in the Jewish experience transcend the narrower institutional definition of a European Community which is itself bound to change in the course of time. Yet, if the goal is a pragmatic assessment of society, the existing institutional context cannot be ignored, since in the end it is the one that determines the actual constraints and opportunities of Jewish life.

---

[6]Federico Chabod, *Storia dell'idea d'Europa* (Bari, 1964); Robert T. Anderson, *Modern Europe: An Anthropological Perspective* (Pacific Palisades, 1973); Luigi Barzini, *The Europeans* (New York and London, 1982); H. Seton-Watson, "What Is Europe, Where Is Europe?" *Encounter*, July-Aug. 1985, pp. 9–17; William Wallace, *The Transformation of Western Europe* (London, 1990).

[7]These concepts are discussed in greater detail in U.O. Schmelz and Sergio DellaPergola, "World Jewish Population 1990," AJYB 1992, vol. 92, pp. 484–512.

One further major difficulty in organizing a coherent analysis derives from a chronic lack of data sources on many important aspects of Jewish life in Western Europe, and the fragmentary and inconsistent nature of the sources that are available. Before World War II, official censuses and reports of vital statistics in some EC countries provided information on the respective Jewish populations. In the postwar period, such information has become extremely rare.

Under these circumstances, the bulk of documentation on EC Jews in recent years has been provided by sources internal to the Jewish communities.[8] One tool is the routine compilation of vital statistics (marriages and divorces, male births, and burials) and the analysis of membership registers in synagogues and other Jewish institutions. Such efforts have been successfully implemented in the United Kingdom, the Netherlands, Italy, Germany, and to a limited extent in Belgium, Greece, and a few more places. More significantly, special surveys of representative samples of the Jewish population were undertaken in certain countries or localities—in France, Italy, Denmark, and in selected locales of the United Kingdom. Over the years, the latter efforts have provided integrated views of the demographic, socioeconomic, and Jewish behavioral and attitudinal characteristics of the surveyed Jews. Moreover, repeated international surveys of Jewish education conducted in the 1980s have provided quite a detailed and accurate picture of this significant aspect of Jewish life.[9]

Unfortunately, limited coordination between these efforts makes it difficult to provide systematic comparisons and syntheses. Nor has there been any serious attempt to update the information collected in the past on a European scale. Yet the need for a systematic approach is greater now than ever, in the context of the EC integration process under way and in light of emerging social developments. Ideally, a European Jewish Population and Community Survey would be an instrument for assessing the different communities within the EC-12, based on a common set of definitions and research agenda. But this would require a far more coordinated Jewish organizational structure than that which exists at present within the European Community.

---

[8]For inventories of sociodemographic sources, see Sergio DellaPergola, "Recent Demographic Trends Among Jews in Western Europe," in Stock, *European Jewry: A Handbook*, pp. 19–62; Sergio DellaPergola and Leah Cohen, eds., *World Jewish Population: Trends and Policies* (Jerusalem, 1992), pp. 154–56.

[9]See below in the section on Jewish education.

Jewish Community Organization in the EC

Just as the main frame of reference of collective life in Europe has long been the nation-state, the form taken by Jewish life in each country has been shaped along lines that reflect the different character of the various nations. In the modern period, the standing of the Jews vis-à-vis the majority society and institutions has typically been that of a religious group. The alternative possibility of definition as an ethnic-national group was not conceivable, given the ethnocentric and culturally homogeneous character of most nation-states. In the French tradition, which exerted strong influence throughout the continent, Jews were indeed granted equal civil rights as individuals, not as a corporate group. Consequently, the development of organizations to represent Jews before the general polity reflected a balance between the basic needs of Jewish communities and the somewhat limited ways in which the majority was able to conceive of the Jewish presence.[10]

The three major types of concern reflected by Jewish community organization can be defined as political representation, religious functioning, and the provision of social and educational services. In a more distant past, individual Jews or small groups sought to carry out these functions on the basis of their own special standing and influence with public authorities. In the course of modernization, the character of Jewish community organization tended to become less personal and elitist, with a more democratically selected leadership to some extent replacing charisma and color. Based on the circumstances in each country and community, slightly different forms of community organization evolved for dealing with the three major areas of communal concern (see table 1).

In France, the main religious organization, the Consistoire, long served as the central Jewish representative body. However, needs emerging in the social sphere, notably in connection with the absorption of Jewish refugees and other immigrants, led to the emergence of a powerful central lay community organization, the Fonds Social Juif Unifié (FSJU). At a later stage, the need to provide unified representation to all of the major Jewish organizations—often representing quite different constituencies and interests within the same Jewish community—led to the creation of a central roof political organization, the Conseil Représentatif des Institutions Juives de France (CRIF). With different degrees of complexity, these major functional divisions exist in Belgium, the Netherlands (which lacks a central Jewish political representative organization), and Germany (where there is no central Jewish religious body).

The major alternative model is that of the central, all-inclusive represent-

---

[10]For more detailed discussion of the topics in this section, see Stock, *European Jewry: A Handbook,* and Elazar, *People and Polity.*

ative body, such as the Board of Deputies of British Jews. In this case, even if the major functions are technically split among different organizations, the main entity plays a pivotal role in all or most areas of Jewish life. The central representative organization is usually elected by, or composed of delegates from, local Jewish communities and institutions. Variations of the centralized Jewish community model exist in Italy and Spain (where the emphasis of the central body is on political representation), Greece, Ireland, and Denmark (actually the Jewish community of Copenhagen where most Jews live). Small communities that lack the scale to develop more than one function, such as Luxembourg or Portugal, have only a religious body.

With regard to both major models, the "centralist" and the "pluralist," an important distinction exists between activities of national and local scope. Where the main purpose of the unified central representative body is political, religious and service activities are usually the province of local Jewish communities. Where several central organizations coexist nationally, they may maintain branches at the local level. `

Another important area of Jewish community activity is all that concerns the State of Israel, the Zionist movement, and the many related fund-raising bodies. Other organized activities within the Jewish community address culture, recreation, and the representation of specific sectorial interests. All or several of these options operate in one form or another in the various EC communities. The result is a rich and complex patchwork of national and local institutions, of either broad or limited purpose.

The core of leadership and the main activists involved in these different groups often overlap significantly, while a large share of the Jewish public may not be involved at all. Indeed, the proportion of fee-paying members of a community varies substantially.[11] In Italy, where until 1984 paid membership in a Jewish community was compulsory under state law, the proportion formally affiliated may be above 90 percent. In the United Kingdom, in 1990, probably as many as 70 percent of the Jewish households were synagogue members. In France, the overall rate of belonging to any Jewish organization probably approaches 40 percent; in a 1988 survey, 22 percent of the respondents were frequent participants in Jewish community activities, 29 percent participated rarely, and 48 percent never or nearly never attended.[12]

The major problem of Jewish community organization in the 12 EC countries is the remarkable lack of coordination, the fact that there is no

---

[11]See DellaPergola, *Anatomia*; Doris Bensimon and Sergio DellaPergola, *La population juive de France: socio-démographie et identité* (Jerusalem-Paris, 1984); Marlena Schmool and Frances Cohen, *British Synagogue Membership in 1990* (London, 1991).

[12]Erik H. Cohen, *L'Etude et l'éducation juive en France ou l'avenir d'une communauté* (Paris, 1991).

central representative organization of the Jews of the 12 EC countries. There are several significant Jewish organizations operating at the continental level, such as the European Jewish Congress, the European Council of Jewish Community Services, and the Conference of European Rabbis. But in each of these instances, "Europe" is understood in the broader and, we would argue, somewhat anachronistic perspective extending from Lisbon to Vladivostock, rather than in the restricted and operative EC-12 definition. It is one thing to foster a sense of solidarity and interchange among Jewish communities continentally, or for that matter, globally; it is another to be able to conduct focused activity, such as lobbying, at the level of the central EC institutions in Brussels, Luxembourg, or Strasbourg, and to be regarded by those official European institutions as their functional Jewish counterpart. Failure to provide coordinated planning and representation of the different Jewish communities in a clearly delimited EC framework could seriously hinder the ability to defend or promote Jewish interests in a rapidly changing environment.

Demographic Trends, 1939–1991

Both the size of the Jewish population throughout the territory of the current European Community and its geographic distribution have been shaped by a complex of factors, some imposed from the outside by the majority society, others reflecting internal conditions and needs of the Jewish community.[13] Political, economic, and cultural forces determined quite different and changing rates of demographic growth among Jewish populations across the various regions and provinces of Europe, within the EC and outside of it. Over time, most communities, countrywide and locally, experienced alternating periods of sustained growth and sudden collapse, due to large-scale in- or out-migration or actual physical destruction. A high degree of geographic mobility also influenced the changing size and distribution of Jewries in Europe, as did differing intensities of demographic patterns such as marriage, fertility, mortality, and natural increase. Secessions from, or accessions to, Jewish communities on religious or ideological

---

[13]The demographic data in this section are adapted from Jacob Lestschinsky, "Die Umsiedlung und Umschichtung des judischen Volkes im laufe des letzten Jahrhunderts" *Weltwirtschaftliches Archiv* 30 (1929), pp. 123–56, and 32 (1930), pp. 563–99; Moses Moskowitz, "Distribution of the Jewish Population on the European Continent," AJYB 1941–42, vol. 43, pp. 662–73; U.O. Schmelz, *World Jewish Population: Regional Estimates and Projections* (Jerusalem, 1981); Sergio DellaPergola, "Changing Patterns of Jewish Demography in the Modern World," *Studia Rosenthaliana* (special issue) 23, no. 2, 1989, pp. 154–74; and U.O. Schmelz and Sergio DellaPergola, "World Jewish Population," appearing each year in AJYB since vol. 82, 1982. The latest update is "World Jewish Population 1991," AJYB 1993, vol. 93.

grounds were yet another component of Jewish population change, generally resulting in net losses to the Jewish side.

HISTORICAL TRENDS

In comparison with the total European population, European Jewry experienced a much earlier pace of rapid growth. From an estimated 719,000 Jews in 1700, the total of Jews in Europe (Western and Eastern together) rose dramatically to 2,020,000 in 1800, 8,766,000 in 1900, and 9,500,000 in 1939. Between 1700 and 1939 the Jewish population multiplied by a factor of above 13, while the total population of the continent passed from 125 million in 1700 to 575 million in 1939—a growth factor of 4.6. As a consequence of its early and powerful demographic "takeoff," European Jewry increased its numerical and cultural dominance over other sections of the Diaspora. By 1860, European Jewry's share of the world's total Jewish population approached 90 percent. Continuing intense Jewish population growth in Eastern Europe and the buildup of strong social pressures there ultimately led to mass emigration, which played a crucial role in the formation of major new Jewish centers in America and other extra-European countries, and also produced some growth in Western European Jewries.

Quite a different picture emerges when one tries to reconstruct the historical demography of the Jewries in what today are the 12 EC countries. It can be roughly estimated that the total Jewish population in EC countries increased from some 180,000 in 1700 to 1.3 million in 1939, a factor of 7.2. In addition to the immigration from Eastern Europe mentioned above, a continuous though small trickle of Jewish immigrants arrived from various parts of the Mediterranean area. However, the share of total world Jewry held by Jewish communities in the EC area declined steadily over the same period, from more than 16 percent to less than 8 percent. At this stage, when the Jewish population of Western Europe had already reached slower demographic growth and was headed toward stagnation, the Holocaust resulted in irreversible losses. Beyond the direct consequences of physical destruction, other demographic effects of the Holocaust included emigration, conversion from Judaism, and the scanty numbers of the generation born during the war. Because of the consequent rapid aging and the additional effects of assimilation, current Jewish population estimates are, and are bound to remain, substantially lower than on the eve of World War II. In 1945, an estimated 843,000 Jews lived in the present EC countries, representing about 7.8 percent of world Jewry (see table 2). The overall trend has since been one of moderate increase, the total estimate for EC Jewry in 1991 being 987,000 persons, still only 7.6 percent of the world's Jewish population.

Over time, significant changes occurred in the geographic distribution of Jews in Europe, and more specifically within the present EC. Looking at the changing size of Jewish communities over the last two or three centuries according to present-day political boundaries, three basic profiles emerge: (a) substantial growth and then dramatic decline, as happened in most Eastern European and Balkan countries as well as in Western European countries such as the Netherlands, Belgium, Germany, and Austria; (b) growth in more recent generations and then stabilization, as in the United Kingdom and France; and (c) relative stability in the long run, as in the case of Italy and smaller communities such as Switzerland, the Scandinavian countries, and Spain.

PRESENT-DAY JEWISH COMMUNITIES

In the perspective provided by contemporary events, four major groups of European Jewish communities may be singled out: the 12 EC member countries, other non-EC-member countries in Western Europe, the new independent republics which until 1991 formed part of the Soviet Union, and other countries in Eastern Europe. For most of the historical span considered here, Eastern European Jewish communities were clearly preponderant. After World War II the demographic center of gravity of European Jewry moved westward.

At the end of 1991, the total Jewish population of Europe was estimated at 2,010,000, or 2.6 per 1,000 total inhabitants of the continent. Roughly one million Jews lived in the 12 EC countries, less than 900,000 remained in the seven European countries of the former USSR, and smaller numbers were found elsewhere—44,000 in Western Europe outside the EC, and 111,000 in Eastern Europe and the Balkans. The recent emigration from the former USSR is leading to a rapid decline of the Jewish population in that region. Most of the emigrants are headed to Israel or to the United States and other overseas countries, but Germany is drawing its share, providing some demographic reinforcement to the Jewish population in that country and in the EC more generally. Significantly, since the exodus from the former USSR that began in the early 1990s, and for the first time in modern history, more Jews can be found in Western than in Eastern Europe.

As to the internal distribution of Jewish population within the EC itself, before World War II it was much more equally spread across different countries than it is today. After the initial decline of German Jewry through large-scale emigration, already by the late 1930s the United Kingdom had the largest Jewish population of any EC country. This held true until the early 1960s when, following the decolonization of North Africa, the mass immigration of close to 250,000 Jews gave to France its new standing as flag bearer of the Jewish presence in Western Europe. Since the late 1960s, the size of French Jewry (referring to the "core" Jewish population) can be realistically estimated at about 530,000, a figure that has remained quite stable until now.[14] Higher figures that have been circulated periodically may refer to the enlarged Jewish population of Jews, ex-Jews, and non-Jewish household members, but certainly appear to be inconsistent with the known historical development of the Jewish population.

By contrast, the United Kingdom has traditionally been a country with substantial emigration, and that has included several thousands of Jews. Based on a recent reconsideration of the vital statistics regularly collected by the Jewish community, the estimate of the Jewish population of the United Kingdom was reassessed downward to about 300,000, and in all likelihood will continue to decline in the near future.[15]

The third largest Jewish population in the EC has now become Germany, which after World War II was reduced to a scant and heterogeneous community of elderly German Jews, displaced persons from other European countries, and former Israelis. According to the detailed records kept by the Zentralwohlfartsstelle der Juden in Deutschland—the central Jewish social service agency in the country—the Jewish population grew from 27,711 at the end of 1989 to 28,468 in 1990, 33,692 in 1991, and 37,498 at the end of 1992. While there is a lack of certainty about the number of recent immigrants from the former USSR, according to some reports, as many as 20,000 have settled in Germany since the end of 1989.[16] Allowing for some time lag between immigration and registering with the organized Jewish community, the Jewish population in Germany probably passed the 40,000 mark in 1990, and most likely reached a total of 50,000 by the end of 1992. Since many of these migrants appear to have ambivalent feelings about their Jewishness, German Jewry has yet to reach the standing of a consolidated community, such as the one that emerged in France soon after mass immigration, or the more established one in the United Kingdom or smaller communities such as those in Italy, the Netherlands, or Greece. Moreover, if we consider the nature of the interaction between majority society and

---

[14]Bensimon and DellaPergola, *La population juive de France*.

[15]Steven Haberman, Barry A. Kosmin, and Caren Levy, "Mortality Patterns of British Jews 1975–79: Insights and Applications for the Size and Structure of British Jewry," *Journal of the Royal Statistical Society*, ser. A, 146, pt. 3, 1983, pp. 294–310; Steven Haberman and Marlena Schmool, *Estimates of British Jewish Population 1984–88* (London, forthcoming). The earlier revision suggested a central estimate of 336,000 for 1977; the latter brings the estimate down to 308,000 in 1986; hence 300,000 or less at present.

[16]E.g., Judith Winkler in the Israeli daily *Ha'aretz*, Feb. 23, 1993, reports first data from a survey of Jewish immigrants to Germany from the former USSR. The survey was done by the Mendelsohn Center for Judaic Studies of the University of Potsdam and Germany's central Jewish community organization.

Jewish minority—one of the more sensitive factors in the growth or decline of a Jewish community—any judgments about the long-term prospects of a Jewish community in Germany are better left suspended.

Reflecting the interplay of different demographic variables, Jewish population growth rates in EC countries have tended to be generally negative or only marginally positive (table 3). The main exception, apart from postwar France and current Germany, is Spain, which has attracted immigration from various sources, including Latin America. With the exception of France and Spain, the number of Jews per 1,000 inhabitants of each country—and hence their visibility in the broader society—is now much less than it was in 1939. Of all the geographic, political, and socioeconomic factors that help to explain the differences between individual countries, the variable effect of the Holocaust is by far the strongest. Between 1939 and 1945, seven EC countries lost significant portions of their Jewish populations: Greece, 89 percent; Germany, 78 percent; the Netherlands, 77 percent; Belgium (with Luxembourg), 66 percent; France, 44 percent; Italy, 38 percent. (The remaining five EC countries—Denmark, Ireland, Portugal, Spain, and the United Kingdom—had postwar Jewish populations that were the same or larger than before the war.) Here indeed is a melancholy reminder of a tragic chapter in the rich, creative, and often happy history of the Jews in modern Europe.

Recent Geographic Distribution: Patterns and Significance

To gain deeper insight into the present as well as possible future changes, we need to understand the determinants and consequences of Jewish population distribution in individual countries as well as in smaller geographic divisions. We have already mentioned the differential effects of the Holocaust in determining the size of current Jewish populations. It is also important to assess the forces of attraction and repulsion that generate voluntary population movements to and from given regions and cities. A further critical element is the ability of a population to reproduce itself demographically, which, in the case of Jewish communities, may be affected by changing patterns of group identification no less than by the biological facts of birth and death.

In the more distant past, the Jewish presence in a given country, both nationally and locally, was related only in part to a set of rational socioeconomic factors; more often it reflected the willingness or unwillingness of the ruling powers to provide the Jews with the legal and economic conditions required for survival. For the more recent period, European countries and their respective Jewish populations have to be seen as components in a broader, global socioeconomic and political system. The balance of forces operating in such a system tends to attract people toward the "center" of the more developed and stable countries, and away from the "periphery" of the less developed and more unstable nations. Jews, unless political barriers prevented them from doing so, have tended to respond rationally to these forces of push and pull. Indeed, at the world level, the size of Jewish populations in the various countries and their proportion in the total population in those countries tend to be highly and positively correlated with major indicators of socioeconomic development, industrialization, and political freedom.[17]

In the contemporary world, socioeconomic modernization and affluence in a given country have been, more often than not, positively associated with liberal public attitudes that permit Jews to conduct a relatively autonomous communal life. In the post-World War II period, EC countries generally offered both political freedom and affluence, conditions that attracted substantial immigration from other parts of the world. The fact that there are today more Jews in France than in the United Kingdom indicates that the former offered relatively better economic opportunities and therefore was able not only to attract more Jews but to hold on to more of those already there. The major exception to this schematic view of the relationship between Jewish population size and a country's socioeconomic attractiveness is represented by the relatively scarce numbers in Germany, the strongest economic partner in the EC. While the obvious explanation rests with the historical factors already outlined, it is also the case that the Jewish population in Germany is indeed currently growing, fed by immigration from the former Soviet Union.

FACTORS RELATED TO JEWISH PRESENCE

A country-by-country examination of European Jewry illustrates even more clearly the relationship between the Jewish presence and general socioeconomic and sociocultural conditions at the local level. Table 4 presents the detailed distribution of total and Jewish populations (as of 1990) in the 69 main regions into which the 12 EC countries are customarily subdivided.[18] The same table also shows the proportion of Jews per 1,000

---

[17]Sergio DellaPergola, "Israel and World Jewish Population: A Core-Periphery Perspective," in *Population and Social Change in Israel*, ed. C. Goldscheider (Boulder, 1992), pp. 39–63.

[18]Estimates were prepared on the basis of continuous data collection by the Division of Jewish Demography and Statistics at the Avraham Harman Institute of Contemporary Jewry, Hebrew University of Jerusalem. Questionnaires sent periodically to the central Jewish representative organizations in each country yield, among other things, data and estimates on regional Jewish population distribution. The estimates reported here are our adaptation of the original estimates received. Besides sources already quoted in notes 4, 11, 12, and 13, see Dov

inhabitants in each region, and the region's economic status as expressed by Purchasing Power Standard (PPS) per inhabitant, a measure of standard of living. (The PPS consists of the Gross Domestic Product adjusted for market prices.) Table 5 presents a synthetic analysis of the same data, making it possible to compare the distribution of Jewish and general population in five regional strata, based on the economic status of the regions.

The fact that each stratum includes a substantial share of the EC's total population, varying between 13.5 percent and 27.2 percent, indicates that general population size is not clearly correlated with socioeconomic indicators. By contrast, the Jewish population appears to be overwhelmingly concentrated in the upper regional stratum. Around 1990, over 59 percent of the EC-12's total Jewish population resided in the 14 regions of the top stratum; the next two strata of regions each had 19 percent of the Jewish population; and the two bottom strata of regions together accounted for only 2 percent. Accordingly, the proportion of Jews per 1,000 of total population declines from nearly 8 in the upper stratum, to 2–3 in the next two strata, and to 0.2 in the lower two strata.

Further examination of the data in table 4 reveals that even in the 14 European regions included in the top stratum, based on standard of living, there are quite different proportions of Jews per 1,000 inhabitants. The intensity of the Jewish presence is definitely above average in three regions: Greater Paris (310,000 Jews, or 30 per 1,000 population); the United Kingdom's South-East, which includes Greater London (232,000 Jews, or 13 per 1,000); and Greater Brussels (15,000 Jews, or 15 per 1,000). Each of these metropolitan areas is a major world or continental capital whose area of influence transcends the boundaries of a single country. A moderate Jewish presence (1–3 per 1,000 inhabitants) exists in six more regions in the top stratum: Berlin, Hamburg, Hessen (main city: Frankfurt), Denmark (Copenhagen), Lombardy (Milan), and Luxembourg. Again, each of these is a national or regional capital with wide international connections. The five remaining regions in the top stratum have low proportions of Jews (less than 1 per 1,000): Noord (Groningen) in the Netherlands, Bremen and Baden-Württemberg (Stuttgart) in Germany, and Nord-Ovest (Turin) and Emilia-Romagna (Bologna) in Italy. The slight Jewish presence in these latter regions, despite their being among the higher-ranked in living standards, is probably explained by the comparatively less complex and sophisticated socioeconomic and cultural facilities they offer. However, the rela-

---

Liebermann, "Report on the Jewish Community in Belgium," a paper presented at the Conference on Jewish Demography (Jerusalem, 1987); Zentralwohlfahrtsstelle der Juden in Deutschland, *Vierteljahresmeldung uber den Mitgliederstand* (Frankfurt, quarterly); Stanley Waterman and Barry Kosmin, *British Jewry in the Eighties: A Statistical and Geographical Guide* (London, 1986).

tively high standard of living available in these areas may well attract larger numbers of Jews in the future.

While the pull of socioeconomic factors is clearly strong, historical inertia, or the continued presence of a Jewish community in a certain locale, also plays an important role in determining current Jewish population distribution. Relatively large Jewish communities exist in regions whose current socioeconomic situation is just moderately attractive but which had a thriving Jewish life in the past. In the second highest stratum of European regions, six have Jewish populations of 10,000 each and represent at least 2 per 1,000 of the total population: the West (main city: Amsterdam) in the Netherlands, Lazio (Rome) in Italy, Vlaams Gewest (Antwerp) in Belgium, and the Centre-Est (Lyons), Est (Strasbourg), and Sud-Ouest (Toulouse) in France.

In the third stratum of regions, the same conditions of Jewish population size-density are met by four regions: the Mediterranée (Marseilles) in France and the United Kingdom's Scotland (Glasgow), North-West (Manchester), and Yorkshire (Leeds). The same size-density conditions are not met by any region in the two lowest regional strata. Indeed, the scant Jewish presence in some of the more economically depressed regions in the EC, such as Spain, Portugal, Greece, Southern and Insular Italy, Ireland, and the states of former East Germany, supports the general interpretation suggested here.

A further significant feature of Jewish population distribution, shown in table 6, is its overwhelmingly urban concentration. More than half a million Jews (525,000 people, or 53 percent of the total EC Jewry) were estimated in 1990 to live in the two metropolitan areas of Greater Paris and Greater London. In the Paris area, out of a total estimate of 310,000 Jews, about 145,000 lived in the City of Paris, 113,000 in the closer suburban belt (*Petite couronne*), and 52,000 in the more distant suburban belt (*Grande couronne*). In the London area, where overall the Jewish population presented a denser ecological concentration, out of a total estimate of 215,000 Jews, 72,000 lived in the Inner Boroughs and 125,000 in the Outer Boroughs of Greater London, and 18,000 in the more peripheral adjacent Home Counties. Another 258,800 Jews (26 percent of the EC total) lived in 13 cities with 10,000 to 50,000 Jews each; and 131,900 Jews (13 percent) lived in 47 cities with 1,000 to 10,000 Jews. Overall, about 92 percent of all EC Jews lived in cities with an estimated presence of 1,000 Jews or more.

A more sophisticated analysis of the same data, employing multivariate statistical techniques (not presented here in detail), shows that two variables are most prominently associated with the regional distribution of Jews in the EC: the status of a place as a country's capital city and the standard of living. These two variables alone explain about one-third of the statistical variance in Jewish population distribution. This pattern can be better understood by considering the correlation that exists between the general social profile of more developed European regions and the social structure of Jewish populations. On the general side, there is a strong association between a higher standard of living and high population density (as appropriate to large urban areas), the variety of economic activities with an emphasis on services (as contrasted to agriculture and industry), and the quality of available educational, research, and cultural facilities.[19] This major cluster of socioeconomic elements at the regional level fits well with typical socioeconomic characteristics of Jews: high educational attainment and growing specialization in professional and managerial activities (see below).

Even if the correlation between the Jewish presence and the existence of attractive socioeconomic conditions in European regions should be considered with a grain of caution, there can be no doubt that these findings display high internal consistency. The same findings also hint at future trends and adjustments, especially if the process of economic and political integration within the EC continues. The greatly enhanced freedom of travel and employment for EC citizens across country borders, as well as internal migration within countries, will quite probably lead to an increasing correspondence between what a certain place or region can offer, economically and culturally, and the willingness of people to live in such a place. This is the general trend likely to affect the total EC population in the longer run, and there is no reason to believe that EC Jews will not be among those taking advantage of the new opportunities.

Socioeconomic Structure and Mobility

The pattern of Jewish population distribution within the EC that we have just examined reflects the considerable similarities in socioeconomic stratification found in most Jewish populations. Available data on the socioeconomic characteristics of Jews are quite fragmentary, but those that exist show a high degree of consistency. One common trait of nearly all Jewish communities on record is the higher level of education attained by Jews in comparison with the general population. Historically, the trend leads from a relative lack of illiteracy in earlier periods to a significant overrepresentation of university graduates and postgraduates in the present. Today it can be safely assumed that substantially more than one-half of the younger Jewish adult generation is exposed to university education. In other words, while levels of educational attainment have risen among both Jews and

---

[19]Roger Brunet, ed., Les villes "européennes" (Paris, 1989).

non-Jews, the relative gap between the two groups has not tended to disappear.[20]

OCCUPATIONAL PROFILES

Equally significant transformations occurred in the occupational structure and socioeconomic status of the Jewish labor force. Generally speaking, the constraints and—less often—opportunities typical of minority status produced quite similar occupational profiles among Jews in the different EC countries. However, occupational stratification of Jews also reflected particular national economic circumstances. International migration played an important role as well. The occupational structures and mobility paths of the foreign-born and local-born differed, with the foreign-born paying a social price in the process of becoming absorbed in the new country and experiencing, at least initially, a loss of social status. Depending on the general societal circumstances and on the characteristics of the migrants themselves, the latter often eventually recovered some or most of their former status or even improved on it. The local-born had the advantage of beginning their occupational lives in the environment in which they had been socialized, and under normal conditions could expect to improve their socioeconomic standing over that of their immigrant parents.

Between the two world wars, Central and Eastern Europe were the main suppliers of immigrants to Jewish communities in today's EC. After World War II, the immigration of Jews from former colonies in North Africa and elsewhere had the greatest impact and significance. On the largest scale this involved the Jews of the three former French colonies in the Maghreb (Morocco, Tunisia, Algeria) during the 1950s and 1960s. Further examples are the transfers of thousands of Jews from Iraq and India to the United Kingdom in the late 1940s and early 1950s, from Egypt to Italy, France, and to a lesser extent to other countries in the 1950s, from Libya to Italy in the 1960s, and from Iran to Italy in the late 1970s. Still, even with this substantial immigration, the majority of the Jewish population in EC countries is now local-born.

FRANCE

Before looking at the social-mobility trends among Jews in France, it is important to recall that the mass exodus from North Africa involved a split between those choosing France as the preferred country of destination and those choosing Israel. The choice was generally determined by the citizen-

---

[20]Sergio DellaPergola, *La trasformazione demografica della diaspora ebraica* (Torino, 1983).

ship held by North African Jews at the time of decolonization. The overwhelming majority of Algerian Jews, who were French citizens, went to France, while most Moroccan Jews and a majority of Tunisian Jews, who were not, went to Israel. In the process, most of the Jewish upper socioeconomic strata from the three Maghreb communities settled in France, while immigrants to Israel were mostly members of the lower-middle and lower classes.[21]

French Jewry has undergone over the last three generations a thorough socioeconomic metamorphosis,[22] in which the selective character of immigration has figured significantly. The general occupational trend of Jews in France and—as far as the data allow us to ascertain—elsewhere in the EC as well, has been movement away from production and commerce, concentration in the professions and management, and low participation in agriculture, heavy industry, personal services, and public administration. The French case study shows conformity with these trends, though the presence of Jews in public administration is or at least was, until the late 1970s, far higher in France than elsewhere, since many Jews were employed in civil service in the French colonial regime. An interesting consequence for the socioeconomic structure of French Jews after the massive "repatriation" of the early 1960s was that those who were entitled to French government help with tenured jobs and public housing were initially dispersed more widely throughout France and throughout the Greater Paris metropolitan area than those who resettled on their own or with the help of the Jewish community.

Table 7 provides a unique survey of the occupational transformations of French Jewry from the interwar period until 1988. Retrospective data from the 1970s allow a reconstruction of the characteristics of the fathers of contemporary Jewish heads of households, of the foreign-born Jewish labor force on the eve of emigration, and of the current labor force during the 1960s and 1970s. A survey conducted in 1988 provides updated information about the current social characteristics of French Jewry. Fathers of those who were heads of households in the 1970s presumably were economically active during the 1930s. The proportion of "upper cadres"—the French term for higher-status professionals and managers—increased from 9 percent of the fathers of Jewish heads of households living in the Greater Paris area, to 19 percent of the Jewish labor force in the 1960s, and 26 percent

---

[21]Sergio DellaPergola, "Aliya and Other Jewish Migrations: Toward an Integrated Perspective," in *Studies in the Population of Israel in Honor of Roberto Bachi*, ed. U.O. Schmelz and Gad Nathan (Jerusalem, 1986), pp. 172–209; see also Nancy L. Green, "Jewish Migrations to France in the Nineteenth and Twentieth Centuries: Community or Communities?" *Studia Rosenthaliana* (special issue) 23, no. 2, 1989, pp. 135–53.

[22]The following analysis is based on Bensimon and DellaPergola, *La population juive*, and Cohen, *L'Etude et l'éducation juive*.

in the 1970s. It was somewhat lower (15 percent) in French provincial cities in the 1970s where, because of the just mentioned repatriation patterns, one finds a much higher share of "middle cadre" and clerical positions among Jews. In 1988, the proportion of Jewish "upper cadres" was estimated at about 42 percent nationally. Over the period considered here, the proportion of "middle cadres" was fairly stable, around 15–20 percent of the Jewish labor force, while the share of traders and craftsmen declined sharply from 65 percent of the fathers of Jewish heads of households surveyed in the 1970s down to 28 percent of Jews employed in 1988. The blue-collar segment of the Jewish labor force was already small during the interwar period, and remained fairly stable at around or less than 10 percent until the end of the 1970s. From the 1988 data it appears to have declined to less than 2 percent. These data contrast markedly with the general distribution of the total urban French population, which includes lower percentages of "upper cadres" and traders and a substantially higher share of workers in industry and services.

OTHER COUNTRIES

A similar picture emerges from the admittedly scattered data available on the occupational and social-class status of British Jews.[23] Comparisons of different urban and suburban communities, and of different generations within the contemporary Jewish population, indicate an overwhelming predominance of middle-class, professional, technical, and skilled occupations. The upward social mobility of the younger, suburban Jewish population is largely a function of the national expansion of education and training and the increasing diversity of work opportunities in the liberal professions in the United Kingdom. Few Jews can now be found in the traditional working-class occupations, such as the sweated labor in the clothing industry with which immigrant Jews of the London's East End were associated at the beginning of the century.

In countries of the EC with smaller Jewish populations, Jews are less visible in the national socioeconomic context and also have fewer opportunities for occupational differentiation. One of the consequences is a slower pace of social mobility and relatively greater participation in traditional Jewish trades. Even one or two centuries after moving out of the ghetto, there is a strong relationship between occupation, place of residence, and individual behavior. Jewish social interaction tends to be stronger among people who are employed in traditional Jewish economic activities.

One example is Amsterdam, where, during the late 1960s, 47 percent of

---

[23]See Waterman and Kosmin, *British Jewry in the Eighties.*

employed Jews were in occupations that could be termed traditionally Jewish—29 percent in textiles, 9 percent in diamonds, and 9 percent in intellectual professions. These persons displayed more distinctively Jewish behaviors than those found in other types of occupations.[24] There are also examples of significant social-structural differences between Jewish communities within the same country. In Belgium, there is a striking contrast between Antwerp, where the diamond industry has long constituted a prominent enclave of traditional Jewish craftsmanship, and Brussels, the capital city, a more modern environment, where Jews are employed in managerial and professional positions in the bureaucratic economy.[25]

A similar situation exists in Italy, though with reversed roles between cities.[26] In Rome, the capital city, a background of late emancipation from the ghetto has left visible signs of a poorer Jewish economy, long based on peddling and small-scale trade. Although the recent tendency is to move into more ambitious commercial activity, the pace of entry into the professions still lags behind that of other communities. In Milan, a leading international commercial center, a Jewish community with a large immigrant component is heavily engaged in wholesale international trade. At the same time, there has been steady movement into the professions on the part of established Italian Jews and the second generation of immigrant families.

Overall, one can see throughout the EC the meeting of traditional Jewish occupational specialization and know-how in industry, finance, and the professions, based on long experience in the economic life of the Diaspora, with the unique options and opportunities offered by the economy in each specific locale. In the course of time, some trade-off may have occurred between increased occupational prestige and the somewhat diminished prominence of Jewish entrepreneurs. If true, this may have quite mixed consequences for Jewish philanthropy in the long run. In any event, avenues for mobility are greater in the larger and more powerful centers of the world economy than in smaller, more provincial or peripheral localities, and it is in the former that the vast majority of EC Jews reside.

Family Processes and Their Demographic Consequences

To explain the changes that have occurred in the demography of the Jewish family over time, some background on the social characteristics of European Jews will be helpful. One of the main features of European Jewish

---

[24]See Wijnberg, *De Joden in Amsterdam*.

[25]See Liebermann, "Report."

[26]See DellaPergola and Sabatello, "The Italian Jewish Population Study"; Renato Mannheimer, "A Study of the Jewish Community of Milano," in *Papers in Jewish Demography 1989*, ed. U.O. Schmelz and S. DellaPergola (Jerusalem, forthcoming).

demographic trends in the past was the cleavage between east and west. Even though earlier modernization and declining mortality combined with immigration to promote the growth of Western European Jewries, Jewish population grew much faster in Eastern Europe. A common denominator in East and West Europe alike was the distinctively earlier Jewish transition from high to low mortality and fertility levels.[27] Explaining such uniqueness in the context of general demographic trends in Europe requires careful consideration of the Jewish cultural framework, namely, the particular interplay of community, family, and individual in sociodemographic behaviors. Such interaction at different times contributed to reducing morbidity and mortality risks, increased the chances for family formation and reduced the risks of family dissolution, and helped to spread the burdens of family growth. Residential segregation—by region, city, and neighborhood—enhanced the perpetuation of distinctive age-old Jewish demographic and cultural patterns. On the whole, these factors operated less intensively in Western than in Eastern Europe, resulting in less dramatic Jewish population increases.

MARRIAGE AND INTERMARRIAGE

Far removed from these patterns of the past, the Jewish population in the contemporary European Community faces a serious problem of demographic continuity. One leading trend, also present in other Diaspora settings, is the decline of the conventional Jewish family—being currently married, *and* to a Jewish spouse.[28] If the Jewish family of endogamous couple and children was once a cornerstone of corporate Jewish continuity, several relevant indicators point to a process of erosion. These are: a diminished propensity to marry, later marriage, more frequent divorce, less frequent remarriage, low marital fertility, high rate of mixed marriage, and the socialization as Jews of only a minority of the children born to mixed-married couples. Data from a variety of contemporary EC Jewish popula-

[27]See, on the Jewish side: Roberto Bachi, *Population Trends of World Jewry* (Jerusalem, 1976); U.O. Schmelz, "Jewish Survival: The Demographic Factors," AJYB 1981, vol. 81, pp. 61–117; Sergio DellaPergola, "Major Demographic Trends of World Jewry: The Last Hundred Years," in *Genetic Diversity Among Jews: Diseases and Markers at the DNA Level*, ed. B. Bonne-Tamir and A. Adam (New York-Oxford, 1992), pp. 3–30; Barry A. Kosmin, "Nuptiality and Fertility of British Jewry 1850–1980: An Immigrant Transition?" in *Demography of Immigrants and Minority Groups in the United Kingdom*, ed. D.A. Coleman (London, 1982), pp. 245–61. On the general side: Michael W. Flinn, *The European Demographic System 1500–1820* (Brighton, 1981); Ansley J. Coale and Susan C. Watkins, eds., *The Decline of Fertility in Europe* (Princeton, 1986).

[28]These aspects are discussed in detail in Sergio DellaPergola, "Recent Trends in Jewish Marriage," in *World Jewish Population: Trends and Policies*, ed. S. DellaPergola and L. Cohen (Jerusalem, 1992), pp. 65–92.

tions indicate general marriage propensities ranging between 80 and 85 percent of a generation, of whom 10 to 15 percent may be currently divorced at prime reproductive ages, and a rate of outmarriage around or above 50 percent. This implies that considerably less than half the Jewish adults who are at the usual life-cycle stage of child-rearing (roughly ages 30 to 45) find themselves married to another Jew, a status that was once virtually universal.

Contemporary data on mixed marriage, by country, indicate a substantial variation in levels but a consistent pattern of increase. In Germany, the levels reported during the 1970s and 1980s were above 75 percent of the marriages; in Italy and the Netherlands above 50 percent; in France around 50 percent, but still with a significant differential between Jews of longtime European origin and recent immigrants from North Africa—the latter with lower levels but following the general trend toward heterogamy. Conversion in the context of marriage has been much less frequent in Europe than in America, probably because intermarriage generally occurs in a secular environment.

Data from France, Italy, and the Netherlands for the 1960s and 1970s consistently show that a majority of the children of mixed couples are not raised as Jews. Interestingly, in Italy and France, again unlike the trend prevailing in America, the more influential parent in the religious upbringing of a child of mixed marriage is the father. This may produce conflict between the traditional Jewish rules of matrilineal identity transmission and the subjective decisions and feelings in many households. Overall, however, intermarriage is a definite factor in the lowering of the "effectively" Jewish birthrate, which refers to only that part of the newborn generation raised as Jews.

FERTILITY; AGING

Jews in EC countries were among the first to experience an early drop in the birthrate. The data in table 8 illustrate the cases of three countries for which relatively accurate data are available: Germany, Italy, and the United Kingdom. The patterns are similar, although the timing and intensity of the decline in each were quite different, especially as each national experience was differently affected by the Holocaust. In each instance, however, the Jewish birthrate eventually dropped considerably below that of the total population. In the more recent period, the latter too has declined to unprecedentedly low levels.[29]

The same trends are described for France through a reconstruction of the

---

[29]Commission des Communautés Européennes, Cellule de Prospective, *L'Europe dans le movement démographique* (Brussels, 1990).

Total Fertility Rates (TFR) of Jewish and total women over the last 60 years (table 9). The TFR measures the number of children that would be born under the age-specific fertility levels of the observed year. It is a better measure than the crude birthrate, since it is less affected by a population's age structure. Especially since the late 1960s, a marked drop occurred in the TFR among French Jews, and even more significantly, in the "effectively Jewish" fertility level. Among Jewish women in France and presumably most other EC countries, as early as the early 1970s, typical TFRs tended to range around an average of 1.5 children—or 40 percent less than among the French total population. The trend among the total population has since been one of continuing decline, which allows for the presumption that even if the Jewish TFR stabilized and did not continue to decline, it remained extremely low. Similar declining fertility patterns—albeit starting significantly later and somewhat attenuated—have also appeared among Jews who migrated to France in the course of the last few decades from the more traditional Jewish environments in North Africa.

Under contemporary conditions of low mortality, the level required for the replacement of a generation would be 2.1 children per woman. In other words, if—as seems likely—the fertility data for France represent the experience of other countries as well, the estimated average fertility of 1.5 children means that Jewish populations are now experiencing an intrinsic "demographic overdraft" of roughly 25–30 percent of the size of the present generation. This points inevitably to an older age distribution and a smaller population size in the next generation.

Low fertility is indeed a powerful determinant in the process of population aging now visible throughout the EC population in general, and more markedly among the Jews (table 10). Among the Jewish minority, as noted, the general effects of low fertility, combined with attrition in Jewish identification and intensifying intermarriage, are wearing away the younger segment of the age distribution. Table 10 demonstrates the trends and range of variation in age distribution among the Jewish populations in 10 of the 12 EC countries. Nearly without exception, the median age has been increasing, reflecting the declining proportion of Jewish children. Often, the percentage of the latter is lower than that of the elderly aged 65 and over.

Within this general picture, a few differentials are worth noting. The Jewish population in France is significantly younger than that in any other EC country, thanks to the relatively high birthrate that still prevailed in North Africa before the great wave of migration. But a projection of data from the 1970s up to 1990 indicates that aging is a universal trend among European Jews. The degree of aging in larger communities that have attracted immigration tends be somewhat lower than in smaller ones, which may have lost some of their younger adults to the larger centers. Jewish populations tend to be older in central cities than in suburban areas (in table

10, compare the urban Hackney and suburban Redbridge data within the Greater London area, or the central city and suburbs in Greater Paris). Finally, differences in age structure may reflect the different character of local Jewish communities. Such is the case in Belgium, where the more religious community in Antwerp is younger than the more secular one in Brussels.

The end product of the chain of sociocultural and demographic processes that produced an overaged Jewish population structure is an increasing crude death rate and a negative balance between the number of births and deaths (see table 8). One poignant example of this is contained in the vital statistics collected by the Community Research Unit of the Board of Deputies of British Jews.[30] The average annual excess of Jewish deaths over Jewish births in the United Kingdom was 1,674 in 1975–79, 1,840 in 1980–84, 1,108 in 1985–89, and 1,519 in 1990. This corresponds to a Jewish population loss of nearly 25,000 over a period of 16 years, out of a Jewish population estimated at 330,000–350,000 in the mid-1970s and downwardly revised to 300,000 in 1991. While the situation in the UK is quite typical of most other Jewish communities across Europe, it is by no means the most extreme on record. Smaller communities in the EC, as shown by the German and Italian data in table 8, have been experiencing much sharper variations of the same trend.

Low fertility, assimilation, aging, and a negative balance of births and deaths have resulted in what appears to be an irreversible erosion of Jewish population across the EC. Jewish immigration from the crisis-stricken communities in Eastern Europe toward the more affluent and stable communities of the EC can be a palliative, but only as long as no significant reversals take place in the complex of social and demographic factors that determine Jewish population continuity. Jewish family processes within the EC have converged, anticipating to a large extent the current demographic profile of most European societies. Any interpretation of the present pattern and its implications for the future must take into account the transformation of norms, goals, and aspirations of contemporary young adults in the individualistic and secular context of postindustrial European society.[31] As things stand now, the weight of European Community Jewry in the global Jewish picture is clearly diminishing.

[30]The Board of Deputies of British Jews, Community Research Unit, *Annual Report on Vital Statistics* (London, yearly); Marlena Schmool, "Synagogue Marriages in Britain in the 1980s," *Jewish Journal of Sociology* 33, no. 2, 1991.

[31]Ron Lesthaeghe and Johan Surkyn, "Cultural Dynamics and Economic Theories of Fertility Change," *Population and Development Review* 14, no. 1, 1988, pp. 1–45; David A. Coleman, "European Demographic Systems of the Future: Convergence or Diversity?" *Conference Proceedings: Human Resources in Europe at the Dawn of the 21st Century* (Luxembourg, 1992), pp. 137–79.

Aspects of Jewish Identification

As noted earlier, because Jewish identity in Western Europe was predominantly patterned along religious rather than ethnic lines,[32] Jews who were swept up in the extensive secularization of general European society found themselves without alternative avenues for the expression of their Jewishness. One exception was Israel, whose emergence as a state after 1948, and especially with the Six Day War of 1967, provided a powerful new magnet of attraction and a focus for mobilization within the Jewish communities— although, given the complex circumstances of the Middle East, Israel also came to represent a focus of internal dissent.

Based on the actual evidence about the patterns and intensity of Jewish practice and identification, one can describe EC Jewry as being largely secular, having only a minority of intensively practicing Jews, yet with a broad consensus about a necessary minimum of Jewish symbolic interaction. In the European context, this minimum seems to include three elements: interest in Israel—though not necessarily support; performing a Jewish ritual once a year—most likely attending some form of a seder on Passover; and having one's male children circumcised. Not conforming with this bare minimum means intentional self-exclusion from even the loosest definition of a Jewish community, though a residual sense of Jewish identity may take the form of a general interest in Jewish culture, something that is shared today by a significant public of non-Jews.

The whole range of intensity of behaviors and attitudes, from least to most intensive, obviously exists within the Jewish population. Along the intensity continuum one can distinguish three main divisions: a relatively small coherently Jewish subcommunity that remains to a large extent segregated from the majority of general society; a much larger community of those who conform or participate in Jewish communal life in selective ways; and a growing minority of assimilated or absentee Jews. The particular modes of operating and the relative sizes of these major types clearly vary across the different EC countries, but in general terms, this tentative typology seems to apply well to each of them.

SELECTED INDICATORS OF JEWISHNESS

Table 11 reports a selection of data on the frequency of some indicators of Jewishness in three EC countries. The data were compiled from different Jewish population surveys: in France, in the Greater Paris area during the 1970s and in the five major French provincial communities in 1978; in Italy,

---

[32]For a general assessment of the topic, see David Martin, *A General Theory of Secularization* (New York, 1978); Anthony D. Smith, "The Question of Jewish Identity," *Studies in Contemporary Jewry* 8 (New York, 1992), pp. 219–33.

nationally in 1965 and in Milan in 1986; in the United Kingdom, in the Outer London suburb of Redbridge in 1978 and through a survey of the members of the mainstream Orthodox United Synagogue in 1991.[33] Although the data are not as systematic as one might wish, they reveal some significant patterns of similarity as well as variations between the different Jewish communities.

One main element of Jewish identification is the meaning given by the respondents to their attachment to Judaism. In France during the 1970s, this meaning was principally religious, consistent with the already noted European view of Judaism as a religion. Other more secular-ethnic modes of attachment, such as history, community, or the family, played a much smaller role in the Jewish identification of French Jews. A much higher frequency of religious identification in the French provinces than in the Greater Paris area reflects the relatively greater presence in the former of Jewish immigrants from North Africa, who espouse a more traditional view of Judaism. The second most frequently cited meaning of Judaism is a sense of "Jewishness"—something clearly experienced by respondents but neither clearly defined nor necessarily positive in terms of its content.

The Italian data for the 1980s point to a much more secular outlook; the family, Jewish history, and Israel emerge as the principal channels of individual Jewish identification. It is hard to say whether the difference between Jews in Milan in the 1980s and French Jews in the 1970s is due only to the different composition of the respective communities or whether a time effect is at work as well—in other words, that data on French Jews today would be closer to the Italian data reported here.

There is greater consistency between the several sets of data regarding the frequency of Jewish practices such as synagogue attendance, eating matzah on Passover, fasting on Yom Kippur, observing the Sabbath, and keeping kosher. Despite some geographic variation, the distribution of synagogue attendance is quite symmetric in each place, with a plurality attending only on the High Holy Days, festivals, and special family events (such as weddings or bar mitzvahs), and two relatively balanced minorities of people who attend either more often or virtually never. The proportion never attending synagogue appears to be higher in France than elsewhere.

Generally, Passover offers the occasion for the most participation in Jewish observance. Very high proportions of Jewish households (ranging between 79 and 91 percent in the various surveys) say they eat matzah;

[33]See, respectively, Bensimon and DellaPergola, *La population juive*; Cohen, *L'Etude et l'éducation juive*; Renato Mannheimer and Adriana Goldstaub, *Indagine demografico sociologico attitudinale sulla comunità di Milano* (unpublished manuscript; abstracts appeared in *Bollettino della Comunità Israelitica di Milano*, 1988); Barry A. Kosmin and Caren Levy, *Jewish Identity in an Anglo-Jewish Community* (London, 1983); Stanley Kalms, *A Time for Change: United Synagogue Review* (London, 1992).

however, the percentages of those who abstain from consuming leavened bread are significantly lower. Fasting on Yom Kippur tends to be observed by slightly fewer persons than those observing some Passover rituals (with the exception of the Redbridge sample). The levels of observance of the Sabbath and dietary laws are much lower, especially when the distinction is made between casual or occasional observance and strict compliance with Jewish laws and customs. Some Sabbath observance was more frequent in Redbridge (and by reasonable assumption elsewhere in the United Kingdom as well) than in France or Italy. With regard to Belgium, there are no direct data on religious observance; however, counts of the total seating capacity in synagogues and *shtiebels* (prayer rooms) in the 1980s provide one indirect indicator of the demand for Jewish religious facilities. In Antwerp and Brussels, which have Jewish populations of roughly the same size (see table 6), the situation was quite different, with about 9,500 places counted in the former community and about 4,000 in the latter.[34]

While the evidence indicates a significant decline in Jewish religious practice over the past, it also points to some revival among the younger age groups, albeit with some extreme forms of estrangement present as well. Religious practice appears to be strongly affected by the life-cycle stage of a person or household. The changing Jewish character of these stages might be informally described as "youthful enthusiasm," "young-adulthood decline" (in the context of other—mainly economic—cares), "child-rearing revival," and "old-age decline," as physical problems and isolation objectively limit the ability to take part in Jewish observance.

Jewish religious observance tends to decline with rising levels of educational attainment. One of the intervening factors here is the higher rate of mixed marriage that, at least in the past, occurred among better-educated Jews. There is some evidence that the frequency of outmarriage has now increased substantially among the lower social strata of the Jewish population, which in EC countries generally constitute a relatively small minority of the Jewish population. The poorer sections of the Jewish community may feel excluded from organized Jewish life, among other reasons because of the rather high costs entailed in Jewish community membership and participation. Another obstacle to wider Jewish participation is the somewhat elitist character of many programs aimed at deepening familiarity with Jewish culture. At the same time, it should be noted that mass mobilization of Jews did occur in Western Europe whenever Israel was in difficulty and a show of solidarity on the part of Diaspora Jewry was needed.[35]

---

[34]See Liebermann, "Report."

[35]Izhak Sergio Minerbi, Adolphe Steg, and Chaim Perelman, "Western Europe," in *The Yom Kippur War, Israel and the Jewish People*, ed. M. Davis (New York, 1974), pp. 183–218.

RELIGIOUS DENOMINATION

Another significant aspect of Jewish identification is that of religious denomination, which represents an interesting juncture between the individual's needs and preferences and what the Jewish communal structure offers. In this regard, EC communities differ strikingly from North American Jewry, with the Orthodox denomination having a relatively dominant share of the European Jewish public.[36] The counterparts of Conservative and Reform movements exist in some EC countries, such as the United Kingdom, France, Belgium, and the Netherlands, but their share of the total Jewish population is comparatively small. No such congregations exist in Italy, Spain, or Greece.

A likely interpretation of this major difference between EC and American Jewries is that in American society, although it is formally secular, organized religion serves an important function as a primary, albeit nominal, channel both for individual identification and community organization.[37] Thus, changes in personal philosophy and attitudes, or even growing secularization, have not necessarily led to the decline of religious institutions; rather, the institutions have reformulated their content and style, or new churches and similar frameworks have been created. In Europe, on the other hand, civic and religious institutions often found themselves in a situation of conflict, with the success of one working to the detriment of the other. Secularization often led people to drop out from religion altogether. Although the original movement seeking to create Jewish religious institutions that would merge Jewish content with modern ideas and approaches, Reform Judaism, developed in Germany in the 19th century, no comparable movements emerged in postwar Western Europe as serious alternatives to Orthodoxy, on the one hand, and to complete secularism, on the other. As a result, the predominant religious identification of European Jewry is Orthodox, nominal though it is for many individual Jews.

In the United Kingdom, where mainstream Orthodoxy has long been the leading force, there has been a consistent move away from it over recent decades.[38] Between 1970 and 1990, the share of Greater London male synagogue membership held by the United Synagogue declined from 72 to 58 percent; the similarly mainstream small Sephardi Orthodox sector re-

[36]Compare our European data with the situation in the United States in Sidney Goldstein, "Profile of American Jewry: Insights from the 1990 National Jewish Population Survey," AJYB 1992, vol. 92, pp. 77–173.

[37]See Will Herberg, *Protestant, Catholic, Jew: An Essay in American Religious Sociology* (Chicago, 1955); Jack Wertheimer, "Recent Trends in American Judaism," AJYB 1989, vol. 89, pp. 63–162.

[38]See Barry A. Kosmin and Caren Levy, *Synagogue Membership in the United Kingdom 1983* (London, 1983); Schmool and Cohen, *British Synagogue Membership in 1990*.

mained stable at around 4 percent; the right-wing Orthodox sector increased from 3 to 9 percent; the Reform sector (similar to the American Conservative movement) increased from 12 to 18 percent; and the Liberal sector (close to American Reform) increased from 9 to 11 percent. It appears from this that British Jewry is becoming polarized, with the so-called right and left wings gaining at the expense of the center. In France, one indicator of the weakness of the progressive community relative to the mainstream Orthodox Consistorial or right-wing Orthodox is the fact that, during the late 1970s and early 1980s, only about 7 percent of synagogue marriages in the Greater Paris area were celebrated by the Union Libérale.

A 1991 survey of the United Synagogue, the mainstream Orthodox organization in the United Kingdom, confirms the nominal character of a substantial proportion of the membership, with 23 percent labeling themselves weak observers (of these, 4 percent self-described nonreligious Jews, 16 percent just Jewish, 3 percent progressive), 67 percent traditional, and 10 percent strictly Orthodox Jews. Of those who describe themselves as traditional, 88 percent travel on the Sabbath, and 95 percent turn on electric lights on the Sabbath. Overall, the frequency of synagogue attendance among United Synagogue members does not seem to differ substantially from that of a general sample of Jews.

Apart from the religious sphere, other significant paths for expressing Jewish identification do exist and are manifested in EC Jewish communities, as elsewhere in the Diaspora. The level of interest in the Middle East and, by implication, the State of Israel, is extremely high—in fact, the highest of any other indicator of Jewishness (see table 11). The available data show considerable variation in the percentage of visitors to Israel from the different Jewish communities, which can be explained in part by a time effect. An increase in tourism during the last 10–15 years has most probably contributed to raising the percentages of visitors above those reported in the 1970s for France and the UK (where in this respect Redbridge may not be entirely typical), making them somewhat closer to the 80 percent reported for Milan in 1986. High percentages of the Jewish public say they are interested in Judaism, showing their interest through, among other ways, reading books on Jewish topics and Jewish periodicals, following the Jewish press, and keeping up with current developments in Jewish literature, history, and Judaic studies.

GENERAL EUROPEAN TRENDS

To properly understand the data on Jewish identification, we need to view them in the comparative context of general social and intellectual trends in the EC and in European society at large.[39] The historical process of secularization has been accompanied by a decline in religious practice and a lessened willingness of young Europeans to commit themselves to religious vocations. Large-scale surveys, such as the 1981 European Values Study, provide interesting insights into the religious attitudes and practices of the general public. Wherever the data can be analyzed by age groups or compared with similar earlier observations, a conclusion of ongoing erosion in religious and national values is inescapable. At the same time, younger cohorts put more emphasis on a more subjective elaboration of norms and on achieving personal goals. If, as some maintain,[40] a form of secular religion has taken hold, it can be argued that it lacks the binding content and corporate sanction that characterize traditional religion. Facing a general crisis of religious values in contemporary Western societies, efforts are in fact being made by the established religions, chiefly the Catholic Church, to reconquer the lost ground through concerted evangelical activity in Europe.[41]

In 1981, a majority in each of the EC countries investigated said they believed in God, but the frequencies ranged from 58–65 percent in Denmark, the Netherlands, and France; to 72–77 percent in Germany, the United Kingdom, and Belgium; 84–87 percent in Italy and Spain; and 95 percent in Ireland.[42] The proportions attending religious services once a month or more often varied roughly in the same way across the different countries, but the range of variation was much greater, with a minimum of 12 percent in Denmark and a maximum of 88 percent in Ireland. In France, the United Kingdom, and Italy (countries whose Jewish populations are covered in table 11), attendance among the general population at religious services once a month or more was 18 percent, 23 percent, and 52 percent, respectively. Comparing these data with the proportions of Jews attending a synagogue on High Holy Days, festivals, and some Sabbaths, or more often, we can estimate that Jews attend religious services more frequently than the general population in France and the United Kingdom, and less frequently than in Italy. The general population's attendance figure for Italy

---

[39]R. Inglehart, *The Silent Revolution: Changing Values and Political Styles Among Western Publics* (Princeton, 1977).

[40]T. Luckmann, *The Invisible Religion* (London, 1967); John Simons, "Culture, Economy and Reproduction in Contemporary Europe," in *The State of Population Theory: Forward from Malthus*, ed. D. Coleman and R. Schofield (Oxford, 1986), pp. 256–78.

[41]A significant initiative in this sense was the publication in November 1992 of a new, modernized version of basic Catholic doctrine: *Catéchisme de l'Eglise catholique* (Paris, 1992).

[42]Jean Stoetzel, *Les valeurs du temps présent: une enquête européenne* (Paris, 1983); S. Harding, D. Philips, and M. Fogarty, *Contrasting Values in Western Europe* (Basingstoke, 1986).

actually looks quite high, in light of the observed social patterns there during the last decade.

Although there are serious limitations to these comparisons, the impression is that the sweeping secularization process in Western Europe has radically reduced the extent of religious observance among Jews and non-Jews alike, but that a comparatively larger section of the Jewish community seems to have resisted these trends. This is true in terms of both the resilience of the relatively small "hard core" of regularly practicing Jews and the preservation of a minimum of normative or traditional behaviors among a much larger section of the community—no matter how secularized on the whole. This being the case, it may be necessary to reexamine the widespread perception that the fabric of European Jewish communal life is seriously weakened. Such a process is indeed taking place, but it is part of a general European trend of decline in traditional forms of identification that is comparatively even greater.

The recent evidence on changing religiosity patterns in the EC offers strong support for the interpretation offered earlier of marriage and fertility declines. The marriage-and-baby boom of the 1950s and early 1960s and the subsequent decline that started in the mid-1960s and continued into the mid-1970s closely correspond to changes in general religious orientation, as measured by such phenomena as the percentage of Easter communicants in England and Wales and the number of novices entering the clergy in France.[43] As with religion, elementary family processes that once represented the nearly universal norm seem now to have become expressions of highly ideological and optional choices. On the Jewish side, the evidence is accumulating that inmarriage has become the voluntary, conscious expression of a preference for Jewish continuity instead of the automatic, normatively determined behavior it once was.

In summarizing their analysis of French Jewry in the 1970s, Bensimon and DellaPergola estimated that about one-quarter could be considered religious or strongly traditional, one-half otherwise communally involved, and one-quarter quite marginal. In the late 1980s, based on a more recent survey, Cohen evaluated the proportion of observing Jews at 15 percent, with 49 percent considered traditionalists and 36 percent nonobservant.[44] Even if the concepts compared are not identical, the change does not seem to be drastic.

---

[43]See John Simons, "Reproductive Behavior as Religious Practice," in *Determinants of Fertility Trends: Theories Re-examined*, ed. C. Hohn and R. Mackensen (Liege, 1982), pp. 133–145; Guy Michelat, Julien Potel, Jacques Sutter, and Jacques Maitre, *Les Français sont-ils encore catholiques?* (Paris, 1991); Silvano Burgalassi, *Il comportamento religioso degli italiani* (Florence, 1968).

[44]See, respectively, Bensimon and DellaPergola, *La population juive*; Cohen, *L'Etude et l'éducation juive*.

In Italy, similar conclusions can be reached by comparing the data on Jewishness of the 1960s and the 1980s, and comparable observations would probably apply to the Jews in Belgium, Spain, and possibly Germany. It would appear, then, that the Jewish identification of EC Jews has been relatively stable. One important qualification relates to the effects of immigration. In Italy, in the intervening period, substantial Jewish immigration from relatively more traditional backgrounds added fresh blood to the existing community. In France, many immigrants who in the 1960s were too busy coping with the initial stages of integration to be involved in Jewish community activities, by the 1980s were in the forefront of the community.[45]

From World War II to the present, a continuous influx of new forces was instrumental in replenishing EC Jewries and strengthening the Jewish identification of their members. Now, however, apart from the uncertain Jewish impact of possible newcomers from the former USSR, the traditional reservoirs of Jewish immigration are empty. It is essentially with their own existing forces that Western European Jews will have to face the challenges of Jewish continuity in the future.

Ways of Response: The Jewish Educational System

Among the different possible corporate responses of a Jewish community facing the challenge of transmitting a viable Jewish identification, Jewish education is one of the most significant.[46] In Europe, as in other parts of the Diaspora, the role of the Jewish school has been elevated to that of a sort of proxy for the Jewish family, which in many cases and unlike earlier generations lacks the ability to socialize its own children as Jews. As a result, education is now a major item in the overall financial picture of a community. For these reasons, the structural characteristics of the Jewish educational system in the EC merit brief examination.[47]

---

[45]See, e.g., Claude Tapia, *Les juifs sépharades en France (1965–1985); études psychosociologiques et historiques* (Paris, 1986); Martine Cohen, "Les Juifs en France: Renouveau ou assimilation: un faux dilemme," in Michel André et al., *Sortie des religions, retour du religieux* (Lille, 1992), pp. 101–21.

[46]A systematic sociological-historical analysis can be found in Harold S. Himmelfarb and Sergio DellaPergola, eds., *Jewish Education Worldwide: Crosscultural Perspectives* (Lanham, 1989). See there in particular the three articles on Jewish education in Western Europe: Adrian Ziderman, "Jewish Education in Great Britain," pp. 267–300; Yair Auron and Lucien Lazare, "Jewish Education in France," pp. 301–32; Stanley Abramowitz, "Jewish Education in Other Western European Countries," pp. 333–54.

[47]The following analysis is based on a selection of the main sources of data available on the quantitative aspects of Jewish education. Two Censuses of Jewish Schools in the Diaspora have been coordinated by the Project for Jewish Educational Statistics at the A. Harman Institute of Contemporary Jewry of the Hebrew University of Jerusalem. See Nitza Genuth, Sergio DellaPergola, and Allie A. Dubb, *First Census of Jewish Schools in the Diaspora*

Within the network of Jewish educational institutions in EC countries, day schools now play the predominant role. This had been the established pattern in some of the smaller Western European Jewish communities, but not so in the two largest, France and the United Kingdom, where as late as the 1970s the predominant mode of Jewish education was part-time. *Talmud torahs* in the French-speaking communities and *heders* in the English-speaking ones were run largely by the central Jewish institutions responsible for religious affairs, such as the Consistoire Israélite or the United Synagogue's London Board of Religious Education. Their approach reflected the view that the Jew, as an emancipated and equal citizen, would receive his or her basic education in the framework of a country's public education system and would acquire Jewish culture and learning through special supplementary activities.

Historical developments, among which the two principal ones were the anti-Jewish discrimination of the early Holocaust period—when Jews were barred from public schools—and the large postwar Jewish immigration to Western Europe—requiring the integration of many, often deprived, newcomers into the Jewish community—led to growing recognition of a need for Jewish private schools. A more recent factor stimulating the demand for Jewish day schools was disillusionment with a public-school system beset by social, disciplinary, and curricular problems. Over the years, growing proportions of the Jewish public came to accept the inherent value of independent Jewish schooling. Indeed, the interest in developing a Jewish day-school network in different EC countries has increased in intensity in recent years. Initiatives in this area have been taken by central Jewish community organizations, such as the FSJU in France, by ad hoc sponsoring or coordinating bodies, such as the American Jewish Joint Distribution Committee on a continental scale or the Jewish Educational Development Trust in the UK, and by smaller educational networks representing different shades of religious orientation or specific institutions, such as Lubavitch, Otzar Hatorah, and ORT.

FRANCE-UK COMPARISON

Table 12 describes some of the main structural characteristics of Jewish education in France and the United Kingdom between 1981 and 1992. The

1981/2–1982/3; International Summary (Jerusalem, 1985); Sergio DellaPergola, Uzi Rebhun, and Daliah Sagi, *Second Census of Jewish Schools in the Diaspora 1986/7–1988/9; Preliminary Report* (Jerusalem, 1992, mimeo). See also Sergio DellaPergola and Nitza Genuth, *Jewish Education Attained in Diaspora Communities, Data for 1970s* (Jerusalem, 1983). The more recent data are derived from Jewish Educational Development Trust, *Securing Our Future: An Inquiry into Jewish Education in the United Kingdom* (London, 1992); Prosper Elkoubi, *Données sur les écoles juives à plein temps en France* (Paris, 1992, mimeo).

changing enrollment patterns should be understood in the light of the recent Jewish demographic trends noted above. For example, the decline in the overall number of Jewish pupils in the UK reflects the diminishing demographic base of that community; however, it is accompanied by stability or even moderate growth in the enrollment rate per 100 Jewish children of school age (3 to 17). The current Jewish school enrollment is moderately high in the UK, around 55 percent of the potential target population. Taking into account pupils who are exposed to Jewish education for short periods, the rate of those ever enrolled in a Jewish day or part-time school is close to 80 percent. Jewish school enrollment rates in France tend to be lower, in fact the lowest within EC Jewish communities. In France, since the post-World War II period, the effort to develop the Jewish school system has lagged behind the pace of population growth. However, the data for the late 1980s and early 1990s point to substantial increases. Overall, probably more than 35 percent of eligible children were currently enrolled in a Jewish day or part-time school in 1991–92, up from 24 percent ten years earlier. With regard to Jewish schools in other EC countries, data from the early 1980s indicate an intermediate current enrollment rate of around 36–40 percent, on the average.

One significant factor in the impact of Jewish schooling is the duration of exposure. The general tendency in Jewish day schools is a relatively high enrollment at the early elementary level and substantial dropping out with the passage to higher grades, especially at the transition from elementary to high school. The 1980s saw a significant increase in enrollment at the pre-primary level, possibly tied to the expanded participation of women in the labor force. Moreover, there are differences between countries in the emphasis placed on the educational effort at different age levels. In France the major effort has been devoted to post-primary education. In 1986–87, 46 percent of the enrollment in Jewish day schools in France was at ages 12–17, versus 34 percent in the United Kingdom in 1990–91 (see table 12). Part-time Jewish education is concentrated around the ages of bar-bat mitzvah, although enrollment covers the age spectrum between 3 and 17.

The role of different ideological streams is another important facet of the Jewish school system. Since most Jewish day schools, whether sponsored by a central Jewish community body at the national or local level or by a more distinctly ideological organization, service a general Jewish constituency, they tend to have student bodies from heterogeneous Jewish backgrounds. However, in larger communities where several Jewish day schools exist, recent trends point to the growth of schools that hold to more stringent religious standards. In 1986–87, 30 percent of the pupils in Jewish day schools in France attended mainstream Orthodox schools, while 26 percent were in right-wing Orthodox schools—which, among other curricular features, do not allow notice to be taken of Israel Independence Day. In the UK, the student body was split equally between mainstream and right-wing Orthodox day schools, each with 38 percent of the enrollment. The share held by general, nondenominational Jewish community schools has been increasing, too, while the Liberal and Progressive movements are barely represented in the day-school system. Part-time Jewish schools are dominated by the respective mainstream Orthodox movements in the various countries.

Most Jewish day schools are subject to some form of public control. In France, a growing number have obtained some financial support from the government, which regards private schooling as being in the public interest. Similar arrangements exist in several other EC countries. The curriculum of Jewish schools must satisfy the general educational requirements of each country, to which varying amounts of Hebrew and Judaic studies are added. As a result, the variation in the Jewish school curricula between EC countries can be substantial. For example, in 1981–82, a Jewish day-school pupil in the 12–14 age group received an average of 11.1 hours per week of instruction in Hebrew and Judaic studies in France, versus 9.9 hours in the United Kingdom, and 6.2 hours in the rest of the EC countries. These differences reflect, among other things, the different length of the school day in the various locales. Where the general curriculum is based on longer schooling hours, there are more hours for Judaic instruction. On the other hand, the part-time programs are far less intensive, as they are based on one or two weekly sessions, and it can also be assumed that the attendance of pupils is somewhat less regular than in the case of day schools.

Finally, the number and quality of teaching personnel in EC Jewish schools compare favorably overall with those of Jewish schools elsewhere in the Diaspora. The number of teachers in Jewish schools appears to have increased over the 1980s, though some of the increase may simply reflect improvement in the quality of data. Regarding the educational attainment of teachers in Jewish day schools, a fair proportion are college graduates and holders of professional certificates. The level of general and especially Jewish education is lower among teachers in part-time Jewish schools.

The critical question in relation to Jewish education is how it affects the Jewish identification of those who are exposed to it. The evidence available from research in different countries, such as France, Italy, and the United Kingdom, is somewhat mixed. Jewish schooling definitely provides information and intellectual concepts, as well as a solid Jewish environment for the socialization of Jewish youth. All in all, though, the influence of family background appears to be stronger and more lasting than that of formal Jewish education.[48] Also, informal and less expensive Jewish frameworks such as youth movements may prove to be equivalent to formal schooling in their effect on Jewish identification.[49] Still, the plain fact is that Jewish schools now reach the majority—and in some countries the overwhelming majority—of the younger Jewish generation at some time in their lives. At least potentially, therefore, they constitute a powerful instrument in the effort to create a Jewishly aware and educated base for the Jewish community of the future, or at least to counteract the de-Judaizing influences emanating from the general environment. To make the Jewish school system more effective in reaching its objectives is one of the most pressing challenges to the organized Jewish community in the EC, as it is elsewhere.

Some Conclusions and Implications

Our attempt to present a cohesive picture of Jewish population and community in the European Community may be premature, if not naive. What we have been dealing with in this article are two entities which to a large extent do not yet exist: an integrated, functional European Community, and within it an EC-conscious Jewish community. We stressed that the Jewish community in each of the EC member countries essentially functions separately, so that most observers would probably consider the only relevant frame of reference for the analysis of Jewish affairs still to be a national one. Yet, several significant common patterns do exist across EC countries that allow for the formulation of a few synthetic conclusions. On the basis of the trends that have been discussed here, we suggest that European Jewry can be viewed in terms of two alternative models: a "community of presence" vs. a "community of continuity."

Given the devastation and trauma of the Holocaust, it is surely remarkable that the Jews residing in the boundaries of the EC rebounded from their losses and achieved socioeconomic and cultural success, public visibility, and recognition. International migration contributed to the viability of these communities, but that only partially explains their staying power. One may cautiously hypothesize that the size and viability of Jewish populations are significantly associated with, if not entirely explained by, the nature of the societies within which Jews found themselves and with which they interacted. The general socioeconomic forces operating in the European

[48]Stephen Miller, "The Impact of Jewish Education on the Religious Behaviour and Attitudes of British Secondary School Pupils," in *Studies in Jewish Education* 3, ed. J. Aviad (Jerusalem, 1988), pp. 150–65.
[49]Erik H. Cohen, *The World of Informal Jewish Education* (Jerusalem, 1992).

market functioned as powerful poles of attraction or repulsion in the process of settlement of Jewish individuals, and accordingly did or did not generate conditions favorable to a viable Jewish community life. Three apparently essential prerequisites for a successful Jewish presence are a democratic political system, a culture permitting pluralism of expression, and freedom of movement. Based on these criteria, the recent EC experience has been quite favorable for Jews, allowing for the emergence of a lively "community of presence." However, socioeconomic and sociopolitical market forces are mutable by nature; a Jewish presence that relies exclusively or mostly on such premises, should its supporting base topple, may vanish quite rapidly.

A "community of continuity," by contrast, is one that has the strength and capacity to survive in the long run, based on solid demographic processes and the ability to nurture and transmit an original cultural identity from generation to generation. While not necessarily immune to the general market forces operating in society at large, such a community finds major support in an internal value system and the community's own institutional network. The ability to do this—which existed throughout most of the Jewish historical experience—appears uncertain in the light of recent demographic trends in EC Jewish communities, although it surely can be found in particular segments within them. Erosion of the family, assimilation, and the dilution and blurring of Jewish identity at the periphery of the community make the task of demographic and cultural continuity increasingly complicated and uncertain. Still, ways of responding, as shown by the Jewish educational system, exist and can achieve significant results.

How will the Jews fit into the new Europe? At this juncture, it is impossible to suggest a prognosis for the future based on either the past Jewish experience in Europe or the present. The international scene is extremely fluid, and the nature of the emerging European order is shrouded in uncertainty. What is clear is that whatever the thrust of social, economic, cultural, and political change in Europe, it is bound to affect the profile and in fact the very existence of Jewish communities on the continent.

A Europe that is open, pluralistic, and tolerant will offer fertile ground in which Jewish communities can thrive and in turn bestow benefits on society at large. Under such circumstances, the relatively small yet highly selective and geographically concentrated Jewish community might even become significant politically.[50] An interesting case in point is the French

---

[50]On the general significance and trends of Jewish political behavior in some Western European countries, see Dominique Schnapper and Sylvie Strudel, "Le vote juif en France," *Revue française de science politique*, Feb. 1984; Jacky Akoka, "Vote juif ou vote des juifs? Structure et comportement electoral des juifs de France," *Pardes* 1, 1985, pp. 114–37; Geoffrey Alderman, *The Jewish Community in British Politics* (Oxford, 1983); Sergio DellaPergola, *Anatomia*, ch. 15.

vote on the Maastricht treaty on September 20, 1992, in which a scant majority of the total French electorate (less than 51 percent) voted in favor, but Jews (roughly 1 percent of the total population) may have delivered the decisive one percentage point needed to save European economic integration. If this assumption is true, then Jews clearly and resolutely expressed their preference for a manifesto of stability and prosperity in Europe.

If, on the other hand, Europe experiences a revival of ethnic tribalism and national conflicts, or even religious fundamentalism, with the inevitable intolerance for diversity, Jews and other minorities will be in an untenable position. In this regard, the Jews share the fate of many others, such as the large numbers of foreign workers who have entered the EC in recent years, Gypsies, several Protestant and Evangelical minorities in Catholic countries, and most significantly, a rapidly growing Muslim population. At the same time, the uniqueness of their experience has produced heightened sensitivity among Jews. Jews do not need physical violence to put them on the alert; symbolic violence may be enough. Under conditions of crisis, self-defense mechanisms would have to be activated, including complete disentanglement as a last resort. This would of course be a most disruptive and tragic outcome, not only for European Jews but for the European Community itself.

In the light of both historical and contemporary experience, it would seem advisable for European Jews to cultivate an integrated view of themselves. To the extent that a united Europe becomes a permanent reality, the Jews and their institutions will be better off fitting into it rather than ignoring or escaping it. If European Jewry is to take full advantage of the intellectual, socioeconomic, and political weight of its one-million strong constituency, it must find ways to bridge the provincial or particularistic divisions that prevail. Even in the face of a general erosion of traditional norms and beliefs, there seems to be a still unmet demand for Jewish culture and identity, which should be thoughtfully evaluated and satisfied. To slow the pace of demographic erosion, greater resources must be invested in education, and there must be integration between communities continentally. If pragmatic choices have to be made, priority should be given to the larger, stronger centers of greater vitality in an integrated Europe rather than to the smaller, weaker, and dispersed periphery. Moreover, ties should be strengthened between European Jewry and the two major Jewish cultural and demographic centers, in Israel and the United States.

In this respect, it is necessary to mention the need for research that goes beyond the quantitative aspects that constitute the main focus of this essay and that may contribute to an understanding of Jewish sociodemographic and identificational trends and their interplay with general political, socioeconomic, cultural, and institutional variables in the EC. Looking at the unfolding reality of European Jewry with a critical eye and within a coherent analytical frame of reference may help not only to predict the future course of the Jewish experience in the European Community but also to devise Jewish corporate interventions that render that experience more fruitful and rewarding.

TABLE 1. MAIN CENTRAL JEWISH REPRESENTATIVE ORGANIZATIONS IN THE 12 COUNTRIES OF THE EUROPEAN COMMUNITY

Country	Organization	Main Concern
Belgium	Comité de Coordination des Organizations Juives de Belgique (CCOJB)	Political
	Consistoire Central Israélite de Belgique	Religious
	Centrale des Oeuvres Sociales Juives	Service
Denmark	Det Mosaiske Troossamfund i Kobenhaven	All inclusive[a]
France	Conseil Représentatif des Institutions Juives de France (CRIF)	Political
	Consistoire Central des Israélites de France	Religious
	Fonds Social Juif Unifié (FSJU)	Service
Germany	Zentralrat der Juden in Deutschland	Political
	Zentralwohlfartsstelle der Juden in Deutschland	Service
Greece	Kentriko Israelitiko Simvoulio Ellados (KIS)	All inclusive
Ireland	Jewish Representative Council of Ireland	All inclusive
Italy	Unione delle Comunità Ebraiche Italiane (UCEI)	Political
Luxembourg	Consistoire Israélite de Luxembourg	Religious
Netherlands	Nederlands-Israelitisch Kerkgenootschap	Religious
	Stichting Joods Maatschappelijk Werk	Service
Portugal	Comunidade Israelita de Lisboa	Religious[a]
Spain	Federacion de Comunidades Israelitas de España	Political
United Kingdom	Board of Deputies of British Jews	All inclusive

[a]The total country's Jewish population is virtually concentrated in one local community.

TABLE 2. JEWISH POPULATIONS IN EUROPE, 1939–1991 (ROUGH ESTIMATES)

Country[a]	1939	1945	1960	1991
	Absolute Numbers (Thousands)			
World total	16,600	11,000	12,160	12,850
Europe total	9,500	3,800	3,241	2,010
European Community	1,295[h]	843[h]	890	987
Belgium[b]	93	32	36	32
Denmark	6	6	6	6
France	320	180	350	530
Germany	195	45	24	42
Greece	75	8	6	5
Italy	47	29	32	31
Netherlands	141	33	30	26
Spain[c]	6	10	6	13
United Kingdom[d]	345	350	400	302
Other West Europe[e]	130	109[h]	47	44
Former USSR (Europ. part)[f]	3,394	1,989	1,970	868
Other East Europe[g]	4,681	859	334	111
	Percentages			
Jews in Europe as % of world Jewry	57.2	34.5	26.7	15.6
Europe total	100.0	100.0	100.0	100.0
European Community	13.6	22.2[h]	27.5	49.1
Other West Europe	1.4	2.9[h]	1.4	2.2
Former USSR (Europ. part)	35.7	52.3	60.8	43.2
Other East Europe	49.3	22.6	10.3	5.5

[a]Boundaries as in 1990.
[b]Including Luxembourg.
[c]Including Portugal, Gibraltar.
[d]Including Ireland.
[e]Sweden, Norway, Finland, Iceland, Austria, Switzerland.
[f]Belarus, Estonia, Latvia, Lithuania, Moldova, Russia (incl. parts in Asia), Ukraine.
[g]Albania, Bulgaria, Czechoslovakia, Hungary, Poland, Romania, Yugoslavia, Turkey (European part).
[h]Including refugees in transit.
Source: Based on files available at Division of Jewish Demography and Statistics, the A. Harman Institute of Contemporary Jewry, the Hebrew University of Jerusalem.

TABLE 3. JEWISH POPULATIONS IN EUROPE, 1939–1991[a]: YEARLY PERCENT OF
CHANGE AND PROPORTION PER 1,000 INHABITANTS

Country	Yearly Percent Change			Jews per 1,000 Population	
	1939–1945	1945–1960	1960–1991	1939	1991
World total	−6.6	0.7	0.2	7.5	2.3
Europe total	−14.2	−1.1	−1.5	15.6	2.6
European Community	−6.9	0.4	0.3	4.8	2.8
Belgium	−16.3	0.8	−0.4	11.0	3.1
Denmark	—	—	—	1.5	1.2
France	−9.1	4.5	1.3	7.7	9.3
Germany	−21.7	−4.1	1.9	2.8	0.5
Greece	−31.1	−1.9	−0.6	10.1	0.5
Italy	−7.7	0.7	−0.1	1.1	0.5
Netherlands	−21.5	−0.6	−0.5	15.8	1.7
Spain	7.0	−3.8	2.5	0.2	0.3
United Kingdom	0.2	0.9	−0.9	6.9	4.9
Other West Europe	−2.9	−5.5	−0.2	5.4	1.3
Former USSR (Europ. part)	−8.5	−0.1	−2.6	16.7[b]	3.6
Other East Europe	−24.6	−6.1	−3.5	40.4	0.6

[a]See notes to table 2.
[b]Based on total USSR.
Source: as in table 2.

TABLE 4. ESTIMATED JEWISH POPULATION IN THE EUROPEAN COMMUNITY,
ca. 1990: COUNTRIES AND STATISTICAL REGIONS

Country and Region[a]	Total Population[b]	Jewish Population[c]	Jews per 1,000 Population	Purchasing Power Standard[d]
Total European Community	341,560,000	999,600	2.9	100
Belgium	9,845,000	31,800	3.2	102
1. Bruxelles	975,000	15,000	15.4	155
2. Vlaams Gewest	5,681,000	15,000	2.6	102
3. Région Wallonne	3,206,000	1,800	0.6	84
Denmark	5,143,000	6,400	1.2	117
France	56,138,000	530,000	9.4	111
1. Ile-de-France	10,231,000	310,000	30.3	165
2. Bassin Parisien	10,145,000	13,000	1.3	103
3. Nord-Pas-de-Calais	3,929,000	4,000	1.0	91
4. Est	5,019,000	30,000	6.0	100
5. Ouest	7,379,000	10,000	1.4	92
6. Sud-Ouest	5,821,000	35,000	6.0	98
7. Centre-Est	6,849,000	38,000	5.5	105
8. Méditerranée	6,382,000	90,000	14.1	96
Germany	77,573,000	40,000	0.5	114
1. Baden-Württemberg	9,618,000	2,200	0.2	120
2. Bayern	11,221,000	7,600	0.7	113
3. Berlin	3,410,000	9,300	2.7	128
4. Bremen	674,000	100	0.1	146
5. Hamburg	1,626,000	2,500	1.5	187
6. Hessen	5,661,000	9,000	1.6	129
7. Niedersachsen	7,284,000	800	0.1	97
8. Nordrhein-Westfalen	17,104,000	6,500	0.4	111
9. Rheinland-Pfalz	3,702,000	500	0.1	101
10. Saarland	1,065,000	300	0.3	107
11. Schleswig-Holstein	2,595,000	100	0.0	95
12. Brandenburg	2,641,000	450	0.2	67
13. Mecklenburg-Vorpommern	1,964,000	100	0.1	67
14. Sachsen	4,901,000	350	0.1	67

TABLE 4.—*(Continued)*

Country and Region[a]	Total Population[b]	Jewish Population[c]	Jews per 1,000 Population	Purchasing Power Standard[d]
15. Sachsen-Anhalt	2,965,000	50	0.0	67
16. Thuringen	2,684,000	150	0.1	67
Greece	10,047,000	4,800	0.5	57
1. Voreia Ellada	3,196,000	1,300	0.4	54
2. Kentriki Ellada	5,853,000	3,200	0.5	59
3. Anatolika-Nisia	847,000	300	0.4	52
Ireland	3,720,000	1,800	0.5	65
Italy	57,061,000	31,200	0.5	104
1. Nord-ovest	6,271,000	1,700	0.3	128
2. Lombardia	8,879,000	9,000	1.0	133
3. Nord-est	6,468,000	1,600	0.2	109
4. Emilia-Romagna	3,935,000	400	0.1	131
5. Centro	5,818,000	2,200	0.4	110
6. Lazio	5,109,000	16,000	3.1	110
7. Campania	5,671,000	200	0.0	73
8. Abruzzi-Molise	1,586,000	0	0.0	84
9. Sud	6,770,000	50	0.0	71
10. Sicilia	5,098,000	50	0.0	71
11. Sardegna	1,641,000	0	0.0	77
Luxembourg	373,000	600	1.7	124
Netherlands	14,951,000	25,700	1.7	107
1. Noord	1,591,000	500	0.3	151
2. Oost	2,949,000	2,200	0.7	87
3. West	6,809,000	22,000	3.2	112
4. Zuid	3,222,000	1,000	0.3	94
Portugal	10,285,000	300	0.0	52
1. Norte	5,354,000	0	0.0	43
2. Sul	4,333,000	300	0.1	63
3. Ilhas	521,000	0	0.0	52

TABLE 4.—*(Continued)*

Country and Region[a]	Total Population[b]	Jewish Population[c]	Jews per 1,000 Population	Purchasing Power Standard[d]
Spain	39,187,000	12,000	0.3	72
1. Noroeste	4,502,000	0	0.0	68
2. Noreste	4,168,000	0	0.0	86
3. Madrid	4,863,000	4,000	0.8	83
4. Centro	5,388,000	0	0.0	63
5. Este	10,468,000	5,000	0.5	80
6. Sur	7,847,000	2,900	0.4	57
7. Canarias	1,433,000	100	0.1	65
United Kingdom	57,237,000	315,000	5.5	104
1. North	3,080,000	2,000	0.6	92
2. Yorkshire-Humberside	4,899,000	16,500	3.4	95
3. East Midlands	3,920,000	2,000	0.5	98
4. East Anglia	1,992,000	3,000	1.5	102
5. South-East	17,265,000	232,000	13.4	123
6. South-West	4,543,000	2,000	0.4	97
7. West Midlands	5,181,000	6,000	1.1	94
8. North-West	6,374,000	37,000	5.8	97
9. Wales	2,821,000	2,000	0.7	88
10. Scotland	5,121,000	11,500	2.2	98
11. Northern Ireland	1,567,000	1,000	0.6	80

[a]Regional divisions are NUTS 1, the higher geographical level used by the Statistical Office of the European Communities to break down countries into statistical regions. *Source:* Eurostat, *Regions; Nomenclature of Territorial Units for Statistics—NUTS* (Luxembourg, 1991).
[b]Total EC population based on country figures. Total populations of European regions are 1986 averages. Data for Germany refer to 1989; for Greece, to 1984. *Source:* Eurostat, *Regions; Statistical Yearbook 1989* (Luxembourg, 1990).
[c]*Source:* as in table 2.
[d]The Purchasing Power Standard (PPS) is an index of standard of living. It is based on gross domestic product per inhabitant, adjusted for market prices.

TABLE 5. EUROPEAN COMMUNITY'S TOTAL AND JEWISH POPULATION DISTRI-
BUTION BY LEVEL OF REGIONAL STANDARD OF LIVING, ca. 1990

Stratum of Regions, by Standard of Living[a]	Total Population	Jewish Population	Jews per 1000 Population
Total n.	341,321,000	999,600	
Total %	100.0	100.0	2.9
1 (highest)	22.2	59.4	7.9
2	27.2	19.1	2.1
3	19.5	19.0	2.8
4	17.6	1.5	0.2
5 (lowest)	13.5	1.0	0.2

[a]The 69 statistical regions in table 4 were ranked according to Purchasing Power Standard per inhabitant (see last column and note [d] in table 4), and then regrouped into five strata, from highest (stratum 1) to lowest (stratum 5). Strata 1–4 include 14 regions each; stratum 5 includes 13 regions.

TABLE 6. EUROPEAN COMMUNITY CITIES WITH A JEWISH POPULATION OF 1,000 AND OVER, ca. 1990 (ROUGH ESTIMATES)

Country and City	Jewish Population	Country and City	Jewish Population
Belgium		Germany	
Antwerp	15,000	Berlin	9,300
Brussels	15,000	Frankfurt	7,000
		Munich	5,000
Denmark		Hamburg	2,500
Copenhagen	6,000	Cologne	1,500
France		Greece	
Paris region	310,000	Athens	2,900
Paris city	145,000	Saloniki	1,100
*Petite couronne*a	113,000		
*Grande couronne*b	52,000	Ireland	
Marseilles	45,000	Dublin	1,800
Lyon	26,000		
Toulouse	25,000	Italy	
Nice	20,000	Rome	15,800
Strasbourg	15,000	Milan	8,500
Bordeaux	8,000	Turin	1,200
Grenoble	7,000	Florence	1,100
Metz	3,000		
Aix-en-Provence	2,500	Netherlands	
Avignon	2,500	Amsterdam	17,000
Lille	2,500	The Hague	2,000
Nancy	2,500	Rotterdam	1,500
Villeurbanne	2,000		
Cannes	1,500	Spain	
Le Havre	1,500	Barcelona	5,000
Montpelier	1,500	Madrid	4,000
Mulhouse	1,500		
Belfort	1,000		
Colmar	1,000		
Compiègne	1,000		
Dijon	1,000		
Nimes	1,000		

TABLE 6.—*(Continued)*

Country and City	Jewish Population	Country and City	Jewish Population
United Kingdom		Hull	1,500
London region	215,000	Newcastle-upon-Tyne	1,500
Inner London	72,000	Blackpool	1,000
Outer London	125,000	Edinburgh	1,000
Adjacent Home Counties	18,000	Luton	1,000
Greater Manchester	30,000	Nottingham	1,000
Leeds	14,000	Reading	1,000
Glasgow	11,000	Sheffield	1,000
Brighton	10,000		
Birmingham	6,000		
Liverpool	5,000		
Southend	4,500		
Bournemouth	2,000		
Cardiff	2,000		
Southport	2,000		

[a]Départements 92, 93, 94.
[b]Départements 77, 78, 91, 95.
Source: as in table 2.

TABLE 7. JEWISH POPULATION OF FRANCE, BY SOCIAL STATUS, ca. 1930s–1988 (PERCENTAGES)

Socio-economic Status	Jews						Total France Urban 1975[d]
	Greater Paris				Provinces 1978[b]	France 1988[c]	
	Fathers of House-hold Heads[b]	Foreign-born Before Migrat.[b]	1960s[b]	1972–6[b]			
Total	100.0	100.0	100.0	100.0	100.0	100.0	100.0
Upper cadre[a]	8.7	13.3	19.3	25.7	15.2	41.7	12.2
Middle cadre[a]	18.8	16.1	14.6	17.8	52.7	18.1	17.5
Clerical		27.2	30.3	25.1		11.1	25.0
Traders	64.7	36.6	26.8	15.4	22.2	19.4	5.8
Craftsmen				5.6		8.3	2.1
Other blue-collar	7.8	6.8	9.0	10.4	9.9	1.4	37.4

[a]The French term "cadre" applies to managers and professionals. The upper cadre group in this table also includes a small number of industrial entrepreneurs.
[b]Retrospective data relate to people who were employed in the 1970s.
Source: D. Bensimon, S. DellaPergola, La population Juive de France: sociodémographie et identité (Jerusalem-Paris, 1984).
[c]Source: E.H. Cohen, L'Etude et l'education juive en France ou l'avenir d'une communauté (Paris, 1991).
[d]INSEE, Recensement général de la population 1975.

TABLE 8. BIRTH AND DEATH RATES AMONG JEWISH POPULATIONS IN THREE
EUROPEAN COMMUNITY COUNTRIES, 1930–1990 (RATES PER 1,000)

Country	Period Around	Birthrate		Death Rate		Balance	
		Jewish	Total	Jewish	Total	Jewish	Total
Germany	1930	7	15	16	11	−9	+4
	1950	3	18	21	11	−18	+7
	1970	5	13	20	12	−15	+1
	1990	5	11	20	11	−15	—
Italy	1930	15	28	15	17	—	+11
	1950	14	22	16	11	−2	+11
	1970	11	17	15	10	−4	+7
	1990	10	10	15	9	−5	+1
United Kingdom	1930	15	19	7	12	+8	+7
	1950	20	16	9	12	+11	+4
	1970	10	16	13	12	−3	+4
	1990	11	14	15	12	−3	+2

Source: as in table 2.

TABLE 9. TOTAL FERTILITY RATES AMONG THE JEWISH AND TOTAL POPULA-
TIONS OF FRANCE, 1932–1991

Year	Total Fertility Rates[a]				% Difference Jewish-Total
	Jewish Population[b]				
	European-Born	North African-Born	Total	Total Population	
1932–36	1.54	4.58	1.67	2.07	−19
1937–41	1.97	4.52	2.08	2.07	+0.5
1942–46	1.37	4.47	1.72	2.34	−27
1947–51	2.54	3.97	2.65	2.94	−10
1952–56	2.02	3.66	2.37	2.70	−12
1957–61	2.15	3.52	2.44	2.73	−11
1962–66	1.68	2.58	2.15	2.83	−24
1967–71	1.18	1.65	1.43	2.54	−44
1972–76				2.12	
1977–81				1.90	
1982–86				1.83	
1987–91				1.79	

[a]Average number of children expected at the end of a woman's reproductive span under the age-specific fertility levels of the indicated period.
[b]Retrospective data for Jewish women who lived in Greater Paris, 1972–78, irrespective of where the reported births took place.
Sources: D. Bensimon, S. DellaPergola (1984); *Vingt et unième rapport sur la situation démographique de la France, Population,* 47, 5, 1992, pp. 1113–86.

TABLE 10. JEWISH POPULATIONS IN TEN EUROPEAN COMMUNITY COUNTRIES, BY AGE, 1961–1991 (PERCENTAGES)

Country	Year	Total	0–14	15–29	30–44	45–64	65+	Median Age
Belgium								
Brussels	1961	100.0	16.0	16.0	16.0	42.0	7.0	44.1
Brussels	1987	100.0	15.0	15.0	16.0	28.0	26.0	50.0
Antwerp	1987	100.0	25.0	25.0	17.3	16.7	16.0	30.0
Total	1987	100.0	20.0	20.0	16.7	22.3	21.0	40.0
Denmark								
Total	1968	100.0	17.0	20.0	17.0	30.0	16.0	41.5
France								
Paris city	1972–4	100.0	18.0	25.2	16.0	27.3	13.5	36.8
Paris suburbs	1976	100.0	23.9	24.9	19.5	23.3	8.5	31.0
Total Gt. Paris	1972–6	100.0	20.5	25.1	17.5	25.5	11.4	34.1
Rest of country	1978	100.0	17.1	28.1	18.0	22.6	14.2	34.0
Total-projected	1990	100.0	17.2	18.6	26.0	23.0	15.2	37.7
Germany (West)								
Total	1970	100.0	11.0	17.0	16.0	35.0	21.0	48.9
Total	1987	100.0	12.8	18.4	24.0	21.1	23.7	41.0
Total	1991	100.0	12.6	14.9	22.2	25.0	25.3	45.2
Greece								
Total	1969	100.0	15.0	20.0	15.0	36.0	14.0	44.9
Saloniki	1981	100.0	11.7	18.6	17.4	25.0	27.3	46.5
Ireland								
Total	1961	100.0	21.6	17.4	18.9	31.5	10.6	39.6
Italy								
Total	1965	100.0	17.6	18.2	19.2	27.4	17.6	41.7
Total	1985–6	100.0	14.0	23.3	18.2	25.8	18.7	40.5
Rome	1985	100.0	19.0	22.7	20.1	23.8	14.4	36.3
Milan	1986	100.0	13.0	24.6	18.7	26.0	17.7	40.4
Turin	1985	100.0	7.0	22.7	13.9	32.1	24.3	48.8

TABLE 10.—*(Continued)*

| Country | Year | Age | | | | | | Median Age |
		Total	0–14	15–29	30–44	45–64	65+	
Luxembourg								
Total	1970	100.0	15.5	17.4	16.0	31.4	19.7	45.8
Netherlands								
Total	1966	100.0	16.0	21.0	14.0	33.0	16.0	45.3
United Kingdom								
Edgware	1963	100.0	26.0	22.0	23.0	24.0	5.0	31.4
Hackney	1971	100.0	20.0	18.0	14.0	29.0	19.0	43.2
Sheffield	1975	100.0	17.0	15.0	15.0	29.0	24.0	47.6
Redbridge	1978	100.0	19.0	22.0	18.0	30.0	11.0	37.0
Total	1975–9	100.0	19.9	21.2	17.6	23.2	18.1	36.9
Total	1984–8	100.0	16.9	18.9	18.7	21.6	23.9	41.3

Source: as in table 2.

TABLE 11. SELECTED INDICATORS OF JEWISHNESS IN THREE EUROPEAN COMMUNITY COUNTRIES, 1972–1991 (PERCENTAGES)

	France		Italy		United Kingdom	
	Greater Paris 1972–6	Provinces 1978	Total 1965	Milan 1986	Redbridge 1978	United Synagogue 1991
Meaning of attachment to Judaism			a			
Religion	34	58	33			
Community	10	5	9			
History	7		47			
Family	14	8	51			
Israel	b	b	44			
Jewish reality	31	27	33			
None	4	2	1			
Synagogue attendance						
Weekly or more	9	21	12	17	10	9
Holy days, some Sabbaths	29	40	25	16	17	32
Main holy days, events			38	44	52	53
Yom Kippur only	32	20	13	10	10	
Never	30	19	12	13	11	7
Eat matzah on Passover	82	91	88	90	79	
Thereof: no bread at home	57	73	66	69		
Fast on Yom Kippur	65	84		77	82	
Observe the Sabbath	37	57	35	46	70	
Thereof: regularly			15	14	26	
Observe Kosher rules	36	54	31	46		
Thereof: regularly			10	25		
Interested in Judaism	86	82	87			
Read Jewish books, papers	63	78	86			

TABLE 11.—*(Continued)*

	France		Italy		United Kingdom	
	Greater Paris 1972–6	Provinces 1978	Total 1965	Milan 1986	Red- bridge 1978	United Synagogue 1991
Interested in Middle East	97	95		98		
Visited Israel	49	47		80	26	

Ns as follows: Greater Paris—1,256 households, corresponding to 3,808 individuals; Provinces—172 households, 479 individuals; Italy nationally—2,123 households, 6,516 individuals; Milan—559 households, 1,664 individuals; Redbridge—464 households, 1,418 individuals; United Synagogue—816 households.
[a]Multiple answers allowed; total = 218%.
[b]Not asked.
Sources: D. Bensimon, S. DellaPergola (1984); S. DellaPergola, *Anatomia dell'ebraismo italiano* (Roma/Assisi, 1976); R. Mannheimer, A. Goldstaub, *Indagine demografico sociologico attitudinale sulla comunità di Milano,* unpublished manuscript; abstracts appeared on *Bollettino della Comunità Israelitica di Milano,* 1988; B.A. Kosmin, C. Levy, *Jewish Identity in an Anglo-Jewish Community* (London, 1983); S. Kalms, *A Time for Change: United Synagogue Review* (London, 1992).

TABLE 12. JEWISH EDUCATION IN FRANCE AND IN THE UNITED KINGDOM, 1981–82 TO 1991–92: SELECTED INDICATORS

	France			United Kingdom		
	1981–82	1986–87	1991–92	1981–82	1986–87	1990–91
Schools						
Total	216	307		259	271	
Day schools	68	88		82	106	90[a]
Part-time	148	219		177	165	
Pupils						
Total	20,664	25,483		30,248	27,507	26,962
Day schools	12,638	15,907	21,000	15,346	15,120	16,005
Part-time	8,026	9,576		14,902	12,387	10,957
Pupils per 100 Jewish school-age population (3–17)						
Total	24	32	(36)	55	55	56
Day schools	15	20	24	28	30	33
Part-time	9	12		27	25	23
Percent distribution of pupils, by age level						
Day schools, total	100	100		100	100	100
Ages 3–5	20	22		11	31	20
Ages 6–11	43	32		52	44	46
Ages 12–17	37	46		37	25	34
Part-time, total	100	100		100	100	
Ages 3–5	2	4		3	10	
Ages 6–11	82	65		79[b]	67	
Ages 12–17	16	31		18[c]	23	
Percent distribution of pupils, by school's ideological orientation						
Day schools, total	100	100		100	100	100
Right-wing Orthodox	}	26		}	38	43
Mainstream Orthodox	} 75	30		} 98	38	56[d]
Conservative and Reform	—	—		0	1	1
Communal and other	25	44		2	23	d

TABLE 12.—*(Continued)*

	France			United Kingdom		
	1981–82	1986–87	1991–92	1981–82	1986–87	1990–91
Part-time, total	100	100		100	100	
Right-wing Orthodox		3			—	
Mainstream Orthodox	100	73		61	57	
Conservative and						
Reform	—	7		39	43	
Communal and other	—	17		0	—	
			Teachers			
Total	1,648	2,660		1,991	2,709	
Day school	1,282	1,897		1,046	1,486	
Part-time	366	763		945	1,223	

[a]Including double counts of schools with multiple educational levels.
[b]Ages 6–12.
[c]Ages 13–17.
[d]Communal and other included in mainstream Orthodox.
Sources: Adapted from N. Genuth, S. DellaPergola and A. Dubb, *First Census of Jewish Schools in the Diaspora 1981/2–1982/3; International Summary* (Jerusalem, 1985); S. DellaPergola, U. Rebhun, D. Sagi, *Second Census of Jewish Schools in the Diaspora 1986/7–1988/9; Preliminary Report* (Jerusalem, 1992, mimeo); Jewish Educational Development Trust, *Securing Our Future: An Inquiry into Jewish Education in the United Kingdom* (London, 1992); P. Elkoubi, *Données sur les écoles juives à plein temps en France* (Paris, 1992, mimeo).

Review
of
the
Year

UNITED STATES

Civic and Political

Intergroup Relations

J EWISH GROUPS GENERALLY SUPPORTED American military intervention in the Persian Gulf at the start of 1991, consistent with a UN resolution authorizing "all necessary means" to force Iraq to withdraw from Kuwait. Later in the year, disturbances in Brooklyn and the remarks of a black professor, Leonard Jeffries, fueled heightened anxieties among American Jews with respect to anti-Semitism, even as Jewish security in the United States remained essentially strong. The announced presidential candidacies of Patrick J. Buchanan and David Duke raised concern in the Jewish community about right-wing influence in politics. Some tension occurred in Catholic-Jewish relations—particularly regarding the visit to the United States of Polish cardinal Jozef Glemp—but in the end, ties between the organized Jewish community and the National Conference of Catholic Bishops were strengthened. In the area of the separation of church and state, both "establishment" and "free-exercise" protections were at risk. The Civil Rights Act of 1991 was passed by the Congress and signed into law by President George Bush.

The Gulf War

The first decision facing the 102nd Congress in January was whether to commit troops to war in the Persian Gulf. Despite a spate of diplomatic initiatives that followed Iraq's invasion of neighboring Kuwait on August 2, 1990, the elements for a major war were in place by January 1. Nearly one million troops were poised along Kuwait's border with Saudi Arabia. On November 29, 1990, the UN Security Council had adopted Resolution 678, an ultimatum to Iraq, setting a January 15 deadline and authorizing member states "to use all necessary means" to force Iraq to withdraw from Kuwait.

As the new Congress convened, its Democratic leaders spurned President George Bush's invitation for an open-ended vote of support for military intervention. The leadership, fearful of undermining final attempts at a diplomatic solution, also urged members to delay congressional action. But the Congress, with the Senate in the lead, haltingly began debate on January 4.

In the House of Representatives, two approaches emerged. A resolution offered by Rep. Richard Gephardt (D., Mo.) asked that additional time be given to the economic sanctions policy—economic pressure put on Iraqi leader Saddam Hussein—before using the military option. A resolution spearheaded by Rep. Stephen J. Solarz (D., N.Y.), who characterized the Gulf crisis as "one of the transcendental issues of our time," "authorize[d] the use of United States armed forces pursuant to United Nations Security Council Resolution 678." On the Senate side, the most prominent, and perhaps most unexpected, voice of restraint was that of Sen. Sam Nunn (D., Ga.), the relatively conservative chairman of the Armed Services Committee, who argued forcefully for continuing tough economic sanctions rather than resorting to a quick use of military force.

The Jewish membership within each House of Congress was divided. With voting for the most part along party lines—Democratic members in large numbers preferring the continued use of economic sanctions to war—Rep. Solarz was noteworthy in his active support of the administration position. In the Senate, Joseph Lieberman (D., Conn.) was a cosponsor of the parallel resolution. In the weeks following the vote, two Democratic House members from New York—Charles Schumer and Nita Lowey—faced serious revolts in their districts from Jewish constituents. Schumer—whose Tenth District in Brooklyn was at the time threatened with redistricting into Solarz's Thirteenth—later recanted. At a meeting with Jewish activists, he said that he had made a mistake in voting against the House bill.

A sharply divided Congress voted on January 12—three days before the expiration of the UN deadline—to go to war against Iraq if the Kuwait occupation was not ended. The congressional action marked the first time since World War II that Congress had directly confronted the issue of sending large numbers of American forces into combat. The Senate voted for the resolution by a 52–47 margin, with ten Democrats joining a virtually unanimous Republican delegation in support of the resolution. Minutes later, the House approved identical legislation by a vote of 250–183. The resolution was signed by President Bush on January 14, and on the evening of January 16 a resolute president told the nation of his decision to transform the massive military deployment known as "Operation Desert Shield" into the war known as "Operation Desert Storm."

During the period of the congressional debate, Jewish groups affirmed their support of UN Resolution 678. Although a number of groups had expressed initial reluctance to support a resolution that would almost certainly lead to military action, Jewish organizations all across the political spectrum ultimately felt that they had no alternative but to support it, given the circumstances. (See "Jewish Communal Affairs," elsewhere in this volume, for more on the Jewish debate.)

As for anti-Semitic fallout from the Gulf War, the view that American Jews were pressing for the war solely for Israel's interest—a variation of the "dual loyalty" charge—found little support among most Americans, who were, in any case, overwhelmingly supportive of the war. Within the antiwar movement itself, however, there were resonances of anti-Semitism, much of it fueled by extremist anti-Semitic organizations (see "Anti-Semitism," below).

RELIGIOUS DIFFERENCES

Among Jewish religious groups, the sentiment was overwhelmingly prowar. The Synagogue Council of America (SCA), an umbrella organization of the rabbinical and congregational bodies of the Orthodox, Conservative, and Reform movements, passed a resolution on December 19, 1990, characterizing military action as "justifiable" in order to "effectively deter or end Iraq's capacity to threaten other nations," even as peaceful means to end the conflict needed to be explored. The SCA view was in marked contrast to that of various Christian and other religious bodies that questioned the use of force and called for reflection and ongoing dialogue to resolve the situation.

The sweeping antiwar language of the National Council of Churches (NCC), articulated in its November 15, 1990, "Message on the Gulf and Middle East Crisis" (see AJYB 1992, p. 178), resulted, in the view of observers of Christian affairs, from pressure to find a rhetorical common denominator embracing all of its 32 denominations. According to Dale Bishop, Middle East director for the NCC, "Some are opposed to any war on fundamental theological grounds; others would say that war is justified in some circumstances, but not under the current circumstances." The NCC message drew a sharp rebuke from a range of Jewish organizations over "the equation drawn [in the NCC message] between Iraq's aggression and Israel's occupation of the territories" and other points. The NCC, in a statement reported on February 22, reaffirmed its opposition to the war: "We opposed this war on moral grounds and remain opposed to it now." But there was no unanimity among Protestant clergy, and a number of Christian voices around the country expressed support for the war.

By contrast, the National Conference of Catholic Bishops/U.S. Catholic Conference was not officially declared as opposed to the war. Nevertheless, its president, Archbishop Daniel Pilarczyk of Cincinnati, said, "We are deeply disappointed it has come to war." And in a subtle but not unimportant shift, on February 14, Pope John Paul II rejected his previous stand of "peace at any cost," articulated in more than 40 previous public statements, and called for a "just peace." Analysts interpreted the pope's new formulation as a response to criticism that he had identified himself too closely with the pacifist cause.

Notwithstanding their opposition to U.S. involvement in the Persian Gulf War, Christian groups were united and vocal in their condemnation of Iraq's attacks on Israel. "There is a reservoir of good will for Israel," said the American Jewish Committee's national interreligious director, Rabbi A. James Rudin, even though "Israel's behavior during the *intifada* was seen by many Christians as using up a lot of that good will."

After the war ended, leaders of the Reform movement's Union of American Hebrew Congregations (UAHC) and the National Council of Churches amicably resolved the sharp differences that divided them during the Gulf crisis and issued, on April 22, a joint statement about Israel and the Palestinians. The statement expressed the hope "that all nations in the Middle East will be able to pursue peace through negotiation," and called on Israel's neighbors "to recognize her legitimate right to exist within internationally recognized borders." The single point of disagreement between the two religious groups was over who ought to negotiate with Israel: "The UAHC supports a process of open elections in the West Bank and Gaza. The NCC advocates the right of the widely dispersed Palestinian people to freely select their own representatives."

ARAB-AMERICANS

Concern was expressed during January by Jewish groups over reports that the Federal Bureau of Investigation planned to conduct interviews with Arab-Americans for the purpose of seeking information about possible Iraqi terrorist activity. The FBI, for its part, asserted that its interviews had the additional purpose of warning Arab-Americans about possible reprisals. Recalling the internment of Japanese-Americans in World War II, David A. Harris, executive vice-president of the American Jewish Committee, warned, "This could happen again," that "Arab-Americans could be unfairly linked to Iraq, whether or not they have supported the Iraqi invasion of Kuwait." He went on: "Necessary actions taken by our law enforcement authorities to protect U.S. security must at the same time be protective of the civil rights and liberties of Arab-Americans." Jewish community relations organizations maintained that, while governments have an obligation to prevent terrorist activity, insinuations of dual or diminished loyalty or any other intimidation based on ancestry or ethnic background were unacceptable.

Anti-Semitism and Extremism

EVALUATING ANTI-SEMITISM

While polling data continued to indicate that the level of negative attitudes toward Jews was at a low ebb, developments during 1991 deepened concern among most American Jews. Nonetheless, as measured by most major criteria for assessing anti-Semitism, the security of Jews in the United States remained strong.

A significant help in evaluating the picture was a new study, "What Do Americans Think About Jews?" prepared for the American Jewish Committee by Tom W. Smith of the National Opinion Research Center (NORC) of the University of Chicago and released in December. The study was based on data collected by NORC's General Social Survey, which studied in detail 57 ethnic groups in the United States, as well as data gleaned from a number of other studies and polls. Smith analyzed this profusion of data specifically for findings with respect to American Jews. The study concluded: "Today anti-Semitism in America is neither virulent nor growing. It is not a powerful social or political force." Nonetheless, Smith cautioned that "anti-Semitism is not a spent force . . . [it] has not disappeared. In both latent and manifest forms it remains part of contemporary American society."

Some confirmation of this could be found in statistics compiled by the Anti-Defamation League (ADL), which reported 1,879 incidents of anti-Semitism in 1991. This figure represented the highest level of discrete anti-Jewish acts in the 13-year history of ADL's annual audit and an 11-percent increase over the number of incidents reported in 1990. It was the fifth straight year of increase in these forms of behavioral anti-Semitism. Further, the ADL reported that for the first time since the statistics were compiled, there were more attacks on Jewish individuals than against their property. Of the 1,879 incidents reported, 950 were incidents of anti-Semitic harassment, threats, and physical assault, as compared to 929 acts of vandalism. Moreover, the physical assaults—60 in all, double the 1990 figure—included one murder, that of Yankel Rosenbaum during the Crown Heights disturbance in August. (See below, "Anti-Semitism in the Black Community.") The number of serious crimes—arson, bombing, and cemetery desecration—was 49, a 29-percent increase over the previous high of 38 noted in both 1989 and 1990.

As noted above, relatively little expression of anti-Semitism was generated by the Persian Gulf War, although the Anti-Defamation League did report that approximately one-half of all anti-Semitic acts reported nationwide between January 16 and February 14—52 incidents—were linked to the war. One disturbing element was the use of anti-Semitic rhetoric in the antiwar movement. One of the major peace movements, the Coalition to Stop U.S. Intervention in the Middle East, reportedly permitted representatives of extremist anti-Semitic groups, such as the Liberty Lobby and the LaRouche organization, to speak on its behalf. Coalition organizers subsequently repudiated such activity.

The larger number of incidents reported by the ADL clearly suggested, in the eyes of analysts, that inhibitions and taboos against such expressions were eroding, together with a rising level of interethnic conflict in general in the United States. One area of growing concern during 1991 was the use of the electronic media—particularly "talk radio" and public-access cable television—as forums for anti-Semitic expression. Reports by the American Jewish Committee ("Hate on Talk Radio") and the Anti-Defamation League ("Electronic Hate: Bigotry Comes to T.V.") explored both the extent of the problem and the relevant Federal Communications Commission rules and First Amendment issues.

EXTREMIST GROUPS

There was a continuing decline in most extremist groups, in both membership and activity, during 1991. A report prepared by the Anti-Defamation League, "The KKK Today: A 1991 Status Report," released in February, placed the total membership of the different factions collectively known as the Ku Klux Klan at 4,000 (down from a peak of 11,500 in 1981). The report discussed the ten-year decline of the Klan and concluded: "There is little prospect of the Klan once again becoming a significant force." Factors contributing to the decline in Klan membership—and that of other extremist groups as well—were the implication of members in violent crime, highly publicized civil and criminal trials, and the passage of hate-crimes legislation in numerous states. The ADL placed the membership of all hate groups in the United States at fewer than 20,000, approximately the same as in 1990; the Center for Democratic Renewal, an organization monitoring extremist-group activity, estimated that it was in excess of 25,000. According to Klanwatch, a project of the Southern Poverty Law Center, the number of discrete hate groups in the United States in 1991 totaled 346.

White supremacist Tom Metzger, a former Klan leader who headed the racist organization White Aryan Resistance (WAR), was once again in the news. Metzger, who lost in a $12.5-million verdict in 1990 in *Engedaw Berhanu v. Tom Metzger et al.*, was tried in August for his participation in a cross-burning ceremony in a Los Angeles suburb. On December 3—eight years to the day after 15 men joined in shouting racist slogans, giving Nazi salutes, and burning three large crosses in a Los Angeles canyon—Metzger was sentenced to a prison term of six months.

ANTI-SEMITISM IN THE BLACK COMMUNITY

The major source of anxiety among American Jews during 1991 with respect to anti-Semitism was anti-Semitism among African-Americans. This anxiety was fueled, in large measure, by two events: a speech by Prof. Leonard Jeffries, Jr., in July, and a riot in Crown Heights in August.

The Jeffries matter provoked a fire-storm of reaction from the Jewish community and counterreaction from the African-American community. The uproar was occasioned by a speech delivered on July 20 by Professor Jeffries, chairman of black studies at the City College of New York, at the Empire State Black Arts and Cultural Festival, held in Albany, New York. Jeffries framed his speech as a defense of the commission appointed by Thomas Sobol, New York State commissioner of education, to rewrite the public-school curriculum to include material of significant "multicultural" content. In his two-hour speech, however, Jeffries for the most part picked on the Jews and, to a lesser extent, the Italians. The speech included anti-Semitic swipes at Diane Ravitch, an assistant secretary of education, sociologist Nathan Glazer of Harvard, former New York City mayor Edward I. Koch, and City University of New York historian Arthur Schlesinger, Jr., whom Jeffries mistakenly identified as a Jew. An antiblack "conspiracy, planned and plotted and programmed out of Hollywood" by "people called Greenberg and Weisberg and Trigliani" was responsible for blacks being denigrated in films, asserted Jeffries. On slavery, Jeffries asserted in his July 20 speech that a Jewish conspiracy was the driving force behind the slave trade. In general, Jeffries accused "Russian Jewry" of conspiring with the Mafia to "put together a system of destruction of black people."

Knowledgeable observers pointed out that the effort to promote Africa and African studies as part of the central public-school curriculum is not *a priori* anti-Semitic and is, by and large, without an anti-Semitic component. On the extreme end of the multicultural movement, however, are those "Afrocentrists" who claim the superiority of all things African to anything non-African; many of these individuals have used anti-Semitic rhetoric—as well as anti-Catholic and anti-Muslim rhetoric.

The Jeffries speech did not come to public attention until August 5—two weeks before the Crown Heights disturbances—when it was first reported in the *New York Post*. While Jewish and other groups, a number of newspapers, and white elected officials, including New York governor Mario Cuomo, vigorously denounced Jeffries' bigotry, black officials were largely silent on the matter. *The Amsterdam News*, a black newspaper, rallied to Jeffries' defense. Jewish groups expressed appreciation at the overall level of public criticism of Jeffries but found the reluctance of black leadership to repudiate racism and anti-Semitism in their midst increasingly disturbing.

Jewish groups such as the American Jewish Committee, the American Jewish Congress, and the Anti-Defamation League immediately called upon City University chancellor W. Ann Reynolds to distance the university from Jeffries' views. The executive committee of the faculty senate of the City College of New York, however, citing freedom of expression, declined to recommend censure. And City College president Bernard Harleston, a black, said on November 4 that, while he considered Jeffries to be "anti-Semitic," he would defend keeping the professor in his position because dismissing him would "deepen the sense of crisis on campus." On November 6, he said that statements undermining racial or ethnic groups were "deplorable," but did not mention Jeffries or the speech, instead simply defending freedom of expression, in principle. Following an administrative review of the situation, the City University board of trustees voted on October 28 to reappoint Jeffries as chairman of black studies for a probationary period of one academic year, rather than dismiss him outright or extend his chairmanship by the customary three-year term. The Jewish Community Relations Council of New York termed the board's decision "validation of Jeffries' anti-Semitic and racist views." The fact that "a racist can help to create tension and then use it to intimidate a major public institution proves that there is something drastically wrong with the process." The American Jewish Committee criticized the City College trustees for saying, in effect, "that the preaching of hatred should not disqualify the bestowing of honors, that political expediency is more important than a strong stand against bigotry."

The disturbance in August in the Brooklyn neighborhood of Crown Heights evoked equally strong concern but was a far more complex situation. Although cries of "Kill the Jew!" were heard in the streets, and the murder of Australian student Yankel Rosenbaum seemed clearly motivated by anti-Semitism, some analysts suggested that the root of the problem was not black anti-Semitism per se but the unique dynamics of the Crown Heights situation. Crown Heights is home to some 25,000 Jews—most of whom are Lubavitcher Hassidim, who began arriving in the neighborhood in the 1930s—and 100,000 blacks, including a sizable population of Caribbean blacks. Deep-seated "tribal rivalries" over land, housing, political power, and culture—and not anti-Semitism—were at the heart of the Crown Heights manifestations, suggested sociologist Jonathan Rieder in the *New Republic* (October 14, 1991). These rivalries, however, "easily upset the delicate balance between pluralism and difference," said Rieder, resulting in an atmosphere of profound misunderstanding during crisis situations, such as the one that occurred in August.

The August 19 events were ignited when a car driven by Yosef Lifsh, a Hassid who was driving in a motorcade escorting the Lubavitcher Rebbe, Menachem Mendel Schneerson, through Crown Heights, jumped a curb and struck seven-year-old Gavin Cato, killing the black child and injuring his cousin. A private Jewish ambulance service, Hatzolah, arrived within minutes of the accident—almost simultaneously with a New York City ambulance. As a crowd of 100 to 150 was gathering, police advised the Hatzolah ambulance to remove Lifsh, who was already being beaten by blacks in the crowd, from the scene. It was widely believed that the Jewish ambulance ignored the injured black children because they were black and treated the Hassidim because they were Jews, though subsequent investigation failed to confirm this. In the ensuing riot, cries of "Get the Jews" and "Jews! Jews! Jews!" were heard.

Three hours after the accident, and three blocks from the scene, 29-year-old Yankel Rosenbaum, an Australian Hassid who had come to New York to study anti-Semitism, was stopped in his car by a gang, assaulted, held down, and stabbed. Rosenbaum died later that night. The riots lasted three days and resulted in injuries to 65 civilians and 158 police officers, as well as significant property damage.

Blacks from outside the community, most notably the Reverend Al Sharpton and Sonny Carson (a longtime black activist), were instrumental in fomenting the riot. Also of significance, in the view of most observers, was the role played by the press. Looking for a "story," press reports tended to downplay—or not cover at all—constructive statements of some black leadership, focusing instead on the violence.

Lingering questions remained afterward about the role played by black leaders—and by Jewish groups—during the riot. "We may have had unrealistic expectations of a black leadership that simply didn't exist—a naked emperor playing no role in the community," commented one Jewish official. At the same time, mainstream Jewish organizations were noticeably hesitant in their own initial responses: none mentioned anti-Semitism in its public statements the first few days after the disturbances. One element in the slow Jewish response was undoubtedly the fact that mainstream Jewish organizations were generally distant from the Hassidim and ambivalent toward them. They also hesitated to disrupt the already fragile black-Jewish coalition in the city. Indeed, it was not until 11 days after the riot's eruption that the ADL characterized the black reaction as "anti-Semitic." ADL national director Abraham H. Foxman, on August 30, explained his agency's "self-imposed restraint" as "a desire not to hurt those who were hurt in the past," referring to the blacks.

Even as Jewish groups acknowledged the reality of anti-Semitism as a factor in the Crown Heights situation, several Jewish leaders expressed the view that there would be no peace in Crown Heights—and little hope for a lessening of black-Jewish tensions—until root causes of those tensions were examined. "It's not too late," suggested Albert Vorspan of the Union of American Hebrew Congregations. "Charges of preferential treatment [made by blacks of Jews in the neighborhood] need to be thoroughly examined." Vorspan further noted that the Crown Heights confrontation constituted the first instance in American Jewish history in which there was a physical confrontation between black and Jewish populations.

While some observers believed that Crown Heights was unique, that the conditions underlying the violence there were not present elsewhere, others saw Crown Heights as a symbol of the breakdown of the black-Jewish relationship in general. Author Jim Sleeper, a white, Jewish analyst of black-Jewish affairs, argued that if Jews and blacks were "the closest of strangers before," the riots tore the communities farther apart than ever. "The relationship," asserted Sleeper, "is dead. The silence of the black leadership really killed it. But the romance had been one-sided for some time. I sense that on the part of the blacks it's been dead for a lot longer."

Jewish leaders differed in their assessments of black anti-Semitism in the aftermath of Crown Heights. To ADL's Foxman, the Crown Heights riots may have been the catalyst the Jewish community needed to overcome its deep reluctance based on "color consciousness" to address the specter of "anti-Semitism that is all over the place in Crown Heights" and on the rise elsewhere.

Henry Siegman, executive director of the American Jewish Congress, had a different view. The issue, suggested Siegman, was more one of black-white race relations in the society at large than of anti-Semitism in Crown Heights. "It is strategically dumb and factually incorrect," said Siegman, "to insist that the violence in Crown Heights is essentially a black-Jewish problem. It is not. It is essentially a black-white problem, and it seems to me that for Jews to insist that it is a black-Jewish problem is to take the monkey off the back of white Americans and to put it on our own back." Echoing this view from a black perspective, Princeton University scholar Cornell West suggested that "black anti-Semitism is a species of anti-whitism." As such, it could conceivably be interpreted as black anger directed at the most visible manifestation of white power in the neighborhood. Knowledgeable observers suggested that the true nature of "black anti-Semitism" would not be understood until there was a serious ethnographic study in the street.

Several conclusions could be drawn from the Crown Heights events. First, while animosity toward Jews per se played a part, long-standing, deep-seated community rivalries clearly lay at the root of the riots. Second, a seriously distorted picture of the event was reported in the media. Blacks and Jews were consistently portrayed as antagonists throughout the affair, yet constructive efforts by blacks and Jews, working together in the neighborhood, kept tensions from building further than they did. Third, although several black leaders denounced the violence, questions remained about the responses of both black and Jewish influentials as well as the roles played by community organizations, the police, and other government institutions.

Jewish groups called upon the U.S. Justice Department to look into possible civil-rights violations that may have been committed during the disturbances.

POLITICAL ANTI-SEMITISM

Controversy continued to swirl around syndicated columnist Patrick J. Buchanan over his remarks in August 1990, during the Gulf crisis, referring to American Jews in relation to Israel as the "amen-corner." In late December of this year, three weeks after Buchanan announced his candidacy for the presidency, he was the subject of a "case study" in a special issue of the *National Review*, a conservative weekly edited by William F. Buckley, Jr., entitled "In Search of Anti-Semitism" (December 30, 1991). Buckley found it "impossible to defend Buchanan against the charge that what he said during [the Gulf crisis] amounted to anti-Semitism, whatever it was that drove him to say it; most probably an iconoclastic temperament." Nonetheless, Buckley suggested that critics of Buchanan at the time may have overreacted.

The activities of former Ku Klux Klan leader David Duke were again a matter of concern as he continued his quest for electoral legitimacy. Duke, who had garnered 44 percent of the vote in a 1990 Senate race in Louisiana, ran for governor of Louisiana on the Republican ticket. He qualified for the runoff in the 1991 gubernatorial race by placing second in a nonpartisan primary election in October. In the runoff election on November 16, Duke received some 700,000 votes—39 percent of the total, including 55 percent of the white vote. The 96 percent of the African-American vote against Duke assured victory for Duke's runoff opponent, Edwin W. Edwards.

Duke, who was a Klan leader from 1975 to 1980 and who associated with neo-Nazi groups throughout the 1970s, made an effort during the campaign to shed his Klan and racist image and ran his campaign in the guise of a devout Christian. He skillfully exploited voter hostility to "big government," and many voted for him despite his racial views. According to exit-polling conducted by Voter Research Surveys and interpreted by Melman and Lazarus, 27 percent of voters supported Duke because of his views on the state's economy, 39 percent because of government corruption, and only 12 percent because of the candidate's views on racial issues.

President George Bush and other Republican leaders disavowed Duke after the October primary, but the president issued a more vigorous denunciation on November 6, ten days before the runoff election: "When someone has an ugly record of racism and bigotry, that record simply cannot be erased by the glib rhetoric of a political campaign."

Jewish communities within Louisiana worked within the framework of the Louisiana Coalition Against Racism and Nazism, a broad-based intergroup political action committee, in countering Duke's candidacy. Most national and local Jewish groups were constrained from becoming involved by the absolute ban on political activity imposed by Sect. 501(c)(3) of the Internal Revenue Code. The Duke election evoked concern about the willingness of the large numbers of Americans who are not anti-Semitic—indeed for whom Jews are not an issue—to vote for a candidate who appeals to them on issues of concern, even if the candidate espouses racist and anti-Semitic views. There was little evidence, however, of an emergent political anti-Semitism during 1991 elsewhere in the country.

HOLOCAUST REVISIONISM

Holocaust revisionism—the denial of the Holocaust or of its extent, often by pseudo-scholars—found its main expression in 1991 in a series of advertisements offered for placement in campus newspapers around the country. In November, Bradley R. Smith, head of the revisionist Committee for Open Debate on the Holocaust, began submitting the ads, which claimed that the "myth of the Holocaust" was created by Zionist organizations in order to promulgate anti-German propaganda. The ads did appear in some newspapers but were rejected by a majority of editorial boards and advertising directors. University-based Hillel groups played a major role in exposing the false content of these advertisements. Indeed, observers noted that the publication of the ads and the attendant controversy raised awareness on a number of campuses of the anti-Semitic agenda of the revisionists.

Fred A. Leuchter, Jr., a Massachusetts builder and repairer of execution equipment and author of a 192-page document claiming that gas chambers were never used for execution during the Holocaust, lost considerable credibility this year as a self-appointed expert witness on the subject. He was forced to sign a consent agreement on June 11 with the Massachusetts Board of Registration of Professional Engineers and Land Surveyors, admitting that he was not an engineer and agreeing to "cease and desist" from commenting authoritatively on gas chambers.

ANTI-SEMITISM ON THE CAMPUS

The number of anti-Semitic incidents on college campuses slightly increased in 1991, with 101 acts reported at 60 campuses, as compared to 95 in 1990. Overall, according to Melanie Schneider of the National Jewish Community Relations Advisory Council, while most Jewish students on campuses around the country felt secure, "many among the Jewish student leadership are feeling increasingly uneasy." Nonetheless, most incidents on college campuses occurred around "flash points," such as invited speakers who carried an anti-Zionist or anti-Semitic message. One such speaker, Kwame Toure (black activist Stokely Carmichael), continued his rounds of the campuses in 1991. Following Toure's speech at Amherst College in Massachusetts in February, an Israeli flag owned by Jewish students was set on fire. City College of New York professor Leonard Jeffries (see above) was on the campus speaking circuit as well during the autumn of 1991.

In Los Angeles, after months of shilly-shallying and amid rising indignation in the Jewish community, the administration of the University of California, Los Angeles, took action on May 23 against a black student magazine, NOMMO, for its persistent "highly offensive and blatantly anti-Semitic statements," withdrawing student-affairs advertising from the magazine. *NOMMO* had, in February, approvingly cited excerpts from *The Protocols of the Elders of Zion* and Henry Ford's *The International Jew: The World's Foremost Problem*, and continued to publish anti-Semitica in May. The university action came in response to a campaign spearheaded by the Los Angeles Jewish Community Relations Council, Anti-Defamation League, and the Los Angeles Hillel Council that included a faculty "teach-in."

LEGISLATIVE AND JUDICIAL ACTIVITY

Following passage in 1990 of the Hate Crimes Statistics Act, on January 1 the Federal Bureau of Investigation began collecting statistics on crimes based on prejudice against race, religion, ethnicity, or sexual orientation. The Justice Department's Civil Rights Division reported that through March 1991 the department had indicted 139 defendants in 26 states for "hate crimes" under the Religious Violence Act (passed in 1990) and other legislation; of these, 126 resulted in convictions.

In 1991, 47 states, in addition to the federal government, had some form of hate-crimes, ethnic-intimidation, or bias-motivated violence laws. Three of these states passed new statutes and four strengthened existing law during 1990 and 1991. However, the constitutionality of such laws was challenged in a number of states as well as in the U.S. Supreme Court in *R.A.V. v. City of St. Paul* (see AJYB 1992, p. 189). No decision was reached during 1991 on this case. Challenges to hate-crimes laws—on the grounds that they violate free-speech or due-process protections—were mounted in federal and state courts in California, Florida, Georgia, Ohio, Vermont, Virginia, Washington, Wisconsin, and the District of Columbia. In Ohio two courts of appeal arrived at different conclusions regarding the constitutionality of that state's ethnic-intimidation statute. *Ohio v. Wyant* found that the law was not overbroad and therefore did not violate freedom-of-expression protections. *Ohio v. van Gundy* ruled that the Ohio statute was both overbroad (and therefore violates First Amendment free-speech rights) and vague (thereby violating the due-process clause of the First Amendment). Both cases were appealed to the Ohio Supreme Court. The Anti-Defamation League filed an *amicus* brief in *Ohio v. van Gundy*. Another hate-crimes-law case that reached its state's highest court in 1991 was *State of Wisconsin v. Todd Mitchell*, in which an appeals court in June upheld the constitutionality of Wisconsin's statute.

There were further developments in the so-called Merchant of Venice case, *Weiss v. United States*, in which a federal prosecutor on a Medicare and mail-fraud case repeatedly referred to Shakespeare's *A Merchant of Venice* and harped on defendant Steven Weiss's greed, clearly invoking the character of Shylock, a classic and libelous anti-Semitic stereotype. While the U.S. Second Circuit Court of Appeals in New York was troubled by the prosecutor's remarks, it rejected a new trial for Weiss based on those remarks. In August the Anti-Defamation League, the American

Jewish Congress, and Agudath Israel of America joined in an *amicus curiae* brief in support of a petition of *certiorari* asking the U.S. Supreme Court to review the case.

OTHER MATTERS

For the fourth year in a row, the National Alliance, a racist and anti-Semitic neo-Nazi group that owned 100 shares of stock in the American Telephone and Telegraph Company, submitted a proposal to the AT&T annual shareholders' meeting on April 17 calling on shareholders to stop providing products and services to Israel. The AT&T board of directors recommended against the proposal, characterizing it as "lacking credibility and misleading, given the consistent anti-Semitic bias of the proponent." Jewish groups were nuanced in their approach on this issue, however. "We never want to give these groups the visibility they don't deserve," said the National Jewish Community Relations Advisory Council, reflecting the view shared by most Jewish groups. "At the same time," said the group's spokesman, "our long experience has taught us that the best counteraction against groups such as the National Alliance is public exposure . . . they are repudiated by the American body politic and individual Americans." As expected, 96 percent of AT&T shareholders voted against the proposal.

Congressional resolutions introduced by Sen. Alfonse D'Amato (R., N.Y.) and Rep. Ray McGrath (R., N.Y.) called upon the German and Austrian governments to "halt the distribution of neo-Nazi computer games and prosecute those in possession of those materials." The measure was passed in both Houses as an amendment to the Foreign Aid Authorization Bill. There were no reports of the video games—which bore such names as "KZ Manager" and "Aryan Test"—having been distributed in the United States. A troubling matter of free-speech protection came to the fore when it was learned that Prodigy Services, an on-line computer service owned by IBM and Sears, permitted subscribers to post anti-Semitic messages on its computer "bulletin board" while disallowing responses to those messages. Representations made by the Anti-Defamation League in October resulted in an agreement by Prodigy to amplify its guidelines to consumers of the service, in which the company requested Prodigy members not to post offensive notes. At the same time, Prodigy asserted that these forms of expression constitute protected behavior.

Rock star Madonna angered Jewish groups with her song "The Beast Within," released in late December 1990, which included a verse from the New Testament Book of Revelations (2:9): " . . . and the slander of those who say they are Jews, but they are not, they are a synagogue of Satan." Jewish groups noted that the "Jew-as-Satan" image was a notorious piece of anti-Semitica. Madonna responded on January 4, asserting that she had no anti-Semitic intent, and that her message was "pro-tolerance and about love."

In November, the Anti-Defamation League and the B'nai B'rith of Canada

League for Human Rights convened a conference in Montreal on worldwide anti-Semitism, bringing together scholars, journalists, and community leaders in an effort to assess the changes in levels of anti-Semitism in various countries.

Political Affairs

BUCHANAN AND DUKE

The electoral off-year 1991 was noteworthy in terms of what it presaged for 1992, a presidential-election year. Two right-wing figures announced their candidacies for the presidency: David Duke, who was defeated in November in the gubernatorial race in Louisiana, but garnered 39 percent of the vote; and syndicated columnist Pat Buchanan. Duke, declaring his candidacy on December 4 for the Republican party nomination, highlighted in his declaration speech the undermining of "Christian society." The National Jewish Coalition, a group of Jewish Republicans, arguing that Duke was a "bipartisan problem," suggested that Duke's candidacy would not cost President George Bush—or any other Republican candidate—Jewish votes in November 1992.

The candidacy of Patrick J. Buchanan, on the other hand, announced on December 10, clearly complicated the Republican party's quest for the Jewish vote. Analysts—recalling the history of 1984 and 1988, when the Reverend Jesse Jackson ran for the Democratic nomination—suggested that Buchanan in the race would make it more difficult to convince Jewish voters that the Republican party was not hostile to their interests. While Buchanan was considered to be more respectable than Duke, he had in the past questioned the dual loyalty of American Jews to Israel and America, shown some sympathy for suspected Nazi war criminals, and supported the presence of the Carmelite convent at the Auschwitz/Birkenau death-camp site.

Most of the announced contenders for the 1992 Democratic nomination—Sen. Tom Harkin of Iowa, former Sen. Paul Tsongas of Massachusetts, Gov. Bill Clinton of Arkansas, Gov. Douglas Wilder of Virginia, former Gov. Jerry Brown of California, and Sen. Bob Kerrey of Nebraska—had strong pro-Israel records and generally supported Jewish communal positions on domestic issues. A question mark about Kerrey concerned his absence from the majority of senators supporting loan guarantees for immigrant resettlement in Israel.

The election in Pennsylvania on November 5 of interim senator Harris Wofford to the three-year unexpired term of the late John Heinz, defeating former U.S. attorney general Richard Thornburgh, was greeted with relish by Jewish Democrats. Although Wofford and Thornburgh were equally supportive of Israel, many pro-Israel activists preferred Wofford over Thornburgh. Morris Amitay, former director of the American Israel Public Affairs Committee (AIPAC), said that support of Wofford was justified because Thornburgh, who served under President Bush, "owed the president too much to break with him on any issue," spelling possible trouble if Bush continued to block the loan-guarantee package.

In one of the two off-year races for the House of Representatives, Lucien Blackwell, a Democrat, defeated three candidates to win the seat vacated by Rep. William Gray, who resigned from Congress to become president of the United Negro College Fund. Gray, who represented a Philadelphia district, had close ties to the Jewish community in that city and to Jewish groups nationally. Also in Philadelphia, Edward Rendell was elected the city's first Jewish mayor.

LEGISLATIVE DEVELOPMENTS

A change was made in the passport law that affected travelers to both Israel and Arab countries. Legislation introduced by Sen. Frank Lautenberg (D., N.J.) and Rep. Howard Berman (D., Calif.), as part of the 1992 State Department Appropriations Bill (passed and signed into law in October), barred the use of passports stamped with the words "Israel only." Consular officials had issued such passports as a service to citizens wishing to travel to both Israel and Arab countries, which routinely denied entry to those carrying passports with Israeli visas. (Indeed, in March, the Saudi and Kuwaiti governments had denied visitors' visas to Sen. Lautenberg because his passport contained Israeli entrance stamps.) The change was made because the practice was seen as reinforcing Arab ostracism of Israel.

REDISTRICTING AND REAPPORTIONMENT

Jewish groups expressed concern over the possible consequences of electoral redistricting based on the 1990 census. New York, Illinois, Michigan, Ohio, Pennsylvania, New Jersey, and Massachusetts—all states with concentrations of Jews—were among those states that lost seats, according to figures released by the Census Bureau in July.

Of particular concern was the application of the Voting Rights Act of 1965 and the 1982 amendments to the act which, as interpreted by the U.S. Supreme Court, served as a mechanism for guaranteeing minority representation. A harbinger of the kind of problem that could arise developed in New York in 1991. Consistent with interpretations of the provisions of the Voting Rights Act amendments—that the race of communities be considered in the carving up of electoral districts—the New York City Districting Commission in June passed a plan for the city that would have gerrymandered at least one Jewish City Council member out of her district. Jewish groups reacted vigorously to the "mirror-image" representation scheme. In a July 15 letter to the Justice Department's Voting Rights Section, the American Jewish Congress, the Anti-Defamation League, B'nai B'rith District 1, the National Council of Jewish Women, the Union of Orthodox Jewish Congregations of America, the Workmen's Circle, and the New York Jewish Community Relations Council charged that the plan was "illegal under both the Voting Rights Act and the Constitution." The point was underscored by Washington attorney Nathan Lewin, a longtime participant in Jewish legal affairs: "The Constitution doesn't permit any government agency to determine the race of an elected official." The Justice Department on July 23 rejected the idea that the Voting Rights Act required minority electoral districts to elect minority representatives and sent the commission back to the drawing board. At year's end a number of redistricting and reapportionment plans under consideration around the country were being monitored by Jewish groups.

OTHER MATTERS

Among the long-awaited and eagerly welcomed public-affairs actions of 1991 was the repeal on December 16 by the United Nations of Resolution 3379, which said that "Zionism is a form of racism and racial discrimination." Repeal of Resolution 3379, passed in 1975, had been a cornerstone of Jewish public policy for more than a decade and a half. In November, in anticipation of the UN vote, the U.S. Senate passed a resolution, 97–0, calling upon the United States and the Soviet Union to lead an effort to repeal the measure. (See "The United States, Israel, and the Middle East," elsewhere in this volume, for more on the subject.)

A flap surrounding White House chief of staff John Sununu's misuse of government transportation for private travel spilled over into the Jewish community in June. An unsourced item in the June 21 *Wall Street Journal* reported, "Israel supporters quietly campaign against him [Sununu], spreading their complaints about his ties to Arab-American groups." The story gathered steam when Rowland Evans and Robert Novak (*Washington Post*, June 24) cited unnamed sources who said that Sununu believed the "attacks . . . have come because he is a second-generation Lebanese-American who is not fully supportive of Israel's demands on the United States." In other words, Sununu believed that the Jewish community was out to get him because of his Middle East views. Matters were further complicated by the appearance on June 27 of a column, "Sununu Blames the Jews," by William Safire in the *New York Times*; and a news article by David Twersky in the English-language *Forward*, which criticized Sununu for his involvement in the creation of a new organization, the Arab-American Council.

Sununu immediately denied that he blamed Jews and other supporters of Israel for the controversy raging over his unreimbursed travel and other questionable practices. In a telephone call to the Conference of Presidents of Major American Jewish Organizations on June 26, Sununu replied to a letter from Malcolm Hoenlein, Presidents' Conference executive director, and Shoshana Cardin, conference president, and said that he never made the allegations. On June 27, Sununu held a conference call with American Jewish Committee executive vice-president David Harris, Anti-Defamation League national director Abraham H. Foxman, Meyer Mitchell of AIPAC, and George Klein, a leading Jewish Republican, in which he advised the Jewish leaders of a statement he was releasing that read, in part: "I am not blaming anybody but myself for the flurry of recent events nor am I engaging at all . . . to suggest any involvement by any one or any groups in what has taken place or been reported." And in letters to Hoenlein and Foxman, Sununu recalled his "good and productive working relationship" with Jewish organizations and expressed his intention to "continue working with all of you in an accessible and forthright manner." Many Jewish leaders, who had been uneasy about Sununu since President Bush named him chief of staff, were privately outraged that Sununu may have sought, despite his denials, to blame Jews for some of his problems. At the same time, as Kenneth Jacobson of the ADL noted, "our principal role was to make clear, on the one hand, that scapegoating Jews was intolerable; and on the other hand, that accusations against an official for activities based only on his ethnic ties were also unacceptable."

Finally, various Jewish groups expressed support for the plight of some 7,000 Haitians who fled Haiti, most in small boats headed toward the United States, after a military coup deposed democratically elected Haitian president Jean-Bertrand Aristide on September 30. The Bush administration's policy of returning refugees to Haiti was temporarily restrained on December 3 by a federal district court judge in Florida, whose ruling was overturned on December 17 by a federal appeals court in Atlanta. Supreme Court review was expected. A statement of support for the plight of the Haitian refugees first came from a coalition of Hassidic groups in the Crown Heights, Williamsburg, and Boro Park sections of Brooklyn, New York, in early December. Statements of support soon followed from other groups, including the American Jewish Committee, the Jewish Labor Committee, the Union of Orthodox Jewish Congregations of America, the American Jewish Congress, the Hebrew Immigrant Aid Society, and the Anti-Defamation League, all of whom called upon the administration to reverse its repatriation policy.

Soviet Jewry

The resettlement in Israel of Jews from the former Soviet Union was a major area of Jewish public-policy activity. The specific focus was Israel's request to the United States to guarantee, by acting as a co-signatory, a loan for $10 billion to assist in absorption of the immigrants. (It was estimated in early 1991 that approximately one million new immigrants, mostly from the Soviet Union, were expected to arrive in Israel over the next three to five years.) Jewish groups attempted to make the case to the administration and the Congress that the absorption of Soviet immigrants was not simply a "Jewish" issue but a humanitarian concern shared by the United States. Moreover, argued Jewish groups, the loan-guarantee program, far from being a drain on American resources, would yield economic benefits, such as profits to American financial institutions servicing the loans, increased Israeli purchases of American goods and services, and so on. The administration, however, saw the question in the context of settlement building in the West Bank, which it strongly opposed, and as a possible obstacle to a Middle East peace conference.

The formal request from Israel to Secretary of State James Baker for the guarantees came on September 7, after—and despite the fact that—President Bush announced that he would ask the Congress not to act on the Israeli request for 120 days, in order to allow the planned peace conference to get off the ground. The request was for a total of $10 billion in five annual installments of $2 billion each for fiscal years 1992 through 1996. On September 11, the president said that he was not committed to supporting the $10-billion guarantee.

On September 12, more than 1,000 activists converged on Washington from communities around the country to lobby the Congress to act swiftly on Israel's request. The president, at a hastily convened news conference, repeated his request for a 120-day delay in congressional consideration, in order to "avoid a contentious debate." Jewish groups were upset, however, more by the president's words and tone than by his political message. In the televised news conference, the president unleashed an unprecedentedly sharp attack on the Jewish community leaders who had come to Washington, characterizing the activists as "powerful political forces" and himself as "one lonely little guy down here." Jewish groups strongly criticized the president, both for his decision to postpone consideration of the guarantees and for the nature of his remarks, which echoed classic anti-Semitic charges of Jewish power and manipulation. In a letter sent on September 17 to Shoshana Cardin, chairwoman of the Conference of Presidents, the president asserted that his remarks were not meant to be pejorative. "I have great respect for the exercise of free expression in the democratic process," he wrote. "Politically organized groups and individuals are a legitimate and valued part of the decision-making process in a democracy." Nonetheless, many observers continued to view the September 12 remarks as a hostile expression.

The options before Congress during the last three months of 1991 included amending the foreign operations appropriations bill to include the loan guarantees; introducing clean bills; or following the president's request to wait until January to introduce the legislation approving the guarantees. The ambivalence of many members of Congress came into play during this crucial period. While a clear majority in the Senate supported the guarantees, there was no willingness, in the words of one Jewish official, "to stand up and fight once the president called for a delay." On October 2, senators who had been working on behalf of the loan guarantees formally acceded to the president's 120-day-delay request. At year's end, the proposal awaited the beginning of the Second Session of the 102nd Congress. Jewish groups continued making the case for loan guarantees as a humanitarian issue.

In recognition of the steady flow of immigrants from the Soviet Union, on June 3, President Bush extended the temporary waiver of the Jackson-Vanik Amendment granted in December 1990 for a one-year period. (Jackson-Vanik, passed in 1974 as an amendment to the U.S. Trade Act of 1974, imposed restrictions on U.S. trade with the Soviet Union and linked "most-favored-nation" status to Soviet-Jewish immigration.) The waiver of Jackson-Vanik was a prelude to congressional passage in November, and presidential approval on December 9, of a U.S.-Soviet agreement that included MFN status for the USSR. The president had held off submitting the pact, signed in June, to Congress for ratification until the Soviet legislature passed a law guaranteeing Soviet citizens the right to emigrate freely. The legislature adopted such a law on May 20.

Black-Jewish Relations

Notwithstanding the tensions surrounding Crown Heights and other events, or declarations about the demise of the black-Jewish coalition, there were some positive developments to report. A recent study commissioned by the American Jewish Committee found that Jews had more positive attitudes toward blacks and a greater commitment to equal opportunity than did other white Americans. The study, "Jewish Attitudes Toward Blacks and Race Relations," by Tom W. Smith, director of the General Social Survey of the University of Chicago's National Opinion Research Center, found "no evidence of a Jewish backlash against the goal of racial equality or against blacks as a group, either as part of a general movement away from liberalism or as a specific result of racial conflicts with blacks."

In Kansas City, the city's first black mayor, Emanuel Cleaver, credited the Jewish community with playing a "major role" in his victory in an April election. While the community's agencies were proscribed from articulating formal support of any candidate, Jewish support "added credibility to the campaign." And in many communities faced with municipal budget cuts, intergroup coalitions formed to make their collective voice heard in city councils and state houses around the country.

Common Road to Justice: A Programming Manual for Blacks and Jews, published by the Religious Action Center of Reform Judaism, outlined programmatic initiatives that had been undertaken in hundreds of communities around the country. The manual was the result of a project cosponsored by the National Association for the Advancement of Colored People and the Union of American Hebrew Congregations, a parent body of the Religious Action Center.

In a public-policy area with long-standing implications for black-Jewish relations, Jewish groups were divided on the Bush administration's decision on July 10 to lift the economic sanctions imposed on South Africa by Congress in 1986, over President Reagan's veto. The National Jewish Community Relations Advisory Council (NJCRAC), arguing that the legal criteria for lifting sanctions had not been met, urged Jewish organizations to lobby the Congress to block President Bush's decision; and failing congressional action, to challenge the decision in the courts. Other Jewish groups took different positions. The Anti-Defamation League supported the president's action, accepting Bush's "assessment that South Africa has met the conditions for change embodied in the sanctions act." The Union of Orthodox Jewish Congregations, while not immediately adopting a position on the matter, raised questions about the NJCRAC stance, suggesting that the views of South African Jewry needed to be considered.

A meeting between African National Congress president Nelson Mandela and representatives of four national Jewish organizations, held in Washington on December 5 at Mandela's request during the South African leader's second U.S. trip, resulted in declarations on Mandela's part that the UN resolution equating Zionism with racism "has done much harm," but that he could not support the effort to repeal the resolution until further discussions with his ANC colleagues took place. Mandela reaffirmed the long-standing affection and cooperation between the ANC and South African Jews.

Catholic-Jewish Relations

The close, cooperative relations that existed between American Jews and American Catholics, on the national and local levels, were both tested and enhanced by developments this year.

POLAND: CARDINAL GLEMP; AUSCHWITZ

The visit of the Polish primate, Jozef Cardinal Glemp, to the United States—to visit Polish-American communities in 15 cities in September and October—provoked significant controversy within the Jewish community. The controversy dated back to August 1989, when Glemp delivered a homily at the Jasna Góra monastery in Czestochowa, Poland—the site of the "Black Madonna" shrine and therefore the focal point of Polish Catholic nationalism and religion—harshly criticizing the Jews, asserting that Jews controlled the mass media, "got peasants drunk," and felt "superior" to other people. He further accused New York rabbi Avraham Weiss and Weiss's followers, who had trespassed on the grounds of the Carmelite convent at Auschwitz, of plotting the "killing of our sisters." Cardinal Glemp's remarks were criticized by many Catholic religious leaders, especially by bishops in the United States and Europe, and his planned pastoral visit to the United States had to be put off. The 1991 visit to the United States was his rescheduled visit.

In the view of Jewish interreligious leaders, Glemp had never adequately apologized for his words. Thus, when the National Conference of Catholic Bishops (NCCB) in August invited Jewish leaders to a meeting with Glemp on September 20, a number of groups insisted that the cardinal first apologize for his Czestochowa remarks. On August 12, following a series of consultations between Jewish leaders and the NCCB, Cardinal Glemp, at the urging of Archbishop William Keeler of Baltimore, vice president of the NCCB, sent a letter to Archbishop Adam Maida of Detroit. In his letter to Maida, Glemp enumerated some of the Polish Catholic church's initiatives in Polish-Jewish affairs, but he did not repudiate his August 1989 remarks. Still, Jewish leaders by and large agreed that a meeting with Glemp could be a vehicle for further clarification of his views and for discussing other matters on the Polish-Jewish agenda.

Cardinal Glemp did not fully retract his 1989 remarks at the September 20 meeting in Washington, nor at a meeting with Jewish leaders on October 6 in New York. In a prepared statement read at the September 20 meeting, he asserted that he regretted the pain caused by his comments, but said that these comments "were in many aspects based on mistaken information." Nonetheless, the view expressed by most Jewish groups was that the meeting as a whole constituted a step forward and could lead to progress in Polish-Jewish relations in a number of areas discussed: anti-Semitism in Poland, curricula on Judaism in Polish seminaries, the condition of Jewish cemeteries in Poland, the timely implementation of the Auschwitz convent agreement.

Analysts of Catholic-Jewish relations took the position that what Cardinal Glemp believed with respect to Jews was far less important than his actions. They suggested that he was shrewd enough politically to understand the benefits that might accrue to his Polish Catholic flock, from the American government and elsewhere, through adherence to the teachings of Vatican II on the Jews. The Glemp meeting also served to enhance Jewish relations with the National Conference of Catholic Bishops, which from the outset—and particularly Archbishop Keeler—wanted the meeting to take place.

The issue that lay close to the heart of the Glemp matter was that of the Carmelite convent abutting the Auschwitz/Birkenau death-camp site. Construction of the interfaith "study center" and quarters for the Carmelite nuns was completed in 1991, but serious inflation in Poland during the year wiped out much of the capital that had been raised for completion of other facilities, including a new convent, several hundred meters from—and out of sight of—the death camp. At year's end the nuns were yet at their old convent. In July the newly elected superior-general of the Carmelite order, Father Camilo Maccise, said that the nuns would move no sooner than October 1992.

A signal development in Polish-Jewish relations—and in Catholic-Jewish relations generally—was the reading in Polish churches, during Sunday services on January 20, of a bishops' pastoral letter on anti-Semitism and Christian-Jewish relations. The letter, signed by all of Poland's bishops, including Cardinal Glemp, was a detailed statement on Jews and Judaism, anti-Semitism, and the Holocaust. It expressed "sincere regret for all the anti-Semitism committed at any time or by anyone on Polish soil" and asserted, "We must ask for forgiveness." The Polish bishops' pastoral was viewed as an important follow-up to the September 1990 "Prague Declaration" by Catholic and Jewish leadership on anti-Semitism in Eastern Europe. "As a pastoral letter, and not merely a statement," said Rabbi Leon Klenicki of the Anti-Defamation League, "the document carries weight."

THE VATICAN

There were encouraging signs this year on the question of establishing full and formal diplomatic relations between the Holy See and the State of Israel. New York's John Cardinal O'Connor visited Lebanon, Egypt, Jordan, and Israel from December 27 to January 7, 1992, and reported to Jewish groups upon his return, "There is a definite change in the Vatican's orientation toward Israel." Most significantly, with respect to diplomatic relations, said O'Connor, "The issue is no longer the status of Jerusalem, but guarantees of free access to Jerusalem's holy shrines to Christians, Muslims, and Jews; and the protection of Christian communities in the Middle East." Commenting on the political dynamics of the situation, Rabbi Marc Tanenbaum, a longtime observer of Vatican-Jewish relations, said, "[The Vatican] is not a player now and it needs to find a way to get to the negotiating table, or the fate of Jerusalem will be decided without them. The Vatican now realizes it needs diplomatic relations with Israel far more than Israel needs diplomatic relations with the Vatican." The Vatican had earlier asserted that there was no theological bar to full normalization of relations, and also that it recognized the State of Israel on a *de facto* basis.

Questions were raised by Jewish groups about a papal encyclical (*Redemptoris Missio, The Church's Missionary Mandate*), issued January 22, in which Pope John Paul II called for more active missionary efforts among non-Christians. The encyclical did not specifically mention Jews and reportedly reflected church fears that Catholicism was lagging behind Islam in expansion in Asia, Africa, and the Middle East. Nonetheless, according to Rabbi Leon Klenicki, interfaith affairs director of the ADL, "The language of Christian supersessionism and triumphalism resonates in the encyclical."

Finally, Jewish groups worldwide were exercised when, on June 4, Pope John Paul II, while on a visit to Poland, delivered a stinging condemnation of abortion, comparing it to the Nazi Holocaust.

OTHER MATTERS

Various Catholic bodies supported the movement for repeal of the 1975 UN resolution equating Zionism with racism. (When the original resolution was passed in 1975, Joseph Cardinal L. Bernardin of Chicago, then archbishop of Cincinnati and president of the U.S. Catholic Conference (USCC), the public-affairs arm of the Catholic Church in America, issued a statement expressing the conference's "profound disagreement" with the UN vote. The USCC position was reaffirmed in 1986 by Bishop James W. Malone of Youngstown, then USCC president.) In May of this year, the Roman Catholic archdiocese of Miami issued a call for repeal of the resolution, characterizing it as "offering a cloak to bigoted anti-Semitism around the world." And following the UN vote to repeal, in December, the U.S. Catholic Conference hailed the successful vote.

Within the American bishops' conference there were some indications of a growing impatience with Israeli government policy and performance. In an October 4 letter to President George Bush, welcoming U.S. efforts to bring about a Middle East peace conference, NCCB president Archbishop Daniel E. Pilarczyk of Cincinnati asserted that "legitimate and necessary assistance to Israel [should] not be used to foster a settlements policy which our government opposes and which could undermine prospects for peace." The suggestion of "linkage" of foreign aid to settlements went significantly beyond the 1989 NCCB statement, *Toward Peace in the Middle East: Perspectives, Principles, and Hopes*, in which the conference, in an otherwise positive analysis, called for Palestinian "sovereignty."

On the domestic public-affairs agenda, despite disagreement over the Religious Freedom Restoration Act (RFRA) (see "Church-State Issues," below), Catholic and Jewish groups continued to make common cause in statehouse advocacy around the country for a range of social-service and other programs.

Finally, the move to have Queen Isabella of Spain considered for sainthood in the Roman Catholic Church appeared to have fizzled when, in March, the 40 bishops on the Pontifical Council for Christian Unity unanimously passed a resolution recommending against it, stating that the proposed beatification contradicted current church teachings on the freedom of conscience. Queen Isabella, who in March 1492 signed the edict of expulsion of Jews from Spain, is viewed as a despot by both Jews and Muslims. American Jewish groups, and many American bishops as well, regarded the sainthood proposal as harmful to interreligious relationships.

Protestant-Jewish Relations

Protestant-Jewish relations in 1991 were characterized by disquiet on the national denominational level over the policies of the government of Israel and by cooperation on the local level—"in the pews"—on a range of issues on the domestic agenda.

On the national level, Protestants continued to express critical—sometimes harsh—positions on Israel and the Middle East and positive statements on Jews, Judaism, and Christian-Jewish relations. One significant departure from the pattern of blanket criticism of Israel was the statement adopted in June by the annual meeting of the General Assembly of the Presbyterian Church (USA), the main denominational body for American Presbyterians, which was more balanced with respect to the Arab-Israeli conflict and exhibited some concern for Israel's situation. The Presbyterian Church (USA) did not call for a cutoff in U.S. aid to Israel (as it had in 1990) and, in language that Jewish groups viewed as positive, asserted that "any peaceful resolution of the Israeli-Palestinian conflict must be accompanied by peace between Israel and the Arab states" through direct negotiations.

The General Board of the National Council of Churches (NCC), the 32-member umbrella group comprising traditional mainline Protestant and Orthodox denominations, which in November 1990 had issued a message on the Gulf crisis that called for the withdrawal of Israeli forces from the West Bank and for the convening of an international conference to resolve the Israeli-Palestinian issue, issued no significant statement in November 1991. Indeed, the professional leadership of the National Council of Churches indicated to Jewish leaders its intention to continue its effort to pursue a "moderate" stance on Israel.

The General Convention of the Episcopal Church adopted a Middle East resolution on July 13 that was highly critical of Israel. The resolution urged the U.S. government "to hold in escrow aid to Israel by an amount equal to any expenditures by the Government of Israel to expand, develop, or further establish Israeli settlements in the West Bank, Gaza, and East Jerusalem and only release the aid from escrow if proof is given that settlements are not being established." Jewish groups sharply criticized the Episcopal resolution. Rabbi A. James Rudin, national interreligious director of the American Jewish Committee, said the resolution was "one-sided in that it makes demands solely on Israel and not on those who have been at war with Israel for 43 years." The resolution notwithstanding, a July 29 letter to his fellow bishops by Bishop John H. Burt, chairman of the Church's Presiding Bishop's Committee on Christian-Jewish Relations, reflected the intense debate within the church on the resolution. It called upon Episcopalians to "understand and recognize" the "risks Israel must take" and the "virtues of the Jewish State along with its warts."

On the local level, Bishop Charles Vache of the Episcopal Diocese of Southern Virginia created a flap in May when he compared the treatment of Palestinians under the Israeli government to that of Jews in Nazi Germany. "We were sinfully silent then. . . . We must speak out now," said Vache. Jewish groups characterized Vache's comments as "arrogant, ignorant, and offensive." Noted the local ADL representative, Ira Gissen, "In the 1930's the churches were actively teaching contempt, which created the climate in which the Holocaust was possible; perhaps the bishop is trying to relieve his own guilt by making this ludicrous comparison."

The Evangelical Lutheran Church, the nation's largest Lutheran denomination, passed a resolution at its biennial churchwide assembly in August calling for the delay of U.S. loan guarantees to Israel "until and unless the construction and expansion of settlements in the occupied territories is stopped." Finally, the 7th Assembly of the World Council of Churches (WCC)—the WCC meets every seven years—met in February and issued a statement on the Gulf War, the Middle East, and the threat to world peace. Conspicuously missing from the WCC statement was any reference to threats to Israel during the war.

The New York Jewish Community Relations Council (JCRC) was victorious in 1991 in two lawsuits brought against it by Jews for Jesus, a Hebrew-Christian missionary group. In January the Appellate Division of the New York State Supreme Court upheld a lower court's ruling that Jews for Jesus was not a victim of discrimination when the JCRC, in February 1985, circulated a warning about its activities, encouraging rabbis to ask local restaurants and catering halls not to rent their premises to the group. And on July 31, in *Jews for Jesus v. Jewish Community Relations Council of New York*, a federal district court judge in New York ruled that objections raised by Jewish organizations to Jews for Jesus holding its annual convention at a kosher resort were protected under First Amendment free-speech guarantees. Jewish organizations had objected to the practice of Jews for Jesus misrepresenting themselves as "Jewish," and had said that they would not hold their meetings at the facility. Jews for Jesus announced that it would appeal the district court decision.

Although there was a continuing decline in the growth of most Protestant denominations, including many evangelical churches, during 1991, one notable exception was the Assemblies of God, a pentecostal group that proselytized aggressively, was politically and religiously conservative, and was generally supportive of Israel. In general, whatever growth was occurring in the Protestant community was in large measure among the theologically and politically more conservative. Jewish groups viewed with some concern the changes taking place in the Southern Baptist Convention, the nation's largest Protestant denomination, which in 1991 saw its offices and seminaries dominated by fundamentalist conservatives. In the decade-long struggle between "moderates" and "conservatives" for control of the Southern Baptist Convention, the battleground now shifted to the Baptist Joint Committee, a respected public-policy voice in Washington that had long enjoyed a close working relationship with Jewish groups.

Federal Judiciary

Changes in the federal judiciary, especially the U.S. Supreme Court, seemed likely to influence the arena of constitutional protections, particularly First Amendment guarantees of the separation of church and state. A signal development was the resignation, on June 27, of Associate Supreme Court Justice Thurgood Marshall, the first black justice in the High Court's history and the present court's most consistent liberal. Clarence Thomas, a conservative black judge on the U.S. Court of Appeals for the District of Columbia Circuit, was named by President Bush on July 1 to succeed Marshall. It was not until October 23, however, that Thomas took the oath as a Supreme Court justice, following several weeks of explosive confirmation hearings—including last-minute hearings on allegations of sexual harassment—that culminated in his narrow (52–48) confirmation on October 15 by the Senate. At 43, Clarence Thomas became the youngest justice on the Rehnquist court.

Jewish groups expressed concern over Thomas's views on a variety of issues, especially employment discrimination, affirmative action, and church-state separation. Among the Jewish groups that took positions in opposition to Thomas's confirmation were the American Jewish Congress, the National Council of Jewish Women, the Jewish Labor Committee, New Jewish Agenda, the Union of American Hebrew Congregations, and the Workmen's Circle. Agudath Israel of America and the National Council of Young Israel, two Orthodox Jewish congregational bodies, endorsed Thomas. Other groups did not adopt formal positions on Thomas; nonetheless, these organizations raised questions with respect to the nominee's qualifications and his positions on civil liberties.

Another judicial nomination that evoked criticism was that of Florida federal district court judge Kenneth L. Ryskamp, in April 1990, to fill a vacancy on the U.S. 11th Circuit Court of Appeals. Jewish groups, together with civil-rights and civil-liberties organizations, raised questions with respect to Ryskamp's positions on civil-rights issues, his membership in a club that reportedly discriminated against blacks and Jews, and his comments from the bench that indicated an insensitivity to discrimination issues. The Anti-Defamation League, the American Jewish Committee, and the American Jewish Congress delivered testimony at Senate Judiciary Committee hearings on Judge Ryskamp in March. On April 11, the committee voted 6–5 to kill the nomination.

Through 1991, 115 Bush nominees to the federal judiciary had been confirmed, with 50 nominations pending and 30 vacancies on the federal bench yet to be filled. Analysts such as Marc Stern, co-legal director of the American Jewish Congress, suggested that, with the changing contours of the federal judiciary resulting from the unusually large number of Reagan-Bush appointees, the federal courts might be less reliable guarantors of fundamental constitutional rights for the foreseeable future. According to Stern, "Even without Clarence Thomas, the Supreme Court— and other federal courts—would be on a course that's very inhospitable toward using judicial power as a check on government action. The Jewish community needs to revisit its strategy of looking toward the federal courts. We need to go to the Congress for legislative action to ensure our rights, to state constitutions, and to state courts and legislatures."

Church-State Issues

"ESTABLISHMENT-CLAUSE" MATTERS

The U.S. Supreme Court on March 18 agreed to review a Rhode Island case, *Lee v. Weisman*, which would test whether public-school graduation ceremonies that include prayers violate the establishment clause and are therefore illegal. Daniel and Vivian Weisman of Providence objected in the mid-1980s, and again in 1989, when prayers were offered at graduation ceremonies at their daughters' graduations from the Nathan Bishop Middle School, a public school. A federal appeals court agreed with the Weismans. The Bush administration, in requesting that the Supreme Court hear *Lee v. Weisman*, urged the court to replace the existing standard, the so-called *Lemon* test,[1] with a new test: whether anyone not choosing to participate in the practice at issue would feel coerced.

Almost all Jewish groups were opposed to the substitution of a stricter "coercion" test for the three-part *Lemon* test. "We haven't always agreed with where the courts have come out when they use *Lemon*," said Marc Stern of the American Jewish Congress, "but without *Lemon* it will be impossible." A broad coalition of organizations filed an *amicus curiae* brief, urging the Supreme Court to affirm the appellate-

---

[1]In order to be constitutional under the *Lemon v. Kurtzman* guidelines, a statute or governmental activity must satisfy at least one of three conditions: it must have a secular legislative purpose; its principal or primary effect must be one that neither advances nor inhibits religion; and it must not foster an excessive government entanglement with religion. Violation of any one of the three prongs of this test renders the act or activity unconstitutional. The *Lemon* test has been the one most often applied since it was first articulated in the 1971 decision.

court decision holding the prayer unconstitutional, and retaining the *Lemon* test as "an elaboration of the fundamental rule that government must be neutral with respect to religion." One group that was not opposed to revising or removing *Lemon* was Agudath Israel of America. Abba Cohen, Washington representative of Aguda, asserted that "[*Lemon's*] impact has been devastating [for religion]. Such hostility has never been required by the Constitution."

Questions related to religion in the schools—long a heated battleground in the church-state area—came up on a number of fronts in 1991. President Bush set the tone for the administration stance in an address on January 27 to the convention of the National Religious Broadcasters, whom he told that he had not lessened his "commitment to restoring voluntary prayer in the schools."

A development that was noted with growing concern was the resurgence of the evangelical religious right and the move to renew the social agenda of fundamentalist groups. Pat Robertson's Christian Coalition, founded in 1989, a political-action group whose agenda for America was "a return to moral strength," by 1991 had 125 chapters in 43 states and announced a ten-year plan to become "the most powerful political organization of its kind." The most likely long-term impact of the evangelical resurgence, in the view of analysts of the field, was in two areas touching on public-school education: "equal access," with its increased possibilities for proselytizing; and teaching about religion. In fact, largely as a result of evangelical complaints, many texts were being rewritten to include material on religion.

"Equal access"—allowing noncurriculum-related student-run clubs in public schools to meet during noninstructional hours—was still in the courts during 1991. On August 14, a federal district court in Washington, reconsidering *Garnett v. Renton*, ruled that the 1984 federal Equal Access Act could not require activity that the state's constitution prohibited, specifically, the use of school premises for religious clubs and the appropriation of public money for religious purposes. At the close of 1991 the district court ruling was on appeal to the Ninth Circuit. Precisely the opposite conclusion was reached in a similar situation in Idaho. In *Hoppock v. Twin Falls School District*, a federal district court ruled in September that the Idaho state constitution could not overrule the Equal Access Act. These cases, particularly *Garnett*, suggested to Jewish groups that they ought to look to state constitutions, in addition to, or even rather than, the federal courts, in developing tactical approaches to such issues.

Recognizing the reality that the Equal Access Act was not likely to be repealed or overruled in the foreseeable future, two Jewish groups, the American Jewish Committee and the American Jewish Congress, joined with 19 Protestant, Catholic, and educational organizations in publishing *The Equal Access Act and the Public Schools: Questions and Answers*, in order to provide guidance in the implementation of the act, to ensure that religious groups receive "equal, and not preferred, treatment," and as an aid in guiding against proselytizing. A number of Jewish groups, believing that the guidebook implicitly sanctioned the act, declined to participate in the project.

One area in which the establishment clause crossed swords with other constitutional guarantees—notably freedom of expression—involved the distribution of religious literature in public schools. A number of cases involving this issue arrived in federal courts in 1991, indicating that the problem was no longer an isolated one. *Berger v. Rensselaer Central School District*, before the U.S. Seventh Circuit Court of Appeals, tested the constitutionality of distribution by the Gideons, a Christian religious organization, of various items of sectarian literature to primary-school students. A range of Jewish groups joined in broad coalitions in submitting *amicus* briefs in this case. In *Wauconda v. Hedges*, a federal district court in Illinois upheld a ban on student distribution of religious literature. And in *Roberts v. Madigan*, the Tenth Circuit Court of Appeals, in a split decision, affirmed a district court decision prohibiting an elementary-school teacher from displaying religious materials—a Bible, Christian religious books, and a religious poster—in his classroom. Observers noted that case law in this area remained mixed and was likely to remain so until a religious-literature case reached the Supreme Court.

A continuing battleground was public aid to parochial schools and aid for remedial programs in schools. Of particular concern to Jewish groups was the Bush administration's "Choice for Education" plan, which offered federal incentives for school "choice" programs, giving parents the option of sending their children to any school, public or private, secular or parochial. Jewish groups questioned the proposal on two grounds: diverting federal funds from public to private schools would further erode the already inadequate pool of resources for public education (for which the Jewish community had long articulated support); and the use of public funds for religiously sponsored schools violates the establishment clause. The Bush plan for choice did not move forward during the First Session of the 102nd Congress in 1991. In a few states, measures that included voucher plans and tuition-tax-credit systems were considered by legislatures; in one state, New Hampshire, a voucher plan put forth by the town of Epsom was invalidated in the courts. Budget crunches in many states undoubtedly inhibited consideration of programs that required additional expenditures.

On the related issue of public-sector aid to remedial programs, the U.S. Eighth Circuit Court of Appeals ruled, in *Pulido v. Cavazos*, that publicly funded off-premises remedial programs for private and parochial schools were permissible. Jewish groups were divided on this issue, the American Jewish Congress, for example, sanctioning the use of off-premises vehicles for such activity. Regarding programs conducted on school premises, the U.S. Supreme Court had previously ruled, in a 1985 case, *Aguilar v. Felton*, that use of funds under Chapter I of the Elementary and Secondary Education Act of 1965 to aid auxiliary services provided in religiously related schools was unconstitutional.

Two federal court cases, in California and Illinois, dealt with the subject of religious symbols in public parks—which are considered "open forums" and are thus arguably different from government-owned buildings. The Ninth U.S. Circuit Court of Appeals ruled in *Hewitt v. Joyner* that government ownership of a park containing statues depicting scenes from the Christian Scriptures violated the establishment clause. And in June, the Seventh Circuit, in a similar case, *Doe v. Small*, ruled that Ottawa, Illinois, could not display in a public park 16 large paintings depicting events in the life of Jesus. The full (*en banc*) Seventh Circuit Court was expected to rehear *Doe v. Small*. Jewish groups participated in these cases as "friends of the court" and applauded the decisions.

The Lubavitch organization continued to erect Hanukkah menorahs in a number of communities around the country, generally in proximity to Christmas trees or other artifacts, in an effort to satisfy the technical requirements laid down in recent Supreme Court decisions. One long-standing dispute, simmering since 1987, over placement of a menorah in Cincinnati's Fountain Square, ended with a federal appeals court permitting the Chabad menorah. Most Jewish groups viewed placement of religious symbols—including placement together with other religious symbols or secular artifacts—as a violation of the establishment clause.

The constitutionality of designating Good Friday a legal state holiday was upheld, for the first time, by the U.S. Ninth Circuit Court of Appeals in early May. The 2–1 decision in *Cammack v. Waihee*, declaring Good Friday a Hawaii state holiday, was surprising to knowledgeable observers. Analysts suggested that if the Hawaii statute were ultimately upheld by the Supreme Court, such a ruling could sanction the closing of public schools on the Jewish High Holy Days. Although the Jewish community had not traditionally opposed this practice—currently done in many school districts for administrative reasons—it had never advocated it officially. Hawaii was one of 12 states that currently designated the Friday before Easter, a Christian holiday commemorating the crucifixion of Jesus, as a state holiday. State courts in California and Connecticut in previous years ruled that Good Friday cannot be a state holiday.

Finally, in October, the Fourth U.S. Circuit Court of Appeals upheld a lower-court decision in *North Carolina Civil Liberties Union v. Honorable H. William Costangy* that it was unconstitutional for a state-court judge to open his court sessions with a 15-second, self-composed, nonsectarian prayer.

"FREE-EXERCISE" MATTERS

In the aftermath of the April 1990 U.S. Supreme Court decision in *Employment Division of Oregon v. Smith*, the so-called peyote case, which rejected the "compelling-state-interest" standard in use since 1963 in free-exercise cases, no fewer than 33 federal cases, through 1991, were decided using the new standard articulated by Justice Antonin Scalia in his majority opinion in *Smith*. (See AJYB 1992, pp. 201–02.) Seeking to reverse that decision with legislation, on July 26, the Religious Freedom Restoration Act (RFRA) was introduced anew in the 102nd Congress by Rep. Stephen J. Solarz (D., N.Y.). (Solarz's original bill had died without coming to a vote in the 101st Congress.) Drafted by a broad coalition of religious groups, RFRA was considered one of the highest legislative priorities of Jewish groups across the political and religious spectrum. The measure aimed to codify the principle that no governmental body may restrict a person's free exercise of religion unless it can demonstrate a compelling state interest to do so.

Although the language of RFRA was neutral on the issue of reproductive choice, some prolife groups, including the National Right to Life Committee and the U.S. Catholic Conference (USCC), the public-affairs arm of American Catholic bishops, alleged that the bill implicitly supported abortion, and that it would be used to establish a religiously based right to abortion were *Roe v. Wade* to be overturned. (The USCC also maintained that RFRA would be used to challenge "parochiaid" proposals and religious organizations' tax-exempt status.) Movement on RFRA was stalled in 1991; indeed, by year's end companion legislation had not been introduced in the Senate.

Jewish groups, concerned about the potential erosion in religious liberty and practices made possible by the Scalia opinion in *Smith*, played an active role in drafting the legislation and in its advocacy. Even the Union of Orthodox Jewish Congregations of America and Agudath Israel of America, congregational bodies of Orthodox Judaism normally aligned with "prolife" forces, were vigorous advocates of the measure.

As Jews continued moving into areas new to Jewish population, the decision to build a synagogue sometimes resulted in disputes related to local zoning regulations. In some cases, questions were raised as to whether houses of worship had to adapt to the same land-use regulations as other community institutions. In others, zoning authorities attempted to regulate the scope and extent of a congregation's activities. This relatively new area was a difficult one for Jewish groups. "While zoning laws perform an important function, and synagogues cannot legitimately expect routinely to supersede these laws in the name of religious liberty," said American Jewish Committee legal director Samuel Rabinove, "these laws must not be permitted to stifle religious practice, diversity, and change."

In New York state, in May, a number of suits were brought in federal district court challenging the creation of a new village, Airmont, within the town of Ramapo, New York, whose zoning regulations would ban worship services in private residential dwellings. The proponents of the newly created village did not hide the fact that their motivation was to discourage Orthodox Jews from living in the community. On December 14, the U.S. Justice Department joined in the fray, filing its suit, *United States v. Village of Airmont*, against the new village and the town from which it was formed, alleging violation of the Orthodox residents' rights under federal fair-housing laws. At year's end, *U.S. v. Airmont* and other cases were pending in the district court.

On appeal before the Pennsylvania Supreme Court was a child-custody case, *Zummo v. Zummo*, arising from the divorce of an interfaith couple who made competing claims regarding the children's religious training and education. An appellate court in Pennsylvania permitted the father, during visitation periods, to take his children to religious services in a faith different from the mother's Jewish faith. *Zummo* raised constitutional issues—not resolved to date—which were perhaps overshadowed by strong emotional and religious issues.

Civil Rights

DISCRIMINATION

The U.S. Supreme Court ruled on March 26 that federal law barring discrimination in employment—Title VII of the 1964 Civil Rights Act—does not apply to Americans overseas. The 6–3 decision in *Equal Employment Opportunity Commission v. Aramco* upheld a federal appeals court ruling. The American Jewish Committee, the Anti-Defamation League, and the American Jewish Congress joined in a single *amicus curiae* brief in the case. American Jewish Committee legal director Samuel Rabinove, calling for legislation to remedy *Aramco*, asserted that "language can be formulated quite easily to say that Title VII does apply to American citizens working for American companies abroad." Indeed, a provision of the Civil Rights Act of 1991 (see below), signed into law on November 21, permitted American workers abroad to sue their U.S.-based employers for discrimination, reversing the Supreme Court ruling in *Aramco*.

CIVIL RIGHTS ACT OF 1991

The embattled Civil Rights Act of 1991 finally achieved passage in the 102nd Congress. The measure was a compromise bill, two years in the making, that had become a flash point in the relationship between President George Bush and black Americans and a battleground over racial preference involving the Jewish community as well.

The Civil Rights Act of 1991 was the first successful effort on the part of Congress to reverse the work of the conservative Rehnquist Supreme Court. Six U.S. Supreme Court decisions handed down during the 1988–89 term (and four other High Court rulings since 1985 involving awards in civil-rights cases) had restricted the reach and remedies of federal laws involving gender, racial, religious, and ethnic discrimination in hiring, promotion, and termination. Passage of this legislation, which would make it easier for a plaintiff to prove the discriminatory effect of employment practices and require employers to defend the legitimacy of such practices—and not the other way around—had been frustrated since first introduced early in the 101st Congress. President Bush had, in 1990, vetoed an earlier version of the bill, contending that it would induce employers to hire certain numbers of minorities and women in order to avoid lawsuits. His warning played to the belief of some whites that race preferences had cost them jobs; this administration view did not help to lessen political wrangling, which stretched out over a period of months and continued into the 102nd Congress.

Among the provisions of the final compromise bill, passed by the Senate in October (93–5) and the House in November (381–38), was one permitting American workers abroad to sue their U.S.-based employers for discrimination, reversing the earlier U.S. Supreme Court ruling, *Equal Employment Opportunity Commission v. Aramco*. President Bush signed the bill on November 21.

In the sharp debate that unfolded during the year over the proposed bill, almost all Jewish groups supported the legislation, notwithstanding questions involving the "quota" issue that had been played out in the extended 1990 debate over the bill. (See AJYB 1992, pp. 204–05.) But the discussion within the Jewish community in 1991 was more nuanced, and the administration took advantage of the slight differences in levels of support of Jewish groups for the bill. Early in the debate—on January 16, the day the Gulf War began—representatives of the Anti-Defamation League, the American Jewish Committee, and the Agudath Israel of America were wooed by administration representatives at a White House meeting called to discuss the views of Jewish communal organizations, ranging from the AJCommittee's enthusiastic support, through ADL's somewhat reluctant middle course of support, to Aguda, which had opposed the 1990 bill, supporting the president's position that the bill would promote the use of quotas. Ultimately, the Union of Orthodox Jewish Congregations of America, a centrist Orthodox congregational body, decided in May, after lengthy deliberations, to oppose the bill, asserting its belief that the bill "includes provisions that might lead employers to conclude that they should use racial, religious, or gender quotas," and joining Agudath Israel in that view. Twelve national organizations articulated joint support for the measure: the American Jewish Committee, the Anti-Defamation League, the American Jewish Congress, the National Council of Jewish Women, Hadassah, Women's American ORT, the Jewish War Veterans, the Jewish Labor Committee, the congregational bodies of Conservative and Reform Judaism in America, B'nai B'rith, and the Women's League for Conservative Judaism. The basis for their support was articulated by the American Jewish Committee: "The Civil Rights Act is about fairness and opportunity . . .[it] has nothing to do with quotas."

A number of Jewish groups voiced strong objections to last-minute amendments to the House bill, including one that could arguably be interpreted as permitting quotas when used to hire or promote only "qualified" applicants. The American Jewish Committee and the National Council of Jewish Women expressed "reservations" about the measure, suggesting that the "cap" provisions for punitive damages weakened the bill, and that "undue obstacles" in the way of discrimination claims were yet in place. Nonetheless, final passage of the Civil Rights Act was welcomed by most Jewish groups as a major step in remedying the 1988–89 Supreme Court decisions, one that sent a strong message to the High Court that the intent of Congress in earlier civil-rights legislation had to be taken seriously in judicial interpretation.

Nazi War Criminals

Through 1991, the U.S. Justice Department Office of Special Investigations (OSI), charged with the investigation of individuals suspected of being Nazi war criminals and alleged to have lied when they entered the United States or applied for citizenship, had stripped 35 Nazi war criminals of their citizenship. Legal action of some sort—deportation and extradition—had been taken against 75 people since the office was created in 1979. During 1991, OSI had approximately 500 cases of suspected war criminals under investigation.

The citizenship of Anton Baumann, 79 years old, was revoked in May by a federal district court in Milwaukee, on the grounds that Baumann had illegally concealed his service as a member of the Death's Head Battalion of the SS, as a guard at the Stutthof and Buchenwald concentration camps, when he sought entry into the United States after World War II. In October the U.S. Supreme Court denied an appeal from Michael Schmidt, who was stripped of his citizenship in 1990 for concealing wartime service as a guard at the Sachsenhausen concentration camp. Observers noted that it was routine for the Supreme Court to refuse to hear such appeals. But in December the U.S. Sixth Circuit Court of Appeals did block the government from deporting Leonid Petkiewytsch, 68, who admitted, when he applied for U.S. citizenship, to having served at the Kiel-Hassee labor camp during the war. He had been living in the United States on an immigrant visa since 1955. The court said that the government had failed to prove that Petkiewytsch had abused prisoners. At year's end the government had not decided whether to appeal the ruling to the Supreme Court.

DEMJANJUK CASE

New evidence submitted by John Demjanjuk's defense attorney during 1990 raised questions about the identity of the 65-year-old Demjanjuk, who was in prison in Israel, as "Ivan the Terrible." (Demjanjuk, accused of having operated the gas chambers at the Treblinka death camp, was extradited to Israel by the United States in 1986. After a lengthy and often contentious trial, he was convicted on April 18, 1988, of crimes against the Jewish people, crimes against humanity, war crimes, and crimes against persecuted people. On April 25, 1988, Demjanjuk was sentenced to death. In 1989, the Israeli High Court of Justice, which had planned to hear an appeal of Demjanjuk's conviction and death sentence, granted a six-month delay, based on reported new defense evidence that Demjanjuk was a victim of mistaken identity.) In August 1991, Demjanjuk's lawyer appealed to the High Court for Demjanjuk's immediate release on the grounds that the prosecution withheld from the defense exculpatory evidence about Demjanjuk's identity. Demjanjuk's Israeli lawyer, Yoram Sheftel, claimed that the testimony—in the form of statements, found in the Soviet Union, from former Treblinka prison guards—identified another Treblinka guard, Ivan Marczenko (or "Marchenko") as Ivan the Terrible. (Sheftel had made the same claim during Demjanjuk's trial; the prosecutor had countered by maintaining that "Marczenko" was the maiden name of the defendant's mother, which he sometimes used as his own.) The Israeli High Court of Justice on August 14 rejected the Demjanjuk application; the court, however, agreed to hold a hearing on the evidence in December. The hearing was held on December 23. The court then said that it would hear "new evidence" on the appeal from both sides in the case in January 1992.

OTHER MATTERS

The First International Gathering of Hidden Children took place in New York at the end of May. The gathering, sponsored by the Anti-Defamation League and Child Development Research (an organization that studies the psychological effects of persecution on children), brought together 1,600 child Holocaust survivors from around the world who survived the Holocaust in hiding or by being rescued by non-Jews.

The Pollard Case

On September 11, Jonathan J. Pollard filed an appeal with the U.S. Court of Appeals for the D.C. Circuit to reverse a 1990 district court decision denying his motion to have his plea of guilty set aside. (Pollard had pleaded guilty, was convicted in June 1986 of spying for Israel, and was serving a life sentence. Pollard's attorneys contended that the government had violated a number of promises made in the plea-bargain agreement, chiefly not to seek a life sentence.) Were the district court decision reversed and the motion granted, Pollard would be entitled to a trial on the espionage charges. A decision was expected on the appeal during 1992. In August President Bush said "there is no consideration" for presidential commutation of Pollard's sentence.

Pollard's appeal generated increased activity throughout the year on the part of his family and a cadre of activists on his behalf. The stance of most Jewish groups was articulated by the National Jewish Community Relations Advisory Council (NJCRAC), in a statement issued on behalf of NJCRAC's member agencies in June: "The NJCRAC has supported the call for full, open, and fair hearings, before appropriate tribunals, on the question of whether the fact that Mr. Pollard was an American Jew who spied for Israel may have had an improper influence in his sentencing." However, said NJCRAC, "there is no demonstrable indication that factors related to [Pollard's] standing as a Jew entered into the determination of his sentence." Most Jewish groups did not join as *amici* in the appeal of *U.S. v. Pollard*. Jewish organizations continued exploring with government officials and with Pollard's attorneys allegations of discrimination, civil-rights and civil-liberties abuses, and institutional anti-Semitism.

JEROME A. CHANES

The United States, Israel, and the Middle East

T HE YEAR 1991 BEGAN WITH an imminent threat of war in the Middle East and ended with the first stirrings of hope for peace between Arabs and Israelis. It was a year of great highs and lows in relations between the United States and Israel, highs in the American-led defeat of Iraq's Saddam Hussein and the opening of Middle East negotiations in Madrid, lows in the off-and-on contention between the Bush administration and the Shamir government, highlighted by bitterness over Israel's request for loan guarantees from the United States. Above all, it was a year of change—in the Middle East, in U.S. involvement in the area, in U.S.-Israeli relations—which reflected the wider change in the world brought about by the fall of the Soviet Empire and the ensuing ambivalence about America's role in the world.

The Gulf War

On the first day of the new year, President George Bush met with his senior advisers to discuss military and diplomatic strategies that might avert war in the Persian Gulf. Five months had passed since Saddam Hussein invaded and overran Kuwait. Nothing had budged the Iraqi leader, not the formation of a coalition of nations (including a number of Arab states) led by the United States, not a series of United Nations resolutions instituting sanctions against Iraq, not a variety of diplomatic approaches by the United States and others, and not a U.S. buildup of forces in Saudi Arabia. In place was the critical Security Council resolution of November 29 which demanded that Iraq leave Kuwait by January 15, 1991, or face possible war.

An unnamed senior official had told the *New York Times* on December 31 that Secretary of State James A. Baker III would likely make a trip to the Gulf as the deadline approached, leading to speculation that a much-discussed meeting between Baker and Foreign Minister Tariq Aziz of Iraq might yet come off. The negotiations about such a meeting, which had begun in December 1990, had stalled when the Iraqis insisted that Baker could visit Baghdad only on January 12, a date that the administration rejected as being too close to the deadline. The Baker trip's purpose, as described by an official, was "to hold the coalition together, to seek a peaceful solution, and if Saddam Hussein fails to accept the message that he must unconditionally leave Kuwait, we want to consider the use of force."

Meanwhile, the foreign ministers of the European Community (EC) had agreed on December 30, 1990, to meet in Luxembourg on January 4, 1991, to consider an independent initiative to persuade Iraq to withdraw from Kuwait. There seemed to be no consensus among the countries, however, as to whether the EC should simply reiterate the demand for an end to Iraq's occupation of Kuwait or offer some face-saving formula that might ease a withdrawal. British foreign minister Douglas Hurd cautioned against any independent move, saying that if there were any chance for peace, however slim, it lay in Saddam's knowing that "if he stays in Kuwait, he will be attacked, and that if he withdraws completely and unconditionally, he will not be attacked."

Early January also brought a greater urgency to the question of Congress's role in events in the Gulf. Some commentators and newspapers criticized the administration for not bringing Congress into the decision-making process; others accused Congress of shrinking from its constitutional duty to debate the issue. Robert Dole (R., Kan.), Senate minority leader, and Les Aspin (D., Wis.), chairman of the House Armed Services Committee, indicated that Congress would be unwilling to support a war until it had been persuaded that all opportunities for a peaceful settlement had been exhausted, making it clear that they looked for further efforts beyond the January 3 U.S. deadline to arrange a Baker-Hussein meeting.

And, indeed, as January 3 arrived, a new initiative was taken. Saying "I am ready to make one last attempt to go the extra mile for peace," the president offered to send Baker to Geneva on January 7, 8, or 9 during his Middle East trip to meet with Aziz. The proposal was described by administration officials as an effort by the White House to reassert Bush's leadership on the diplomatic and domestic political fronts in the face of potential independent peace initiatives abroad and congressional grumbling at home. That evening Baker indicated in an ABC television interview that he was "not as optimistic about the possibility" of a diplomatic settlement as he had been even the week before, but he expressed the hope that the Iraqis would pick up on this offer "because this will be the last such proposal we will make." Congressional reaction to the proposal was generally positive, with Democratic leaders saying there should be no debate pending the outcome of Baker's mission.

In spite of the new administration offer, the Europeans held their scheduled emergency meeting the following day in Luxembourg. Halfway through the closed-door session, word came that Aziz had agreed to travel to Geneva on January 9 to meet with Baker. One official said the news brought "an audible sigh of relief" to the room. By day's end, the EC members had issued a statement reiterating "their firm commitment in favor of the full and unconditional implementation of the relevant resolutions of the UN Security Council," welcoming the agreement for a Baker-Aziz meeting, inviting Aziz to meet with EC representatives on January 10, but also asserting their commitment, once the present crisis was settled, "to contribute actively to a settlement of the other problems of the region," a clear reference to the Arab-Israeli conflict. The latter was seen as a French victory, part of the ongoing French effort to mount an approach independent of the United States by suggesting an incentive for Iraq to withdraw from Kuwait. However, on January 5, Aziz declined the European invitation for a meeting, saying that Iraq resented "the submissive policies" of some European governments to the United States.

In announcing Iraqi acceptance, over state-run television, of the U.S. offer for a meeting, Aziz said he would press for "justice and fairness" for the Palestinians, including the "right of the Palestinian people in establishing its free state on the land of Palestine with Jerusalem as its capital."

In his own announcement of the agreed-upon meeting, President Bush told the news conference on January 4 that there "can be no compromise or negotiating on the objectives contained in those UN resolutions." When asked by a journalist whether Baker would also talk in Geneva about the Palestinian problem, as the Iraqis wanted, the president said: "There will be no linkage on these questions."

The following day the president addressed the nation over radio. He told the country that "time is running out," that 11 days from then, Saddam Hussein "will either have met the United Nations deadline for a full and unconditional withdrawal, or he will have once again defied the civilized world. This is a deadline for Saddam Hussein to comply with the United Nations resolution, not a deadline for our own armed forces."

On Sunday, January 6, prior to taking off for his trip to Europe, Baker told ABC News that he considered the French approach to resolving the crisis—Iraq to withdraw from Kuwait with the understanding that there would later be an international conference to try to settle all outstanding conflicts in the Middle East—as unacceptable: "You cannot make promises that would constitute linkage. We think that is a terrible mistake." He added that the only thing he would offer Aziz was that if they complied with the UN resolutions, "they can expect that force will not be used against them. And if they don't, then, in all probability, force will be used against them."

Baker also indicated that the administration would now welcome even a 60–40 congressional vote backing the use of force. This was a change in the administration's position, which had previously treated anything less than overwhelming congressional support as likely to send a message of weakness to Iraq. On the same ABC show, House Speaker Thomas Foley (D., Wash.) and Republican Senate leader Dole indicated that Congress would take up the issue after the Baker-Aziz meeting, and that votes in support of the use of force were likely.

A *Washington Post*-ABC News poll released on January 7 showed strong support—67 percent—for the president's handling of the crisis. In addition, there were majorities calling for Bush to get congressional approval before using force as well as for Congress to give more support to the president.

On January 8, one day before Baker's meeting with Aziz, Bush sent a letter to Congress calling for a resolution supporting the use of force to "help dispel any belief that may exist in the minds of Iraq's leaders that the United States lacks the necessary unity to act decisively in response to Iraq's continued aggression against Kuwait." The letter was the first presidential request for congressional backing for offensive military action since President Lyndon Johnson asked for the Gulf of Tonkin resolution on the Vietnam War on August 5, 1964.

On January 9, Baker and Aziz met for six hours in Geneva. Although expectations were high, Baker dashed hopes when he announced to the press immediately afterward that he had "heard nothing that suggested to me any Iraqi flexibility whatever." Baker indicated that he had offered Aziz assurances that if Iraq were to comply with UN resolutions and leave Kuwait, it would not be attacked by U.S. forces. The secretary said that when Aziz raised the idea of an international conference on the Middle East, he told the Iraqi that "rewarding Iraq's aggression with a link to the Arab-Israeli peace process would really send a terrible signal." When Aziz insisted that Iraq was trying to help the Palestinians, Baker said that Iraq had invaded Kuwait "for its own aggrandizement." Baker indicated as well that he had rejected Aziz's invitation to come to Baghdad as a stall and warned the Iraqi "not to miscalculate the resolve of the American people."

At a separate press conference, Aziz complained about Baker's "threats" and reiterated the old Iraqi theme that the peace of the whole region was the real issue. When asked about a possible war, Aziz said Iraq would defend itself in "a very bold manner" and pledged that Iraq would "absolutely" target Israel for attack.

Aziz's threat to attack Israel raised the question of Israel's role should war break out. On January 8, Hosni Mubarak told a gathering of writers in Cairo that Egypt would "not permit an Israeli involvement or a military involvement in the Gulf crisis. I do not think Israel would get involved, but if it did, Egypt would take a different position." Three days later, Mubarak told CNN that if Iraq launched an attack against Israel, "she will have the right to retaliate. Every country has a legitimate right to defend itself." But he added that he doubted Israel would have to do so since the United States had the ability to destroy Iraqi Scud missiles. On January 10, President Bush called Prime Minister Yitzhak Shamir to tell him that he was sending Deputy Secretary of State Lawrence Eagleburger to Israel to discuss Israel's role; he urged Israel to "lie low" and "stay out" of the conflict.

After two days of talks in which Eagleburger reportedly asked Israel to let the United States handle any response to an Iraqi attack, Israeli defense minister Moshe Arens made clear that "if we are attacked, we will respond." Shamir was reportedly more equivocal in his response, not saying explicitly that Israel would strike back at Iraq but only that it "will determine its response if attacked." It was also reported that Eagleburger and his team were unable in the two days of talks to conclude arrangements on tactical coordination between the Israeli military and U.S. forces in the Gulf.

In Baghdad, meanwhile, Saddam told a conference of Islamic leaders that he was preparing for a holy war against the U.S.-led military alliance, and that if international law and legitimacy were the issues, "let us start with Palestine." He threatened that "whether they solve the problem according to international law or not, Palestine will return to the Palestinians."

On January 12, after debating for three days, Congress passed a resolution authorizing the president to use military power to force Iraq from Kuwait. The resolution passed the Senate 52–47 and the House 250–183. The voting was largely partisan: Republicans supported the resolution 42–2 in the Senate and 164–3 in the House; Democrats opposed it, 45–10 in the Senate and 179–86 in the House. The debate saw 268 members of the House and 93 senators take the floor, and many referred to the vote as the most important of their careers. Bush, reacting after the vote, said that it "unmistakeably demonstrates the United States' commitment to enforce a complete Iraqi withdrawal from Kuwait."

As the possibility of war drew closer, three key aspects of Israel's approach to the crisis emerged. First, while preemptive action was historically central to Israel's defense policies, Israel seemed ready to rule it out and to risk absorbing an Iraqi missile strike because of larger strategic and political concerns—keeping the coalition together and maintaining good relations with the United States. Second, while Israeli leaders were reluctant to oppose a negotiated settlement publicly, they clearly saw such a possibility as dangerous because it would leave the Iraqi arsenal intact, would invite linkage between the Iraqi occupation and Israel's, and would make inevitable a future Middle East war in which Israel, rather than the United States, would have to face Saddam. Third, it was understood that the flip side of the government's decision to accept a first strike would be an automatic counterattack. As one Israeli official told the *Washington Post*: "This government would never be able to explain to Israelis why it allowed them to be attacked, then didn't even respond to the attack. It would be political suicide here."

As the January 15 deadline arrived, France brought an initiative to the Security Council in a last-minute effort to defuse the crisis. The initiative called for Iraqi troops to withdraw from Kuwait, to be replaced by an international Arab force and international observers, and for an international conference to find a solution to the Israeli-Palestinian conflict. The United States and Britain expressed severe reservations; Shamir's spokesman, Avi Pazner, said Israel viewed the initiative as "extremely negative" since it "gives a prize for aggression." Noting these reactions, the French let it drop.

Meanwhile, in a briefing in Tel Aviv, Israeli Air Force chief Avihu Bin-Nun indicated that Israel planned a major retaliation should Iraq send planes or missiles. On the question of coordination with the United States, Bin-Nun left a mixed message, saying, "We have no promises and no coordination with the United States at all," but predicting that "when it comes to actuality, I think we'll have the necessary coordination."

AIR WAR BEGINS

On January 16, the U.S.-led coalition let loose a massive air attack on Iraq. There were reports in Israel that U.S. planes first attacked surface-to-surface missile launchers in western Iraq targeted at Israel. Israel declared a state of emergency minutes after the war began, with authorities closing schools and advising people to stay home and to prepare gas masks and chemical-warfare kits. Israeli sources indicated that U.S. and Israeli military officials had finally succeeded in working out basic arrangements for coordinating their actions in the event that both Israeli and U.S. planes were striking Iraq simultaneously.

Reaction to the U.S. attack in the Arab world was restrained or supportive, with the exception of Jordan and the PLO. Crown Prince Hassan of Jordan expressed "horror and shock" at the large-scale raids, as well as anxiety about a tidal wave of refugees fleeing to Jordan. The PLO, in a statement from Tunis, urged Muslims and Third World countries to pool their resources in the face of what it called a "bold-faced and treacherous aggression against Iraq."

On the second night of the war, Israel's worst fears were realized. Iraqi Scud missiles carrying conventional warheads hit Israel in an area running from Tel Aviv to Haifa. The army reported seven injuries and extensive property damage. Chief of Staff Dan Shomron said on Israel Television that the attacks "cannot go without a response." When asked if Israel could respond in view of the American need to maintain its coalition with Arab partners, Shomron said that it "doesn't alter the principle that the protection of the civilians of Israel is the responsibility of the State of Israel."

President Bush said he was "outraged" at the Iraqi attack on Israel, and Secretary Baker was reportedly urging the Israelis not to engage in any large-scale retaliation that might be used by Iraq to transform the Gulf War into an Arab-Israeli conflict. Israel's ambassador to the United States, Zalman Shoval, indicated at a Washington news conference that Israel "reserves the right to respond in any way it deems fit." He declined to specify, but he pointed out that Israel, in seeking to accommodate Washington, had refrained from launching a preemptive strike against the Iraqi missile batteries and had now paid the price.

Israel, however, did not retaliate. Instead it accepted an American offer to have U.S. technicians make two Patriot antimissile systems, already in Israel, operational, as well as a commitment to establish a liaison between the Israeli military and the U.S. Central Command in Riyadh.

On January 19, as the U.S. assault on Iraq continued, a second barrage of Iraqi Scuds struck Israel. President Bush called Prime Minister Shamir twice during the night to express concern about the attacks and his continuing hope that Israel would let the United States retaliate on its behalf. Marlin Fitzwater, the White House spokesman, reported that the president told the Israeli leader: "I understand the anguish of your people and your Government. We will use every resource possible to suppress and destroy the mobile Scuds." The president, according to Fitzwater, thanked Israel for its "restraint" and explained in detail to Shamir what American forces were doing to seek out and destroy the mobile missile launchers in western Iraq. After two more batteries of Patriots and American crews arrived in Israel on the 19th, Pete Williams, Pentagon spokesman, said the missiles would be operated by the Americans as long as it took to train Israelis. Williams called the provision of American crews to Israel "an extraordinary step taken in view of the unconscionable attacks" by Iraq on residential neighborhoods in Israel.

Still, Israel's leaders were keeping their options open. The deputy foreign minister said during a news briefing, "We're not saying what we will do, when we will do it, where or how we will do it." Immediately, Eagleburger returned to Israel to shore up Israel's commitment to restraint in the face of Iraqi attempts to draw it into the war. This American activity—the Bush calls, the Eagleburger visit—clearly sprang from American anxiety over what Israel would do. Israeli officials chose to focus on the positive. Yossi (Yosef) Ben-Aharon, the prime minister's chief of staff, explained Israel's position this way: "Restraint is not always negative. It all depends on your capacity, your intentions and your potential for achieving your goals in a confrontation. At this time, the United States and its coalition partners are pouring hundreds, if not thousands, of tons of bombs and missiles on Iraq." Coming from a key figure, these comments reflected Israel's understanding of the consequences of retaliation.

Commentators noted the striking improvement in U.S.-Israeli relations, in light of the previous two years of mounting tension. On the personal level alone, four telephone conversations between Bush and Baker and Shamir in several days seemed to have established mutual trust that had not existed before. The perception existed on both sides that the other could be depended upon more than it had previously believed. The United States, critical of Israeli actions in Lebanon, the West Bank, and the peace process, now saw Israel showing concern for American interests by its restraint; and Israel, which had questioned Bush and Baker's commitment to Israel, now saw the United States swiftly sending Patriot teams to its aid.

At a news conference in Jerusalem, after two days of talks, Eagleburger articulated these new warm feelings. "We have a common cause with Israel now," he said. He said the United States recognized and respected the right of every sovereign state to defend itself and had "never questioned Israel's right to respond to attack." But, he added, "we also recognize and respect Israel's desire not to get drawn into this conflict, and greatly admire Israel's restraint." For his part, Shamir said after one meeting with Eagleburger, "We are working together. We are thinking together how to do it better." Nothing demonstrated the new mood better than an Eagleburger tour of sites in Tel Aviv struck by an Iraqi missile the previous Saturday morning. Crowds mobbed and cheered the U.S. representative and he, in turn, shouted: "Good for you! The people of Israel live." An Israeli poll published on January 21 by *Yediot Aharonot* showed 91 percent of Israelis in favor of a policy of restraint.

That policy, however, was put to its most severe test when the third Iraqi Scud attack took place on Tuesday, January 22. Evading the Patriots, the missile slammed into a Tel Aviv suburb, leaving 3 dead and 96 hurt and damaging some 20 apartment buildings. The White House again praised Israel's "remarkable restraint in the face of this aggression." The next day, following a morning meeting of the government's most senior members, it became clear that immediate retaliation was not contemplated. Unnamed officials pointed out that for Israeli retaliation to be worthwhile, it would have to reduce or remove the Iraqi threat to Israel, not endanger the coalition, and be coordinated with the United States. For the moment, there would be no action.

Back in Washington, Secretary Baker said that while Israeli retaliation "might not" fracture the American-Arab alliance, Israel's continuing restraint was "very much appreciated by the United States." Baker also indicated that the administration would consider any Israeli request for additional financial aid to deal with the war and the absorption of Soviet Jews. Earlier, Israel's finance minister, Yitzhak Modai, had suggested to Eagleburger that Israel would need $13 billion in extra economic assistance over five years.

As the rocket attacks on Israel continued, Chancellor Helmut Kohl of Germany announced that his government would send $165 million to Israel as "immediate humanitarian aid." In a news conference in Bonn on January 23, Kohl said that the missile attacks filled Germans "with deep outrage," describing them as "a clear blow against Israel's integrity and right to exist, for which we Germans have a special responsibility." The following day, German foreign minister Hans-Dietrich Genscher visited Israel. At a news conference with David Levy, he said, "We have come at an hour of danger for Israel . . . You can count on the Germans." He also indicated that besides the announced aid, Germany would tighten its laws to prevent export of materials and technology that could be used to produce weapons such as chemical and biological warheads. Levy, however, voiced strong criticism of Germany's export policy, saying that Saddam was threatening to burn Israel, and that his chemical and other weapons of mass destruction "are all coming from German soil." Several days later, Kohl announced a $666-million defense package, including funds to build two submarines and a battery of Patriots, "in accordance with the special responsibility which [Germany] . . . feels toward Israel."

The attacks on Israel and Israel's restraint generated much comment about the future impact on U.S.-Israeli relations and the Middle East. Clearly, some of the old sympathy for Israel as the beleaguered underdog was reemerging. The administration and Congress as well as the public were depicted as viewing Israel in a new light. It was argued that these factors were key elements in Shamir's decision to forego a military response. As for the impact of the war on the Arab-Israeli conflict, there seemed to be greater recognition that Arab hostility to Israel generally, beyond the Palestinian issue, was indeed a core issue, and that the PLO had hurt itself immeasurably by its support of Saddam.

The missile attacks continued almost daily, and tens of thousands of Tel Aviv residents moved away from town. On January 25, the fifth night of bombardment, Patriot missiles were reported to have intercepted seven Scuds fired at Haifa and Tel Aviv. Parts of the missiles fell, however, killing one person and wounding 42. Property damage was extensive. Despite the fact that the Patriots were not completely destroying the Scuds, Israelis were described as extraordinarily grateful for U.S. help, with dozens of people every day bringing cookies and gifts to the American soldiers operating the batteries outside Tel Aviv. And the policy of restraint was holding, as Chief of Staff Shomron told Israel Television on January 25: "We have the ability to hit back, but we have a long-term interest in holding back now. If we try to be rational, there's no other way." Shomron also dismissed the notion that Israel could do better against the Scud launchers in Iraq, saying "anyone who thinks Israel could do a quick job and finish it is mistaken."

Two days later, the Israeli cabinet reaffirmed the policy of postponing any military action, this despite continued attacks, despite much damage, frayed nerves, and some pressure from several hard-line members of the cabinet for action. The vote was seen as reflecting an appreciation of the political and diplomatic rewards the government appeared to be reaping both at home and abroad. At the same time, government officials expressed concern over renewed threats by Saddam to use nonconventional weapons against Israel. "So far, he has done everything that he said he was going to do and so we are taking this very seriously," said one unnamed official.

Another night of Scud attacks appeared to snap Israel's patience. A different tone emerged. Shamir spokesman Avi Pazner said on January 28: "We are quite fed up with what's going on here. Maybe we can do the job. Our main constraint is military coordination." Moshe Arens told the Knesset: "Israel can contribute to the removal of the missile threat on the condition that it is done with total coordination with the United States."

On January 29, in an interview on Israeli television, Arens heard the interviewer express his own frustration: "The Americans keep bombing launchers but haven't been terribly effective. Meanwhile, Americans are watching the Super Bowl, and Israelis are sitting in shelters and sealed rooms." To which Arens responded: "The situation you described isn't going to continue—not two months, and not a month. I simply estimate that a situation in which we'll be neutral or not active, and their ability to launch missiles against us isn't eliminated, it won't continue for a long time." Meanwhile, the director-general of Israel's Ministry of Defense, David Ivri, spent two days in Washington talking with Pentagon officials about possibly improving the Patriot missile so that it could prevent an Iraqi chemical missile attack on Israel.

U.S.-SOVIET STATEMENT

While the U.S.-led onslaught on Iraq continued and Israeli frustrations grew, a brouhaha developed over a joint U.S.-Soviet communiqué about the war. It was issued on January 29, following a meeting between Secretary of State Baker and Soviet foreign minister Aleksandr Bessmertnykh, and was released, according to officials, without the president's knowledge. The document said: "The two ministers continue to believe that a cessation of hostilities is possible if Iraq would make an unequivocal commitment to withdraw from Kuwait." Critics saw this as a softening of Bush's vow that there would be "no pause for negotiations" in the war. The communiqué also said that the Soviet Union and the United States would work with the countries of the Middle East after the war to resolve other regional disputes. This was read as a move toward the "linkage" between Iraq's withdrawal from Kuwait and the Palestinian question that Bush had sought to avoid.

Indeed, the Kremlin hailed the document as a significant shift in Washington's position. Bessmertnykh, speaking on Soviet television on January 30, described the document as "important," calling it the first U.S.-Soviet statement on Arab-Israeli issues since 1977. He said that he and Baker had tried to "look beyond the boundaries of the war in Kuwait" to consider the broader Mideast crisis. Soviet commentators saw the document as a sign of U.S. acceptance of indirect linkage, the longtime Soviet position.

In Jerusalem, Shamir and other Israeli leaders sharply criticized the document. The prime minister complained about the lack of consultation: "A political act that involved us, our fate, our future, was taken without consulting with us, without even telling us beforehand." The White House sought to calm the storm. Spokesman Fitzwater said the statement had been "widely and wildly" misinterpreted as a change of policy, and White House officials admitted that the affair had been handled clumsily. Clearly, though, the document served both sides' purposes: the Soviets were eager to demonstrate that they remained major players, with the ability to influence U.S. policy; and the State Department wanted to ensure that the Soviet Union remained an active and supportive member of the coalition. It was also a means of strengthening the new foreign minister, who had recently replaced Eduard Shevardnadze.

In Iraq, Saddam's efforts to turn the war into a struggle against the Zionists were not limited to his almost nightly Scud attacks. In an interview with Peter Arnett on CNN on January 28 he charged that the forces attacking Baghdad were all due to the "Zionist influence" in the corridors of the U.S. administration: "This war that is being waged against us is a Zionist war. Only here, Zionism is fighting us through American blood, through your blood . . . in order to be the dominant power in the area once the war has come to an end."

As January was coming to a close, Israeli leaders, while still inclined not to retaliate against the missile attacks, were signaling Washington that they could not indefinitely absorb such strikes, particularly if Iraq used a chemical warhead. In Washington, on January 31, Israel's defense attaché, Rear Admiral Avraham Ben-Shoshan, told reporters that American coordination with Israel had improved since the war began, including information about the military situation in western Iraq where Iraq had fixed Scud missile sites and mobile launchers. On the other hand, Israeli officials indicated that Washington had withheld daily electronic identification codes used by the allied forces bombing Iraq. This meant that if Israel suddenly wanted to enter the fray, its pilots would not be able to tell friendly aircraft from Iraqi aircraft.

Israeli military officials began to sound more optimistic about the situation early in February. On the 1st, army chief of staff Shomron said that "even if Saddam Hussein has chemical warheads, they are very primitive and the damage will not be that great." And Air Force commander Avihu Bin-Nun indicated in an interview that with every passing day the war in the Gulf was working in Israel's favor: "Because of the American activities in the gulf, Israel can see itself as more secure today than two weeks ago." The fact that Iraq had launched four missiles at Israel during the last days of January and first days of February and all fell far short of Israel's civilian population centers generated hope that U.S. efforts were having an effect.

As U.S. air attacks continued, President Bush told a White House news conference, on February 5, that he was "somewhat skeptical" that air power alone would force Iraqi troops to leave Kuwait. He announced that he was sending Secretary of Defense Richard Cheney and Chief of Staff Gen. Colin Powell to Saudi Arabia to consult with local commanders before he determined whether to order a ground offensive or continue the air campaign alone. The president was buffeted by conflicting political pressures as he considered a ground war. Pressure to move quickly stemmed from concern that a growing tide of sympathy for Saddam in the Arab world could in time create serious domestic problems for Arab allies. Pressure to go slowly came from many in Congress anxious to minimize U.S. casualties.

For Israel, even as Iraqi missile attacks were diminishing, the deeper ramifications of its position of restraint were causing concern. As one unnamed Israeli official told the *Washington Post*: "We have to think about what other Arab leaders will think in the future if they remember there was an attack on Tel Aviv and Israel did not act." Or, as a Shamir aide put it: "Our whole conception of ourselves is that no one will be able to attack us and go unpunished. And we feel strongly that to do nothing is not healthy for us in the long run."

On February 9, Israel once again experienced casualties as a result of a Scud attack. The missile was said by Israeli authorities to have been hit by a Patriot, but burning debris struck buildings in a residential area of Tel Aviv, badly damaging property and hurting 15 residents. This was the 11th Iraqi missile attack on Israel since the war began, but the first in two weeks to cause any significant damage or injuries. Reports from Israel indicated that the Israeli public understood Saddam's game of trying to goad Israel into responding and continued to support the government's policy of restraint as being in Israel's self-interest.

Meanwhile, Secretary Cheney and General Powell returned from Saudi Arabia and met with the president on February 10. Afterward, Bush told reporters that the air war, which "has been very, very effective," would continue "for a while," but added that he was prepared to move to a ground phase when Cheney, Powell, and Gen. Norman Schwarzkopf, commander of the U.S. military force, suggested doing so: "If they come to me and say there needs to be another phase, then I will make that decision because that is a decision for the President of the United States."

On February 11, Arens came to Washington for a hastily arranged one-day visit. He had meetings with Bush, Baker, and Cheney and reportedly told the president in his 30-minute meeting in the Oval Office that Israel was suffering heavy damage and could only go on so long. The visit's intent was perceived to be as much as anything to impress the administration with the sacrifice Israel was making, in the hope that this would elicit a more favorable response to Israel's increased economic needs. When reporters at the Pentagon asked Arens if Israel could be counted on to show restraint indefinitely, he said: "I don't think we can make any such commitments."

On the diplomatic front, Iraq's ruling Revolutionary Command Council issued a surprise statement on February 15, suggesting for the first time that Iraq would withdraw from Kuwait if the terms were right. The Iraqi statement expressed "appreciation" to the Soviets for their diplomatic efforts. This was clearly related to the visit to Baghdad, two days earlier, of Soviet envoy Yevgeny Primakov, bearing a private message from Gorbachev to Saddam. Later he said that Saddam had given him "cause for hope" for a diplomatic solution. Subsequently, Tariq Aziz visited Moscow and received from Gorbachev a new Soviet peace plan, all of which was seen as a last-minute effort to prevent a U.S. ground war. President Bush was clearly cool to the Soviet move, saying that the Soviet initiative would be "thoroughly explored" but that "as far as I'm concerned there are no negotiations." The plan reportedly promised some "progress on the Palestinian issue" after an Iraqi pullout, but this was seen by administration officials as too much "linkage."

Meanwhile, on February 22, as the United States considered the next critical move, Israel's prime minister made clear what he believed the war should accomplish: "It would be very bad for us if Saddam Hussein remained in power in Iraq with a substantial part of his large army still intact." And he noted that if Saddam's army were left intact, it might lead Israel to abandon its policy of restraint: "If the conditions will change, it will change our behavior. Our army is ready." Israeli leaders, however, stopped short of directly advocating the launching of an allied ground offensive to destroy the Iraqi army.

THE END OF THE WAR

On February 23, the U.S.-led forces launched a ground offensive in addition to the air war in Iraq and Kuwait. Prime Minister Shamir, speaking on Israeli television, said that the end of the Iraqi regime was near and praised the Americans: "Our hearts are with the fighters and all the soldiers in the large coalition who are fighting against the tyrannical Iraqi tyrant. We wish them a decisive and quick victory." Shamir aide Avi Pazner added that the outcome of the war had to be "the removal of Saddam Hussein from power in Baghdad and the dismantling of his military machine." Israelis wondered, in the meantime, whether the ground war would provoke Hussein into firing chemically tipped Scuds at Israel.

By February 27, the allied forces had liberated Kuwait, routed Iraqi forces, and gone deep into Iraq. That day President Bush announced that the allies would suspend military operations against Iraq: "Kuwait is liberated. Iraq's army is defeated. Our military objectives are met." On the following day, in a letter from Tariq Aziz transmitted to the Security Council, Iraq agreed to comply with all the UN resolutions that formed the allies' mandate in the war.

On March 3, U.S. general Norman Schwarzkopf met with Iraqi military commanders at a captured Iraqi airfield to arrange the terms of a formal cease-fire. One day earlier, the Security Council passed Resolution 686 setting the terms, including a reaffirmation of the 12 previous resolutions. Included were calls on Iraq to rescind its annexation of Kuwait, return Kuwaiti property, and disclose data on chemical and biological weapons and materials possibly stored in Kuwait or allied-occupied Iraq. On March 3, Aziz informed the Security Council that Iraq had agreed "to fulfill its obligations" under the resolution, while pointing out that the new resolution "ignored the Iraqi people's suffering" from the war.

Meanwhile, on February 28, Purim, Israel lifted its state of emergency and advised citizens to resume normal lives. While jubilant Israelis ripped the plastic sheeting off their windows and tossed their gas masks into closets, thoughts were already turning to the impact of the war on future Israeli relations with its Arab neighbors and the United States. Chief of Staff Shomron focused on Israel's greatly improved security situation: "The central building block of the eastern front—the Iraqi military—has been destroyed. The threat from the east, for years I hope, will be much smaller." Shamir, however, told the *Boston Globe* that he was deeply disappointed that the coalition had not driven Saddam from power: "It is clear that as long as he will be in power in Iraq he will look for opportunities to attack us. It could be in a year, or in three years, or in five years. He is always an enemy." Moshe Arens, on Israeli radio, expressed the hope that the cease-fire "will involve in time the destruction of all missile capability, and monitoring that would assure us that there would not be rejuvenation of that capability."

In the days following the end of the war, Washington addressed the issue of Israel's request for additional U.S. aid to meet Israel's costs from the war. Israel had asked for $1 billion. On March 5, in agreement with the administration, the House Appropriations Committee voted to spend $15.8 billion to begin paying the U.S. share of the war costs, including $650 million in aid for Israel.

As the weeks passed, a strange relationship developed between the UN forces in Iraq and Saddam Hussein, involving agreements, broken agreements, sanctions, accusations, and recriminations. That the end of the war would remain an issue of controversy was reflected in General Schwarzkopf's television interview with David Frost on March 27. The general said that he had recommended to the president to "continue the march" into Iraq to annihilate Iraq's armed forces, but that, as a result of the cease-fire ordered by Bush, significant elements of Iraq's army and Republican Guard escaped. The following day, the president rebutted the general, saying, "All I know is there was total agreement in terms of when this war should end." Clearly, there was concern within the administration about criticism that the United States missed an opportunity to remove Saddam from power, and having the military hero Schwarzkopf play into this criticism could not be allowed.

Concerns about Saddam were somewhat alleviated by the Security Council resolution passed on April 3, stipulating terms for a permanent end to the war. This resolution, 687, set forth stern financial and military conditions to limit Iraq's ability to make war on its neighbors. Included were new demands: UN monitoring of a demilitarized zone to be created on the Iraq-Kuwait border; destruction of all Iraqi chemical, biological, and nuclear weapons, to be supervised by a UN commission; destruction of all but short-range missiles; and a renunciation of international terrorism. On April 6, Iraq accepted the terms for a permanent cease-fire. Three days later, the Security Council authorized development of a 1,440-member peace-keeping force to patrol a demilitarized zone along the Iraq-Kuwait border. Meanwhile, the United States began withdrawing its forces from Iraq.

The Peace Process

The crisis in the Gulf had a mixed effect on the Arab-Israeli peace process. On the one hand, official diplomatic efforts were set aside as the struggle against Saddam consumed the Western world. On the other hand, the Arab-Israeli conflict was never far from the surface, whether the issue was Israel's involvement in the war, or efforts to link the Gulf conflict to the Arab-Israeli conflict, or, most significantly, what opportunities for movement in the peace process might appear after resolution of the Gulf War.

Leading up to the January 15 deadline, the United States resisted efforts by Saddam, as well as by France and the Soviet Union, to link the Gulf struggle to the Arab-Israeli struggle. With the war in full tilt, the administration focused its efforts, as noted, on keeping Israel out of the conflict. However, on January 28, in a speech perceived to be a move to reassure the Arab world, the president told the National Association of Religious Broadcasters that, when the war was over, Washington would take the lead in efforts "to bring peace to the rest of the Middle East." Marlin Fitzwater later explained that the administration intended to pursue some "initiatives" in the Middle East after the war ended. Other officials, unnamed, told the *New York Times* that the Bush statement was intended to signal that "Israeli restraint now is not being purchased at the price of forsaking our interest in pushing along the peace process later," and that after the war there would be "increased pressure to focus on the Palestinians and a great desire to show that this coalition against Iraq can do something on the other front." This proved to be the opening shot leading to the postwar fireworks.

Following the joint U.S.-Soviet declaration that generated strong reaction (see above), Israeli foreign minister David Levy, on January 31, told the *Washington Post* that Israel would resist any joint move by the powers to structure a comprehensive solution to the Arab-Israeli conflict, especially if it involved an international conference. Levy focused instead on the need for the Arab states finally to engage in direct bilateral talks with Israel. "Once we start face-to-face negotiations with the Arab countries," he said, "we will at the same time negotiate with the Palestinians." He added that a successful peace process depended on a total Iraqi defeat; this, he said, would leave the United States as the sole superpower and put it in a position "to end the Arab state of war against Israel, because the Arab states, for the most part, need the United States and the West more than the United States needs them, both politically and economically."

On February 4, the European Community ministers meeting in Brussels indicated that they would approach Washington to devise a joint U.S.-European strategy about how to deal with the Arab-Israeli conflict as well as Gulf issues. British foreign minister Douglas Hurd said that Israel had a "right to expect security and acceptance of her right to exist," but added that "Israelis above all should understand the position of the Palestinians who see themselves as dispossessed."

That night, Shamir, in an address to the Knesset, reacted to the growing clamor for something to be done after the Gulf War. He warned the West that it had better take into account the lessons learned from the Gulf War before pressing Israel to accept any new Middle East peace plans: "We hope that now, more than in the past, the complexity of the problems in the Middle East—the cruelty of dictatorial regimes here, and that of Saddam Hussein is today the worst and cruelest of all, but not the only one—has been better comprehended, and the need for us to exercise care in our political moves better understood." Shamir went on to lay out basic tenets of Israel's approach to any new peace plan, including opposition to an international conference and rejection of any PLO role. Most importantly, like Levy, he stressed the need for the Arab nations to end their belligerency toward Israel if there was to be progress on the Palestinian issue.

The Gulf War clearly did refocus attention on the Arab war against Israel, a perspective that had been lost in the focus on the Palestinian issue in recent years. Thus, the *New York Times* in an editorial on February 11, "Plan Now for Peace," noted that the war "gives dramatic evidence that Israel is an integral part of the Middle East," and "Arab states will have to recognize it as such."

One focus of the renewed emphasis on the Arab states was Syria. Long held to be one of the most intractable and extreme of the Arab states, in light of its place in the U.S.-led coalition against Saddam, Syria was now being viewed as a potential partner for peace talks. Reportedly, early in February Baker had suggested to Israeli ambassador Shoval that an Israeli commitment to demilitarization of the Golan might be part of a rapprochement between Israel and Syria. On February 13, German foreign minister Hans-Dietrich Genscher visited Damascus. After meeting with Syrian foreign minister Farouk Sharaa, he said, "Syria realizes that the recognition of the right of self-determination for the Palestinians also means that the right of Israel to exist is recognized and assured."

The government of Israel was quick to make its own position clear on these matters when, on February 14, it released a telegram from the prime minister to Jewish settlers in the Golan Heights assuring them that Israel would not accept demilitarization of the territory or any other change in its status. The message was seen as an effort to forestall any U.S. move to have Israel pay a political price for Arab participation in the U.S.-led coalition.

Meanwhile, the Arab countries that had joined the allied coalition to fight Saddam met in Cairo on February 16 and reaffirmed the right of Palestinians to self-determination and an independent state. They noticeably omitted any reference to the PLO, which was seen as a reaction to PLO support for Saddam, and omitted the usual call for an international conference.

As the ground war against Saddam brought victory for the allies into sight, Prime Minister Shamir reportedly told Likud members of the Knesset, in a closed meeting on February 25, that the end of the war would bring a new "period of trial" for Israel. The *Jerusalem Post*, in an account of the session, quoted the prime minister as warning what was ahead: "The end of the Gulf War will be followed by the usual attempt to establish a new pattern of Middle East arrangements. There will be an effort to use political means to snatch from Israel what could not be snatched from us by force. We shall stand firm and not retreat. If negotiations do take place, we shall go into them with a number of advantages, and weather them successfully."

Late in February, consistent with reports that President Bush wanted to move quickly to the Arab-Israeli issue following the Gulf War, it was announced that Secretary Baker would soon make his first trip to Israel. While Shamir's chief of staff, Yossi Ben-Aharon, indicated that the government still stood behind its own initiative of February 1989, calling for elections in the territories, Foreign Minister Levy continued to argue that Israel should come up with its own new plan before the Americans tried to impose one, adding that Israel needed to demonstrate that it was not running away from peace. On the other side, Labor leader Shimon Peres offered his own plan, calling for a demilitarized West Bank and unilateral withdrawal from Gaza.

The likely effect of the war on the peace process also evoked mixed views. Some focused on increased U.S. prestige, improved U.S.-Israeli relations, new Arab dependence on the United States, the decline of the PLO, and the new emphasis on the Arab states' role in the Arab-Israeli conflict as factors providing opportunities for a breakthrough. Others pointed to Israelis' heightened resentment of the Palestinians as a result of the war and the weakness of both the Palestinians and the right-wing Israeli government as factors inhibiting any movement.

Speaking on NBC's "Meet the Press" on March 3, Secretary Baker said he believed Arabs and Israelis would display "goodwill" in trying to resolve differences following the Gulf War. He emphasized that the United States had no intention of trying to impose a solution and that he was going to the region merely to consult. He said he would press for a "two-track approach"—finding a way for Arab states and Israel to make peace, as well as Israelis and Palestinians. Baker's comments on an imposed solution and the two-track approach were viewed as intended to soothe Israeli concerns. At the same time, Baker and National Security Adviser Brent Scowcroft ruled out a PLO role because of Arafat's early outspoken support of Saddam. Baker said Arafat's standing among Arab states that had backed him in the past was "seriously and substantially hurt." As for King Hussein and the sympathy he showed for Saddam, Baker made clear that the United States wanted "to see him continue in power," and suggested that the Jordanian ruler might still "become an important player" in the peace process.

On the evening of March 6, President Bush addressed a special joint session of Congress to celebrate the victory in the war. Basking in the ovation from members of Congress, Bush said he would immediately begin bringing American troops home from the Gulf and pledged to redouble efforts to solve the Arab-Israeli conflict. "Our commitment to peace in the Middle East does not end with the liberation of Kuwait. The time has come to put an end to the Arab-Israeli conflict." In his address, Bush made a series of comments which were seen as hinting pressure on the Shamir government. He spoke of the need for "compromise" in the region. He noted that "we have learned in the modern age geography cannot guarantee security and security does not come from military power alone." He said that a comprehensive peace must be grounded in UN Resolutions 242 and 338 and in "the principle of territory for peace." At the same time, he spoke of the two-track approach, of the need to close the gap between Israel and the Arab states as well as that between Israel and the Palestinians.

BAKER'S TALKS: FIRST ROUND

On the flight to the Middle East on March 7, Secretary Baker and his aides told reporters that they did not expect peace initiatives to emerge quickly but were seeking to secure modest goodwill gestures from the Israelis and Arabs to establish a measure of trust. On March 10, Baker was in Riyadh to meet with Arab foreign ministers from the Gulf states, Egypt, and Syria. While the diplomats endorsed Bush's approach to Middle East security, including the presence of American naval forces and occasional visits of U.S. ground troops, on the conflict with Israel there appeared to be little change, the group calling for Israel to end the occupation, and as of old, for an international conference under UN auspices as the only way to negotiate with Israel. Baker indicated that "this is not the appropriate time" for such a conference, and unnamed officials described it as a "total non-starter" since Israel would never attend. Acknowledging that he was not "overly optimistic" about the peace process, Baker added, prior to leaving for Israel: "Please don't declare it dead until it's actually dead—I happen to think it's at least alive until we explore the concept and the possibilities with the leadership of Israel."

Baker arrived in Israel the next day for his first visit since becoming secretary of state in 1989. He immediately went to Yad Vashem where he laid a wreath. After meeting with Foreign Minister Levy, Baker emphasized that he did not come with any plan or intention to impose peace but "to listen, to cajole, to plead and to offer our good offices to see if we can seize this opportunity to make progress for peace." He said that he had seen "signs of new thinking" in the Arab world. Levy said that Baker's report left him with the impression that the Arab states were "beginning to show signs of change."

On March 12, Baker met with Shamir for over an hour and later held talks with ten leading Palestinians from the West Bank and Gaza. According to U.S. officials, Baker asked Shamir to take specific steps to engage the Arab states and the Palestinians in a new peace process. These included a halt to settlements, stopping deportations of Palestinian militants, and not ruling out an exchange of land for peace. Shamir reportedly did not reject anything outright, but this was seen to reflect a desire not to be viewed as negative more than anything else. In Baker's controversial meeting with the Palestinians, which they tried to claim was equivalent to meeting with the PLO, the Palestinians insisted that the PLO must be included in any peace process and called for a Palestinian state and an international conference. Baker, according to reports, told the Palestinians that they had a great deal at stake now and should not squander the opportunity by continuing to rely on the PLO leadership, which had alienated the Arab states by its support of Saddam.

The Baker visit was as important for its tone as for its substance. The secretary clearly was interested in building trust, as seen in a helicopter tour he took to allow Israelis to show him how narrow the country was within its pre-1967 boundaries, and a visit to the cemetery where four Israeli women killed by a Palestinian on March 10 were buried. As Baker left Israel to move on to Syria for meetings with Hafez al-Assad, officials in Jerusalem were reportedly relieved that the pressure from Washington had not materialized, this despite the fact that Baker had asked Israeli leaders to commit themselves to the concept of "land for peace."

In Damascus, on March 13, Baker met with Assad for seven hours, the third time the two had met since the beginning of the Gulf crisis. In a press conference with Syrian foreign minister al-Sharaa the next day, Baker said that he and Assad agreed that they must take advantage of the "window of opportunity" that existed after the Gulf War to produce a comprehensive Arab-Israeli settlement. When asked whether he heard any "new thinking" about Israel from Assad, as he said he had heard from Arab leaders in Saudi Arabia, he could not point to anything other than the commitment to be active in the peace process.

In Ankara, on March 16, at the end of ten days in the Middle East, Baker told reporters that he was sufficiently encouraged to begin presenting specific proposals the following week to see if "old stereotypes" and "rigid positions" would give way to "new thinking." "I think that what makes the situation a little bit different now is that there has been a significant change in the region and that has presented us with an opportunity to act as a catalyst. The Soviets were responsive and I think that there is a basis for us to continue to work together."

During the following ten days, as part of Baker's commitment to follow up on his Middle East trip, he met in Washington with Israeli ambassador Shoval, Osama Baz, national security adviser to Mubarak, and Adnan Abu Odeih, foreign policy adviser to King Hussein; other State Department officials were reported to have been in touch with Saudi diplomats and some of the Palestinians Baker had met in the Middle East. As the month drew to a close, reports began to surface that the administration was exploring the possibility of convening regional peace talks, with the United States and Soviet Union as hosts, that would serve as the opening for direct negotiations between Israel and the Arabs. Under that proposal, the United States and the Soviets would invite Israel, Palestinian representatives, Egypt, Jordan, and Syria and possibly others to a ceremonial opening that would be followed by direct talks.

In this same period, strains between the Bush and Shamir governments began to reemerge. Reports circulated of unhappiness in Washington concerning a series of Israeli moves that seemed ill-timed: a tour by Ariel Sharon of the territories, shortly after Baker's visit, in which he urged further settlement activity; Israel's announcement that it planned to deport four Palestinians; and Shamir's rejection of talks with Palestinians with whom Baker had held a meeting on his trip.

SECOND ROUND

On Friday, April 5, Baker suddenly announced that he was leaving for a second round of Middle East meetings because of concern that whatever momentum had been generated by the war was in danger of evaporating. On April 8, one day before scheduled talks between Baker and Shamir in Jerusalem, Israel's Defense Ministry announced that it would free more than 1,000 of the approximately 14,000 Palestinian prisoners held for actions connected with the *intifada*. Israeli officials maintained that the move was timed for the end of the Muslim fasting month of Ramadan and was not connected with the Baker visit. Nonetheless, the step was seen as responding to Baker's request for confidence-building measures from both sides.

Baker's talks in Israel with Shamir, Levy, and Arens, as well as with Palestinian representatives, brought into the open the idea of a regional conference as the centerpiece of the post-Gulf War effort to rekindle the peace process. The one-time regional conference was seen by American officials as a useful vehicle to bridge the gap between the Arab demand for international cover for any talks with Israel and Israel's demand for direct talks with the Arabs. Levy, following his meeting with Baker, told the press, with Baker at his side, that the two sides had reached an "agreed position" on how such a parley might be organized, but there were still "many details that have to be addressed and looked at and ironed out." One major issue that remained to be settled was the conference's structure—whether it should be ongoing or not; have Soviet participation or not; consider proposals for autonomy only or the final status of the territories as well. Second was the old question of who should represent the Palestinians; and third was the question of the terms of reference, whether Israel should commit itself to an interpretation of UN Resolution 242 that left open the possibility of trading land for peace.

Meanwhile, Baker also met with a group of Palestinians from the territories, led by Faisal al-Husseini and approved by the PLO. Afterward, the Palestinians said they were disappointed by what they described as American pressure to "forget about" bringing the PLO into any regional talks and by Baker's failure to promise to do anything about expanded Israeli settlement activities. However, Husseini indicated that the regional conference idea was new, one that "we would like to know more about and that the PLO is interested in." When Baker moved on to Cairo, he received the same vague positive response, Foreign Minister Ahmad Esmat Abdel-Meguid indicating that Egyptians were "open to discuss any way to find a practical solution."

On April 11, Baker met with Saudi foreign minister Saud Faisal in Cairo and reportedly sounded him out on Saudi willingness to provide economic and political support for a new leadership of the Palestinians, in light of the Saudi break with the PLO over the Gulf War. They also discussed the regional conference plan, about which Faisal asked numerous questions. Later in the day, Baker moved on to Damascus, where he met with President Assad for six hours but failed to get any definitive response to his ideas. In Damascus, as elsewhere, the host apparently sought to convince the American official of good intent. However, after Baker left Syria, Sharaa announced that Syria "opposes" the Israeli-backed "regional" conference idea.

At the end of this latest swing through the region, the Baker party reportedly believed that a consensus had developed for an Arab-Israeli conference, but that differences were unresolved on what would happen at such a meeting. It was also reported that, in focusing on the conference, Baker would put aside efforts to get each side to offer confidence-building measures. Shamir had told Baker that he had no intention of halting settlements, and it was unclear what gestures the Arabs were willing to make. Returning to Washington, Baker consulted with Bush about developments. Within days, on April 15, it was announced that Baker would return to the Middle East after going to Luxembourg on the 16th. The decision was seen as reflecting a sense of urgency to pin the parties down soon or risk falling back.

On April 16, a small group of Israeli settlers opened a new settlement on the West Bank, called Revava, three days before Baker's scheduled visit. While the settlement had been planned for years, its timing was seen as symbolic defiance of the United States. The White House called it an "obstacle to peace" and through the U.S. embassy in Tel Aviv asked the Israeli government for an explanation. Even some Likud leaders raised questions, David Levy saying that building should be done quietly, without any "unnecessary declarations that will only bring pressure on Israel," and Health Minister Ehud Olmert wondering whether it might have been better to delay the settlement for a couple of days because of Baker's visit. Shamir, visiting in London, said settlements were not relevant to the peace process: "We have explained many times to our American friends that it does not make any difference if there will be in these disputed territories 100 settlements or 120 settlements because a permanent political solution will be accepted outside this fact."

THIRD ROUND

Baker arrived in Israel on April 18, amid new concern over a reported comment by the secretary that there would not be any movement toward a peace conference unless the United States was willing to press for an agreement. On the day of Baker's arrival, Shamir cautioned, in an Israeli radio interview, against any U.S. pressure, saying that anyone who knew Israel knew "that pressure doesn't yield flexibility— just the opposite." In the interview, Shamir also reiterated his opposition to any UN role in a peace meeting or participation by East Jerusalem Palestinians, but indicated that a European role was not excluded. The mood of anxiety in Israel was reflected in reports in the Israeli media that Israel's ambassador in Washington, Zalman Shoval, suspected the administration of backing off from earlier reported agreements about the conference.

On April 19, Baker and Shamir met for four hours, during which the secretary presented a series of questions to the prime minister in an effort to find a compromise position on the conference. The questions posed reportedly referred to whether the proposed conference should have some permanent character without allowing it to act collectively or impose decisions; whether Israel would accept participation by the European Community or the UN; and whether Israel would allow Palestinians who were dual residents of East Jerusalem and the West Bank to participate in the negotiations.

As Baker moved on to Saudi Arabia, and reports circulated of new troubles in U.S.-Israeli relations, Shamir stated after an April 21 cabinet meeting, "There was no atmosphere of ultimatum in our talks with Baker" and "It's exaggerated to say there's a crisis." Meanwhile, Levy acknowledged that there were differences between the U.S. and Israeli positions, some procedural, some substantive.

After meetings in Cairo, Baker disclosed the administration's strategic plan. Asked by reporters why Saudi Arabia, which was supposed to have changed its posture toward Israel after the Gulf War, would not be taking part in any talks with Israel, Baker indicated that he was trying to organize a two-phase conference. The core conference, he said, would involve Israel, Jordan, Syria, Egypt, Lebanon, and the Palestinians; the second phase would focus on regional issues like water, arms control, and economic development, in which the Saudis and others might all take part. Baker described the Saudis as "a significant part of the peace process," whether in attending wide regional talks or broadly trying to promote the process. Significantly, he mentioned that the Saudis could help end the Arab boycott of Israel, provided that Israel agreed to halt the building of settlements.

On April 23, as Baker's travels continued, the secretary held almost ten hours of talks with Assad in Damascus. Baker reportedly tried to persuade Assad to limit his demands concerning the conference, including questions of a UN role, a permanent structure for the conference, and Syria's insistence on a prior commitment from Israel to abide by UN resolutions calling for land for peace. A news conference made clear that little had been accomplished. Foreign Minister Sharaa sought to blame Israel for the stalemate and to identify Baker with that view, saying he agreed with Baker's assessment that "the difficulties and obstacles remain in Israel." Baker interjected, "Well, now, that is not exactly what I said." But the secretary did have some strong words about a new Israeli settlement established on Tuesday, April 23: "I have to say to you that we were very disappointed to learn this morning that there is yet another settlement that has been established in the occupied territories. I think that probably points up rather visibly that it is easier to obstruct peace than it is to promote it and that the establishment of those settlements certainly doesn't help the efforts of those who are interested in peace."

From Syria, on April 25, the Baker road show moved on to the Soviet Union, where the secretary met his Soviet counterpart, Bessmertnykh, at the Black Sea resort of Kislovodsk. The talks seemed to restore some momentum to Baker's efforts as the Soviets formally announced that they were prepared to cosponsor a Middle East peace conference with the United States.

The next step was a return to Israel, where Baker was going to make another effort at a breakthrough. However, reports filtering back to Israel of what had taken place on other stops of the road show generated pessimism. Moshe Arens spoke of learning that the Arab states "are trying to take this instrument, this one-time meeting, and turn it into an international conference which I don't think could be a forum that would lead us to peace." He added, "I doubt the intentions of any state that isn't prepared to sit down with us at the negotiating table."

These latest talks did not go well. Following a meeting with Shamir on April 26, Baker issued a statement, saying: "Questions remain here in Israel. We still need some answers from the Israeli government relating primarily to modalities before we can move this process forward." The comments were widely perceived to be a slap at Israel, especially in contrast to the situation two days earlier in Damascus, when Baker said nothing about Syria's refusal to modify its hard-line terms for peace talks.

While the question of Palestinian representation continued to be at the heart of the administration's difficulties with Israel, the issue of whether the conference could reconvene after an opening session became a subject of intense division among Israel's top leaders. In his meeting with Baker, Levy reportedly left open the possibility that a conference might be reconvened periodically to monitor progress in Arab-Israeli talks (but only if Israel and the others agreed in advance). Later in the day, however, after objections from several cabinet ministers, Shamir notified Baker that Israel would stick to its original insistence that only one ceremonial meeting of the conference be held. And two days later, a cabinet majority agreed that Levy's accord with Baker was invalid since it had not received formal government approval. Shamir said that the government was opposed even to a qualified permanent conference, "because if there are subsequent sessions of the same meeting or conference, we'll never get to direct negotiations." As for the status of Baker's efforts, Shamir indicated that even if the dispute over the conference was resolved, "there are other differences of opinion that we haven't yet touched upon. Not only matters of procedure, but of substance." As to U.S.-Israeli relations, he said, "I don't think we are on the verge of a crisis."

A mini-crisis, however, did occur in connection with the visit at this time of Housing Minister Ariel Sharon to the United States. When Secretary Baker, who was still angry at Israel for establishing new settlements on the eve of two of his trips, learned on April 25 that Sharon had arranged a meeting with Secretary of Housing and Urban Development Jack Kemp, he raised questions with the White House about the meeting. According to spokeswoman Margaret Tutwiler, the White House let Kemp know that Sharon should not be received officially. And so Kemp met Sharon on May 1 at the Israel embassy in Washington, instead of at Kemp's agency. Sharon, in a radio interview broadcast to Israel on May 2, urged the Israeli government to "respond swiftly and firmly to this attack on it," adding that "no independent state with any self-respect would accept such an attack." And as journalists and politicians in Israel expressed concern that the slight of Sharon might be Washington's way of putting full blame on Israel for failure to get peace talks going, the government delivered an uncommon protest to the United States, complaining about the "inappropriate way that the Administration behaved" in the Sharon affair.

With pessimism in the air following Baker's third swing through the region, the secretary suddenly announced on May 5 that he would return to the Middle East, again out of a sense that another push might get the parties to the table. His goal, he said, was still to arrange a conference "that would see direct face-to-face discussions and negotiations between Israel and each of its neighboring Arab states, as well as direct face-to-face discussions between Israel and the Palestinians. And in that sense, it would be a very, very broad conference of a nature and type that has never before taken place." This trip was to be unique in that Soviet foreign minister Bessmertnykh would also be touring the region, and the two planned to join forces. On May 8, the president told a news conference, "I think there's reason to be optimistic."

On May 8, Bessmertnykh opened his tour in Damascus by trying to reassure the Arabs of his support, despite warming Soviet ties with Israel: "The Soviet Union has been and is going to be a strong supporter of the Arab cause, the supporter of the rights of the Palestinians." He added that the PLO "should undoubtedly play a role in the quest for a resolution of the Middle East conflict." In Amman the following day, Bessmertnykh continued his pro-Arab comments, saying, after meeting with King Hussein, that he could not "conceive or accept a situation where a peace conference is in session while the settlements are being built."

The next day the Soviet foreign minister was in Israel for the highest-level visit ever to the Jewish state by a Soviet official. While Israeli officials anticipated difficulties, the visit was notable mostly for the lack of conflict. Bessmertnykh offered nothing but platitudes and praise: "We agreed that no state should try to pressure or impose something on another country. No pressure, because this process will yield fruit only once we all try to achieve the objectives we have set for ourselves." Issues such as settlements and the PLO appeared not to have been discussed, and he made clear that Jewish emigration was not tied to Israeli positions on the peace process: "The immigration of Soviet Jews to Israel is the result of democratization in our country, both in internal policy and foreign matters. The immigration from the Soviet Union isn't only to Israel, but to any place where our citizens want to live."

FOURTH ROUND

As Baker embarked on his fourth trip to the region on May 10, the Gulf Cooperation Council announced that it would be ready to participate only "as an observer in the forthcoming peace conference through representation of its secretary-general." The statement went on to say that if peace talks occurred, the Gulf states would participate in discussions on regional issues such as arms control, water resources, and protection of the environment. Reports indicated that the administration exerted some pressure on the Gulf states, including a Bush call to King Fahd, in which it was pointed out that it would be impossible to get arms sales through

Congress without approval. In Damascus on May 12, Baker met once again with Assad. The talks lasted five and one-half hours and were reported to have been unsuccessful, as reflected in the cancellation of the usual postmeeting news conference. The sticking points were said to be Syrian demands for a UN role and a permanent conference, both of which Israel had rejected.

Baker's meeting with King Hussein on May 14 also did not appear to achieve any breakthrough, with Jordan hedging on whether it would move forward if Syria did not. The secretary's decision to go by car, rather than plane, from Amman to Jerusalem, the first time any secretary of state had done so, made more news than the talks with Hussein. The drive was even depicted as symbolic, Baker noting in Jerusalem that "you realize when you drive like that, rather than flying, just how short the distances are and how important, therefore, it is to promote peaceful coexistence."

In Israel, Baker seemed to make no progress in finding a compromise on the outstanding issues of a UN role and a continuing conference. It was said that Baker's compromise involved a UN "observer" at the talks, and that the conference would reconvene periodically, provided both sides were amenable, to hear reports of progress but not to interfere in the talks in any way.

As the fourth trip was drawing to a close, Baker indicated in Jerusalem that he and President Bush would consult upon his return to see where they were and what they should do next. He pointed out that he had obtained general agreement on several key issues: that there should be a peace conference; that the Saudis and Gulf states would attend as observers; and that the Palestinians would likely be represented by a Jordanian-Palestinian delegation. Baker left Israel in a more upbeat mood than the last time, expressing some hope, without assigning blame and saying that he was "not disappointed, because I do think we are making progress." Later, Shamir spoke on Israel Television in optimistic tones: "There's a basis for my hope. We agreed on several things that still can't be made public—things that lay the groundwork for Baker to come into close and serious contact with the other parties."

On May 17, after meeting with Baker, the president said that he saw "real cause for optimism" and pledged the administration would "just keep plugging away," despite what appeared to be a lack of visible progress. He refused to discuss any details of the process on the grounds that the "way to solve this conundrum is not to get these parties positioned by public statements." When asked if a fifth Baker mission was planned, Bush replied, "If there is reason to go back, he will."

Four days later, at a ceremony marking the start of a new settlement in the Golan Heights, Ariel Sharon vowed to "at least double" the Jewish population there and said that the "component of settlement" in the territories was "a component of security in Israel."

The following day, in testimony before a House Foreign Affairs subcommittee, Secretary Baker cited Israeli settlement building as a particular problem: "Nothing has made my job of trying to find Arab and Palestinian partners for Israel more difficult than being greeted by a new settlement every time I arrive. I don't think that there is any bigger obstacle to peace than the settlement activity that continues not only unabated but at an enhanced pace." Baker did point out several areas of Arab-Israeli agreement: the conference would aim to achieve a comprehensive settlement through direct talks between Israel and the Arabs and Israel and the Palestinians; negotiations between Israel and the Palestinians would first address an interim self-government solution and then the permanent status of the territories; and Palestinians would be represented by leaders from the territories. He reiterated that the issues of a UN role and a permanent conference remained unresolved.

Israeli leaders reacted angrily to Baker's comments about settlements. They blamed the Arabs for the slow pace of Baker's initiative and rejected his claim of settlements as the largest obstacle to peace. Yosef Ben-Aharon summed up the government's view, saying that to keep the territories "clean of Jews pending a settlement would mean, in effect, relinquishing the territories before negotiations."

A number of American senators, including Alfonse D'Amato (R., N.Y.), Robert Kasten (R., Wis.), Frank Lautenberg (D., N.J.), and Arlen Specter (R., Pa.), charged that Baker was unfair to single out Israel. They said he had failed to cite Saudi Arabia's failure to move, Syria's missile buildup, and Jordan's ambivalence about the talks. And the Conference of Presidents of Major American Jewish Organizations said it was "shocked and dismayed" by Baker's remarks. President Bush, however, defended Baker: "I'm backing the man. I'm stating the policy of the United States of America and so was the Secretary. We would like to see those settlements stopped."

Despite this latest brouhaha over Israeli settlements, the administration pushed forward on the peace process. At the beginning of June, President Bush sent personal letters to the leaders of Israel, Syria, Jordan, Egypt, and Saudi Arabia emphasizing his personal commitment to Middle East peacemaking and spelling out what he considered to be a fair compromise of each party's conditions for peace talks. The letters reportedly also made clear to the parties that the president would have a hard time understanding if they refused his compromises. To Syria, he reportedly focused on the need for talks as the only way to change the post-1967 status quo in the Golan Heights; to Israel, he spoke of his proposal as providing the direct negotiations Israel had always wanted. In each case he argued that the technicalities of a UN role and reconvening of the conference should not stand in the way of important achievements.

Foreign Minister Levy, in Paris on June 5 for talks with European Community representatives, predicted that the impasse over the conference would soon be broken and that the conference could be approved in a matter of weeks. However, Shamir's response to the Bush letter, delivered to the president on June 7, was broadly characterized as a rejection of Bush's appeal, with the Israeli leader suggesting that the procedural issues at stake—the UN and the reconvening of the conference—were really attempts by the Arabs to continue their refusal to deal directly with Israel. In Washington, the White House maintained a low-key posture, saying that Israel had "other ideas" about a formula for Mideast talks, but that this would not derail American efforts.

Several days later, in an interview with Israeli journalists, Shamir reintroduced the question of Palestinian representation as a sticking point in the discussions. He indicated that Israel would insist on approving the names of any Palestinians named to the proposed conference's joint Jordanian-Palestinian delegation. A senior official said that Shamir felt the need "to make this point now so there will be no misunderstandings later." Some, however, interpreted the Shamir comments as a new condition, because when Baker left Jerusalem on May 16 there were signs that he and the Israelis had come to an agreement on how Palestinian delegates would be chosen, and there seemed to be no demand for a veto. In addition, all the focus in recent weeks had been on the UN and reconvening issues, leaving the impression that the Palestinian representation matter was no longer in contention. In Washington, on June 12, State Department deputy spokesman Richard Boucher said pointedly that "Palestinians must choose those who will represent them in negotiations."

The next day, David Levy, in the States on a private visit, met with James Baker. The secretary's message to Shamir was that "Israel should try to be a bit more flexible." For his part, Levy continued to sound optimistic, saying that despite the apparent stall, "the process is not stuck." He added, however, that Israel had made many concessions and that "it is time for Syria and the Arab countries to make concessions." Regarding Shamir's remarks on Palestinian representation, Levy said that this had been Israel's position all along: "Israel will not sit down with parties it refuses to sit down with."

On July 1, at a press conference outside his summer home in Maine, President Bush indicated that his patience was beginning to wear thin over the Middle East stalemate. Israel had rejected his compromise proposals, and Syria, more than a month after receiving his letter, had not even bothered to respond. He strongly suggested that he might have to press the issue publicly: "I have invoked quiet diplomacy and the need for confidentiality, but I can't do that forever. I just simply can't do it. I owe it to the American people and I think the people around the world to say, 'Hey, here is what the United States thinks is a good formula.' "

With the process apparently stalled, cynics wondered whether this was just one more in a long line of Middle East initiatives heading for failure. On July 14, however, a surprise development occurred when Assad finally responded to Bush's proposal and stated that the plan was "an acceptable basis for achieving a comprehensive solution." Baker, speaking at the State Department, said, "I do believe it is fair to characterize the response as positive. I do not see anything expressed specifically as conditions." He added that, overall, the response "moves the Syrian government further than they have been willing to move in any peace process effort."

The president, in London for the annual economic talks of the seven major industrial powers ("G-7"), hailed the Syrian response and characterized it as a "very positive breakthrough." He added that he hoped that Israel would "get on board," that Israel had "been wanting to talk with people in the area, and if all goes well here, that is exactly what will happen . . . so here will be a good test."

The Syrian response highlighted divisions in Israel. The government issued a statement on July 15 that it "would stand on all the positions expressed in the Prime Minister's letter to President Bush." Defense Minister Arens said that the Syrian letter would be important only "if the Syrians have indeed expressed a willingness to sit down and negotiate directly on a peace treaty with Israel," suggesting that compromise proposals would not do. By contrast, Shimon Peres said the government "will have to deal with this or appear as the only rejectionist on the scene." And one Israeli newspaper said in an editorial that "this is the moment of truth for Shamir's government."

On July 16, the G-7 leaders issued a communiqué strongly endorsing Bush's peace efforts and supporting "the principle of territory for peace." Coming just before Baker's fifth trip to the region, the message was seen as presaging pressure on Israel.

FIFTH ROUND

Two days later, after three hours of talks with President Assad in Damascus, Secretary Baker announced that Syria had accepted the U.S. proposal for a peace conference that would open direct talks between Israel and its Arab neighbors. Baker called it "an extraordinarily important and positive step." Sharaa indicated that Syrian acceptance of compromise on a UN role and a limited reconvening of the conference was based on several assurances: commitment by Moscow and Washington to keep the UN secretary-general "fully informed" of progress in the talks; U.S. reaffirmation that it had never recognized Israel's de facto annexation of the Golan Heights; and U.S. support for the interpretation of Resolution 242 as applying to "all fronts" from the 1967 war.

By the time Baker arrived in Jerusalem on July 21, he had commitments from five Arab countries—Syria, Jordan, Lebanon, Egypt, and Saudi Arabia—to take part in the conference. In his visits to Riyadh, Amman, and Cairo following his stay in Damascus, he also heard offers from the three to suspend the Arab boycott of Israel if Israel would suspend building settlements. Shamir was perceived to be in a bind—to say yes to the conference he risked collapse of his government; to say no, he risked alienation from the United States and others.

After two days of meetings between Baker and Shamir, Israel's approach had clearly changed. Baker told the press that in light of recent Syrian, Lebanese, and Jordanian commitments, Israel was rethinking its position and would respond shortly. A close adviser to Shamir, Yossi Achimeir, indicated that Shamir had told his cabinet after hearing from Baker that there appeared to be a "revolutionary change" in Syria's position, even if it was only for tactical reasons. Baker labeled it a "moment of historic opportunity," saying that "direct negotiations are the only way to solve problems." And later that evening, Shamir told a reporter for Israel Television, "It's very possible that talks could be held in the framework of peace negotiations between us and the Arab world."

When Baker reported on the proposal—endorsed by Saudi Arabia and Egypt—to exchange an end to the boycott for suspension of settlement building, he said that Shamir was "not enthusiastic about that approach. That may be an understatement. We have a disagreement on that issue which is quite separate and apart from the peace process." This was the first acknowledgment by the Americans that the process could proceed irrespective of Israeli settlement policy. Baker also met in Jerusalem with three Palestinian representatives and reportedly told them that, while he sympathized with their plight, the realities of power in the Mideast now were such that if they wanted to take part in negotiations, they would essentially have to accept the Israeli conditions.

The president, flying back from Ankara to Washington, spoke by phone with Baker, and according to Brent Scowcroft, national security adviser, was "encouraged that there wasn't a rejection." Scowcroft also indicated that the president wished for an Israeli response by the time of his summit meeting in Moscow on July 30 and 31, which would allow him and Mikhail Gorbachev to announce the conference and issue invitations.

On July 24, in a television interview, Shamir focused on the question of Palestinian representation as the main stumbling block. He said that Israel would only be ready to attend the U.S.-designed conference if no Palestinians from East Jerusalem or with connections to the PLO were present. He then went on to speak in optimistic tones: "Something has happened in the Middle East in the past few days. I wouldn't say it's already time to turn swords into plowshares . . . but there will be peace." He also said that Baker had promised Israel it would not be forced to negotiate with anyone it did not want to and said he was waiting for a list of names of Palestinians from U.S. officials.

Meanwhile, Yasir Arafat told Radio Monte Carlo the same day that he rejected the U.S. plan for a regional peace conference because it "ignores the Palestinian people's national rights and completely leaves out the question of East Jerusalem."

Hope for a breakthrough mounted when Moshe Arens, in an interview on ABC's "This Week," on July 28, said that Israel had "reached agreement with the United States over the Jordanian-Palestinian delegation. . . . I think we are very close to a general agreement that will allow an initial meeting to take place and then break up into bilateral talks." He called a public Israeli declaration to attend "no more than a formality." When asked later in the day about Arens's comments, Bush said he heard Arens "was very upbeat and we view that as positive, but there has been no official word from Mr. Shamir yet." The next day, Shamir told the Knesset's Foreign Affairs and Defense Committee that with one more visit by Baker, "we will manage to settle all the remaining questions."

On July 29, King Hussein of Jordan appealed to the leadership of the PLO to refrain from raising unnecessary problems over Palestinian representation that might delay the convening of the peace conference. In an interview at the royal palace, he described the American initiative as a "last chance," warning that without an agreement, large-scale Jewish settlement in the occupied territories might soon result in the territories being effectively merged into Israel.

The same day Bush arrived in Moscow for a summit meeting with Gorbachev to explore relations in the post-cold-war era. Reports circulated that Soviet officials were pressing the United States to issue invitations to a Middle East conference as a means of stepping up pressure on Israel, but that Baker and others expressed reluctance to do so. As the summit began, it was clear that no invitations would be issued at that time.

During the summit, a series of messages were exchanged between U.S. and Israeli officials, and there was a report that the United States had given Israel private assurances that it would support Israel's insistence that no Palestinians from East Jerusalem or linked to the PLO would be allowed to attend the talks. This was based on two factors: that the previous year's peace effort had failed because Israel could not agree to these points, and that the Palestinians were now the weakest party in the equation and desperately needed a change in the status quo. While in Moscow, Baker spoke to Shamir by phone on two occasions in an effort to seal the agreement. The Baker message reportedly was again that Israel should consent to the conference even if all details of who would be included in a joint Jordanian-Palestinian delegation had not been worked out.

The next day, Bush announced in Moscow that he was sending Baker to Israel immediately to obtain an official Israeli statement expressing its willingness to attend a conference in October. In a joint statement, Bush and Gorbachev declared that there was a "historic opportunity" in the Middle East that "must not be lost." They indicated that invitations to the conference would be issued "at least ten days prior to the date the conference is to convene." In Israel, reaction to the upcoming Baker visit was low-keyed; Avi Pazner, Shamir's spokesman, talked of progress but said the question was "not yet solved."

SIXTH ROUND

On August 1, Baker and Shamir met in Jerusalem for the sixth time. After the meeting, Shamir announced that Israel would join in Middle East negotiations as long as its conditions on the composition of a Palestinian delegation were met. Standing next to Shamir when the announcement was made, Baker said he thought that "the prospect of Arab-Israeli peace discussions are no longer simply a dream. I think we should all recognize that there is still some work to be done, but I think that the announcement today by the Government of Israel is extraordinarily positive and significant." When asked by reporters whether he had received the response he was hoping for, Baker said, "That is the 'yes' we were hoping for from the Israelis, yes sir." At the same time, there were many reports indicating that Israel had demanded a number of concrete assurances from the United States that were yet to be worked out, on such matters as the organization of the talks, the Palestinian delegation, and an affirmation of existing agreements and understandings between the two countries.

On August 4, by a 16–3 vote, the Israeli cabinet approved Shamir's agreement to attend the conference. Most notable in opposition was Ariel Sharon, who called it a "trap." Ehud Olmert, health minister, reflected the feeling that underlay the relative lack of resistance to this, as opposed to other, peace initiatives over the years: "I think that the damage that might have been caused to Israel had we answered negatively was much greater than the risk involved." The next day, Baker made his pitch to the Palestinians, meeting in Jerusalem with Faisal al-Husseini, Hanan Ashrawi, and Zakaria al-Agha. Baker later reported that he tried to impress on the Palestinians that they "have more to gain from a viable and active peace process than do almost anyone else," and "have the most to lose if there is no process." Ashrawi made clear that the group was "not empowered to say 'yes' or 'no,' " but described the PLO as having a "positive inclination." Husseini emphasized that the notion that Israel could veto anyone on a Palestinian delegation would be unacceptable.

On August 4, with Baker in Tunisia to seek Tunisian support for the conference, Bassam Abu Sharif, a spokesman for Arafat, told reporters that the Palestinians were "ready to attend the peace conference," and that no obstacle was "big enough" to prevent it. It didn't take long for the official PLO news agency to disavow Abu Sharif's remarks. The next day the agency said that "these statements do not represent the view of the PLO nor express its position."

On August 6, in an interview, Arafat talked tough, saying that the United States must ask him to choose the Palestinian delegation, otherwise the Palestinians would not attend: "I want the same terms as being given to the other participants because the Palestinians are the main factor in the Middle East peace equation. It's a matter of principle. Why are only the Palestinians treated in this way?"

The Moscow coup on August 19 caused international attention to shift away from the Middle East. The dramatic and historic events of the next few days and their residual effects left the Middle East process on hold for weeks. And U.S.-Israeli relations suffered a blow early in September when President Bush rejected Israel's request for $10 billion in loan guarantees as long as Israel continued building settlements in the territories. (See below for a full discussion of this issue.)

SEVENTH ROUND

On September 16, James Baker embarked on a new round of visits to Middle East countries to try to get final agreement for the conference. While the loan-guarantee crisis had strained relations, Shamir insisted the guarantees had nothing to do with the peace process and therefore Israel still planned to take part in it, as long as the Palestinian delegation met its approval. On September 19, however, in a meeting with visiting members of Congress, he questioned U.S. impartiality and raised questions about the impact of the guarantee delay on the Arab world and the peace process: "Now there is euphoria in the Arab world because of the Arab perception that the United States stands on their side. And thus this is not advancing peace but rather making it more distant."

Meanwhile, Baker invited the three Palestinians he had met with in Jerusalem in August to see him in Amman on September 19. At first they refused to do so, which was widely interpreted as a PLO show of dissatisfaction with the U.S. approach to the issue of Palestinian representatives that Baker had presented to them in Jerusalem. On the same day, Baker and King Hussein held a joint news conference in which they both implored the Palestinians not to miss the opportunity to attend the conference, tentatively scheduled for October. For the Palestinians, said Baker, "this is the best opportunity that has presented itself for a long, long time, and I also think that it is going to be a long, long time before the bus ever comes by again." And King Hussein, for his part, said: "Time is short. The opportunity may not come again—ever." The next day, Hanan Ashrawi showed up in Amman to meet with Baker and made clear she was doing so at the PLO's behest.

On September 20, flying to Ireland after a week of talks which failed to produce final confirmation for a conference, Baker suggested that if the parties did not stop "fiddling" over terms for attending talks, Washington might simply issue invitations to them. Baker's frustration stemmed from the fact that each party had asked for advance assurances about terms and objectives of the conference and about American policy on sensitive issues. None was ready to accept fully the draft letters of assurance that Baker presented during his seventh swing through the region. Talks were scheduled to continue the following week in New York, when the foreign ministers of Jordan, Israel, and Syria would attend the UN opening session. And the PLO's parliament-in-exile was scheduled to meet in Algiers at the same time, where it was hoped a decision would be reached.

Although Bush's tough stance on the loan guarantees did not derail Israel's commitment to move forward in the peace process, it did raise serious questions in Israel about the U.S. role at the conference. Foreign Minister Levy reflected these concerns when he commented, on September 19, "We are going toward a situation where we are almost alone. What is our security? It is that every Israeli feels that the United States will treat Israel with special sensitivity. If this trust is broken, we go into the unknown without any security."

Meanwhile, the search for the final piece of the conference puzzle turned to Algiers on September 23, where 450 delegates of the Palestine National Council (PNC) met to discuss Palestinian participation. This was the first meeting of the PNC since November 1988, when the group issued a conciliatory statement that presaged moderate comments by Arafat to a UN meeting in Geneva that in turn led to the opening of U.S.-PLO talks. Arafat told the gathering, "We renew our readiness to work with all the international parties to make the peace conference successful." He called the gathering "a decisive point in the history of the Arab cause." And he indicated that "we are ready to remove the obstacles which continue to prevent the holding of this peace conference, hoping that other parties also will make the same efforts. These efforts are entering an extremely delicate and serious phase."

Despite reports that a consensus was building at the meeting to give a go-ahead to a conference in which there would be no direct role for the PLO, the voices of the hard-liners, opposed to any agreement, continued to dominate. On September 26, Hanan Ashrawi and Faisal Husseini, the two key Palestinians from the territories, addressed the meeting, with an eye to boosting Arafat's support for the negotiations. The two were welcomed with enthusiastic applause, and Ashrawi urged the council members to push for a solution that was "badly needed" by Palestinians living under occupation. The conspicuous role of leaders from the territories at this crucial PNC meeting highlighted some of the changes that had taken place within the Palestinian movement as a result of the *intifada*—chiefly the PLO's loss of status by virtue of its support for Saddam Hussein and the fundamental interest in movement toward a solution by residents of the territories, as compared to those outside.

The next day, the PNC concluded its meeting by issuing a statement that seemed to endorse the conference. It declared that the PLO maintained the "right" to form its delegation from Palestinians in and outside the territories, including Jerusalem, but did not specify whether it would exercise that right. The statement was interpreted as a vague go-ahead for the effort to form a joint Jordanian-Palestinian delegation and at least left open the possibility that the PLO would stay in the background, which would allow the conference to proceed.

October began in an atmosphere of optimism that the conference might indeed take place that month. David Levy, addressing the UN General Assembly on October 2, expressed the hope that face-to-face Arab-Israeli negotiations would take place "in a few weeks." Egyptian foreign minister Amre Moussa added that he was "cautiously optimistic" about the prospects. (Moussa's predecessor, Abdel Meguid, had been elected secretary-general of the Arab League on May 15.) On October 4, in Jerusalem, Yitzhak Shamir said that the chances were "very good" that a peace conference would start late in October. And Hosni Mubarak went even further, telling Egyptian newspaper editors flatly that day that the talks would be held by the end of the month. French foreign minister Roland Dumas added to the chorus with a similar prediction, saying the conference site would be a European city. Only President Bush sought to dampen such talk, telling reporters that the Dumas statement "sounded to me a little more firm than where we are right now." He indicated that no dates had been set. In fact, it was clear that the effort to work out remaining questions regarding the joint Jordanian-Palestinian delegation would require another visit to the region by Baker.

Four days later, on the 8th, it was announced that Baker would indeed embark on his eighth trip to the region. This announcement came on the same day as revelations that the administration had sent a strongly worded private protest to Israel after Israeli F-15 fighters flew over northern Iraq on Friday, September 25. The administration letter expressed two concerns: that the flights risked a new military confrontation with Iraq that could interfere with UN efforts to disarm Saddam's regime, and that such a military confrontation could wreck chances for a Middle East peace conference. According to reports, four Israeli jets flew into Iraqi air space because of continuing Israeli "grave concerns" about the threat from Scud missiles in western Iraq. Israeli officials made no public response to the U.S. protest, but Israeli public opinion was notably unhappy with the American criticism.

On October 10 and 11, Ashrawi, Husseini, Sari Nusseibeh, and Zakaria al-Agha met in Washington with Baker, who reportedly told them that they should go immediately to Amman and set up the joint delegation "in the right way" to ensure that the conference could begin before the end of October. Baker told the press prior to the meeting that Bush and Gorbachev had made it clear they wanted a conference in October, which required "some decisions taken across the board, across the region." He warned that, as the parties got closer to a decision, there would be a tendency by "rejectionists and extremists across the region to take actions designed to disrupt the possibilities for peace." The two days of talks ended in a mood of cautious optimism that the Palestinians would indeed begin formal discussions with Jordan on forming a joint delegation.

EIGHTH ROUND

On October 13, Baker arrived in Cairo to begin his eighth trip—possibly the decisive one—to the Middle East since the end of the Gulf War. Meanwhile, the new Soviet foreign minister, Boris Pankin, was also coming to the region during the Baker stay, with rumors circulating that he might announce the establishment of full diplomatic relations with Israel.

The next day, Baker was in Amman, conferring with King Hussein on ways to persuade Palestinians to take part. At a news conference following the meeting, Baker sought to prod the Palestinians by warning them that Washington's patience had limits: "The bus is not going to come by again. The Palestinians have more to gain and more to lose from this process than anyone else." Baker was reportedly annoyed that upon his arrival in Amman, rather than seeing non-PLO Palestinians working to form a delegation with Jordan, as they had assured him they would, a PLO delegation led by Yasir Abed Rabbo was there. Baker made clear that "it is not our objective to get Israel into a dialogue with the PLO." The next day, however, as Baker departed for talks in Damascus, the three Palestinian leaders—Ashrawi, Husseini, and al-Agha— met with Jordanians and announced that they had reached some basic understanding with Jordan on the framework of the joint delegation.

Meanwhile, Secretary Baker met with President Assad over a two-day period. Afterward, at the usual joint conference with Sharaa, Baker indicated that "we are still on course to hold a peace conference in this month of October." He indicated that Assad had agreed to attend the formal conference, scheduled for a European location October 29–31, and to join ensuing face-to-face negotiations between Israel and its Arab neighbors. But he acknowledged that during 12 hours of talks he had been unable to overcome Assad's refusal to participate in a third stage, the multilateral talks. When asked whether he would shake hands with Levy at the conference, Sharaa, showing how deep the hostility was, said: "I will tell you frankly no. This very hand is very guilty. It is a hand which occupies our lands, ignores Palestinian rights, and for the last decades, we have been suffering from this occupation. So why do you ask me to shake hands with them unless and until they prove they are not guilty?" Sharaa explained Syrian opposition to the multilaterals on the grounds that Israel's position was "intransigent," and Syria "wanted first" to test the Israeli intentions in the peace conference before even considering multilaterals, which it clearly saw as a concession to Israel.

On the 16th, Baker flew to Jerusalem for talks with Israelis and Palestinians. Reports were circulating meanwhile that, if an agreement were not immediately forthcoming, the Americans and the Soviets might just issue invitations for the conference and force the parties to either accept the assurances they had already received or risk isolation by staying away from such talks. A flurry of diplomatic activity took place, with both Baker and Pankin meeting with Palestinians in an effort to get a list of delegates for the joint group, a list that would be approved by the PLO but would not include members of the PLO or Palestinians from East Jerusalem.

On the 17th, Baker spent six hours with Shamir and his key aides. The talk reportedly focused on a U.S. letter of assurances to Israel about the conference. Meanwhile, the PLO reportedly approved participation by seven Palestinians from the territories in the joint delegation. A compromise solution was in the works on participation of East Jerusalem Palestinians—a separate committee, in addition to the negotiating delegation, which would operate as a "decision-making" body. It would include several Palestinians from East Jerusalem, among them Husseini and Ashrawi.

Friday, October 18, was a historic day in the region. At a joint news conference in Jerusalem, Baker and Pankin announced that their two governments had issued invitations to Israel, its Arab neighbors, and the Palestinians for a Middle East peace conference to convene October 30 in Madrid. The parties had until 6 P.M. Eastern time, Wednesday, October 23, to respond officially. Reportedly, the invitations were sent after Baker was told by Palestinians in East Jerusalem that they were prepared to send representatives who were neither formal members of the PLO nor residents of East Jerusalem. When Baker communicated that to Shamir, the Israeli leader indicated that he would recommend to his cabinet that it approve Israel's participation. He said the conference offered the first opportunity to negotiate directly and that he would recommend yes to the government, "because I don't see a better alternative." Baker said these talks held "the hope of a new era in the Middle East."

While officials reported that all issues had still not been resolved, including that of Palestinian representation and how the second phase of direct negotiations would be conducted, Washington reportedly decided to issue the invitations in hopes that no one would dare to stay away, even if the terms were not 100 percent satisfactory. One unnamed senior official described the decision: "We just thought if we don't make it happen in October, it very likely won't happen, this being the Middle East."

According to the invitations, the conference would be opened by Presidents Bush and Gorbachev. The opening session would last three days, to be followed at some point by two phases—direct talks between Israel and each of the various Arab parties and multilateral talks on several issues, bringing together regional and other concerned parties.

Simultaneously, foreign ministers Pankin and Levy announced that Israel and the Soviet Union had restored full diplomatic relations. Pankin called the long rupture a "historic mistake." He indicated that in the past the Soviets tended to side with the Arabs, while the United States sided with Israel, and this "did not bring any tangible fruit."

Responses to the invitations started to come in the following day. Jordan announced that it would attend, and Assad's comments after a meeting with Pankin were interpreted as his approval. On October 20, the Israeli cabinet voted 17–3 to approve Shamir's decision to attend. Sharon led the opposition in a seven-hour debate, but the vote was overwhelming. Reports of the discussion indicated that the cabinet members were not necessarily optimistic but felt that Israel had no alternative, since it had been saying for decades that what it wanted above all was face-to-face negotiations. Justice Minister Dan Meridor summed it up: "It is a turning point in Israeli politics. It will not be easy, but we are taking a path whose essence is to bring peace." In fact, it was noted, that, because Washington feared that otherwise Israel would not attend, the peace talks were constructed largely on Israel's terms: Palestinian representatives had to be acceptable; there was no commitment to territorial concessions; Israel did not have to promise a freeze on settlements; and the conference would not be ongoing.

PRECONFERENCE MANEUVERING

Meanwhile, the issue of Palestinian representation continued to fester. As it became clear that the delegates would not officially be representatives of the PLO, statements were being made to reassert the PLO presence. The leader of the proposed delegation, Dr. Haidar Abdel-Shafi of Gaza, put it bluntly: "Certainly, we are not going to refrain from affirming we are PLO supporters." On October 22, the official Palestinian delegation of 14 men was announced, all living in the occupied territories but none from Jerusalem. Israeli officials expressed satisfaction with the delegation, but said they were "most unhappy" with a six-person advisory panel, whose members all violated Israel's guidelines, that would also be in Madrid and would serve as a conduit between the official Palestinian delegation and the PLO. Shamir, in Strasbourg on a visit to the European Parliament, said that Israel "will not speak with these advisers," and "they will not be present in the room during the deliberations of the conference."

On October 23, Shamir announced that he would personally head the Israeli team at Madrid. Since the conference invitations called for negotiations at the "ministerial" level, and since no Arab head of government had said he would attend, the Shamir decision was seen as a slap at David Levy and a determination by the prime minister to show that he was in charge of the process. Soon thereafter, Levy announced that he would not attend the conference at all. (See "Israel," elsewhere in this volume.)

The Arab side held a meeting the same day in Damascus to unify its position before sitting down with Israeli representatives the following week. Among the issues discussed were the location of the bilateral talks, whether to attend multilateral talks, and how to prevent the signing of separate peace agreements. The next day the participants expressed agreement in a joint statement to "guarantee a unified Arab stand throughout all the phases of the conference and the talks that complement it." Opposition to separate deals was the main point of agreement, while Syria failed to convince other Arabs to promise to boycott the multilateral talks.

For the Palestinians, the decision to attend Madrid reflected their coming to grips with new realities. In Jerusalem on October 23, Faisal al-Husseini explained the change to a theater full of local residents: "Today we are entering a new phase. We are heading toward political discussions, a new reality." He said that this was a stage "which follows many catastrophes," referring to the *intifada* as well as Palestinian support for Iraq in the Gulf War. He said that the mistake they made "was facing powers that were much stronger than us," and he spoke of a "new world order" and urged his compatriots "to understand the rules of the new game so that we can face the challenge and reach our goal." It was noted that the Palestinians had moved toward a more realistic posture in several areas: talking to Israel, accepting negotiations without any guarantee of how they would end up, and acceding to a shift in representation away from the PLO toward residents of the territories. Elias Freij, Bethlehem mayor and one of the delegates, summed it up: "The Palestinians now realize that they will not win a military victory, that time is now on the side of Israel, which can build settlements and create facts, and that the only way out of this dilemma is face-to-face negotiations."

At the same time, as the opening of the conference neared, it was clear that Arab leaders believed that a new attitude had developed in the Bush administration. Nabil Shaath, adviser to Arafat, reflected this view: "The Arabs now see that there is more divergence between the interests of the United States and Israel, which allows the United States for the first time to do some things more than before." And Sharaa of Syria indicated that, since the United States would be the "moving force" at the conference, "we are confident we will arrive at the desired results." Arab leaders pointed to Bush's statement to Congress in March on "territory for peace"; his stand on the loan guarantees; and Baker's continuous talks with Ashrawi and Husseini, even as their coordination with the PLO became increasingly overt.

Meanwhile, Shamir expressed greater optimism as the talks neared. In an interview on October 24 he said that the talks offered hope for "revolutionary change," and that, while things could easily go wrong, "there are many chances for success." He expressed doubts about Washington's impartiality in light of the loan-guarantee and other spats, but he said there was a need for an "honest broker" and "there's not a better candidate for playing this role" than the United States. An Israeli poll showed that Israelis overwhelmingly supported the decision to take part in the negotiations, with 57 percent believing they might actually produce significant results.

Israel announced its delegates to the talks, naming Yosef Ben-Aharon to lead negotiations with Syria and Elyakim Rubinstein, the cabinet secretary, to lead negotiations with the Jordanian-Palestinian team.

At a White House news conference on October 25, President Bush stressed that the United States would serve as a catalyst to bring people together but would not try to "impose a settlement." Secretary Baker indicated that the plans for the conference were proceeding on schedule. He noted, too, that the Americans and Soviets hoped to prevent the opening conference from getting bogged down in procedural disputes, so that the parties could move to the direct bilateral negotiations which were the key to progress.

On October 28, participants in the peace conference began to arrive in Madrid, including Mikhail Gorbachev, making his first trip out of the Soviet Union since the failed coup. Palestinian delegates arrived in Madrid bearing olive branches and chanting "Palestine is Arab." And the first dispute of the opening conference surfaced when Israeli officials criticized the fact that the official Palestinian delegation was going to have equal speaking time at the conference with all other delegations. The Israelis argued that the Palestinians were part of a joint delegation and should split the time with the Jordanians.

On the eve of the opening of the historic talks, Bush, in Madrid, refused to reiterate the "land for peace" formula, saying again that "we're not here to impose a settlement" and "I don't want to give anybody reason to walk away or make additional conditions because of anything I say." It was as if, after all the years of disappointment and false starts, there was a lurking fear that another nasty surprise could still be in store for everybody. During the day, Shamir held a private meeting with Gorbachev, which again showed how much the world had changed on all sides.

On issues, on October 29, Israel agreed that Palestinians and Jordanians would each be permitted 45 minutes for their opening statements, although they were part of the same delegation. Regarding the direct talks, still unresolved were the questions of venue after the initial talks in Madrid—Israel wanted a Middle East location, the Arabs wished to stay in Madrid—and a continuing U.S.-Soviet role—Syria wanted their presence in direct talks, Israel was opposed.

PEACE CONFERENCE OPENS

And so, in Madrid, on October 30, Israel and the Arab states that surround it met face to face for peace talks. Representatives from Israel, Jordan, Syria, Lebanon, and the Palestinians sat around a T-shaped meeting table in the Hall of Columns at Spain's Royal Palace. Presidents Bush and Gorbachev gave the opening speeches. Bush used his speech to tell the Israelis that "territorial compromise is essential for peace," but balanced that declaration by telling the Arabs that they must make real peace, not just end the state of war, to gain any territorial concessions. Gorbachev said that all should seek a shared victory over a "cruel past." Reporters noted that the Israeli and Arab delegates were cold to each other in public but that during the breaks, several Israeli delegates quietly exchanged greetings with members of the Palestinian, Jordanian, and Lebanese teams. There was no contact, however, between Israelis and Syrians.

Baker, for whom the talks represented a personal triumph, said afterward that the "old taboo that Arabs and Israelis cannot meet and cannot talk is now something that we want to relegate to history." He added, "The road to peace will be very long and it will be very difficult. We have to crawl before we walk and we have to walk before we run, and today I think we all began to crawl." It was noted ironically by some commentators that, while this conference should have been a political triumph for George Bush back home, as a logical extension of the victory over Saddam, in fact, with the end of the threat that an Arab-Israeli conflict could escalate into a U.S.-Soviet nuclear war and with no imminent risk of an oil embargo, most Americans saw the development as distant and unlikely to influence their own well-being at home.

On the second day of the opening conference, each participant had an opportunity to present its perspective on the struggle. On the third day, each party had time for rebuttal. Shamir directed sharp attacks at Syria, charging that it was "the home of a host of terrorist organizations that spread violence and death to all kinds of innocent targets" and "merits the dubious distinction of being one of the most oppressive, tyrannical regimes in the world." The prime minister saved his softer remarks for Jordan, noting that Israel maintained a "situation of de facto non-belligerency" with Jordan, as well as that Israel had no designs on Lebanese territory. Sharaa of Syria struck the most strident note of the day, holding up a picture of Shamir when he was a member of the Jewish underground and claiming that Shamir "himself recognized that he was a terrorist. . . . He killed peace mediators."

The conference concluded with an address by James Baker in which he sought to dampen the effects of the harsh rhetoric: "I said often that the parties would probably stake out maximum positions, especially as they get closer to negotiations. This is not surprising, especially in a public forum." He called it a "good start, an historic start that has broken taboos," but cautioned that "you must not let this start become an end," and added, "We cannot want peace more than you."

On his return to Jerusalem on the same day, Shamir reiterated his commitment to the process, despite the vituperative comments by the Syrian representative and despite the dispute over where to hold the direct talks. Early on, the Jordanian-Palestinian group had agreed to meet with the Israelis on November 3 to discuss unresolved details, including the site of further talks. Hanan Ashrawi, speaking for the Palestinians, said that procedural matters should not be allowed to hold up the start of the bilateral talks, reflecting the sense that the Palestinians saw a prospect for immediate tangible gains from the talks.

The Syrian insistence on Madrid was seen as reflecting their fear that other bilateral talks would yield greater results than their own, which in their view depended on Israel's willingness to return the Golan Heights. Sharaa indicated in his press conference that Syria would not agree to normalize ties with Israel and said he would not even shake hands or talk with Israelis until "after the withdrawal from the Golan." By November 3, however, the Syrians had given in and met the Israelis for the first time in direct talks. Reportedly, the Saudis and Egyptians had weighed in against the Syrian position, and the Palestinians had made it clear that they would not hold back, so the Syrian hold over Arab negotiating positions had been broken. Minus Soviet backing, Syria's weakness was exposed; it capitulated by showing up for the talks, though several hours late. After the sides met for five hours, Ben-Aharon, head of the Israeli delegation, indicated that the talks were "not fruitful at all," with the Syrians repeating the question: "When will you withdraw from the territories?" The Syrian chief delegate, Muwaffaz al-Allaf, also expressed dissatisfaction, claiming that the Israelis "wanted to make gains without giving anything in return."

In contrast, the Israeli-Jordanian-Palestinian talks were said to have been held in a good atmosphere with friendly exchanges. They ended with a joint statement saying that Israelis and Palestinians would soon begin negotiations for self-rule in the territories. Baker expressed pleasure with the quality of these talks and added that he hoped they would lead "within a year" to limited self-rule for the Palestinians. Elyakim Rubinstein, heading the Israeli delegation on the Jordanian-Palestinian talks, said "there is still a long way to go," but "there surely is an historic feeling here." The real success of the talks was that they had taken place at all, and that the Palestinians and Jordanians had put themselves on separate tracks from the Syrians, thus limiting the Syrian ability to dominate.

AFTER MADRID

With the end of the Madrid phase of the talks, it was unclear where and when they would continue. The Israelis sought Middle East venues on the grounds that it would be easier for government leaders to consult with their delegates, as well as for the recognition of Israel that would be implicit in such meetings. While the Arabs continued to argue on behalf of Madrid or other European spots, it was reported that Baker would seek to resolve the dispute by inviting the parties to Washington sometime in December.

Back in Washington, Baker held a news conference on November 5 in which he urged Israel and Syria to reach an agreement within two weeks on a location for the bilateral talks. "If there's no agreement," he said, "we will feel free to submit proposals." When asked about Israel's announcement of a new settlement in the Golan Heights the day before, he said that he could not see how such a move could help the process and expressed concern about provocative steps by any party.

Days passed without any resolution of the question as to where future talks should be held. Shamir's visit to the United States to speak to the annual assembly of the Council of Jewish Federations provided an opportunity for him to consult with Bush and Baker on the matter. On November 21, Shamir told the Council of Jewish Federations meeting in Baltimore that Israeli security required that Israel maintain control of the West Bank and Gaza because there is "no room for two states in such a small area." Later in the day he met with Baker in Washington; after the meeting Baker said they had made progress regarding the site. Shamir, when asked if Israel was now ready to come to Washington to continue the talks (Washington was increasingly mentioned as the compromise site), would only say, "We have discussed this question of venue together with other questions and we have not yet decided."

The following day, November 22, only hours before Shamir was to meet with President Bush, the State Department issued invitations to the parties to begin their next round of peace talks in Washington on December 4. Shamir reportedly still tried to convince Bush in his meeting that he should bring more pressure to bear on the Arab states to hold the talks in the Middle East. Two hours later, however, spokeswoman Tutwiler announced that the invitations had gone out: "After waiting three weeks for the parties directly involved to work out among themselves the question of venue for additional bilateral talks, we proposed that the parties meet here in Washington on December 4."

Yitzhak Shamir returned to Israel on November 24, amid a storm of accusations that Washington had humiliated the prime minister in the way it fixed the next round of talks. Shamir himself sought to play down the dispute, insisting that, despite the obvious disagreements with Washington, "there is no crisis of confidence, not personal and not any other kind."

The Israeli government's concerns about the U.S. attitude were heightened by some of the suggestions for bridging differences between the parties contained in the invitation. Included in it was language suggesting that Israel ask the Syrians what they would give in return if Israel were to withdraw from the Golan. Such references to withdrawal reportedly created an uproar in Shamir's office.

On November 26, the informal deadline for response to the U.S. invitations, three parties—Israel, Syria, and the Palestinians—had not yet responded. The administration indicated that it would not consider any changes in its invitations and told Israel and the Arab parties, "The ball's in your court." The issues of concern to the parties were: for Syria, its desire for a prior commitment from Israel to consider withdrawing from the Golan; for the Palestinians, admission of PLO representatives to the United States to observe the talks; for Israel, the venue.

On November 27, the government of Israel issued a statement indicating that, "out of respect for the United States," it was prepared to conduct one or two meetings in Washington, with subsequent talks to be held in the Middle East or close by. It proposed that the first talks take place on December 9. Later in the same day, sensing an opportunity to score a propaganda coup over the Israelis, Syria and the Palestinians quickly dropped their resistance and agreed to show up on December 4. Tutwiler indicated that the U.S. invitation stood and that the State Department would "have the negotiation facilities ready and open on December 4."

On November 29, Shamir explained to reporters why his government was so intent on having the talks in the region and separately. Both positions, he said, were designed to dispel assumptions by the Arabs that they could bypass Israel and deal only with the Americans. He indicated that, while Bush and Baker told him that "the Arabs are making a complete mistake if this is what they think," he remained concerned about American intentions. Despite reports of possible compromise, Israel stuck to its guns about not appearing until December 9, apparently ready to take a public-relations setback in order to make the point that Jerusalem would not allow Washington to dictate procedural details, because that might lead the United States to dictate substantive measures.

While the United States refused to give in to Israeli requests to delay the talks, it did make a concession to Israel by barring photographers and reporters from the negotiating rooms until all the participants were in place, presumably to avoid a publicity barrage showing empty Israeli chairs. In two other developments perceived partly as U.S. efforts to heal the latest Israeli wounds, Washington announced, on December 3, a large-scale international meeting for January 28–29 in Moscow, to discuss Middle East regional issues. The administration indicated as well that it would press harder for repeal of the UN resolution equating Zionism with racism.

December 4 came and Israeli delegates did not appear. Syrian, Lebanese, Jordanian, and Palestinian negotiators gathered at the State Department but quickly departed. Tutwiler said it was "disappointing" that Israel did not show up. Meanwhile, Benjamin Netanyahu held a news conference in Washington in which he explained Israel's absence as a signal to both the Arabs and the United States that there could be no talks without Israel, and that Washington should not have issued the invitations without first insisting that the Arabs directly discuss the issue with Israel. By the next day, the Palestinians showed unhappiness that the American response to Israel's absence was not sharper. Ashrawi accused the United States of "avoiding confrontation with Israel and allowing Israel to stall." After much wrangling, the two sides agreed to begin the Washington talks on December 10.

On that date, after Syrian and Israeli negotiators met for 2½ hours, Syrian officials complained that Israel was "trying to talk about everything except for withdrawal from the territories, rejecting the possibility of land for peace," while Israel was trying to determine whether the Syrians were "willing to accept Israel's right to exist and its legitimacy."

Meanwhile, the Israeli-Jordanian-Palestinian talks, deemed the ones most likely to produce some sort of agreement in the future, became bogged down in a procedural dispute. Israel insisted that the talks open with a joint Jordanian-Palestinian delegation, and only after the opening would the Israelis and Palestinians separate into working groups. While Israel pointed out that the invitation to the talks required a joint delegation, it also wanted to highlight its view that a solution must be in the Jordanian context. For their part, the Palestinian delegates insisted on separate talks from the outset to underscore their view as to where the talks should lead.

By the end of the first week of talks, observers noted that the gulf between the sides was too wide to permit any quick, dramatic agreements, but that the parties were willing to show just enough flexibility to avoid dooming the talks to failure. One of Israel's negotiators was quoted as saying, "If you ask me where we will be a year from now, I would predict that we will have not reached any agreements. But I also believe that we will still be negotiating."

Bush met with Levy on December 17, and officials reported that the president had called on Israeli and Arab negotiators to resolve the procedural wrangling. Two days later, with the round of talks over and scheduled for resumption on January 2, Bush said he was "disappointed" at the lack of progress, but insisted that when the talks resumed, the United States would "continue to have the same role, as a catalyst, not attempting to dictate solutions." These comments were seen as siding more with Israel, which argued that the Arabs would not be forthcoming as long as they believed Washington would intervene, than with the Arabs, who sought a more active U.S. role to break the deadlock. On December 21, Shamir, talking to 3,000 members of Likud's Central Committee, congratulated Israel's negotiating team and said that their mission was to achieve peace without giving up land.

Loan Guarantees

Aside from the Gulf War and the beginning of the peace conference, the major issue facing the United States and Israel in 1991 was Israel's request that the U.S. government cosign a loan for $10 billion over five years to help Israel absorb Soviet Jewish immigrants. The impetus for Israel's request was the fact that Soviet Jews, alarmed by the collapse of the Soviet economy as well as fear of growing anti-Semitism, were rushing to leave the USSR by whatever means possible for the one country willing to take them immediately. In December 1990 alone the figures were close to 40,000, a record for immigration to Israel; officials of the government and Jewish Agency were predicting 200,000 to 400,000 for 1991. Simcha Dinitz, chairman of the Jewish Agency, summed up the mood: "We are going to get them out as quickly as we can, regardless of the difficulties it creates here. Because if we wait, the doors could close and it could be too late."

In 1990, when the Soviets loosened restrictions on emigration and the number of immigrants began to climb, Israel requested and received a commitment for a $400-million loan guarantee from the United States. Final approval, however, had been held up by the administration's desire for written assurance that the money would not be used to build housing units in the occupied territories. Although Israel submitted a letter signed by David Levy, making explicit promises to this effect, on October 2, 1990, the State Department continued to raise questions about Israel's spending plans regarding road building and settlements.

On February 13, 1991, Ambassador Shoval handed the State Department answers to its last three questions on Israel's plans. The following day, Secretary Baker read an article in the *Washington Post* suggesting that Israel had secret plans to build 12,000 new housing units in the territories. He instructed his aides to find out from the ambassador whether this was official policy or not. That afternoon, Shoval, in a Reuters interview, accused Washington of giving his country the "runaround" on its request for loan guarantees, and complained that Israel had so far received no compensation for losses incurred as a result of the Gulf War.

The administration reacted with an unusual rebuke of the ambassador in the form of a White House statement on February 15: "Public statements made yesterday by Israeli Ambassador Zalman Shoval criticizing the United States are outrageous and outside the bounds of acceptable behavior by the ambassador of any friendly country. The Secretary of State made this clear to the Ambassador yesterday, and the President protested to Prime Minister Shamir by cable this morning. We deserve better from Israel's Ambassador." Administration officials made clear that Israel understood that Washington was prepared to release the $400 million as soon as the Israelis provided the information they had promised, and therefore the "runaround" claim was dishonest.

On February 17, at the National Jewish Community Relations Advisory Council meeting in Miami, Shoval apologized for his criticism, saying, "I did say some things which diplomats are not supposed to say and I am sorry for that." Clearly trying to smooth over the flap with the administration, Shoval called the dispute a "squabble between friends, and mistakes on my part can be overcome." Finally, on February 20, Baker telephoned Levy to inform him of Washington's decision "to release the $400 million." Reports were already circulating, however, that Israel would come back to the United States for further assistance, as well as seeking additional support from world Jewry and from other governments in the form of guarantees.

On May 6, ending months of speculation, Ambassador Shoval said in a speech to the American Jewish Committee that Israel would soon request $10 billion in loan guarantees and urged the United States not to link the aid to "political considerations of the moment." He indicated that Israel would not ask the administration for the additional guarantees until September (reportedly because of an agreement giving Israel $650 million in emergency aid at the end of the Persian Gulf War and mandating that there would be no additional Israeli aid requests until Labor Day). Shoval also indicated that once Washington agreed to grant the guarantees, Israel hoped that Europe and Japan would follow suit with additional assistance. He suggested that the world owed Israel and the Jewish people "a debt to normalize Jewish history."

Concern began to mount in Israel and the Jewish community as stories circulated that the administration was going to take a tougher stand on a new request, seeking concessions on the peace process or on settlements. Tom Dine, executive director of the American Israel Public Affairs Committee (AIPAC), declared in a speech on June 9 that the "paramount challenge this year" to American Jews would be to persuade Congress and the administration to grant the loan guarantees: "We must fight any attempt to imperil this vital program by linking it to the explosive ideological issue of settlements, or the peace process. This is something we will fight with all our being." On June 26, Israeli defense minister Arens said in a talk to the

Washington Institute for Near East Policy that Israel would fiercely resist any effort to link the loan guarantees to a halt in settlement building, saying that he found it "hard to believe anybody would tie together these two incommensurate things which would deprive Soviet Jews of needed help."

Reports also circulated that Shoval had sent a message to Jerusalem warning that additional settlement activity would seriously jeopardize efforts to secure the loan-guarantee package. In Israel, the government was pushing ahead with a massive building program in the territories. Thousands of housing units were under construction, and Sharon promised to build 12,000 new units over the next two years, which would increase the Jewish population in the territories by up to 50 percent.

On Monday, July 1, Bush addressed Israel's concern, saying that he did not think the loan guarantees should be a "quid pro quo." While Israeli officials said they were "happy" with Bush's statement, there still was concern that linkage would occur. Israel Radio's correspondent in Washington, Oded Ben Ami, said on July 2, "One must be blind to think there will not be a linkage; there will be one." And in an interview with Israel Radio, Shoval laid it on the line: "The government of Israel will have no choice but to decide if it is more important to continue settlement-building in Judea, Samaria, and Gaza, or obtain American aid for the absorption of Soviet immigrants." He stressed that he took no position but intended only to lay out the problem facing the government: "There is no escape from this choice. If the government refuses to freeze the settlements, it must know whether it is capable of absorbing the immigrants without U.S. aid."

As an open struggle began to loom between the administration and Israel, commentators looked at the third side of the triangle, Congress. It was noted that Capitol Hill would not want to do anything to undermine the administration's efforts to get a peace process started; at the same time, few members would want to pressure the Israeli government, particularly as it struggled to deal with the tide of new immigrants. Most significantly, it was pointed out that Congress would have to deal with the potential budgetary impact of the loan guarantees, the varying estimates of the money that would have to be set aside.

As the summer moved along and the September date for Israel's formal request neared, there was some hope that Israel's acceptance of the Baker peace initiative might lead the administration to back off from any thoughts of linkage. In September, as the day approached when Shoval would present Israel's request, Baker reportedly tried to persuade Shamir to defer the request until the peace conference opened in October. Shamir told Baker that he could not delay the request because the aid was too important and because he did not want to look weak before the Arabs. On September 4, having gotten nowhere with Shamir, Baker said at a news conference that he hoped Congress would defer the loan matter in order to give the peace conference a chance. Sen. Patrick Leahy (D., Vt.), chairman of the Senate appropriations subcommittee on foreign operations, said, after meeting with Bush and Baker on September 4, that he had decided to delay consideration of the foreign operations aid bill, which would include the loan guarantees.

On September 6, the day that Shoval would formally present Israel's request, Bush took the unusual step of summoning reporters into the Oval Office to announce that he would ask Congress not to act on the Israeli appeal for 120 days. This meant that it would only be dealt with after the opening of the peace conference. Bush said, "I think the American people will strongly support me in this. I'm going to fight for it because I think this is what the American people want, and I'm going to do absolutely everything I can to back those members of the United States Congress who are forward-looking in their desire to see peace." While Bush was making it clear that Shamir must take the administration seriously, that he could not have everything, Israelis and American Jewish leaders argued that in demanding a freeze on settlements, Bush was prejudicing himself as a cosponsor for the peace conference by insisting that Israel make a prior commitment on a matter that should be negotiated with the Arabs.

Several hours after Bush's meeting with reporters, Shoval presented Israel's request to Baker.

On September 10, Bush met in the White House with Senate supporters of Israel—Robert Kasten (R., Wis.), Daniel Inouye (D., Hawaii), and Patrick Leahy—and appealed to them to back his request for a four-month delay. All the senators promised him, however, was a two-week delay "to avoid confrontation if possible." The president told them that he would not seek any further delays in taking up the issue after January but gave no assurances that he would support the guarantees after the delay.

On September 11, Bush told reporters that it was "simply . . . not correct" to say, as one anonymous Israeli official had said in Jerusalem the day before, that the administration was breaking a vow on the loan guarantees. The president said, "I'm not committed to any numbers and never have been. I'm committed to seeing that they get considered. And we generally have been quite supportive of the idea of absorption" of Soviet Jews into Israel. While reports told of a president angered over Israel's insistence on pushing forward, he limited his public remarks on the 11th to the fact that he had seen comments from abroad "that I didn't particularly appreciate."

On September 12, as part of the American Jewish community's effort to win approval for the loan guarantees, more than a thousand people came to Washington from across the country to lobby members of Congress. While the community leaders were gathering in the capital, the president called a hurriedly scheduled nationally televised news conference in which he urged, in unusually vehement terms, that Congress delay debate on Israel's loan-guarantee request and threatened to use his veto to block any early congressional action on the matter. He expressed how upset he was that Congress was moving forward and reiterated his concern that a "contentious debate" on the issue "could well destroy our ability to bring one or more of the parties to the peace talks." The president spoke of his commitment to help Soviet Jews but said that he had "absolutely not" made any commitment to support the loan-guarantee request, even at the end of 120 days.

Even more than the policy decision of the president, the words and the tone of his remarks created an uproar in Israel and the American Jewish community. He conjured up old anti-Semitic stereotypes of excessive Jewish power when he said that "powerful political forces" were at work against him, while "we've got one lonely little guy down here doing it." He said that he heard "there were something like a thousand lobbyists on the Hill working the other side of the question." He talked of how American soldiers "risked their lives to defend Israelis" in the face of Iraqi Scud missiles but made no mention of the Israeli policy of restraint in support of the U.S. war effort in the face of those same Iraqi missiles. And he referred to U.S. aid to Israel in terms that those who propagandize against aid to Israel employ: "nearly $1,000 for every Israeli man, woman, and child" (as if the money were simply given to individual Israelis rather than assisting a nation considered crucial to U.S. interests).

The following day, Shamir, returning to Israel from a trip to Paris, responded defiantly to the Bush threat to veto a loan guarantee, saying that his government saw "no reason to change our position" on the issue. He seemed to encourage American Jews to press forward when he said, "Our friends have brought this . . . problem before the Congress, and the Congress will discuss it and take its decisions." Earlier, in a meeting with French Jews, he stressed that American Jews "have learned a lesson from the Holocaust and they are now united and very active, to the surprise of political circles in their country."

On September 15, things got nastier. Cabinet minister Rehavam Ze'evi, from the far Right, called George Bush an anti-Semite and a liar. Moshe Arens later repudiated this attack in an interview on ABC, and Shamir reportedly urged his ministers to "calm the atmosphere and watch our words." Shamir, however, was also quoted by officials as having said: "We will not retreat . . . we will stick by our position." Meanwhile, the official Syrian daily *Tishreen* said that if the United States submitted to Israeli pressure for loan guarantees—labeled Israeli "blackmail"—it risked destroying peace efforts and threatening U.S. interests.

Commentators on the Middle East pointed out that the conflict between Bush and Shamir was far deeper than just over loan guarantees. From Israel's side, it was noted, there were general anxieties about American attitudes now that the Cold War had ended, as well as questions about linkage of U.S. aid to settlements and nervousness that Israel would be isolated in the difficult negotiations. The American perspective, in turn, was seen as conflicted: on the one hand, the desire to coax or pressure the Arabs to come to the table so as to produce a change in Israeli behavior; on the other, a sense that without U.S. pressure, the Shamir government would never truly change.

On September 16, Secretary Baker visited Israel and spent two days of talks in Jerusalem. According to reports, Baker offered the Israelis a six-point compromise proposal that included an administration commitment to address the loan guarantees in principle after the four-month delay; it did not include a promise of the full $10 billion in guarantees or a way to avoid any linkage to a halt in settlements. Israeli officials reportedly told Baker that they would agree to a delay if the administration promised an eventual full guarantee without any linkage. On the plane to Cairo, Baker called together reporters accompanying him and reportedly indicated that the administration would not give Israel the loan guarantees without an Israeli agreement to halt further settlements.

The following day, however, at a news conference in Damascus after talks with Assad, Baker said he had not "discussed either publicly or privately a settlement freeze" in connection with the loan guarantees. Instead he said: "We have asked for a delay, because we want to avoid the question of linkage, not to promote it. It is not new information that the Administration believes that when Congress debates the issue of absorption aid to Israel in the form of guarantees or otherwise, we have a right to know and a right to ask how that aid and how those guarantees would be used." Syrian foreign minister Sharaa used the occasion to warn that if Washington granted the loan, "then that will be a major obstacle to peace, certainly." In Israel, Shamir told a group of visiting congressmen, on September 19, that the U.S. decision on loan guarantees was creating "euphoria in the Arab world, and that this fact cannot advance peace."

Meanwhile, in Washington, President Bush sought to calm the uproar in the Jewish community over his September 12 remarks by sending a conciliatory letter to Shoshana Cardin, chairwoman of the Conference of Presidents of Major American Jewish Organizations. While standing by his decision calling for a 120-day delay of consideration of the loan guarantees, Bush expressed recognition that some of his comments had "caused apprehension within the Jewish community," and said that his reference to "lobbyists and powerful political forces was never meant to be pejorative in any sense." He believed, he said, that "politically organized groups and individuals are a legitimate and valued part of the decision-making process in a democracy."

At the same time, key members of Congress were seeking a compromise to avoid confrontation. Senators Kasten and Inouye sponsored a proposal to approve the guarantees without reference to a 120-day delay but indicated that they would wait for Baker's return in hopes of reaching agreement. Senator Leahy summed up congressional opinion: "Even those who disagree with the President would like to avoid a fight, feeling that no one would win—not Israel, not the United States." Commentators noted that the president saw the persistence of Israel and the Congress over this issue as a challenge to his control over foreign affairs and believed that he had public backing.

As discussions continued about possible congressional compromise, increasingly there were reports that the lawmakers would not oppose the president on his desire for a 120-day delay. A key figure, David Obey (D., Wis.), chairman of the House Appropriation Committee's subcommittee on foreign operations, supported the president: "I don't care if you tell me that Daffy Duck has a proposal. Proposals are very interesting, but in the end they've got to get the money, and they have to get the money through my committee. And that's not going to happen until January." With an election year coming and the country in a recession, there was ambivalence in Congress and unwillingness to confront the president over an issue perceived to be one of foreign aid. Inouye, for one, said, on September 23, that he believed most of his colleagues "do not want to frustrate the President in his role in conducting the nation's foreign policy. I don't think there's any doubt about the 120 days. In fact, it may be longer."

One proposal that received a good deal of attention and seemed to address the administration's concern that money lent to Israel would free other money to build settlements ("fungibility"), was circulated by Senator Leahy. This would link the guarantees to settlements by deducting a dollar from the guarantees for every dollar Israel invested in settlements in the territories.

On September 25, Levy and Baker met in Washington, and the Israeli foreign minister told reporters afterward that a "better climate" had been achieved. This improvement in atmosphere was understood to mean not any substantive understandings but rather a growing sense that a fight with the White House in Congress was not realistic.

On October 2, the key senators working for the loan guarantees, Kasten and Inouye, formally acceded to the president's request for a 120-day postponement. State Department spokeswoman Margaret Tutwiler said the congressional decision was "a welcome affirmation of the President's judgment that a pause" would be "in the best interests of historic opportunity for peace that lies before us." She indicated that the administration would support the guarantees the following year, "provided terms and conditions acceptable to the Administration are worked out."

At the opening session of the Knesset, on October 7, Shamir took his strongest stand yet against the administration: "The pain and disappointment are especially great because the American Administration chose to take a step that damages the deepest foundations of Jewish and Zionist existence." While praising Bush for his past efforts on behalf of Soviet and Ethiopian Jews, Shamir said that the administration had neglected to recognize the decades of Arab opposition to Jewish immigration to Israel.

On November 12, Bush met with Jewish leaders and reportedly told them that he was troubled that some of his remarks "hurt some people." He refused, however, to discuss the loan guarantees, saying that he would take up the matter in January. Visiting Washington in November, Shamir chose not to raise the loan-guarantee issue with the president, apparently having been advised that it would not be a good idea. However, the prime minister was said to be angry at the lack of discussion on a matter of such importance to Israel.

"Zionism Equals Racism" Resolution

Amid the difficult struggles to start a peace process and to evaluate loan guarantees to Israel, the Bush administration took a major initiative to have the United Nations repeal its infamous resolution of 1975 equating Zionism with racism. Speaking to the UN at its opening session, on September 23, Bush called for repeal, saying that the UN "cannot claim to seek peace" until it does: "We should take seriously the charter's pledge to practice tolerance and live together in peace with one another as good neighbors. Resolution 3379, the so-called Zionism-is-racism resolution, mocks this pledge and the principles upon which the United Nations was founded."

The administration had been committed in principle for two years to such a move, but had delayed because of the Gulf War. Although the president now stressed that the measure would promote the cause of peace, it was also noted that it was intended to heal the strains with Israel over the loan guarantees. Still, John Bolton, assistant secretary of state for international affairs, indicated that the United States was far from ready to put repeal to a vote because, while there was probably a majority in favor of repeal, it was not strong enough to risk a vote. The following day, September 24, Soviet foreign minister Boris Pankin joined Bush in calling on the UN to "once and for all leave behind the legacy of the ice age like the obnoxious resolution equating Zionism to racism." The change in the Soviet position was seen as one more indicator of the new world created by the fall of Communism, holding out hope that repeal was not a pipe dream.

While other nations began to express their support for repeal, Arab leaders refused to budge. Syrian foreign minister Sharaa told the UN, on October 1, that Bush's call was premature, that first the causes that prompted passage in 1975—Israel's occupation of Arab lands and treatment of the Palestinians—must be dealt with.

After the initial flurry of activity following the president's speech, the campaign for repeal seemed to stop dead, and in Israel there was some criticism of Bush for having let the issue drop. Early in December, however, U.S. diplomats engaged in an extensive campaign in capitals around the world to secure support for repeal of the resolution. By December 5, U.S. and Israeli officials reported that at least 85 and possibly 100 of the General Assembly's 166 members were ready to vote for repeal. Meanwhile, on that day, 21 Arab members of the UN, including Egypt, decided that the repeal resolution was unacceptable because it offered nothing to the Palestinians. On December 8, the 45-nation Organization of the Islamic Conference approved a resolution condemning Zionism as racist.

Momentum for repeal continued to build. On December 9, it was revealed that Japan had decided to vote for it, the decision seen as part of a broader Japanese effort to improve relations with Israel.

Finally, on December 16, the General Assembly voted overwhelmingly to revoke the resolution. The vote was 111 in favor of repeal, 25 against, with 13 abstaining and 17 not taking part in the voting. The heavy vote was interpreted as a demonstration of U.S. diplomatic power as well as of the shifting political currents following the collapse of Communism and the Gulf War. All the former Soviet Bloc nations voted for repeal; many Asian and African nations, including India, Nigeria, Singapore, and the Philippines, which had voted for the resolution in 1975, reversed themselves. Among the Arabs, none voted for repeal, but Bahrain, Egypt, Kuwait,

Morocco, Oman, and Tunisia were all absent from the vote.

As the result of the vote flashed on the big electronic board in the General Assembly, applause broke out and delegates rushed to congratulate Israel's foreign minister Levy. Later, Levy described the vote as "removing a terrible blot" and said the world community was "sobering up." Lawrence Eagleburger, speaking for the United States, summed up the situation: "We believe that with the world's and this body's passage into a new era, it is more than time to consign one of the last relics of the Cold War to the dustbin of history."

KENNETH JACOBSON

Communal

Jewish Communal Affairs

T HE GROWING TENDENCY OF American Jews to focus more of their
attention on domestic communal concerns was temporarily sidetracked by the Gulf
War of 1991, when Iraqi Scud missiles seemed to threaten the very existence of the
Jewish state, and the American need to shore up an Arab anti-Iraq coalition raised
the possibility that the United States might push Israel toward territorial compromise. But once that crisis passed, American Jewish concern with its own viability
reasserted itself, especially in light of accelerating intermarriage, low rates of affiliation, and internal conflict over values and life-styles.

American Jews and Israel

THE GULF WAR

As 1991 began, the world waited for news of Iraqi intentions in the Persian Gulf.
The Security Council of the UN had given Iraq until January 15 to withdraw its
forces from Kuwait, which it had invaded five months earlier, or face armed attack
by the United States and its allies.

With President Saddam Hussein of Iraq threatening to attack Israel if the United
States used force against his country, Jewish groups rallied behind the administration of President George Bush. The Conference of Presidents of Major American
Jewish Organizations announced support for U.S. policy in the Gulf and lauded the
administration's "refusal to accept any linkage of the occupation of Kuwait with the
Palestinian issue." In contrast to the National Conference of Catholic Bishops and
the National Council of the Churches of Christ, both of which questioned the use
of force in this case, the Synagogue Council of America justified military action to
restore Kuwaiti independence and "effectively deter or end Iraq's capacity to
threaten other nations." And experts on Jewish law from all branches of Judaism
were virtually unanimous that a war against Saddam Hussein's Iraq was Jewishly
permissible, perhaps even mandatory.

The support for military action did not come without serious soul-searching.

169

"You have people who were dovish on Vietnam and passionate about peace, but Israel's survival played a very powerful role in the decision," said Albert Vorspan, vice-president of the ordinarily dovish Union of American Hebrew Congregations, the congregational body of the Reform movement, one of the first organizations to issue a statement in 1990 in favor of military action. Vorspan and others argued that it was simplistic to assume that opposition to the Vietnam war necessitated opposition to a war in the Gulf, that the two situations were hardly comparable. Elements of the Israeli Peace Now movement in the United States also acknowledged a need to defeat Iraq.

Other groups on the Jewish "left"—the New Jewish Agenda and the Shalom Center—disagreed, however, and strongly opposed military action. In a statement that ran in a number of national and Jewish newspapers across the country in January, the Shalom Center asserted, "It is most likely that invasion or bombing of Iraq by U.S. forces would be likely to undermine our goals, not advance them," and called for economic sanctions and embargoes instead. *Tikkun* editor Michael Lerner at first appeared to support the use of force—"if and *only* if the U.S. had first tried to do everything in its power to dismantle Iraq's offensive military capacity through other means"—but quickly decided that Bush had failed to explore all available means and therefore the war was not justified (January/February 1991).

Jewish members of Congress were divided. On January 12, when both Houses voted to authorize President Bush to use force against Iraq, most Democratic legislators voted—together with their party allies—in favor of continued use of economic sanctions rather than war. Notable exceptions were Sen. Joseph Lieberman of Connecticut, the only Jewish Democrat in the Senate to back the administration, and Rep. Stephen Solarz of New York, a sponsor of the House resolution authorizing force.

With war imminent, the Conference of Presidents set up a "crisis response center"—a toll-free hotline to apprise local Jewish federations about the latest news of the Gulf crisis—and the Council of Jewish Federations made its satellite network available for communication between Israel and American Jewish leaders. Concerned that pro-Iraqi terrorists might attack American Jewish institutions, Jewish leaders in many communities met with local police officials to discuss security precautions. When the U.S. bombardment of Iraq began on the night of January 16, Shoshana Cardin, chairwoman of the Conference of Presidents, announced that American Jewry backed the president's policy and "is grateful that Israel is not involved in this." The next night, when Iraqi missiles landed in Israel, the Conference of Presidents called it "an act of war" and saluted Israelis' courage "in confronting the great challenges they face." The Synagogue Council of America issued a statement urging Jewish congregations to conduct special services to pray for the safety of American soldiers. (The council deliberately left out any mention of Israel so as not to appear to link the crisis in the Gulf with the Jewish state.) The United Jewish Appeal (UJA) and State of Israel Bonds launched emergency campaigns to solicit funds for Israel that would, within two weeks, raise $90 million for UJA and

$100 million for Bonds. And on Sunday, January 20, Jewish communities all over the country held prowar and pro-Israel rallies.

To the great disappointment of Israelis, many American Jews who found themselves in Israel before the war made sure to leave before the January 15 deadline. However, some American Jewish leaders began to come to Israel while the war was still on, as a sign of solidarity. Among the first was a three-person delegation from the American Jewish Committee that arrived on January 22 and, an hour after landing, was ushered into a sealed room when the air-raid sirens sounded. A week later, the Conference of Presidents sent a 51-person delegation. Chairwoman Cardin explained: "It is important for us to see this. . . . It is difficult for Americans to understand what this means just by looking at it on television." She pledged to "tell Israel's story in depth" and to "remind American political leaders of the role of Israel as an ally" upon her return.

THE PEACE PROCESS

On January 31, Cardin and other American Jewish leaders met with the president and then with State Department officials to explore whether the administration had any plans to impose a settlement of the Arab-Israel conflict as part of a resolution of the Gulf War. They came out of the meetings assured that there was no linkage between the two issues.

In February, American Jewry reacted angrily when President Bush harshly criticized Ambassador Zalman Shoval of Israel for publicly complaining that a promised $400-million loan guarantee for Israel was being delayed. The delay, it appeared, was due to American suspicions that the loans might fund Israeli settlement of new immigrants in the West Bank and Gaza Strip. Eager to smooth over this hitch in U.S.-Israeli relations, the plenum of the National Jewish Community Relations Advisory Council (NJCRAC), meeting in Miami, passed, by a very close vote, a resolution urging the Israeli government not to direct immigrants to these territories. After receiving Israeli assurances that the loan money would indeed not be spent on the territories, the administration approved the guarantees a few days later.

In March, with the Gulf War over and Kuwait liberated, there was rising apprehension among American Jews about the administration's intentions regarding Israel. Addressing Congress on national television on March 6, President Bush called for an end to the Arab-Israeli dispute on the basis of "land for peace." Fearing pressure on Israel, both the Conference of Presidents and NJCRAC issued statements that praised the president's commitment to peace while also putting the onus on the Arab world for the current state of affairs. The approach of these umbrella organizations was challenged by a delegation of dovish American Jews sponsored by Project Nishma—including Theodore Mann, a former chairman of the Conference of Presidents, Hyman Bookbinder, the former Washington representative of the American Jewish Committee, and three former NJCRAC chairmen—that issued a statement in Jerusalem backing the American administration and accusing the Israeli government of not being serious about peace. Mann claimed that "our views truly represent the majority views of American Jews."

An extensive survey of American Jewish public opinion, conducted during the summer and released in October, showed that the Conference of Presidents was probably closer than Project Nishma to the views of most American Jews. *After the Gulf War*, prepared by Prof. Steven M. Cohen for the American Jewish Committee, indicated how Iraqi aggression against Israel had moved American Jewish attitudes to the right. Whereas a similar 1989 poll had shown just 25 percent of Jews favoring the expansion of Israeli settlements in the territories, the figure rose to 30 percent in 1991. While 23 percent had said that American Jews should not publicly criticize Israeli policies in 1989, 30 percent felt that way two years later. And the percentage of American Jews who felt that the PLO was determined to destroy Israel rose in those years from 62 percent to 83 percent.

Another indicator that the Gulf War and prospects of a new peace process had strengthened American Jewish solidarity and ties with Israel was the decision by the American Jewish Committee in March to join the Conference of Presidents of Major Jewish American Organizations. For 23 years the AJCommittee had sought to assert a position of independence through maintaining only observer status at the conference. Sholom Comay, the committee's president, explained that, while this independence would continue: "We feel that we are at a historic point in approaching some of the most vexing concerns of our generation, and we are at a time when the unity of the American Jewish community must be maximized—not only because of the Middle East but also because of the challenges world Jewry faces in other areas."

On May 22, after an unsuccessful trip to the Middle East to get the peace process started, Secretary of State James Baker asserted publicly that no obstacle to peace was greater than Israeli settlement activity. The Conference of Presidents responded swiftly, saying it was "shocked and dismayed" at Baker's singling out Israeli actions for condemnation.

LOAN GUARANTEES

It was in this atmosphere that American Jewry geared up for a massive campaign to convince the president and Congress to approve a request for an additional $10 billion in loan guarantees that Israel was to submit in September. Since the loans would be used for the absorption of Soviet immigrants in Israel, and the administration clearly opposed settlement in the disputed territories, proponents of the guarantees faced the daunting task, once again, of preventing a linkage between the issue of humanitarian help for immigrants and the political question of the disposition of the territories.

One way to do so was to convince the Israelis to ease up on settlements. Echoing a warning given to his countrymen by Israeli ambassador Zalman Shoval, Abraham Foxman, director of the Anti-Defamation League, publicly warned Israel in June that the establishment of more settlements "is a provocative act" in the eyes of the American administration, and that Israel would have to choose between settlements and loan guarantees. The same message was conveyed to the Israeli government privately by other American Jewish leaders. On August 1, it was with a great deal of relief that American Jewish organizations hailed Israel's acceptance of a U.S. proposal for Middle East peace talks, a concession likely to win points with the White House.

Another American Jewish strategy to secure approval of the loan guarantees was a public education campaign. Over and over, Jewish organizations sent out the word that the guarantees, which would enable Israel to borrow from banks on favorable terms, were not a grant, and would cost the American taxpayer virtually nothing. They also stressed that much of the money to be borrowed would be spent in the United States, helping the American economy, and that Americans, who had done so much to gain the freedom of Jews in the former USSR, now had a moral obligation to help them resettle. Much was made as well of Israeli cooperation with American strategy in the Gulf War: despite Scud attacks on their cities, the Israelis had helped the United States maintain the anti-Iraq coalition intact by not retaliating.

On September 6, despite pleas from both Secretary Baker and President Bush to delay the request, Israel formally submitted its application for the guarantees. That same day, numerous Jewish organizations issued statements calling on Congress for quick approval. On Thursday, September 12, over a thousand people came to Washington to lobby for the loan guarantees. To their dismay, President Bush convened a press conference at which he asserted that precipitous approval might upset the delicate negotiations under way for Middle East peace negotiations, and asked for a 120-day delay to give the peace process a chance to get off the ground. In words that many Jews felt conjured up old anti-Semitic stereotypes of sinister behind-the-scenes Jewish manipulation, he referred to himself as "one lonely little guy" and to the loan-guarantee activists as "some powerful political forces." Pounding on the lectern for emphasis, Bush called on the American people to back him up in opposing immediate approval.

At first, Jewish leaders refused to budge. That same day, Shoshana Cardin reasserted to reporters the humanitarian case for the loan guarantees, pledging that "we will carry forward our effort with our senators and representatives." She also sent a letter to the president voicing concern that his remarks about "powerful political forces" unjustly impugned the right of American citizens to organize in support of policies they believed in. But when it became clear that the congressional forces supporting loan guarantees did not have enough votes to block the inevitable presidential veto, plans to introduce the legislation were postponed to January.

This was a humiliating defeat for Israel's supporters in the United States, and it led to considerable soul-searching by American Jewish leaders. To prevent a repetition of the debacle, on September 20 a number of American Jewish leaders met privately with the Israeli ambassador hoping to convey to the Israeli government the need to reach an accommodation with Washington on the settlement issue. Meanwhile, failure to obtain the loan guarantees encouraged those elements of the American Jewish community that had long opposed Israeli settlements policy. Project Nishma's executive board issued a public statement on October 2 urging Israel to institute a temporary freeze on the expansion of settlements in the territories "in the interest of larger national goals: immigration absorption, a stronger economy, and progress toward security and peace." And the next day, 50 members of Americans for Peace Now came to Washington to urge lawmakers to combine support for loan guarantees—when it came up again in January—with an insistence on an Israeli freeze on settlements.

Alarmed at the volume of anti-Semitic mail he received approving his stand on the loan guarantees, President Bush sought to mend relations with American Jews by inviting Jewish leaders to meet with him on November 12. In a discussion that lasted over an hour, Bush expressed regret for any of his September 12 remarks that might have been construed as attacks on the pro-Israel lobby. Stating his support in principle for humanitarian aid to resettle Soviet Jews in Israel, he nevertheless refused to commit himself on the loan guarantees. "It's open in January," he said. "We'll take it up at that time."

Although President Bush's handling of the loan guarantees was disappointing, his success in arranging peace talks between Israel, the Palestinians, and the Arab states—the first session opened in Madrid on October 30—drew praise from Jews. After the first meeting, Shoshana Cardin expressed gratification: "The fact that everyone sat down together in itself was an accomplishment." The new mood engendered by the peace initiative even enabled two groups of Jewish leaders, one from the American Jewish Congress, the other from the Conference of Presidents, to hold separate meetings, on November 18, with Prince Bandar Ibn Sultan, the Saudi Arabian ambassador to the United States. Cardin commented: "For the first time, the barrier was removed and we engaged in dialogue."

Israeli prime minister Yitzhak Shamir's scheduled appearance at the General Assembly of the Council of Jewish Federations on November 21 provided a focus for renewed debate over Israel's settlements in the territories. Hoping to confront Shamir with evidence that American Jewish leadership disagreed with his policies, on the day before his arrival Project Nishma and the Wilstein Institute of Jewish Policy Studies publicized the results of a poll indicating that federation leaders overwhelmingly backed a freeze on settlements and territorial compromise. That same day, Americans for Peace Now released an open letter to Shamir signed by 235 rabbis, asserting that "continued settlement activities are not only detrimental to the peace process, but also to the successful absorption of the new *olim* in Israel."

Shoshana Cardin downplayed the representativeness of these views. Citing her travels around the country, Cardin remarked that she rarely heard anyone in the audiences she addressed call for a settlement freeze. And on November 21, when Prime Minister Shamir spoke to the General Assembly and castigated those who urged his country to give back land taken in a defensive war, the volume of applause from federation leaders was impressive.

On December 16, the General Assembly of the United Nations rescinded its 1975 resolution identifying Zionism as a form of racism by a 111–25 vote. American Jewish organizations, which had struggled for years to accomplish this, were overjoyed. For the U.S. government, which had exerted considerable political muscle to secure this result, this was another example of help for Israel that American Jews would have to weigh in the balance when it came time to assess the Bush administration's record on issues of concern to Jews.

Soviet Jewry

The daily lunchtime vigil of Soviet Jewry activists outside the Soviet embassy in Washington that had taken place without fail since 1970 came to an end on January 27, 1991. On that day, Jewish leaders joined with local dignitaries and Soviet officials in a final ceremony marking freedom of emigration for Soviet Jews. While the USSR had not yet enacted legislation codifying the new liberal emigration policy—a condition Jews insisted upon for full waiver of the Jackson-Vanik Amendment provisions barring most-favored-nation trade status—over 180,000 Soviet Jews had emigrated in 1990, more than had left the USSR in the 21 previous years combined.

With many American Jewish communities still seeking to collect pledges made to the 1990 Operation Exodus campaign to resettle Soviet Jews in Israel—which raised $420 million—the UJA's board of trustees decided on March 7 to open a new campaign to raise an additional $450 million. Working in tandem with UJA, the Council of Jewish Federations asked its member federations to guarantee an additional $900 million in loans for resettlement. Despite opposition from some federations that feared the consequences of massive default, the proposal was approved overwhelmingly. Shoshana Cardin explained, "I think that the American Jewish community realized we don't have an option. This is an opportunity, and maybe the only opportunity, to bring *klal Yisrael* to Israel."

On May 20, the Soviet Parliament passed a liberal emigration law, but the Union of Councils for Soviet Jews (UCSJ) criticized its vagueness and the fact that its provisions would not go into effect until January 1993. While the UCSJ asked President Bush to continue to deny the Soviets most-favored-nation status, the National Conference on Soviet Jewry announced support of a one-year waiver in recognition of the new Soviet liberality, a position that President Bush espoused on June 1.

The attempted coup in the USSR in August aroused great anxiety among American Jews for the fate of Soviet Jewry. The National Conference on Soviet Jewry reacted with a call for the new leadership in the Kremlin to "adhere scrupulously to all of the Soviet Union's international and constitutional obligations, particularly in the area of human rights, and to continue to allow Soviet Jews to emigrate freely." The quick reversal of the coup brought expressions of relief. In December, as the USSR began to dissolve into its component republics, American Jewish organizations began to consider the prospect of dealing with 12 separate countries over the emigration of their Jews rather than one regime in Moscow.

The Pollard Case

Since Jonathan Pollard was sentenced to life imprisonment in 1987 for having passed classified military documents to Israel, his family had sought to reopen the case on the grounds that the severity of the sentence was grossly disproportionate when compared to the shorter jail terms meted out to others convicted of similar crimes. In 1991, the drive to help Pollard received a new lease on life when his lawyer, renowned trial attorney and Harvard professor Alan Dershowitz, announced plans for an appeal. If granted, it would enable Pollard to withdraw his original guilty plea—which had been part of a bargain that Pollard's supporters said had not been kept by federal authorities—and demand a new trial.

In preparation for the appeal, scheduled for September, Pollard's family launched a drive to mobilize Jewish opinion, based on the argument that anti-Semitism, particularly on the part of former secretary of defense Caspar Weinberger, lay behind the harsh sentence. In the wake of the Gulf War, they also sought to mitigate the crime with the claim that some of the information Pollard passed to Israel had enabled the Israelis to minimize loss of life in the Iraqi Scud attacks. In his sister's words, "The information he gave Israel ensured that Israel was prepared."

The first well-known Jewish leader to rally to Pollard's cause was Seymour Reich, the immediate past chairman of the Conference of Presidents, who visited Pollard's prison cell in April and came out pledging to use his influence to help. Then, the American Section of the World Jewish Congress issued a statement asking that Pollard's sentence be commuted to time already served. The Central Conference of American Rabbis was next, declaring that an "injustice" had been done to Pollard. Also backing the pro-Pollard position were the heads of the three major rabbinical seminaries, the Simon Wiesenthal Center, and Agudath Israel of America.

The campaign for Pollard in the Jewish community put considerable pressure on the National Jewish Community Relations Advisory Council, which, three years earlier, had set up an ad hoc committee on the case. Phil Baum of the American Jewish Congress, who chaired the committee, was not impressed. There was no evidence, he said, to support the allegation of anti-Semitism. "We don't intervene just because a defendant is Jewish," Baum explained. "There are many Jewish criminals who claim to be innocent." Not one of the major Jewish organizations expressed an interest in filing a friend-of-the-court brief in Pollard's appeal.

The motion for appeal was filed on September 11, and a decision was expected early in 1992.

Do Jews Need More Chutzpah?

For Pollard's lawyer, Alan Dershowitz, the reluctance of the organized American Jewish community to involve itself in the case was symptomatic of a more general mood of fear, passivity, and lack of self-respect that pervaded the American Jewish establishment. The Pollard case, in fact, occupied close to 30 pages of Dershowitz's book, *Chutzpah*, which appeared in 1991. Part autobiography and part polemic, *Chutzpah* chronicled the author's boyhood in Brooklyn, his early experiences of anti-Semitism as a student at Yale Law School, applicant for a job at prestigious law firms, and faculty member at Harvard Law School, and his involvement in defense of Jews and Jewish interests in the United States and around the world. All of these experiences had taught him that "despite the unmistakable contributions of Jews to the American success story, we seem willing to accept less than first-class status. We still seem fearful of offending the 'real' Americans—in the face of the reality that we are no longer guests in someone else's America."

Dershowitz's critique of American Jewry for its lack of sufficient *chutzpah* struck a sensitive nerve among many Jews, putting his book at the top of the best-seller list. But it evoked mostly ridicule from Jewish reviewers. Writing in *Commentary* (September 1991), Ruth Wisse charged Dershowitz with possessing an "arrested, narcissistic conception of 'assertiveness.'" Leon Wieseltier (*New Republic*, July 29, 1991) called the book "shrill and platitudinous," and accused Dershowitz of "chasing ambulances through Jewish history" and grossly exaggerating anti-Semitism in the contemporary United States. Albert Vorspan (*Reform Judaism*, Winter 1991), slyly suggested that Arnold Schwarzenegger "play Dershowitz in the movie version—'The Chutzpadik Terminator'—in which all the anti-Semites die in the last scene from subpoena envy."

While Dershowitz could shrug off such academic insults, the threat of a lawsuit from Henry Siegman, executive director of the American Jewish Congress, was another matter. In *Chutzpah*, Dershowitz claimed that he had gotten Jozef Cardinal Glemp of Poland to agree to issue an apology for anti-Semitic remarks he had made. But then, Dershowitz alleged, after Siegman met with Glemp and refrained from criticizing the remarks, the cardinal backed off. Denying that this had happened, Siegman accused Dershowitz of "an arrogance fueled by personal hubris and self-promotion." The controversy between the two men went on all summer, but mutual threats of lawsuits, either before the civil courts or before a rabbinical tribunal, were never carried out.

In all the hue and cry about Dershowitz's account in *Chutzpah* of his role as public defender of the Jews, little attention was paid to what he wrote about the evolution of his private Jewishness. Having grown up as an observant Jew in an Orthodox Brooklyn neighborhood, Dershowitz gradually discarded Jewish ritual practice as he became more and more of an activist for Jewish causes. And he now wondered wistfully what kind of Jews his children, having grown up with minimal religious training, would become. Many other American Jews were pondering the same question in 1991.

Demographic Dangers

A sense of crisis over the potential demographic erosion of American Jewry pervaded communal discussions throughout the year, as the full implications of the

1990 National Jewish Population Survey, commissioned by the Council of Jewish Federations (CJF), became clearer.

In early June, the CJF officially released the results of the survey in summary form, *Highlights of the CJF 1990 National Jewish Population Survey*.[1] Among its more significant findings: the Sunbelt was now home to many more American Jews than was the case 50 years before; there were proportionally far more old people and fewer young people in the Jewish community than in the United States at large; only 14 percent of American Jewish households fit the traditional definition of a Jewish family—mother and father, both Jewish, married for the first time, with children; nearly half of American Jews considered themselves politically liberal and only one-fifth identified as conservative; Jews had an exceptionally low birthrate, although this could rise as more baby boomers became parents; Jews had a far higher rate of college graduates and members of the professions than non-Jews; and observance of certain Jewish rituals—such as attendance at a Passover seder and lighting Sabbath candles—had increased in families where both parents were Jewish.

A unique feature of the survey was its adoption of a new, broader definition of the Jewish population, one that tracked not only "core" Jews, that is, those born of Jewish parents who currently identified as Jews, plus converts to Judaism, but also people with other kinds of Jewish attachments. It was clear from the data that the core Jewish group—some 5,515,000—was barely reproducing itself, and if not for Jewish immigration into the country, might actually have declined since 1970.

An astounding 625,000 respondents—a total equal to more than one-ninth of the number of core Jews—said they were born Jewish but now considered themselves members of another religion, having either converted to, or assimilated into, another faith. Undoubtedly, many of these were Jews who had married non-Jews. And their children and grandchildren surely made up the bulk of the 700,000 individuals of Jewish descent under age 18 that the survey found were being reared in other religions.

The extent of this Jewish crossover into Christianity and other religions was buttressed by another study released in 1991, commissioned by the Graduate Center of the City University of New York. This survey focused on the demography of American religions. Of those in the sample who said their ethnic background was Jewish, over one-third did not now identify with the Jewish religion, 12 percent identifying with some form of Christianity, and another 22 percent claiming either no religious identity or adherence to a non-Christian faith.

The CJF study also included a category for adult non-Jews living in Jewish households, most of whom would be unconverted non-Jews married to Jews, and possibly their relatives who had moved in. While some eyebrows were raised over the inclusion of data about out-and-out Gentiles in a survey of Jews, the rationale

---

[1]See also Sidney Goldstein, "Profile of American Jewry: Insights from the 1990 National Jewish Population Survey," AJYB 1992, pp.77–173.

given was that these individuals might be considered Jews for certain purposes, such as voting and support of Jewish-backed causes, and purchasing ethnic products.

AN INTERMARRIAGE CRISIS

The survey highlight that created headlines was the news that over half of young American Jews were marrying non-Jews: the intermarriage rate for Jews who had married since 1985 was 52 percent. (The data in this section are from *Highlights*, mentioned above.) For all married Jews—including those who married years before, when intermarriage was rare—the percentage of those with partners who were not born Jewish was now almost one-third. Furthermore, very few of these born non-Jews were becoming Jewish: 4 percent of all married Jews had spouses who were originally not Jewish but now considered themselves Jewish, and the figure for those marrying since 1985 was only 5 percent. Roughly 30 percent of these Jews by choice had never been formally converted. What is more, the bulk of American Jewry had apparently made peace with the new reality: asked if they would accept the marriage of their child to a non-Jew, approximately 90 percent of the sample said Yes.

Clearly, the future of American Jewish life depended heavily on whether the children of the growing number of mixed marriages would identify as Jews. Here, the data did not offer much encouragement. Only 28 percent of the children in the mixed-married families surveyed were being raised as Jews, 41 percent were being raised as non-Jews, and the other 31 percent were being brought up with no religion. (In the relatively small number of conversionary families, 99 percent of the children were being raised as Jews.) A clear difference emerged between patterns of religious observance in entirely Jewish households and those with a Gentile spouse: the likelihood of attending a Passover seder, lighting Sabbath and Hanukkah candles, contributing to Jewish charities, and belonging to a synagogue was far less in the mixed-religion families. The summary report concluded that "there will probably be net losses to the core Jewish population in the next generation."

The bad news—especially the over-50-percent intermarriage rate that some observers saw as a tipping point in the collective psyche of American Jewry—set off a tidal wave of commentary. Since the planners of the CJF survey had decided to devote the bulk of the project's resources to data gathering and leave analysis for later, the media, scholars, communal leaders, and spokespersons for the various Jewish movements had a veritable field day reporting, criticizing, commenting upon, bemoaning, or agonizing over the data.

For journalists, all this was big news. On June 7, as soon as the survey summary was released, the *New York Times* ran a long story on it, complete with interviews and graphs depicting the major findings. On July 22, *Newsweek* published a report on "The Intermarrying Kind: A Gloomy Study Leads Jews to Fear for Their Future." On August 8, it was the turn of the *Wall Street Journal*, whose front-page story "Keeping the Faith: Marriage and Family No Longer Are Ties That Bind to Judaism" featured the efforts of a rabbi in Alexandria, Virginia, to deal with the new demographic trends. Jewish newspapers across the country seized upon the story as well, usually reporting the survey results along with the reactions of local rabbis.

Although the demographers who had designed and conducted the study carefully avoided passing sweeping judgments on the Jewish community and, in their public presentations, always balanced the bad news with whatever good they could glean from the data, most other social scientists came to pessimistic conclusions.

Prof. Samuel Z. Klausner of the University of Pennsylvania entitled an essay on the apostasy data "The Conversion of the Jews" (*Jerusalem Letter*, August 1, 1991). He suggested that "the soaring rate of intermarriage . . . almost inevitably leads to non-Jewish grandchildren," and that the over one million respondents calling themselves secular Jews were in reality characterized by attitudes and practices little different from those of the majority Christian culture. "Cultural assimilation," he concluded, was leading to "societal conversion" and, over time, there would be "an increasing number of Christians who are two or three generations removed from Jewish forebears."

Daniel Elazar, who divided his time between Israel and the United States as both president of the Jerusalem Center for Public Affairs and professor at Temple University, drew from the CJF survey the conclusion that American Jewry was losing its demographic preeminence on the world Jewish scene (*Jerusalem Letter*, September 15, 1991). In 1948, he noted, the new State of Israel had only one-tenth the Jewish population of the United States; in 1990, however, "the ratio of U.S. Jews to Israeli Jews is about 3 to 2 and approaching parity." Furthermore, said Elazar, the Jewish communities emerging in Europe and the former USSR were far more likely to line up with Israel than with American Jewry on issues of world Jewish concern. He concluded that American Jews would have to shift their attitudes toward other Jewries from a posture of philanthropy to one of cooperation between equals.

Prof. Sergio DellaPergola of the Hebrew University was prepared with a projection of exactly when there would be more Jews in Israel than outside it. Speaking in Los Angeles in May, the Israeli demographer suggested that, if current American intermarriage and low-birthrate trends continued, and immigration and the Israeli birthrate held steady, Israel would be home to the majority of world Jewry by the year 2020. Even a diminished *aliyah*, he noted, would merely postpone the date till later in the century.

Edward Norden, an American-born Israeli, meditated on the demographic erosion of American Jewry in the pages of *Commentary* magazine (October 1991):

> The Jews in the U.S. today are comparable to a wee cube of sugar or grain of salt floating in a soothing bath of continental dimensions. As the sugar or salt melts, the bathwater is rendered ever so slightly sweeter or zestier. If the water temperature stays pleasantly warm, the little bit of stuff will eventually melt altogether, or be reduced numerically to a religiously committed kernel.

While this scenario gave Norden no comfort—"only the most primitive Zionists," he wrote, "the most unthinking deniers of the Diaspora, ever looked forward to its liquidating itself"—he saw no alternative.

Virtually the only social scientist rejecting the new picture of American Jewry offered by the CJF survey was Prof. Steven M. Cohen of the City University of New York, who severely attacked it on methodological grounds. Presenting his objections in a public forum at Brandeis University in November, Cohen said that his own analysis of the completed CJF questionnaires yielded far different conclusions: the intermarriage rate was around 40 percent, roughly what it had been for the last generation. "American Jewish life may be shallow and superficial," he said, "but it's not getting any worse."

Cohen presented his own alternative picture of American Jewry in *Content and Continuity: Alternative Bases for Commitment*, commissioned by the American Jewish Committee and published in 1991. Rather than project trends for the community as a whole, Cohen delineated three distinct groups: roughly a quarter of American Jews who are "committed both to Jewish continuity and to Jewish content of one sort or another," half the population who feel deeply committed to Jewish continuity but have only a vague sense of what its content should be, and the other quarter whose Jewishness is "peripheral." Cohen suggested that the insistence of the first two groups on remaining "Jewishly connected to other Jews" gave grounds for guarded optimism.

COMMUNAL STRATEGIES

For those American Jews who took the new CJF survey data at face value, the question was what to do about the demographic threat. Already in the *New York Times* story reporting the survey, battle lines were drawn. Asked to comment, sociologist Egon Mayer stressed the futility of trying to stem intermarriage. "Stop the angst," he urged, "and let's devote ourselves to outreach." But Alvin Schiff, executive vice-president of the New York Board of Jewish Education, insisted that the ancient taboo on intermarriage had to be retained: "Throughout history, Jews have never given up the fight. If they had, there would be no Jews left today."

Striving to strike a balance between the two extreme positions, the American Jewish Committee developed a policy statement on intermarriage. Calling the rising rates "a serious risk to the vitality of the Jewish community, Jewish continuity and identity," the document called for greater emphasis on programs that would make it easier for young Jewish men and women to meet each other, carefully targeted outreach efforts to intermarried families with the goal of conversion, and more willingness on the part of the Jewish community to make converts to Judaism feel at home in their new faith.

Of the Jewish religious movements, Reform was overwhelmingly in favor of outreach to the intermarried, a posture it had adopted years before, and one that left it open to the charge that it had virtually abandoned opposition to intermarriage. Indeed, some Reform leaders asserted that high rates of Jewish-Christian marriage presented a potential opportunity for the Jewish community. Dru Greenwood, director of the movement's Commission on Reform Jewish Outreach, said that bringing such families into the synagogue not only enhanced Jewish numbers but also gave American Judaism "new energy and commitment, profoundly affecting our sense of ourselves as a community of Jews." Across the country, Reform congregations had instituted courses, workshops, discussion groups, and children's programs for mixed-religion families.

What was the aim of such initiatives? Rabbi Alexander Schindler, president of the Union of American Hebrew Congregations (UAHC), said, "We need to be more assertive in our conversion efforts. Judaism has always been and should continue to be a missionary religion." Yet it was clear that the drop in conversions to Judaism was at least partially due to the Reform acceptance of patrilineal descent as sufficient for Jewish identification without formal conversion. Furthermore, a survey conducted by the Commission on Reform Jewish Outreach showed widespread acceptance of unconverted non-Jews, most of them married to Jews, in Reform Jewish life: 88 percent of temples granted them membership; 62 percent allowed them to vote on synagogue matters; 27 percent did not bar them from holding office; and more than one-fifth called them to the Torah for *aliyot*. The most surprising statistic was the three-quarters of Reform congregations for whom all such rules were academic, since they did not keep track of the religion of their members.

If Reform Jews sought to cope with the demographic danger through accelerated outreach, much of Orthodox Jewry saw outreach as part of the problem. By blurring the distinction between Jew and non-Jew, editorialized the *Jewish Observer* (November 1991), such programs encouraged the notion that "we're really not all that different," and gave a green light for others to contemplate intermarriage. Recalling with some nostalgia the era when parents refused to countenance the marriage of a child to a non-Jew and even performed the mourning rituals in anguish over it, the *Observer* suggested "avoiding the crisis before the fact" by exposing marginal Jews to the experience of traditional Jewish life, "instead of attempting spiritual resuscitation after the fact."

But this was not the only voice coming from the Orthodox camp. In December, the Rabbinical Council of America Roundtable, a group of centrist Orthodox rabbis eager to apply Jewish law to contemporary issues, produced an analysis of whether a Jewish man married to a non-Jew might be counted in a *minyan*. Based on classic Jewish legal sources, the paper showed that an affirmative argument could be made, and the authors, citing the possibility of "rescuing souls," clearly sympathized with the lenient position. Furthermore, the Roundtable forthrightly criticized "an Orthodox Fortress Philosophy" that writes off the intermarried as "not our problem." While appended to this document was a statement that it did not represent the policy of the Rabbinical Council of America (RCA), Rabbi Marc Angel, RCA president, indicated that it "reveals the deep sense of responsibility" his organization felt for the broad Jewish community.

It was the Conservative movement, with its commitment to Jewish tradition coupled with an openness to innovation, that had the most difficulty facing up to the implications of the CJF data on intermarriage. While Reform congregations had no qualms about accepting mixed-religion couples, noted Rabbi Gilbert Kollin at the Rabbinical Assembly (RA) national convention in April, the Conservative movement, with its ambivalent stance, "has buried its head in the sand." But how was Conservative Judaism to maintain opposition to intermarriage while at the same time welcoming these families?

Dr. Steven Bayme, director of Jewish Communal Affairs for the American Jewish Committee, sought to provide an answer in the keynote address he delivered at the RA convention. He challenged the movement to end its vacillation on the subject of the status of mixed-religion families. Urging the Conservative rabbis not to follow the Reform path which, he felt, had destroyed the incentive of the non-Jews to become Jewish, Bayme proposed outreach initiatives geared to encouraging conversion and ensuring that the children are brought up as Jews. This, he said, should be combined with a clear message that intermarriage is destructive of Jewish continuity and insistence on a demarcation between Jews and non-Jews in synagogues and religious schools.

But the Rabbinical Assembly was not ready to deal with the problem. Resolutions proposed by some of the more liberal members, calling on congregations to make mixed-married families "feel welcome in the synagogue" even if there was not an immediate interest in conversion, to accept the children of such families in Conservative schools and youth programs, and to "consider ways" to involve unconverted spouses in life-cycle events in the synagogue were all tabled. The only resolution on intermarriage to pass was one urging the establishment of *keruv* (outreach) committees on all levels of the movement and training programs for synagogue professionals as well as lay leaders on how to deal with interfaith couples.

Interdenominational tensions over what stance to take toward the intermarried erupted in open conflict in April, when the Covenant Foundation, a Chicago-based fund set up to reward excellence in Jewish education and encourage innovative programming, hired an intermarried Jewish woman as executive director. Expressing the Orthodox consensus, Rabbi Marc Angel of the RCA said: "She's a bad role model. If the foundation's purpose is to promote Jewish values, its leader should reflect Jewish values." Angel felt so strongly about this that he recommended that no one accept grants from the foundation. Leaders of Conservative Judaism backed the Orthodox view. But Reform rabbi Daniel Syme, vice-president of the UAHC, called their reaction "totally ridiculous" and "utter stupidity." Sociologist Egon Mayer, perhaps the leading proponent of aggressive outreach, commented, "The bigots have come out of the closet," and charged the traditionalists with hypocrisy, claiming that "there is not a major Jewish organization that doesn't have among its leadership those who are intermarried or whose children are intermarried." The problem was resolved when the foundation changed the woman's title and responsibilities.

The Council of Jewish Federations devoted an entire day of its 1991 General Assembly—November 20—to a discussion of intermarriage. That the federation world, traditionally averse to getting embroiled in debates with potentially divisive religious overtones, proved willing to focus on the issue was attributed by some observers not only to the magnitude of the problem but also to the incidence of intermarriage among the children and grandchildren of the federation leaders themselves.

All the speakers at the sessions favored greater involvement by federation-funded agencies in outreach programs for the intermarried. Setting the tone was Egon Mayer, who characterized the traditional Jewish rejection of intermarriage as a reflection of "anger, fear, guilt, and no small measure of ambivalence." He called for a massive campaign to "enhance the self-image of Jews" through the media, in school textbooks, museum exhibits, and theatrical offerings as a way of increasing the chances that interfaith couples would choose Judaism. David G. Sacks, president of the New York UJA-Federation, compared the argument that outreach encourages more intermarriage to the notion that supplying condoms encourages promiscuity and made light of the argument that funds directed to programs for the intermarried would cut into the monies currently allocated for programming for affiliated Jews. For the first time in its history, the CJF adopted a mission statement on the subject of Jewish continuity. It voted unanimously to urge federations to work with local "religious, cultural, social service, and educational" institutions to "preserve and foster" Jewish values and Jewish identity.

Life-styles and Gender Roles

Demographic statistics were not the only signs of change in the American Jewish community. "Equally explosive," commented Daniel Elazar, "were the changes in the status of women and non-heterosexuals in Jewish life" (*Jerusalem Letter*, September 15, 1991).

As Elazar observed, the community's treatment of gay Jews had become "a litmus test for the dominant liberal ideology of American Jewry." Encouraged by the recent decisions of the Reform and Reconstructionist movements to ordain homosexual rabbis, gay Jews became increasingly vocal about what they perceived as discrimination against them by the Jewish community, and articles about them began to appear with some regularity in Jewish newspapers and periodicals. The first Jewish Community Dialogue on Gay and Lesbian Issues, held in Washington early in the year, drew 200 Jews. Discussion groups for Jewish homosexuals, often sponsored by gay synagogues (some 30 around the world were affiliated with the World Congress of Gay and Lesbian Jewish Organizations) became popular. Feeling especially aggrieved were men and women of a Jewishly traditionalist bent who could only maintain their Orthodox or Conservative affiliations by disguising their sexual orientation. And across the denominational spectrum, Jewish gays said that they were reluctant to open up to their rabbis for fear of rejection.

Further evidence that Jewish homosexuals had entered a new era of assertiveness was a letter sent in the spring to Jewish publications across the country which began, "We are lesbian and gay rabbis from across North America. We are Conservative, Orthodox, Reconstructionist, and Reform. We are proud to be Jewish and proud to be gay and lesbian." It was signed by eight rabbis willing to identify themselves, and "21 other gay and lesbian rabbis" who did not want their names used. The letter described the strains involved in functioning as professionals while hiding evidence about their sexual preferences: "What distresses us is the demand that we separate our personal lives from our rabbinic careers. It is time to be accepted for who we really are: committed Jews and rabbis who are also lesbians and gay men."

Soon after the release of the letter, the New York *Jewish Week* (April 26–May 2, 1991) ran a long article on gays in the rabbinate, based on interviews with many of those who signed it. The phenomenon of homosexual rabbis, they all agreed, was far more widespread than commonly believed. "Most people think they've never met a gay rabbi," said one, "but they probably have." Particularly moving were the accounts provided by gay rabbis who were Orthodox, forced to live secretive, double lives in order to maintain their religious credentials in a movement that condemned their sexual behavior.

Indeed, Orthodox antagonism toward any religious legitimization of homosexuality caused a rift in the Jewish community of Washington, D.C. In June, the local Jewish Community Council, an umbrella body for Jewish organizations in the city, approved the membership application of Bet Mishpachah, a gay and lesbian synagogue, despite a request by the Orthodox Rabbinical Council for a delay to consider the matter from the standpoint of Jewish law. When the gay congregation was admitted, several of the Orthodox constituents of the council threatened to walk out. Efforts to arrive at a compromise were still under way as the year ended.

The question of whether homosexuals might marry in a Jewish ceremony was given prominence by a lawsuit against the state of Georgia. In July, a female Emory University law student who had been offered a job in the state attorney general's office had the offer withdrawn once it became known that she had been married, in a Jewish ceremony, to another woman. As the law student and her ACLU lawyers prepared their case against the Georgia law banning sexual relations between people of the same sex, the attention of many Jews focused on rabbinic attitudes. The rabbi who performed this particular wedding, Sharon Kleinbaum, was a graduate of the Reconstructionist Rabbinical College and worked for the Reform movement's Religious Action Center in Washington. This was the first homosexual union she had solemnized, but, she promised, it would not be the last. "The Jewish community condemns gays for promiscuity, not having a stable relationship," she complained, "yet at the moment they want to religiously sanctify their relationship and create a family, the attorney general punishes them."

Interviews with Reform rabbis revealed considerable support for Kleinbaum's act. Typical was the reaction of Rabbi Alvin Sugarman of The Temple in Atlanta, who said he had never yet officiated at such a marriage but considered lesbian lovers no different from any other couple. "These are two human beings saying that 'we care deeply for one another and want in a sacred context to respect that. . . ,' " he said. "If they were members of The Temple, I would sit down with them and talk about what it meant to them."

With the Reform rabbinate largely acquiescent and Orthodoxy firmly opposed, once again—as in the debate over the role of the intermarried in Jewish life—the Conservative movement found itself in the eye of the storm. On December 11, the Rabbinical Assembly's Law Committee—the supreme halakhic authority for Conservative Jews—sought to develop its own Jewish approach to homosexuality that would provide guidelines for resolving the questions of ordaining gays and performing same-sex marriages. So sensitive did the committee members deem this discussion that they barred outsiders from the session, and only at the last minute decided to allow students of the Jewish Theological Seminary to attend.

Staking out the traditional position was Rabbi Joel Roth, professor of Talmud at the seminary. His 140-page paper argued that the biblical categorization of homosexuality as "abomination" was "not open to any real doubt," and he denied that modern science had proven otherwise. Furthermore, whether or not a same-sex relationship was warm and caring was irrelevant from the standpoint of Jewish law. "It must follow," Roth reasoned, "that the halakhically committed Jewish community cannot . . . take any act or espouse any action which can reasonably be understood to imply the co-equality, validation or acceptability of a homosexual lifestyle." No acknowledged gay or lesbian should serve in any official position within the Conservative movement, he stated, and neither gay synagogues nor gay marriages were legitimate. Roth even went so far as to declare that a heterosexual rabbi who condoned homosexuality as Jewishly valid behavior should himself be disqualified from religious leadership.

At the other extreme was the view of Rabbi Bradley Artson, who argued that the biblical abhorrence of homosexuality no longer applied, since it referred only to relations that are "oppressive, coercive or idolatrous." If gay sexuality is part of "a mutually exclusive, committed, adult relationship," it was Jewishly equivalent to heterosexuality. Thus Artson supported both the ordination of homosexual rabbis and the performance of Jewish wedding ceremonies for gay couples.

No decision was reached at the meeting, and several committee members expressed the hope that some compromise might be reached before the next session, scheduled for February 1992.

THE ROLE OF WOMEN

"Call it a bloodless revolution," wrote Orthodox feminist Blu Greenberg in the pages of the *Jewish Monthly* (February 1991), "call it a reformation, call it a social movement, feminism has profoundly affected the life of every woman, no matter the age or orientation—and the life of every man as well." Disputing the common notion "that nothing is happening in the Orthodox community," Greenberg listed women's prayer groups, institutions where women study Talmud, and increased activity by organizations dedicated to enhancing the status of women under Jewish divorce law. But in 1991, the major issue confronting women in Orthodox Judaism was whether one might serve as president of a synagogue.

At a congregation with no rabbi in West Bloomfield, Michigan—a suburb of

Detroit—a woman who had served as vice-president was nominated for president. Two local Orthodox rabbis were consulted about this step; one said it was absolutely forbidden, the other that there was no law against it. Since the congregation was a branch of the National Council of Young Israel, a large network of Orthodox congregations generally identified with the centrist wing of the movement, the question was referred to national headquarters in New York.

The response, that the woman could not be president, was explicitly limited to the particular case at hand. The rabbis involved in the decision indicated that there was little precedent to follow, since only recently had women expressed interest in such posts. They said that the key issue was what a particular congregation expected of its president. In synagogues where the presidency was a purely administrative responsibility with no religious functions, there would be no objection to the selection of a woman.

For women in the Conservative movement, 1991 saw the final resolution of a divisive battle that had plagued it for three years—acceptance of women as cantors. In May, when the Cantors Assembly inducted its first 14 female members, its executive vice-president said: "We could no longer have a part in the duplicity of recruiting women to study for the cantorate, encouraging them in their studies, providing them with scholarship assistance, helping them with repertoire and advice, and then admit the men and bar the door to the women." As an indication of its wholehearted welcome, the Cantors Assembly commissioned Conservative cantorial works for soprano and alto voices.

But the movement paid a price for admitting women cantors. Dissidents in the Cantors Assembly, who considered acceptance of women one more piece of evidence of a general Conservative drift away from Jewish tradition, broke away and founded the International Federation of Traditional Cantors. Explained one, "There's a disenchantment, to put it mildly, within the Conservative movement. . . . They're getting closer and closer aligned with Reform." It appeared likely that the new organization would establish ties with the Union for Traditional Judaism, a rabbinic and educational group that split away from the Conservative movement several years before, when the latter began to ordain women rabbis.

Denominational Developments

Although issues of demography, sexual orientation, and feminism drew considerable attention from the Jewish religious movements, other concerns were not ignored. Orthodox, Conservative, Reconstructionist, and Reform Jews continued to address a number of ideological and theological matters.

ORTHODOXY

Centrist Orthodoxy, still feeling the influence of the more insular Orthodox, underwent two wrenching disputes in 1991. The first involved rabbis who were members of the Rabbinical Council of America who had also joined the Fellowship of Traditional Orthodox Rabbis (FTOR), a more liberal organization formed in 1987, many of whose members served in congregations where men and women sat together, contrary to Orthodox teachings. On the grounds that such dual membership conferred unwarranted legitimacy on the newer group, the RCA sent letters to eight of its members in May, notifying them that so long as they continued in FTOR, they were no longer RCA "members in good standing." This action had potentially severe consequences: the men might lose their pulpits, have difficulty finding new ones, and could have trouble getting their divorces and conversions recognized.

The controversial rabbis managed to win reinstatement by threatening a lawsuit and publicly branding the treatment they received as coercive, authoritarian, and a breach of their rabbinic prerogatives. In June, the RCA's executive committee reinstated these rabbis, and the organization's president assured them that the concerns that had led them to join FTOR would be addressed by the RCA.

The second conflict that roiled centrist Orthodoxy was a battle over the fate of Yeshiva University's Bernard Revel Graduate School. In December, the university announced the "restructuring" of the Revel School; instead of offering master's and doctoral degree programs in Jewish history, philosophy, literature, Bible, Semitics, and Talmud, it would have only a nondegree program in Orthodox Jewish thought. The reason given for the change was financial: the small number of students in the degree programs did not justify the cost of running the school.

Neither consulted nor informed in advance of the decision, faculty and students reacted angrily, pointing out that since Revel was the only graduate division of the university where Jewish texts were studied using modern critical methodology, dismantling the school's programs would effectively make the institution's Jewish studies curriculum identical to that of a European-style yeshivah. Furthermore, since Revel programs were open to women, the announced change would end the only opportunity that Orthodox women had to pursue Jewish studies on the graduate level in an Orthodox institution. On December 19, 300 students rallied in front of the office of the university president, carrying a petition with 1,100 names that declared: "An institution that prides itself on *Torah U-Maddah* (religious studies along with secular knowledge) must have a place for its students to integrate Jewish studies with the best ideas of modern scholarship." But as the year ended, the Yeshiva administration held firm to its plans.

In the more stringently Orthodox community, the Gulf War provided the backdrop for intensified messianic expectation centered around the Lubavitch Hassidic movement. Rabbi Menachem Mendel Schneerson, the 90-year-old charismatic leader of Lubavitch, having declared the Hebrew year 5751 a "year of great wonders," made repeated references in his public discourses to the imminent coming of the Messiah and urged his followers to increase their prayers, Torah study, and good deeds to accelerate the process. Lubavitch Hassidim seized upon a 13th-century midrash predicting the Messiah's arrival at a time of war between "Persia" and

"Arabia" as a reference to the Gulf War and, once the war ended, claimed that Schneerson had correctly predicted it would be over by Purim. In May, Lubavitch leaders ran a full-page ad in Jewish newspapers that began: "We must sincerely realize that the Gulf War and its accompanying miracles mean the imminent arrival of Maschiah," and in June a full-page ad in the *New York Times* proclaimed: "The Time for Your Redemption has Arrived!" While his lieutenants carefully avoided outright claims that Schneerson was himself the Messiah, they hinted at it by remarking that he was the "likeliest candidate." The violence that erupted in Crown Heights during the summer, after a car in Schneerson's entourage accidentally struck and killed a black boy, was interpreted as Satan's last, desperate attempt to derail the messianic process. (See "Intergroup Relations," elsewhere in this volume.)

CONSERVATISM

Buffeted by conflict between traditionalists and liberals over the religious role of women, the place of mixed-married families in Jewish life, and what approach to take toward gay marriages and gay rabbis, the Conservative movement struggled to assert a unified, principled position that would dispel its image as an untidy compromise between Orthodoxy and Reform.

It chose opposition to patrilineal descent as an issue that could clarify its religious identity. Although the Conservative movement had consistently opposed Reform and Reconstructionist recognition of the children of Jewish men and non-Jewish women as Jews with no need to convert, it went further in 1991. The biennial convention of the United Synagogue of America resolved that, since conflicting definitions of Jewishness affected the future of all Jews, Reform and Reconstructionism should reconsider their acceptance of the patrilineal criterion and require conversion for the offspring of non-Jewish mothers. United Synagogue president Alan Tichnor cited the CJF survey of American Jews as proof that mixed-religion families without conversion were unlikely to produce Jewishly identified children. The two liberal movements quickly rebuffed the Conservative suggestion.

Rabbi Jerome Epstein, executive vice-president of the United Synagogue, suggested paying less attention to what the other movements were doing and more to what Conservative Jews were not doing. "Many Jews choose the Conservative synagogue with the mistaken belief that there are no standards," said Epstein. "Well, there are . . . we are reticent about telling people what to do—about what is expected of them. And we go on calling ourselves Conservative Jews without any commitment to climb the ladder of Jewish living."

As a step toward clarifying its institutional identity, the United Synagogue of America changed its name to the United Synagogue of Conservative Judaism. Epstein explained: "We want people to be proud of being Conservative Jews because we believe we are the authentic approach to Judaism, the normative approach."

RECONSTRUCTIONISM

A number of issues vital to the future direction of the Reconstructionist movement—now in its 36th year as an autonomous branch of American Judaism—were
debated in the pages of the Spring 1991 issue of its journal, *Reconstructionist*.

One controversial item was the legacy of Mordechai Kaplan, the movement's
founder, who had preached a naturalistic, scientific, rationalistic world view. Prof.
Emanuel Goldsmith defended Kaplan's legacy from the growing popularity of
mysticism within Reconstructionism. "We seek to purge our religious thoughts and
emotions of superstition, literalism, and illusion," he asserted. "We should not want
our movement to grow if that entails growing out of our devotion to the Kaplanian
heritage."

Another subject of debate was the particular attractiveness of Reconstructionism
for Jewish radicals and advocates of alternative life-styles. Rabbi Sheila Peltz Weinberg lauded the movement for opposing the class system created by capitalism and
espousing the causes of gays and lesbians, Jews-by-choice, "recovering people who
have been powerfully influenced by the Twelve-Step culture," and the ecologically
enlightened. But Rabbi Sidney Schwartz warned Reconstructionists not to take
"single issues with particular constituencies and make them the most visible agenda
of a national religious movement."

A consensus did emerge on the imperative to enlarge the movement by creating
more Reconstructionist congregations across the country. Noting that the Reconstructionist Rabbinical College was ordaining many more rabbis than there were
Reconstructionist pulpits to fill, Rabbi Arnold Rachlis warned that "no business can
survive, let alone thrive, having created two to three times as much product as its
market could bear." Rabbi David Teutsch agreed: "Outreach represents the next
step in fulfilling the mission of our movement as most people understand it, which
is to transform the lives of Jews, to transform Jewish life."

REFORM

For Reform Judaism, confirmed by the new CJF survey of American Jews as the
most popular Jewish denomination, the problem was not quantity but quality. As
the least ritually demanding expression of Judaism and the one most open to
mixed-marrieds and homosexuals, was Reform becoming a minimalist Judaism, a
lowest common denominator for marginal Jews?

This question was publicly debated in the pages of *Reform Judaism* (Spring 1991).
Rabbi Alexander Schindler, president of the Union of American Hebrew Congregations (UAHC), expressed optimism. Calling Reform "a growth industry" in both
quantitative and qualitative terms, he predicted that the growth would continue, and
that social activism would become integrated into Reform spirituality. "I believe,"
he wrote, "that our evolutionary form of Judaism shall surpass a grasping Orthodoxy in its claim to 'authenticity.'"

Rabbi Mark Winer was less sanguine. The growing proportion of Reform members who were products of mixed marriage, he felt, "could comprise a kind of 'Trojan horse' which dilutes the compelling character of Jewish identity." Winer cited evidence showing that even when a non-Jewish spouse converts to Judaism, the family tends to score low on measures of Jewish communal identification, such as commitment to Israel and social relationships with other Jews. Sheer numbers, concluded Winer, "say nothing about the inner content or spiritual quality of 21st-century North American Judaism."

Whether Reform indeed had any identifiable "inner content" became a practical issue in 1991 when a "humanistic" congregation in Cincinnati, which had excised all mention of God from its liturgy, applied for membership in the Union of American Hebrew Congregations. The matter was referred to the Committee on Responsa of the Central Conference of American Rabbis (CCAR), a body whose authority was advisory rather than prescriptive. An 11-person majority of the committee reasoned that while "persons of various shadings of belief or unbelief, practice or non-practice, may belong to UAHC congregations *as individuals*. . . . *it is different when they come as a congregation whose declared principles are at fundamental variance with the historic God-orientation of Reform Judaism.*" But three committee dissenters did not believe that denial of God should bar a congregation from UAHC membership.

The controversy set off considerable debate over Reform attitudes about God. One issue of *Reform Judaism* (Winter 1991), which was largely devoted to the topic, provided a panorama of the different positions within the movement. Rabbi W. Gunther Plaut, chairman of the Committee on Responsa, advised Reform Jews "to fill our common God language with an attitude that begins to shed the assumptions of scientism and the trappings of 'civil religion.' " Rabbi Roland Gittelsohn, in contrast, declared himself a "religious naturalist," certain that God, bound by the laws of nature, "exists within the universe rather than operating it from outside." Rabbi Rebecca Alpert suggested that only a radical recasting of traditional male language about God could make the concept meaningful to feminists like herself.

The fall convention of the UAHC focused on the issue of ideological and religious coherence in the movement. Rabbi Plaut complained that "in the name of openness and tolerance, we are stressing Reform at the expense of Judaism." Agreeing, CCAR president Rabbi Walter Jacob said: "We need a greater sense of discipline and sense of direction. Build-your-own Judaism is absurd." And Rabbi Schindler suggested that the time had come for Reform to convene a synod that would draw up a body of doctrine and ritual—nonbinding, to be sure—that might give the movement some sense that Reform Judaism did have boundaries.

LAWRENCE GROSSMAN

Jewish Population in the United States, 1992

$\mathbf{B}$ASED ON LOCAL COMMUNITY counts—the method for identifying and enumerating Jewish population that serves as the basis of this report—the estimated size of the American Jewish community in 1992 was 5.8 million. This is about 5 percent more than the 5.5 million "core" Jewish population estimated in the Council of Jewish Federations' 1990 National Jewish Population Survey (NJPS).[1]

The difference, small though it is, between the national and aggregated local figures is probably explained by the lag in data gathering and reporting on the local level, as well as definitional problems. As more local communities conduct studies over the next few years, declines and increases that have already occurred will be documented, and the updated statistics will show national and regional patterns more in line with NJPS findings. Based upon trends revealed in NJPS data, declines can be expected to be reported in Connecticut, New York, New Jersey, Pennsylvania, and most of the Midwestern states. Higher community totals are anticipated for Colorado, Arizona, and the Pacific Northwest.

The NJPS used a scientifically selected sample to project a total number for the United States, but could not provide accurate information on the state and local levels. Therefore, as in past years, in this article we have based local, state, and regional population figures on the usual estimating procedures.

While the Jewish federations are the chief reporting bodies, their service areas vary in size and may represent several towns, one county, or an aggregate of several counties. In some cases we have subdivided federation areas to reflect the more natural geographic boundaries. Some estimates, from areas without federations, have been provided by local rabbis and other informed Jewish community leaders. In still other cases, the figures that have been updated are from past estimates provided by United Jewish Appeal field representatives. Finally, for smaller communities where no recent estimates are available, figures are based on extrapolation from older data. The estimates are for the resident Jewish population, including those in private households and in institutional settings. Non-Jewish family members have been excluded from the total.

The state and regional totals shown in Appendix tables 1 and 2 are derived by summing the individual estimates shown in table 3 and then making three adjustments. First, communities of less than 100 are added. Second, duplicated counts within states are eliminated. Third, communities whose population resides in two or more states (e.g., Kansas City and Greater Washington, D.C.) are distributed accordingly.

---

[1] See Barry A. Kosmin et al., *Highlights of the CJF 1990 National Jewish Population Survey* (New York, Council of Jewish Federations, 1991).

Because population estimating is not an exact science, the reader should be aware that in cases where a figure differs from last year's, the increase or decrease did not come about suddenly but occurred over a period of time and has just now been substantiated. Similarly, the results of a completed local demographic study often change the previously reported Jewish population figure. This should be understood as either an updated calculation of gradual demographic change or a correction of a faulty older estimate.

In determining Jewish population, communities count both affiliated and nonaffiliated residents who are "core" Jews as defined in NJPS.[2] In most cases, counts are made by households, with that number multiplied by the average number of self-defined Jewish persons per household. Similarly to NJPS, most communities also include those born and raised as Jews but who at present consider themselves as having no religion. As stated above, non-Jews living in Jewish households, primarily the non-Jewish spouses and non-Jewish children, are not included in the 1992 estimates presented in the appendix below.

Local Population Changes

Nine communities reported increases of greater than 1,000 this year. The community reporting the largest numeric increase was that of the suburban Cherry Hill-Southern New Jersey area, which includes Camden, Burlington, and Gloucester counties. The new population figure of 49,000, which results from a recently completed Jewish population study, is nearly double the old estimate of 26,000.

Only one other community reported a Jewish population increase of more than 10,000—the Chicago metropolitan area. A new study in Chicago showed a Jewish population of 261,000, up 13,000 from the previous estimate of 248,000 in a similar study a decade ago. While the geographic area covered in the new study is larger than that in the previous study, other factors in this modest increase of about 5 percent are an influx of immigrants from the former Soviet Union and in-migration from smaller Midwestern communities.

Three of the seven other communities with Jewish population increases of greater than 1,000 were in Florida: Sarasota, Naples-Collier County, and Ft. Myers-Lee County. Sarasota's increase is based upon a recently completed demographic study; in Naples, a recently established Jewish federation was able to identify many new as well as previously unknown Jewish households. The other four communities with large increases were Raleigh, North Carolina; Somerset County, New Jersey; Norfolk-Virginia Beach, Virginia; and St. Paul, Minnesota. In the latter, a recently completed demographic study found a larger Jewish population than previously believed.

The remaining communities with significant increases in Jewish population were

---

[2]Born Jews who report adherence to Judaism, Jews by choice, and born Jews without a current religion ("secular Jews").

primarily in the South and in the West. These include Prescott, Arizona; Fresno, Monterey, Riverside, Salinas, and San Bernardino, California; Key West, Gainesville, Ocala, Tampa, and Tallahassee, Florida; Savannah, Georgia; Frederick and Harford counties, Maryland; Las Vegas, Nevada; Eugene, Medford, and Salem, Oregon; Greenville, South Carolina; Knoxville, Tennessee; Lubbock, Texas; Salt Lake City, Utah; Fredricksburg, Virginia; and Bellingham, Olympia, and Tri-Cities, Washington. Other places with significant increases outside of the South and West are New Milford, Connecticut; Greenfield, Massachusetts; Hoboken, New Jersey; Ithaca, New York; Rochester, Minnesota; Bennington, Vermont; and Appleton, Wisconsin. Finally, there are three communities listed for the first time: Redwood Valley and South Lake Tahoe, California; and Manchester, Vermont.

No community reported a significant loss of Jewish population. However, continuing the trend of recent years, the largest declines were reported in the Northeast, Midwest, and interior South. In the Northeast, Jewish population dropped in New Haven and Stamford, Connecticut; Buffalo, New York; and Passaic, Bergen, and Northern Hudson counties in New Jersey. The Bergen and Passaic losses reflect the decline in the Jewish population reported by the North Jersey Jewish Federation, which serves portions of these two counties. Other smaller losses in the Northeast were in Colchester, Connecticut; Augusta and Bangor, Maine; Amsterdam and Binghamton, New York; and Chambersburg, Pennsylvania. Losses were reported in the Midwest and interior South in Joliet, Illinois; Fort Wayne, Indiana; Alexandria and Lake Charles, Louisiana; Jackson, Michigan; Greenville and Jackson, Mississippi; Lincoln, Nebraska; and Toledo and Lima, Ohio. Decreases in other parts of the country were reported in Albany, Georgia; Stockton and Tulare-Kings counties, California; and Waco, Texas. In California, the reduction in the Orange County figure is based upon a reevaluation of the community lists.

BARRY A. KOSMIN
JEFFREY SCHECKNER

APPENDIX

TABLE 1.   JEWISH POPULATION IN THE UNITED STATES, 1992

State	Estimated Jewish Population	Total Population*	Estimated Jewish Percent of Total
Alabama.	8,500	4,089,000	0.2
Alaska	2,400	570,000	0.4
Arizona	72,000	3,750,000	1.9
Arkansas	1,700	2,372,000	0.1
California.	920,000	30,380,000	3.0
Colorado	51,000	3,377,000	1.5
Connecticut	100,000	3,291,000	3.1
Delaware	9,500	680,000	1.4
District of Columbia.	25,500	598,000	4.2
Florida.	599,000	13,277,000	4.5
Georgia	74,500	6,623,000	1.1
Hawaii	7,000	1,135,000	0.6
Idaho	500	1,039,000	(z)
Illinois	268,000	11,543,000	2.3
Indiana.	18,000	5,610,000	0.3
Iowa.	6,000	2,795,000	0.2
Kansas.	14,000	2,495,000	0.6
Kentucky.	11,500	3,713,000	0.3
Louisiana	15,500	4,252,000	0.4
Maine.	8,000	1,235,000	0.6
Maryland	212,000	4,860,000	4.4
Massachusetts	275,000	5,996,000	4.6
Michigan	107,000	9,368,000	1.1
Minnesota	32,500	4,432,000	0.7
Mississippi	1,400	2,592,000	0.1
Missouri.	61,500	5,158,000	1.2
Montana.	500	808,000	0.1
Nebraska	7,000	1,593,000	0.5
Nevada.	21,000	1,284,000	1.6
New Hampshire	7,000	1,105,000	0.6
New Jersey	443,000	7,760,000	5.7
New Mexico	6,000	1,548,000	0.4
New York	1,643,000	18,058,000	9.1

State	Estimated Jewish Population	Total Population*	Estimated Jewish Percent of Total
North Carolina	17,500	6,737,000	0.3
North Dakota	600	635,000	0.1
Ohio	130,000	10,939,000	1.2
Oklahoma..........	5,500	3,175,000	0.2
Oregon	17,000	2,922,000	0.6
Pennsylvania	329,000	11,961,000	2.8
Rhode Island	16,000	1,004,000	1.6
South Carolina......	8,500	3,560,000	0.2
South Dakota.......	350	703,000	(z)
Tennessee..........	18,000	4,953,000	0.4
Texas	109,000	17,349,000	0.6
Utah	3,500	1,770,000	0.2
Vermont...........	5,500	567,000	1.0
Virginia............	68,500	6,286,000	1.1
Washington	33,000	5,018,000	0.7
West Virginia.......	2,500	1,801,000	0.1
Wisconsin..........	35,000	4,955,000	0.7
Wyoming	500	460,000	(z)
U.S. TOTAL.....	**5,828,000	252,177,000	2.3

N.B. Details may not add to totals because of rounding.
*Resident population, April 1, 1991. (*Source:* U.S. Bureau of the Census, *Current Population Reports,* series P-25, no. 1044.)
**Exclusive of Puerto Rico and the Virgin Islands, which previously reported Jewish populations of 1,500 and 350, respectively.
(z) Figure is less than 0.1 and rounds to 0.

TABLE 2. DISTRIBUTION OF U.S. JEWISH POPULATION BY REGIONS, 1992

Region	Total Population	Percent Distribution	Jewish Population	Percent Distribution
Northeast	50,976,000	20.2	2,828,000	48.5
New England	13,197,000	5.2	411,000	7.1
Middle Atlantic	37,779,000	15.0	2,416,000	41.5
Midwest	60,225,000	23.9	680,000	11.7
East North Central . .	42,414,000	16.8	557,000	9.6
West North Central . .	17,811,000	7.1	122,000	2.1
South	86,916,000	34.5	1,188,000	20.4
South Atlantic	44,421,000	17.6	1,017,000	17.5
East South Central . . .	15,347,000	6.1	39,000	0.7
West South Central . .	27,148,000	10.8	132,000	2.3
West	54,060,000	21.4	1,133,000	19.4
Mountain.	14,035,000	5.6	154,000	2.6
Pacific	40,025,000	15.9	979,000	16.8
TOTALS.	252,177,000	100.0	5,828,000	100.0

N.B. Details may not add to totals because of rounding.

TABLE 3. COMMUNITIES WITH JEWISH POPULATIONS OF 100 OR MORE, 1992
(ESTIMATED)

State and City	Jewish Population	State and City	Jewish Population	State and City	Jewish Population
ALABAMA		**CALIFORNIA**		Ontario (incl. in	
*Birmingham	5,100	Antelope Valley	700	Pomona Valley)	
Decatur (incl. in		Bakersfield-Kern		Orange County	75,000
Florence total)		County	1,400	Palmdale (incl. in	
***Dothan	150	Berkeley (incl. in Contra		Antelope Valley)	
Florence	150	Costa County, under		Palm Springs[N]	9,850
Huntsville	750	S.F. Bay Area)		Palo Alto (incl. in South	
**Mobile	1,100	Carmel (incl. in		Peninsula, under S.F.	
**Montgomery	1,000	Monterey Peninsula)		Bay Area)	
Sheffield (incl. in		*Chico	500	Pasadena (incl. in L.A.	
Florence total)		Corona (incl. in		Metro area total)	
Tuscaloosa	300	Riverside total)		Petaluma (incl. in	
Tuscumbia (incl. in		***El Centro	125	Sonoma County, under	
Florence total)		*Eureka	500	S.F. Bay Area)	
		Fairfield	800	Pomona Valley[N]	6,750
ALASKA		Fontana (incl. in		*Redding area	145
**Anchorage	2,000	San Bernardino total)		Redwood Valley	200
*Fairbanks	180	*Fresno	2,500	Riverside	2,000
Juneau	100	Lancaster (incl. in		Sacramento[N]	12,500
Ketchikan (incl. in		Antelope Valley)		Salinas	750
Juneau total)		Long Beach (also		San Bernardino area	
		incl. in Los Angeles			3,000
ARIZONA		total)[N]	13,500	*San Diego	70,000
Cochise County	260	Los Angeles Metro Area		San Francisco Bay	
*Flagstaff	250		501,000	Area[N]	210,000
Lake Havesu City	100	*Merced County	190	Alameda County	
*Phoenix	50,000	*Modesto	500		32,500
Prescott	250	Monterey Peninsula		Contra Costa County	
Sierra Vista (incl. in			2,300		22,000
Cochise County)		Moreno Valley (incl. in		Marin County	18,500
*Tucson	20,000	Riverside total)		N. Peninsula	24,500
***Yuma	100	Murietta Hot Springs		San Francisco	49,500
			400	San Jose	33,000
ARKANSAS		*Napa County	450	Sonoma County	9,000
Fayetteville	150	Oakland (incl. in		S. Peninsula	21,000
Hot Springs	130	Alameda County,		*San Jose (listed under	
**Little Rock	1,300	under S.F. Bay Area)		S.F. Bay Area)	

[N]See Notes below. *Includes entire county. **Includes all of 2 counties. ***Figure not updated.

State and City	Jewish Population	State and City	Jewish Population	State and City	Jewish Population
*San Luis Obispo	1,450	Cheshire (incl. in Meriden total)		Westport (incl. in Norwalk total)	
*Santa Barbara	5,000	Colchester	300	Willimantic area	700
*Santa Cruz	1,200	Danbury[N]	3,500		
Santa Maria	300	Danielson	100	DELAWARE	
Santa Monica (also incl. in Los Angeles total)	8,000	Darien (incl. in Stamford total)		Dover[N]	650
		Greenwich	3,900	Wilmington (incl. rest of state)	9,500
Santa Rosa (incl. in Sonoma County, under S.F. Bay Area)		Hartford[N]	26,000		
		Hebron (incl. in Colchester total)		DISTRICT OF COLUMBIA[N]	
Sonoma County (listed under S.F. Bay Area)		Lebanon (incl. in Colchester total)		Greater Washington	165,000
South Lake Tahoe	150	Lower Middlesex County[N]	1,475	FLORIDA	
*Stockton	1,200	Manchester (incl. in Hartford total)		Boca Raton-Delray Beach (listed under Southeast Fla.)	
Sun City	200				
Tulare & Kings counties	300	Meriden[N]	3,000	Brevard County	3,750
		Middletown	1,300	*Crystal River	100
Ukiah (incl. in Redwood Valley total)		New Britain (incl. in Hartford total)		**Daytona Beach	2,500
***Vallejo	400	New Haven[N]	24,000	Fort Lauderdale (listed under Southeast Fla.)	
*Ventura County	9,000	New London[N]	4,000		
		New Milford area	600	Fort Myers-Lee County	5,000
COLORADO		Newtown (incl. in Danbury total)		Fort Pierce	500
Aspen	250	Norwalk[N]	9,500	Gainesville	1,600
Boulder (incl. in Denver total)		Norwich (also incl. in New London total)	1,750	Hollywood (listed under Southeast Fla.)	
Colorado Springs	1,500			**Jacksonville	7,300
Denver[N]	46,000	Rockville (incl. in Hartford total)		Key West	500
Evergreen	100	Shelton (incl. in Valley area)		*Lakeland	800
*Ft. Collins	1,000	Southington (incl. in Meriden total)		*Miami-Dade County (listed under Southeast Fla.)	
*Grand Junction	250				
Greeley (incl. in Ft. Collins total)		Stamford/New Canaan	9,600	Naples-Collier County	2,500
Loveland (incl. in Ft. Collins total)		Storrs (incl. in Willimantic total)		Ocala-Marion County	500
Pueblo	250	Torrington area	580	Orlando[N]	18,000
Telluride	100	***Valley area[N]	550	Palm Beach County (listed under Southeast Fla.)	
Vail	100	Wallingford (also incl. in Meriden total)	500	**Pasco County	1,000
CONNECTICUT		Waterbury[N]	2,700	**Pensacola	775
Bridgeport[N]	13,500			*Port Charlotte-Punta Gorda	400
Bristol (incl. in Hartford total)					

State and City	Jewish Population
*St. Petersburg-Clearwater.....	9,500
**Sarasota......	12,000
Southeast Florida	515,000
Miami-Dade County	189,000
Hollywood[N] ..	66,000
Ft. Lauderdale[N]	140,000
Boca Raton-Delray Beach......	60,000
Palm Beach County (excl. Boca Raton-Delray Beach)	60,000
Stuart-Port St. Lucie	3,000
Tallahassee	1,640
*Tampa........	13,000
Venice (incl. in Sarasota total)	
*Vero Beach	300
Winter Haven (incl. in Lakeland total)	

GEORGIA

State and City	Jewish Population
Albany...........	190
Athens...........	300
Atlanta Metro Area	67,000
Augusta[N].......	1,400
Brunswick........	100
**Columbus	1,000
**Dalton..........	180
Fitzgerald-Cordele .	125
Macon...........	900
*Savannah.......	3,100
**Valdosta........	110

HAWAII

State and City	Jewish Population
Hilo.............	280
Honolulu (includes all of Oahu) ...	6,400
Kauai...........	100
Maui	210

IDAHO

State and City	Jewish Population
**Boise	220
Lewiston (incl. in Moscow total)	
Moscow..........	100

ILLINOIS

State and City	Jewish Population
Aurora area.......	500
Bloomington-Normal	230
Carbondale (incl. in S. Ill. total)	
*Champaign-Urbana	1,300
Chicago Metro Area[N]	261,000
**Danville.........	100
*Decatur	200
***DeKalb........	200
East St. Louis (incl. in S. Ill.)	
Elgin[N]	600
Freeport (incl. in Rockford total)	
*Joliet	500
***Kankakee.......	200
*Peoria...........	900
Quad Cities[N]....	1,250
**Quincy..........	105
Rock Island (incl. in Quad Cities)	
Rockford[N]......	1,000
Southern Illinois[N]..	815
*Springfield......	1,000
Waukegan........	400

INDIANA

State and City	Jewish Population
Bloomington	1,000
Elkart (incl. in South Bend total)	
Evansville	520
**Ft. Wayne.......	880
**Gary-Northwest Indiana	2,200
**Indianapolis...	10,000
***Lafayette.......	500
*Michigan City.....	280
Muncie...........	160
South Bend[N]....	1,900
*Terre Haute.......	250

IOWA

State and City	Jewish Population
Ames (also incl. in Des Moines total).	200
Cedar Rapids	420
Council Bluffs (also incl. in Omaha total)	150
Davenport (incl. in Quad Cities, Ill.)	
*Des Moines.....	2,800
*Iowa City	1,200
**Sioux City.......	590
*Waterloo	170

KANSAS

State and City	Jewish Population
Kansas City (incl. in Kansas City, Mo.)	
Lawrence.........	175
Manhattan........	100
*Topeka...........	500
Wichita[N]	1,300

KENTUCKY

State and City	Jewish Population
Covington/Newport (incl. in Cincinnati, Ohio total)	
Lexington[N]	2,000
*Louisville.......	8,700
Paducah (incl. in S. Ill.)	

LOUISIANA

State and City	Jewish Population
Alexandria........	150
Baton Rouge[N]...	1,200

State and City	Jewish Population	State and City	Jewish Population	State and City	Jewish Population
Lafayette (incl. in S. Central La.)		Athol area (also incl. in Worcester County total)	300	New Bedford[N]	3,000
Lake Charles area	200	Attleboro	200	Newburyport	280
Monroe	525	Beverly (incl. in Lynn total)		Newton (also incl. in Boston total)	34,000
**New Orleans	12,000	Boston Metro Region[N]	228,000	North Adams (incl. in N. Berkshire County)	
*Shreveport	915	Brockton[N]	8,000	North Berkshire County	750
South Central La.[N]	250	Brookline (also incl. in Boston total)	26,000	Northampton	700
MAINE		Cape Cod-Barnstable County	3,000	Peabody (incl. in Lynn total)	
Augusta	200	Clinton (incl. in Worcester County)		Pittsfield-Berkshire County	3,100
Bangor	1,000	***Fall River	1,780	Plymouth area	500
Biddeford-Saco (incl. in S. Maine)		Falmouth (incl. in Cape Cod)		Provincetown (incl. in Cape Cod)	
Brunswick-Bath (incl. in S. Maine)		Fitchburg (also incl. in Worcester County total)	300	Salem (incl. in Lynn total)	
Lewiston-Auburn	500	Framingham (incl. in Boston total)		Southbridge (also incl. in Worcester County total)	105
Portland	3,900	Gardner (incl. in Athol total)		Springfield[N]	11,000
Rockland	110	Gloucester (also incl. in Lynn total)	450	Taunton area	1,300
Southern Maine (incl. Portland)[N]	5,500	Great Barrington (incl. in Pittsfield total)		Webster (also incl. in Worcester County total)	125
***Waterville	300	*Greenfield	1,100	Worcester area[N]	10,100
MARYLAND		Haverhill	1,500	*Worcester County	13,700
*Annapolis	2,000	Holyoke	600	MICHIGAN	
**Baltimore	94,500	*Hyannis (incl. in Cape Cod)		*Ann Arbor	5,000
Cumberland	265	Lawrence (incl. in Andover total)		Bay City	200
*Frederick	900	Leominster (also incl. in Worcester County total)	400	Benton Harbor area	450
*Hagerstown	325	Lowell area	2,000	**Detroit Metro Area	94,000
*Harford County	1,200	Lynn-North Shore area[N]	25,000	*Flint	1,725
Howard County	7,200	*Martha's Vineyard	260	*Grand Rapids	1,500
Montgomery and Prince Georges Counties	104,500			**Jackson	200
Ocean City	100			*Kalamazoo	900
**Salisbury	400			***Lansing	2,100
Silver Spring (incl. in Montgomery County)				*Marquette County	150
Upper Eastern Shore[N]	130				
MASSACHUSETTS					
Amherst	750				
Andover[N]	3,000				

State and City	Jewish Population	State and City	Jewish Population	State and City	Jewish Population
Midland	100	*Las Vegas	19,500	Cherry Hill-Southern N.J.[N]	49,000
Mt. Clemens (incl. in Detroit total)		**Reno	1,400	Edison (incl. in Middlesex County)	
Mt. Pleasant[N]	100	Sparks (incl. in Reno total)		Elizabeth (incl. in Union County)	
*Muskegon	220			Englewood (incl. in Bergen County)	
*Saginaw	150	**NEW HAMPSHIRE**		Essex County[N] (also incl. in Northeastern N.J. total)	76,200
		Bethlehem	100	North Essex	15,600
MINNESOTA		Claremont	150	East Essex	10,800
**Duluth	500	Concord	450	South Essex	20,300
*Minneapolis	22,000	Dover area	600	Livingston	12,600
Rochester	550	Exeter (incl. in Portsmouth total)		West Orange-Orange	16,900
**St. Paul	9,200	Franconia (incl. in Bethlehem total)		Flemington	900
Winona (incl. in La Crosse, Wis. total)		Hanover-Lebanon	360	Freehold (incl. in Monmouth County)	
		*Keene	150	Gloucester (incl. in Cherry Hill-Southern N.J. total)	
MISSISSIPPI		**Laconia[N]	270		
Biloxi-Gulfport	150	Littleton (incl. in Bethlehem total)		Hoboken (listed under Hudson County)	
**Greenville	160	Manchester area	2,500	Hudson County (also incl. in Northeastern N.J. total)	12,800
**Hattiesburg	130	Nashua area	1,000	Bayonne	2,500
**Jackson	550	Portsmouth area	950	Jersey City	5,700
		Rochester (incl. in Dover total)		Hoboken	1,100
MISSOURI		Salem (also incl. in Andover, Mass. total)	150	North Hudson County[N]	3,500
Columbia	400			Jersey City (listed under Hudson County)	
Hannibal (incl. in Quincy, Ill. total)		**NEW JERSEY**		Lakewood (incl. in Ocean County)	
Kansas City Metro Area	19,100	Asbury Park (incl. in Monmouth County)		Livingston (incl. in Essex County)	
*St. Joseph	265	*Atlantic City (incl. Atlantic County)	15,800	Middlesex County[N] (also incl. in Northeastern N.J. total)	58,000
**St. Louis	53,500	Bayonne (listed under Hudson County)			
Springfield	300	Bergen County (also incl. in Northeastern N.J. total)	83,700		
		Bridgeton	200		
MONTANA		Bridgewater (incl. in Somerset County)			
*Billings	240	Camden (incl. in Cherry Hill total)			
Butte	110				
Helena (incl. in Butte total)					
NEBRASKA					
Grand Island-Hastings (incl. in Lincoln total)					
Lincoln	800				
Omaha[N]	6,500				
NEVADA					
Carson City (incl. in Reno total)					

State and City	Jewish Population	State and City	Jewish Population	State and City	Jewish Population
Monmouth County (also incl. in Northeastern N.J. total)	33,600	Toms River (incl. in Ocean County)		Ellenville	1,600
Morris County (also incl. in Northeastern N.J. total)	33,500	Trenton[N]	6,000	Elmira[N]	1,100
		Union County (also incl. in Northeastern N.J. total)	30,000	Fleischmanns	120
Morristown (incl. in Morris County)		Vineland[N]	2,200	Fredonia (incl. in Dunkirk total)	
Mt. Holly (incl. in Cherry Hill-Southern N.J. total)		Warren County	400	Geneva area	310
		Wayne (incl. in Passaic County)		Glens Falls[N]	800
Newark (incl. in Essex County)		Wildwood	425	*Gloversville	380
New Brunswick (incl. in Middlesex County)		Willingboro (incl. in Cherry Hill-Southern N.J. total)		*Herkimer	180
Northeastern N.J.[N]	365,000			Highland Falls (incl. in Orange County)	
Ocean County (also incl. in Northeastern N.J. total)	9,500	NEW MEXICO		*Hudson	500
		*Albuquerque	4,000	*Ithaca area	1,700
Passaic County (also incl. in Northeastern N.J. total)	17,000	Las Cruces	525	Jamestown	100
		Los Alamos	250	Kingston[N]	4,300
Passaic-Clifton (also incl. in Passaic County total)	8,000	Santa Fe	900	Lake George (incl. in Glens Falls total)	
Paterson (incl. in Passaic County)		NEW YORK		Liberty (also incl. in Sullivan County total)	2,100
		*Albany	12,000		
Perth Amboy (incl. in Middlesex County)		Amenia (incl. in Poughkeepsie-Dutchess County)		Middletown (incl. in Orange County)	
Phillipsburg (incl. in Easton, Pa. total)		Amsterdam	170	Monroe (incl. in Orange County)	
Plainfield (incl. in Union County)		*Auburn	115	Monticello (also incl. in Sullivan County total)	2,400
Princeton	3,000	Beacon (incl. in Poughkeepsie-Dutchess County)		Newark (incl. in Geneva total)	
Somerset County (also incl. in Northeastern N.J. total)	9,000	*Binghamton (incl. all Broome County)	2,600	Newburgh (incl. in Orange County)	
Somerville (incl. in Somerset County)		Brewster (incl. in Putnam County)		New Paltz (incl. in Kingston total)	
		*Buffalo	17,000	New York Metro Area[N]	1,450,000
		Canandaigua (incl. in Geneva total)		Bronx	83,700
		Catskill	200	Brooklyn	379,000
Sussex County (also incl. in Northeastern N.J. total)	4,100	Corning (incl. in Elmira total)		Manhattan	314,500
		*Cortland	200	Queens	238,000
		Dunkirk	100	Staten Island	33,700
				Nassau County	207,000
				Suffolk County	100,000

State and City	Jewish Population
Westchester County	94,000
Niagara Falls......	400
Olean	120
**Oneonta........	250
Orange County	10,000
Pawling	105
Plattsburg	260
Port Jervis (also incl. in Orange County total)	560
Potsdam..........	200
*Poughkeepsie-Dutchess County........	6,500
Putnam County..	1,000
**Rochester.....	22,500
Rockland County	83,100
Rome............	205
Saratoga Springs...	600
Seneca Falls (incl. in Geneva total)	
**Schenectady....	5,200
South Fallsburg (also incl. in Sullivan County total)	1,100
Sullivan County .	7,425
Syracuse[N]	9,000
Troy area........	800
Utica[N]	1,900
Walden (incl. in Orange County)	
Watertown........	120
Woodstock (incl. in Kingston total)	

NORTH CAROLINA

Asheville[N]	1,300
**Chapel Hill-Durham	3,000
Charlotte[N]	4,000
Elizabethtown (incl. in Wilmington total)	

State and City	Jewish Population
*Fayetteville	320
Gastonia	190
Goldsboro	120
*Greensboro	2,700
Greenville	240
*Hendersonville	200
**Hickory	100
High Point (incl. in Greensboro total)	
Jacksonville (incl. in Wilmington total)	
Raleigh-Wake County	4,250
Whiteville (incl. in Wilmington total)	
Wilmington area...	500
Winston-Salem	440

NORTH DAKOTA

Fargo............	500
Grand Forks......	130

OHIO

**Akron	6,000
Athens...........	100
Bowling Green (also incl. in Toledo total)	120
Butler County.....	900
**Canton........	2,400
Cincinnati[N]	23,000
**Cleveland[N] ...	65,000
*Columbus	15,600
**Dayton........	6,000
***Elyria..........	200
Fremont (incl. in Sandusky total)	
Hamilton (incl. in Butler County)	
*Lima	210
Lorain	600
***Mansfield.......	180
Marietta (incl. in Parkersburg, W.Va. total)	

State and City	Jewish Population
Marion...........	125
Middletown (incl. in Butler County)	
New Philadelphia (incl. in Canton total)	
Norwalk (incl. in Sandusky total)	
Oberlin (incl. in Elyria total)	
Oxford (incl. in Butler County)	
**Sandusky........	130
Springfield	200
*Steubenville.......	150
Toledo[N]	5,500
Warren (also incl. in Youngstown total)	400
Wooster..........	135
Youngstown[N] ...	4,000
*Zanesville........	100

OKLAHOMA

Norman (also incl. in Oklahoma City total)	350
**Oklahoma City .	2,500
*Tulsa	2,750

OREGON

Ashland (incl. in Medford total)	
***Corvallis	150
Eugene.........	3,000
Grants Pass (incl. in Medford total)	
**Medford.......	1,000
Portland.......	12,000
**Salem..........	530

PENNSYLVANIA

Allentown	6,000
*Altoona	350

State and City	Jewish Population
Ambridge[N]	350
Beaver Falls (incl. in Upper Beaver County)	
Bethlehem	800
Bucks County (lower portion)[N]	14,500
*Butler	250
**Chambersburg	125
Chester (incl. in Phila. total)	
Chester County (also incl. in Phila. total)	4,000
Coatesville (incl. in Chester County)	
Easton area	1,200
*Erie	800
Farrell (incl. in Sharon total)	
Greensburg (also incl. in Pittsburgh total)	425
**Harrisburg	6,500
Hazleton area	300
Honesdale (incl. in Wayne County)	
Jeanette (incl. in Greensburg total)	
**Johnstown	415
Lancaster	2,100
*Lebanon	350
Lewisburg (incl. in Sunbury total)	
Lock Haven (incl. in Williamsport total)	
McKeesport (incl. in Pittsburgh total)	
New Castle	200
Norristown (incl. in Philadelphia total)	
**Oil City	100
Oxford-Kennett Square (incl. in Chester County)	

State and City	Jewish Population
Philadelphia area[N]	250,000
Phoenixville (incl. in Chester County)	
Pike County	300
Pittsburgh[N]	45,000
Pottstown	650
Pottsville	250
*Reading	2,800
*Scranton	3,100
Shamokin (incl. in Sunbury total)	
Sharon (also incl. in Youngstown, Ohio total)	260
State College	550
*Stroudsburg	400
Sunbury[N]	200
Tamaqua (incl. in Hazleton total)	
Uniontown area	250
Upper Beaver County	200
**Washington (also incl. in Pittsburgh total)	175
Wayne County	500
Waynesburg (incl. in Washington total)	
West Chester (also incl. in Chester County)	300
Wilkes-Barre[N]	3,200
**Williamsport	350
York	1,500

RHODE ISLAND

State and City	Jewish Population
Cranston (incl. in Providence total)	
Kingston (incl. in Washington County)	
Newport-Middletown	700

State and City	Jewish Population
Providence area	14,200
Washington County	1,200
Westerly (incl. in Washington County)	

SOUTH CAROLINA

State and City	Jewish Population
*Charleston	3,500
**Columbia	2,000
Florence area	220
Georgetown (incl. in Myrtle Beach total)	
Greenville	1,100
Kingstree (incl. in Sumter total)	
**Myrtle Beach	425
Rock Hill (incl. in Charlotte, N.C. total)	
*Spartanburg	330
Sumter[N]	160

SOUTH DAKOTA

State and City	Jewish Population
Sioux Falls	135

TENNESSEE

State and City	Jewish Population
Bristol (incl. in Johnson City total)	
Chattanooga	1,350
***Johnson City	210
Kingsport (incl. in Johnson city total)	
Knoxville	1,630
Memphis	8,800
Nashville	5,600
Oak Ridge	200

TEXAS

State and City	Jewish Population
Amarillo[N]	150
*Austin	5,000
Bay City (incl. in Wharton total)	
***Baytown	300
Beaumont	800

State and City	Jewish Population	State and City	Jewish Population	State and City	Jewish Population

*Brownsville 325
College Station-Bryan
. . . . 400
*Corpus Christi . . 1,400
**Dallas. 35,000
El Paso 4,900
*Ft. Worth 5,000
Galveston. 800
Harlingen (incl. in
Brownsville total)
**Houston[N]. 42,000
Kilgore (incl. in
Longview total)
Laredo 160
Longview 150
*Lubbock. 480
Lufkin (incl. in
Longview total)
Marshall (incl. in
Longview total)
*McAllen. 475
Midland-Odessa . . . 150
Port Arthur. 100
*San Antonio . . . 10,000
Tyler 400
Waco[N] 300
**Wharton 100
***Wichita Falls. . . . 260

UTAH
Ogden 150
*Salt Lake City. . . 3,300

VERMONT
Bennington 300
*Brattleboro 350
**Burlington 3,000
Manchester area . . . 250
Montpelier-Barre . . 550
Newport (incl. in St.
Johnsbury total)
Rutland 550
**St. Johnsbury 100

VIRGINIA
Alexandria (incl.
Falls Church,
Arlington, and Fairfax
counties) 35,100
Arlington (incl. in
Alexandria total)
Blacksburg. 300
Charlottesville . . . 1,000
Chesapeake (incl. in
Portsmouth total)
Colonial Heights (incl.
in Petersburg total)
Fredericksburg[N] . . . 500
Hampton (incl. in
Newport News total)
Harrisonburg (incl. in
Staunton total)
Lexington (incl. in
Staunton total)
Lynchburg area. . . . 275
**Martinsville 100
Newport News-
Hampton[N] 2,000
Norfolk-Virginia Beach
. . . . 19,000
Petersburg area. . . . 550
Portsmouth-Suffolk
(also incl. in Norfolk
total) 1,900
Radford (incl. in
Blacksburg total)
Richmond[N] 8,000
Roanoke. 1,050
Staunton[N] 370
Williamsburg (incl. in
Newport News total)
Winchester[N] 200

WASHINGTON
Bellingham 400
Ellensburg (incl. in
Yakima total)

Longview-Kelso (incl.
in Portland, OR total)
*Olympia. 450
Port Angeles 100
Pullman (incl. in
Moscow, Idaho total)
*Seattle[N] 29,300
Spokane. 750
*Tacoma 1,100
Tri Cities[N]. 300
Vancouver (incl. in
Portland, OR total)
**Yakima 100

WEST VIRGINIA
Bluefield-Princeton
. . . . 200
*Charleston. 950
Clarksburg. 110
Fairmont (incl. in
Clarksburg total)
Huntington[N] 300
Morgantown 175
Parkersburg. 100
**Wheeling 275

WISCONSIN
Appleton area 400
Beloit 150
Fond du Lac (incl. in
Oshkosh total)
Green Bay 320
Janesville (incl. in
Beloit total)
*Kenosha. 180
La Crosse 120
*Madison. 4,500
Milwaukee[N]
. . . . 28,000
Oshkosh area. 170
*Racine 375
Sheboygan 140

State and City	Jewish Population	State and City	Jewish Population	State and City	Jewish Population
Waukesha (incl. in Milwaukee total)		WYOMING		Laramie (incl. in Cheyenne total)	
WausauN	240	Casper	100		
		Cheyenne	230		

Notes

CALIFORNIA

Long Beach—includes in L.A. County: Long Beach, Signal Hill, Cerritos, Lakewood, Rosmoor, and Hawaiian Gardens. Also includes in Orange County: Los Alamitos, Cypress, Seal Beach, and Huntington Harbor.

Palm Springs—includes Palm Springs, Desert Hot Springs, Cathedral City, Palm Desert, and Rancho Mirage.

Pomona Valley—includes Alta Loma, Chino, Claremont, Cucamonga, La Verne, Montclair, Ontario, Pomona, San Dimas, and Upland. Portion also included in Los Angeles total.

Sacramento—includes Yolo, Placer, El Dorado, and Sacramento counties.

San Francisco Bay Area—North Peninsula includes northern San Mateo County. South Peninsula includes southern San Mateo County and towns of Palo Alto and Los Altos in Santa Clara County. San Jose includes remainder of Santa Clara County.

COLORADO

Denver—includes Adams, Arapahoe, Boulder, Denver, and Jefferson counties.

CONNECTICUT

Bridgeport—includes Monroe, Easton, Trumbull, Fairfield, Bridgeport, Shelton, Stratford, and part of Milford.

Danbury—includes Danbury, Bethel, New Fairfield, Brookfield, Sherman, Newtown, Redding, Ridgefield, and part of Wilton; also includes some towns in neighboring Putnam County, N.Y.

Hartford—includes most of Hartford County and Vernon, Rockville, Ellington, and Tolland in Tolland County, and Meriden area of New Haven County.

Lower Middlesex County—includes Branford, Guilford, Madison, Clinton, Westbrook, Old Saybrook. Portion of this area also included in New London and New Haven totals.

Meriden—includes Meriden, Southington, Cheshire, and Wallingford. Most included in Hartford total and a portion also included in New Haven total.

New Haven—includes New Haven, East Haven, Guilford, Branford, Madison, North Haven, Hamden, West Haven, Milford, Orange, Woodbridge, Bethany, Derby, Ansonia, and Cheshire.

New London—includes central and southern New London County. Also includes part of Lower Middlesex County and part of Windham County.

Norwalk—includes Norwalk, Weston, Westport, East Norwalk, Darien, Wilton, part of Georgetown, and part of New Canaan.

Valley Area—includes Ansonia, Derby, Shelton, Oxford, Seymour, and Beacon Falls. Portion also included in Bridgeport and New Haven totals.

Waterbury—includes Middlebury, Southbury, Naugatuck, Watertown, Waterbury, Oakville, and Woodbury.

DELAWARE

Dover—includes most of central and southern Delaware.

DISTRICT OF COLUMBIA

Greater Washington—includes Montgomery and Prince Georges counties in Maryland, Arlington County, Fairfax County, Falls Church, and Alexandria in Virginia.

FLORIDA

Ft. Lauderdale—includes Ft. Lauderdale, Pompano Beach, Deerfield Beach, Tamarac, Margate, and other towns in northern Broward County.

Hollywood—includes Hollywood, Hallandale, Dania, Davie, Pembroke, and other towns in southern Broward County.

Orlando—includes all of Orange and Seminole counties and part of Lake County.

GEORGIA

Augusta—includes Burke, Columbia, and Richmond counties and part of Aiken County, South Carolina.

ILLINOIS

Chicago—includes all of Cook and Du Page counties and a portion of Lake County.

Elgin—includes northern Kane County, southern McHenry County, and western edge of Cook County.

Quad Cities—includes Rock Island, Moline (Ill.); Davenport and Bettendorf (Iowa).

Rockford—includes Winnebago, Boone, and Stephenson counties.

Southern Illinois—includes lower portion of Illinois below Carlinville, adjacent western portion of Kentucky, and adjacent portion of southeastern Missouri.

INDIANA

South Bend—includes St. Joseph and Elkhart counties and part of Berrien County, Mich.

KANSAS

Wichita—includes Sedgwick County and towns of Salina, Dodge City, Great Bend, Liberal, Russell, and Hays.

KENTUCKY

Lexington—includes Fayette, Bourbon, Scott, Clark, Woodford, Madison, Pulaski, and Jessamine counties.

LOUISIANA

Baton Rouge—includes E. Baton Rouge, Ascencion, Livingston, St. Landry, Iberville, Pt. Coupee, and W. Baton Rouge parishes.

South Central—includes Abbeville, Lafayette, New Iberia, Crowley, Opelousus, Houma, Morgan City, Thibodaux, and Franklin.

MAINE

Southern Maine—includes York, Cumberland, and Sagadahoc counties.

MARYLAND

Upper Eastern Shore—includes towns in Caroline, Dorchester, Kent, Queen Annes, and Talbot counties.

MASSACHUSETTS

Andover—includes Andover, N. Andover, Boxford, Lawrence, Methuen, Tewksbury, Dracut, and town of Salem, New Hampshire.

Boston Metropolitan Region—includes all towns south and west of Boston within approximately 30 miles, and all towns north of Boston within approximately 20 miles. All towns formerly part of Framingham area are now included in Boston total.

Brockton—includes Avon, Brockton, Easton, Bridgewater, Whitman, and West Bridgewater. Also included in Boston total.

Lynn—includes Lynn, Saugus, Nahant, Swampscott, Lynnfield, Peabody, Salem, Marblehead, Beverly, Danvers, Middleton, Wenham, Topsfield, Hamilton, Manchester, Ipswich, Essex, Gloucester, and Rockport. Also included in Boston total.

New Bedford—includes New Bedford, Dartmouth, Fairhaven, and Mattapoisett.

Springfield—includes Springfield, Longmeadow, E. Longmeadow, Hampden, Wilbraham, Agwam, and West Springfield.

Worcester—includes Worcester, Northborough, Westborough, Shrewsbury, Boylston, West Boylston, Holden, Paxton, Leicester, Auburn, Millbury, and Grafton. Also included in the Worcester County total.

MICHIGAN

Mt. Pleasant—includes towns in Isabella, Mecosta, Gladwin, and Gratiot counties.

NEBRASKA

Omaha—includes Douglas and Sarpy counties. Also includes Pottawatamie County, Iowa.

NEW HAMPSHIRE

Laconia—includes Laconia, Plymouth, Meredith, Conway, and Franklin.

NEW JERSEY

Cherry Hill—includes Camden, Burlington, and Gloucester counties.

Essex County—East Essex includes Belleville, Bloomfield, East Orange, Irvington, Newark, and Nutley in Essex County, and Kearny in Hudson County. North Essex includes Caldwell, Cedar Grove, Essex Fells, Fairfield, Glen Ridge, Montclair, North Caldwell, Roseland, Verona, and West Caldwell. South Essex includes Maplewood, Millburn, Short Hills, and South Orange in Essex County, and Springfield in Union County.

Middlesex County—includes in Somerset County, Kendall Park, Somerset, and Franklin; in Mercer County, Hightstown; and all of Middlesex County.

Northeastern N.J.—includes Bergen, Essex, Hudson, Middlesex, Morris, Passaic, Somerset, Union, Hunterdon, Sussex, Monmouth, and Ocean counties.

North Hudson County—includes Guttenberg, Hudson Heights, North Bergen, North Hudson, Secaucus, Union City, Weehawken, West New York, and Woodcliff.

Somerset County—includes most of Somerset County and a portion of Hunterdon County.

Trenton—includes most of Mercer County.

Union County—includes all of Union County except Springfield. Also includes a few towns in adjacent areas of Somerset and Middlesex counties.

Vineland—includes most of Cumberland County and towns in neighboring counties adjacent to Vineland.

NEW YORK

Elmira—includes Chemung, Tioga, and Schuyler counties. Also includes Tioga and Bradford counties in Pennsylvania.

Glens Falls—includes Warren and Washington counties, lower Essex County, and upper Saratoga County.

Kingston—includes eastern half of Ulster County.

New York Metropolitan Area—includes the five boroughs of New York City, Westchester, Nassau, and Suffolk counties. For a total Jewish population of the New York metropolitan region, please include Fairfield County, Connecticut; Rockland, Putnam, and Orange counties, New York; and Northeastern New Jersey.

Syracuse—includes Onondaga County, western Madison County, and most of Oswego County.

Utica—southeastern third of Oneida County.

NORTH CAROLINA

Asheville—includes Buncombe, Haywood, and Madison counties.

Charlotte—includes Mecklenburg County. Also includes Lancaster and York counties in South Carolina.

OHIO

Cincinnati—includes Hamilton and Butler counties. Also includes Boone, Campbell, and Kenton counties in Kentucky.

Cleveland—for a total Jewish population of the Cleveland metropolitan region, please include Elyria, Lorain, and Akron totals.

Toledo—includes Fulton, Lucas, and Wood counties. Also includes Monroe and Lenawee counties, Michigan.

Youngstown—includes Mahoning and Trumbull counties. Also includes Mercer County, Pennsylvania.

PENNSYLVANIA

Ambridge—includes lower Beaver County and adjacent areas of Allegheny County. Also included in Pittsburgh total.

Bucks County (lower portion)—includes Bensalem Township, Bristol, Langhorne, Levittown, New Hope, Newtown, Penndel, Warrington, Yardley, Richboro, Feasterville, Middletown, Southampton, and Holland. Also included in Philadelphia total.

Philadelphia—includes Philadelphia City, Montgomery, Delaware County, Chester County, and Bucks County. For a total Jewish population of the Philadelphia metropolitan region, please include the Cherry Hill, Salem, and Trenton areas of New Jersey, and the Wilmington area of Delaware.

Pittsburgh—includes all of Allegheny County and adjacent portions of Washington, Westmoreland, and Beaver counties.

Sunbury—includes Shamokin, Lewisburg, Milton, Selinsgrove, and Sunbury.

Wilkes-Barre—includes all of Lucerne County except southern portion, which is included in Hazleton totals.

SOUTH CAROLINA

Sumter—includes towns in Sumter, Lee, Clarendon, and Williamsburg counties.

TEXAS

Amarillo—includes Canyon, Childress, Borger, Dumas, Memphis, Pampa, Vega, and Hereford in Texas, and Portales, New Mexico.

Houston—includes Harris, Montgomery, and Ft. Bend counties, and parts of Brazoria and Galveston counties.

Waco—includes Mclellan, Coryell, Bell, Falls, Hamilton, and Hill counties.

VIRGINIA

Fredericksburg—includes towns in Spotsylvania, Stafford, King George, and Orange counties.

Newport News—includes Newport News, Hampton, Williamsburg, James City, York County, and Poquoson County.

Richmond—includes Richmond City, Henrico County, and Chesterfield County.

Staunton—includes towns in Augusta, Page, Shenandoah, Rockingham, Bath, and Highland counties.

Winchester—includes towns in Winchester, Frederick, Clark, and Warren counties, Virginia; and Hardy and Jefferson counties, West Virginia.

WASHINGTON

Seattle—includes King County and adjacent portions of Snohomish and Kitsap counties.

Tri Cities—includes Pasco, Richland, and Kennewick.

WEST VIRGINIA

Huntington—includes nearby towns in Ohio and Kentucky.

WISCONSIN

Milwaukee—includes Milwaukee County, eastern Waukesha County, and southern Ozaukee County.

Wausau—includes Stevens Point, Marshfield, Antigo, and Rhinelander.

Review
of
the
Year

OTHER COUNTRIES

Canada

National Affairs

THE GULF WAR

WITH THE OUTBREAK OF THE GULF WAR in January 1991, Canada became an integral member of the coalition that was arrayed militarily against Iraq. Indeed, three Canadians ships and a number of planes participated in the conflict. Although opinion within the country was divided with regard to the question of whether military action was justified at that particular time, the government was forthright in its determination to proceed with the military option once the decision was made. Most MPs supported that position, with the House of Commons voting 217–47 on January 22 to support the United Nations efforts. In the opposition, New Democratic party (NDP) leader Audrey McLaughlin opposed the war as being an inappropriate way to end an international dispute, but Liberal opposition leader Jean Chrétien and most of his party did support the war after considerable soul-searching.

The unprovoked Iraqi missile attacks on Israel were roundly condemned by Canadians of all backgrounds and political persuasions. Prime Minister Brian Mulroney's government denounced the attacks and expressed strong support for Israel, as did many other politicians. The significance of the war for Israel was assessed sympathetically by *Montreal Gazette* editor Norman Webster in a widely disseminated column in which he concluded that the Israelis "will rely on none but themselves. They will do whatever is necessary. Masada shall not fall again."

SEPARATISM VS. NATIONAL UNITY

Since the failure of the Meech Lake package of constitutional amendments in 1990, Canada had been troubled by renewed threats of Quebec separatism. The government of Quebec was actively exploring constitutional options and had committed itself to a referendum by October 1992. Thus the year 1991 was spent investigating the issues and testing mass and elite opinions on the subject. One focus for such activity was Quebec's Belanger-Campeau Commission. Three broadly

215

based Jewish organizations in Quebec—Canadian Jewish Congress (CJC-Quebec Region), Allied Jewish Community Services (AJCS), and the Communauté Sépharade du Québec (CSQ)—submitted a joint brief to the commission on behalf of the community. The brief reflected the general Jewish preference for the maintenance of Quebec as part of Canada in some form, a commitment of the community to remain in Quebec, and a desire for the recognition of minority rights regardless of the constitutional outcome. The community representatives who presented the brief to the commission were very careful to tone down the strong federalist leanings of their constituents, in order not to be seen as simply in opposition to Quebec's nationalist aspirations. The entire exercise of producing the brief made evident the contradictions with which Quebec's Jews were living.

Later in the year, the Quebec Region of CJC launched a campaign to make Jews across the country aware of the stakes in the national-unity struggle. The same body also undertook an initiative with comparable Greek and Italian organizations to sensitize their respective members to the constitutional issues from the perspective of Quebec minorities. The three groups later endorsed the idea of "distinct society" status for Quebec while maintaining federal links and sent representatives on a cross-country tour to meet with politicians and community leaders in order to promote their views on renewed federalism.

Within the Montreal Jewish community, differences on the national-unity issue between Ashkenazim and Sephardim remained a source of possible tension, despite efforts to have a unified front for external purposes. For example, CSQ president Salomon Oziel stated publicly that separation "would be a non-event, in the same way as when Norway separated from Sweden." He contended that the mainly francophone Sephardim were much more comfortable with Quebec's evolution than their mainly anglophone Ashkenazi counterparts.

ELECTIONS

As Canadians began to look ahead to the next federal election, expected in 1993, the alignment of political parties was shifting. For the first time, a separatist party, the Bloc Québécois, was expected to contest the election in Quebec. Out west, the populist Reform party was becoming a major force, threatening to attract votes in Ontario, the largest province. The right-wing character of the group led Jews and other minority groups to express concerns about possible racism and anti-Semitism. These allegations were denied strenuously by party leader Preston Manning, who told a Jewish audience in Calgary in July, "I despise racism in general, and anti-Semitism in particular. . . ." He promised that his party would be insulated against extremism and invited Jews to participate in its activities.

In the British Columbia general election in October, the New Democratic party won a strong majority, including two Jews: legislative newcomer Bernie Simpson and Dr. Tom Perry, who was appointed minister of advanced education, training, and technology. Attorney Douglas Christie, who represented accused anti-Semites such as Ernst Zundel, James Keegstra, and Malcom Ross, lost in his effort to be elected as a candidate for the Western Canada Concept party.

Municipal elections were held in Ontario and Quebec in November. Mel Lastman was elected to a record ninth straight term as mayor of North York, Ontario. In Outremont, Quebec, Sydney Pfeiffer was elected to the city council. An Orthodox Jew, he claimed that he was drafted by several Hassidic sects to represent their interests in a Montreal suburb that has had several confrontations in recent years between Hassidim and French Quebecers or municipal officials. Zoning regulations were a matter of particular contention, and Pfeiffer was hopeful that increased dialogue between the Hassidim and non-Jews would help to improve the situation.

OTHER MATTERS

After a great deal of pretrial maneuvering, Patricia Starr, a prominent member of the Toronto community, pleaded guilty to charges of fraud and breach of trust based on her political activities while directing the Toronto section of the National Council of Jewish Women (NCJW). She was sentenced to two concurrent six-month terms. However, all charges against the organization were dropped. Between 1986 and 1988 Starr had applied to an Ontario government ministry for certain grants that were supposed to have been matched by the NCJW but never were. In addition she pleaded guilty to having diverted some $33,000 from the NCJW's charitable foundation's trust fund for personal use. She also was convicted separately on eight counts of violating Ontario's Election Finances Act by using NCJW money for political campaign purposes. She was fined $3,500 for those offenses.

Relations with Israel

In the aftermath of the Gulf War there was a flurry of diplomatic activity, during which major policy differences surfaced between Prime Minister Mulroney and Secretary of State for External Affairs Joe Clark. In their conviction that the defeat of Iraq had created a remarkable opportunity for peacemaking, Canadian officials turned their attention to the Arab-Israeli conflict, with the prime minister advocating an international conference to deal with what he referred to as "the most worrisome fault line" in the Middle East. He also asked that the "legitimate interests of the Palestinians be respected." Clark visited Israel in March and called upon the Israelis to be prepared to trade territory for peace. He argued that the Gulf War had demonstrated both the inadequacy of conventional defenses and the necessity for negotiated settlements. In meetings with Prime Minister Yitzhak Shamir and Foreign Minister David Levy, Clark praised Israel for its restraint in the face of severe provocation.

The crucial difference between Clark's and Mulroney's positions was over the role of the PLO in any future peace negotiations. Clark maintained that "the PLO retains an important role in these matters," despite a diminution of its authority as a consequence of its role in the Gulf War, while Mulroney responded that "the PLO and its leader, Mr. Arafat, have been substantially if not completely discredited as a result of their own actions." He added that "our enthusiasm for the present PLO leadership is zero," while stressing the necessity of Palestinian participation. It was unclear exactly how much effect the public rebuff had on Clark's standing, but he was replaced by Barbara McDougall at the end of April, in a move that was generally welcomed by Canada's Jews. On the issue of the PLO, the Canada-Israel Committee (CIC), the community's official representative on Israel-related matters, had called for an end to Canada-PLO relations in light of Arafat's support for Saddam Hussein.

At the annual parliamentary dinner of the CIC in March, Barbara McDougall, then employment and immigration minister, reaffirmed Canada's inalienable friendship for Israel in the context of an argument that the end of the Gulf War presented an unusual opportunity to move toward Arab-Israeli peace. The NDP's Audrey McLaughlin made an effort to persuade the Jewish community that her party's position was balanced and not definitely tilted toward the Arabs, while Liberal Sheila Copps tried to compensate for her party's initial ambivalence about the Gulf War by strongly urging repeal of the UN resolution on Zionism as racism and backing fundamental pro-Israel principles with regard to the peace process. When the repeal of the UN resolution was passed in December, Canada was among the majority. Mulroney and McDougall were commended by the CIC for their leadership on the issue.

When McDougall was named later to succeed Clark as external affairs minister, the appointment was well received within the Jewish community. CJC president Les Scheininger described her as "a strong supporter of Israel and, I think, more reflective of the Prime Minister's own position. . . ." In a speech delivered just before assuming her new post, she strongly resisted the idea of an imposed settlement in the Middle East.

The government appointed Michael Bell as ambassador to Israel. In Ontario, the Canadian Arab Federation protested plans to twin the town of Vaughan with the Israeli town of Ramla.

Canada hosted a controversial UN meeting in Montreal in June, the Eighth Annual North American NGO Meeting on the Question of Palestine. This was the first such meeting outside the United States. Nongovernmental organizations that wished to participate had to subscribe to a number of pro-Palestinian positions. Backers of the conference, which was vigorously opposed as one-sided by the Jewish community, viewed it as an opportunity to raise consciousness in Canada and to encourage Canada to take a position different from that of the United States. The conference attracted about 250 delegates and observers but did not receive the media attention that its organizers had anticipated.

OTHER MATTERS

In Israel, Yasser Hijazi, a Hamas member from a West Bank town, was convicted in the bombing murder of Marnie Kimelman of Willowdale, Ontario, on an Israeli beach in 1990. Hijazi was sentenced to life in prison. He said that his sentence was "a great honor." A former PLO official's request for political asylum in Canada was turned down by the Department of Immigration on the grounds that he was a security threat. Mahmood Abo Shandi, who arrived in Montreal from Norway in October, claimed to have been a high-ranking member of al-Fatah. A new Canadian Parliamentary Group for Syrian Jewry was formed with representation from all political parties, based on the model of a similar group that aided Soviet Jewry.

Anti-Semitism

The long-running cases of Ernst Zundel, James Keegstra, and Malcolm Ross continued to wind their way through courts and other legal bodies. (See previous volumes of AJYB.) Zundel, who was appealing his conviction in Canada, ran into trouble in his native Germany. He was convicted in Munich of denigrating the memory of the dead and inciting racism and was fined about $7,500. The actions that prompted the charges involved an extension of his Canadian Holocaust-denial activities. As a result of his German convictions, CJC and B'nai Brith asked Canadian authorities to consider whether he had violated the terms of his bail, which were in effect while his appeal was pending. Meanwhile, prosecutors decided to retry Keegstra on hate-mongering charges. After a conviction and a successful appeal on technical grounds, Keegstra had to face a new trial in the light of a 1990 Supreme Court of Canada decision upholding the constitutionality of the antihate statute.

The Malcolm Ross case, involving his fitness to teach in the public schools of New Brunswick because of the anti-Semitic attitudes that he had expressed in print, finally reached a conclusion. The human-rights board of inquiry decided in August that the school board, by employing Ross, fostered a climate of discrimination. Ross, who had written books denying the Holocaust and contending the existence of an international Jewish conspiracy, asked a court to review the board's decision. In a December court hearing, attorney Douglas Christie depicted his client as a victim of persecution and an "inquisition." In the meantime, the school board relieved Ross of his teaching duties at the beginning of the academic year and made him a program developer.

British writer David Irving, whose books also questioned accepted views of the Holocaust, again encountered difficulties in carrying out a speaking tour of Canada. Both the Marriott and Novotel hotels in the Toronto area canceled planned events in October, when the nature of the speaker was made clear to management by Jewish groups. Earlier in the tour, he had encountered similar difficulties in Vancouver after addressing a surreptitious meeting in Victoria that was chaired by Christie. Irving did manage to speak in Kitchener but found his Ottawa meeting canceled.

B'nai Brith Canada's League for Human Rights found that the number of anti-Semitic incidents in 1990 was 19 percent higher than in 1989, with a total of 210 recorded. There was another 20-percent increase in 1991, to a total of 251, of which 201 were classified as harassment and 50 as vandalism. The most incidents by far were in Toronto, with 130. Furthermore, there were signs of greater use of violence. The Gulf War spawned a series of incidents, especially in the Toronto area. In the first four weeks of the war, some 60 incidents were reported in metropolitan Toronto alone. There were synagogue and school desecrations, bomb threats, and harassment of children. Karen Mock of B'nai Brith contended that economic conditions and increased immigration helped to produce a climate in which hostility toward minority groups was more likely to come out.

Among the anti-Semitic incidents that occurred during 1991 were the fire-bombing of a Jewish memorial chapel in Calgary and the desecration of a Jewish cemetery in Sherbrooke. A teenager was arrested in Hamilton for a series of cemetery desecrations carried out in 1990. In another case from 1990, five Quebec teenagers convicted of attacking Hassidic Jews in Outremont were sentenced to 35 hours of community service plus seven hours to be spent getting to know the Jewish community.

A special national survey of attitudes toward six minority groups, commissioned by B'nai Brith and carried out by Environics, showed that anti-Semitic attitudes were more prevalent in Quebec than elsewhere in Canada, and particularly among francophones. Moreover, unlike the rest of the country, in Quebec the incidence of such attitudes did not decline with higher education. In commenting on the survey, Prof. Stephen Scheinberg, chairman of the League for Human Rights, pointed out that the existence of anti-Semitic attitudes constituted a "latent" problem, and that overt anti-Semitism was not a cause of immediate concern in Quebec.

Nazi War Criminals

Despite efforts by the government to move ahead with war-crimes prosecutions, the attempt to bring alleged criminals to justice appeared to be far from realization. The greatest success was achieved in the case of Jacob Luitjens, who was accused of having been a Nazi collaborator in his native Holland. Based on evidence that Luitjens had belonged to Nazi organizations and had participated in shootings and arrests, a judge of the Federal Court ruled that his Canadian citizenship should be revoked. Shortly after the court decision, the federal cabinet stripped Luitjens of his citizenship, and deportation proceedings were initiated.

Former Nazi rocket scientist Arthur Rudolph was barred from entering Canada by an immigration adjudicator. He was found to have committed war crimes and crimes against humanity through the use of slave labor at a V-2 rocket factory. Subsequently, Rudolph was allowed to appeal the ruling to the Federal Court.

A procedural decision by the judge in the trial of Michael Pawlawski constituted a major setback to the prosecution. The Crown wanted to send a commission to gather evidence in Russia and Germany, but was turned down by the judge. Pawlawski had been charged with four counts of murder for actions in the Minsk area in 1942.

Imre Finta, who was acquitted in a war-crimes trial in 1990, faced an appeal of the verdict by the Crown. A panel of the Ontario Court of Appeal heard arguments as to whether to order a new trial. Among the grounds for the appeal were the status of certain evidence and allegedly inflammatory statements by defense counsel Christie.

Stephen Reistetter, who had been accused of kidnapping Czech Jews and sending them to concentration camps while a member of the paramilitary Hlinka Guard, was released when the Crown decided that it lacked the necessary evidence to prosecute. Sol Littman, Canadian representative of the Simon Wiesenthal Center, expressed doubts about the government's commitment to the prosecution of war criminals. Speaking about the Justice Department, he claimed that "they opposed prosecution for 40 years and when told by Parliament to go ahead, they did it without any sincerity and zeal." Other Jewish spokespersons were less harsh but nonetheless disappointed, especially since the charges had been dismissed with prejudice, meaning that they could not be brought again should fresh evidence materialize. The decision on how to proceed was made by Justice Minister Kim Campbell on the advice of the war-crimes unit.

JEWISH COMMUNITY

Demography

Canada conducted its decennial census on June 1, 1991; information on ethnicity and religion was expected to be released early in 1993. In the Canadian census, "Jewish" has usually been an option both under religion and under ethnicity, with people counted as Jewish who list their religion as Jewish or list no religion but claim Jewish ethnicity. While this method has provided the community with a wealth of information, it has also caused some confusion about the exact number of Jews in the country. In the 1991 census, instead of asking an individual to specify his or her own ethnic identity, the question asked about the ethnic identity of ancestors. In the 1981 census, the total of Jews came to 312,060.

The Council of Jewish Federations (CJF) planned to use the census to create a data bank on social and demographic trends within the community. Prof. Jim Torczyner of McGill University, who was analyzing the data for the CJF, said that he expected the census to show increasing poverty among Jews, increased migration from Montreal to points west, and more elderly Jews than in the previous census.

In late 1990, the CRB Foundation commissioned a major survey of Canadian Jewry that was carried out by the Goldfarb polling organization. The sample consisted of 409 people in Toronto, 352 in Montreal, and 210 elsewhere, for a total of 971. An analysis of the data by Steven Cohen, a consultant to the CRB Foundation, showed that Canadian Jews are more traditionally observant and more highly organized than American Jews. They are also more Zionistic, more closely identified with Israel, and more conversant with Hebrew and Yiddish. Goldfarb noted that 55 percent of Canadian Jews do not feel totally accepted in Canadian society, despite the fact that "Jews have participated in virtually every stream of Canadian society: in every field and at every level. We participate fully, but we still have feelings of anxiety that it will not always be that way."

Allied Jewish Community Services (AJCS) in Montreal carried out further analysis of the CRB data. Their study showed that Montreal Jews come out even more strongly than the Canadian Jewish average on most measures of Jewish identity, involvement, and practice. Among the more noteworthy statistics: 71 percent have visited Israel, 60 percent work as volunteers in Jewish community organizations, and 86 percent fast on Yom Kippur. According to AJCS official Nancy Rosenfeld, "The sense of philanthropy, attachment to Israel, strong support of Jewish education and commitment to Jewish life continue to be the main factors which make Montreal one of the top Jewish communities in North America."

On the other hand, despite its evident virtues, the Montreal community continued to suffer from an exodus of younger people due to economic, linguistic, and political considerations. The CRB survey indicated that about half of the Jews between the ages of 20 and 40 and about 40 percent overall were considering leaving Quebec. AJCS expected the 1991 census to show a decline of Quebec Jews from 96,000 in 1986 to about 90,000. There was also growing concern that the departure of young Jews entering their productive years would leave the community with an inadequate base to support the young and elderly in the dependent age groups. The president of AJCS, Maxine Sigman, estimated that about 44 percent of Quebec Jews were either under 18 or over 64 years of age. Both she and her successor, Harvey Wolfe, indicated that the community might reconsider its funding allocation to national and overseas causes because of the pressing local needs caused by demographic shifts. Immigration, perhaps of Soviet Jews, was seen as one option for rebuilding the community. Wolfe also made youth retention one of the top priorities for his administration.

The CRB data additionally showed that only about 5 percent of Montreal Jews support Quebec independence; 73 percent of Ashkenazim and 69 percent of Sephardim claim to be bilingual; and some 19 percent live below the poverty line.

Growth continued in the Sephardic community in Montreal. The Sephardim had a higher birthrate than their Ashkenazi confreres and a younger age distribution. The Communauté Sépharade du Québec (CSQ) estimated that there were about 25,000 Sephardim in the province, accounting for nearly 30 percent of the Jewish population.

Jewish Immigrant Aid Services estimated that 1,000 to 1,200 Soviet Jews came to Canada in 1990, about 150 of them settling in Montreal. Most went to the Toronto area. Some additional Soviet Jews came to Canada as tourists and then sought refugee status. Meanwhile, Montreal Jewish community representatives and the Quebec minister of immigration, Monique Gagnon-Tremblay, were exploring ways to encourage Soviet Jewish immigration to the province, which both parties saw as a means to bolster sagging population. On a visit to Moscow, the minister met with Soviet Jews to discuss immigration possibilities.

Communal Affairs

The economic recession weighed heavily on the Canadian Jewish community, with a serious impact on fund-raising and budgeting. The budget crunch was exacerbated by the needs of Operation Exodus for the resettlement of Soviet Jews in Israel, compelling policymakers to reexamine priorities carefully. National organizations, which often depend on the local federations for support through the National Budgeting Conference (NBC), were particularly vulnerable in the competition for funds between local agencies and services, on the one hand, and Israel needs, on the other.

At the local level, the Toronto federation, then known as Toronto Jewish Congress, had to make program cuts because of a diversion of funds to Operation Exodus. There was also a budget crunch in Vancouver, and Ottawa had to streamline its operations. In Montreal, local agencies had to absorb cuts of about 6 percent. The Jewish Community Center in Toronto had trouble making payments on its nearly $7-million debt, which was incurred during an expansionary phase. B'nai Brith Canada also felt the pressure and decided to cut its funding of the B'nai Brith Youth Organization.

Despite the financial difficulties, a number of new projects were under way. In Vancouver, a Holocaust Center, to be attached to the Jewish Community Center, was started. The initial funding came from survivors and their children, who had been accumulating money for that purpose for some years. In Winnipeg, Congregation Rosh Pina, with funds contributed by the Manitoba government, built a senior citizens' home at a cost of about $4.5 million. The Jewish community in Kelowna decided to build the Okanagan Jewish Community Center to serve the Okanagan Valley area in the interior of British Columbia. About 40 percent of the funding came from the provincial government. The new Mount Sinai Hospital in Cote St. Luc, Quebec, was opened by Health Minister Marc-Yvan Cote in October. The hospital, which moved from St. Agathe, specializes in respiratory care.

In Montreal there were two closings. The Davis Branch of the YM-YWHA in suburban Cote St. Luc was shut down and the property sold to the Hebrew Academy. The building was subsequently demolished and a new school erected. In addition, the Jewish Introduction Service ran out of money and closed. It was a nonprofit matchmaking service that was unable to obtain regular community funding and relied on private support.

The Communauté Sépharade du Québec had been playing an increasingly active role in community affairs, was a constituent agency of AJCS, and was active in the Sephardi division of the Combined Jewish Appeal. The CSQ helped to develop a second campus for Ecole Maimonide, in St. Laurent, complementing the existing facility in Cote St. Luc. One measure of the increasing importance of the largely French-speaking Sephardi community was the introduction of regular French articles, written by French-speaking reporters, in the *Canadian Jewish News*. The CSQ election of a new board of directors in November was marked by some discord. An insurgent group headed by Michel Abessera denounced the "antidemocratic practices of a small clique" that had dominated the community for 25 years, charges that were denied vigorously by Salomon Oziel and other leaders of the CSQ.

The decision by the administration of the Jewish Family Services Social Service Center in Montreal (JFSSSC) to remain open on Shemini Azeret, Simhat Torah, the seventh day of Passover, and the second day of Shavuot highlighted the dilemma of Jewish institutions increasingly dependent on government funding. In a city where community bodies generally are closed on all Jewish holidays, the decision created an uproar, especially in the rabbinate. JFSSSC director-general Leon Ouaknine defended the announced policy on the grounds that "staying closed has caused a lot of problems. Social service care . . . [is] just as important as medical care." Rabbi Yonah Rosner, president of the Rabbinical Council of Canada's eastern region, described the decision as a "desecration" and contended that it amounted to JFSSSC "dissociating itself" from the community. Eventually the center decided to remain closed for the two holidays in the fall of 1991, with further discussions to follow. Ouaknine claimed that the problem was primarily financial, based on the center's obligations regarding vacation pay under collective agreements.

Canadian Hadassah-WIZO formally affiliated with Hadassah International, a six-year-old grouping of Hadassah organizations outside the United States.

Israel-Related Activity

Although Canadian Jews were generally pleased with their country's role in the Gulf War, they continued to be divided and in many cases apprehensive regarding Canada's general policy toward Israel and the Arab-Israeli conflict. Canadian Jewish Congress, holding its first national executive committee meeting in Israel, in January, heard Israeli deputy foreign minister Benjamin Netanyahu criticize Canada's UN voting record, especially support for hostile resolutions. Defense Minister Moshe Arens echoed the theme in very strong terms, calling for an improvement in relations. Labor party leader Shimon Peres also expressed concern about Canada's UN positions.

McGill University professor Ruth Wisse delivered a strongly worded speech in June in which she attacked Jewish critics of Israel for serving Arab or anti-Semitic ends. Speaking to the annual meeting of the Association of Jewish Community Organization Personnel meeting in Montreal, she contended that the worst thing for Jews to do was to focus attention on alleged Israeli misdeeds rather than persistent Arab hostility. She was particularly critical of fellow academics who were "crawling under their chairs" to avoid the political fight on behalf of Israel, and firmly opposed

Diaspora Jews engaging in divisive and demoralizing debate on Israeli policy.

In the economic sphere, businessman Charles Bronfman's Claridge Investment Ltd. bought one-third of Osem, the Israeli food company. In addition, it was announced that the success of a $4-million private loan fund that Bronfman developed to help Israeli small businesses had stimulated the Israeli government to carry the idea further with a loan fund of its own. In his capacity as honorary chairman of Canada-Israel Securities Ltd., Bronfman was also involved in Israel's launch of the first Canadian-dollar Israel Bonds issue. The variable interest rate would be slightly less than on Canadian government bonds of similar maturities.

Education

Existing conditions in Jewish education continued as in the past. Toronto Jewish schools maintained their growth but remained unsuccessful in the long quest to obtain government funding. Legal actions based on contention of unequal treatment were contemplated. The twelve elementary schools and eight high schools in Metro Toronto increased their enrollment from 9,258 to 9,608. With 5,996 students in supplementary programs, the total of 15,604 receiving Jewish education was at a record level. Some of the schools were among the largest on the continent, with over 3,000 students in Associated Hebrew Day Schools and over 1,000 each in the United Synagogue Day School and Eitz Chaim. But educators were concerned that about half the students left Jewish schools by ninth grade, and only 10 percent completed Jewish high schools. The three government-supported schools in Alberta enrolled a total of 766 students.

In Montreal, the total day-school enrollment at the primary and secondary levels was 6,623, with 1,084 students in supplementary schools. These figures were virtually identical to the previous year's in the case of the day schools, with the supplementary schools down slightly. The venerable Montreal day-school system, United Talmud Torahs, turned itself around with managerial and financial help from the federation and then began an expansion and renovation of one of its two campuses.

In Vancouver, the federation increased its support of the three day schools, and the British Columbia government provided support at 35 percent of the public-school cost per student. There were 649 students in day schools and 594 in supplementary schools, for a total of 1,243.

There were at least two negative notes on the educational scene. The Torah Academy in the South End of Winnipeg closed at the end of the school year because of declining enrollment. The federal government's Heritage Language Program was reduced, thereby eliminating subventions for Hebrew and Yiddish instruction for nearly 23,000 children in Jewish schools. Tuition increases were necessary to offset the shortfall.

Community Relations

Mordecai Richler's September 23 *New Yorker* article about the foibles of Quebec's language policies became a cause célèbre during September and October, threatening to disrupt relations between Jews and French Quebecers. The prominent novelist's sharp pen and satirical style produced a penetrating critique of the evolution of Quebec politics and public policy since the election of the Parti Québécois in 1976. In a society that is exceptionally sensitive about public criticism, especially to an external audience, this was seen as a serious betrayal. Even though Richler was writing on his own account, the fact that he is Jewish led to calls for the Jewish community in Quebec to disavow his views, thereby creating a major community relations problem for communal agencies, especially Canadian Jewish Congress. The problem was compounded by Richler's contention that anti-Semitism is an integral component of modern Quebec nationalism, even though the evidence he cited was regarded by many as out of date. The flap over his accusations of anti-Semitism, which were in fact a relatively minor part of a lengthy article, distracted attention from his main message. This was that the language laws were petty and silly, and that nationalist policies in Quebec exceeded the bounds of common sense and now constituted a danger to the well-being of the country. He charged that non-francophones felt unwelcome in his native province and would continue to move away regardless of the outcome of the referendum that was scheduled for October 1992.

The response in the French media was surprisingly intense. Lise Bissonnette, publisher of *Le Devoir*, suggested that legal action might be taken against the writer. A Quebec diplomat in New York was quoted in the same newspaper as saying that Richler's opinions were not surprising and were "largely known and shared by the New York Jewish milieu." Jewish themes were prominent in many of the attacks on Richler, thereby artificially creating a Jewish issue when Jewish matters were really peripheral to Richler's argument. Thus Hy Goldman, a founder of the Jewish-French Dialogue St. Urbain, stated that Richler was "in a time warp" on the question of anti-Semitism and lamented the author's attempt to connect the anti-Semitism of the 1930s and 1940s with contemporary Quebec nationalism. CJC issued a carefully crafted public statement defending Richler's right to express his views but taking issue with him on the anti-Semitism question.

Richler was unrepentant in several media appearances, attacking his critics for "intellectual dishonesty, hysteria, and vulgarity" and reiterating his contempt for Quebec's language policies. Furthermore, he contended that the anti-Semitism element of his argument was essential because we must understand "our roots. . . . The point is we are riding dark, tribal horses. It could be unpleasant. . . . We are playing dangerous games." McGill University professor Ruth Wisse carried that theme further by arguing that Quebec seemed to be departing from the model of tolerance that characterized North America, in contrast to Europe. "Quebec is the first place in North America to use the 'protection of the collectivity' as an excuse to limit certain rights of its citizens. . . . Quebec, then, may be a test case of minority influence in North America" (*Canadian Jewish News*, October 10, 1991).

Sunday shopping persisted as an issue, particularly in Ontario, which had quite strict prohibitions and a long history of contention over them. The legal developments in 1991 included a decision of the Ontario Court of Appeal in March overturning a lower court decision that had invalidated the existing law. By the end of the year, the legislature passed a new law, which made some modifications but still prohibited Sunday store openings in most cases. Thus Sabbath-observing consumers remained inconvenienced. Moreover, store owners who wanted to close on Saturday and open on Sunday were still compelled to make a religious declaration to the government. Jewish organizations remained dissatisfied but were hopeful that continued consumer pressure might bring about changes in the future.

There was a brief flurry of interest in *shehitah* (ritual slaughter) in Quebec and Ontario. For a time in the spring there was some indication that the Quebec government might go along with an interest group's recommendation on an animal-protection law that would effectively ban kosher slaughter, but prompt and vigorous Jewish community action helped to forestall any action. In the Ontario government sector, two Jewish employees succeeded in their fight against the supervisors' refusal to grant them time off without pay to observe Rosh Hashanah. The Ontario Crown Employees Settlement Board ruled that they had suffered discrimination. In another case, an Orthodox woman denied a term job with an Ontario ministry because of her Sabbath observance received an apology from the minister.

Ontario's Science Center was found guilty in April of violating an antidiscrimination law by virtue of its contract with Oman for a children's science exhibit that called for a boycott of Israeli goods and services. The center was ordered to cease and desist in any such action, make public all relevant documents, and ensure through administrative changes that there would be no recurrence. The center also agreed to mount an exhibit showing the contributions of different cultural groups to science and how science can help to overcome discrimination.

Religion

The issue of the role of women in the synagogue remained contentious. Several Ontario members of the Conservative Cantors Assembly broke away from that body and formed a new group to protest the assembly's decision to admit female cantors to membership. They claimed that a woman leading public prayer was a violation of Jewish law. Cantor Eliezer Kirshblum was one of the leaders of the traditionalists; other prominent Toronto cantors involved were Louis Danto, David Bagley, and Paul Kowarsky.

Montreal's Conservative Shaare Zion Congregation inaugurated an alternative Sabbath service in which women were allowed to read the Torah and have *aliyot*, which was not the practice in the main service. Rabbi Lawrence Perlman saw an openness to alternatives "within the framework of Jewish law" as a sign of spiritual growth in the congregation.

A conference on the future of Reform Judaism in Canada, held at Ottawa's

Temple Israel in October, discussed the possibility that a decline in interest in Orthodoxy in the country would create greater opportunities for Reform. Rabbi Elyse Goldstein called for Reform to redefine the meaning of *mitzvot*, while Rabbi Daniel Gottlieb urged Reform Jews to take greater responsibility for their institutions.

Culture

A number of films of Jewish interest appeared this year. Among the most noteworthy was *Deadly Currents*, directed by Toronto filmmaker Simcha Jacobovici and produced by Ric Bienstock and Elliot Halpern and winner of the Grand Prix gold medal at the International Documentary Festival of Nyon in Switzerland. The film, which was shown on CBC television as well as in theaters, explores the conflict between Israelis and Palestinians from the perspectives of both groups within the context of the *intifada*. Another documentary, by Montrealers Howard Reitman and Sid Goldberg, is a record of the 1990 March of the Living, which focuses on the 340 Canadians among thousands of Jewish youngsters who march from Auschwitz to Birkenau and visit several other death camps in Poland.

Two films set in Montreal attempt to make the lives of Hassidim more relevant to viewers in a period when tension between them and Québécois neighbors has become an important issue of community relations. *Moïse*, written by Michelle Allen, produced by Ina Fichman, and directed by Howard Goldberg for the National Film Board and Radio Quebec, tries to break down the stereotypes and illuminate the inner lives of the Hassidim of Outremont through the story of a young Hassidic couple. The documentary *Bonjour! Shalom!* directed by Gary Beitel, which has a similar purpose, contains interviews with both French Quebecers and Hassidim as well as scenes of Hassidic life. The juxtaposition of a group of Jews trying to preserve their traditions while living among Québécois intellectuals and artists who have thrown off religious constraints and see themselves as the avantgarde of their society is particularly graphic.

The Quarrel, a Canadian production with Canadian actors and an Israeli director, is based on a story by Chaim Grade. The film depicts the ongoing argument between two old friends who survived the Holocaust, were reunited in Montreal, and there resumed the intense dialogue that had characterized their friendship in prewar Poland. Fundamental theological and philosophical issues raised by the destruction of European Jewry are brought to life in spirited disputation between the two friends, one who remained devout and the other who rejected religion. Sondra Gotlieb's book about Winnipeg in the 1950s was made into the film *True Confections*, written and directed by Gail Singer. It is the story of a young Jewish girl's coming of age and her struggle against the conformity of her family. The late Montreal artist Sam Borenstein is the subject of a documentary by his daughter, Joyce Borenstein, *The Colours of My Father*. The film shows how the painter's art enabled him to overcome tremendous adversity in life.

In theater, *Bitter Friends* by Gordon Rayfield opened in Toronto in January. It is a fictional drama based loosely on the Pollard case. Arthur Milner's controversial *Masada* had its premiere in Toronto in April.

Seymour Mayne and Shel Krakofsky launched a new magazine, *Parchment*, for Jewish creative writing, with Krakofsky as editor. Israeli-Canadian poet Rafi Aaron gave readings of his poetry in several North American cities, including Montreal, Toronto, New York, and Los Angeles during a 45-day tour in January and February. Much of the material came from his recently published collection *The Lost and Found*.

In commemoration of the 500th anniversary of the expulsion of the Jews from Spain, André Elbaz created a series of 23 silk screens, entitled *Of Fire and Exile*, that were exhibited at the University of Ottawa. They depict the history of the Inquisition and the exile and their impact on Spanish Jewry.

The new Musée des Réligions in Nicolet, Quebec, which seeks to promote greater understanding and tolerance between religions, contains a considerable amount of Jewish material, much of it donated by Jewish institutions and private individuals in Montreal. Another Quebec institution, the Musée du Québec, purchased 28 works of art by five Montreal Jewish artists who worked in the 1930s and 1940s.

Yehuda Elberg served as writer-in-residence for the Yiddish Studies program at Oxford University, England. The National Library selected Cheryl Jaffee to be curator of the Jacob M. Lowy Collection of Hebraica and Judaica. The J.I. Segal Awards of Montreal's Jewish Public Library were conferred on Sylvia M. Gelber and Sam Simchovitch. Arlazar Eliashiv won the Jacob Zipper Education Prize.

Publications

The almost legendary Samuel Bronfman, founder of the Seagram's liquor business and one of the great leaders of Canadian Jewry, is the subject of *Mr. Sam: The Life and Times of Samuel Bronfman* by Michael Marrus, a comprehensive biography by a noted historian, who was given access to Bronfman's personal papers by his family. Marrus examines the personality of Bronfman, his business style, generous philanthropy, confrontations with anti-Semitism, his central role in the building of the Canadian Jewish Congress and later, after the Six Day War, his role in raising large amounts of money for Israel. In the author's view, "He was a mythic figure, a business genius. . . . He was a kind of Jewish prince."

The saga of another Montreal Jewish businessman named Sam, who built his family grocery business into one of the major retailing operations in central Canada, is related in *Steinberg: The Breakup of a Family Empire* by Ann Gibbon and Peter Hadekel. The book chronicles the family feud that led to the business being sold to outside interests after Steinberg's death.

Mordecai Richler collected a number of his essays, reviews, and articles and published them as *Broadsides*. Most of the book consists of his views on other writers. Richler himself is the subject of Rachel Feldhay Brenner's *The Response to the Holocaust in Mordecai Richler's Writing.* She analyzes the tension between the particularism due to the effects of the Holocaust and the writer's attempt to identify with universal values.

Other noteworthy new works this year were: Rabbi Dow Marmur's *The Star of Return: Judaism After the Holocaust; Burn This Gossip* by Sheldon and Judith Godfrey, a biography of the 19th-century Canadian Jewish politician George Benjamin; *Gathering Rosebuds* by Abraham Lieff, an autobiographical memoir by a former Ontario Supreme Court justice, which also provides much information on the history of the Ottawa Jewish community. *From Lebanon to the Intifada—The Jewish Lobby and Canadian Middle East Policy* by Ronnie Miller concludes that "the *intifada* intensified the divisions within the Jewish community which first emerged in 1982," in an alignment roughly parallel to what exists within the Israeli political system. In *Les Partis Réligieux en Israël*, a study of those parties from the founding of the state until the present, Julien Bauer confronts the problems of trying to accommodate religious interests in a formally secular state. Jacques Langlais and David Rome collaborated on *Jews and French Quebecers/Two Hundred Years of Shared History.* The authors take pride in what they see as a model of cooperative living between different peoples, despite the existence of anti-Semitism in the society. Louis Levendel wrote a comprehensive history of a surprisingly diverse subject in *A Century of the Canadian Jewish Press 1880–1980.* A much longer historical story, this one of a prominent Jewish symbol, is told by Rabbi W. Gunther Plaut in *The Magen David.*

Harold M. Waller and Daniel J. Elazar received the National Jewish Book Award in the United States for *Maintaining Consensus: The Canadian Jewish Polity in the Postwar World.* The Central Jewish Community of Mexico presented the Fernando Jeno International Award of Literature to Nachman Shemen for *Batziung Tzu Mensch.* The Toronto Jewish Congress Book Committee Awards were presented to Ibolya Grossman and Martin Lockshin.

Personalia

Dr. Victor Goldbloom was appointed commissioner of official languages for the federal government. Stephen Bornstein became Ontario's senior representative in Quebec. Rose Wolfe assumed the post of chancellor of the University of Toronto, and Stephen Fienberg became vice-president (academic affairs) of York University. Bernard Ostry was reappointed as chairman and CEO of TV Ontario and was elected chairman of the Shaw Festival. Murray Koffler and the late Ray Wolfe were elected to the Junior Achievement Canadian Business Hall of Fame. The Order of British Columbia was presented to Jack Diamond, Dr. Vivien Basco, and Jack Bell.

David Rome received the Prix d'Excellence du Québec for his work in fostering intercultural relations. The Metro Toronto Council presented the Gardiner Award for community service to Susan Cohon. Jean Charles-Chebat was awarded the Prix Jean-Jacques Rousseau by the Association Canadienne Français pour L'avancement des Sciences.

In the community, Maureen Molot became the first female president of Ottawa's Jewish community council, the Vaad Ha'ir. Gloria Levitt was elected president of B'nai Brith Women/Canada, and Esther Matlow assumed the presidency of Hadassah-WIZO. J. Stephen Lipper was elected president of Canadian Friends of the Hebrew University. In Montreal, Harvey Wolfe became president of Allied Jewish Community Services and Stephen Vineberg president of the Jewish General Hospital. Canadian Jewish Congress presented the Samuel Bronfman Medal to Barbara Stern for her outstanding work on behalf of that organization. Dr. Harvey Sigman received the Samuel Bronfman Award from AJCS for his service to the Montreal Jewish community.

Among leading Jews who died in 1991 were the following: Moe Abramowitz, longtime YMHA basketball player and coach, in January, aged 87; William Gittes, fund-raiser and community leader, in January, aged 95; Marie Berdugo-Cohen, author of a book on the Jewish experience in Morocco, in February, aged 63; Col. Yehoshua Bar-Am, JNF *shaliah*, in February, aged 60; Ann Steindel, historian of the Winnipeg community, in March, aged 80; Dr. Joseph Sternberg, nuclear medicine pioneer, in March, aged 79; Nina Cohen, former president of Hadassah-WIZO, in March, aged 84; Min Heft, community leader, in April, aged 86; David Peters, former president of the Toronto Zionist Council, in May, aged 79; Luciano della Pergola, music professor, opera singer, and cantor, in May, aged 80; Sen. David Croll, trail-blazing politician and member of Parliament, known as Canada's social conscience, with three Jewish "firsts" in Canada—mayor, provincial cabinet member, and senator—in June, aged 91; Rabbi Chaim Denburg, noted scholar and synagogue leader, in August, aged 73; Max Federman, prominent labor union organizer, in August, aged 89; Walter Hess, executive vice-president of the United Israel Appeal and former educator, in September, aged 53; Allan Grossman, former Ontario cabinet minister and the first Jew in a Conservative government in Ontario, in September, aged 80; Dr. Jack Shekter, Hamilton physician and community leader, in October, aged 67; Fagel Gartner Krolitzky, pianist, teacher, and choir director, in October, aged 79; Dr. Tovi Cheryl Comet-Walerstein, physician, researcher, and lecturer on Jewish and medical topics, in November, aged 38; Shmuel Isackson, educator and former principal of Herzliah High School in St. Laurent, Quebec, in December, aged 61; Dr. Levi Jacober, a founder and former principal of the Associated Hebrew Day Schools in Toronto, in December, aged 88; and Patricia Appleton, organizational volunteer, in December, aged 47.

HAROLD M. WALLER

Western Europe

Great Britain

National Affairs

IN 1991, THE CONSERVATIVE GOVERNMENT of John Major sought both to strengthen the country's economic position and to regain the popularity forfeited by imposition of the community charge (poll tax) in 1990. As early as January the government announced an alleviation of the community charge; in March came a surprise announcement that much of the burden of the community charge would be transferred from the individual to the central government, which would recoup most of the cost through an increase in value-added tax.

The British economic picture remained decidedly mixed. Interest and mortgage rates declined; inflation dropped from 9 percent in February to 6.4 percent in April; and unemployment showed a rising trend, reaching 7.6 percent in May.

The electorate expressed its frustration in a sensational Liberal Democrat victory in the Ribble Valley by-election in March as well as in parliamentary by-elections in April and May and local elections in May (in England and Wales), when both Labor and the Liberal Democrats scored a number of sensational gains against the Tories. The main themes in all these contests were the community charge, the economic situation, and the National Health Service, Labor alleging that the government's health reforms were in fact subordinating clinical to commercial considerations. Urban riots in August and September in Birmingham, Newcastle, and Oxford underscored the government's failure to deal with persistent social problems, and its popularity remained low.

Relations with Israel

THE GULF WAR

Following the outbreak of the Gulf War in January, Israel's policy of restraint won warm support in Britain. Prime Minister John Major described Iraqi missile attacks on Israeli cities as "utterly deplorable" and "wholly unforgivable." "The remarkable restraint which Israel has shown so far is a sign of strength not weakness and will be widely recognized as such," he said in the House of Commons in January. After Iraq's third missile attack on Israel, Foreign Secretary Douglas Hurd told the House that the government had "nothing but admiration and respect" for Israel and urged the Israeli government to continue its policy of nonretaliation. (Sympathy notwithstanding, at the end of January the Foreign Office revealed that the government had decided to continue its nine-year-old embargo on arms sales to Israel.) In February, Defense Secretary Tom King wrote to Chief Rabbi Lord Immanuel Jakobovits expressing sympathy with the feelings of British Jews at the "barbaric attacks against Israel with Scuds." "The use of such indiscriminate weapons of terror against innocent civilians," he said, "shows clearly the nature of Saddam Hussein's regime." The Labor party, the Trades Union Congress (TUC), and 17 individual trade unions sent messages of support and solidarity to their Israeli counterparts.

The government's attitude to the PLO hardened in view of its support for the Iraqis. It had behaved in a "discreditable and foolish manner in the Gulf conflict," Foreign Office minister Douglas Hogg told Parliament. Although it was impossible to discount the PLO's importance as a representative of the Palestinians, he said, its assurances that it accepted Israel and rejected terrorism would have to be "treated with a great deal of caution." Foreign Secretary Hurd played down the option of Palestinian statehood prior to visiting Cairo in February. His view, which Prime Minister Major supported, envisaged flexible political arrangements for the West Bank and Gaza, which took account of Israel's concern for security.

Although Natan Meron, outgoing minister at London's Israeli embassy, said in September that he was "very happy with our relations with Britain now," old criticisms of Israeli policy in fact resurfaced in the months following the war. On a visit to Israel and the occupied territories in May, Foreign Secretary Hurd expressed disapproval of the West Bank settlements; in November, the Foreign Office's Hogg described Israel's policy in the occupied territories as "wrong and destructive." He told a meeting organized by the Institute of Jewish Affairs that Israel's future security depended on it reaching a peace agreement with the Arabs. Without compromising Israel's security within borders recognized by all other states in the area, he said, the Palestinians had "the right to self-government and political rights, and the British government believes, too, must have land to make a reality of these rights." In December Hogg rejected calls for government action against Israel for alleged denial of human rights, but expressed the government's deep concern about the condition of the Palestinians in the occupied territories and Gaza strip. "For the moment at least," he told Parliament, "I should prefer to rely on the process of negotiation."

Israel also came under pressure for its "hostage" policy. During talks with Prime Minister Yitzhak Shamir of Israel in London's Downing Street in April, Prime Minister Major appealed to Israel to encourage the freeing of Western hostages held in Lebanon by releasing Muslim cleric Sheikh Abdul Karim Obeid, who had been abducted from Lebanon by the Israelis two years previously. In June Britain played a mediating role in London discussions and negotiations with Israeli officials aimed at securing a deal with Lebanon to free Israeli and Western hostages in exchange for Obeid and other Israeli-held prisoners. In response to Major's request that Israel free some of its Shi'ite prisoners, Israel stated its determination to do nothing until it received solid information about missing Israeli soldiers.

Foreign Minister Farouk-al-Sharaa of Syria held talks in London in February with Foreign Secretary Hurd, the first such high-level contact since diplomatic relations between Britain and Syria were reestablished in November 1990. The Board of Deputies of British Jews protested to the Foreign Office in July when minister Hogg, after talks with European Community ministers in Luxemburg, stated that Britain would be "willing to see" the arms embargo against Syria lifted. Britain itself "did not anticipate selling arms to Syria," he explained.

Fears that the PLO might be regaining international recognition were aroused in November by Hogg's statement that the time would undoubtedly come when Britain would want to resume contact with the PLO at a ministerial level. But Prime Minister Major reassured the Board of Deputies that no immediate upgrading of Britain's relations with the PLO was contemplated. The PLO, he said, had been sidelined in the Middle East equation, and the government intended to keep it that way. However, meetings between senior PLO members and Foreign Office officials continued to take place.

Both the Conservative Friends of Israel (CFI) and Labor Friends of Israel (LFI) sponsored visits to Israel by groups of MPs. CFI appointed a campaign director to promote understanding of Israel among local councils and constituencies and announced plans to campaign in the next parliamentary elections on behalf of Tory MPs in marginal seats who supported Israel.

In May a group of MPs led by Labor's Jimmy Wray criticized a proposed loan package, comprising a subsidized loan of £111.5 million to Israel and a grant of £41.8 million to the occupied territories, because of Israel's "unlawful appropriation of Palestinian lands" and "overt defiance of UN resolutions." In September shadow foreign secretary Gerald Kaufman praised American president George Bush for withholding a $10-billion loan guarantee to Israel until after a Middle East peace conference. Kaufman, who was elected for the first time to Labor's national executive, was addressing the pro-Palestinian Labor Middle East Council during the Labor party's Brighton conference. A Labor government, said Kaufman, would dedicate itself to a peace settlement in the Middle East that gave Palestinians the right to self-determination and also ended Israel's chronic insecurity. The conference supported a Poale Zion resolution urging support for a negotiated peace between Israel and the Palestinians under the terms of UN Security Council resolutions 242 and 338, but with an amendment calling on the party to support the right to Palestinian self-determination, not excluding a Palestinian state.

Nazi War Criminals

The War Crimes Bill allowing the prosecution of alleged Nazi war criminals currently living in Britain became law in June. It passed the House of Commons in March by a majority of 166 on a free vote, after the House had voted 177 to 17 to block the possibility of amendment. In the House of Lords, two amendments were presented, one postponing implementation of the bill for six months, the other extending it to cover war crimes committed in territory held by Japan in World War II and by Iraq between July 1, 1990, and March 12, 1991. The bill passed directly to the Queen for royal assent after the Lords had rejected it, in a form incorporating the first amendment, in April, and the government overruled the Lords by invoking the Parliament Act—only the second time it had done so since 1945.

A seven-member special war-crimes unit at Scotland Yard, set up under the authorization of the home secretary and led by Detective Chief Superintendent Edward Bathgate, immediately began investigations. In November Bathgate was in the former Soviet Union making contact with war-crimes investigators there. Also in Russia at the time were legal experts from the special casework section of the Crown Prosecution Service. Following Bathgate's visit, government officials in the former Soviet republics pledged to help the British detectives in their search for evidence. Other members of the unit were in Israel working with officials of Israel's war-crimes unit.

In November Prime Minister Major told a Board of Deputies delegation that the government's commitment to bringing alleged war criminals to justice remained, but that finding sufficient evidence to prosecute remained a problem. In December Attorney-General Sir Patrick Mayhew informed the Commons that no decision could yet be made on when to begin prosecutions.

Anti-Semitism and Racism

Both in early January, following Britain's expulsion of 75 Iraqis suspected of involvement in planning terror attacks on British targets, and during the Gulf War, the Community Security Organization (CSO), the Board of Deputies' security arm, warned the Jewish community and Zionist and communal organizations of possible attacks by pro-Iraqi terrorists and also by extreme right-wing groups using the war to exploit racial tensions. Heightened activity by extreme right-wing groups was in fact reflected in Board of Deputies' statistics issued in June, which showed 50 percent more anti-Semitic incidents in the first five months of 1991 than in the same period in 1990.

In January the Holocaust Memorial in London's Hyde Park was daubed; tombstones were desecrated at Fawcett Road cemetery, Portsmouth (January), and at Exeter and Grimsby (September); arson attacks and vandalism were reported against Hasmonean Boys' School, Hendon, and synagogues in Birmingham and Staines (January), Greenford (April), Wanstead and Woodford, northeast London

(June). A pig's head was nailed to the door of the small Sunderland synagogue on Yom Kippur. Kosher food suppliers also experienced arson attacks: in Tottenham, North London, in January, and Israeli-owned Bis-Bas in November. The appearance in February of a series of anti-Semitic leaflets and posters in many areas, alleging that a Jewish conspiracy controlled the war, suggested that the far-right British National party (BNP) and neo-Nazi Colin Jordan's "Gothic Ripples" group had joined the campaign. In May the Tyne and Wear Anti-Fascists Association reported increased activity against minorities by extreme right-wing groups in northeast England, one of the targets being Gateshead's ultra-Orthodox community.

Active attempts were made throughout the year to combat the threats of racism and neo-Nazism. Among such activities was a mass demonstration in London's East End in March, organized by Anti-Fascist Action, to demand an end to weekly gatherings of the National Front (NF) and British National party (BNP) newspaper-sellers; in May, antiracist groups called on the government to outlaw the BNP and also demanded that Home Secretary Kenneth Baker ban a BNP march through Thamesmead Estate, south-east London. Although the police also requested the ban, Baker refused on the grounds that the event did not meet the specific requirements of the Public Order Act. In June the Manchester city council canceled an NF meeting and march following a protest campaign, in which Manchester Jewish students were prominent. In York, in November, a 600-strong picket, many from the Union of Jewish Students, formed a human wall across the entrance to Clifford's Tower, scene of a medieval Jewish massacre, to prevent a BNP meeting.

Growing awareness of the need for public education in this area was also evident. The National Union of Teachers' national conference in April adopted a policy calling for teachers to challenge anti-Semitic remarks by pupils and staff, give equal treatment to Jewish culture and festivals in multicultural education, include the Holocaust in the curriculum, and support general protests against anti-Semitism. In June the Trades Union Congress's national education center agreed to include anti-Semitism in its "Tackling Racism at Work" course. In July a British branch of the Inter-Parliamentary Council Against Anti-Semitism was formed, its aim to monitor and inform parliamentarians and the public of signs of anti-Semitism and react to anti-Semitic attacks. The council, which was linked to groups in more than 30 international parliaments, also wanted to promote education about the Holocaust.

In August the Commonwealth Jewish Council meeting in Jerusalem established a London-based "rapid response unit" to help remote Jewish communities around the world combat anti-Semitism and anti-Zionism.

Racist literature continued to cause concern. In January some 20 Jewish organizations received copies of the *Holohoax* by "Simon Weaselstool"; in March *Zionism and Internal Security*, a book containing extracts from *The Protocols of the Elders of Zion*, was for sale at the Moslem Information Center in Islington, North London. There were indications that the authorities were taking the problem more seriously than in the past. In September the Crown Prosecution Service asked the police to make inquiries about a booklet, *The Longest Hatred: An Examination of Anti-Gentilism*, with a foreword by Lady Birdwood, that had been sent to MPs in July. In September *Lord Horror* by David Brent, published by Savoy Books and based on the life of British World War II traitor William Joyce ("Lord Haw-Haw"), was banned under the Obscene Publications Act, though no reason was given.

The first prosecutions for the distribution of anti-Semitic material ordered by the attorney general under section 3 of the Public Order Act (1986) resulted in a guilty verdict against Francis Patrician Walsh, aged 66, in September, for possessing anti-Semitic and racially inflammatory material likely to stir up racial hatred. Walsh, who was arrested for displaying two racist placards in Bethnal Green, North London, was fined £10 for obstructing the highway and was legally bound to keep the peace for a year, on pain of receiving a stiffer £100-penalty. In October, 78-year-old Dowager Lady Birdwood was found guilty of ten charges of distributing and possessing thousands of anti-Semitic leaflets. She was sentenced to two years' conditional discharge plus £500 costs and warned that she would be sent to prison if she continued to break the law. Lady Birdwood, who lived in West London, in 1973 founded the anti-immigration "Choice" organization whose newspaper carried the slogan "Racialism Is Patriotism." In November she entered an appeal of her sentence.

In October the BNP was fined £300 for defacing tourist information signs with anti-Muslim slogans. In December Andrew Benjamin, the Jewish former owner of Cut Down, a West End record and video store, was jailed for two months for behavior likely to stir up racial hatred by selling "offensive and abusive" material.

On the legal front, a call to change public-order legislation came in June from Metropolitan Police Commissioner Sir Peter Imbert following the government's refusal to ban the BNP Thamesmead march. "The time may have come," he said, "to reexamine the difficult question of balancing the right to march with the right of the community to live without malign provocation." MP Greville Janner began a movement in Parliament for tougher measures against anti-Semites. He also sent a parliamentary question to the home secretary asking that the government's record on banning demonstrations by racists be made public.

Efforts were made to prevent the entry into Britain of extreme right-wing activists, particularly in light of reports that London might become a center for their activities. In July, when it was reported that 15 Euro MPs from extremist parties in Germany, France, and Belgium, including Jean-Marie Le Pen, head of France's National Front, were to meet in Britain, Home Secretary Baker rejected the Board of Deputies' request that Le Pen be refused entry. Members of the European Parliament, he said, were free to meet in any member state. Nevertheless, Greville Janner entered a motion in Parliament condemning the visit, and Le Pen faced a demonstration by the Union of Jewish Students, the Association of Jewish Ex-servicemen and Women (AJEX), the Board of Deputies, and antifascist groups, when he spoke at Queen Elizabeth Conference Center, Westminster, central London.

In September, following a National Union of Students' (NUS) campaign and appeals by the Board of Deputies and AJEX, Home Secretary Baker banned the entry to Britain of American Fred Leuchter on the ground that his "deeply repugnant" views were an offense to British Jews and "his presence here would not be conducive to the public good." Leuchter, author of a report claiming that no death chambers existed, had been invited by right-wing revisionist historian David Irving to address meetings in Britain. But Baker said he could not grant AJEX's request to use his powers under the Public Order Act to deny entry to French revisionist historian Robert Faurisson, as Faurisson held dual French and British citizenship. However, if Faurisson came, he would be "subject to the law on matters such as incitement to racial hatred."

In November, when it was confirmed that Le Pen would again visit Britain, a "Stop Le Pen" drive was organized by the Campaign Against Fascism in France, supported by 60 MPs who signed an early-day motion calling for the visit to be canceled and pledging to "chase, hound and disrupt" it. Hundreds of angry demonstrators greeted Le Pen's arrival and waved banners and chanted slogans when he met with far-right members of the European Parliament at a Knightsbridge, West London, hotel. In December the Board of Deputies pledged to oppose a planned visit to Britain by the American Black Muslim leader Louis Farrakhan, based on his record of anti-Semitic rhetoric.

Although Jewish and nonwhite communities cooperated in attempts to combat racist hostility, Jewish youth workers in May voiced concern that racism toward blacks among Jewish youngsters had reached "disturbing" proportions. In June the Jewish Council for Community Relations announced plans for an antiracism resource center for teachers and youth leaders and a training program for educators. By July, Orthodox and Reform educators were working with the council to introduce antiracist projects in Jewish schools, youth clubs, and Hebrew classes.

On the other side, in January, Leeds police were asked to investigate an outbreak of anti-Semitic abuse against Jewish students by local Asian youths, and in May, black youths were accused of conducting a terror campaign against Edgware and Golders Green youngsters. In June it was reported that elements in the large Luton, Bedfordshire, Muslim community were harassing and abusing Jews en route to synagogue. In December the National Union of Students launched an inquiry into campus anti-Semitism after Jewish students complained of verbal abuse and physical intimidation by members of the radical Black Students' Caucus at NUS's Blackpool conference. "We have no problem with black students generally," said Union of Jewish Students (UJS) organizer Simon Pollock. "In fact most of the positive work against racism and fascism we do on campus is in conjunction with black students."

In December UJS announced plans to join the Reform Synagogues of Great Britain and the Board of Deputies to lobby against the government's Asylum Bill, designed to limit the number of political refugees allowed into Britain.

JEWISH COMMUNITY

Demography

Britain's Jewish community had shrunk to 300,000 in 1988—from 330,000 in 1985—the lowest figure since the beginning of the century and comparing with a peak of 430,000 in the 1950s. This according to an estimate published in the *Jewish Chronicle* in September and based on figures prepared for a Board of Deputies report to be issued in 1992. The drop was attributed to the imbalance between births and deaths as well as to "social erosion," including emigration and a sharp decline in synagogue marriages.

A slight increase in synagogue marriages was recorded in 1990—a total of 1,098 compared with 1,057 in 1989—according to the Board of Deputies' Community Research Unit. Marriages under both centrist Orthodox and Liberal auspices increased (centrist Orthodox to 722 in 1990 from 679 in 1989; Liberal to 58 from 43); while there were fewer right-wing Orthodox weddings: 103 against 118. Other groups were virtually unchanged.

Some 261 religious divorce decrees were issued by both Orthodox and Reform *batei din* (rabbinical courts) in 1990, compared with 228 in 1989 and an annual 1987–1990 average of 254. Total births estimated on the basis of circumcision registration were 3,341 in 1989, compared with an annual 1985–88 average of 3,608. Burials and cremations under Jewish religious auspices rose to 4,615 in 1990 from 4,535 in 1989.

Communal Affairs

During the Gulf War, Jewish organizations and the community rallied round Israel with expressions of support and large-scale fund-raising efforts. More than 300 British Jews expressed solidarity by joining the Joint Israel Appeal's (JIA) "Exodus 1991" mission to Israel at the end of January. That month the Board of Deputies and JIA agreed on a division of responsibility: the board to watch over Jewish defense; JIA, which stepped up its £40-million campaign, to spearhead all fund-raising for Israel.

In June, 70-year-old Judge Israel Finestein was elected president of the Board of Deputies of British Jews for three years, beating fellow board vice-president Eric Moonman by 196 votes to 116. Finestein, a former president of Norwood Child Care and founder of the B'nai B'rith Hillel Foundation in the United Kingdom, succeeded Dr. Lionel Kopelowitz, who retired after serving the maximum of six consecutive years. His first duty, said Finestein, would be to enlist the energies and talents of deputies, particularly younger members and those from the provinces. His tasks would include promoting the training of young lay leaders, strengthening ties between Jews and other ethnic groups, and addressing the problems of provincial communities. In July Rosalind Preston became the board's first woman vice-president. Aubrey Rose was the other vice-president.

Jewish Care—Britain's major Jewish welfare organization, formed by the merger of the Jewish Welfare Board (JWB) and Jewish Blind Society (JBS)—entered its second year in a climate dominated by the recession. Government funding was being cut back, and donors were also feeling the pinch. With layoffs affecting many Jewish families, a record 3,500 requests for help were dealt with in 1990, 25 percent more than in 1989. At the same time, the number of elderly clients was increasing, as hard-pressed local authorities referred unprecedented numbers of cases. New referrals to the association in the first quarter of 1991 were 12.25 percent higher than in the same 1990 period, while re-referrals rose 22 percent. In March, Care executive director Melvyn Carlowe reported signs of poverty in the community at large. "We are seeing the emergence of a growing underclass of people who are the antithesis of the image the Jewish community usually enjoys," he said. Over 25 percent of Care's work was with mentally frail elderly people, the majority suffering from Alzheimer's disease.

Soviet Jewry

The movement to help Soviet Jews operated on two fronts this year, helping new immigrants settle in Israel and assisting Jews remaining in the Soviet Union/ Commonwealth of Independent States.

Financial help for new immigrants was provided through the Joint Israel Appeal (JIA)'s Campaign Exodus '91, launched in March; an art show of works by eight leading Russian Jewish artists, sponsored in April by British ORT; and the "One to One" program launched in February by the 35s, the Women's Campaign for Soviet Jewry, in conjunction with Refusenik, a group that twinned British families with newly arrived Russian families in Israel to offer financial and moral support. In January a group of Tory MPs, led by Conservative Friends of Israel chairman Michael Latham, carried clothing parcels to new Russian immigrants in Israel.

To aid in the revival of Eastern European Jewish life, the Institute of Jewish Education at Jews' College, Hendon, hosted seminars in June for Russian Jewish teachers brought to London by British groups working for Soviet Jews. In September the Student and Academic Campaign for Soviet Jewry (SACSJ) opened an office in Leningrad to help that Jewish community reestablish its religious life. The Bournemouth Committee for Soviet Jewry recruited international legal help in a program to combat Russian anti-Semitism, advise in Soviet law cases, and help ensure safe passage to all Soviet Jews wishing to emigrate. In December the London-based Central British Fund launched a "Food for Life" campaign to send supplies to Jews in Russia and the Ukraine.

The second eminent persons group visited Moscow in February, under the auspices of SACSJ, to monitor the progress of human rights in the Soviet Union. Returning in March, participants told Prime Minister Major they were not satisfied that the conditions for Britain to attend the upcoming human rights conference in Moscow had been met, especially in view of lack of progress on emigration legislation. The group welcomed the progress made in respect of human rights but was struck by the extent of abuse that still persisted.

Religion

No chief rabbi had had "so profound an effect on the life of the nation," ex-prime minister Margaret Thatcher told a dinner honoring retiring chief rabbi Lord Immanuel Jakobovits, given in February by the Jewish Educational Development Trust (JEDT) and the Chief Rabbinate Council. His leadership had shown "an unyielding commitment to principle, a refusal to seek easy popularity at the expense of integrity, and a fearless statement of values." He had left his successor "a Jewish community whose standing and confidence had never been higher," she averred.

In March Lord Jakobovits was awarded the £410,000 Templeton Prize for progress in religion. The money would be used to establish a Jakobovits Foundation for advancing the ideal of *Torah im Derech Eretz* (Torah and modern culture), particularly through projects that would promote authentic Jewish religious teaching as applied to modern conditions.

The last months of Lord Jakobovits's chief rabbinate were marred by discord. In an interview in Toronto in May, he criticized Israeli policy, which the London *Evening Standard* reported under the headline "Chief Rabbi Shames Israel." In the interview, the chief rabbi allegedly described the plight of the Palestinian refugees as "a stain on humanity," although he said that the Jews were not to blame for creating the problem. "We can not for ever dominate a million and a half Arabs," he was quoted as saying. "This blinkered attitude is self-destructive."

The interview, which Lord Jakobovits had stipulated should appear only after his retirement, aroused protest, the cancellation of fund-raising dinners under the chief rabbi's patronage, and the resignation of Michael Levy, a JIA vice-president, from the Jakobovits Foundation board. Board of Deputies president Lionel Kopelowitz described the comments as "unhelpful" at a time when total solidarity with Israel was needed. "On these matters the Chief Rabbi speaks for himself," he said, "not as a representative of Anglo-Jewry. But inevitably the world will regard his statement as authoritative and representative." Matters reached a climax when businessman and JIA vice-president Cyril Stein wrote in an open letter to the chief rabbi: "The foolishness of your latest outburst is beyond comprehension. Your statements have been seized upon by Israel's enemies. . . ." In June, following threats by the Israeli Kach party to mount public protests, Lord Jakobovits canceled a planned trip to Israel to attend a fund-raising dinner for the Horeb schools, saying that he did not want the schools to become embroiled as innocent victims in an irrelevant squabble.

Incoming chief rabbi Dr. Jonathan Sacks told the *Jewish Chronicle* that he supported any rabbi's right to speak on a matter of principle. "I admire his moral courage," he said. "My views are not significantly different from his own." Sacks seemed to emphasize this point when in June he named Jonathan Kestenbaum as executive director of his office. Kestenbaum's controversial diary of a period of reserve duty in the Israeli army, which was published in the *Jerusalem Post* in 1988, was critical of his colleagues' treatment of the Palestinians. Sacks said the diary had no relevance to Kestenbaum's qualifications for his new position and stressed his resolve "to fight against the politicization of Jewish life." "His work and mine," he explained, "will be primarily in the field of Jewish education, Jewish spirituality and Jewish leadership." At his induction as chief rabbi at St. John's Wood Synagogue, north-west London, in September, Sacks called for "a decade of Jewish renewal."

A total of 356 congregations with a membership of 101,239 household units existed in the United Kingdom in 1990, according to a report by the Board of Deputies' Community Research Unit. Of the total households, 67.9 percent belonged to the centrist Orthodox group (comprising the US, the Federation of Synagogues, and independent Orthodox congregations); 16.9 percent to Reform congregations; 6.3 percent to Liberal; 5.7 percent to right-wing Orthodox; and 3.2 percent to Sephardi congregations.

Although centrist Orthodoxy remained the major synagogue movement, the report noted shifting balances within the Orthodox grouping as a whole: centrist Orthodoxy's share of total Orthodox male membership fell nationally from 92 percent in 1977 to 87 percent in 1990; and in London from 91 percent in 1970 to 82 percent in 1990. Conversely, the right wing's share of total Orthodox male membership rose from 4.4 percent nationally in 1977 to 9.2 percent in 1990; and in London from 3.2 percent in 1970 to 12.4 percent in 1990.

At the beginning of the year, new *mikvaot* (ritual baths) opened in Edgware and Wimbledon. By September, three north-west London US synagogues—at Edgware, Hendon, and West Hampstead— were running "alternative" minyans designed to attract single people and young married couples.

The United Synagogue's financial problems continued. In April, Edgware, its third-largest constituent synagogue, refused to pay the required contribution toward US's central services. Members unanimously voted a payment of £74,000, instead of the £110,000 requested, on the grounds that membership income was declining and almost a quarter of its 1,174 male and 603 female members were in arrears.

The Liberal Jewish Synagogue in St. John's Wood, north-west London, reopened in January after a £5-million renovation. At the Union of Liberal and Progressive Synagogues (ULPS) conference in May, plans were unveiled for a new prayer book to replace the 1967 *Sacred Heart*. The aim, according to editor Rabbi John Rayner, was "to produce a better balanced, more mature and more progressive Jewish liturgy than any currently available." Acceptance of the East Anglia and Peterborough congregations as affiliates of ULPS in September brought the total number of its congregations to 30. As of June, the Reform Synagogues of Great Britain (RSGB), which was preparing to celebrate its 150th anniversary in 1992, had 41 congregations.

Attention was drawn to a shortage of rabbis within the Reform and Progressive networks by RSGB's executive director Raymond Goldman. In a July statement he said that nine small Reform communities, comprising about 950 of RSGB's 18,000 family units, had no rabbi, though five had some part-time rabbinic support. Rabbi Sidney Brichto, ULPS executive vice-president, reported that three ULPS synagogues were without ministers.

Talks collapsed in April in the *shehitah* (ritual slaughter) dispute, with no solution to the rift caused in 1989 when the US split from the other two constituents of the London Board for Shechita—the Federation of Synagogues and the Spanish and Portuguese Congregation—to set up its own organization. In May the US preempted the London board and set up a joint authority with the Manchester Shechita Board under the supervision of London and Manchester *batei din*. By using one instead of two abattoirs in London and reducing the number of *shohetim* (slaughterers), the arrangement would save the US £250,000, said US *kashrut* head Michael Gross, and bring down the cost of kosher meat as well. In September Manchester and the US formed a new company, Shechitah UK, with a view to creating a national organization. Meanwhile, the London board, prevented since the rift from carrying out *shehitah* because the majority of its staff defected to the US, resumed meat production in Manchester in June, using local slaughterers working free-lance against the wishes of the Manchester board. The London board brought the meat from Manchester to its new north London manufacturing and retailing outfit, Mehadrin Meats.

Education

In April Chief Rabbi Jakobovits's Jewish Educational Development Trust (JEDT) set up a think tank to examine the financing and development of Jewish education in Britain over the next 20 years.

Government approval was obtained in June for the first state-aided Jewish secondary school in Redbridge, north-east London, on a site next to Ilford Jewish primary school. The US-sponsored school, scheduled to open in September 1993, will eventually have 900 pupils. With nearby Barkingside Jewish youth center, the two schools will form London's first Jewish educational campus, comparable to Harold House and the King David School campus in Liverpool. In July the government approved state aid for a 480-pupil Jewish primary school to open in Southgate, north London, in September 1992, serving an area containing some 5,000 Jewish families.

Hendon, one of the US's largest congregations, in July closed its part-time religious school, which had been reduced to 40 pupils both by the increasing age of the community and the growing popularity of Jewish day schools. The move was part of US's general reorganization of its part-time system through closing or merging small religious schools.

A record 38 graduates received degrees and diplomas from Jews' College in March, at which time an honorary doctorate was awarded businessman and philanthropist Stanley Kalms for his contribution to the "recent transformation of the

Anglo-Jewish educational scene." It was announced in April that Jews' College B.A. degrees would be awarded by London University instead of the Council for National Academic Awards, which validates polytechnic degrees. Also in April, the college announced that it had admitted the first women students to its B.A. program, following the introduction of a broader range of courses.

In May, Leo Baeck College, the Progressive rabbinical training institute, announced that it would offer M.A. and Ph.D. degrees in Jewish studies. As a result of a major recruitment drive, seven students registered for its five-year rabbinical training course in September; this compared with an average intake of two in the preceding few years.

Prof. Robert Wistrich of the Hebrew University of Jerusalem was appointed in May to the Jewish Chronicle Chair of Jewish Studies at University College, London. The chair, established to commemorate the *Jewish Chronicle*'s 150th anniversary, was the first full-time, permanent chair in Jewish studies created in Britain in over 160 years.

A fellowship in Talmud and rabbinics was established in February at the Oxford Center for Post-Graduate Hebrew Studies by the New London Synagogue, in the name of its minister, Rabbi Dr. Louis Jacobs.

Publications

H.H. Wingate/Jewish Quarterly literary prizes for nonfiction went to Bertha Leverton, editor with Shmuel Lowensohn of *I Came Alone* (a series of recollections by *kindertransport* refugees) and Anthony Rudolf for *At an Uncertain Hour* (a work on Primo Levi); for poetry to Liz Cashdan for *The Tyre-Cairo Letters*; and for fiction to Bernice Rubens for *Kingdom Come*, her novel about the false messiah Shabbetai Zevi.

Works of fiction published this year included a new novel by Bernice Rubens, *A Solitary Grief*; *The Hidden I: A Myth Revised* by Frederic Raphael; *Hidden in the Heart* by Dan Jacobson; *New Beginnings* by Maisie Mosco (bringing her *Almonds and Raisins* saga up to the present); *Labyrinth* by Thomas Wiseman; *The Man Before Yesterday* by Lionel Goldstein; *Steps: Selected Fiction and Drama* by Gabriel Josipovici; *Jump and Other Stories* by Nadine Gordimer; *The Lights of Manchester* by Tony Warren; *A Night with Casanova* by Wolf Mankowitz; and *A Closed Eye* by Anita Brookner. Fictional works with Holocaust themes were *Postscripts* by Claire Rayner; and *Anton the Dove Fancier and Other Tales of the Holocaust* by Bernard Gotfryd. Three books by Israeli novelists—*The Court Jesters* by Avigdor Dagan, *The Smile of the Lamb* by David Grossman, and *To Know a Woman* by Amos Oz—were also published this year.

Among biographies and autobiographies of Jewish interest were *Herzl* by Steven Beller; *Billionaire: The Life and Times of Sir James Goldsmith* by Ivor Fallon; *The Junk Bond Revolution* by Fenton Bailey, mainly based on the activities of Michael Milken; *Spring Remembered* by Evelyn Cowan; *Edward VII and His Jewish Court* by Anthony Allfrey; and two books about Jewish artists: *Zvi Ribak: A Jewish Artist*, paintings with a foreword and text by Jay Weinstein, and *Bernard Meninsky* by John Russell Taylor.

New works on religious themes included *Tradition and Unity*, a collection of sermons in honor of the retiring archbishop of Canterbury, Dr. Robert Runcie, edited by Rabbi Dan Cohn Sherbok; *Issues in Contemporary Judaism* by Dan Cohn Sherbok; *The Festivals: A History of Jewish Celebration* by Chaim Raphael; *Orthodoxy Confronts Modernity*, a collection of essays edited by Chief Rabbi Jonathan Sacks; *Structure and Form in the Babylonian Talmud* by Louis Jacobs; *A Rabbi's Bible* by Jonathan Magonet; and *A Dictionary of Jewish Lore and Legend* by Alan Unterman.

New studies of Jewish history were *The Sephardi Story* by Chaim Raphael; *1492: The Year and the Era* by Barnet Litvinoff; *An Atlas of Modern Jewish History* by Evyatar Friesel; *Second Chance: Two Centuries of German-Speaking Jews in the United Kingdom*, edited by Werner E. Mosse with Julius Carlebach, Gerhard Hirschfield, Aubrey Newman, Arnold Paucker, and Peter Pulzer; and *Jews and Messianism in the Modern Era*, edited by Jonathan Frankel.

New publications related to the Holocaust included *The Genocidal Mentality: Nazi Holocaust and Nuclear Threat* by Robert Jay Lifton and Eric Markusen; *Kristallnacht: Unleashing the Holocaust* by Anthony Read and David Fisher; *The Gestapo and German Society: Enforcing Racial Policy, 1933–1945* by Robert Gellately; *The Auschwitz Chronicle, 1939–1945* by Danuta Czech; *Children of the Flames: Dr. Josef Mengele and the Untold Story of the Twins of Auschwitz* by Lucette Matalon Lagnado and Sheila Cohn Dekel; *Escape from the Holocaust: Illegal Immigration to the Land of Israel* by Dalia Ofer; *There Was Life Even There* by Mina Tomkiewicz; and *Final Letters*, selected by Reuven Dafni and Yehudit Kleiman. Two books devoted to war-crimes trials were *Ivan the Terrible: The Trial of John Demjanjuk* by Tom Telcholz; and *Uncertain Hour: The French, the Germans, the Jews, the Klaus Barbie Trial, and the City of Lyons, 1940–45* by Ted Morgan.

Among new books about Israel were *Israel's Secret Wars: The Untold History of Israeli Intelligence* by Ian Black and Benny Morris; *Among Arabs and Jews: A Personal Experience, 1936–1990* by P.J. Vatikiotis; *The Israeli-Palestinian Conflict: A Documentary Record, 1967–1990*, edited by Yehuda Lukacs; *The Last Option: After Nasser, Arafat and Saddam Hussein* by David Kimche; *Ploughshares into Swords? Israelis and Jews in the Shadow of the Intifada* by Colin Shindler; *Alarms and Excursions* by Naomi Shepherd; and *Trial and Error* by Tom Gilling, concerning the trial of Mordechai Vanunu.

Among new collections of poetry were *Bridge Passages* by George Szirtes; *City Music* by Elaine Feinstein; *For Anne Frank* by Nick Naydler, with paintings by Greg Tricker; *Words on a Faded T-Shirt* by Norman Silver; *Clouds of Glory over Soho Rooftops* by Chaim Lewis; *The Self as Fighter* by Shlomo Kalo; and *Berlin Proposal* by Thomas Land.

Works of general Jewish interest were the annual publication *A Survey of Jewish*

Affairs, 1990, edited by William Frankel; *A Sense of Belonging: Dilemmas of British Jewish Identity*, written by Howard Cooper and Paul Morrison to accompany a television series assessing the Anglo-Jewish family in the 1990s; and *The Really Jewish Food Guide*, published by the United Synagogue.

Personalia

Knighthoods went to Harry Solomon, chairman and founder of Hillsdown Holdings, one of the world's largest food manufacturing companies, and to Ivor Harold Cohen, chairman of Remploy, which provides work under sheltered conditions for people with mental and physical handicaps.

Among British Jews who died in 1991 were Sir Rudolph Lyons, eminent lawyer and Leeds communal personality, in January, aged 79; Ruth Rabbinowitz, educator, in January, aged 90; Sir Monty Finniston, eminent scientist, industrialist, chairman of the British Steel Corporation (1973–76), Zionist, and Jewish communal figure, in February, aged 78; Cecil Kahn, chairman, Nightingale House (1953–77), in February, aged 89; Irene Sala, founder president of Hadassah Medical Relief Association, UK, in February, aged 61, in a plane crash in Chile; Nat Levy, a Jewish civil servant who worked for the Board of Deputies for 50 years, in March, aged 83; Julian du Parc Braham, professional soldier, in March, aged 69; Sam Golding, educator, in March, aged 98; Jack "Kid" Berg, boxer, in April, aged 81; Samuel Dimson, pediatrician, in April, aged 83; Henry Lipson, emeritus professor of physics, Manchester University, in April, aged 81, in Israel; Bernie Winters, comedian, in May, aged 58; Sadie Levine, longtime *Jewish Chronicle* women's page editor, in May, aged 82; Alexander Margulies, communal figure, philanthropist, and patron of the arts, in May, aged 88; Sir Isaac Wolfson, internationally prominent businessman and philanthropist, in June, aged 93, in Israel; Rafael Hirsch, for over 46 years secretary of the Orthodox Hebrew Congregations (Adath Yisroel) and the Joint Kashrus Commission, in June, aged 71; Erwin Rosenthal, emeritus reader in Oriental Studies, Cambridge University, in June, aged 86; Peter Sontar, theater production manager, in June, aged 68; Hyman Diamond, national communal personality, in July, aged 77, at a Board of Deputies election meeting; David Shiffer, Leeds communal personality, in July, aged 91; Max Jaffa, violinist, in July, aged 78; Sir Bernard Waley-Cohen, major communal and civic figure, in July, aged 77; Regina Kapeller-Adler, geneticist, in August, aged 91, in Edinburgh; Harry Brooks, boxer, in August, aged 85; Hyman A. Simons, notable Anglo-Jewish personality and historian, in August, aged 80; Ruth Cohen, principal, Newnham College, Cambridge, 1954–72, first Jewish head of an Oxbridge college, in August, aged 84; E. Alec Colman, real-estate developer and philanthropist, in August, aged 88; Sir Leo Schultz, Hull Labor city councillor for 57 years, in September, aged 91; Theo Cowan, theater and film publicist, in September, aged 75; Alex Alfred, for 20 years chairman of the Haven Foundation, in October, aged 79; Bernard Homa, authority on circumcision and president of Machzikei Hadath for 37 years, whose autobiography, *Footprints on the Sands of Time*, appeared this year, in October, aged 91; Robert Maxwell, media magnate, in November, aged 68, at sea; Etta Topel, Yiddish actress, in November, aged 80; Anne, Lady Chain, biochemist, in November, aged 70; Mort Shuman, songwriter, in November, aged 52; Cyril Barnet, Lord Salmon, judge, in November, aged 87; Francis Mann, international lawyer, in November, aged 84; Isaak Goldberg, Yiddish scholar and writer, in December, aged 92; Maurice Abbey, supporter and organizer of Jewish sports, in December, aged 78; Sam Rabin, artist, in December, aged 88.

MIRIAM & LIONEL KOCHAN

France

National Affairs

AT THE START OF 1991, France's attention was focused on the crisis in the Persian Gulf. Although, as a major supplier of arms to Iraq, France was in a difficult position, President François Mitterrand had no alternative but to support the United States and the multinational force seeking to oust Saddam Hussein from Kuwait. On February 2, the Socialist party's steering committee reaffirmed its support for President Mitterrand's policy in the Middle East, though members of the party's left wing either abstained or did not take part in the ballot.

Relations with Israel

In the period leading up to the Gulf War, France tried to avert hostilities and to maintain its ties with the PLO, which it had been cultivating as a "moderate" force in the Middle East. PLO support for Saddam, however, forced French leaders to reevaluate their position. After Jean Kahn, president of CRIF (the Representative Council of French Jews), met with Mitterrand on February 26, he indicated that he felt a lessening of conflict between France and Israel was possible. The CRIF president, who carried a message from Prime Minister Yitzhak Shamir of Israel to Mitterrand, suggested that there were renewed bases for relations between the two countries, despite conflicting views over a European role in the peace process. Kahn mentioned that the PLO had lost favor at the Elysée, due to its support for Saddam Hussein during the Gulf War, and added that Mitterrand was genuinely concerned with Israeli security.

In April, Minister of Foreign Affairs Roland Dumas, a longtime supporter of the PLO, was the first Western official to meet PLO leader Yasir Arafat after the end of the Gulf War. At their meeting in Tripoli, Dumas asserted that although Arafat supported Saddam Hussein, he "remains the only person who truly represents the Palestinians." On April 25, the PLO leader was a special guest on "La Marche du siècle" on public TV, channel FR3, and PLO's representative in Paris, Ibrahim Souss, appeared on "L'Heure de vérité" (the French "Meet the Press") on Antenne 2, the other state-owned TV station.

A cabinet reshuffle in early May was expected to bring about a warming in France-Israel relations. Although the new prime minister, Edith Cresson, apparently had no strong views on the Arab-Israeli conflict, pro-Israel partisans were optimistic. Their hopes were dampened, however, when, contrary to expectations, Dumas remained as foreign minister. Dominique Strauss-Kahn, a French Jew, was appointed minister of industry and external trade, and hope was expressed that he would help fight the Arab boycott, especially in the L'Oréal affair (see below). On the negative side, the Jewish community lost an important ally when Lionel Stoléru, former minister of planning, left the government.

In mid-June, an official of the Ministry of External Affairs met with two representatives of the Democratic Front for the Liberation of Palestine (DFLP), Fahed Suleiman and Souheil Natour, who were in Paris seeking increased European and French support in the form of economic aid for the population of the occupied territories. Suleiman and Natour also met with the national secretary of the Socialist party, Gérard Fuchs, Communist Maxime Gremetz, and representatives of the Green party.

Pro-Israel and pro-Palestinian supporters clashed in the press at the end of June. A letter published in the daily Le Figaro from Michel Habib-Deloncle, president of the French-Arab Chamber of Commerce, used the terms "racist" and "expansionist" to describe the State of Israel. André Monteil, minister under General de Gaulle and now vice-president of the France-Israel Friendship Association, responded to Habib-Deloncle, advising him to look to Baghdad for expansionism and to Damascus for racism.

Faisal Husseini, a Palestinian leader from the occupied territories, paid a short and discreet visit to Paris the same month, meeting with two former prime ministers, Michel Rocard and Pierre Mauroy. It was the first such contact between Husseini and Socialist party officials. Husseini's visit was followed in September by that of Radwan Abu Ayash, another Palestinian leader from the occupied territories, who held talks with the Foreign Ministry's secretary-general, François Scheer. Abu Ayash claimed that France would support Palestinians and the PLO in opposing the Americans' "inadequate" peace plan.

Even as France's relations with Palestinians intensified, the French authorities, for the first time in decades, and following repeated contacts between French and Israeli cabinet ministers, decided to offer a guarantee of $500 million to French public-works contractors willing to do business with Israel, for the building of a housing project for Soviet Jews in the Beersheba area. The guarantee, as usual, was valid only for one year, ending in October, and Israel wondered whether the agreement would be kept. According to officials of the French Public Works Office, any delay could be explained by technical and legal difficulties. Some observers noted that the Israeli officials in charge of the housing project were not eager to work with French companies.

Yasir Arafat's visit to Paris on October 21—the fourth in three years—did little to comfort the Jewish community. Arafat came to the French capital to meet with Foreign Minister Boris Pankin of the Soviet Union, who, only a week before, had reestablished diplomatic relations between the Soviet Union and Israel. President Mitterrand did not receive the PLO leader at the Elysée Palace, to avoid "creating suspicion" before the peace conference on Middle East. He indicated, however, that he wished to meet Arafat at a later date, "since it is normal that France hold discussions with participants in the peace process." Arafat did, however, meet with Foreign Minister Dumas, who declared on October 27 that the EC embargo against Libya should be lifted.

Extremism, Racism, Anti-Semitism

Municipal and parliamentary by-elections on January 27 and February 3 confirmed the rising popularity of Jean-Marie Le Pen's National Front (FN). In Paris's 15th precinct, candidate Serge Martinez, editor of the extreme right-wing *Minute* magazine, received 9 percent of the vote, a slight increase over the 1988 parliamentary elections. In the Rhone constituency, Bruno Gollnisch, member of the FN scientific council and former member of Parliament, won 25.5 percent in the second round, a gain of 2.3 percent. FN candidates made gains in all urban constituencies, even against diversionary candidacies, such as that of the CNI (Far Right) in Lyons. All this despite Le Pen's isolationism in the Gulf War, which alienated some of his more militant supporters.

On February 5, enormous posters (three by four meters) appeared on public billboards bearing the following slogan: "Le Pen, *Maher*," a translation into Hebrew of the FN's usual slogan, "Le Pen, now," with *Maher* written in Hebrew letters. The poster was part of a campaign, with text in Arabic and Chinese to follow the one in Hebrew, aimed at making Le Pen's image more acceptable and statesmanlike.

The Versailles Court of Appeals handed down a judgment against Jean-Marie Le Pen on March 18, increasing the penalties imposed in an earlier trial. He had been sued for declaring in 1987 that the existence of Nazi gas chambers was a subject of debate among historians and "a detail in the history of World War II." The FN described the fine of 1.2 million francs, which Le Pen was ordered to pay to nine organizations representing deportees, as an attempt to "financially asphyxiate" the far-Right movement. Another court fined Le Pen 10,000 francs for insulting a government minister in 1988, with a pun—"Durafour-crématoire"—linking the minister's name with the Nazi gas chambers.

The controversial issue of immigration came to the fore on June 19, when the leader of the right-wing opposition, Jacques Chirac, declared at a public dinner that the "overdose of foreigners" in France was mostly perceptible in the municipal housing projects, where "noise and odor" signaled their presence. President Mitterrand denounced the statement but that did not prevent another leader of the Right, a former president of France, Valéry Giscard d'Estaing, from expressing his views on the immigration "invasion" in the *Figaro-Magazine*, proposing to replace the basis for acquiring citizenship from residency to blood, i.e., having French parents. Statements by France's new prime minister, Edith Cresson, were a welcome contrast to the intolerant statements of other politicians. On December 21, Cresson appealed to the French people to oppose the far Right, especially the demagogy of the FN.

A poll published on October 25 in *Le Monde* dramatized the extent of anti-immigration sentiment in France. It indicated that whereas 65 percent of the French population considered the National Front a threat to democracy, 32 percent agreed with Le Pen's ideas, an increase of 14 percent compared to the preceding year. Perhaps encouraged by the results, the FN struck again on November 16, proposing 50 new measures to "solve the immigration problem," among them limiting immigration to EC citizens, imposing immigrant quotas in schools, and prohibiting the construction of more mosques. The latter proposal was in accord with at least some public sentiment, as evidenced by the case of the city of Libercourt's inhabitants, in the Pas de Calais region, where 83 percent of the voters rejected a referendum on expansion of their city's mosque. Only 55 percent of these eligible took part in the vote, but their message of intolerance was surprising, considering that religious liberty is assured in the French constitution.

The second annual report of the Human Rights Advisory Commission, submitted to the prime minister on March 21, contained both quantitative data on racism and anti-Semitism and a qualitative, detailed analysis of political movements espousing exclusionary ideologies. Polls including items on the image of Jews showed a decline in anti-Semitism: 94 percent of those interviewed saying that "Jews are as French as others," as against 37 percent in 1946. However, in 1990, 24 percent thought Jews in France were too numerous, as against 17 percent in 1977. The results also showed 9 percent saying that Jews had too much power, and 20 percent that references to the Holocaust were excessive. According to the authors of the report, those who are more prejudiced against Jews tend to be of lower socioeconomic status, elderly, or sympathetic to either the far Right or the Communist party.

A number of right-wing groups engaged in activity that, if not overtly anti-Semitic, was clearly offensive to many Jews. The National Union for Christian Europe (UNEC) went to Auschwitz in the spring to pray and demonstrate against the new "genocide," abortion. The ecumenical union was composed of fundamentalist Catholics close to Msgr. Marcel Lefebvre (the dissident archbishop who broke with the Church over Vatican II, who died in Switzerland in March at the age of 85) as well as some Protestants and an Orthodox priest as a member of its honorary committee. Other participants included Martine Lehideux, an FN Euro MP, the pro-Lefebvre French bishop Tisser de Mallerais, and the Belgian FN leader Dr. Daniel Ferret. The UNEC is part of the Confederation for French Renewal (Confédération du Renouveau français), which includes groups situated to the right of the FN, and is open only to "French citizens, white and Christian."

In the same vein, FN militants and former World War II collaborators gathered on April 20 in Paris to pay tribute to Saint-Loup, a far-Right writer and former editor-in-chief of the World War II collaborationist newspaper *La Gerbe*. Members of a self-styled "Jewish Action Group" (Groupe d'Action juive) invaded the meeting place and did not hesitate to use force. Nazi flags, tapes and records of Nazi music produced by Le Pen's company for war memorabilia, and pictures showing one of the participants in Nazi uniform were reportedly found. One elderly woman was badly wounded in the fracas. Two suspects, reportedly members of the Herut-France youth organization Tagar, were later arrested and released on bail. When the wounded woman finally regained consciousness, the two were brought to court on minor charges and released.

The Barroux Benedictine monks in the Vaucluse region (southeastern France) published a new missal, calling on the faithful to pray for "perfidious Jews" so that they "recognize Jesus Christ," thus ignoring the fact that this language had been explicitly suppressed by Vatican II.

In June, the Green party held its general assembly and took up the case of Jean Brière, who, as spokesman for the Green party during the Gulf War, charged that "Israel and the Zionist lobby" were responsible for the war. Brière also referred to Israel as "a racist, militaristic, theocratic and expansionist state with a policy based on permanent war." Brière was suspended in April as party spokesman, but it was left to the Lyons branch, which he represented, to decide his fate. Despite protests from within the party, Brière refused to resign, insisting that he "said the truth." "If the truth is anti-Semitic, then I am anti-Semitic," he concluded. Brière later asserted that if he was condemned for racism, the other 56 million French citizens were equally deserving of prison. In December the Green party announced Brière's definite suspension from any office in that movement.

Holocaust-Related Matters

France was still attempting to deal with ghosts from the past, but the ghosts were not easily laid to rest. The 17th Court of Summary Jurisdiction in Paris ordered three staff members of the left-oriented weekly news magazine *Nouvel Observateur*, Claude Perdriel, Serge Raffy, and Marie-France Ethegoin, to pay Maurice Papon 10,000 francs for having defamed him in an article by emphasizing his role in the wartime Vichy regime. Papon was one of the three French who had been indicted for crimes against humanity, especially the deportation of tens of thousands of Jews during the war. As a wartime official of the Vichy government in Bordeaux, Papon was accused of having ordered the arrest and deportation of 1,690 Jews, among them 230 children, in 1943 and 1944. Almost all of them were exterminated by the Nazis.

Families of deported French Jews had lodged 17 complaints against Papon and his superior, René Bousquet, wartime commander of Vichy's police, in May 1990. In April 1991, Bousquet was officially indicted on the basis of new documents brought by Serge Klarsfeld, especially a 1942 ordinance issued by Bousquet that made it easier to arrest certain Jewish children living in the so-called Free Zone. But proceedings against Bousquet, like those against Papon, appeared to have come to a dead-end, thanks to widespread reluctance in France—including leading politicians and judges—to pursue these cases.

An exception was Albert Cardinal Decourtray, archbishop of Lyons, who instituted a commission to study the links between the Catholic Church and Paul Touvier, head of the Lyons collaborationist militia during the war. His initiative was not universally appreciated, however. One of the cardinal's consultants on Jewish affairs and a member of the commission, Dr. Charles Favre, was kidnapped on June

21. He was freed a few hours later, but his abductors succeeded in stealing some of the commission's working documents.

On July 11, the Paris Court of Appeals released Paul Touvier, who had been arrested in 1989, because of health problems, although the charge of crimes against humanity against the former collaborator still stood. (Touvier had been sentenced to death in 1945, for his activities as head of the militia in Lyons in 1943–44, but managed to escape and to remain in hiding, with the help of conservative clerics and a pardon by President Georges Pompidou in 1971, in an effort aimed at "national reconciliation." (See AJYB 1991, pp. 264–65.)

With all these proceedings, the only Nazi to have been judged, condemned, and imprisoned in France to this date was Klaus Barbie. But less than five years after being given a life sentence, the "butcher of Lyons" died of leukemia in prison on September 25, at the age of 77. He had been extradited from Bolivia in 1983 through the efforts of the Klarsfeld couple. Before his death, Barbie tried to take last-minute revenge against Resistance heroes Raymond and Lucie Aubrac, who embarrassed him in 1943 by organizing a prisoners' escape in Lyons. The former Gestapo officer accused Raymond of being responsible for the arrest of resistance fighters in Caluire in June 1943, one of the most controversial episodes in the history of the resistance, during which Jean Moulin, de Gaulle's envoy in occupied France, was caught and tortured.

On November 12, Nazi hunter Serge Klarsfeld announced that after a search of many years, researchers had found the files containing names of 140,000 Jews who had registered with the local police stations, as required by the racial laws instituted by the Vichy regime in 1940. The files were used in 1941 and 1942 by the French police to round up and deport the Jews. The files, which were said to have been destroyed or lost, were found in the archives of the Ministry of Veterans Affairs, and there were grounds to believe that some authorities in fact knew of their existence and whereabouts. The discovery was not expected to reveal the identities of those responsible for the deportations but would provide useful information about the victims. Klarsfeld asked that the Jewish files be transferred to the Jewish Contemporary Documentation Center (CDJC), which had been collecting material relating to the Holocaust since 1943.

The Court of Summary Jurisdiction found Vincent Reynouard and Rémi Pontier guilty of disseminating Holocaust revisionist literature in front of Caen University and fined them 10,000 francs (approximately $2,000), to be paid to four refugee and human-rights organizations.

On October 13, a ceremony took place at the Nice central station, in remembrance of the Jews who were deported from that city to the camps at Drancy. Simone Veil, former minister of health, participated in the commemoration, and described the circumstances of her own arrest in 1944.

On October 23, as part of its educational program, the CRIF conducted a day trip to Auschwitz for Toulouse high-school students, an activity that CRIF director Jacqueline Keller considered the most effective way to inform young people—Jews and non-Jews—about the Holocaust. This year's program, the fourth, was financed by the Education Ministry, whose head, Lionel Jospin, had been actively involved in helping to establish the activity in the curriculum. Some 200 students participated in 1991, accompanied by history teachers and four former camp inmates.

L'Oréal Affair

In May, Jean Frydman, a shareholder and officer of Paravision, a subsidiary of L'Oréal, charged the world's leading cosmetics firm with trying to force him to resign in order to comply with the Arab League boycott of Israel. Frydman refused, instead taking the offensive himself. His first act was to publicize the name of Jacques Corrèze, president of Cosmair, which markets L'Oréal products in the United States, as the individual directly responsible for Frydman's removal. Corrèze had been associated with the Nazis during the occupation and with the group that blew up Paris synagogues in 1941 and requisitioned Jewish shops. His boss in the prewar right-wing Revolutionary Social Movement (Mouvement social révolution-naire), Eugène Schueller, made his fortune during the war and floated L'Oréal. L'Oréal general manager François Dalle replied to Frydman's revelations by accusing him of financial blackmail. "He takes advantage of the Holocaust to make money," said Dalle, who justified the attempt to fire Frydman by claiming that the latter had been involved in dangerous transactions.

David Frydman, Jean's brother, instituted legal proceedings at two levels, civil and penal, against L'Oréal. In penal court, Frydman and Frydman accused the company of "counterfeiting documents and of racial discrimination." The civil suit aimed at collecting damages and getting the right to sell the Paravision company so that Jean Frydman could claim what he regarded as his share of the enterprise. But the penal suit received more attention; it would be the first attempt to punish a boycott action since the French Parliament passed an antiboycott law in 1977. The law, in fact, had essentially been ignored. According to Arieh Gabay of the Israel embassy in Paris, none of the 200 biggest French companies had any direct dealings with Israel.

On June 26, Jacques Corrèze died of cancer. Before his death, he expressed "his sincere regrets for the acts committed 40 years ago and their consequences, even indirect." Corrèze had consistently maintained, since the affair was made public, that he had no connection with the Paravision subsidiary nor with the internal conflict involving Frydman, "whom he did not know."

In November, Dalle was charged with racial discrimination by Judge Jean-Pierre Getti. When David Frydman heard the news, he described it as a "second Dreyfus affair." To the surprise of many, the year ended with an out-of-court agreement between Dalle and Frydman, after Judge Getti insisted on a compromise for the "common good of the nation." The agreement called for the appointment of an expert who would determine whether there had been a boycott action or not. Although Frydman withdrew his penal charge, he did obtain the three conditions he was asking for: Jacques Corrèze's resignation, François Dalle's apology, and an investigation of the boycott allegation by an independent expert on the boycott, Jean-Louis Bismuth. His report was due in March 1992, but the delay would not permit any subsequent penal procedure. The civil suit continued, however.

JEWISH COMMUNITY

Demography

The estimated Jewish population of France remained around 550,000, with some claiming the figure to be slightly lower or higher.

Communal Affairs

As the UN ultimatum to Saddam Hussein expired on January 15, the French Jewish community gathered for prayer and speeches at Paris's main synagogue on Rue de la Victoire. Israeli ambassador Ovadia Soffer and community leaders joined in reaffirming the unity of the Jewish people. Some community events were canceled or postponed for the duration—such as a private showing of a new exhibition from Israel's Museum of the Diaspora—and shops closed as fear spread over rumored terrorist acts in the Jewish neighborhood of Le Marais.

Contrary to expectations, the Jewish community received neither comfort nor support from *SOS Racisme*, the movement created several years earlier by Arab and Jewish youths to fight racism. Harlem Desir's organization opted for a pacifist position in the Gulf War, thus joining the far-Right and far-Left camps. As a consequence, *Globe* editor Georges-Marc Benamou, Bernard-Henri Lévy, Guy Konopnicki, and Elie Wiesel dissociated themselves from the antiracist group. According to Marc Rochmann, president of the French Jewish Students' Union, by adopting a pacifist stance, *SOS Racisme* opened the door to young North African Arabs wishing to fight beside Saddam Hussein.

SOS Racisme vice-president Eric Ghebali, a Socialist activist, also rejected the organization's antiwar stand. Returning from a short visit to Israel, Ghebali insisted that the organization take a stand opposing Iraqi bombings of Israel. When Harlem Desir, who in the meantime created "Paix maintenant" (Peace Now, no link with the Israeli movement), maintained that war could not solve the problem and called instead for an embargo, Ghebali sought to make public the difference of opinion within the movement and called on Benamou and Lévy for help.

Some 2,000 people took part in a demonstration of support for Israel later in January in front of the Israel embassy. Members of the Jewish community did not all approve the action, claiming that it could be harmful to the Jewish state, which had been keeping a low profile since the beginning of the conflict. Some charged the organizers—French Herut, the Zionist Federation, Tagar, Betar—with merely wanting to gain partisan political advantage, though most demonstration participants undoubtedly only wanted to show their support for Israel.

As the war neared an end, French Jews turned to internal concerns, such as intermarriage and education.

Many within the Jewish community put the blame for the high rate of intermarriage (according to various assessments, about half the weddings) on the Paris Consistoire's attitude toward conversion. According to the rules of the Paris Beth Din, a conversion associated with marriage was not "sincere" and could not be accepted. The Consistoire's requirements for a "bona fide" conversion were regarded as so out of reach that most Jews wishing to marry a non-Jew either turned to one of the two Reform synagogues in France, or abandoned any hope of conversion and left the community altogether. Benny Cohen, president of the Paris Consistoire, argued in the May 16 edition of *Actualité juive* that "if a man or woman wishes to convert to Judaism, there is no problem. The door is open without animosity to everybody. But the Torah remains law. If someone respects it, this person is part of the Jewish people. It is impossible to modify the law in a particular case."

A counterargument was presented by Robert Binisti, a retired lawyer and author of a book on intermarriage and rabbinic fundamentalism. The law never says that it is forbidden to marry a non-Jew, he asserted, or that children of a mixed union are non-Jews, even if they have had a Jewish upbringing. He saw in Cohen's words not an "open door," but merely gratuitous hostility.

The debate over intermarriage reflected deepening tensions between religious and secular elements in the Jewish community. In May, a conference took place of ten nonreligious organizations seeking to challenge the dominance of Orthodox Jewry, not only in religion (conversion was controlled by the Consistoire, and, as noted, there were only two Reform congregations in France) but in political and cultural life as well. Although these groups had memberships numbering only in the hundreds, they claimed that most French Jews were either secular or only nominally Orthodox and that the community offered no alternative avenues for participation in Jewish life. The conference proposed creating community centers and informal educational and cultural programs to try and attract young Jews who want nothing to do with the Consistoire.

In May, Jean Kahn, president of CRIF, succeeded Dr. Lionel Kopelowitz of Great Britain as president of the European Jewish Congress. Kahn said he would focus his activity on solidarity with Israel and on the struggle against racism and anti-Semitism in France.

Education and Culture

The results of a study of all-day Jewish schools in France were released this year. The study's author, sociologist Erik Cohen, reported that parents of children attending the schools were generally satisfied with their children's experience, though 10 percent of them were disappointed with an academic standard they judged insufficient and with the sectarianism of the schools. Some 68 percent of surveyed Jewish parents said they would send their children to such schools if they met three conditions: proximity, limited financial burden (the average cost of Jewish schools was 1,700 francs a month, except for those having association contracts with the state), and quality. Thirty-one percent believe that children cannot receive an adequate Jewish education if they do not go to all-day Jewish schools.

Popular education, along with entertainment, was offered by the four Jewish radio stations in France: Radio Shalom, Radio Communauté, Radio J, and Judaiques FM, which all celebrated their tenth anniversary this year. The first all-Jewish radio station to broadcast in France, Radio J, was created by Michael Zlotowski, with the help of *Renouveau Juif*, Henri Hajdenberg's organization that functions as a secular Jewish lobby. Zlotowski also founded Judaiques FM. After years of bitter feuding, the four stations finally came to an agreement to share the same frequency, 94.8 FM, in Paris, on which they broadcast 24 hours a day, six days a week. The Gulf War crisis increased their audience, since the stations served as a focal point of identification and a link between different elements in the community. Stimulated by their success, the Paris Consistoire proposed opening a wholly denominational station, an idea that was not well received by the existing Jewish stations, who were reluctant to give up airtime and feared that pluralism within the community would suffer. For the same reason, they were skeptical regarding a merger of Jewish stations, preferring to operate cooperatively, which they also saw as a way of increasing professionalism.

Publications

A number of new works on the Holocaust period were published this year. They included *Le camp des Milles* ("The Tile Factory Camp") by André Fontaine, a leading writer for the daily *Le Monde*, which reveals previously unpublished details about this notorious detention center for foreigners in France. *Une mauvaise histoire juive*, by Bernard Fride, offers new evidence of discrimination during the occupation, even among Jews. Fride investigated the history of a commemorative tablet in Nancy which mentions only two names, those of local representatives of UGIF (Union Générale des Israélites Français, the umbrella organization of the Jews in France, whose role during the Nazi occupation is still the subject of controversy) who had been interned in Auschwitz. The plaque ignores the hundreds of immigrant Jews who were also deported. Gustave Nordon, one of the two named men, appears to have been implicated in the arrest and internment of Jewish children.

De Drancy à ces camps dont on ne parle pas by Etienne Rosenfeld is a highly personal Holocaust memoir. It offers a vivid picture of life in the concentration camps, from today's perspective and also through letters he wrote to his wife at the time, as well as drawings he made which are included in the book. *Pivert: Histoire d'un résistant ordinaire* by Daniel Goldenberg is the biography of Raymond Kojitsky, one of the "ordinary" heroes of World War II. The subject speaks—through

the author's pen—of his wanderings as a 16-year-old Jewish resistance fighter, of
the fear and anguish he felt once his parents had been rounded up by Vichy police,
"when he had no other choice than to fight in order to survive."

Other Holocaust-related works were *La propagande sous Vichy, 1940–1944*, on
Vichy propaganda; *Le statut des Juifs sous Vichy*, published by FFDJF and CDJC,
articles gathered under Serge Klarsfeld's direction on the subject of the Jews' status
under the Vichy regime; *Histoire de la jeunesse sous Vichy* by Pierre Giolitto, a
700-page book covering Marshal Philippe Pétain's genocide policy; and *Le Syn-
drôme de Vichy de 1944 à nos jours* by Henry Rousso, which explores the controversy over the Vichy government, in the past and the present.

Other new works this year included *Un visionnaire nommé Herzl, la résurrection
d'Israël* by André Chouraqui, which traces the Zionist theoretician's evolution
through his works as journalist, playwright, and writer. *De Génération en Génération . . . être Juif* by Jacques Ouaknine contains questions and answers on subjects
of current concern to Jews, among them intermarriage, conversion, artificial insemi-
nation, and euthanasia. The European Union of Jewish Students (UEEJ) published
a work by Melitina Fabre and Bernard Suchecky, "The Christianization of Auschwitz." The 130-page report traces the origins of the Carmelite nuns' settling in the
Auschwitz camp in 1985, which the authors claim is part of the church's strategy
to appropriate Holocaust martyrdom to itself and through it gain recognition of the
supremacy of Jesus. In *Mitterrand, Israël et les Juifs*, Yves Azéroual and Yves Derai
examine Mitterrand's relations, contacts, and experiences with Israel and its people.
Mémoires d'un hérétique by Léon Chertok relates the author's years as a French
resistance fighter and an agent of Stalin as well as later experiences with
psychoanalysis and hypnosis.

Personalia

Edmond Jabès, poet and writer, died on January 2 at the age of 78. An Egyptian
national of Jewish origin, Jabès was forced by Nasser's nationalist policy to leave
his country in 1957. He emigrated to France and dedicated himself to writing, where
he was often quoted as saying that the "book is to the refugee what the universe
is to God." His works, which are hard to classify, employ poetry, mystical philosophy, and fiction. His major work, the seven-volume *Livre des Questions, Le Livre
des ressemblances, Le Livre du dialogue, Le parcours, et Le Livre du portage* deals
with the themes of violence, death, love, and Judaism. A book on Jabès's life, by
Didier Cahen, was published in July.

Popular songwriter and singer Serge Gainsbourg (né Lucien Guinzburg) died at
the beginning of March, at the age of 63. The Paris-born entertainer produced only
one work related to his Jewishness, the album *Rock Around the Bunker*, in which
he recalled memories of anti-Semitism in France during the occupation.

Georges Wellers, renowned historian of the Holocaust, died on May 2, at age 86. A physiologist before being deported, he turned to the study of gas chambers and genocide victims after his return from Drancy and Auschwitz. After 1946, he wrote a number of important books and published the *Monde Juif* magazine.

MICHAEL M. ZLOTOWSKI

ANNICK GOULET

The Netherlands

National Affairs

THE COALITION GOVERNMENT OF CHRISTIAN DEMOCRATS (CDA) and Labor (PvdA), headed by Rudolf Lubbers (CDA) as premier and Willem Kok (PvdA) as vice-premier and minister of finance, held together throughout 1991, despite differences in ideology, in particular on economic issues. To deal with the sizable deficit in the government budget, most of the Labor cabinet ministers, first and foremost Kok, as well as the Labor president of the Netherlands State Bank, Willem Duyzenberg, favored stringent cuts in all government departments, increases in certain taxes and excise duties, limitations on wage increases, and abolition of a considerable number of subsidies. This program was announced as part of the interim government budget on February 19 and reiterated in greater detail in the annual address from the throne on the third Tuesday of September. Though most Labor ministers had, after lengthy deliberations, agreed to the plan, the rank-and-file Labor electorate showed little understanding of it. In elections for the provincial councils on March 6, Labor lost spectacularly, dropping by over a third.

The announcement by the government that it wanted to restrict the number of persons receiving permanent disability payments led to major unrest throughout the summer and fall. Some 900,000 persons, out of a total Dutch population of barely 15 million, had been declared medically unfit for work and were receiving up to 70 percent of the last wages earned, until age 65, when they became eligible for old-age pensions. To reduce the numbers of disability recipients—a far larger proportion of the population than in the surrounding countries—the government proposed that all those under 50 years of age should be reexamined medically and offered work they were capable of doing. The status of those 50 years and over would not be affected. Despite enormous protests, inspired primarily by the Netherlands Federation of Trade Unions (FNV), and a mass demonstration in The Hague in the middle of October, with a turnout of some 200,000 persons, the government stuck to its decision.

Although the government appealed for moderation in wages, there were numerous strikes this year, usually for higher wages. One of the longest, of a month's duration, was in the harbor of Rotterdam and caused considerable economic damage. Unemployment stood at some 330,000, largely affecting unskilled persons and so-called *allochthones*, members of ethnic, primarily Third World, minorities. At the same time, since minimum wages were only a little higher than unemployment payments, unskilled labor was hard to find.

The number of those demanding political asylum in the Netherlands in 1991 was some 23,000, all of whom were entitled to Dutch government support in special absorption centers while their cases were before the courts. The constant arrival of new persons seeking political asylum—from countries like Somalia, Ethiopia, Zaire, and Sri Lanka—and the lengthy stay in absorption centers of most of them, necessitated the opening of ever more such facilities.

The integration of ethnic minorities from Third World countries—mostly from Morocco, Turkey, Suriname (former Dutch Guiana), and the Netherlands Antilles—continued to arouse public concern. Now numbering about 700,000, minorities constituted nearly 5 percent of the entire population of the country; in the large cities—Amsterdam, Rotterdam, and The Hague—they constituted some 25 percent overall and, among children up to age 18, almost 50 percent. Public debate over the *allochthones*, many of whom were unskilled, knew little Dutch, and were unemployed or held low-level jobs, focused on whether there was active discrimination and racism or just "normal" tensions between the original residents and the ever larger percentage of *allochthones* in certain districts in the large cities. Affirmative action was advocated and sometimes practiced, particularly in the case of women, and in some instances job quotas were imposed.

THE GULF WAR

In September 1990 the Netherlands had sent two navy frigates to the Gulf of Oman to help enforce the UN embargo against Iraq; in December they were relieved by two other frigates and a supply vessel. In January 1991 the Netherlands supplied Turkey—as a NATO member—with eight Patriot systems of the older type to help protect its frontier with Iraq as well as with a number of Hawk aircraft. It also supplied an emergency hospital, with staff, for the British forces in Saudi Arabia, and established a large camp in Syria for potential refugees from Iraq, who, however, never arrived. The Dutch suffered no casualties in the conflict.

Demonstrations against Dutch participation in the Gulf War, mostly organized by the KAGO or Committee Against the Gulf War, with the participation of the Green Left party, usually drew no more than several hundred demonstrators, among whom were many Iraqis and Kurds. The demonstrations were directed both against the United States and against Israel.

Premier Lubbers placed Patriot systems of the older type at the disposal of Israel, with instructors, but they arrived in Israel too late to be of use. The entire Second Chamber of Parliament approved the decision to send Patriots, with the exception of four of the six members of the Green Left party who argued against the use of all weapons, including defensive ones. At the same time, it was announced that, in addition to the 3 million Dutch florins (some $1.75 million) which the Netherlands had given in December 1990 for food to the Palestinians in the occupied areas, it would give another F. 2 million (some $1.25 million) for this purpose, as well as 10,000 gas masks for Palestinians.

In a public-opinion poll conducted by a Dutch daily at the end of February, 87 percent of all those interviewed approved the sending of Patriots to Israel, and 11 percent opposed. Two percent had no opinion.

The minister for development aid, Jan Pronk, put F. 2 million ($1.25 million) at the disposal of Israel for the repair of damage caused by the Scuds, and F. 1 million for humanitarian support for Ethiopian Jews in Israel. He also made F. 3 million available for humanitarian help to the Kurds. Within the framework of allied humanitarian help to the Kurds, Holland maintained 120 Dutch commandos in northern Iraq.

The Dutch firm Delft Instruments, with 2,500 employees, of whom 1,800 were in the Netherlands, was placed on the boycott list by the United States because it had supplied so-called night-watch viewers to Iraq. The boycott meant that Delft could not receive spare parts for its medical instruments, which formed 85 percent of its production.

Relations with Israel

Foreign Minister Hans van den Broek visited Israel in March as a member of the EC "troika" (the outgoing, the present, and the future chairpersons of the EC Foreign Ministers Council) and again in May as Dutch foreign minister, to explore the prospects for a peace conference. While in Jerusalem, he received a medal from the World Jewish Congress for the role played by the Dutch embassy in Moscow for 23 years in providing exit visas for Soviet Jews. Van den Broek held a meeting with a Palestinian delegation and later visited President Hafez al-Assad of Syria. A delegation of the Dutch parliamentary Foreign Affairs Committee paid a weeklong visit in May to various Middle East countries, including Israel, to discuss the proposed peace conference. Such a conference had originally been scheduled to take place in The Hague, as the Netherlands was at the time president of the European Community. But owing to the objections of Syria—because the Netherlands had not lifted its arms embargo against it and because it had no full embassy in The Hague—the meeting was transferred to Madrid, much to the relief of the Dutch authorities.

Anti-Semitism

There were few cases of overt anti-Semitism this year. Two women who were sentenced by a Dutch court had been sentenced earlier for similar offenses. The Gospel preacher Jenny Goeree, who had been sentenced previously to two months' probation for alleging in her small paper, *Evan*, that the Jews had called the Holocaust upon themselves for rejecting Jesus as the Messiah, continued to make the same allegation. She was sentenced by the Zwolle district court to two months' imprisonment plus the earlier two months' probation. Flora Rost van Toningen, the widow of a leading Dutch Nazi, Meinout Rost van Toningen, and a neo-Nazi in her own right, continued to publish Holocaust-denial material and was sentenced to a fine of 5,000 florins (some $3,000). Because she was well over 70, no prison term was imposed.

In his book *De Uitbuiting van de Holocaust* ("The Exploitation of the Holocaust"), Flemish author Giel van den Berghe analyzed a number of neo-Nazi, so-called revisionist, groups, largely Belgian, some of whose publications found their way to Holland.

JEWISH COMMUNITY

Demography

Of the estimated 25,000 Jews in the Netherlands, in a total population of just over 15 million, less than one-third were members of any official Jewish community. The Ashkenazi community (Nederland Israelietisch Kerkgenootschap, NIK) had nearly 6,000 members, the Sephardi community (Portugees-Israelietisch Kerkgenootschap, PIK) some 500 members, and the Liberal Jewish community some 2,250. By far the largest Ashkenazi community was that of the Amsterdam area, with over 3,000 members. Rotterdam had 375 and The Hague 400 members. The other members were scattered over 30 congregations, which together were under the aegis of the Inter-Provincial Chief Rabbinate, or IPOR, with its seat in Amersfoort. The Sephardi community had one significant congregation only, in Amsterdam. The Liberal Jewish community had two congregations with full-time rabbis and four others with part-time rabbis.

The number of Jews coming directly from the Soviet Union to Holland and asking for political asylum rose to over 400 this year. Like others seeking political asylum, they were placed in absorption centers until their applications were acted on, which could take up to two years. The Dutch government took care of their physical needs, and the Jewish Social Welfare Foundation (JMW), with volunteer assistance, attended to social and other needs. The religious needs of Russian Jews in absorption centers were looked after by the IPOR. A different policy was followed with regard to Russian Jews who came to Holland from Israel, claiming that they had been discriminated against there. Their applications for political asylum stood no chance of being accepted, and JMW did not take care of them.

Communal Affairs

The introduction to the 1991 annual report of the Ashkenazi community, NIK, analyzed why only a minority of all Jews in the Netherlands were members of any organized Jewish community and suggested the following reasons: widespread secularization, with only about half of the non-Jews in the Netherlands belonging to any church; assistance to the poor no longer the responsibility of religious institutions but of the government, along with other social services; high synagogue membership fees, even though they are often progressive; the growing number of mixed marriages; the existence of Jewish social activities outside synagogues; and the fact that synagogue membership is no longer required for involvement in B'nai B'rith or agencies such as the Jewish Social Welfare Foundation. Twenty years earlier, many Jews remained members of a Jewish community in order to be buried in a Jewish burial ground, but with the increase in cremation, this reason too lost its force. Last but not least, the Ashkenazi community of Amsterdam had taken on an increasingly Orthodox character—under the influence of its present rabbis, who had come from abroad or were at least trained abroad—which may have acted as a deterrent to some.

The strict interpretation of Jewish law by the Amsterdam rabbis led to what became known as the "Carla van Klaveren case" (not her real name). A young non-Jewish woman who had been close to Jewish affairs and Israel for many years was converted to Judaism by the Israeli rabbinate. When she wanted to marry a young Jewish man in Amsterdam, the rabbis refused to approve the marriage, saying they did not recognize Israeli conversion. They also refused to accept her conversion in Holland because she indicated that she would not keep all the 613 commandments. The couple subsequently married on a visit to Israel.

Both the Sephardi community of Amsterdam and the Liberal Jewish communities of Amsterdam and The Hague confronted the need for costly repairs to their synagogues, which they could not afford. The Friends of the Portuguese Synagogue of Amsterdam Foundation, with a board consisting partly of non-Jews, was engaged in raising funds both in the Netherlands and abroad for the restoration—which started in February—of the famous 300-year-old Sephardi synagogue of Amsterdam. One of the donors was the Prince Bernhard Fund. Princess Margriet, a sister of Queen Beatrix, and her husband and two of their sons attended a fund-raising function in New York, on November 7, organized by the American Friends of the Portuguese Synagogue of Amsterdam. A souvenir shop selling items relating to the "Esnoga" and the Sephardi community of Amsterdam opened in a small house adjacent to the synagogue.

Societies of friends were formed to raise funds for the restoration of the Liberal synagogue in Amsterdam, which was constructed only in 1966, and that in The Hague, which occupied the former Sephardi synagogue that had been completely renovated and reopened in 1976.

The strictly Orthodox "Cheider" school—comprising a kindergarten, an elementary, and a secondary school—which had been founded in 1973 and had started with only a few pupils saw its enrollment rise to about 300, for which its existing premises were now too small. By contrast, the Leo Baeck School of the Liberal Jewish community, which opened in 1989, had to close down in the autumn of 1991, as only 20 pupils and a few teachers were left.

The Hatikva kosher restaurant, formerly at the Amstelveenseweg, moved to the ground floor of the new Beth Shalom Old Age Home in Buitenveldert; the Mouwes kosher delicatessen, formerly in the center of Amsterdam, moved to the vicinity of the Beth Shalom.

The Inter-Provincial Chief Rabbinate (IPOR) subsidized a Torah seminar in Moscow and school projects in Kharkov and Tashkent. At a summer seminar in Moscow for some 200 Jewish teachers, organized by the Vaad of Russian Jews, an educator sent by the Dutch community gave a series of lectures on modern methods of teaching Jewish subjects. Liberal rabbi Abraham Soetendorp and his wife spent some months in Moscow during the summer, teaching about Judaism.

Israel-Related Activity

As early as the beginning of August 1990, various Dutch-Jewish organizations, with the Netherlands Zionist Organization (NZB) as the coordinator, had drawn up an emergency plan of action in the event of war in the Persian Gulf and possible Israeli involvement. When war did break out in January, the plan had only to be put into action. During the second half of January the Zionist office was open 24 hours a day to answer questions and accept offers of assistance.

On January 21, a mass demonstration of solidarity with Israel was held in Amsterdam, attended primarily by Jews. The speakers included Minister of the Interior Ina Dales, the chairpersons of the four main parliamentary political parties, representatives of the Protestant communities, and Dr. Emanuel Wikler, chairman of the NIK, on behalf of the Jewish community. A motion of solidarity with Israel was adopted.

On January 24, a large Jewish delegation, including representatives of Jewish welfare organizations such as JMW, met with the minister of the interior and other officials to request increased police protection for Jewish community buildings in the Netherlands against possible terrorist attacks. Dales expressed the Dutch government's readiness to give humanitarian help to Israel.

At the initiative of Abraham Soetendorp, the rabbi of the Liberal Jewish community of The Hague, and of Ronny Naftaniel, the director of the CIDI, the Center for Information and Documentation on Israel, a meeting of Jewish representatives and members of the board of the three main Muslim organizations in the Netherlands—of Moroccans, Turks, and Surinamese—took place on January 29. On the Jewish side were representatives of the three Jewish communities, of the CIDI, and of the Jewish Social Welfare Foundation (JMW). The object of the meeting, which received considerable media attention, was to examine how tolerance between Jews and Muslims could be maintained in Holland, and how the followers of both religions, minorities in Holland, could learn from each other's experiences—while avoiding all mention of religion or politics. The first meeting hardly got past the introductory stage; at the second meeting, some of the Muslims were absent; and no third meeting followed. In Muslim circles, doubts were expressed about the ability of lay members of the boards of three Muslim organizations to adequately represent the Muslim masses.

February 24 was the date picked for "A Chain of Hope," an expression of solidarity between Christians, Jews, and Muslims. That date is the anniversary eve of the so-called February strike, the abortive strike on February 25–26, 1941, of

Amsterdam workers protesting the deportation of the first 400 young Jews. The event was initiated by Rabbi Abraham Soetendorp and the priest of the so-called Moses and Aaron Church, a Roman Catholic church in what was once the Jewish quarter, which stands almost opposite the Esnoga and the Jewish Museum and is now mainly a center for the underprivileged, such as illegal immigrants and immigrants from Third World countries. Very few Jews attended and only one Muslim, a Dutch convert to Islam. Preceding the demonstration, a lecture on Islam was given in the Jewish Museum, which stressed the relatively peaceful relations of Jews and Muslims in the Middle East before the 20th century.

At an extraordinary conference held on June 27, the Netherlands Zionist Organization voted to reorganize itself into a federation of Zionist political parties and to allow other pro-Israel Jewish organizations, such as WIZO, to join the federation. A commission was appointed to work out the details—legal, financial, and otherwise—of this transformation. The United Israel Appeal (Collective Israel Actie) this year raised a record F. 11 million, or F. 2 million more than the previous year.

Holocaust-Related Matters

The persecution of the Jews in the Netherlands during the German occupation of 1940–45 was commemorated by non-Jews as well as Jews in various settings and forms, for its own sake and also as an object lesson.

The commemoration in Amsterdam on February 25 of the 50th anniversary of the February strike, which was attended by Queen Beatrix and Prince-Consort Claus and Minister of Welfare and Culture Hedy D'Ancona, was used as a warning about discrimination against Muslims and Arabs on account of the Gulf War. Similar warnings were voiced at the Yom Hashoah observance on April 10 at the Hollandse Schouwburg, the former Amsterdam theater that served as a collecting center for Jews who had been rounded up for transfer to Westerbork, between July 1942 and 1944.

On May 4, Dutch Memorial Day, and May 5, Liberation Day, the wartime persecution of the Jews was featured in articles and special radio and TV programs. A documentary by Dutch-Jewish filmmaker Willy Lindwer, *A Jewish Wedding in 1942*, was shown by the TROS Broadcasting Company. The film is based on a recently discovered short film of a wedding made by an amateur photographer. Of the many persons who attended the wedding, only the bride and a then eight-year-old nephew survived. The VPRO Broadcasting Organization showed three of a total of fifteen interviews made in cooperation with the Anne Frank Foundation in a series called "Child of the War."

The Conference of Hidden Children, held in New York in June, was attended by some 40 to 50 Jews who had been saved in Holland during the German occupation. The event received considerable attention in the Dutch media.

An exhibition was shown in Westerbork transit camp of paintings and drawings made in the camp by the young Dutch-Jewish artist Leo Kok (1923–1945). A book containing the works, with text in both Dutch and English, was published on this occasion by Jaap Nijstad. (For other books published this year on the persecution of the Jews in Holland, see below.)

The Jewish Social Welfare Foundation (JMW) organized a conference on November 28 on the problems of the Jewish postwar generation. In October it organized a weekend to bring together members of this generation who had lost all contact with Judaism and Jews. It also subsidized so-called Jewish cafes, monthly, in various towns, for young Jews.

Monuments to deported Jews were unveiled in Enschede, in the east of the Netherlands, and at Schoorl, north of Amsterdam.

Controversy arose over ownership of a menorah in Alphen-on-the-Rhine, a village east of Leyden. The menorah had been hidden under the floor of the synagogue by a local Jewish couple during the German occupation, prior to their deportation. Nearly all the Jewish inhabitants of the village perished, and after the war the synagogue was sold to a Protestant congregation. In 1980, during repair work, the menorah was discovered and given a prominent place in the now church. Rabbi Lody van de Kamp, Ashkenazi rabbi of Amsterdam—and head of the Jewish Heritage Foundation established to reclaim such property—demanded return of the menorah on behalf of the town's only surviving former Jewish inhabitant, who now lived in Israel. At the same time, the only surviving relative of the couple, who himself had not been a resident of Alphen, declared that the Protestant church— which refused to give up the menorah—could keep it. The dispute, which was given considerable publicity, was eventually resolved by the Israeli ambassador in The Hague, Michael N. Bawly. He proposed that the Protestant congregation donate the menorah to Israel, in return for which it would receive an Israeli menorah.

Culture

Within the framework of several general exhibitions on relations between the cities of Amsterdam and Venice, in particular in the 17th century, an exhibition on the ghetto of Venice was held in the Jewish Historical Museum, largely organized by guest curator Julie-Marthe Cohen, with a fine accompanying catalogue. The same museum also presented an exhibition on the Sephardi Esnoga in Amsterdam, accompanied by a book on the subject, edited by Raphael Shibboleth and Marianne Stroo. Simultaneously, an exhibition of photographs of a small group of Marranos still living in Belmonte in northeast Portugal was shown, along with videotaped interviews with group members.

An exhibition about the life and career of Dutch-Jewish trade-union leader Henri Polak (1868–1943), founder of the Diamond Workers Trade Union (ANDB), was held in the former building of the ANDB, which housed the offices of the Netherlands Federation of Trade Unions after 1945 and had recently been turned into a trade-union museum. The building is situated in what until 1945 was called the Plantage Franselaan but was then renamed the Henri Polak-laan. The new museum and the Henri Polak exhibition were opened officially by Queen Beatrix on, appropriately, May 1.

Apart from the above-mentioned documentaries in connection with the Holocaust, another documentary of Jewish interest was a two-hour TV film, made by Emile Fallaux, on the Dutch-Jewish poet and journalist Jacob Israel de Haan (1881–1924). A most complicated character, de Haan, who was born of Orthodox parents, originally espoused socialism but later became a Zionist and settled in Jerusalem, where he became ultra-Orthodox and an anti-Zionist, which views he expressed as the Jerusalem correspondent of the *London Daily Express*. He was also a well-known homosexual. He was murdered in Jerusalem in June 1924 by Zionists. The documentary contains interviews with, among others, Abraham Tehomi, who murdered de Haan on behalf of the Haganah and who, at the time of the interview, was living in California, and with Rabbi Menachem Porush of the Agudath Israel party in Jerusalem, who had been among de Haan's admirers.

There was continuing interest in Yiddish, especially among non-Jews. An International Yiddish Festival was held in Amsterdam, November 24–30, with the participation of theatrical companies and Klezmer groups, in particular from the United States, and with the showing of several Yiddish films, from before 1940 and more recently. The festival was organized by Mira Rafalowitz, the daughter of Polish-Jewish parents who had been great advocates of Yiddish in Amsterdam, and who herself had studied Yiddish at the YIVO Institute in New York. The festival was widely publicized, and most performances were sold out well in advance. It was opened by Minister of Welfare and Culture D'Ancona. Several mainly non-Jewish musical groups also performed Yiddish songs and Klezmer music in Holland during the year.

The Amsterdam Summer University offered two courses of Jewish interest, one about East European Jewry and one about Dutch Jewry. Both were attended by persons from Holland and abroad.

The Netherlands Society for Jewish Genealogy had over 400 members, of whom over 50 were in the United States and Israel. Its members included many non-Jews or persons with a remote Jewish ancestor. Its thoroughly professional quarterly, *Misjpoge*, had a special issue on Jewish burial grounds in the Netherlands. The society also published *Trouwen in Mokum* ("Marrying in Amsterdam"), a listing of 15,300 Jewish marriages registered in Amsterdam between 1598 and 1811, compiled by Dave Vordooner, an officer of the society, and Harmen Snel, of the Amsterdam Municpal Archives.

Publications

In addition to new works on Jewish themes already mentioned above, the following should be noted. In connection with the Holocaust: *Vervolging, vernietiging, literatuur* ("Persecution, Annihilation, Literature"), a series of essays by Sem Dresden; *Voorbij de Verboden Drempel. De Shoah in ons Geschiedbeeld* ("Past the

Forbidden Threshold: The Shoah in Our View of History") by H.W. von der Dunk; *Om het Joodse Kind* ("About the Jewish Child") by Elma Verhey, on the struggle over Jewish war orphans in the Netherlands in the first years after liberation; *Grenzen aan de solidariteit* ("Limits to Solidarity") by Paul Vigeveno and Ton van der Meer, a series of lessons for schools; *Joodse vluchtelingen in Nederland, 1938–1949* ("Jewish Refugees in the Netherlands, 1938–1949," documents on their admission and refusal) by Corrie K. Berghuis; *De Zoektocht* ("The Search") by Gerhard L. Durlacher, the story of a 16-year-old boy who survived Auschwitz and went to search for fellow survivors in Israel; *Zwijgende Stenen* ("Silent Stones") by Shmuel Hacohen, a translation from Hebrew of the author's experiences in Amsterdam during the German occupation of the Netherlands and afterward in Israel; *Tralievader* by Carl Friedman, a work about the problems of the second generation. The well-known short novel about Westerbork by the late Jacques Presser, *De Nacht der Girondijnen*, originally published in 1957, was issued in a new edition with an introduction written by the late Primo Levi. Translations of this edition were published in Italian, English, French, and German.

Several histories of Jewish communities appeared this year, among them of Aalten, by Peter Lurvink; of Assen, by F.J. Mulder; of de Pekela's, by E. Schut; and of Oldenzaal, by G.J.J.W. Wensink. Robert Cohen's *Jews in Another Environment: Surinam in the Second Half of the 18th Century* also appeared this year, as did a collection of some 30 essays in honor of David Goudsmit, a former librarian of the Etz Hayim Library of the Portuguese synagogue in Amsterdam, on his 80th birthday.

Personalia

Mrs. R. Musaph (née Andriesse) received a Silver Carnation from Prince Bernhard for her work on behalf of Jewish culture in the Netherlands, including chairing the Foundation of Friends of the Jewish Historical Museum. The queen's birthday list, on April 29, included Judith Belinfante, director of the Jewish Historical Museum; Bloeme Evers (née Emden), chairwoman of the Jewish women's group "Deborah"; Robert Goudsmit, chairman of the Foundation of the Jewish Invalid and of the Foundation for Jewish Daytime Education; and Frieda Menco-Bromet, a past chairwoman of the Liberal Jewish community.

Raphael Evers was officially installed as rector of the Netherlands Ashkenazi Rabbinical and Teachers Seminary, of which he had been director for several years. Leo Palache retired on June 1 as director of the United Israel Appeal, which office he had held for exactly 40 years.

Among prominent Dutch Jews who died this year were Siegfried ten Brink, vice-chairman of the Netherlands Zionist Organization, editor of its periodical, and for many years a member of the executive of the Liberal Jewish community of Amsterdam, aged 65; Hans Evers, a leader in the Amsterdam Ashkenazi community and the Netherlands Zionist Organization and OJEC, aged 67; Robert Goudsmit, chairman of the Foundation of the Jewish Invalid, the Foundation for the Jewish Elderly Beth Shalom, and the Foundation for Jewish Daytime Education, aged 69; Liesbeth van Weezel, editor of the Dutch-Jewish weekly *Nieuw Israelietisch Weekblad* in the 1960s, aged 83.

HENRIETTE BOAS

Italy

National Affairs

ITALY'S POLITICAL SITUATION remained relatively stable in 1991, although a mini-crisis occurred when Prime Minister Giulio Andreotti (Christian Democrats, DC) resigned on March 30, following the withdrawal of the Socialist party (PSI), led by Bettino Craxi, from the coalition government. But the crisis was quickly resolved, and Andreotti formed a new government—his seventh—that was approved on April 19. The new coalition, like the former one, included the Christian Democrats, Socialists, Social Democrats, and Liberals; the Republicans, who had been part of the previous government, resigned in a dispute over the assignment of cabinet posts.

An increasingly outspoken President Francesco Cossiga expressed disappointment that the "reshuffling" had produced no significant policy change, and observers generally bemoaned the continuing sclerosis of Italy's political system. A referendum on political reform in June produced a large turnout and an overwhelming vote in favor of reducing the number of candidates voters must choose among in the elections for the lower chamber. While the change is a small one, it was hailed as a step toward a thoroughgoing reform of the system. It also made politicians and the public aware that the workings of Italian democracy are not cast in stone.

In February the Communist party of Italy, once the largest Communist party in the West, changed its name to the Democratic Party of the Left (Partito Democratico della Sinistra, PDS). Under Secretary Achille Occhetto, the party had abandoned much of its traditional line and become more social-democratic in outlook. The decision was rejected by the most extreme wing of the party, which broke away and formed the Communist Refoundation party (Rifondazione Comunista, PRC). Another political development of note was the growth of the Lombard League and associated Northern League, parties in the north of the country that advocate greater regional autonomy and have rightist leanings.

Although Italy participated in the Gulf War (see below), criticism of its forces by an American general was a blow to public pride and served to spotlight the military's serious deficiencies, including use of outdated hardware and an unprofessional, largely conscript army, plagued by the same patronage system that characterizes the rest of Italy's public sector.

Italy faced growing problems related to the recent influx of Albanian refugees and other migrant groups. The UN appealed to Italy not to expel the Albanians, most of whom were living in makeshift camps and being helped by volunteer organizations. African and Arab workers protested in Rome in mid-May over work and

271

housing conditions. Milan experienced a number of anti-immigrant strikes over the presence of migrant encampments in the city. There were protests over the announcement that non-EC immigrant nurses would be allowed to work in Italian hospitals, to fill a serious shortage.

Although political terrorism had virtually ceased, organized crime—a long-standing problem in southern Italy—was viewed as a serious national problem, with Mafia activity spreading to other parts of the country. Political leaders, investigating officials, and police involved in trying to curb the Mafia were murdered, and there was a substantial increase in the overall number of murders attributable to organized crime. The government had relatively little success in fighting it, in part due to the inefficiency of the legal system.

The economy was somewhat sluggish after almost a decade of buoyant growth. A chronic unemployment rate of over 11 percent and the public-sector deficit were the major underlying problems. The inflation rate had remained at above 6 percent since 1989, some 1 to 3 percentage points higher than in France, Germany, the United States, and United Kingdom, which hurt Italy's competitiveness. Another long-term problem was Italy's dependence on oil imports for almost 80 percent of its energy needs, higher than any other EC country.

THE GULF WAR

During the entire seven months of the Gulf crisis and the "Desert Storm" military operation, the Italian government was actively involved in finding ways to "save the peace." At the same time, it acceded to the request of the United States to join the coalition against Saddam Hussein and sent five ships and eleven combat planes to the Gulf, without placing any limitations on their use. Both Prime Minister Andreotti and Foreign Minister Gianni De Michelis engaged in active diplomacy up to the last minute, in an attempt to avoid war. Andreotti was about to leave for Baghdad when hostilities began on January 16. De Michelis, who was in close contact with Nemer Hammad, PLO representative in Rome, urged that Palestinians appeal to Saddam Hussein to withdraw from Kuwait, in exchange for the Italian government's commitment to work for an international peace conference on the Middle East to deal with the Palestinian problem.

In the Italian Parliament, pacifists on both Left and Right, ready to appease Saddam Hussein, clashed with supporters of UN intervention. Achille Occhetto, leader of the Communist party, called the war "an adventure without return," urged both dialogue with Iraq in order to preserve the peace and an international meeting on the Middle East. Raniero La Valle of the Sinistra Indipendente, a group of independent leftists, quoting a Catholic source, stated that the war against Saddam Hussein was a crime and accused the West of failure to understand Islam. Giovanni Russo Spena, secretary of Proletarian Democracy (DP), supported the Iraqi version of the Kuwait crisis, and the neo-Fascist Italian Social Movement (MSI; the most right-wing party in Parliament) accused the Italian government of "not having given enough support to European-Arab dialogue" and defined as a political priority the defense of Palestinian rights.

By contrast, Renato Altissimo, leader of the Liberal party (PLI), denounced the PLO for its political attitude toward the war, and Bettino Craxi of the Socialist party (PSI) reminded political leaders and the Italian public that "Saddam Hussein attacked an Arab country and wiped it off the map, an act that had no connection at all to the Israeli-Palestinian question."

The Radical party (PR) was in a quandary: generally opposed to military intervention, in this situation it supported the political objectives of the war. Deputy Emma Bonino stated that "as a nonviolent person," she was not prepared to accept "any violation of human rights"; her party colleague Roberto Cicciomessere, quoting Ghandi, affirmed that "everyone is free to choose between cowardice and violence, but in this particular case violence is better." Giovanni Spadolini, of the moderate left Republican party (PRI) and president of the Senate, was among the first to express sympathy with Israel.

The outspoken opposition of Pope John Paul II to allied intervention in the Gulf helped to swell an already substantial peace movement in the country (close to 74 percent opposed the war, in a late-January opinion poll). During an Angelus in St. Peter's Square on January 24, the pope berated the "terrible logic of war" and called for a peace conference to resolve all problems in the Middle East, particularly the Palestinian question.

The pope's stance caused a serious rift with the Christian Democratic party (traditionally regarded as the Vatican's political wing), brought the Vatican into unaccustomed alliance with the Communists, and caused a split in the Christian Democratic party itself. Support for intervention came from the party's higher echelons, particularly the prime minister, while more Catholic and liberal elements followed the pope's lead and agitated against their own leadership. Even conservative cardinals were displeased with the pope. Camillo Cardinal Ruini, one of the pope's pro-vicars, said he would "absolve the Italian government and all those who voted for the war."

The pope's position enraged Italy's Jewish community. Chief Rabbi Elio Toaff of Rome called the Vatican line "politically unsustainable and morally unjustified . . . and an invitation to anti-Semitism" and challenged the pope to "look Israel in the face and say these things."

On January 27, while Israel was under attack by Iraqi missiles, the director-general of the Italian Foreign Ministry, Bruno Bottai, paid a one-day visit to the country to express his government's solidarity. He brought with him a letter of support from President Cossiga.

Relations with Israel

At the end of February, Foreign Minister De Michelis called for broad international support for the establishment of a Helsinki-type conference on security and cooperation in the Mediteranean and the Middle East, to deal with the aftermath of the war in the Gulf, in particular to create a framework within which to deal with the Israeli-Palestinian conflict. He even claimed to have the support of some Israelis for the idea.

Various Italian political leaders visited Israel throughout the year. On April 28, Achille Occhetto, secretary of the Democratic Party of the Left, made his first trip to Israel, as part of a Middle East study tour. This visit reflected a virtual turnabout in the policy of the PDS toward the State of Israel, a result, largely, of Israel's self-restraint during the war. Occhetto was generally regarded as sympathetic to Israeli interests but opposed to the Likud government's policy on the territories. The Italian delegation met with Israeli prime minister Yitzhak Shamir as well as with Palestinian leaders. The PDS officials also took part in a memorial ceremony on Jerusalem's Mount Herzl for Italian Jewish Communist leader Umberto Terracini, who died a few years earlier.

A delegation from the Italian Senate, headed by Socialist Michele Achilli, chairman of the Foreign Affairs Committee, visited Israel in June, meeting with Foreign Minister David Levy, Speaker of the Knesset Dov Shilansky, and Yitzhak Rabin, former defense minister, among others.

Foreign Minister De Michelis paid an official visit to Israel on September 4, during which he met with Israeli political leaders and a West Bank Palestinian delegation. The purpose of the visit was to discuss the proposed Middle East peace conference that Washington was trying to organize as well as Israel's economic relations with Europe after the unification of the European Community in 1992. (De Michelis was responsible for initiating the idea of including Israel in European economic plans after unification.) De Michelis aroused some ire over an interview with the daily Ha'aretz, in which he said that "Eretz Yisrael no longer exists," referring to Israel's conflict with the Palestinians over "Greater Israel." He went on to say: "It would be hard for Israel to remain isolated in its attitude that self-determination was fine for all nations—for the Ukrainians and Moldavians—but not for the Palestinians."

Leaders of the new PDS, Piero Fassino and Carlo Leoni, together with Janiki Cingoli, director of the Italian Center for Peace in the Middle East, visited Israel and the West Bank in November. The same month, an Italian Socialist delegation came to Tel Aviv to observe the Israel Labor party congress.

Defense Minister Virginio Rognoni arrived in Israel on December 26 for an official visit, as the guest of his counterpart, Moshe Arens. The Italian met with Prime Minister Shamir and Foreign Minister Levy as well. Rognoni stressed the importance of the Israeli-Arab peace process and predicted a strengthening of Israeli economic ties with Italy and with the European Community as a whole.

Cultural and trade relations between Italy and Israel remained strong. According to the Israel Central Bureau of Statistics, exports from Italy for 1990–1991 totaled $935 million, with imports from Israel of some $503 million. The Italian exports were mainly industrial machinery, motor vehicles, metal products, and electrical and electronic items. The imports from Israel were largely chemical and agricultural products, fertilizers, and electrical wares.

On March 3, right after the Gulf War, a delegation of some 200 residents of Milan, led by Mayor Paolo Pilitteri, arrived in Israel for a visit. The delegation, which included Cobi Benatoff, the president of the Milan Jewish community, was received by Tel Aviv mayor Shlomo Lahat, Jerusalem mayor Teddy Kollek, and Deputy Minister of Foreign Affairs Benjamin Netanyahu. The delegation expressed the support of the Italian people for Israel and donated funds for a school building to replace one that had been seriously damaged during the Iraqi missile attacks on Israel.

A Friendship for Israel Parliamentary Association was founded in March by the deputies Oscar Luigi Scalfaro and Gerolamo Pellicano, president and secretary of the new organization, and by Parliament members Alfredo Biondi of the Liberal party, Emma Bonino of the Radical party, Laura Finacato of the Socialist party, and Filippo Caria of the Social-Democratic party. Some 200 deputies and senators participated in the first meeting. In the same period, the Union of Italian Jewish Communities (Unione delle Comunità Ebraiche Italiane, UCEI) and the Italy-Israel Friendship Association—a group open to the general public—held a joint meeting at the Villa Pamphili Hotel, where they were addressed by Israeli ambassador Mordechai Drory, MPs Scalfaro and Andrea Cifarelli (Republican party MP and former president of the association), president of the Rome Jewish community Sergio Frassineti, and UCEI president Tullia Zevi. At another meeting organized by the association, on June 19, held at the Chamber of Deputies, Mrs. Zevi asserted that Italy, by virtue of its history and geographic position, could play a key role as mediator in the conflicts troubling the Mediterranean basin.

An Italian scientific delegation visited the Weizmann Institute in Rehovot on April 30, to review recent work in cancer research and other fields. The scientists also discussed plans for the "Mediterranean School for Polymer Science and Technology," which was being promoted by the Italian National Research Council. Participants included Arab as well as Italian and Jewish scientists.

A group of 30 Italian intellectuals—artists, scholars, and journalists—visited Israel in May, seeking to deepen their understanding of the country and its problems. They met with Israeli political leaders, scholars, and writers, and participated in debates and seminars at various political and cultural institutions. The trip was arranged by the Rome Jewish community.

On June 7, the Italian ambassador in Israel, Pierluigi Rachele, attended the annual convention of the Italian-Israeli Chamber of Commerce. He told a large group of Israeli and Italian tour operators that, during 1990–91, economic and commercial relations between Italy and Israel showed an upturn, and that the prospects for further growth were encouraging. In his speech, Rachele noted that Italy was Israel's fourth largest trading partner in the world and the third largest within the European Community. He stressed the fact that trade had increased in the first quarter of 1991, despite the negative effects of the Gulf War.

Avi Pazner, the spokesman for Prime Minister Yitzhak Shamir, was appointed Israeli ambassador to Italy in July, replacing Mordechai Drory.

Anti-Semitism

During 1991, the Milan-based Center for Contemporary Jewish Documentation (Centro di Documentazione ebraica contemporanea, CDEC) continued to survey the media for evidence of prejudice against minorities in general and against the Jews in particular. CDEC and the Union of Italian Jewish Communities (UCEI) organized an educational program about anti-Semitism in Italian high schools. CDEC scholars and researchers participated in a number of meetings and conferences on anti-Semitism. A seminar took place for WIZO-Italy's youth organization, AVIV, in Milan on May 8, organized by Adriana Goldstaub, on "Anti-Semitism in Italy After the Second World War." In Turin, on November 23, Liliana Picciotto Fargion spoke on "Coming Back from the Lager." Michele Sarfatti and Liliana Picciotto Fargion spoke at an AVIV meeting in Milan, in January, on "Persecution Against the Jews in Italy 1938–1945."

JEWISH COMMUNITY

Demography

Some 31,000 Jews were affiliated with their local Jewish communities. The total number of Jews in Italy, taking into account those not affiliated, was believed to be around 35,000.

Communal Affairs

The Gulf War and events in the Middle East were of great concern to the Italian Jewish community.

On January 14, a rally for peace began at Rome's Great Synagogue, where the chief rabbi of Rome, Elio Toaff, led "a prayer for peace." The rally continued that evening with an enormous demonstration organized by the Jewish Students Cultural Movement (Movimento culturale studenti ebrei, MCSE), with the participation of Rabbi Toaff, Israeli ambassador Mordechai Drory, and the president of the Rome Jewish community, Sergio Frassineti.

On January 16, the Jewish Youth Council (Comitato Giovanile Ebraico, CGE) invited a prominent Italian Jewish journalist, Fiamma Nirensztein, correspondent of the popular Italian weekly *Epoca*, to discuss developments in the Persian Gulf. On January 20, in reaction to the first missile attacks on Israel and Saudi Arabia, Angelo Pezzana, president of the Italy-Israel Association, called a solidarity sit-in outside the Israeli embassy in Rome. Participants included representatives of the

Radical party (with its deputies Emma Bonino and Bruno Zevi), the Republican party and its youth organization, the Liberal party, the Social-Democratic party, the Evangelical Churches Association, and the Association of Christians Against Anti-Semitism. The Israeli ambassador thanked the participants for their support.

On January 24, at Palazzo Chigi in Rome, Tullia Zevi and Dario Tedeschi, representing the UCEI, met with Prime Minister Andreotti to discuss the tense situation in Israel caused by the Gulf War. The two UCEI representatives asked Andreotti to intervene with the European Community to renew a program of scientific collaboration between the EC and Israel, to use his influence with the Vatican in regard to Vatican diplomatic recognition of the State of Israel.

At the first session of the new council of the UCEI, in January, Tullia Zevi was confirmed president by acclamation. The vice-president was Giuseppe Viterbo of Florence; the other members of the council committee were Amos Luzzatto (Venice), Alda Segre (Turin), Dario Tedeschi (Rome), and Elio Toaff as representative of the Rabbinical Council. The council devoted particular attention to questions concerning Jewish education and culture, relations among the Jewish communities, the preservation of the Italian Jewish artistic heritage, and relations between the Jewish community and the Italian state.

Tullia Zevi represented the Italian Jewish community at a number of Jewish communal meetings in Europe and Israel: at the executive committee of the European Jewish Congress (EJC), on January 13, in Paris, which heard a careful analysis of the Gulf crisis and considered concrete ways to support Israel in the crisis; at the meeting of the executive of the World Jewish Congress in Jerusalem, February 11 and 12, during which she met with Yitzhak Navon, former president of Israel, and several professors of the Hebrew University to discuss plans for the 1992 observance of the 500th anniversary of the expulsion of the Jews from Spain. Zevi also took part in EJC meetings in Jerusalem, May 4–5, and the plenary assembly of the WJC, immediately following. Zevi was joined by Giorgio Sacerdoti, Dario Tedeschi, and Federico Steinhaus, members of the UCEI Council. In July, Zevi participated in an executive meeting of the EJC in Paris, at which the main topics for consideration were anti-Semitism, the situation of Judaism in Eastern Europe, Jewish-Christian relations, the European organizations, and the State of Israel.

On October 16, in Rome, Tullia Zevi, Sergio Frassineti, and the mayor of Rome took part in ceremonies commemorating the deportation of Rome's Jews in World War II. The ceremonies were held at the Great Synagogue, at the Mausoleum of the Fosse Ardeatine, at the city cemetery, in the Rome Ghetto, and at the Vittorio Polacco primary school.

The 90th anniversary of the Italian Zionist Federation (FSI) was observed in Milan in November, with a special exhibition and celebrations.

Community Relations

The final decision regarding the teaching of Catholic religion in public high schools was handed down by the Italian Constitutional Court on January 14. The court ruled that secondary students who do not elect religious instruction are allowed to leave the school; however, it did not reach a decision concerning the teaching of Catholic religion in kindergarten and the primary grades.

A ceremony took place on June 20, in the Chamber of Deputies, on the anniversary of the death of the Jewish antifascist and scholar Eugenio Colorni. The gathering was arranged by the World War II partisans' association ANPI, the Eugenio Colorni Club, and the UCEI.

Jewish-Christian Relations

As noted above, the Gulf War strongly affected relations between the Jewish community and the Vatican, and Jewish officials were critical of Pope John Paul II's antiwar stance. On February 3, the Rome Jewish community organized a peaceful demonstration in St. Peter's Square, asking, in a dignified way, for full recognition of the State of Israel by the Vatican.

Rabbis Toaff and Piattelli and Tullia Zevi participated in a celebration of the 23rd anniversary of the founding of the community of St. Egidio, a highly influential Catholic organization involved in peace work, on March 2, in Rome. The mayor of Rome, members of the government, and Edward Cardinal Cassidy, president of the Political Council for Promoting Christian Unity, were present at the ceremony.

On July 4, Tullia Zevi met with Cardinal Cassidy to discuss, among a number of issues, the Carmelite convent in Auschwitz and a meeting to be held between a delegation of the EJC and Carlo Maria Cardinal Martini, bishop of Milan, before the Special Assembly of the European Synod of Bishops.

Speaking at the opening of the Assembly of the Federation of Evangelical Churches in October, Tullia Zevi invited the federation to work more closely with the UCEI for the improvement of relations between the two communities.

On November 19, Jean Kahn, president of the EJC, together with Gerhart Riegner and Tullia Zevi, president and vice-president of the EJC's commission for interreligious relations, delivered a letter of protest to Cardinal Martini, in his capacity as president of the Council of European Episcopal Conferences. The letter criticized statements made by the pope in the document prepared for the upcoming Synod of European Bishops, in which he described his program for the "evangelization of Europe, a continent that can find its unity only in Christian values." In their memorandum, the EJC representatives reaffirmed the importance of Jewish culture in European history and the suffering of European Jewry during the centuries as a warning for the future.

In fact, the persecution of the Jews was recalled several times during the meeting of European bishops, which took place in the Vatican the first week of December.

Camillo Cardinal Ruini, in his introduction, stated the value and the importance of the dialogue between Jews and Christians. He also affirmed that the Jewish faith and culture represented "a constitutive moment in the development" of Western civilization and said that the tragedy of the Shoah showed "how far the perversion of the European conscience can reach." A few days later, during mass at St. Peter's, there was a symbolic "confession of sins," in which the German bishops acknowledged their passivity in the face of the persecution and extermination of the Jews. The final document of the synod stated that the effort to achieve understanding between Jews and Christians could have enormous significance for the future of Europe.

Culture

In a solemn ceremony on March 21, in Rome, representatives of the CDEC and leading Italian Jews presented to Francesco Cossiga, the president of the Republic, the first copy of Liliana Picciotto Fargion's volume *Il libro della memoria. Gli ebrei deportati dall'Italia (1943–1945)*, a listing of the Jews deported from Italy and from the Aegean Islands during World War II. In her remarks, Luisella Mortara Ottolenghi, president of the CDEC, underscored the moral and pedagogic value of the work. Tullia Zevi stressed the importance of such works in countering revisionist attempts to deny the facts of the Holocaust. A similar presentation was made on June 12 in Rome, at Palazzo Giustiniani, to the president of the Senate, Giovanni Spadolini. After Spadolini's speech, Simon Wiesenthal, Serge Klarsfeld, Prof. Renzo De Felice, and Luisella Mortara Ottolenghi spoke on various aspects of the Italian Jewish experience during the Nazi period. The German ambassador and Johannes Cardinal Willebrands, former president of the Vatican Commission for Relations with the Jews, participated in the ceremony.

The first meeting of the Primo Levi Cultural Center took place in Genoa, on April 11, at the municipality building. The new organization planned to promote and support a variety of programs for the study and dissemination of Judaism and Jewish culture.

In April, in honor of Israel Independence Day, all-day study sessions were arranged by the UCEI's cultural department in Ancona and in Trieste, on the subject "Yom Ha'atzmaut: From Exile to Redemption." The two events were sponsored by the ADEI-WIZO and the Federation of Italian Jewish Youth (FGEI).

On June 5, in Soncino, a small town in northern Italy, near Cremona, a special gathering marked the publication of *La Menorah nella Rocca* ("Rocca's Menorah") by Ermete Rossi, a scholarly work about the Jews of Soncino in the 15th and 16th centuries. On the same occasion, plans were discussed for the creation of a Jewish music section in the National Jewish Bibliographical Center in Rome, with the involvement of the School of Music Paleography in Cremona, the District of Cremona, the Hebrew University of Jerusalem, the UCEI, and the Lauder Foundation. (Cremona was the site of a school for lutists in the first half of the 16th century, which had its headquarters in the shop of a Jewish lute seller, as well as the home of many of the world's most famous makers of stringed instruments.) On September 22, the Soncino municipality organized a gathering of the descendants of the Soncino family of Jewish printers, who produced the Soncino Talmud and other important Jewish books in the Middle Ages.

A planning meeting for the archaeological exhibition *Antichita' ebraiche a Roma* (Jewish Antiquities in Rome) took place on July 16. The participants were Dr. Gherpelli, deputy mayor of Emilia Romagna Council; the cultural attachés of the U.S. and Canadian embassies; Tullia Zevi; and various specialists. The exhibition was scheduled to open in the winter of 1993 in Jerusalem and later to travel to New York, Toronto, and Rome.

An exhibition opened in July in Riva del Garda, a small town near Trent in northern Italy, about the Hebrew printing press that was active there, 1557–1563, and the physician-printer, Jacob Marcaria, who ran it.

Publications

Several new studies on the history of Italian Jewry were published this year.

In *Libri e scrittori nella Roma ebraica del Medio Evo* ("Authors and Books in the Jewish Rome of the Middle Ages"), Giulio Busi describes the intense cultural life of the Jewish community of Rome during the 13th and 14th centuries, as seen in the numerous manuscripts produced in the city in those years. *Processi contro gli ebrei di Trento (1475–1478)* ("Trials of the Jews of Trent 1475–1478"), by Anna Esposito and Diego Quaglioni, analyzes the tumultuous and terrifying events that led to the martyrdom and beatification of the young Simon of Trent, allegedly murdered by Jews, in a famous case of blood libel.

Cesare Colafemmina, a scholar who has devoted his career to the study of the Jewish presence in southern Italy, edited a new volume of essays on the history of the Jews in the area of Apulia, *Documenti per la storia degli ebrei in Puglia nell'Archivio di Stato di Napoli* ("Documents on the History of Apulian Jewry in Naples State Archives"). It was issued by the Regional Council of Apulia and by the St. Nicola Ecumenical Institute.

Liliana Picciotto Fargion's *Il libro della memoria. Gli ebrei deportati dall'Italia (1943–1945)* ("The Book of Memory: The Jews Deported from Italy, 1943–1945") is the culmination of several decades of research started in 1944 by Massimo Adolfo Vitale, president at that time of the CRDE (Comitato Ricerche Deportati Ebrei) and finally completed by the author. As noted above, the volume catalogues the victims of the Holocaust in Italy, including brief biographical entries, a historical review, statistical tables, and footnotes.

Michele Luzzati's *Ebrei di Livorno tra due censimenti (1841–1938). Memoria famigliare e identità* ("Leghorn Jews Between Two Censuses, 1841–1938: Family Memory and Identity") presents an intimate view of the life of the Jewish community of Leghorn and of some of its leading families (Castelli, Orefice, Belforte) at the end of the 19th and beginning of the 20th centuries.

The eighth volume of *Processi del S. Uffizio contro Ebrei e Giudaizzanti (1587–1698)* ("St. Uffizio Trials Against Jews and Crypto Jews, 1587–1698"), edited by Pier Cesare Ioly Zorattini, is part of a monumental work started by the author in 1980, which uses dramatic stories of individuals to document the accusations made against Jews and those charged with behaving like Jews in 16th- and 17th-century Venice.

Roberto Bonfil's latest work, *Gli ebrei in Italia nell'epoca del Rinascimento* ("The Jews of Italy in the Renaissance"), presents a fascinating picture of the Jewish community, with its cultural, economic, and social ties to the Gentile world.

Personalia

Italian composer Luciano Berio was a co-winner this year of the prestigious Israeli Wolf Prize for the arts, which he shared with Sir Yehudi Menuhin. Berio is a well-known musical scholar, writer, and conductor. The prize was personally presented in May by Chaim Herzog, president of the State of Israel.

Bar-Ilan University in Israel conferred an honorary degree on Elio Toaff, the chief rabbi of the Italian Jewish community, citing his historical achievements in the area of Jewish-Christian relations and his dynamic spiritual leadership of Italian Jewry. The ceremony was attended by the Italian ambassador in Israel, Pierluigi Rachele, and Israeli minister of education Zevulun Hammer.

World-renowned physicist Salvador Luria died in Lexington, Massachusetts, in February, at the age of 79. Luria, a pioneer in modern genetics and winner of the Nobel Prize for medicine and physiology in 1969, was born in Turin in 1912. After the passage of the 1938 Italian racial laws, he left for Paris and then for the United States, where he joined the faculty of the Massachusetts Institute of Technology.

Emma Cantoni, aged 88, died in Israel in September. Born in Florence in 1903 to an educated, upper-class Jewish family, she emigrated to Palestine in 1936, where she worked as a nurse and became deeply involved in the work of Youth Aliyah. In 1951 she married Raffaele Cantoni, one of the most important and charismatic leaders of Italian Jewry, and joined her husband in Rome. They were actively involved in the Keren Hayesod, the Italian Zionist Federation, and the Jewish Medical Organization (OSE). She returned to Jerusalem to live after her husband's death.

M. M. CONSONNI

Federal Republic of Germany

National Affairs

THE EVENTS OF 1991 IN GERMANY were dominated by the process of unification. The two German states had been formally reunited on October 3, 1990, and the first all-German national elections were held in December. The resounding victory for the incumbent Christian Democrats and Liberals (CDU/CSU-FDP) led to the reelection of Helmut Kohl as the first all-German chancellor since 1945, on January 18. Despite its strength in the national elections, the conservative CDU did poorly in local elections that followed, largely to the advantage of the Social Democrats (SPD). Some of the strength of the SPD, however, simply derived from a weakening of the CDU, because in several of these elections, the Christian Democrats lost voters to stronger radical right parties. This became especially apparent in Bremen, where in the September state elections the Deutsche Volksunion (DVU), the right-wing party led by the notorious Gerhard Frey, made surprising gains.

With the opening of the East German market, the West German economy experienced a boom. At the same time, major changes in industry took place in Germany's so-called Five New Länder, the states of the former German Democratic Republic. In April, the last GDR automobiles—Trabant and Wartburg—rolled off the assembly lines. Volkswagen assembly plants were scheduled to open in Mosel and Chemnitz in 1993. In the same month, the East German airline Interflug made its last flight and was then taken over by Lufthansa. The shutting down of most large industrial and agricultural units in the east led to massive unemployment—which climbed to over a million, or 12.1 percent, in July—and underemployment. In February and March, large demonstrations protesting closings and layoffs and demanding higher wages took place in Mecklenburg-W. Pomerania (Vorpommern), Chemnitz, Erfurt, Halle, Leipzig, and East Berlin.

Throughout the year, migration—especially of young people—from the former GDR to the west averaged 10,000 per month. In April, the lifting of visa requirements for Polish citizens crossing into Germany aggravated the increasing competition between unemployed East Germans and foreign workers and asylum seekers. Right-wing radical attacks on foreigners reached new highs in late April (Hitler's birthday) and early October (the first anniversary of unification). (See below, "Anti-Semitism and Extremism.")

With unification and the end of the Cold War, Bonn attempted to put its relations with Eastern Europe on a new footing. In March, Kohl met with Prime Minister Jan Bielecki of Poland in Bonn after the German government had formally recognized its border with Poland as final; and in June—after opening the border with

Poland in May—the German-Polish "good neighbor" treaty was formally signed. In November, Russia's Boris Yeltsin visited Germany, a visit which clearly consolidated the relationship between the two countries and reaffirmed Germany's commitment to Russia.

In June, by a narrow majority of 17 votes, the Bundestag decided that the future seat of government should be moved from Bonn to Berlin over a 12-year period; this move was supported by most of the (older) leadership of the major parties except the Bavarian Christian Social Union; many of the younger parliamentarians, however, opted for Bonn. The cost of moving to Berlin was estimated at 15 billion Deutsch marks.

The Gulf War; Relations with Israel

Outside the Middle East itself and possibly the United States, nowhere did the Gulf War arouse as much heated debate as in Germany. This debate between "pacifists" and "militants," between those supporting UN intervention and those opposed to it, cut across virtually all parties, from the Christian Democrats to the Greens. Israeli politicians were quick to criticize the "anti-American" sentiments underlying the German antiwar movement, as well as the neutral stance taken by German politicians and media and the cessation of visits to Israel by parliamentarians, unionists, and leftists. In January, in front of the German embassy in Tel Aviv, Holocaust survivors protested the "hypocrisy of German citizens who are now demonstrating against the Americans" and the complicity of German firms in the armaments buildup in Iraq.

A report by the Hamburg-based news magazine Der Spiegel indicated that numerous German firms had assisted in the development of the Iraqi Scud-B missile. The article identified several firms that were under investigation in this regard, including the Düsseldorf-based Thyssen AG. In March the State Prosecutor's Office in Darmstadt (Hesse) brought charges against 12 business executives and one corporation for having broken the law on arms exports to Iraq. In reaction to international criticism of the involvement of German firms in armaments exports, the Bundestag approved changes in the foreign trade law regulating such exports.

The Central Council of Jews in Germany (Zentralrat der Juden in Deutschland) demanded that Germany "stop its reticence and get actively involved in protecting Israel." The German government, according to the Zentralrat, knew full well about the shipments of poison-gas equipment and arms of mass destruction to Iraq but had not taken any action. The Social Democrats and the Christian Democrats were both internally divided over the war. The biggest controversy by far erupted when the leader of the Green party in Bonn, Christian Ströbele, visited Israel in February, where he stated in effect that he opposed the sale of Scud missiles to Israel because Israel's own policies had brought the Iraqi attacks upon it. In the uproar that followed, Ströbele was forced to resign his position, and the party leadership apologized to Israel for Ströbele's statements.

Indeed, by that time, the tide of German public opinion had begun to turn in Israel's favor. Already on January 24, Foreign Minister Hans-Dietrich Genscher, Minister for Economic Cooperation Carl-Dieter Spranger, and CDU general secretary Volker Rühe had flown to Israel, bringing a promise of $250 million in financial aid, plus a DM 5-million contribution toward the reconstruction of Scud-damaged Tel Aviv neighborhoods. Apart from signaling support in the Gulf conflict, this move was also meant to indicate continued support for Israel after unification—the fact that the close political relationship between the two states was unchanged.

In this period, a number of demonstrations in support of Israel took place, often initiated by Jewish groups. The Federation of Jewish Students demonstrated in front of the Iraqi embassy in Bonn and against anti-American demonstrators; church groups working with the Stuttgart Jewish community organized an event in solidarity with Israel; 12,000 demonstrated in Berlin, with sponsorship from the Jewish community and the established political parties; similar demonstrations took place in Frankfurt, Düsseldorf, and other centers. In early February, a delegation led by the speaker of the Bundestag (parliament), Rita Süssmuth, left for Israel; and a Zentralrat delegation went to visit in mid-February. Meanwhile, Germany made a promise to Israel of $670 million in military aid, it supported the allied war effort with a pledge to the United States of $5.5 billion, and it sent military goods and gas masks valued at DM 100 million. Bonn did not send troops, however, because the German constitution excludes military involvement outside NATO.

Bonn's moves vis-à-vis Israel were complemented by meetings with major international Jewish organizations. Already in January, Kohl met with Kent E. Schiner, president of B'nai B'rith, who praised Bonn's show of solidarity with Israel; Chancellor Kohl, in turn, expressed his appreciation for B'nai B'rith's positive stance on German unification. And in March, Kohl received a delegation of the American Jewish Committee, reassuring them as well of Bonn's continued support for Israel.

A major crisis occurred in late October when harbor police in Hamburg discovered that an Israeli ship was carrying 14 tanks and other military materiel instead of its declared cargo of agricultural equipment. The armaments were Soviet in origin and came from the army of the former GDR; the shipment was engineered by the German secret service (BND); its intended recipient was the Israeli Mossad. Defense Minister Stoltenberg and his state secretary denied knowledge of this shipment, but in early December, the state minister in the Chancellery, Lutz Stavenhagen, was forced to resign over the incident.

The Israeli consulate in Berlin, which opened in October, served as a focus of Israel-oriented activity. The major outreach organization, the Deutsch-Israelische Gesellschaft (Germany-Israel Society), which was established in West Germany in 1966, took over the GDR-Israel Society and opened chapters in Chemnitz, Dresden, Erfurt, Leipzig, and Rostock. The founding of chapters in Magdeburg and Halle was planned for 1992.

One indication of the positive orientation of important segments of East German society toward Israel was the fact that Konrad Weiss (Alliance 90) of East Berlin was the only German politician in Israel on January 15, the date of the ultimatum which marked the beginning of the Gulf War. (Alliance 90 is a coalition of former dissidents who were active in the 1989 revolution and is somewhat akin to the West German Greens.) Over the course of 1991, the speakers of the parliaments of three eastern states—Brandenburg, Thuringia, and Mecklenburg-W. Pomerania—visited Israel, as did the ministers of culture of Saxony, Saxony-Anhalt, and Mecklenburg-W. Pomerania. Preliminary talks were held regarding the possibility of student and teacher exchanges between Israel and the East German states; the major impediment appeared to be lack of financing. Some personnel exchanges and demonstrations of solidarity were organized by church groups in the east (see Jewish-Christian Relations below). In November, the Jüdische Volkshochschule (Jewish Adult Education Program) in Berlin organized a weekend seminar for teachers from East Berlin and Brandenburg to inform them about Israel.

In March, Gregor Gysi, president of the PDS (the renamed former GDR Communist party), led a party delegation on its first visit to Israel. Gysi and his entourage were invited by Shimon Peres, head of the Labor party. They also spoke with representatives of the Likud bloc, the Communist party, and the trade unions. In July, Gysi met with Yasir Arafat in Tunis to demonstrate solidarity with the PLO.

CULTURAL RELATIONS

The first East German-Israeli symposium was held in May at the Charité, the medical faculty of Humboldt University in East Berlin. The symposium, attended by 70 students from all over Europe, grew out of the agreement signed by Humboldt University and the Hebrew University in Jerusalem in 1990. A student exchange between the two universities was in the planning stages.

The Jewish Cultural Festival in Erfurt, in June, featured the Israeli film *Aviya's Summer* and performances by the Batsheva Dance Company of Tel Aviv. In November, a weekend youth seminar on "The Possibilities and Risks of Peace in the Middle East" was held in Leipzig. In December, German president Richard von Weizsäcker traveled to Israel with the Dresdener Staatskapelle to perform a benefit concert. This event, originally scheduled for February, had been postponed because of the Gulf War. Other Israel-oriented cultural events included a number of exhibits of contemporary Israeli art. "Israeli Art 1990," shown from January to March at the prestigious Städtische Kunsthalle in Düsseldorf, was the largest exhibit of Israeli art ever to be shown abroad. Israeli artist Dorit Ya'acoby had an exhibit in October in Bad Salzhausen, later shown in Berlin and Munich.

Anti-Semitism and Extremism

In 1991, 2,368 racially motivated incidents were recorded in Germany, ten times as many as in 1990. The German Intelligence Service estimated the number of right-wing extremists to be about 40,000, organized particularly in the DVU and the National Democratic (NPD) parties. A further estimate speaks of 4,500 militant neo-Nazis. In the east, Saxony and Saxony-Anhalt became centers of neo-Nazi and racist activity which peaked in late September-early October, around the first anniversary of German unification. Bernd Wagner, director of the security division of the General Länder Criminal Authority, estimated that there were 1,500–2,000 neo-Nazi militants in the east, but he emphasized that accurate figures were impossible to come by. This was due to the enormous volatility of the mood, especially in the east, as well as the cooperation between East and West German neo-Nazis. A good example is Rainer Sonntag (see below). He grew up in East Germany, moved to West Germany in 1987, then came back to the east after the border was opened in 1989 and assumed a leading role in the radical right.

Most of the racism in the east in 1991 was aimed, not at Jews, but at Vietnamese and black Africans who had been guest workers in the German Democratic Republic under Erich Honecker and at refugees and asylum-seekers from Eastern Europe and the Third World. On New Year's Day in Görlitz a group of neo-Nazis shouting *"Dieses Jahr brennt die ganze Oder-Neisse Linie"* (This year the whole Oder-Neisse line will burn) tried to cross the border and enter Poland, but were held back by police. In April, neo-Nazi riots marked Hitler's 102nd birthday in Magdeburg, Dessau, Dresden, Leipzig, Erfurt, Chemnitz, and East Berlin. In June, Heinz Galinski, president of the Central Council of Jews in Germany and of the Jewish Community of Berlin, criticized Harald Wagner (CDU), mayor of Dresden, for allowing 1,500 neo-Nazis to organize a funeral procession for their leader Rainer Sonntag, slain May 31 in a street riot.

By far the most serious incident occurred in late September in Hoyerswerda (northern Saxony), where, for five days, several hundred young East Germans attacked barracks housing Vietnamese, Mozambiquans, and Gypsies (Sinti und Roma) from Romania. Five hundred local residents stood by and applauded as the German youths threw bottles and Molotov cocktails at the buildings housing the unarmed foreigners. On the fourth day, a convoy of autos organized by citizens' committees and the Alliance 90 political party in Berlin arrived in Hoyerswerda to protect the victims, thereby serving to enlarge the melee. Rudolf Krause (CDU), Saxony's minister of the interior, appealed to local residents to avoid the scene of the conflict, which he attributed to abuse by foreigners of Germany's liberal asylum law.

In January Heinz Galinski reported receiving threatening mail daily because of his efforts on behalf of Soviet Jewish refugees seeking admission to Germany. In February Soviet Jewish immigrants were attacked in Brandenburg, Glauchau, and Rostock. In April a plaque on the Grosse Hamburger Strasse (in East Berlin), dedicated to the 50,000 Berlin Jews murdered by the Nazis, was damaged. In August three neo-Nazis sprayed "Schluss mit dem Holocaust" (Enough about the Holocaust) on directional signs at the former Sachsenhausen concentration camp. And November 9—the anniversary of the *Kristallnacht* pogrom of 1938 and of the opening of the Berlin Wall in 1989—saw clashes between neo-Nazis (800 in Halle) screaming "Ausländer und Juden Raus" (Foreigners and Jews out) and demonstrators protesting violence and hostility to foreigners. On the other hand, in Cologne, Berlin, and elsewhere, rallies commemorating *Kristallnacht* drew hundreds of thousands of protesters demonstrating against the increasing hostility to foreigners.

JEWISH COMMUNITY

Demography

The year 1991 was one of considerable flux in the Jewish population of Germany, especially in the five eastern states. A complicated and confusing element of the demography, particularly in the east, was the immigration of the Soviet Jews. Because many Soviets entered Germany on tourist visas and later tried to regularize their status, and moved frequently after they arrived, the statistics fluctuated and administrative categories changed. (Indeed, the Zentralwohlfahrtsstelle, the Central Welfare Board of Jews in Germany, in contrast to previous years, was still compiling its demographic data for 1991 at the time this report was being written.)

At the start of 1991, the number of Jews in unified Germany—Jews as registered members of *Gemeinden* (central communal organizations)—could be conservatively estimated at 32,000 to 34,000. Of these, some 4,000 were recent arrivals from the former USSR. During the year, an estimated 5,000 additional Soviet Jews entered the country, raising the official Jewish population at the end of 1991 to an estimated 37,000–39,000. Estimates of unaffiliated Jews, including many Soviet Jews, ranged from 10,000 to 35,000. The largest single community was that of united Berlin, which at the end of 1991 had grown to about 9,000, from 6,411 in 1990.

Some reorganization of the official Jewish communal bodies occurred in former East Germany. On January 1, the Jewish communities of East and West Berlin officially merged; the 209 members of the East Berlin community were absorbed into the West Berlin community to form a new united Jewish community. The Jewish community of Schwerin was disbanded; in September, a new Jewish community organization was established in Potsdam; and the remaining six communities registered increases, largely through the admission of newly arrived Soviet Jews.

As of December 1991, 408 Jews belonged to the seven Jewish communities in the east (*not* including East Berlin): 53 members in Erfurt, 98 in Dresden, 46 in Chemnitz, 54 in Leipzig, 40 in Potsdam, 75 in Magdeburg, and 42 in Halle. An estimated 4,000 East German citizens of Jewish or partly Jewish ancestry did not belong to any organized Jewish community, and there were, in addition, several thousand new Soviet arrivals (see below). Additionally, in East Berlin, Adass Jisroel, legally recognized as a corporate body but not as a religious community, reported having 200 members who met halakhic requirements. The Jewish Cultural Association, a community service organization, reported that its 400 members (including 100 Soviets) claimed to be Jewish or of partly Jewish ancestry.

Soviet Jews

Throughout 1991, policy on the admission of Soviet Jews was a point of heated contest between Germany, the Zentralrat, and the Israeli government. The Central Council of Jews in Germany supported the right of Soviet Jews to seek refugee status; the Israeli government sharply criticized this position of the German Jewish leadership, which had actually become somewhat stronger after their earlier vacillation on this issue (see AJYB 1992, pp. 367–68); and the German government sought to limit Soviet Jewish immigration, partly because of the strains placed on the housing and job markets, and partly because of strong pressures emanating from Jerusalem.

Officially, Jews were considered admissible as so-called *Kontingentflüchtlinge* (a special status enabling them to be admitted immediately as refugees, without having to go through bureaucratic and legal procedures). However, in the early months of 1991, the government applied a series of changing categories and statuses to try and limit the immigration—ultimately unsuccessfully, though it was more successful in minimizing the extent of the immigration to the German public. In the course of the year, Bonn's attitude moved gradually in the direction of acceptance of these refugees.

Starting in January, Jews arriving from the Soviet Union were admitted only to Berlin, where they were "tolerated," i.e., allowed to remain but with no clear legal status and no rights. At one point, 100 immigrants were arriving each day, and approximately 11,000 in the Soviet Union had applied to German consulates for visas. By the end of January it was reported that 4,000 Soviet Jews had arrived "in recent weeks"; 3,500 were housed in temporary quarters—barracks or dormitories—in or near East Berlin. At the end of February, 1,516 Soviets were living in 25 camps in former East Germany, in addition to the 3,500 Soviet Jews in Berlin. Because of this concentration, Ingrid Stahmer, Berlin's social services minister, announced that Jews arriving from the USSR would be admitted only on 90-day tourist visas. Subsequently, in December, Minister of the Interior Schäuble agreed to award refugee status to all Soviet Jews who had arrived in Germany before November 10—altogether 23,218 since spring 1990. (This figure, which seems high, includes many who were not Jewish according to Halakhah or who never joined the Jewish community.) This concession was seen as resulting at least partly from expressed fears of a new outbreak of anti-Semitism in the former USSR in the wake of the failed putsch attempt in August and the resulting dissolution of the Soviet Union.

After the outbreak of the Gulf War, in January, about 270 Soviet Jews arrived on flights from Tel Aviv, without visas, prompting the Israeli government to insist that Jews arriving from Israel should under no circumstances be considered "refugees," and that they should be returned to Israel. In Germany, on the other hand, advocacy groups insisted on the right of these Jews to remain.

Problems of dealing with immigrants, many of them of marginal Jewishness, and of verifying identity papers, plagued the admission process throughout. Such problems were no doubt exacerbated by the reluctance of immigration officials—sensitive to the Nazi past—to appear to be questioning the identity of anyone who claimed to be a refugee from anti-Semitism—a fact that was understood and exploited by various illegal organizations that, for a fee, arranged for Soviets to enter Germany. Officials of the Berlin Jewish community, often acting on behalf of the Central Jewish Welfare Board, attempted through personal interviews to determine the halakhic status of the immigrants. Many did not qualify but were permitted to remain in Germany nevertheless.

There were several reasons for the concentration of Jews in the east. For one thing, the Jewish community hoped that the immigrants, with their children and teenagers, would settle into and rejuvenate the virtually geriatric existing Jewish communities and establish new ones in this all but *judenrein* region. The latter applied most notably to Potsdam, the new capital of the state of Brandenburg. For another, the Zentralrat was interested in claiming former communal Jewish property in the east for its own use, rather than let unused properties, which hitherto had not been dealt with in restitution agreements, fall into the hands of the Jewish Restitution Successor Organization. The latter, by agreement, would acquire the properties unless it could be shown that a presently existing Jewish community could make use of the synagogue or school building in question. Finally, on a purely practical level, disbanded army camps and other GDR government installations were available in the east for temporary housing, in contrast to the west.

Jews arriving from the Soviet Union were looked after by the Central Council of Jews in Germany, by the Jewish Central Welfare Board, and by the local Jewish communities. The Central Welfare Board, housed in Frankfurt and Berlin, which in the early postwar years had had a pivotal role in German Jewish life, assumed renewed importance. In the east, Soviet Jewish immigrants were placed without regard to the existence of a Jewish community and were supported, from a distance, by the Central Welfare Board. In East Berlin they were also cared for by Adass Jisroel, the recently reestablished neo-Orthodox congregation, the Friedländer Multinational Language School, and the Jewish Cultural Association. All these were, to a degree, competing with the larger established Jewish institutions and with organizations such as the Brandenburg RAA (Regional Workshop for Problems of Foreigners) and the Berlin FIS (Support Group for Immigrants from the USSR).

Hundreds of immigrants were dispersed to Jewish communities throughout West Germany. In contrast to the situation in the east, those sent to the west were placed into the direct charge of local Jewish communities, which had greater resources and ability to absorb immigrants more easily. The numbers, however, remained small. Frankfurt/Main agreed to take 400; other communities took in between 200 (Munich) and 60 Jews (Hamburg). Hamburg also took some responsibility for immigrants in Rostock, in the eastern state of Mecklenburg-W. Pomerania.

Official statistics were notably hard to come by, but by the end of October, these figures were released for the five new states of former East Germany: 595 Jewish immigrants from the Soviet Union in Brandenburg, 383 in Mecklenburg-W. Pomerania, 1,201 in Saxony, 628 in Saxony-Anhalt, and 506 in Thuringia. Of the 2,000 Soviet Jewish immigrants in East Berlin, 773 had joined the Berlin Jewish community. Of the Soviets in East Berlin and the east not registered with the Jewish communities, some were in the process of applying for admission to the Jewish communities; others, presumed either uninterested in Judaism or non-Jews with false papers, received help from the Jewish communities and then disappeared into the larger population.

The Central Council of Jews in Germany continued to insist on the right of the arriving Soviets to refugee status, even as problems developed, some of them originating in the behavior of the immigrants themselves. A number of Soviet Jews, admitted as political refugees, made visits to the USSR and reentered Germany with cars full of goods for sale. And police raids on the quarters where the Soviets were being housed turned up copious commodities of unknown origin.

Leaders of the Jewish communities who were working with the Soviet Jewish immigrants complained that the Soviets found it hard to learn German and that they tended to stick together, which impeded their ability to find jobs and to make contact with the German population. In the east, especially, local Jewish leaders attempted to disperse the Soviets to facilitate their integration and to avoid the formation of "ghettos" that could become targets for increasingly active neo-Nazi youth gangs. Another source of tension was that the arriving Soviets had little or no knowledge of Judaism and often resisted efforts of the Jewish communities to "educate" them. The Jewish communities were also irritated that the Soviet Jews expected the communities to provide them with money, cars, and television sets but were unwilling to participate in community activities or to take on positions of responsibility within the Jewish communities.

Still, the community took seriously its responsibility for the immigrants. In January the Yiddish Cultural Festival in East Berlin ended with a benefit concert for Soviet Jews, featuring Soviet Jewish instrumentalists. Another benefit featured Wolf Biermann, a highly acclaimed singer whose father had perished in Auschwitz. In February, the East Berlin theater Die Volksbühne, in cooperation with the Brandenburg RAA and the Friedländer Language School, organized a weekend of cultural events to raise money for Soviet Jews and provide exposure for newly arrived Soviet Jewish artists. In June, the Jewish Cultural Festival in Erfurt included an exhibit and sale of works of Soviet Jewish artists. In the west, numerous Hanukkah and Purim parties were designed to welcome and integrate the newcomers, and in October, Heinz Galinski opened an exhibit in the Jewish Community Center of Berlin, featuring Russian émigré artists.

Community Relations

A major item on the agenda of the Central Council of Jews in Germany was the negotiation of agreements with state governments in the east to regularize Jewish community-provincial relationships. Two primary areas for discussion were restitution for formerly Jewish property "Aryanized" by the Nazis and protection of the generous pensions enjoyed by victims of Nazism and by resistance fighters in the GDR.

Over the course of the year, the Central Council signed agreements with each of the five eastern states (contracts with the western states had been signed in the 1980s). The state governments undertook to repair and maintain the numerous Jewish cemeteries within their borders; to provide financial support for their Jewish communities, as well as social support and housing for Soviet Jewish immigrants; and to help locate and effect the return of formerly Jewish property. Throughout the year, though, complaints were heard from the eastern Jewish communities that the state administrations, financially strapped and overwhelmed by the demands of national unification and economic collapse, failed to allocate flats and jobs for Soviet immigrants or, for example, adequate quarters for the new Jewish community organization in Potsdam.

The Central Council retained attorney Simona Reppenhagen, a member of the Berlin Jewish Community Council, to locate and pursue claims to formerly Jewish communal property in the east. Claims were filed for the return of 477 properties (including 13 synagogues) in East Berlin; 176 properties (including 63 synagogues and 86 cemeteries) in Brandenburg; 109 properties (including 42 synagogues and 58 cemeteries) in Mecklenburg-W. Pomerania; 103 properties (including 32 synagogues and 47 cemeteries) in Saxony-Anhalt; 293 properties (including 21 synagogues and 10 cemeteries) in Saxony; and 112 properties (including 39 synagogues and 43 cemeteries) in Thuringia.

A confrontation took place in October between the Central Council and the federal government in Bonn, which attempted to reduce pensions awarded to resistance fighters and victims of Nazism in the east. Bonn hoped to equalize eastern pensions with the lower pensions awarded to these categories in the western states and to initiate a case-by-case review of pension recipients in the east to exclude persons who had transgressed human rights under the Communist government. These measures would have affected 10,000 pensioners and saved the government 90 million marks.

The Central Council argued that, in contrast to those in the east, victims of Nazism in the west had already been compensated for their lost property. An agreement was reached in November. Pensions for resistance fighters in the east were lowered from DM 1700 to DM 1400 per month, while pensions for victims of Nazism remained at DM 1400 per month. Individuals in the east who, for political reasons, were excluded from these categories could apply to have their status recognized. The case-by-case review was scrapped, but major abusers of human rights were scheduled to be excluded—the category "major abuser of human rights" was left undefined for the time being.

Holocaust-Related Matters

After the unification of Germany, nothing more was heard about the restitution payments promised Israel by the GDR. In December, a television report on the question of these payments brought a flood of hate mail to Jewish communities.

Over the summer, the town of Fürstenburg (in Brandenburg) became a scene of confrontation when it was revealed that a Kaisers supermarket and a Renault dealership were being built on the outskirts of nearby Ravensbrück concentration camp, where 90,000 women and 1,000 children were murdered by the Nazis. The Association of Ravensbrück Survivors protested, as did the Central Council of Sinti und Roma (Gypsies). The only local resident to join the protest was the Protestant minister Eberhard Erdmann. Residents of the town told journalists they wanted a modern supermarket; the mayor felt it was time for "normal life here." A compromise was reached: the auto showroom and the supermarket parking lot were moved several meters to keep commerce off the historic road leading to the camp. Heinz Galinski, president of the Central Council of Jews in Germany, and Manfred Stolpe (SPD), prime minister of Brandenburg, agreed that, in the future, the Central Council of Jews in Germany would be represented on all Brandenburg commissions dealing with historical monuments.

Jewish-Christian Relations

National unification reduced the role of the Lutheran Church's Arbeitskreis für Christen und Juden (Workshop for Christians and Jews) in the east. Founded in 1981, it was for many years the only nongovernment group that provided information about Israel and Judaism to those outside the GDR's Jewish communities. It also served as a framework for the church and the Jewish communities to pool scarce resources, such as guest speakers and printed documents. Since 1990, the Jewish communities and the church had been preoccupied with their own restructuring. Moreover, other institutions—e.g., DIG (Deutsch-Israelische Gesellschaft) and the universities—had begun to administer Jewish culture programs and exchanges with Israel. Most important, young Christians and Jews were emigrating west and were busy reestablishing their own lives, leaving little time or inclination for interfaith activity.

Despite these changes, programs to bring Christians and Jews together continued. In the east, because of its size and location, East Berlin was able to provide the richest offerings; but in smaller cities lacking an active Jewish community the Workshop for Christians and Jews often provided the only contact with Judaism for the larger public. In 1991 a delegation of 42 members of the workshop visited Israel for two weeks. Money was raised and Hanukkah presents were sent to Neve Chanah, a home in Kiryat Gat for children from broken families. The Berliner Domkantorei (a Lutheran choir) organized a benefit concert on November 9 (*Kristallnacht*) to raise money for handicapped children at Migdal Yam Kinneret. And four lectures on Jewish subjects were offered, with speakers from East and West Berlin.

In Greifswald, a commemorative prayer service was held on November 9; and a seminar was organized on "Jewish Concepts of the Messiah." In Saxony two lectures took place: "The Fiftieth Anniversary of the Yellow Star" and "Rashi." In Thuringia, the workshop organized the rededication of the synagogue in Berkach. And in Dresden, in June, in the wake of increasingly violent activity by right-wing radical youth gangs, the Lutheran church sent social workers to the area to work with the juveniles.

Communal Affairs

On January 1, the official Jewish communities of East and West Berlin merged. Two immediate problems were the Jewish old-age home in the east (in which only non-Jews were living and which did not conform to the new building code), and maintenance and repair costs for Jewish community property in the east—estimated at DM 1.4 million—which pushed the projected budget deficit for 1991 to DM 1.9 million. The mayors of East and West Berlin assumed responsibility for East Berlin's extensive and dilapidated Jewish cemeteries at Weissensee and Schönhauser Allee.

By April, many Jewish community services, such as lectures and rabbinical counseling, were being offered in the east, but the largely western functionaries complained that members in East Berlin made limited use of them. In June, the Jewish community opened a club for art, culture, and leisure in East Berlin. Organized to integrate the Soviet immigrants, it contains a café with kosher cuisine, a video theater, and space for art exhibits and dance performances.

Construction of the dome and facade of the New Synagogue Berlin-Centrum Judaicum was completed in September, in time to mark the 125th anniversary of the building. The center is expected to serve as a Jewish museum and research and conference center, after completion of the total reconstruction in 1995.

The existence of a unified, if not streamlined, Jewish communal life continued to be challenged by two alternative Jewish organizations in East Berlin. The Jüdische Gemeinde Adass Jisroel had attained legal corporative status under the de Maizière government, and the Jüdische Kulturverein (Jewish Cultural Association) was recognized for its secular work. Both, however, served largely East Berliners and Soviet immigrants who were uncomfortable with the cool, bureaucratic, and anti-Communist tone of the established Jewish community.

Adass Jisroel considered itself Orthodox and claimed to have 200 members (from both parts of the city) who met halakhic requirements. Throughout the year, it offered a program of religious and cultural services and opened a kosher dairy café. Over the spring and summer months, it conducted a campaign for full recognition as Berlin's second Jewish community; this recognition would have made it eligible for government funding and enabled it to have undisputed title to valuable pieces of real estate. Adass's strategy included a well-publicized exhibit of enlarged documents and photographs of demolished synagogues, along with indisputable evidence that, in the postwar decades, with the cooperation of both official Jewish communities, East and West Berlin blew up many synagogues that had survived the war. (The facts, while accurate, fail to take account of the circumstances at the time: many of the buildings were damaged beyond feasible repair; there were too many synagogues for the existing Jewish population; money that could have been spent on restoration was desperately needed for housing and other necessities; and so on.)

The Galinski-led Berlin Jewish community charged that Adass Jisroel was not a Jewish community but a private enterprise and that the Offenberg family which in effect controlled Adass did not represent the surviving members of the prewar Orthodox Jewish community of the same name to which Adass claimed to be heir. By deploying theatrical tactics—i.e., publicly comparing Berlin Jewish community president Heinz Galinski to the Romanian dictator Ceausescu—Mario Offenberg escalated the conflict into a public scandal. In the meantime, the Berlin Senate began legal action aimed at rescinding Adass Jisroel's status as a legal corporate body with special privileges.

The Jewish Cultural Association, which is not a religious community but a community service organization, claimed to have 400 members who are Jewish, partly Jewish, or "friends of Jewish culture." It sponsored regular cultural programs—lectures, films, holiday celebrations, and get-togethers—in German and Russian. Though it considered itself secular, it regularly invited ultra-Orthodox rabbis from Israel as guests and maintained a kosher kitchen. The Jewish Cultural Association was officially administered by an elected board of directors, but in fact, Irene Runge, a writer and former sociology lecturer with an acknowledged Stasi (state security) past, was in charge. Many of the group's members came from institutions central to the former East German state—i.e., the state prosecutor's office, the university, the foreign ministry, and the media.

Elsewhere in the east, the tiny aged Jewish communities were overwhelmed by the demands of national unification: these included communal reorganization, looking after the newly arrived Soviet immigrants and processing their applications for admission to the communities, as well as developing a new and higher public profile. Functionaries reported that the Jewish communities had become more respected; for example, they were now invited to send representatives to sit on many provincial and local civic committees. But, as many younger Jews emigrated west or became preoccupied with reorganizing their own lives, these new responsibilities fell on the shoulders of a handful of pensioners. The social and financial chaos in the larger society made everything more difficult and less certain.

In Leipzig, for the first time in 40 years, there was no seder; the newly expanded community did not have enough money, tables, or chairs. The Jewish community in Halle was struggling to keep its old-age home in operation; the future of its four cemeteries remained unclear. In September, a new Jewish community was founded in Potsdam: almost all members were recently arrived Soviet immigrants. Despite generous promises by the province of Brandenburg, it was functioning with great difficulty in three rooms (80 square meters), with no adequate space or furnishings for prayer or for social gatherings. Officeholders of the Jewish communities in the east appealed for help, particularly for a trained itinerant Hebrew teacher and rabbi.

Culture

Jewish themes figured prominently in German cultural and academic life this year, continuing a trend of several years. In the academic sphere, two highlights were a conference at the Salomon-Ludwig Steinheim Institute of Duisburg entitled "Social Utopias and Religious-Cultural Traditions: Jews and the German Labor Movement Until 1933" and an international symposium, "The Jewish Woman in Germany," in Heidelberg, organized by the College for Jewish Studies and the Leo Baeck Institute of London. The first chair in Yiddish language in Germany was inaugurated at the University of Trier.

A number of exhibitions of Jewish photographers and artists were mounted this year: photographs by Benjamin Katz were shown in Berlin and those of Lotte Jacobi in the Folkwang Museum in Essen; oils and gouaches by Marc Chagall were on view in Munich's Hypo-Kulturstiftung, and Chagall's murals made for the Moscow Jewish Theater were shown in Frankfurt. The Leipzig Art Museum organized an exhibit of five representatives of the Vienna School, "Die Phantasten": Arik Brauer, Ernst Fuchs, Rudolf Hausner, Wolfgang Hutter, and Anton Lemden, the first three of whom were Jews. Stuttgart held a retrospective of the work of Otto Dix, later to be shown in Berlin and Friedrichshafen, and works by the Polish painter Maurycy Gottlieb were shown in the Jewish Museum of Frankfurt. Other exhibits were devoted to Ilex Beller (Giessen; on the Polish shtetl), Max Ernst (Stuttgart), Ludwig Meidner (Darmstadt), Georg Meistermann (Cologne), and the German-Jewish sculptor Leopold Fleischhacker (Düsseldorf), as well as Motke Blum (Frankfurt, with "Pictures of Jerusalem"). The 200th birthday of composer Giacomo Meyerbeer was the occasion for an exhibit at the Dahlem Museum in Berlin.

Exhibitions on local Jewish history included the following: "Die vergessenen Nachbarn. Juden in Frankfurter Vororten" (Jews in Frankfurt suburbs) at that city's Jewish Museum; "Joods," a photodocumentary by the Dutch photographer Jenny Wesly, in Cologne's Germania Judaica; pictures and documents of Berlin synagogues at the Berlin Jewish Museum; an exhibit about Jewish émigré life in Prague before and during Nazi persecution, in Frankfurt's Deutsche Bibliothek; and "Breslau Jews, 1850–1945," in Wiesbaden and Stuttgart.

Under the patronage of North-Rhine Westphalia's premier, Johannes Rau, an Else Lasker-Schüler Society was founded in Wuppertal, the city where this Jewish German poet was born. The Ulrich Becker Archive was taken over by the "Exilarchiv," devoted to émigré writers, of the Deutsche Bibliothek Frankfurt.

In theater, George Tabori's Jewish western, "Weisman and Redface," played in East Berlin. An impressive one-woman show, "Jonteff," by Adriana Altaras, was presented in an "off-Broadway" theater in West Berlin. In it, the young Jewish actress reflected on her life's journey from Sarajevo and Italy to Germany and her difficulties as a Jew in Germany.

This year saw an expansion of Jewish cultural offerings in the east and some export of East German Jewish culture to the west. The Leipziger Synagogalchor, an amateur choir founded in 1962, performed in Karlsruhe in March and in Frankfurt in April. In Berlin, the Jüdische Volkshochschule (Jewish Adult Education Program) organized events to acquaint (West) Berlin Jews with Jewish cultural activities in the east. In September, it sponsored an excursion to the Jewish Museum in Gröbzig; in May, Sylvia Schlenstedt of East Berlin and Erwin Märtin of Leipzig gave lectures, and Jürgen Rennert of East Berlin read from his translations of Yiddish literature.

The fifth annual Yiddish Cultural Festival, organized by Jalda Rebling, took place in East Berlin, in January. In June, for the first time, a Jewish Cultural Festival—with 35 events on the program—was produced in Erfurt. A public discussion of Soviet Jewish literature was held at the Literaturcafé Wolkenbügel in East Berlin. And in October, an exhibit on Berlin Jewish cemeteries was mounted in East Berlin.

The nonaffiliated East Berlin Jewish organizations Adass Jisroel and the Jewish Cultural Association organized regular cultural programs—in German and Russian—featuring films, lectures, readings from new books, and celebrations of Jewish holidays.

Holocaust Commemoration

As in the past, a number of communities invited former citizens back for visits. Participants this year included the villages of Hachenburg and Gangelt, the towns of Hamm, Wetzlar, Fürth, Schweinfurt, Braunschweig, and Koblenz, and large cities such as Mannheim-Ludwigshafen, Düsseldorf, Frankfurt, and the state of Schleswig-Holstein.

Exhibits in Mülhausen, Erlangen, Ichenhausen, and Berlin-Kreuzberg portrayed Jewish life in a world gone by. Former Jewish citizens of the town of Mühlhausen (Thuringia) who returned for a visit attended the openings of two exhibits: "Jews in Mühlhausen" and "Traces of a Minority." The documentation center situated at the site of the Gestapo headquarters in Berlin, Topographie des Terrors, featured an exhibit, "War Against the Soviet Union." Two Anne Frank exhibitions were mounted: "The World of Anne Frank, 1929–1945," with previously unpublished photos, at Herford's, and one sponsored by the SPD's Friedrich Ebert Foundation, which traveled to a number of East German cities. Marl, a town in Westphalia, showed an exhibit on the Star of David called "Sign of Shame, Symbol of Hope," which coincided with the 50th anniversary of the decree requiring Jews to wear a yellow star. A Christian-Jewish Brotherhood Society in Koblenz organized an exhibit on "One Hundred Years of German Racism," and the Congress of German Pharmacists presented an exhibit on the "Expulsion and Annihilation of Jewish Pharmacists in the Third Reich."

In May, an exhibit was opened in Steckelsdorf (near Rathenow) to commemorate the 50th anniversary of the deportation of Jews from Rathenow and from the Zionist camp in Steckelsdorf where, in the late 1930s, young German Jews received agricultural training as preparation for immigration to Palestine; almost none of them survived the Holocaust.

In July, a former synagogue in Aschenhausen (Thuringia) was restored and transformed into a site for "discussion and remembrance." The renovation costs— DM 300,000—were covered by the federal, provincial, and district administrations.

In September, a commission of historians in Weimar held a conference to discuss reorganizing the informational aspect of Buchenwald concentration camp so as to recognize that not only Communists were killed there, and that after 1945 it became a Soviet internment camp. It was decided to invite representatives of all groups of victims—including Jews—to participate in the deliberations.

A plaque was unveiled in Chemnitz, in November, in memory of Hermann Fürstenheim, director of the Jewish department store H. and C. Tietz. In December, a lecture series on Jewish life in Saxony was held in Leipzig, in conjunction with an exhibit at the University of Leipzig on the murder of Jews during the Third Reich. Both the lectures and the exhibit were sponsored by Fischer Pocket Books (a West German publisher, which published the book based on the exhibit), the Ephraim Carlebach Foundation in Leipzig, and the department of history of the University of Leipzig.

Beginning with the *Kristallnacht* commemorations of 1988, individual cities and towns in the east began to publish—following a long-standing practice in the west— chronologies and documentation of their Jewish communities or former Jewish communities. New publications in this category included: Günther Kunge, *Juden in Schönebeck* ("Jews in Schönebeck"), published by the Kreismuseum Schönebeck (near Magdeburg), and Roland Otto, *Die Verfolgung der Juden in Görlitz unter der faschistischen Diktatur 1933–1945* ("The Persecution of the Jews in Görlitz Under the Fascist Dictatorship 1933–1945"), published by the city of Görlitz.

Publications

National unification affected the operations of the publishing business in former East and West Germany. Works of East Germans appeared in the catalogues of West German publishing houses and vice versa; and some major East German publishers were taken over by West German enterprises. Still, although the official division between east and west no longer existed, differences in markets and issues persisted.

A new literary genre emanating from the east was the critical or self-critical (auto)biography of Jewish Communists or socialists. New works in this category included: Helmut Eschwege, *Fremd unter meinesgleichen: Erinnerungen eines Dresdner Juden* ("A Stranger Among My Peers: Memories of a Dresden Jew"), and Annette Leo, *Briefe zwischen Kommen und Gehen* ("Letters Between Coming and

Going"), annotated letters of her grandfather, a Jew who was forced out of the Communist party in the 1920s because of his dissident views.

Important new works relating to German Jewry included: F. Hager, ed., *Geschichte Denken: Notizbuch für Leo Löwenthal* ("Thinking History: A Notebook for Leo Löwenthal"), an interview and essays in a dialogue with the last remaining representative of the Frankfurt School (the critical social-science tradition founded in the 1920s by Max Horkheimer and Theodor W. Adorno); A. Lixl-Purcell, ed., *Erinnerungen deutsch-jüdischer Frauen 1900–1990* ("Memories of German Jewish Women 1900–1990"); Peter Weiss, *Briefe an Hermann Levin Goldschmidt und Robert Jungk 1939–1980* ("Letters to Hermann Levin Goldschmidt and Robert Jungk, 1939–1980"), letters of young, unknown Jewish writers trying to establish themselves in exile; Nea Weissberg-Bob, ed., *Der dumme Fuß will mich nach Deutschland tragen—Eine Auseinandersetzung um Deutschland. Gespräche, Gedichte, Briefe* (a literary anthology about the problem of Jewish existence in Germany); Horst Göppinger, *Juristen jüdischer Abstammung im Dritten Reich. Entrechtung und Verfolgung* ("Lawyers of Jewish Descent in the Third Reich"; second, fully revised edition); Ellen Presser and Bernhard Schossig, eds., *Junge Juden in Deutschland. Protokoll einer Tagung* ("Young Jews in Germany: Conference Proceedings"); Gerd Stolz, ed., *Zwischen Gestern und Heute—Erinnerungen jüdischen Lebens ehemaliger Schleswig-Holsteiner* ("Jewish Life in Schleswig-Holstein Remembered"); Wolfgang Benz, ed., *Dimension des Völkermords. Die Zahl der jüdischen Opfer des Nationalsozialismus* (A new calculation of the number of victims of the Shoah by country), by the new director of the Institute for Research on Anti-Semitism in Berlin; Claus Stephani, *War einer Hersch, Fuhrmann. Leben und Leiden der Juden in Oberwischau* (portrait of rural Jewish life); Ralph Giordano, *Israel, um Himmels willen Israel* ("For Heaven's Sake, Israel"), mildly critical notes from a visit to Israel; Heinz Knobloch, Alfred Etzold, Joachim Feit, and Peter Kirchner, *Die jüdischen Friedhöfe in Berlin* ("Jewish Cemeteries in Berlin"); Hans Küng, *Das Judentum—Die religiöse Situation der Zeit* ("Judaism and the Religious Situation of Today"); Fritz Fischer, *Hitler war kein Betriebsunfall* ("Hitler Was No Accident"); Wolfgang Benz, ed., *Das Exil der kleinen Leute. Alltagserfahrungen deutscher Juden in der Emigration* (everyday experiences of average German Jewish émigrés); Michael Wolffsohn, *Spanien, Deutschland und die "jüdische Weltmacht."* Über Moral, Realpolitik und Vergangenheitsbewältigung (essays on Jewish "world power" and coming to grips with the past); Dan Diner, *Krieg der Erinnerungen. Deutsche und Israelis im Ernstfall* ("The War of Memories: Germans and Israelis in the Gulf War"); Micha Brumlik, *Weltrisiko Naher Osten. Moralische und politische Perspektiven in einem Konflikt ohne Ende* (moral and political issues in relation to the Middle East).

A work by Thea Altaras, *Synagogen in Hessen—was geschah seit 1945?* (a complete register of synagogues in Hesse and their history after 1945) received an award from the state of Hesse.

Personalia

The federal state of Hesse honored the president of the Jewish community of Frankfurt, Ignatz Bubis, for his involvement in Jewish affairs. Former lord mayor of Frankfurt Volker Hauff received the silver seal of the Frankfurt Jewish community. A number of Jewish writers and playwrights received prizes this year, among them: György Konrad of Hungary, the Peace Prize of the German booksellers association, Germany's most prestigious literary award; George Tabori, playwright, the Peter Weiss Prize of the city of Bochum, awarded for the first time; Marcel Reich-Ranicki, the Polish-born critic for the *Frankfurter Allgemeine Zeitung*, considered the most influential literary critic in Germany, the Hermann-Sinsheimer Prize of the city of Freinsheim; Jenny Aloni, an Israeli writer who writes in German, the Droste Prize of Meersburg; Georges-Arthur Goldschmidt, who was born in Hamburg and lives in France, the Geschwister Scholl Prize; Irene Dische, who has written on her life in America, the Jeannette-Schocken Prize of Bremerhaven; Wolf Biermann, a singer and songwriter whose father perished in Auschwitz, the important George-Büchner Prize; Ilse Aichinger, on the occasion of her 70th birthday, the literature prize of the Bavarian Academy of Arts; and Carl Amery, the newly created prize for literature of the city of Munich. The award given by the Heinz Galinski Foundation, which is linked to the Berlin Jewish community, was given to Lea Rosh and Irmgard von zur Mühlen. The Israeli writer David Grossman was awarded the Nelly Sachs Prize of Dortmund.

A number of German politicians were honored for work on behalf of Jewish and human-rights causes. Ben-Gurion University in Beersheba awarded an honorary degree to former Bundestag president Annemarie Renger; the former federal commissioner for foreigners in Germany, Lieselotte Funcke, who resigned her position in protest against the government's inaction in this area, was awarded the Carl von Ossietzky Medal of the League for Human Rights for her "untiring and fearless engagement on behalf of foreign citizens in Germany; and the Theodor Heuss Award went to Anetta Kahane, who, together with others from the former GDR, was recognized for her peaceful political activity in the fall of 1989 and for her leadership in integrating Soviet Jewish refugees and other foreign groups in the east.

Novelist Stefan Heym received an honorary doctorate from Cambridge University (England), in June. In August, Nathan Peter Levinson (rabbi of Hamburg and former rabbi of Berlin 1950–52) gave a lecture in the building in East Berlin which used to house his office. Levinson was also awarded the Augsburg Peace Prize for his work in Christian-Jewish relations. Elie Wiesel spoke at graduation ceremonies at Humboldt University in East Berlin.

Among prominent German Jewish émigrés who died this year were the artist Gitta Alpar, 87, who died in Palm Springs, California; Brigitte Bermann-Fischer, 86, co-owner of the S. Fischer Verlag publishing house in Switzerland; and two distinguished rabbis: Hans Chanoch Meyer, 82, and Manfred Lubliner, 81. Meyer, who was born in Crone (Posen), later lived in Berlin and from 1938 in Palestine.

In 1958 he returned to Dortmund and later taught Jewish history at Bochum University. He subsequently lived in Haifa but returned frequently to Germany. Lubliner was born in Halle, was a rabbi in Cottbus, fled to Chile in 1938, and returned from there to Berlin in 1970, where he was a highly respected and popular figure. Two other deaths of note were those of the publisher and journalist Marian Gid, 85, who wrote for French papers and published what was for many years the only Yiddish paper in Germany, the *Naie Yiddishe Zaitung*, in Munich; and Richard Löwenthal, 83, a Berliner, a major intellectual figure in the Social Democratic party. In the Nazi period, he belonged to a group of former Communists who came together in the resistance group New Beginning; he left for Britain and returned to Germany in 1945 as a journalist with the *Observer*; beginning in 1961 he occupied a chair of political science at the Free University of Berlin. He was a critic of the student movement of 1968 and later on of the new social movements, as well as of the Vietnam War and some armament policies of Chancellor Schmidt.

Y. MICHAL BODEMANN
ROBIN OSTOW

Eastern Europe

Soviet Union

National Affairs

IN 1991, AFTER NEARLY 75 YEARS OF RULE, the Communist party of the USSR began to lose power, and the Soviet state itself began to dissolve. These unexpected and dramatic developments were triggered by a failed coup d'état in August, when a group of conservative Communists, led by politician Gennadi Yanaev, Defense Minister Dmitri Yazov, and KGB head Vladimir Kryuchkov, attempted to head off the planned signing of a treaty which would have loosened the ties among the Soviet republics. Arguing that the economic and political deterioration in the country, and her waning power and prestige abroad, had to be halted, they attempted to seize power in Moscow on August 19. They arrested President Mikhail Gorbachev at a summer resort in the Crimea and called troops out into the streets of Moscow. However, they failed to arrest Gorbachev's rival, Russian president Boris Yeltsin, or to align the military and other security forces solidly behind them. They also appear to have had little support in the republics. As a result, Yeltsin was able to rally opposition to the "putschists," arrest them, and emerge as a political hero. Gorbachev was released, but it became clear that he would now take a secondary position to Yeltsin.

Within a few days of the coup attempt, the Baltic states of Estonia, Latvia, and Lithuania reaffirmed their earlier declarations of independence and moved to implement them on the grounds that the coup had demonstrated the fragility of both the democratization processes stimulated by Gorbachev and any new relationship among the republics. In early September, the Soviet State Council recognized the independence of the Baltic states. The European Community and the United States followed suit. This set off the breakup of the Union of Soviet Socialist Republics. A new "union treaty," which Gorbachev had fought to formulate over several months, was to have been signed on August 20, but it was now a dead letter, as were the results of a referendum in March—boycotted by the Baltic republics, Georgia, Armenia, and Moldavia—in which 77 percent of the rest of the population voted to preserve the union. Belorussia, renaming itself Belarus, several Central Asian republics, and Moldavia, renamed Moldova, declared independence. On December 1, a referendum was held in Ukraine, where a majority voted for independence, thus creating a new state of over 50 million people.

On December 8, the leaders of the three Slavic republics, Russia, Belarus, and Ukraine, declared that the Soviet Union had ceased to exist. They proclaimed a "Commonwealth of Independent States" (CIS) open to all the former Soviet republics. Later in the month, five Central Asia republics—Uzbekistan, Tajikistan, Kirghizia (renamed Kyrgyzstan), Turkmenistan, and Kazakhstan—agreed to join. Altogether, eleven republics constituted the CIS: the eight mentioned plus Moldova, Armenia, and Azerbaijan. Georgia and three Baltic republics declined to join. On December 25, Mikhail Gorbachev resigned as president of the Soviet Union. The Soviet flag over the Kremlin was lowered, and the Russian flag was raised in its place. The USSR was no longer.

The coup attempt in August came against a background of economic, political, and social crisis. Rapid inflation, declining productivity, shortages of consumer goods and energy, mounting international debts, and agricultural shortfalls had made the USSR a supplicant and debtor state. Rivalries between Yeltsin and Gorbachev and leadership struggles in several republics, along with a wave of political demonstrations, and the formation and re-formation of political parties and movements, signaled political instability. Political and economic troubles fed social tensions that were exacerbated by continuing ethnic violence in Moldova, Central Asia, and the Caucasus and more benign conflict in the Baltics, Ukraine, and Russia itself. In January, the federal government had sent troops to Lithuania and Latvia, where they seized buildings and killed 15 people in Vilnius in an attempt to keep these republics from leaving the USSR. Crowds in Moscow protested these actions, which Gorbachev was hard put to defend. Referenda in the Baltic republics showed majority support for independence.

Political disaffection was manifested in the decline in Communist party membership. In the year before the coup, about four million people, 20 percent of all party members, had resigned from the party. Each of the 15 republics had declared sovereignty, meaning that its laws took precedence over federal laws. The proposed union treaty would have given the republics more power vis-à-vis the center, but it aroused little enthusiasm, even among those leaders willing to sign it.

During the coup attempt, three people were killed in Moscow, including Ilya Krichevsky, a young Jew. Funerals for the three were scheduled as public events on a Saturday. The proposal to give Krichevsky a Jewish funeral ran into difficulty as Jewish law forbids burial on the Sabbath, but a leader of the new Reform Jewish community of Moscow agreed to conduct Jewish services, which were broadcast nationally.

Soviet Jews were generally pleased by the breakup of a system and state that had persecuted them, but they wondered about their futures in the newly independent states, especially those, such as Georgia, Moldova, Ukraine, and the Baltic states, where they might be caught in rivalries between residents of warring nationalities.

Some also expressed fears that the nascent Soviet Jewish community, just beginning to organize, would be split along republic lines and would thus be weakened. An era had ended and the future appeared highly uncertain.

Relations with Israel

Soviet relations with Israel continued to improve. In January, an Israeli consulate opened in Moscow, replacing the "interests section" established in 1988 after diplomatic relations had been severed by the USSR in 1967. By October, the consulate had been elevated to the status of an embassy. Arye Levin, who held the rank of ambassador, became Israel's ambassador to the USSR. The restoration of full diplomatic relations was apparently linked to Israel's agreement to attend a Middle East peace conference in Madrid, which the USSR cosponsored with the United States.

Direct charter flights began between Israel and the USSR, but at the latter's insistence they were to be used only by tourists and business travelers, not by Soviet immigrants to Israel. However, the Jewish Agency signed an agreement with Aeroflot, the Soviet national airline, allowing that company and El Al to fly immigrants to Israel on El Al's subsidiary, Transair.

The Hebrew University and National Library in Jerusalem signed an agreement with the Lenin Library in Moscow whereby the former could microfilm many of the latter's rich Judaica holdings, including Hebrew manuscripts and incunabula held in the Baron Ginzberg and other collections. The University and National Library was working with Rabbi Adin Steinsaltz's Aleph Society in this endeavor.

Anti-Semitism

Some of the newly unfettered media carried many and virulent anti-Semitic messages. Dmitri Vasiliev, a leader of the extreme Russian nationalist and anti-Semitic organization Pamyat, inaugurated a radio program in September that could be heard all over the country. Titled "Fatherland, Pamyat and We," it broadcast the *Protocols of the Elders of Zion*. The latter was reprinted and distributed in several major cities. Magazines such as *Molodaya Gvardiia* and *Nash Sovremennik*, both monthlies, and the newspapers *Sovietskaya Rossiya* and *Literaturnaya Rossiya* consistently carried anti-Semitic articles. There were calls to curb Jewish emigration and Zionist activity in the USSR and to eliminate Jews from "control" of the government and media. Some authors presented a range of conspiracy theories suggesting that the Jews aimed at controlling the country. Konstantin Smirnov-Ostashvili, a Pamyat leader sentenced in October 1990 to two years in prison for fomenting ethnic hatred, died suddenly on April 26. Vasiliev, leader of a rival Pamyat fraction, blamed Zionists for Smirnov's death. "The Zionists threaten no one personally: they sit somewhere in the Bahamas and pass the order by radiotelephone. Today the order was to eliminate [Smirnov] Ostashvili" (quoted in *Sovetish haimland*, no. 8, p. 37). The leading journal of military history, which had published excerpts from Adolf Hitler's *Mein Kampf*, was scheduled to publish the *Protocols of the Elders of Zion.*

A conference on anti-Semitism was held in Moscow in September, at which the results of a poll taken in ten cities in October 1990 were released. Among 4,200 people interviewed, over half expressed a desire to see all Jews leave the country. A Jewish newspaper, *Evreiskaya Gazeta*, published a list of 38 newspapers and 7 magazines it claimed consistently published anti-Semitic materials. Almost all were published in Russia.

The president and executive director of the American National Conference on Soviet Jewry met with President Gorbachev on October 2 and asked him to issue a statement condemning anti-Semitism. He declined on tactical grounds. However, three days later, a historic statement by Gorbachev was read by his adviser, Alexander N. Yakovlev, at ceremonies commemorating the Nazi slaughter of Jews in Kiev's Babi Yar in 1941. Gorbachev admitted that Stalin had used anti-Semitism as a policy tool, and that it survived in the present on the grass-roots level. He expressed regret at the ongoing Jewish emigration. He concluded: "This ceremony . . . is a mournful event, but it inspires hope that we are renovating our society, are capable of learning lessons from the tragedies and errors of the past" (*New York Times*, October 7, 1991).

JEWISH COMMUNITY

Demography

The census taken in January 1989 showed 1,445,000 people declaring themselves Jews. Since about 345,000 Jews emigrated after the census was taken, the number of Jews in the Soviet Union might have been about 1,100,000 by the end of 1991. However, as emigration proceeded, more and more people claimed or reclaimed Jewish nationality in order to leave the country. Thus, the number of self-described Jews may have stayed closer to the census figure than might be expected.

In the large cities, the number of those claiming Yiddish as a mother tongue continued to decline. *Sovetish haimland* (no. 4, p. 113) noted that, in the 1989 census, only 9,525 Jews in Moscow (5.5 percent of the city's Jewish population) gave Yiddish as their mother tongue. Of the 628 Mountain Jews living in Moscow, 82 percent listed a Jewish language (presumably Tat) as their mother tongue. In Kiev, 4,685 Jews (4.7 percent of all Jews) gave Yiddish as their mother tongue, and in Minsk, 2,130 (5.5 percent). However, in territories annexed to the USSR in 1939–40, the proportion of those giving Yiddish as their mother tongue was much higher. It was 37.3 percent in Vilnius, 22.7 percent in Riga, and 22.2 percent in Kishinev.

Data gathered in 1989 showed that mixed marriages were frequent among Jews, whose rate of intermarriage was exceeded only by that of Germans. In 1989, 57.5 percent of Jewish males entering marriage and 46.6 percent of Jewish females married people of a different nationality (Mark Tolts in *Megapolis-Continent*, August 7–13, 1991). This was a very slight decline from the proportions of mixed marriages in 1988.

Emigration

In 1991, 179,720 Jews left the Soviet Union permanently. Of those, 145,005 went to Israel (a drop from 1990's record 181,759), and 34,715 (an increase from 5,056 in 1990) went to the United States. Of the latter, 36 percent were from Ukraine, 21 percent from Russia, and 10 percent each from Belarus and Moldova. Of those who went to Israel, 30 percent were from Russia, 27 percent from Ukraine, 13 percent from Central Asia, and 11 percent each from Belarus and Moldova.

The decline in emigration was attributed to resettlement difficulties in Israel, especially in employment, and a lessening of the panic that had driven so many out of the USSR when they feared it was lapsing into anarchy. The increase in the number of immigrants to the United States was explained by the clearing away of American and Soviet bureaucratic obstacles to processing immigration applications. In the fiscal year 1991, 40,000 slots had been allotted to Soviet Jewish refugees, but only 26,680 Jews immigrated to the United States, largely because of "processing problems" in both countries. Since the quota was not used up, it was decided to increase the fiscal 1992 quota for Soviet refugees from 50,000 overall to 61,000, of whom presumably about 50,000 would be Jews. A substantial number of Soviet Jews, perhaps as many as 1,500, settled in the Federal Republic of Germany where, it was estimated, 5,000 had already arrived before 1991. In January the German government and its 16 federal states agreed not to limit the number of Soviet Jews allowed to resettle in Germany. Some international Jewish organizations criticized Germany's Jews for pressing for this agreement, while others maintained that a safe haven for endangered Jews was the main consideration. The Union of Councils for Soviet Jews in the United States called for emergency admission of up to a quarter of a million Soviet Jews to the United States on the grounds that they were in imminent danger. The Va'ad in the USSR, the National Conference on Soviet Jewry (USA), and Israeli circles rejected this idea, asserting that Soviet Jews were not in immediate danger, and that such a policy would cause many of them not to immigrate to Israel but to wait in the USSR in anticipation of admission to the United States.

Advocates for Soviet Jewry estimated that there were still several hundred "poor relative" refuseniks and about 40 "secrecy" refuseniks left in the USSR. Gorbachev agreed in his October meeting with the NCSJ leaders to review 355 refusenik cases.

Seven hundred Jews of Tskhinvali, Ossetia, fled to Tbilisi and Gori in Georgia as a result of the Georgian-Ossetian war. They left behind 38 men to guard communal property, including the most recently built (1969) synagogue in the USSR.

In May the Supreme Soviet failed for a third time to pass a new Law on Entry and Exit from the USSR that had been first proposed in 1989, but after two weeks of debate the law was finally passed. It was scheduled to go into effect on January 1, 1993. American president George Bush extended the waiver of the Jackson-Vanik Amendment in recognition of the planned liberalization of emigration. As of July 1, Soviet authorities permitted émigrés to retain Soviet citizenship. They could now leave on Soviet passports and retain them, rather than renouncing citizenship and going abroad stateless. However, the Soviet authorities announced that those who took Israeli government jobs or served in the Israel Defense Forces would lose their Soviet citizenship.

Cultural and Organizational Life

The second congress of the Va'ad, the umbrella organization for local Jewish cultural associations, took place in January. Several hundred delegates, representing up to 400 organizations from 86 cities, registered. Debate focused on the Va'ad itself, one group advocating that it be a strong, centralized organization with one president, rather than the three leaders it had, and another advocating a loose federation, the central body dealing with only a few issues. The latter camp prevailed, reflecting the general tendency toward greater power devolving on republics and regions. Three people were elected to the Va'ad's presidium: Mikhail Chlenov of Moscow, Yosef Zissels of Chernovtsy (Ukraine), and Samuil Zilberg of Riga.

According to the newly established Jewish Information Agency in Moscow, some 42,000 people were participating in activities of local Jewish associations, only 2,000 of them in Moscow. In 47 cities there were well-organized Hebrew study groups, involving over 800 teachers. All told, there were said to be about 22,000 people studying Hebrew, the great majority in preparation for immigration to Israel. In the larger cities there were often several Jewish organizations. Thus, in Kiev there were ten organizations and three Jewish newspapers: *Einikeit* (Unity), *Vozrozhdenie* (Rebirth), and *Evreiskie Vesti* (Jewish News), the latter published by the Ukrainian Republic Society of Jewish Culture headed by Ilya Levitas. The cochairman of the Sholem Aleichem Jewish Cultural and Educational Society, Oleksander Burakovskyi, was also vice-chairman of Rukh, the Ukrainian national organization, and chairman of its Council of Nationalities.

Foreign Jewish organizations were active in assisting the reconstruction of Jewish communities. B'nai B'rith claimed 13 lodges in the USSR, and the Agudas Yisroel and Lubavitch Orthodox movements were sending many emissaries to serve as religious functionaries. The American Jewish Joint Distribution Committee had several representatives in residence in larger cities. It was training cantors, supplying kosher food packages for holidays, and beginning to establish social services, such as assistance to the elderly. On Passover, JDC sponsored 52 seders in 28 cities, serving approximately 15,000 people. By March the Jewish Agency had 31 emissaries working in 22 cities. It had permanent offices in Vilnius, Tbilisi, Odessa, Kishinev, Baku, Leningrad, Kiev, and Chernovtsy. The YIVO Institute and the Jewish Theological Seminary in New York opened a four-year course in Judaica at the

Russian State University of the Humanities (formerly the Moscow Historical-Archival Institute), which trains historians, librarians, and archivists. The World Union for Progressive Judaism assisted the Hineni Congregation in Moscow, a Reform group, and was active in other cities. The Memorial Foundation for Jewish Culture held its Nahum Goldmann Fellowship Program, involving 40 Soviet participants and an equal number from Western and Eastern Europe, outside of Moscow. The two-week seminar continued uninterrupted during the attempted coup in August.

Departments of Hebrew were approved by the Ukrainian Ministry of Education for the universities of Kiev and Odessa. In Ukraine efforts were made to reexamine Ukrainian-Jewish relations and bring out into the open sensitive issues that had been covered over in the Soviet period. In June, Kiev was the site of a three-day conference, with many participants from abroad, on Ukrainian-Jewish relations. The conference was sponsored by the Ukrainian Republic Organization of Ukrainian Specialists, headed by former dissident Ivan Dzyuba, and several local Jewish organizations. Over 70 papers were presented.

A more highly visible series of events took place in Kiev in September. To mark the 50th anniversary of the Babi Yar massacre, on September 29–30, 1941, when the Nazis murdered about 35,000 Kievan Jews, local authorities organized photographic exhibitions, a scholarly conference, ceremonies at Babi Yar, musical performances, and other events. Main streets of Kiev were strung with banners recalling the tragedy, and the photos of some of the victims were displayed on the streets. A commemorative volume was published. Leonid Kravchuk, chairman of the Ukrainian Supreme Soviet, Minister of Education Zvulun Hammer of Israel, the chairman of the German Bundestag, and other dignitaries addressed a large audience at Babi Yar, where a new monument, in the form of a menorah, was dedicated. Yevgenii Yevtushenko read his famous poem "Babi Yar," which had been condemned by Nikita Khrushchev and conservative Soviet writers.

By contrast, the Lithuanian government pardoned 35,000 Lithuanians who had been convicted by Soviet courts of collaboration and other war crimes, on the grounds that Soviet justice was politically directed and that this charge had been used to dispose of opponents of the Soviet regime or nationally minded Lithuanians. The Lithuanian courts refused pardons to 400 people who clearly were active collaborators in murdering Jews and others. Israeli and Jewish officials protested the blanket pardons, in which cases were not examined individually. Rehabilitation of those convicted was stopped, and a parliamentary commission, to be advised by foreign experts, was set up to examine the pardons. The U.S. Department of Justice announced that it had identified 2,000 people who should not be rehabilitated, according to *Izvestiia* (September 11, 1991). Lithuanian president Vytautas Landsbergis said that the KGB had planted the evidence which the Simon Wiesenthal Center in Los Angeles made public.

In Belarus a weeklong Marc Chagall festival took place in the city of his birth, Vitebsk, in January. Films, television programs, and exhibits of his work were shown under the rubric of the "Return of the Maestro." His works were also shown in an exhibit entitled "Artists of GOSET, 1919–1949" (the State Yiddish Theater, closed in 1949) in Moscow. The exhibit featured artistic works by others, such as Alexander Tishler and Natan Altman, who had also painted scenery for the theater. Recordings and films of performances by Shlomo Mikhoels, actor and director of the theater who was murdered in an "accident" in 1948, were part of the exhibit. However, funds were insufficient to publish a catalogue.

The Yiddish journal *Sovetish haimland* lamented that mass emigration was depleting its readership. "When a Jew emigrates, we lose a reader. The size of our editions is falling catastrophically. . ." (no. 7).

Birobidzhan

Early in 1991 there was talk of declaring the Jewish Autonomous Region, whose center is Birobidzhan, an independent, but Soviet and socialist, republic. There was considerable opposition to the idea. Some pointed out that in 1989 the 8,800 Jewish residents comprised only 4 percent of the population and that there was hardly a need for a Jewish autonomous region (*oblast'*), let alone a republic. Others pointed out that the motivation for autonomy or independence was economic, not national. That is, an independent republic could extricate itself more easily from the Soviet economy.

There were two Jewish cultural societies in Birobidzhan, Mame Loshn, with a Yiddish orientation, and Einikeit, with a more Israeli orientation. The two groups were reported to have no contact with each other. In 1990, about 1,000 Jews emigrated to Israel from Birobidzhan, and it was expected that several hundred others would do so by the end of 1991. There were said to be 200 children in a Jewish Sunday school where they studied Yiddish, Hebrew, Jewish history, and Jewish music and dance. Efforts were being made to train Yiddish teachers in the local pedagogical institute, but they were reported to be more interested in studying English.

Velvel Belinker was appointed the new editor of *Birobidzhaner shtern*, the local Yiddish newspaper, which now added four pages in Russian. Belinker, a 37-year-old native of Birobidzhan, had learned to write and speak Yiddish only three years earlier. In an interview, Belinker asserted that there was a future for Jews in the area because "there are people who are afraid both of pogroms and of emigration. Birobidzhan is for them a compromise" (*Sovetish haimland*, no. 6, p. 119).

ZVI GITELMAN

Eastern European Countries

In their attempts to reconstruct their political and economic systems in 1991, the formerly Communist East European states encountered political instability and rapid change, economic difficulties, and social unrest. Because of the lack of political consensus, many parties vied for office, with the result that almost all governments in the region were coalitions. The transition from socialism to capitalism brought relatively high unemployment and steep inflation. Social tensions increased as people felt uncertain about the political and economic situations. There was an upsurge of nationalism, often accompanied by animosity toward other peoples. Anti-Semitism surfaced even in those countries where there were hardly any Jews. The situation roused unease among Jews living in the region, though they were now able to express themselves culturally and religiously to a greater extent than had been possible under the Communists.

Albania

The economic and political situation in Albania was so uncertain that thousands of Albanians fled to Italy, where most were initially refused admission. Others tried to make their way to Greece and other countries. The Communist party won the first multiparty elections since World War II, held in March, but by June the government had fallen.

The Jews of Albania, mostly of Sephardic and Greek origin and heavily intermarried, had no ties with world Jewry until the fall of Communism. There was no synagogue or rabbi in Albania after World War II. In 1991, 300 Jews emigrated to Israel. In August, Albania established diplomatic relations with Israel, the last former Communist state to do so. It is believed that there are practically no Jews left in Albania.

Bulgaria

The United Democratic Front in Bulgaria, the main opposition to the former Communists (reconstituted as the Bulgarian Socialist party), won the second national election since the fall of the Communist government.

The 5,000 Jews of Bulgaria began to reorganize their communal life. A new organization, Zion, was formed in direct competition with the Shalom organization dominated by former Communist functionaries. Its aims were to revive Jewish culture, reestablish links with world Jewry, assist Jews in need, and forge business links with Jewish communities abroad in an effort to help in the revival of Bulgaria's moribund economy.

309

Czechoslovakia

Czechoslovakia undertook to sell Syria a number of T-72 tanks, which aroused much criticism in Israel and elsewhere. Prime Minister Marian Calfa explained that, though Czechoslovakia did not want to spur Middle Eastern arms competition, her economic problems dictated that she earn hard currency, including from the sale of armaments. Two parliamentary deputies caused controversy when, on the floor of the parliament, they warned against the return of Jewish artifacts to the Jewish community, lest the latter sell them abroad, thus depriving the country of its artistic and religious heritage.

Israeli president Chaim Herzog became the first Israeli head of state to visit Czechoslovakia when he came to Prague in October. He was returning an official visit to Israel in 1990 by Czechoslovak president Vaclav Havel.

The Jewish population, estimated at 5,000, seemed to grow as some people who had hitherto not associated themselves with the Jewish communities identified themselves as Jews. This raised questions about the Jewish *bona fides* of many people who are the children of mixed marriages. The question was not only religious, but raised the issue of who would be officially considered a member of the community and hence eligible to participate in decisions about and access to formerly Jewish properties, which the government was being asked to return to the organized Jewish community. These very valuable properties include former synagogues, schools, and communal buildings, the component parts of the State Jewish Museum and its holdings, and even hotels and other commercial establishments formerly the property of the community. Partly because the issue of Jewish identity came to the fore, a group of younger Czech Jews, most of whom are of mixed parentage, began to explore possibilities of creating a non-Orthodox community and synagogue.

Hungary

In May, Hungarian prime minister Jozef Antall visited Israel, where he urged an expansion of economic ties between the two states. While on a visit to Hungary, Pope John Paul II met with representatives of the Jewish community and condemned anti-Semitism. However, he prayed at the crypt of Jozef Cardinal Mindszenty, who had refused to condemn Nazi killing of Jews and was widely perceived in the Jewish community as anti-Semitic.

In December, a bomb exploded near a bus carrying Soviet Jewish émigrés to the Budapest airport, where they were to embark for Israel. Two Hungarian policemen were seriously injured and four passengers were lightly wounded, but Hungary continued to be a way station for Soviet immigrants to Israel.

The largest Jewish population in Eastern Europe, estimated at between 35,000 and 100,000, continued to develop its educational and cultural institutions. Three Jewish day schools operated in Budapest for a second year, and newly founded or revived Jewish organizations continued their activities. These schools were the Anna

Frank Gymnasium, Yavneh, and Masoret Avot. The Anna Frank school existed throughout the Communist period but its enrollments rose dramatically after 1990 and it now enrolled about 200 high-school students. It had close links with the Jewish Theological Seminary in Budapest, the center of Neolog Judaism. The Yavneh school was secular in orientation and was supported by the Lauder Foundation based in the United States. It enrolled about 200 students. Masoret Avot was an Orthodox school with a Zionist orientation. Funded in part by the Reichmann family of Canada, its Judaic faculty was staffed partly by Hungarian-speaking Israelis, with an Israeli educator, Dr. Efraim Frisch, as principal. The school enrolled about 500 students.

There were 20 functioning synagogues in Budapest and 19 elsewhere in Hungary. Ten rabbis served in Budapest and seven outside the capital. The Jewish hospital and nursing home had 250 beds and a central communal kitchen fed 1,300 elderly Jews. There were three Jewish old-age homes, two in Budapest and one in Szeged.

Poland

In Poland, the polity was so fragmented that in the national election no party won more than 13 percent of the vote.

Though no more than 5,000 identified Jews lived in Poland, anti-Semitism became a much discussed issue. In several Polish cities, anti-Semitic graffiti were found, even in places of Jewish martyrdom during World War II. President Lech Walesa met with members of the World Jewish Congress in March, acknowledged the continued existence of anti-Semitism in Poland, and pledged Poland's support for the repeal of the United Nations resolution calling Zionism a form of racism. He said that Poland would protect Jewish cemeteries and former synagogues and would address the property claims of former Polish Jews. In May, addressing the Israeli Knesset, Walesa apologized for Polish anti-Semitism and called for improved Polish-Jewish relations. Earlier, Walesa had announced the formation of a presidential commission to combat anti-Semitism and xenophobia. Members of the commission included literary critic Jan Blonski; Jerzy Turowicz, editor of the leading Catholic newspaper, *Tygodnik Powszechny*; historians Wladyslaw Bartoszewski and Krystyna Kersten; and Stanislaw Krajewski, representative of the World Jewish Congress in Poland.

Just before a trip to the United States, the primate of Poland, Jozef Cardinal Glemp, apologized for remarks made in 1989 when he accused Jews who had demonstrated at the controversial convent in Auschwitz of wishing to attack the nuns. While in America, Glemp also condemned anti-Semitism, of which he himself had been accused after a homily in which he charged that Jews controlled the media worldwide. However, the cardinal refused to make the same condemnation in Poland itself.

Boleslaw Tejkowski, a politician on the fringes of Poland's fractionated political life, gave an interview in *Gazeta Wyborcza*, the country's most widely circulated newspaper, on July 4. The editor clearly wished to draw him out in order to show the absurdity of Tejkowski's views, and the latter obliged him by asserting that Mikhail Gorbachev, Polish prime minister Krzysztof Bielecki, and the wife of presidential candidate Stanislaw Tyminski were Jews. Tejkowski criticized Walesa for apologizing in Israel for Polish anti-Semitism. He argued that anti-Semitism was justifiable because Jews had fatally injured Poland on several occasions: they had collaborated with Swedish invaders and then with the Soviets. Now they were dominating Poland through their "control" of Solidarity.

Public Jewish activity among the 5,000 or so Jews in Poland continued at a modest level. The one synagogue in Warsaw benefited from the services of Polish-born Israeli Rabbi Jozkowicz and daily services were held. A small group of younger Jews, including journalist Konstanty Gebert and mathematician Stanislaw Krajewski, maintained a Sunday school for young children. Festivals of Jewish culture, featuring music and art, were held in Krakow and a few other cities.

Romania

Prime Minister Petre Roman resigned in September after three days of rioting by dissatisfied miners who had come to the capital, Bucharest.

The Romanian Jewish population was dwindling rapidly as a result of emigration, a low birthrate, and a high mortality rate. It was estimated that the Jews numbered between 15,000 and 18,000 in a general population of over 23 million. Nevertheless, there were many anti-Semitic articles in the press, which blamed the Jews both for Communism and for seizing power after the downfall of Communism. The largest circulation weekly, *Romania Mare*, which had half a million readers, was edited by Eugen Barbu and Corneliu Vadim Tudor, both known for their anti-Jewish views. On May 31, the weekly wrote: "While there are 20,000 Jews left in Romania, 5,000 of them are in the country's leadership. . . . In parliament it rains Jews by the bucket. . . . It's not their fault—domination has been their style since the dawn of time—but can't they let us breathe a little, instead of trampling on us as they have been doing since 1947?"

In April, the 45th anniversary of his execution as a war criminal, parliament paid tribute with a moment of silence to Marshal Ion Antonescu, Romania's wartime dictator and collaborator with Hitler. But on June 4 the government issued a declaration dissociating itself from anti-Semitic articles in the press. President Ion Iliescu did the same at a press conference, but some publications continued their anti-Semitic line.

In July, the 50th anniversary of Romanian pogroms in Iasi and Bucharest was marked. Chief Rabbi Moses Rosen accused the government of cowardice and indifference toward anti-Semitism and warned that Romania's image in the world would suffer if anti-Semitism were permitted to go unchecked. He said that 400,000 Romanian Jews had been killed in the Holocaust, but few Romanians were aware of that or acknowledged it. Some intellectuals issued a statement condemning anti-Semitism, but the country's leading political force, the National Salvation Front, was ambivalent about it.

Yugoslavia

In February, the Yugoslav republics of Croatia and Slovenia asserted the priority of their laws over those of the federal government, and the government was forced to initiate discussions with the republics regarding a further loosening of the Yugoslav federation. But in June, Croatia and Slovenia declared independence. The Yugoslav army moved into both republics in order to prevent their secession. Macedonia then declared independence in September. Germany recognized the independence of its wartime ally Croatia, as well as that of Slovenia. The European Community, prodded by Germany, followed suit at the end of the year. Greek objections to Macedonian independence—the Greeks claimed that "Macedonia" is a Greek name and territory and no other state should use it—blocked recognition by Europe of that republic's independence.

The breakup of Yugoslavia threatened the unity and organizational coordination of the 5,000 Jews in the country. Though small, this community was one of the best organized in the region, sponsoring summer camps, old-age homes, cultural and educational activities, and several publications.

ZVI GITELMAN

Australia

National Affairs

AUSTRALIA IN 1991 WAS DEEP in the grip of a recession, the severest downturn in the economy since the Great Depression of the 1930s. Layoffs, losses, closures, and bankruptcies became common, especially in hard-hit Victoria, and Jewish businessmen were among the casualties. Perhaps the most spectacular and publicized case was that of textile magnate Abe Goldberg, whose empire crashed, leaving a staggering amount in loans outstanding.

For most of the year, the ruling Australian Labor party (ALP) was headed by Prime Minister Bob Hawke. In December, owing to his inability to improve the economy, he was replaced by former treasurer Paul Keating in a ballot among ALP parliamentarians. Keating remained singularly unpopular with voters, who viewed him as the principal architect of the recession and who perceived him to be arrogant and detached, in contrast to the approachable, emotional Hawke.

THE GULF WAR

Both the Hawke government and the opposition coalition of Liberal and National parties led by Dr. John Hewson supported military intervention against Iraq's occupation of Kuwait, and Australia contributed to the allied war effort by sending three frigates to the Gulf. But the relatively unpublicized contribution of joint U.S.-Australian communications bases at Nurringar in South Australia and at the North-West Cape was almost certainly far more significant than that of the frigates. Hawke later acknowledged the bases' importance: Nurringar had helped to provide early warnings of Iraq's missile launches, and the North-West Cape base had been a crucial link in satellite communications.

A resolution passed by the Australian Parliament in January, reaffirming support for allied actions against Saddam, added that "this House . . . deplores Iraq's widening of the conflict by its unprovoked attack upon Israel" and "recognizes, as those with whom we are acting now in the Gulf have recognized, the need to intensify efforts to establish peace and stability in the Middle East, including a just resolution of the Palestinian issue and the continuing security of Israel, once the crisis in the Gulf is resolved." Except for hard-line left-wingers, the ruling ALP supported Hawke's refusal to link the Palestinian situation directly to Iraqi withdrawal from Kuwait. However, Hawke told a television interviewer, "We have made it quite clear, before this conflict started, that there has to be a resolution of the Palestinian problem and that includes their right to contemplate a state. . . ."

The existence of a secret Australian government ban on the sale to Israel of lethal weaponry as well as nonlethal military equipment, in force for several years, was leaked during the Gulf War. Defense Minister Sen. Robert Ray favored continuing the ban, saying: "We are avoiding selling lethal weapons into areas of instability." Yet he admitted that the government had approved a major sale of trainer-aircraft engine parts to Iraq (a sale blocked owing to the UN embargo following the Kuwait invasion). Official sources later confirmed that during the Gulf War Australia provided Israel with top-secret information obtained from the Nurringar communications base, which was involved in monitoring satellite infrared detection of Iraqi missile launches. Noting the virulent opposition to such bases in Australia by a coalition of left-wing groups headquartered in Queensland, Senator Ray told Parliament: "Essentially the [anti-bases] coalition accuses me of allowing the Australian-American facilities at Nurringar to be used to give early warning time to citizens of Israel that missiles are coming. If I am guilty of that . . . that is my proudest moment in politics."

During the Gulf War, overt public prejudice against Muslims in Australia (the majority of whom are not of Arabic origin) increased, with verbal and physical attacks on persons and property highlighted in the media. Australia expelled a top Iraqi envoy for "security reasons" after he repeated Saddam's call for a resort to terrorism, and a Lebanese-born Sydney Muslim was charged with offering to smuggle a bomb aboard an airplane.

Relations with Israel

Prime Minister Bob Hawke, an ALP right-winger, was regarded essentially as a warm friend of the Jewish community and the Zionist cause, despite a perceptible tilting of his government toward the PLO in recent years. In May Hawke was presented with the Shield of Jerusalem award by Zionist Federation of Australia president Mark Leibler, on behalf of Jerusalem's mayor Teddy Kollek and World Zionist Organization chairman Simcha Dinitz, in the presence of Israeli ambassador Zvi Kedar. The award came in recognition of Hawke's personal support for a united Jerusalem, a stance that contrasted with his government's official insistence that East Jerusalem is part of the occupied territories and should be relinquished. However, Hawke's press office barred television camera crews from the ceremony and discouraged media coverage in general, presumably to play down his well-known ties with Jews and Israel and to placate the powerful left-wing faction of the ALP, which his increasingly shaky leadership position was forced to rely on for support against the known ambitions of arch-rival Paul Keating.

The latter, who became prime minister in December, was largely an enigma as far as Jews and Israel were concerned. There was little in Keating's political career to indicate any special sympathy toward Israel or indeed any particular interest in foreign affairs. He enjoyed limited contact with Australia's Jewish community, and his inner Sydney electorate held a sizable number of Muslim voters. (He admitted that he had pressed to help controversial Islamic religious leader Sheik Taj El-Din Hamed Al-Hilaly remain in Australia, despite fervent objections from the Jewish community owing to Hilaly's inflammatory anti-Semitic statements.) Nevertheless, Jewish leaders tended to voice optimism about future Australian policy on Israel and the Middle East under Keating. The new prime minister had the reputation of being a good listener and a pragmatist, and his membership in the right-wing ALP faction was expected to ensure his support for Israel.

At its annual conference in June, the ruling ALP allowed a backroom factional deal to give anti-Israel elements—which included left-wing deputy prime minister Brian Howe—the concessions they sought in a one-sided resolution on the Middle East. The resolution was moved by Foreign Affairs Minister Sen. Gareth Evans (a right-winger) and prominent left-wing parliamentarian Stewart West, long known as an anti-Israel, pro-PLO propagandist. To quote the Sydney-based president of the Executive Council of Australian Jewry, Leslie Caplan: ". . . it is a cause for grave concern that these views were allowed to prevail in an attempt to gain a non-existent consensus on Middle East policy." The resolution highlighted UN Resolutions 242 and 338 as a suitable basis for "the achievement of a just, comprehensive and lasting peace in the Middle East," but made no reference to the need for bilateral recognition and negotiation between Israel and the Arab nations. It singled out the "continued expansion" of Israeli settlements in the occupied territories as "a major obstacle to a broader peace in the Middle East" and supported the involvement of the PLO in peace talks. The resolution condemned Israel's human-rights record but made no mention of human-rights violations by Arab countries or of their trade boycott. Bob Hawke took no part in the debate on the resolution, which now bound his government, but later defended it: "We think the Israeli government could have conducted itself differently in regard to certain aspects of its policies."

In January the Australian government formally downgraded its relations with the Palestine Liberation Organization, in view of the PLO's continuing support of Saddam Hussein. Australia had not followed the United States in cutting off dialogue earlier, because, in the words of a Department of Foreign Affairs spokesperson, "we thought it was better to leave a line of communication open so we could encourage forces of moderation." The government's reduction of contacts with the PLO came a few months after a request from the PLO for a major upgrading of its presence in Australia, where its sole representative was Ali Kazak, an Australian citizen. Kazak had opened a Palestine Information Office in Melbourne about 1982, moved it to Canberra in 1987, and in 1990 had successfully sought government permission to rename it, first, the PLO Information Office, and shortly afterward, the PLO Office. The PLO asked the government for an in-principle agreement that would allow officials in Tunis or in the organization's affiliates overseas to join the PLO Office in Canberra, but the downgrading of contacts appeared to thwart that request. In September Senator Evans told Parliament that Australia did not see a role for the PLO in the Middle East peace process unless the PLO unequivocally recognized Israel's right to exist, preferably by amending its charter, and that nothing since the Gulf War had tempted Australian ministers to initiate contact with the PLO.

ARAB BOYCOTT; UN RESOLUTION

The apparent compliance of some Australian companies and even the Victorian and New South Wales chambers of commerce with the Arab trade boycott of Israel led a delegation drawn jointly from the Executive Council of Australian Jewry (ECAJ) and the Zionist Federation of Australia (ZFA) to hold separate meetings in August with Foreign Minister Evans, Primary Industries Minister Simon Crean, and the opposition spokesperson on foreign affairs, Sen. Robert Hill. A submission prepared by ZFA president Mark Leibler stated that the central boycott office in Damascus continued to circulate questionnaires freely to Australian firms, and that a number of major companies had conspicuously avoided the Israeli market. The submission called on the Australian government to follow the example of the United States and adopt legislation prohibiting companies and individuals from complying with the boycott. It claimed that almost 100 Australian companies were known to have been blacklisted by the boycott office at some time, and stressed that anti-boycott legislation would not affect the vast bulk of Australian exports to the Middle East—primary produce and raw materials—which were exempt from boycott procedures. (Meanwhile, permission in principle was given to El Al for direct, one-stop flights to Australia.)

The Australian government played a significant role in events leading to the repeal in December of the 1975 UN General Assembly Resolution 3379, which equated Zionism with racism. In October 1986 the Australian Parliament led the world by passing unanimously a motion recommending rescission of the resolution, and in the ensuing years Australia worked assiduously to convince other nations to follow her example. In May 1991, following the UN secretary-general's call for revocation of Resolution 3379, Australia stepped up her lobbying efforts among neighboring countries and fellow members of the British Commonwealth of Nations. Parliament reiterated its support for repeal, and in September Foreign Minister Evans pleaded the case before the UN General Assembly. After the repeal resolution had been drafted in October, Australian diplomats worked closely with senior U.S. and Israeli officials and with the ZFA in the Asia-Pacific region, with a view to ensuring a maximum number of affirmative votes and to securing as many cosponsors as possible. Australia was in fact joined in cosponsoring the resolution by ten Asia-Pacific nations (including Japan, South Korea, Singapore, and New Zealand) and in voting for repeal by a further seven. The ZFA worked closely with the government throughout the repeal campaign, and Jewish communal leader Isi Leibler played a pivotal role in efforts to persuade Asian governments to vote for repeal of the resolution.

Anti-Semitism and Anti-Zionism

During and after the Gulf War, anti-Semitic incidents—frequently associated with anti-Zionism—increased sharply. The early months of the war saw a prolonged epidemic of defacement and damage to Jewish premises in various cities, with synagogues across Australia commonly reporting anti-Semitic graffiti and smashed windows. The National Jewish War Memorial Center in Canberra was internally vandalized. Arsonists lit fires of varying severity at a kindergarten attached to the North Eastern Jewish War Memorial Center in the Melbourne suburb of Doncaster, and in Sydney at the North Shore Temple Emanuel School in Chatswood, the Illawarra Synagogue in Allawah, the Bankstown War Memorial Synagogue, and the Sephardi Synagogue in Woollahra, while a gasoline bomb attack on the North Shore Synagogue in Lindfield was foiled by a guard. Moreover, in a continuation of a rising trend detected in earlier years, individual Jews suffered harassment, even physical assaults, and threatening mail and phone calls were received at Jewish homes and institutions. These actions were attributed by police and communal leaders to neo-Nazis. A hoax bomb call, which almost disrupted a mass Jewish pro-Israel rally in Melbourne, led to the conviction of a confirmed neo-Nazi. Names familiar and not-so-familiar, on both ends of the political spectrum, made predictable anti-Semitic or anti-Zionist charges in newspaper correspondence columns.

Former Australian diplomat and veteran Arabist Malcolm Booker published a series of anti-Bush, anti-Israel articles in early 1991, in the *Canberra Times*, long regarded as one of the quality national dailies most hostile to Israel. Coincidentally, Booker was the father-in-law of David Hill, managing director of the Australian Broadcasting Corporation (ABC), whose near-exclusive use of known pro-Arab commentators during the Gulf War caused widespread public indignation (including comments by Prime Minister Hawke and Communications Minister Kim Beazley) as well as protests from Jewish groups. Beazley foreshadowed the implementation of a more effective complaints procedure for the ABC, whose reporting and commentary both on radio and television had often been regarded as slanted by friends of Israel. (By contrast, one of the highlights of the viewing year was ABC-TV's series of six interviews by producer Dagmar Strauss with prominent Australian Jews.)

In January, one of the ABC's favorite commentators, Dr. Michael McKinley, caused an uproar by claiming in an article in the *Australian Financial Review* that in order to boost public support for Australia's naval presence in the Gulf, Jewish or Zionist groups in Sydney might be tempted to bomb an American airline, an act which would be assumed to be the work of Arabs. New South Wales journalist David Bowman extended his repeatedly paraded anti-Zionism into the letters page of the London *Daily Telegraph* in a defense of the ABC's failure to use "commentators who were Zionists" during the Gulf crisis.

During the Gulf War, the Sydney-based Australian Federation of Islamic Councils inserted antiwar advertisements in national newspapers, and the Islamic Egyptian Society in Sydney called for linkage with the Palestinian question. Writers in Arabic-language newspapers, like Ali Kazak and his apologists, continued virulent attacks on Zionism. Sheikh Hilaly, imam of Australia's largest mosque, who in 1988 made a notorious slur on Jews and Judaism, told the *Sydney Morning Herald* that Australian Jews were "supporting war, not peace," and claimed that Zionists were creating problems for the whole world. Describing this outburst as "quite inappropriate, provocative and unhelpful," federal opposition spokesperson Philip Ruddock called on the minister for immigration and ethnic affairs, Gerry Hand, to remonstrate with Hilaly. Bilal Cleland, head of the Islamic Council of Victoria, alleged a clear distinction between Judaism and Zionism. Sydney academic Dr. Ahmad Shboul (one of the ABC's frequent commentators) told the *Australian* newspaper that people who associated Islam with penal practices considered barbaric and with female circumcision should realize that such practices were attributable to "the Old Testament rules," some of which Islam had modified. "So . . . we would also have to accuse Judaism. . . ."

During the year, anti-Semitism in Islam-dominated Malaysia spilled over into Australia, with prominent Australian Jews apparently made scapegoats for Malaysia's fragile relations with Australia. In April an article in Malaysia's principal English-language newspaper, the *Straits Times*, claimed that the Australian Zionist movement was seeking to oust Prime Minister Mahathir bin Mohamad because it was "unhappy with the firm stand taken by Malaysia toward Zionist brutality in Palestine." That same month, the Melbourne-based Australian People's Conference (a shadowy anti-Israel, pro-Iraq group) alleged that Australian Zionists were behind Australia's criticisms of Malaysia. The group cited attacks on Dr. Mahathir and his government by Michael Danby, editor of the Zionist newsletter *Australia/Israel Review*, by Isi Leibler and the Asia Pacific Jewish Association (of which Leibler was chairman), and by Sydney judge Marcus Einfeld, in 1988, during his presidency of the Human Rights and Equal Opportunity Commission in Canberra.

RIGHT-WING GROUPS; HOLOCAUST REVISIONISTS

Conspiracy theories inspired by the right-wing, populist, anti-Semitic Australian League of Rights (the devious machinations of "international finance" is a favorite) were steadily gaining currency in depressed rural areas. Denis Collins, a country grape farmer and Independent member for the outback town of Alice Springs in the Northern Territory (NT) Legislative Assembly, perhaps reflected the league's influence when he made the absurd claim (under the cover of parliamentary privilege, which shielded him from defamation action) that Melbourne brothers Isi and Mark Leibler were linked to the drug and pornography trades and that ADL in the United States, of which Isi Leibler was "the No. 2 man" (*sic!*) "engages in a wide range of activities that are inherently criminal in nature" and is known as "the American drug lobby."

Following complaints from the ECAJ, the *Australasian Post*, an adult tabloid magazine, canceled a series of advertisements promoting a package that described the Holocaust as an "Allied Communist fabrication." A Christian fundamentalist group in Victoria distributed a U.S.-made video describing the Holocaust as a hoax and claiming, inter alia, that the Talmud commands Jews to rape preadolescent girls. Holocaust revisionism was also being peddled, as for many years past, in League of Rights publications, by Melbourne lawyer John Bennett and his associates in the minuscule Australian Civil Liberties Union (not to be confused with the reputable Victorian Union for Civil Liberties) and the West Australia-based periodical *Perseverance*, organ of the fascist Hungarista movement. ECAJ secretary Jeremy Jones urged the Australian Law Reform Commission to make denial of the Holocaust a criminal offense.

Other developments included the distribution of material accusing Jews of cannibalism, human sacrifice, and blood rituals by a Queensland-based group known as Christian Identity Ministries; the appearance on a popular daytime television talk show of a self-proclaimed neo-Nazi "fuehrer" wearing Nazi uniform and claiming that "Zionists" controlled the political process in Australia and that Jews might have been responsible for the recent wave of arson attacks on Sydney synagogues in order to "purify" them and collect insurance money; and the appearance in the Victorian country towns of Geelong and Colac of anti-Semitic and white supremacist pamphlets bearing the imprimatur of the newly emerged White Aryan Resistance (WAR).

OTHER MATTERS

Several Jews, identified as such, made unwelcome headlines during the year, a trend some observers attributed to anti-Semitism. The case of ruined Melbourne-based building tycoon George Herscu, jailed for five years in December 1990 for bribing a Queensland government minister in return for a lucrative business deal, was featured frequently in the media. The prominent developer of Surfers Paradise, Queensland, Eddie Kornhauser, was tried in June on similar charges of bribery, but was acquitted. In May the Perth-based Western Women Management Proprietary, a fledgling feminist financial counseling, banking, and investment group, collapsed amid recrimination and innuendo focusing on its founder, Robin Zara Greenburg. In July the Melbourne *Age* splashed across its front page a sensationalized scoop report on the bankruptcy, enormous debts, and numerous distressed personal creditors of Chaim Serebryanski, a principal benefactor of Melbourne's Lubavitcher movement, who had suddenly departed overseas. Political commentator and former ALP federal minister Barry Cohen, echoing a widespread sentiment, claimed "an iniquitous and subtle change in the media, whereby articles on prominent Jews never fail to point out if they are Jewish when they have done something wrong."

The Melbourne *Age* carried an attack on circumcision by celebrated feminist Germaine Greer which, while not inherently anti-Semitic, revived media debate on the subject and put Jews on the defensive.

Australian Jewish leaders, convinced of the need for federal antiracism legislation, welcomed a report by federal Race Relations Commissioner Irene Moss and lawyer Ron Castan recommending federal laws to combat racial violence, incitement to racial hatred, and religious discrimination camouflaging racism. Subsequently, the Law Reform Commission announced that it had drafted legislation against racist violence. In December the Legislative Assembly of the Australian Capital Territory (ACT), which incorporates Canberra, passed Australia's toughest antidiscrimination legislation. The racial vilification section was introduced as an amendment by a former ACT attorney-general, who spoke of "a very active far right element developing" in the territory.

Federal ALP parliamentarian Clyde Holding, a non-Jew with a large Melbourne Jewish electorate, and noted for his attachment to Jews and Israel, succeeded Peter Baume as Australia's representative on the London-based Inter-Parliamentary Council Against Anti-Semitism.

Nazi War Criminals

In April the federal government announced that its War Crimes Special Investigations Unit (established in 1987 in anticipation of the controversial War Crimes Amendment Act of 1988) was unlikely to be funded beyond June 1992. After that date, a litigation support group was expected to assist prosecutions in progress, but no new investigations would be conducted. News of the probable closure of the unit, which had investigated over 600 suspects and recommended the prosecution of 12, was welcomed by the Ukrainian and Baltic communities and also by certain newspapers and politicians who had deplored the investigations as a waste of taxpayers' money.

In August the High Court of Australia (equivalent to the U.S. Supreme Court) decided by a 4–3 majority that the federal War Crimes Amendment Act was valid. The act had been challenged on several grounds by lawyers appearing for an Adelaide man, Ivan Timofeyevich Polyukovich, the first person indicted under the legislation. Polyukovich faced charges involving the wartime murders in the Ukraine of 24 people and of being implicated in the murders of up to 850 others, mostly Jews. He was charged in January 1990, but the hearing was suspended when his lawyers lodged their challenge in April of that year. (The High Court heard the challenge toward the close of 1990 but announced no decision until 1991.) Reflecting a viewpoint widespread among the public, Polyukovich's lawyers argued that the War Crimes Amendment Act did not fall within the external affairs jurisdiction of Australia; that it was a matter of deeply felt Jewish rather than true international concern; that it operated retroactively to make acts criminal which were not criminal under Australian or international law when they were committed; and that it created new offenses—deportation, internment, and genocide—previously unknown in Australian criminal law. The High Court, in an exhaustive and lengthy judgment handed down in 1991, held that the external affairs power of Australia supported making criminal those acts committed outside Australia, even if at the time the perpetrator had no connection with the country but only subsequently established one. The High Court also held that a crime against humanity was part of the international body of law, which could and did become Australian domestic law if the government exercised its external affairs power to include it. In addition, the retroactive reach of the act was insufficient to invalidate it, and the act's recitation of criminal offenses did not usurp the High Court's judicial powers.

As a result of this finding, committal proceedings (similar to a U.S. grand jury) against Polyukovich resumed in Adelaide in November, when the courthouse was picketed by members of the anti-Semitic League of Rights and others protesting the trial, some of whom carried placards bearing anti-Israel slogans (the most notable protester was Sir Walter Crocker, a former career diplomat and lieutenant-governor of South Australia, a man of part-Jewish ancestry whose publications betray a near-obsessive anti-Israel bias).

In September two other Adelaide residents, Heinrich Wagner and an unnamed man, were also charged with involvement in anti-Jewish atrocities in the Ukraine in 1942.

JEWISH COMMUNITY

Demography

The Jewish population of Australia was estimated at just below 90,000 by some demographers, while others put it at between 90,000 and 100,000. The latter suggested that many Jews—those who consider themselves Jewish in a cultural or ethnic sense and Holocaust survivors fearful that their Jewish identity could be used against them by a future hostile regime—do not reveal their Jewishness on federal census forms.

Numbers were augmented during the year by newcomers from South Africa and the Soviet Union, though the peak period for such arrivals had passed. Jewish leaders continued to fret over the fact that, according to census figures, the community was an aging one, and the year's statistics for Jewish marriages and for bar/bat mitzvahs were taken by some as cause for concern.

According to an Australian Bureau of Statistics report, "Fertility in Australia," the 1986 census showed that Jewish women have fewer children than women of other religions in Australia. The average number of children for Jewish women aged 15–54 was 1.6 compared with 2.3 for Muslim women, 2 for Christians, and 1.9 for Buddhists. (Women who stated no religion had an average of 1.4 children.) Among women aged 45–54, Jewish women had an average of 2.3 children, compared with Muslims (3.8), Buddhists (3.5), Catholics (3.1), and Anglicans or Episcopalians (2.8).

A federal census, the first since 1986, was conducted in August. Communal leaders called upon Jews, whether religiously observant or not, to answer "Jewish" to the question about the religion of each household member. The question was vitally important for the community, since census figures influenced government support levels for educational institutions, welfare services, elderly citizens' clubs, and old-age homes, and even ethnic radio. The census results were not expected to become available until 1992–93.

Israel-Related Activity

The Zionist orientation of the community was fully evident, particularly during the Gulf War. A Solidarity with Israel service at Sydney's Great Synagogue at the end of January, after Iraq's Scud attacks began, attracted over 1,600 people. Some 2,600 Jews attended a comparable rally in Melbourne, which heard messages of support from Prime Minister Hawke and Opposition Leader Hewson. In February the New South Wales Jewish Board of Deputies organized a protest outside the Iraqi Embassy in Canberra, attended by hundreds of Sydney's Jews supported by the Canberra Jewish community and Christian groups. Several prominent Jewish leaders traveled to Israel during the war to demonstrate their solidarity and, like the Australian Jewish press, were critical of those who failed to follow suit. Many other Israel-related activities took place throughout the year, ranging from fund-raising via the United Israel Appeal, WIZO, the National Council of Jewish Women (NCJW), groups of "friends of" Israeli universities, and similar organizations, to lobbying by the ZFA and its constituents, and information activities by Zionist groups and Australia/Israel Publications (publishers of the fortnightly newsletter *Australia/Israel Review*, sent to parliamentarians, journalists, and other policy and opinion-makers nationwide).

The articulate and charismatic Isi Leibler, long one of the world's foremost Soviet Jewry activists, had since turned his considerable zeal and energy to improving the image of Jews and Israel in the Asia-Pacific region. In May he was elected cochairman (with Mendel Kaplan of South Africa) of the governing board of the World Jewish Congress (WJC). In that capacity he undertook missions to Beijing in October and to New Delhi, Singapore, Bangkok, Tokyo, and Seoul in November, meeting foreign ministers and high officials in the presence of Australian envoys. During these missions, which received full encouragement and cooperation from Foreign Minister Evans, he discussed not only repeal of the "Zionism Is Racism" UN resolution but also diplomatic relations with Israel and the Arab boycott.

Australia sent 143 immigrants to Israel in 1991, which gave it one of the, if not the, highest proportional *aliyah* rates of any Western country. A record 186 students from around Australia participated in the Australasian Union of Jewish Students (AUJS) Academy tour of Israel. According to a survey conducted by W.D. Rubinstein for the Australian Institute of Jewish Affairs (AIJA) and AUJS, the overwhelming majority of Australia's Jewish college and university students are strongly pro-Israel (as well as Jewishly-conscious and at least somewhat religious).

Communal Affairs

The vibrancy of Australian Jewry was reflected in its myriad communal organizations and activities. Communal forums addressed by distinguished overseas speakers, most of them brought to Australia by the Australian Institute of Jewish Affairs, drew large audiences. Such speakers included Amos Oz, Chaim Potok, Yehuda Bauer, Rabbi Irving Greenberg and his wife, Blu, Rabbi Shlomo Riskin, Rabbi Sherwin Wine, Brig. Gen. Giora Rom, and U.S. congressman Stephen Solarz. In April Czechoslovak hero Alexander Dubcek received the AIJA Human Rights Award in Melbourne.

Among the year's notable events was the National Outlook Conference on the future needs, prospects, and directions of the community, held in Melbourne in June under the joint auspices of the AIJA and the Executive Council of Australian Jewry. Keynote speaker was Los Angeles Jewish educator Hanan Alexander. The conference emphasized the need for the larger Jewish communities in Australia to give more positive and constructive assistance to their smaller counterparts.

At the ECAJ's annual conference, held in Adelaide in November, Jewish Community Council of Victoria president Joe Gersh forcefully advocated an overhaul of the ECAJ's constitution to ensure the organization's relevance into the next century. Claiming that the ECAJ, whose presidency and secretariat rotate periodically between Sydney and Melbourne, was "irrelevant to Melbourne when it was in Sydney and vice versa," he echoed a widely shared view when he recommended the establishment of "a permanent secretariat which doesn't move with the leadership."

Melbourne's financially straitened Makor Library and Resource Center, a unique and heavily utilized collection of material on Jews and Israel, managed to remain in operation, partly owing to a subsidy from the State Zionist Council of Victoria. Communal leaders formally protested to Special Broadcasting Service heads regarding drastic cuts in Jewish programming on radio stations 2EA in Sydney and 3EA in Melbourne.

In July the Australian Association for Jewish Studies held its annual conference in Melbourne, with papers delivered on various topics by Jewish and non-Jewish academics and nonacademics. A decision was made to change the name of the association's scholarly periodical *Menorah* to the *Journal of the Australian Association for Jewish Studies*.

Religion

Jewish congregations existed in every Australian state (but not the Northern Territory), and most Jews were at least nominally Orthodox. There were thriving communities of Lubavitcher, Adass Israel (mainly Hungarian, strictly Orthodox), and Mizrachists in Melbourne and, to a lesser extent, in Sydney. Progressive (or Liberal, equivalent to American Reform) congregations were to be found in all major centers of Jewish life.

In general, the relations between the Orthodox and Reform rabbinates were either strained or nonexistent. However, tentative steps were taken this year in Melbourne toward dialogue between Progressive and Orthodox Jews. The catalyst was the visit in July of U.S. Orthodox rabbi Irving Greenberg, a pioneer of such dialogue in the United States, who addressed members of Sydney's Temple Emanuel and Melbourne's Temple Beth Israel, both Reform, on the need to persist until dialogue is achieved. At a communal forum devoted to the question of whether there would be "one Jewish people" in the next century, at which Greenberg was the keynote speaker, AIJA chairman Isi Leibler (a Mizrachist) and Rabbi Daniel Schiff of Temple Beth Israel committed themselves to initiate dialogue. Schiff revived the proposals of British Reform rabbi Sydney Brichto, who in 1987 had suggested that Reform rabbis cede authority on conversion and divorce to Orthodox rabbis in return for a guarantee that Halakhah would be administered compassionately and creatively. (The Progressive movement in Australia had offered to adopt the Brichto proposals in 1987, but no Orthodox rabbi accepted.) Schiff believed that the proposals might yet be implemented in Australia, and he urged Orthodox Jews to encourage their rabbis to respond positively. Shortly afterward a group of Orthodox and Progressive lay leaders met in Melbourne with Rabbi Schiff and Temple Beth Israel's senior minister, Rabbi John Levi, to discuss ways to overcome differences between Orthodoxy and Progressive Judaism over divorce, conversion, and personal status. A dialogue group chaired jointly by Isi Leibler and the president of the Victorian Union for Progressive Judaism (VUPJ), Walter Jona, met periodically thereafter to discuss such issues as remarriage when there has been no *get* and conversion procedures.

Several congregations celebrated milestones this year: the Melbourne Hebrew Congregation the 150th anniversary of its founding, the St. Kilda Hebrew Congregation, Melbourne, its 120th, and the Bentleigh Progressive Synagogue, Melbourne, its 40th. The Bentleigh Progressive Synagogue was dogged by internal strife, which culminated in the dismissal of its minister, Rabbi Harold Vallins. With a number of seceding members, Vallins founded a new Progressive congregation, Bet Hatikvah, independent of the VUPJ, the umbrella body of Melbourne's three Progressive congregations. Meanwhile, owing to steadily dwindling membership, the congregation of the long-established Bankstown Synagogue, Sydney, decided to disband.

The year saw a surge in communal activity in the Melbourne district of Waverley, far from the Jewish core area yet home to several hundred Jews. The so-called Waverley Jewish Community, with a nucleus of 25 families, conducted the first ever High Holy Day services in the area and floated a proposal to establish an Orthodox synagogue.

A submission by the ECAJ's Jewish Women's Issues Committee to the Australian Law Reform Commission, seeking to make a Jewish divorce decree (*get*) a condition for civil divorce between Jewish parties, was supported by most sections of the community, including the Association of Orthodox Rabbis of Australia and New Zealand.

Education

Australia's Jewish day schools felt the effects of the economic recession: there were signs that owing to financial pressures some parents were delaying enrolling their children in such schools or withdrawing students already enrolled and sending them to non-fee-paying state alternatives. In an attempt to counter these trends, some Jewish day schools offered subsidies or reduced fees to parents. As more parents could not afford day-school fees, demand increased on the United Jewish Education Board (UJEB) in Victoria—the state most affected by the recession—which provided Jewish students at non-Jewish schools with religious instruction. Ironically, the UJEB was forced to reduce some services owing to a substantial funding shortfall, which left between 40 and 50 Victorian children without any Jewish education. However, the UJEB opened its first Sunday school in the country town of Ballarat to accommodate some 12 children in the district.

Leibler-Yavneh College, Melbourne's Mizrachi day school, appeared to surmount a bitter wrangle over financial management between administrators and major benefactors and embarked on an innovative fund-raising program. Rabbi Bill Altshul succeeded fellow American Steven Lorch as principal of Australia's biggest Jewish day school, Mount Scopus Memorial College, Melbourne.

Jewish-Christian Relations

Six invited Jewish observers (including two Australians, Rabbi Raymond Apple of Sydney's Great Synagogue and Rabbi Brian Fox of Sydney's Temple Emanuel), representing the Executive Council of Australian Jewry, attended the huge World Council of Churches (WCC) Assembly, held in Canberra in February. A statement was adopted criticizing Israel for retaliating against PLO missile attacks from Lebanon, yet a motion to commend Israel for not retaliating against Iraqi Scud attacks failed, even though the General Secretary of the WCC had expressed the hope that any statement on the Middle East would deplore the Scud attacks and commend Israeli restraint. Following objections from Dutch, German, and Swiss delegates, the statement was modified to include an acknowledgment that Jews as well as Muslims have suffered in the Middle East troubles and that the Gulf War had increased anti-Semitism as well as prejudice against Muslims.

In March Bishop Ken Mason of the Sydney-based Anglican Board of Missions called on Anglicans to contribute to an urgent appeal for Palestinians, both Muslim and Christian, living under curfew, even though "the delivery of aid may be hindered by the Israelis." He claimed that the Israeli authorities were denying Palestinians "first-aid and health care." John McKnight, the Sydney Anglican clergyman who converted convicted Israeli traitor Mordechai Vanunu, co-authored (with Tom Gilling) *Trial and Error: Mordechai Vanunu and Israel's Nuclear Bomb* (Monarch Publications).

In May Mark Leibler, president of the Zionist Federation of Australia, wrote to the headmaster of the private secondary Brighton Grammar School, Melbourne, expressing concern about a classroom lesson that emphasized Jewish complicity in the death of Jesus and claimed that Christianity had superseded Judaism. Dissatisfied with the headmaster's response, Leibler took the matter to Anglican archbishop Dr. Keith Rayner. Following a strongly worded exchange of correspondence between the two, a special interfaith committee of Christians and Jews was set up in Melbourne in September to review Anglican teachings that may provoke "feelings of hostility toward Jews." This was the first time Jews and Anglicans in Australia had agreed to work together on a major review of church teachings concerning Jews and Judaism.

The Uniting Church of Australia (a Presbyterian-Methodist-Congregationalist amalgam and third largest Christian denomination in the country) held its sixth assembly in Brisbane in July. For the first time the church invited representatives from the Jewish and Muslim communities, and Rabbi John Levi presented a strong paper on the theology of supersession (the doctrine that Christianity has rendered Judaism obsolete). But in October a serious rift opened between the Jewish community and the Uniting Church, when the latter released to its synods throughout Australia a highly tendentious pamphlet that was heavily weighted toward the Palestinians. The pamphlet unleashed a storm of protest from Jewish leaders throughout Australia and was the subject of a meeting in Canberra between ECAJ president Leslie Caplan and Uniting Church president Rev. Dr. D'Arcy Wood. Dr. Wood said he was "most anxious" to improve dialogue with the Jewish community; however, a subsequent written evaluation by the author of the original pamphlet only served to exacerbate the controversy.

Jewish-Muslim Relations

A few hopeful signs were discernible amidst the considerable hostility that existed between the two communities. Sylvia Gelman, Victorian president of the National Council of Women and a past president of the National Council of Jewish Women, wrote a letter to the Melbourne *Age* condemning racist attacks on Muslim women. Sheik Abdullah Nu'man, prevented by illness from participating in an ecumenical service in Melbourne's St. Paul's Cathedral to pray for peace in the Persian Gulf, was visited in the hospital by Rabbi John Levi. Zia Ahmad, managing director of the newly launched, Sydney-based, multilingual *Australian Muslim Times*, told a Jewish reporter that, the Israel-Arab dispute aside, there were many things Jews and Muslims could learn from each other; nevertheless, an anti-Semitic diatribe full of League of Rights themes and by an apparent non-Muslim soon found its way into Ahmad's paper.

Publications

Several noteworthy Jewish books were released during 1991. The two-volume *The Jews of Australia: A Thematic History* by Hilary and W.D. Rubinstein, commissioned by the AIJA (published by William Heinemann Australia), was launched in March by Liberal party leader Dr. John Hewson, at one of his earliest appearances before a Jewish audience. *Hebrew, Israelite, Jew: The History of the Jews of Western Australia* by David Mossenson (published in 1990 by the University of Western Australia Press) became generally available early in the year. *What God Wants*, a collection of short stories by Lily Brett, was published by the University of Queensland Press. Another creative work, *Jewels and Ashes* by Arnold Zable (Scribe Publications), set in Jewish Bialystok, won the 1991 New South Wales Ethnic Affairs Commission Award and the 1991 National Book Council Lysbeth Cohen Memorial Prize.

Personalia

Peter Baume retired from the federal Senate in January, leaving no Jews in that legislature (his cousin, Sen. Michael Baume, is not Jewish). He became head of community medicine at the University of New South Wales. Melbourne lawyer Ron Castan was appointed a part-time commissioner of the federal Human Rights and Equal Opportunity Commission for a three-year term. Michael Gawenda became editor of *Time* Australia. Aviva Kipen, from Melbourne, became the first Australian woman admitted to the rabbinate when she was ordained at Leo Baeck College, London. Daniel Nevo was named Israel's new consul in Australia.

Australian Jews who died during 1991 included Martha Jacobson of Melbourne, a former state and federal president of WIZO who was prominent also in many other communal organizations, in January, aged 66; Rabbi Dr. Israel Porush, chief minister of Sydney's Great Synagogue (1940–72), a scholar and author who retired to Melbourne and remained until the end of his life a towering figure in the Jewish community, in May, aged 83; University of Melbourne postgraduate student Yankel Rosenbaum, aged 29, in August, in Brooklyn, New York, from fatal stab wounds inflicted by young blacks during an anti-Jewish rampage; and Abram (Abrasha) Zbar, a textile wholesaler and Yiddishist who in 1946 cofounded the Bialystocker Center (a principal Melbourne *landsmanshaft*) and who sponsored the migration of numerous Holocaust survivors to Australia, in December, aged 95. (For the record, influential political scientist Henry Mayer of Sydney, who died in May, was, contrary to the general assumption, not Jewish.)

HILARY RUBINSTEIN

South Africa

National Affairs

D URING 1991, THE PROCESS OF dismantling apartheid and the movement toward democracy continued. Among other developments, the classification of the population into racial categories was abolished; racial restrictions relating to land use and ownership were scrapped; and, as a first step in the unification of the educational system, many white schools were opened to children of other races. At the same time, amendments to the Internal Security Act ending detention without trial and restoring the *habeas corpus* constituted an important step toward the return to the rule of law. Finally, a start was made in releasing political prisoners and facilitating the return of exiles and refugees.

Meanwhile, the government declared its commitment to negotiation as the means of bringing about a just and fair "new South Africa." Apart from the radical Right and Left, this approach was universally endorsed, and, indeed, bilateral and multilateral talks were held between leaders of a number of political groups throughout the year. These contacts were not always easy and were characterized by considerable mutual suspicion; however, recognition that a negotiated settlement was the only feasible approach was given expression in the signing of the National Peace Accord in September. Further progress was registered when, two months later, the multiparty Conference for a Democratic South Africa (CODESA) was formed.

The undoubted progress toward democratization was increasingly acknowledged by the international community. During the course of the year several foreign governments lifted economic sanctions, wholly or partially, and long-suspended diplomatic relations were restored. Organizations that had either not been allowed to operate in South Africa or that had not wished to do so sent fact-finding missions or established offices in the country. International sports bodies ended their boycott and, after 32 years, South Africa received an invitation to participate in the upcoming Olympics.

The most disquieting feature of 1991 was the steep rise in the incidence of violence. Political violence, which was primarily black on black, reflected the animosity between the African National Congress and the largely Zulu Inkatha Freedom party. Criminal violence also increased significantly. While whites were frequently the victims, blacks were not immune. In Johannesburg, which was most severely affected, more and more people routinely began to carry arms for self-protection, while the overall quality of life declined significantly.

The government was apparently unable to control either the political or the criminal violence. On the one hand, it was expected to act decisively but, on the other, the image of the police and army as the brutal upholders of apartheid precluded vigorous and effective countermeasures. Ultimately, in an effort to resolve the dilemma, the government announced the appointment of a Commission of Inquiry into the Prevention of Public Violence and Intimidation, whose brief was to investigate the causes of violence and to recommend measures to contain it. The Commission was headed by Richard Goldstone, a Jew, a high court judge who, in the words of the National Peace Accord, was chosen because he enjoyed "the confidence of a broad spectrum of the South African community."

Although progress on the political front during 1991 did lead to the lifting of sanctions and the reestablishment of political and economic relations with the rest of the world, the hoped-for economic revival did not materialize. On the contrary, according to the South African Reserve Bank in its *Annual Economic Report 1992*, "Structural weaknesses in the economy, a severe drought in the summer rainfall areas, internal social and labor unrest, problems encountered in the political negotiations process, and relatively weak economic growth in most of the major industrialized countries, prolonged the downward movement in economic activity in South Africa. . . ." Thus, during 1991 the gross national product declined, retrenchments increased, and employment opportunities decreased, inflation rose to over 15 percent (27 percent for food), and there was less disposable income.

The instability, uncertainty, and economic recession did not appear to have accelerated emigration, which continued the gradual downward trend of the two previous years. Immigration, on the other hand, was 18 percent lower than in the previous year. Nevertheless, there was a net surplus of over 8,000 immigrants in 1991 as compared with 9,800 in 1990.

Relations with Israel

Unlike previous years, when Israel's alleged military assistance to South Africa ensured that country a fairly high media profile, Israel received relatively little coverage in 1991. The exception, understandably, was during the Gulf War. Reports on the war contained frequent references to Israel, and these, for the most part, were sympathetic and supportive. The press also published both Jewish and Muslim reactions to events in the Middle East, including reports on Jewish solidarity meetings and on Muslim rallies at which the United States and Israel were condemned and their national flags burned. The African National Congress (ANC) also participated in some of these demonstrations, praising the PLO and criticizing the Jewish state. Nevertheless, despite the charged emotional climate, Jews for Social Justice had what they described as a highly successful meeting with a group of Muslims, a channel which, they believed, might be useful in the future.

In June State President F.W. de Klerk addressed the national congress of the South African Jewish Board of Deputies. The event was unprecedented in South Africa except, perhaps, for some of the appearances of the late prime minister Jan Smuts. In his well-researched speech, de Klerk traced the history of Jewish settlement in South Africa and recounted the many contributions that Jews had made in the economic, social, and cultural spheres, stressing the country's debt to the community. He emphasized that Jews were absolutely equal partners in the new South Africa, and that any attempt to drive a wedge between them and the rest of the population would not be tolerated. De Klerk also referred to Israel and criticized that country's imposition of sanctions against South Africa. He recognized, however, that Israel had been subjected to considerable pressure by the United States and expressed his satisfaction that good relations had now been restored. He also showed considerable insight into the Jewish attachment to Israel, asserting that this in no way called into question Jewish loyalty to South Africa.

Toward the end of the year, President de Klerk paid an official visit to Israel, where he was received with great warmth and where he was awarded an honorary doctorate by Bar-Ilan University. At a tree-planting ceremony in his honor, an unexpectedly large crowd of former South Africans heard him express, once again, his appreciation for the Jewish contribution to the development of South Africa and his understanding and respect for the deep roots that bind all Jews to Israel.

JEWISH COMMUNITY

It is probably reasonable to assume that individual Jews reacted to the general situation in South Africa in much the same way as other whites. While some Jews were certainly aware that increased frustration, insecurity, and economic hardship may have brought about a further rise in right-wing anti-Semitism, this did not evoke the level of anxiety that was evident in 1990. Similarly, African National Congress support for the PLO and hostility toward Israel drew far less public protest than in the previous year. This relatively calm response was actively fostered and encouraged by the South African Jewish Board of Deputies and other major Jewish organizations. At the same time, these bodies monitored left-wing activities, were in contact with various members of the government, and maintained communication with leaders of the various African political groupings. Their assessments of the attitudes and activities of these groups were reported to the community on appropriate occasions.

Community leaders—notably, members of the national executive of the Board of Deputies and Chief Rabbi Cyril Harris—increasingly urged Jews, both as individuals and as a community, to become more involved with other communities and to demonstrate their resolve to participate in the new South Africa. At the national congress of the Board of Deputies, the newly elected president, Gerald Leissner, stated: "In the past, the Jewish community has tended to worry about itself and issues such as welfare, education and relations with Israel. While that won't change, we hope that we can now get involved in broader issues as well." (Quoted from *The Star*, Johannesburg, June 6, 1991.)

Demography

The official population census of 1991 did not provide a reliable count of Jews in South Africa since, unlike previous censuses, the question on religion was defined as optional. Thus, whereas in 1980, some 160,000 whites refused to answer the question or responded "no religion," in 1991 the number had increased to 1,048,000—that is, one-fifth of all whites. As is the case with most other religious groups, the figure of 65,406 persons classified as Jews is a considerable underrepresentation.[1] A minimum estimate of the actual size of the community, approximately 82,000, was obtained by augmenting the census findings with an assessment of the probable number of Jews who did not specify their religion.[2] Data from a variety of sources suggest an alternative estimate.[3]

The Jewish population at the 1980 census was 118,000. The ensuing decade saw a negative rate of natural increase (deaths exceeding births), leading to a decline of some 6,000, and a negative immigration balance (emigration exceeding immigration) of 7,000. This gives a total of 105,000 Jews in 1991.

Although the discrepancy between this and the lower estimate may be due, at least partly, to mistaken assumptions, quality of sources, and sampling or other errors, there is another factor that must be taken into account. Israelis living in South Africa are a wild card in any estimate of the Jewish population. Neither the 1980 nor the 1991 census reflected more than a small and insignificant influx from Israel. The probable reason is that most Israelis described themselves to enumerators as visitors or temporary residents and were therefore not counted. On the other hand, in the 1990/91 Sociodemographic Survey of the South African Jewish Population, Israelis were sampled along with local Jews—if they lived in "Jewish" suburbs in Johannesburg, or appeared on the community registers of the other survey centers. It is suggested, then, that the Jewish population is not defined in the census in the same way as in the survey and many other sources, and that this accounts for some of the différence between the two estimates suggested above. What is highly probable, however, is that the indigenous Jewish population decreased by between 20,000

---

[1] All references to the 1991 census are based on the *final, adjusted* results published in a series of reports by the Central Statistical Services, Pretoria. The uncorrected raw count for the Jewish population had been just over 59,000.

[2] It was assumed that the proportion of probable Jews among whites who did *not* specify their religion was similar to that of Jews among whites who did.

[3] These include the 1990/91 Sociodemographic Survey of the South African Jewish Population (conducted by Allie Dubb at the Kaplan Centre for Jewish Studies and Research at the University of Cape Town, and scheduled for early publication), communal records, South Africa's Central Statistical Services, Israel's Central Bureau of Statistics, and immigration records maintained by the Tel Aviv office of the South African Zionist Federation (TELFED).

and 36,000 between 1980 and 1991, but that this was partially offset by returning émigrés, some immigration from other parts of Africa and from Western Europe, and a large but unknown number of Israelis.

The full effects of international migration over the last 20 years have still to be researched. Some demographic consequences are, however, already apparent as, for example, in the age structure. According to the official censuses of 1970, 1980, and 1991, the median age increased from 31.9 to 33.9 to 38.9 This reflects the fact that emigrants were primarily young to middle-aged couples and their children, and young adults. Thus the median age, in 1980, of South Africans who emigrated between 1970 and 1980, was 24.7, while those who emigrated between 1980 and 1991 had a median age of 29.7 in 1991. The 1991 survey suggests that in-migration offset, to some extent, the effects of emigration and that the median age of the community—including Israelis and others who may not have been enumerated in the census—is 34.7.

Looking more closely at the age distribution, we find that the youngest age groups have declined in relative size, and that the oldest have increased. Thus, in 1970, 33 percent of Jews were under 20 years old; by 1980 this had dropped to 29 percent, and by 1991 to 23 percent (or 27 percent according to the 1991 survey). By contrast, the proportion of those aged 65 or over increased from 12 percent to 17 percent to 20 percent in the three censuses. The implications of these figures are important in planning both present and future educational facilities, as well as meeting the needs of seniors in the community.

In addition to international migration, movement from small towns and rural areas to the cities continued during the 1980s, while the movement from the smaller cities to Johannesburg, Cape Town, and, to a lesser extent, Durban gained momentum. As regards immigrants and returning émigrés, it appears that they, too, preferred to settle in the two larger cities.

These changes had serious consequences: whereas Jewish life continued to flourish in Johannesburg and Cape Town, the smaller cities were experiencing difficulties. Thus, in Pretoria, Durban, and Port Elizabeth there were not enough Jewish children to maintain viable nursery and day schools—a situation which, in Durban and Port Elizabeth, had already resulted in a large proportion of non-Jewish pupils. In addition, these communities, together with those still extant in the smaller towns, were finding it increasingly difficult to provide for such amenities as ritual slaughter and circumcision or to employ rabbis and cantors. Some had sold or planned to sell synagogues, country clubs, and other property. In all, the future of these communities seemed bleak.

Community leadership responded to demographic change and its consequences by seeking overall, national-level solutions and by coordinating many aspects of Jewish life in the country as a whole. Thus, although local communities retained their autonomy at some levels, their dwindling numbers, shortage of funds, and inability to provide themselves with many of the essential amenities increased their dependence on the national organizations and their leaders.

Communal Affairs

In view of the changing circumstances prevailing in South Africa, the South African Zionist Federation (SAZF) and the South African Jewish Board of Deputies (SAJBOD) established a Joint Communal Co-ordinating Committee to ensure communal unity, loyalty, and discipline. The new committee comprised the respective national presidents, chairpersons, and executive directors of the SAZF and SAJBOD. In addition, Mendel Kaplan, chairman of both the World Jewish Congress and the Board of Governors of the Jewish Agency, and Chief Rabbi Cyril Harris were coopted onto the committee.

Intensive efforts to establish dialogue with the wider community in general and within the Jewish community continued under the auspices of the SAJBOD. As part of the SAJBOD's "outreach program," contact was made with the nation's largest labor federation, the Congress of South African Trade Unions (COSATU). One of the ideas mooted at the meeting was the development of a code of conduct for Jewish business people that could serve as a national model for business ethics. Representatives of the SAJBOD met with Chief Minister Mangosuthu Buthelezi, leader of the Inkatha Freedom party, in Ulundi, Natal Province. A meeting was also held with Sheila Suttner, a social worker currently residing in Perth, Australia, whose son Raymond headed the Department of National Political Education of the ANC. The Cape Council of the SAJBOD met with political science professor Vincent Mapai, to share insights into South African society. The South African Union of Jewish Students (SAUJS) met with the ANC Youth League and Jews for Justice, an activist Jewish liberal organization, and hosted Albie Sachs, a prominent ANC executive member. Minister of Finance Barend du Plessis was guest speaker at the inaugural dinner of the Jerusalem Club, a project of the Young Adult Division of the Israel United Appeal–United Communal Fund (IUA-UCF). The club, which was formed to involve young Johannesburg Jewish professionals and business executives in Jewish affairs, met four times a year to hear guest speakers on topical issues. Both the Israeli embassy and SAJBOD sent representatives to the opening of the ANC's national conference in Durban.

A number of prominent Jewish visitors met with the SAJBOD this year, among them Rabbi Ben Isaacson of the Harare Hebrew Congregation, Zimbabwe, and Lester Scheininger, national president of the Canadian Jewish Congress. Helen Marr, president of the International Council of Jewish Women, visited South Africa as guest of the Union of Jewish Women and addressed the group's 23rd national triennial conference. The union was involved in a variety of educational activities, including the introduction of adult education, the Home Instruction Program for Pre-School Youngsters (HIPPY), and the MATAL science program designed for deprived black children at the preprimary level.

South African Jewry accepted responsibility for an agreement with the government of Lithuania to strengthen tourist relations between the two countries and to maintain Jewish cemeteries in Lithuania. The agreement was signed by Mendel

Kaplan and Prime Minister Gediminias Vagnorius of Lithuania.

It was decided to erect a permanent South African Jewish National Memorial, commemorating fallen comrades in both world wars, in Heroes Acre in the Jewish section of the West Park Cemetery, Johannesburg.

An exhibition about Franz Kafka—the man, his work, and his native city of Prague—toured major centers. The exhibition was prepared by the Nachum Goldmann Museum of the Jewish Diaspora in Tel Aviv.

The *Johannesburg Jewish Voice* celebrated its first anniversary. Although funded by the Jewish community, the monthly served as a forum for a wide range of political opinion.

Israel-Related Activity

Four days into the Gulf War, in the second half of January, over 1,800 Jews in Cape Town gathered in solidarity and prayer, while in Johannesburg five synagogues held solidarity prayer meetings in support of Israel. An all-night solidarity vigil was held in Johannesburg under the auspices of the SAUJS. During the war, a "solidarity tour" of 70 delegates visited Israel, meeting with citizens of the country, government officials, and other dignitaries in order to boost morale and demonstrate to the people of Israel that world Jewry was behind them.

A delegation of leading South African Jews joined Jewish leaders from other countries in Jerusalem for the ninth plenary session of the World Jewish Congress in May.

Members of Parliament Tony Leon and Lester Fuchs attended the Second International Conference of Jewish Members of Parliament in Jerusalem in June. Harry Schwarz, the South African ambassador to Washington, was one of the guest speakers. The same month, a group of South African journalists visited Israel as guests of the Israel Ministry of Tourism. A seminar promoting Israeli medical products was held in Johannesburg under the joint auspices of the Israel Trade Center and the South African-Israeli Chamber of Commerce.

A number of Israeli public figures visited South Africa this year: Yosef Burg, former Knesset member and cabinet minister; Member of the Knesset Eliyahu Ben Elissar; Avishai Braverman, president of Ben-Gurion University; and, as a guest of the South African Foreign Ministry, Yossi Olmert, director of the Israel Government Press Office.

In the buildup to the Gulf War and following its outbreak, Jews and non-Jews rallied to the cause of Israel through the Israel United Appeal–United Communal Fund (IUA-UCF) solidarity campaign. Unsolicited assistance, in the form of both cash and volunteers, poured in for the first time in years. A sum of three million rands (approximately $1 million) was raised within less than two weeks of the start of the war. The coincidence of the war and the arrival of thousands of Russian Jews in Israel added an unprecedented number of new contributors to the ranks of longtime supporters. Community leaders saw the campaign as demonstrating South

African Jewry's unfailing commitment to Judaism and Zionism.

The 1991 Operation Exodus campaign for Russian Jews was launched by Natan Sharansky in February under the auspices of the IUA-UCF. Sharansky addressed meetings in Johannesburg and Cape Town. In Cape Town he met with Jewish members of Parliament and the Presidents' Council.

Community Relations

The Jewish community found itself in the middle of a bitter conflict between the authorities and a black educational organization when it was offered an empty former state-owned school building in Johannesburg. However, as soon as it became clear that the government move had frustrated takeover of the premises for sorely needed accommodation for black pupils, the Board of Jewish Education indignantly turned down the offer.

Difficulty in finding jobs and housing in Israel led a large number of Russian immigrants to apply for visas to South Africa. Among these were some 250 families who were victims of a scam perpetrated by two "employment agencies" that promised them jobs and other benefits—at a price. On arrival in South Africa, the Russians found themselves completely abandoned and destitute. Hearing of their plight, the Board of Deputies took responsibility for housing and feeding them, while successfully interceding with the government to stay deportation and to give them an opportunity to find work.

Education

The gradual desegregation of South African education had implications for Jewish day schools. With state schools now demanding ever increasing tuition fees and the Jewish day schools considered to be academically superior, more of the relatively few Jewish pupils in state schools were considering the day-school option. In Johannesburg, 61 percent of all Jewish children were enrolled in day schools; of these, 70 percent attended the King David Schools. In Cape Town approximately 75 percent of Jewish pupils attended the United Herzlia Schools. In addition, the Lubavitch Hebrew Academy opened a middle school.

The first multiracial Progressive Jewish day school opened in Johannesburg this year. The Yael Primary School was the latest addition to the Yael Education Project, which operated two nursery and play schools as well as an after-school center. The schools are named after the late Yael Assabi, an Israeli lawyer and the wife of Rabbi Ady Assabi, senior rabbi of the Imanu Shalom Congregation.

The Jewish Students University Program (JSUP) opened a Graduate Law School on its newly renovated Johannesburg campus. JSUP was founded by Rabbi M. Kurstag in 1976 to provide Jewish university students who are unable to attend a full-time university with an environment and facilities similar to those found on residential campuses. The latter include classrooms and lecture halls, a kosher canteen, University of South Africa (UNISA) tutors, selected athletic and cultural activities, and a Jewish curriculum. JSUP combines a UNISA degree of choice with Jewish studies, which are organized on an informal basis and cover subjects such as Bible, Jewish philosophy, history, laws and customs, modern Hebrew, and Talmud. All discussions are in English and no prior knowledge of Hebrew is required.

Religion

The Oxford Synagogue Center, Johannesburg, celebrated Rabbi Norman Bernhard's 25th anniversary as spiritual leader. A new Chabad center was established in Lyndhurst, Johannesburg. Ties were severed between the Imanu Shalom Congregation, led by Rabbi Ady Assabi, and the South African Union of Progressive Judaism (SAUPJ). The former indicated that it wanted to distance itself from both the Left and Right and to pursue an independent and unaffiliated path.

Publications

Two new studies dealing with South African Jewry were published this year: *Founders and Followers: Johannesburg Jewry 1887–1915*, edited by Mendel Kaplan and Marian Robertson; and *Sammy Marks: "The Uncrowned King of the Transvaal"* by Richard Mendelsohn. Mendelsohn's biography of Marks, a turn-of-the-century Jewish industrialist and politician, won the University of Cape Town Book Award.

Personalia

Nadine Gordimer, the daughter of Jewish immigrants, was awarded the Nobel Prize for literature, becoming South Africa's first Nobel laureate for literature. Through her many works of fiction, she criticized the indignities of racism and exposed the chasms of South Africa's divided society to an international readership.

Mendel Kaplan was elected chairman of the World Jewish Congress and reelected chairman of the Board of Governors of the Jewish Agency.

Mervyn Smith was elected national chairman of the South African Jewish Board of Deputies. An attorney, Smith was vice-president-elect of the Association of Law Societies of the Republic of South Africa and an executive member of the board of the Cape Performing Arts Board.

Richard Goldstone was appointed head of a Commission of Inquiry into the Prevention of Public Violence and Intimidation. Goldstone, an active member of the Jewish community, had, since his appointment as a judge in 1980, delivered several landmark judgments in the field of human rights. In 1990 he chaired the commission of inquiry into the Sebokeng shootings, in which 18 people were killed.

Prof. Phillip Tobias of the University of the Witwatersrand Medical School was awarded the LSB Leakey Prize for Multidisciplinary Research in Ape and Human Behavior.

338 / AMERICAN JEWISH YEAR BOOK, 1993

Herby Rosenberg retired as director-general of the South African Zionist Federation. An attorney by training, he accepted the post of executive chairman of the South African Associates of Ben-Gurion University, Israel. He was also named a director of the Lubner Foundation, which assists a wide range of community affairs projects.

Hadassah Sachs retired as editor of *Jewish Affairs*, issued by the SAJBOD.

Rudy Frankel, prominent Jewish industrialist, founder of the giant conglomerate Tiger Oats, died this year.

ALLIE A. DUBB
MILTON SHAIN

Israel

THE YEAR 1991 WAS MARKED by alternating peaks and depths, high hopes and dashed spirits. It was a year of both war and peace—a war unlike any other in the country's history, and a first-of-its-kind peace conference that sparked a glimmer of optimism about the future. Throughout the year, with the brief exception of the Gulf War period, relations between Israel and its major ally, the United States, were often acrimonious. This reflected not only divergent policies but also the growing personal animosity between their two leaders, President George Bush and Prime Minister Yitzhak Shamir. Massive immigration from the crumbling Soviet Union continued to pour into Israel, but the initial euphoria was now tempered by awareness that the absorption of the immigrants would be no less difficult than the efforts to free them in the first place.

NATIONAL SECURITY

The Gulf War

Given the extraordinary circumstances, the people of Israel went to sleep with relative security on the night of January 17, 1991. The war between the U.S.-led international coalition and Iraq had broken out only 24 hours earlier, and the population had been instructed to open the boxes containing gas masks that had been distributed throughout the previous months. But most Israeli analysts, including President Chaim Herzog, a noted military commentator and a former head of Israeli intelligence, had reassured the populace that Iraqi president Saddam Hussein would not dare to attack Israel, and even if he did, the chances that he would damage anything worthwhile were virtually nil. Moreover, initial reports from the Pentagon in Washington indicated an overwhelming success for the massive bombing raids launched by the coalition's powerful air forces. The Iraqi bases H-2 and H-3, where Saddam was believed to have stationed his Scud missile launchers, had been virtually wiped out, the reports said.

At 1:42 A.M., a loud bang was heard by most residents of the Tel Aviv metropolitan area. Those who were awake at the time thought at first that the noise they heard was just another clap of thunder, which had been sounding intermittently throughout the evening. But the first bang was shortly followed by another, and then another, at regular intervals. Some were close by, some farther away. Before the eighth explosion was heard, the harsh wail of the air-raid siren pierced the night.

The people of Israel woke from their sleep and entered a nightmare. They turned on their radios and heard excited announcers urging them to don their gas masks immediately and quickly enter the previously designated sealed rooms. They were told to seal the rooms tightly with heavy-duty, thick plastic adhesive tape. And they were told to await further reports. A few minutes later, the announcers said that what the experts had said would not happen had indeed happened: Saddam Hussein had attacked Tel Aviv with surface-to-surface missiles. It was not clear, at this time, whether the missiles carried conventional or chemical warheads.

For the next six weeks, the population of Israel, especially the people of Tel Aviv, learned to live with this and other uncertainties. Each night was marked by the fear that a missile attack would take place. Each missile attack was punctuated by the dread that this time Saddam had decided to escalate and to employ chemical or even biological warheads. After most attacks, the Americans announced that they were stepping up their efforts to eliminate the missile launchers in western Iraq, once and for all. Usually, a few hours after the coalition forces decreed that their efforts had been successful, they would be proved wrong by another missile salvo landing in the heart of Tel Aviv.

Ironically, during the two weeks leading up to the start of the war, the Israeli government and people were concerned that there wasn't going to be any war at all. From Israel's point of view, that was considered the worst of all possibilities. It was feared that the United States and its partners would back off, leaving Israel to fend for itself against the might of the Iraqi army. Worse, the arrangements being considered for a peaceful resolution of the Gulf crisis, which had begun six months earlier with the Iraqi invasion of Kuwait, always seemed to leave Israel paying a steep price in the form of concessions in its conflict with the Palestinians and the Arab states at large.

The year began with a flurry of diplomatic activity aimed at achieving a last-minute Iraqi withdrawal from Kuwait. While Saddam Hussein told his people that Kuwait had become the "19th Iraqi province," his foreign minister, Tariq Aziz, indicated that a mutually acceptable arrangement could be worked out—provided that the international community accepted the principle of "linkage" between the resolution of the Gulf crisis and the Israeli-Arab conflict. The European Community, and especially France, was particularly active in trying to mediate between Washington and Baghdad. And France, at least, did not hide the fact that it did not think it wise to reject the Iraqi "linkage" out of hand. Even as Israel contemplated the dangers of an arranged withdrawal, widely described in Israel as an "appeasement" of Saddam, the Israeli army was preparing itself for the possibility of an Iraqi air or missile attack, or, even worse, an Iraqi land-based attack through Jordan,

Baghdad's closest ally and dependent in the Arab world.

On January 1, King Hussein of Jordan reshuffled his cabinet, installing seven ministers representing the extremist Islamic movement. Despite repeated Israeli warnings during the previous months, Jordan was slowly moving closer to Iraq. On January 5, the Jordanian army was put on an emergency footing. Israeli intelligence experts said, however, that the heightened state of preparedness seemed to be for defensive purposes only. It appeared that Hussein was just as apprehensive about an Israeli attack against him as Israel was that he would allow the Iraqi army to move through his kingdom. Indeed, on January 12, the Hashemite king announced that he would not allow Jordanian air space to be used for an attack against any of Jordan's neighbors.

The previous month, Israeli prime minister Yitzhak Shamir had met with American president George Bush at the White House. At the meeting, Shamir undertook not to launch a preemptive strike against Iraq. Washington's worst fear was that an Israeli move would disrupt the impressive but fragile coalition which it had assembled, especially its Arab components.

But Israel feared that Saddam Hussein might be getting the wrong impression from Jerusalem's agreement not to strike first. Therefore, a stream of warnings emanated from the government in Jerusalem, informing Saddam of the dire consequences that would ensue from an attack against Israel. The warnings were particularly harsh concerning the possibility that Saddam would use chemical weapons against Israel, as he had in the past against Iran and against his own Kurdish population.

On January 3, Chief of Staff Dan Shomron of the Israel Defense Forces (IDF) said, "Israel has the capability of responding with terrible force, but we have always said that we would not be the first ones to use nuclear weapons. This remains our policy." In fact, what Israel had "always said" was that it would not be the first to "introduce" nuclear weapons to the Middle East. Shomron's subtle use of the word "use" was seen as a dramatic warning to Saddam of just how terrible Israeli retribution might be.

Foreign Minister David Levy introduced yet another element in the Israeli attempt to deter Saddam: his own personal safety. On the same day that Shomron issued his warning, Levy said: "Saddam is enamored with the concept of Iraqi expansion, but more than that he is in love with himself, and this is perhaps what is most dear to him. Before he makes a move against Israel, it would be well for him to remember that the thing he holds most dear is in danger." On January 7, Prime Minister Shamir reiterated that, if attacked, Israel would know how to "react appropriately."

Washington urged two of its main Arab coalition partners, Egypt and Syria, to make clear to Saddam that an attack against Israel would not achieve its aim and would not dismantle the coalition against him. On January 10, Egyptian president Hosni Mubarak stated that if Israel were attacked, it would have every right to react. Syria was less explicit, but it too made clear that Saddam was miscalculating if he believed that an attack on Israel would disrupt the Arab force arrayed against him.

Israel watched with trepidation as Secretary of State James Baker of the United States met with Aziz in Geneva, on January 9. On the eve of the meeting, Shamir telephoned Bush and reiterated Israel's opposition to any linkage between the situation in the Gulf and its own conflict with the Arabs. Reports indicating that the Geneva meeting had failed were welcomed in Israel.

Nonetheless, as the days passed before the expiration of the January 15 deadline set by President Bush, Israeli leaders and commentators were constantly on guard against any proposal that would leave the Iraqi military strength intact. On January 11, the daily *Ha'aretz* wrote that an arrangement with Saddam would leave the Middle East with "a time-bomb, armed to the teeth, a perpetual danger to its neighbors and to the world at large."

On January 12, President Bush dispatched a high-level delegation to Israel, headed by Deputy Secretary of State Lawrence Eagleburger and including Assistant Secretary of Defense Paul Wolfowitz. The delegation tried, unsuccessfully, to keep its visit a secret, so as not to antagonize U.S. coalition partners. Eagleburger tried to secure a commitment from Shamir that Israel would not respond even if attacked, and pledged that the United States would defend Israel and destroy the Iraqi missile sites. Shamir refused to give a blanket commitment promising Israeli inaction; but the assumption was that Israel would not retaliate against Iraqi attacks if these were not chemical and if they did not cause too many casualties—and if the United States lived up to its commitment to destroy the Iraqi missile launchers.

As the deadline approached, the Israeli army was placed in a state of high alert, especially its air force, intelligence, and air-defense system. On January 8, Defense Minister Moshe Arens ordered that gas masks be distributed in rural areas as well as cities. Foreign residents and diplomats, including United Nations personnel, left the country in droves. Most airlines, with the notable exceptions of El Al and the U.S. Tower Air, stopped their regular flights to Israel. On January 16, after the expiration of the deadline but before the start of the actual war, armed forces along the borders were put on full alert. "The Israeli army has never been better prepared for war," military sources told the press.

That same evening, coalition forces launched their massive air and missile attack on Iraqi bases and strategic installations—Operation Desert Storm. Israel was informed a few hours before the start of the bombardment. In the wake of the air strike, Shamir sent Bush a message congratulating American resolve and promising continued Israeli "consultations" with Washington before deciding on any action. Initial reports from the Pentagon indicated a massive success for the first blow against Saddam, and analysts said he might have lost his potential to launch a missile attack altogether. At the same time, there was a flurry of worrying rumors about "Saddam's surprise," such as the report in the *Washington Times* about a high-radiation nuclear device in the Iraqi arsenal. A message sent by Baker to Levy also seemed to indicate that the United States was concerned about Saddam's nuclear capability.

ISRAEL UNDER ATTACK

In the early morning hours of January 18, eight modified Scud-B missiles, dubbed by the Iraqis "El Hussein," fell on Tel Aviv and its environs. Thirty hours later, at 7:20 Saturday morning, another four missiles landed on Tel Aviv. Each of the dozen missiles carried an explosive device weighing about 250 kilograms. All were conventional, none were chemical. About 20 people were injured in the two attacks, hundreds of apartments were damaged, and scores of familes were evacuated to hotels, which were empty of tourists anyway. Although the IDF Spokesman described the damage done by the missiles as "minimal," information about their exact landing sites was censored, so as not to assist the Iraqis in improving their aim.

The United States, worried about possible Israeli retaliation, immediately launched an airlift of advanced Patriot antiaircraft missile batteries, complete with logistical support and crews. It was the first time an Israeli government had agreed to allow foreign soldiers on its soil to protect Israelis. President Bush spoke to Prime Minister Shamir on the phone three times in a period of 24 hours and announced that he was sending Eagleburger back to Israel in order to dissuade it from launching an attack against Iraq. A direct, dedicated phone line was set up, linking Desert Storm headquarters in Washington with the Israeli army command in Tel Aviv.

Relations between the Israeli defense establishment and the Pentagon were tense in the first few days of the war. After the war, *Newsweek* revealed that, following the first missile attack, Arens notified Washington that 12 Israeli planes were on their way to bomb targets in Iraq and demanded the special codes that would allow them to be secure from interference by allied planes. The Americans refused, and the planes were recalled.

On January 20, the commander of the coalition forces, Gen. Norman Schwarzkopf, announced that most of Saddam's missile-launching capabilities had been destroyed. All of his stationary missile-launchers had been destroyed, and only five mobile launchers remained. Israeli sources reacted with the skepticism that was to accompany similar American statements throughout the rest of the campaign.

On January 22, at 8:30 P.M., the skepticism was borne out. Although only one missile fell on the city of Ramat Gan, near Tel Aviv, it did more damage than the preceding dozen. An apartment complex received a direct hit, and 96 people were injured, many seriously. Three people died of heart attacks brought on by the sound of the exploding missile. The next day, another missile was fired at Haifa, and early reports indicated that it had been shot down by a Patriot. But the next day, at 6:00 P.M., another salvo of eight missiles descended on the Tel Aviv area. One person was killed in the attack, and another 45 injured.

By this time, Eagleburger had arrived in Israel. He visited the American soldiers operating the Patriot batteries and was given a tour of the neighborhoods hit by the Scuds. Contrary to his behavior on an earlier visit, Eagleburger did not shy away from the press this time. He said publicly that the United States "respects the right of Israel to defend itself"; however, in his talks with the country's leaders, he continued to urge restraint. On January 23, Bush called Shamir once again and expressed his appreciation for Israel's calm and restraint.

While Shamir was maintaining a public calm in the face of the repeated missile attacks, his defense minister and army generals were pressing him for an Israeli response. On January 27, Arens told the cabinet, "Saddam has crossed the red line." IDF chief of staff Shomron and Air Force commander Avihu Bin Nun presented the cabinet with various scenarios for an attack aimed at finally disabling the Iraqi missile launchers. Arens, who had been in constant contact with his American counterpart, Secretary of Defense Richard Cheney, revealed that, while the United States spoke publicly of its respect for Israel's right to defend itself, in practice it was obstructing Israel from exercising that right. The Pentagon, Arens said, refused to supply Israel with the special IFF codes—"identification friend or foe"—that would allow Israeli planes to attack Iraq without fear of being shot down by coalition planes or of shooting them down. On February 3, Deputy Chief of Staff Ehud Barak announced that Israel had "very good" operational plans to take out the Iraqi missile batteries.

By this time, Iraq had already fired 26 missiles at Israeli territory. Four more missiles were launched separately during the next few days. These, however, missed their mark and fell in uninhabited areas, including, for the first time, in the West Bank. Nonetheless, Israelis were growing tired of the incessant air-raid sirens and the sleepless nights.

At this time there was growing apprehension that an increasingly desperate Saddam might try to force Israel to retaliate by launching a chemical attack against it. On February 2, Secretary Cheney warned in a press conference that if such an attack were carried out, Israel might retaliate with "nonconventional" weapons. Arens, asked to comment on Cheney's extraordinary remark, said that "Saddam indeed has something to worry about." Once again, Israel was coming unusually close to public admission of its nonconventional capabilities.

On February 4, Shamir made his first speech to the Knesset since the start of the hostilities. "We are trying to consider the best response at any given moment," he said. "Sitting on the sidelines and not participating in our own defense runs contrary to our principles, but one must view the complete picture and take the special circumstances into consideration."

Four days later, an Iraqi missile once again found its target. Landing in a Tel Aviv suburb, the missile damaged 500 homes and injured 26 persons. The government announced publicly that the missile attacks would not force it to change its policies, but Shamir, in a letter to Bush, warned once again that Israel would have to respond in case of a chemical attack or a conventional attack that resulted in many civilian casualties.

On February 11, Arens, who supported the army demand for action, came to Washington in an effort to secure American agreement for an Israeli role in the fight against the missiles. He was accompanied by General Barak and by the head of the Israeli Mossad. Arens's meetings with Bush, Cheney, and Baker were unsuccessful, however. Baker told Arens that while the final decision concerning retaliation against Iraq rested with the government of Israel, the government had to consider the possible negative consequences of such a decision. Arens told Cheney, "Israel's patience is wearing thin," but the Americans responded that they were capable of handling the missile problem better than Israel could. In a twist of bitter irony, Arens was called out of a meeting with Baker to receive an urgent telephone call from Israel. A missile had fallen on the neighborhood of Savyon, where Arens lived, and his own house was damaged in the attack. Indeed, this missile was the last to cause serious damage, although several more fell on uninhabited areas before the war was over. The launching of these last missiles, it was clear, was an act of desperation on the part of Iraq: at least two carried warheads full of cement, rather than explosives.

THE END OF THE WAR

The start of the land campaign to liberate Kuwait, in the last week of February, raised renewed fears of a last-ditch Iraqi attack with chemical warheads, but this was not to be. Throughout this time, Israel was concerned that Bush and his allies might end the war prematurely. As far as Israel was concerned, the war had to end with the final removal of Saddam Hussein from power and the dismantling of Iraq's offensive capabilities. By the end of February, however, as the war drew to a close, it was becoming increasingly clear that at least one of these objectives, if not both, would not be achieved. The victory celebrations and speeches, on February 28, were thus greeted by the Israeli population with a mix of relief and disappointment: relief at the end of the six-week siege, and disappointment that the cause of the suffering, Saddam, had not been adequately punished.

President Herzog, in an address to the nation, said that the war would truly be over only when Saddam was toppled from his seat. Security sources, speaking on condition of anonymity, saw the brighter side: the war, they said, seriously diminished the possibility of an effective eastern front against Israel for several years to come.

Foreign Minister Levy dispatched an urgent message to his counterparts in the countries comprising the coalition. He listed Israel's demands for the aftermath of the war: destruction of all Iraqi missiles and missile launchers; destruction of the Iraqi chemical and biological arsenals; limitations on supply of conventional weaponry to Iraq; and securing an Iraqi commitment not to launch any more attacks on Israel.

In the immediate aftermath of the war, questions were asked about the prior knowledge held by the Israeli intelligence services concerning Saddam's intentions and capabilities. Member of Knesset Yossi Sarid told the Knesset's Foreign Affairs and Defense Committee that the intelligence community had fallen short. Arens defended the intelligence services, saying they were among the best in the world—but nonetheless lacked the powers of prophecy. A senior IDF officer summed up the Israeli experience in the war in these words: "Altogether, the main conclusion is that we were very lucky; it was, in fact, nothing short of miraculous."

The continuing tensions throughout the rest of the year between the United States and Iraq elicited repeated concern about the possibility of renewed Iraqi missile attacks on Israel. The reports issued in June by the U.S. administration about Iraq's ambitious nuclear program were seen in Israel as confirmation of its own apprehensions and intelligence assessments, as well as belated acknowledgement that its 1981 bombing raid against the Iraqi nuclear reactor at Osirak was justified. On June 30, Shamir praised President Bush's resoluteness in seeking to eliminate Iraqi nuclear, biological, and chemical capabilities.

The Home Front

While Israeli experts mostly agreed, before the war, that there was very little chance that Iraq would attack Israel, the world, it seemed, thought otherwise. The first two weeks of January saw a massive escape from Israel by tourists and dependents of foreign diplomats. And one by one, the foreign airlines announced that they would stop their regular service to Israel as of January 15, the date of the expiration of the deadline set by President Bush for an Iraqi withdrawal from Kuwait.

In the last days before the start of the war, the supermarkets were emptied of basic foodstuffs. There was an acute shortage of supplies needed for the sealing up of rooms, as mandated by the Israeli civil-defense authorities. The two chief rabbis called for mass prayer and fasting to ensure Israel's emergence from the war without harm. They also ruled that, in case of chemical attack, Jews were not obligated to go to synagogue for their daily prayers.

A group of left-wing professors and other intellectuals, titling themselves "A Moment Before the War," called on the Israeli government to accede to Saddam's demand for "linkage" between the Kuwait problem and the resolution of the Palestinian issue, but they were met with almost universal condemnation and derision. On January 14, Israel's two main government-owned radio networks, the state-run Kol Israel and the army-run Galei Zahal, merged and began broadcasting 24 hours a day. Some of their stations, such as the popular and classical music stations, were shut down.

Just a few hours before the deadline expired, the High Court of Justice convened to hear a petition protesting the fact that the Defense Ministry had failed to distribute gas masks to the Arab population in the West Bank and Gaza. The ministry claimed in court that, even if Israel were attacked, the chances of Saddam aiming his missiles at the Palestinian population in the territories—who were sympathetic to him—were minuscule. The ministry's position was undermined, however, by the revelation that it had distributed masks to the Jewish population in the same areas. During the proceedings, it was also revealed that the ministry had only 173,000 masks left, for a population of over 1.5 million. The court rejected the ministry's arguments, ordering it to distribute all the masks at its disposal and to begin immediately purchasing enough masks for the entire Palestinian population.

On January 16, the authorities declared an emergency civil-defense regime. The population was told to open its gas-mask kits and to stay at home. Overnight, the country came to a standstill; workers stayed away from work, and tourists fled the country. The immediate damage to the economy was estimated at $500 million.

MISSILE ATTACKS

The first two missile attacks, in the very early hours of January 18 and on Saturday morning, January 20, shocked the population, first because they took place at all, and second, because, contrary to the experts' opinions, the missiles appeared to be quite accurate. The first attack created waves of true panic, as it was reported that among the missiles were some carrying chemical warheads.

The signal to enter the sealed rooms and don gas masks, and the sounding of the all-clear signal, came by way of announcements on the radio and television. Usually, the instructions were given by IDF spokesman Nahman Shai, whose calm and reassuring manner turned him overnight into a national hero, the only true hero of the war.

Among other things, the attacks immediately created two distinct economic and social classes: those who could afford to get away from the target area, and those who could not. Thousands of well-to-do Tel Avivians started leaving the city on Sunday, January 21, emigrating in droves to Jerusalem and to the southern port city of Eilat, which were thought to be immune from missile attacks. Despite the fact that by this time there were very few tourists left in Israel, the hotels in Eilat and Jerusalem quickly filled up. Many Jerusalemites recounted that, because of the missile attacks, they renewed friendships with Tel Avivians whom they had not heard from in many years. There were those who decided that Eilat wasn't far enough and decided to go abroad for the duration of the war. The "migration" from the missile-prone areas sparked a typical national debate: Tel Aviv mayor Shlomo Lahat said on January 24 that, in his opinion, "whoever defects from Tel Aviv will ultimately defect from the homeland."

On January 21, the government decided to restart the economy and to allow workers to return to work, on a gradual basis. On January 24, pupils in the upper grades in high schools were ordered back to school, but warned to take their gas masks with them. Children who came to school without the masks were ordered back home. During the day, the country was getting back to normal. At night, however, when most of the missile attacks took place, Tel Aviv, Israel's largest city, resembled a ghost town. Theaters, cinemas, restaurants, and kiosks were all closed, and the streets were empty, except for the occasional security car or ambulance. On February 7, the situation was considered stable enough to allow cinemas to resume operation. More tellingly, the process of reopening schools had reached kindergartens, which were allowed to start functioning again. The process was speeded up in those areas of the country that had not been hit by any missiles; Tel Aviv and its environs were the last in line.

As the missile attacks continued, there was increasing criticism of the army's decision to shield the population in sealed rooms in their apartments, rather than directing them to existing bomb shelters. The sealed rooms had been recommended in anticipation of a chemical attack, but they offered little protection against the conventional explosives delivered by the Iraqi missiles. On February 10, after Israelis had endured a full month of nerve-wracking life in sealed rooms, the army's chief civil-defense officer, Brig. Gen. Uri Manos, stunned the nation when he said in a television interview that, in his opinion, the best option was to head for a sealed bomb shelter. Although he was reprimanded by army commanders, the remarks launched a national critique of the army's civil-defense policy, a debate that would last long after the war was over. Adding to the debate, on February 15, the first insinuations appeared in the Israeli press that the gas masks distributed by the army were inadequate and would not have protected the population had the Iraqis decided to employ chemical weapons.

There was a final week of anxiety at the end of February, when the coalition forces launched their ground campaign to evict Iraq from Kuwait. There was concern that, in his desperation, Saddam might try to escalate the situation with Israel by using chemical weapons. But this did not happen, and on February 28—as it happened, coinciding with the merry festival of Purim—Israelis were finally relieved of the emergency civil-defense regime and were told that they could strip their doors and windows of the ugly brown tape that had been used to seal off the rooms. That same day, most of the foreign airlines operating to and from Israel announced that flights would resume shortly.

AFTERMATH

In the final accounting of the war's effects: 9,000 apartments were damaged, 120 buildings were earmarked for demolition, and close to 2,000 families were removed from their homes to other sites. A study released on March 7 revealed that the two-month-long forced stay at home had improved the domestic situation in many households: 22 percent of the couples said their relationships had improved during the crisis, while only 6 percent said they had deteriorated. The war was also thought to have improved the status of Israeli women, who, according to various studies, were better equipped psychologically and emotionally to handle the kind of stress created by the war.

On March 16, State Comptroller Miriam Ben Porat revealed, in a special report, that close to 1.4 million gas masks given out by the army were either inadequate or defective. She severely criticized Prime Minister Shamir and his government for the faulty decision-making process governing the army's purchase of masks. The army rebutted Ben Porat's assertions, saying she had misread some of the data supplied to her by army authorities. The issue was brought to the Knesset committee in charge of the State Comptroller's findings, which backed her report on gas masks handed out to children, but not her findings on masks for adults.

On June 8, as part of the lessons learned from the war, Defense Minister Arens ordered the army to set up a Civil Defense Command, which henceforth would be in charge of all civil-defense matters.

The Intifada

The dry statistics of the *intifada* for the year 1991 give an accurate portrayal of its evolving nature: mass disturbances, such as riots and rock-throwing, decreased significantly; acts of terror and personal violence, especially the use of firearms, increased dramatically.

According to official statistics compiled by the Israel Defense Forces, the number of disturbances in 1991 declined by over 50 percent: in the West Bank, there were 2,218 disturbances, compared to 5,882 the previous year; in Gaza, 3,730 compared to 8,062. The number of Palestinians killed by the IDF was 78, compared to 93 in 1990 and 270 in 1989; 1,475 were injured, compared to close to 4,000 the previous year. At the same time, 82 hand grenades were thrown by Palestinians, compared to only 8 in 1990. Shots were fired by the Palestinians in 131 incidents, compared to 85 cases the previous year. Sixteen Israeli civilians and two tourists were killed, compared to only one civilian in 1990; the number of wounded soldiers, however, dropped by more than half. The statistics should also be viewed against the backdrop of the Gulf War: For the first two months of the year, the population in the occupied territories was under virtual nonstop curfew. As soon as the curfew was lifted, the violence erupted once again.

Indeed, the war in the Gulf served to further alienate the Palestinian population from most Israelis, including the most die-hard supporters of Palestinian rights. This process had begun in the summer of 1990, when the Palestinians followed the lead of the PLO and openly rooted for Saddam Hussein and his battle against the United States. The Palestinian press, too, took a decidedly pro-Iraqi line. The crisis in the Gulf, Deputy Foreign Minister Benjamin Netanyahu told the Knesset on January 9, is causing the "Saddamization" of the Palestinians and Israeli Arabs as well. The Israeli army, it was reported in the opening days of the war, was considering sending tanks into towns and cities if the inhabitants took to the streets in support of Saddam.

The gap between the two peoples turned into a seemingly unbridgeable chasm during the first days of the war, as Iraqi missiles slammed into Tel Aviv and its environs, and Palestinians were reported to be "dancing on the roofs" in celebration of the damage done to the Israeli civilian population. The Israelis, for their part, grew even more suspicious of the Palestinians, and in several cases, Palestinians were arrested and charged with espionage and attempting to aid the Iraqi war effort.

The January 14 assassination in Tunis of PLO strongman Salah Khalaf, also known as Abu Iyad, touched off demonstrations throughout the territories in which 3 were killed and 60 wounded. The assassination was carried out by a renegade bodyguard thought to be linked with the Abu Nidal organization, but PLO spokesmen intimated that the Israeli Mossad was involved. Other observers believed that

Iraq may have contracted with the Abu Nidal group to carry out the killing because Abu Iyad was thought to have reservations about the PLO's support for Saddam.

On January 29, leading Palestinian activist Sari Nusseibeh was arrested and placed under administrative detention. Nusseibeh was charged with conveying to the Iraqis information about the exact landing sites of their missiles, in order to help improve their aim. The arrest was greeted with some skepticism inside Israel and by worldwide condemnation. The *New York Times* asserted, on February 2, that Nusseibeh's arrest was simply an Israeli ploy aimed at oppressing the legitimate Palestinian leadership and destroying all hopes for a peaceful resolution of the Palestinian-Israeli conflict. Indeed, *Ha'aretz* reported on February 5 that the majority of the recognized Palestinian leaders were either under arrest or under curfew or being called in for interrogation day after day.

Peace groups and foreign governments joined in strongly protesting Nusseibeh's arrest, and the outcry, or the flimsiness of the charges from the outset, made their mark. Nusseibeh was brought before a judge on February 3, just a few days after his original detention, and his sentence was cut from six to three months, with the acquiescence of the prosecution and the security authorities. He was ultimately released on April 8. That same day, however, 10 Israeli Arabs were arrested and charged with serving as Iraqi spies. In the coming weeks, there were several more cases of Palestinians and Arabs arrested on charges of spying, either for Iraq or for its reluctant ally, Jordan.

International attention was also directed at the ongoing curfew in the territories. The extended curfew made a shambles of the West Bank economy and seriously damaged the Israeli economy as well, since tens of thousands of Palestinian manual laborers were prevented from crossing the Green Line and entering Israel to work. But by far the most troubling concern was that the curfew was creating starvation, either because the residents were not being allowed to purchase basic foodstuffs, or because the forced layoffs were depriving them of the means to buy the food in the first place. Doctors in the territories said that the curfew was preventing sick residents from seeking necessary medical attention and from receiving vital medicines.

On January 31, the Defense Ministry gave the United Nations Relief Works Agency, UNRWA, whose brief is usually limited to dealing with refugees alone, special permission to distribute food to the general population. The United States, despite its preoccupation in the Gulf, also found time, on February 3, to urge the Israeli government not to deny food and medical supplies to the population.

On February 4, the curfew was partially lifted, in rural areas and in some cities. In other cities, residents were allowed out for an hour or two during the day in order to stock up on provisions. As the curfew was lifted, however, the violence returned. The impulse to strike out was reinforced by the deep disappointment and despondency created by the defeat of Saddam Hussein, especially after his announcement at the end of February that he would withdraw from Kuwait.

The PLO decision to side with Saddam had been made only a few weeks after the Bush administration severed its dialogue with the organization. Frustrated and ostracized, the Palestinians had pinned their unrealistic hopes on the "latter-day Salah Ad-din." His defeat signaled a triple setback for the Palestinians: their savior turned out to be a false messiah, their international isolation solidified, and even traditional supporters such as the European Community were now backing away from them. Added to that, their brothers and sisters in the Gulf countries were personally bearing the brunt of the post-victory vengeance of the Kuwaitis and the Saudis.

TERRORIST ATTACKS

On February 27, the knifings that had become a permanent feature of the Palestinian attacks against Israel in 1990 resumed. Elhanan Atali, a yeshivah student, was brutally stabbed in Jerusalem's Old City. Defense Minister Arens said, "There are Arabs who haven't learned anything and haven't forgotten anything, either."

At the beginning of March, Palestinians were once again allowed to enter Israel to work. In the first few days, only a few thousand did so, apparently out of concern that the Israeli population would retaliate against them; but the numbers picked up quickly, and by mid-March nearly half of the regular 100,000 workers were crossing the Green Line each morning. The "return to normalcy" led to resumption of the popular resistance to the occupation: on March 9, the first general strike since the start of the war was held.

The American-brokered peace process, in the immediate aftermath of the war (see below), spawned two divergent reactions among the Palestinians. On the one hand, for the first time, mainstream Palestinian leaders openly voiced criticism of Saddam and of the PLO's blind faith in him. These same leaders also quietly ended their unofficial boycott of the United States, imposed after the administration had severed its links with the organization. On the other hand, Secretary of State James Baker's efforts spurred extremist elements to greater acts of terror in the hope of disrupting the diplomatic moves.

On March 10, the day before Baker's arrival in Israel for the first time, a knife-wielding Arab went on a rampage in the Jerusalem neighborhood of Kiryat Yovel, stabbing four women to death at a bus stop: Bela Levitsky, Rosa Alispur, Miriam Biton, and Mercedes Benita. Jewish residents of the city rioted, attacking Arab passers-by and demanding the immediate imposition of the death sentence on terrorists. A few days later, in Gaza, another method of terrorism was employed as an Arab truck purposely drove into a group of soldiers on the side of a road, killing two soldiers and wounding several others.

The violence, once resumed, took on a new momentum. On March 20, a 70-year-old jewelry salesman from Hadera, Mordechai Reuchman, was stabbed to death in his store. On March 26, a Jewish resident of the West Bank settlement of Dolev, Yair Mendelson, was ambushed on his way from Ramallah. The Popular Front for the Liberation of Palestine claimed responsibility for the attack. On March 31, the cabinet approved a new series of measures restricting the entrance of Palestinians into Green Line Israel, including any Palestinian ever convicted of a security offense. On April 30, an Arab stabbed a French tourist to death in Bethlehem. He was apprehended the next day, claiming allegiance to the Islamic Jihad group.

On May 20, Petah Tikvah storeowner Reuven David was stabbed to death in his store; two weeks later, on June 6, a guard at the Petah Tikvah municipal dump, Rafi Madar, was hacked to death with axes. As the stabbings continued and the public's sense of security declined, pressure mounted on the government to take drastic steps. On May 19, a 21-year-old resident of Ramallah wounded three residents of Jerusalem. Prime Minister Shamir, responding to news of the assailant's apprehension, showed signs of the pressure on him. "I'm sorry he got out alive," he said, eliciting criticism even within his own cabinet.

On June 29, the violence continued when a Jewish settler from the Jordan Valley, Avi Oshar, was stabbed to death. A week later, Moshe Bukhris, a resident of the coastal town of Ashdod, was shot to death in Gaza. On July 15, an Arab attacked passers-by in Netanya with an ax (they all survived), and four days later another army soldier was run over purposely by a truck, in Gaza. Concurrently with the violence against Jews, internecine Arab violence continued unabated. A total of 88 Palestinians were killed in 1991 at the hands of their own people, for allegedly "collaborating" with the Israeli authorities.

The continued intercommunal bloodshed, the escalation of violence against the Jews, the aftermath of the Gulf crisis, and the burgeoning hopes that the American-led peace process might yield some tangible results this time around all led to a process of reassessment within the Palestinian community. On June 11, an extraordinary meeting of popular leaders took place in Jerusalem. This group, composed of the recognized political leadership as well as the street-level commanders of the *intifada*, condemned the internal violence and called for a general review of the uprising itself. Two weeks later, a new party was established in the territories, the Palestinian National Union, which distanced itself from the PLO leadership in Tunis and dissociated itself from the principle of "armed struggle" against Israel's existence. The Jerusalem meeting and the new political organization, coupled with the ongoing decrease in the incidents of mass resistance, led *Ha'aretz* to declare, somewhat prematurely, "the *intifada* is over."

On June 21, on Israel Television's Friday evening newcast, representatives of the Israel Defense Forces took the unusual step of disclosing information about one of their top-secret weapons in the *intifada*—the undercover units dubbed "*mist'aravim*." The units consisted of regular army soldiers disguised as Arabs, who mingled with the local population in the territories. Their aim was to apprehend wanted agitators while denying them the benefit of prior warning. Military officers explained that by revealing the existence of the units, they hoped to sow discord and confusion among the Palestinians and, at the same time, dispel allegations that the units acted merely as "death squads" against Palestinian agitators. The political echelons described the exposure as ill-timed and ill-conceived.

In July, an explosive device was detonated inside the Jewish settlement of Atniel, although no one was injured. On August 10, the *intifada* claimed its first victim among new immigrants from the former Soviet Union, as 49-year-old Vladimir Makarov was stabbed to death in Rishon LeZion. On September 26, Shlomo Yihye was stabbed to death in Moshav Kadima, and on October 2, a second tourist fell victim to the violence as a German visitor, sitting in a cafe in Bethlehem, was attacked by a knife-wielding Arab. Ten days later, a car driven by an Arab plowed into a group of army soldiers waiting to hitchhike at one of the busiest intersections just outside of Tel Aviv. Two soldiers were killed and 13 injured. On October 15, an Israeli Druze, Jamil Hasoon, from the village of Daliat el Carmel, was shot to death while shopping in the West Bank town of Jenin. "We are losing control," said a senior IDF officer.

The continuing bloodshed spurred Jewish settlers in the territories to unsanctioned retaliation raids, including, in a few cases throughout the year, unprovoked assaults, sometimes with actual gunfire, against Palestinians.

Responding to the increasing pressure to do something about the rising violence inside the Green Line, the security establishment decided on various measures aimed at limiting the number of Palestinians permitted to cross over into Israel for work. On October 20, the government adopted Arens's proposal to institute the death penalty for terrorists; the proposal, however, was never implemented.

The convening of the Madrid Peace Conference at the end of October brought another burst of violence: two Israeli settlers—Rahel Druck and Yitzhak Rofeh—were killed and five children were injured in an armed confrontation in Samaria, on October 28.

On November 30, Zvi Klein, a resident of the West Bank town of Ofra, was shot dead near the town of El-Bireh. The government decided to tighten security in the territories by forbidding any travel other than on main roads during darkness. On December 16, the security forces announced the uncovering of no less than 100 clandestine terrorist groups operating in the territories. As the year ended, it was all too clear that, despite the historic start of peace talks between Jews and Palestinians, the reality on the ground had not changed, and that more than talk would be needed to bring the violence to an end.

SILWAN-CITY OF DAVID CONFLICT

In October, a new location was added to the troubled map of Jewish-Palestinian tensions: a village in southeast Jerusalem called *ir david*, the City of David, by the Jews and Silwan by the Arabs. On October 9, in a well-planned operation, supposedly without the knowledge of the authorities, Jewish settlers from the territories seized six houses in Silwan, adjacent to the Old City Wall. Jews had not lived in the area since the early 1920s, and the seizures raised concern among Palestinians that the Jews were planning to infiltrate yet another Muslim neighborhood of Jerusalem and to evict the Arab residents from their homes. The settlers, organized in a company called Elad, claimed that the houses they occupied had been legally purchased. Their position was that Jews could not and should not be barred from residing in any part of their own capital.

The Jewish settlement of Silwan attracted international attention and created widespread tension in the territories. The police refrained from evicting the settlers, but did not allow them to complete their plans for occupying additional houses. The matter was referred to the attorney general, who, on November 25, ruled that the Jews indeed had a legal right to remain in some of the houses occupied by them, but that the police could evict them if it was decided that their removal was necessary to maintain the peace. On December 8, however, the government gave retroactive legal sanction to the settling of Silwan, and at the end of the year the entire matter was under review in the courts. It emerged, meanwhile, that Elad had been operating in close coordination with the Ministry of Housing, which had provided most of the funding for the purchase of the houses from a special ministry budget ostensibly dedicated to solving pressing social needs.

LEGAL PROCEEDINGS

Ami Popper, who murdered seven Arab laborers near Rishon LeZion on May 20, 1990, was sentenced to seven terms of life imprisonment, on March 18.

A special military tribunal demoted Lt. Col. Yehuda Meir to the rank of private, on April 23, for ordering his unit to "break the arms and legs" of Palestinians in the villages of Beita and Huwara, during the second month of the *intifada*, in January 1988. The sentence was widely criticized as being too lenient.

On July 18, Jerusalem district court judge Ezra Kama, who had been conducting a judicial investigation of the October 1990 Temple Mount incident in which 18 Palestinians were killed, refuted the government's own findings on the incident and said that the incident was sparked by police incompetence, not by Arab provocation. Kama refrained, however, from recommending criminal proceedings against those responsible.

Peace activist Abie Nathan was sentenced, on October 6, to 18 months' imprisonment for illegally meeting in June with PLO leader Yasir Arafat. Nathan had spent 122 days in prison in 1990 for having contacts with the PLO, following which he embarked on a 40-day hunger strike to protest the Israeli law that forbids such contacts.

Other National Security Matters

JORDAN

On January 6, shots were fired from the Jordanian border into Israeli territory. The incident was an omen of things to come, turning 1991 into one of the most violent years in recent memory on the hitherto tranquil border between the two countries. At the beginning of the year, the escalation was attributed to tensions resulting from Jordan's affiliation with Iraq during the Gulf crisis; as the year passed, however, it became apparent that the border incidents had more to do with internal Jordanian factors, especially the rise of Islamic fundamentalism.

In January, King Hussein decided to distribute arms to Jordan's mass "popular militia." On February 9, three terrorists crossed the border in the southern Arava desert and attacked Israeli buses carrying soldiers, injuring several. Analysts in Israel saw the raid as a sign that King Hussein was losing his grip on his kingdom and proof that his decision to distribute arms was folly.

On February 23, another terrorist squad infiltrated, killing a soldier. The rejectionist Palestinian group Abu Musa claimed responsibility. Two weeks later, six terrorists who had crossed the border ran into an army patrol. All six were killed and three Israeli soldiers wounded in the skirmish. On March 23, another two terrorists crossed the border in the Jordan Salient and were killed. Israel concentrated troops on its border with Jordan, in order to reinforce statements by political and military leaders that the regime in Amman would be held responsible for any further attacks. But on April 18, another terrorist crossed the border near the Allenby Bridge; he was wounded and captured. A second squad was more successful, killing a member of Kibbutz Neve Or.

Prime Minister Shamir asked Secretary of State James Baker, who was in the area on one of his numerous peace shuttles, to warn Hussein that Israel could no longer tolerate the continuing attacks. The warning seemed to have the desired effect: on April 22, it was reported that Hussein had ordered his army to put a stop to the infiltrations; on May 7, the Jordanian army was reported to be establishing numerous posts along the border in an effort to improve their control. On May 30, the daily *Ha'aretz* reported that the Jordanian army had successfully thwarted several attempted terrorist attacks against Israel. But the success was only partial. On May 31, there were two infiltrations; miraculously, they yielded no casualties. In one case the terrorists got into a water park near the Dead Sea, and in the other they actually succeeded in entering an IDF stronghold; in both cases they were killed or captured.

LEBANON

The border with Lebanon was marked by unabated violence. The arena for battle between Israel and the various terrorist groups operating in Lebanon was the so-called security zone established by Israel in southern Lebanon in the wake of the 1982 war, in which the Israeli-backed Southern Lebanese Army (SLA) was active. Israel's main adversary among the groups was the Iranian-backed and Syrian-tolerated Hezballah movement.

On January 12, four terrorists were killed in the security zone. Throughout the month, there were continued confrontations between the terrorists and the SLA, as well as numerous Katyusha rocket attacks against positions and villages in the security zone. The Israel Air Force responded with repeated bombing attacks against the Hezballah. In February, tensions on the border increased as rumors spread of a potential Israeli ground operation across the security zone. Indeed, on February 5, a combined force of the Golani infantry brigade backed by Israeli artillery crossed the border to engage in a search-and-destroy mission of terrorist hideouts in Hezballah-controlled villages north of the security zone.

In May, tensions reached a peak as Lebanon and Syria concluded a "Treaty of Brotherhood, Cooperation and Coordination." Although the document was intended ostensibly to formalize, for the first time, Syria's recognition of Lebanon as an independent state, in effect, it put the official stamp on Syria's domination of Lebanon. Israel warned against a Syrian repositioning of troops and backed up its warnings with troop concentrations just south of the border. Defense Minister Arens, reacting to the treaty on May 21, said that "we could wake up one morning and find the Syrian army on the border with Lebanon—and this does not make us happy." Israel did see some room for optimism, however, as the Lebanese army, in accordance with its agreement with Syria, began moving south to strip the local militias of their arms. The Lebanese were tough with the Palestinians, but decidedly more lenient when it came to Israel's bitterest foe, the Hezballah. In July, following some harsh battles, the army and the PLO reached an agreement by which some of the Palestinian groups would surrender their arms to the advancing Lebanese army.

On June 4, the Israel Air Force launched its heaviest bombing operation since the 1982 war; 15 Lebanese were reported killed and 62 wounded. On July 3, an ominous development took place: for the first time in many years, a terrorist squad originating in Lebanon first crossed the border into Syria and from there launched an attack on an IDF position on Mount Hermon. On September 23, there was another infiltration from Syria, and three Palestinian terrorists were killed.

On July 7, the Lebanese army was deployed on the outskirts of the town of Jezzin, an important northern outpost of the security zone, which was under the control of the Southern Lebanese Army. There were differences of opinion in Israel concerning the proper reaction to this development: on the one hand, there was reluctance to enter into an open confrontation with the Lebanese army and perhaps deflect it from its mission of disarming the militias. On the other hand, the SLA was pressing the IDF for action, and failure to respond, it was feared, would be interpreted in Lebanon as a weakening of the Israelis' backing for their proxy SLA. Ultimately, when it became clear that the Lebanese army had no intention of advancing, the new status quo was allowed to remain in place.

On July 17, three soldiers of the Givati infantry brigade were killed in a skirmish with Hezballah terrorists. It was the 24th major skirmish with that group in just two years. On September 14, a terrorist squad planning to attack the northern Israeli town of Nahariya by sea wound up just north of the border in the Lebanese village of Nequra. One UN soldier was killed and eight others wounded. On September 24, an Israeli soldier in south Lebanon accidently shot and killed a prominent Druze sheikh, Fares Barawi from Hazbaya. Israeli leaders as well as prominent Israeli

Druze sheikhs worked hard to prevent the alienation of the Druze, both in Lebanon and in Israel.

On October 20, three Israeli soldiers were killed when an explosive device detonated near their vehicle on patrol in the security zone. The next few days saw a massive artillery bombardment of villages and strongholds north of the security zone, by both the IDF and the SLA. On December 21, an Israeli squad crossed the border of the security zone and kidnapped three Lebanese; they were released within a few hours, after it emerged that the three were victims of mistaken identity. Israel had apparently sought to kidnap prominent figures in the Hezballah, but wound up instead with innocent civilians, including a baker.

The kidnapping was widely seen as an Israeli move aimed at improving its bargaining position with Hezballah for the return of navigator Ron Arad, lost when an Israeli jet plane was downed in October 1986. In addition to Arad, six other Israeli soldiers were considered missing in action in Lebanon. Three—Zecharia Baumel, Zvi Feldman, and Yehuda Katz—were still missing from the 1982 war, their tank having been destroyed in the tough battle of Sultan Yaakoub, against the Syrians, on June 12, 1982. Samir Assad, an Israeli Druze, was kidnapped near the town of Tyre on March 4, 1983, and was subsequently photographed by Americans. Yosef Fink and Rahamin Alsheikh were captured on February 17, 1986, after a disastrous skirmish with Hezballah.

In the months after the end of the Gulf War, there were persistent rumors of negotiations to free the Western hostages held in Lebanon, and of contacts between Israel and Hezballah on the release of captured Israelis in exchange for terrorists held by Israel and the SLA. In August, Western hostages began to be released. Israel was under pressure to free Hezballah terrorists, in order to facilitate the continued release of Western hostages, but Israel balked at releasing the Shiites it held without getting anything for itself in return. On August 12, Israel proposed releasing Shiites in exchange for information, and a series of contacts was made between UN secretary-general Javier Pérez de Cuéllar and the chief Israeli negotiator on the hostage issue, Uri Lubrani. Throughout the month, there were conflicting reports from various Arab sources about the fate of the Israeli soldiers. Palestinian terrorist leader Ahmed Jibril stated, on August 13, that three were being held by the Hezballah, three were dead, and one was missing. A few days later, Syrian foreign minister Farouk al-Sharaa, basking in the accolades accorded Syria for its role in the release of the Western hostages, said that as far as he knew, "most" of the Israeli hostages had been killed. On August 21, an "official Lebanese source" told the Reuters news agency that navigator Ron Arad was alive. On September 2, a new twist was added when the Islamic Hamas movement announced in Beirut that it was holding Israeli soldier Ilan Sa'adon, who had disappeared in May 1989. Israeli sources discounted the story, saying that Sa'adon had most probably been killed in southern Israel, where he was last seen, and that the Hamas statement was just another facet of the wide-ranging psychological war being waged against Israel in connection with the hostages.

On September 11, the first "breakthrough" occurred: Israel announced that it had received "definite proof" that Alsheikh was dead, but that the information received about Yosef Fink was inconclusive. It was reported that Israel had received, via Syria, dental x-rays and tissue of the two. In exchange, Israel released 51 prisoners from El-Khiam prison in south Lebanon, as well as nine bodies of Hezballah terrorists. The next day, the body of Samir Assad was returned, in Vienna, by the Democratic Front for the Liberation of Palestine (DFLP). In exchange, Israel agreed to allow a prominent DFLP activist, deported from the territories several years earlier, to return to his home near Jerusalem. The next month Israel confirmed that it had received conclusive proof that Fink was dead.

On October 21, the SLA released 14 more prisoners from El-Khiam, and Israel released one Hezballah terrorist, in conjunction with the Hezballah release of American hostage Jesse Turner. In November and December, more Western hostages were released and more Hezballah prisoners as well. Israel was acting on the basis of pledges that its gestures would ultimately bring about a general exchange of prisoners, including Israelis. But on December 9, Hezballah announced that it was not holding Ron Arad at all. Two weeks later, the failed kidnapping attempt took place. The newly appointed UN secretary-general, Boutros Boutros-Ghali, claimed that Israel had now disrupted the flow of negotiations for a successful swap.

SYRIA

Syria was reported to be arming itself with long-range modified Scud ballistic missiles, manufactured by North Korea; Pyongyang was also providing technical know-how for the establishment of a Scud-manufacturing plant in Syria itself. In June it was reported that China would also enhance Syria's ballistic-missile capability, with long-range M-9 missiles.

On August 14, three years of tough and frustrating negotiations between Israel and Syria, through the International Red Cross, finally reached a successful end when Fahan Assad Hamoud, the 21-year-old daughter of a Syrian-Druze brigadier, was allowed to cross the border into Israel in order to marry her loved one, 30-year-old Izat Safadi, a Druze living on the Golan Heights.

TERRORIST INCIDENTS OUTSIDE ISRAEL

On June 26, anti-Indian terrorists in the remote area of Srinagar, in Kashmir, kidnapped eight tourists, including seven Israelis. After releasing one Israeli woman and one non-Israeli, they informed the remaining six that they would be executed. The six, all graduates of elite army units, struggled with their captors; one Israeli, Erez Kahane, was killed, another was wounded, and a third disappeared. For several days the authorities searched for the missing Israeli, Yair Yitzhaki; ultimately it turned out that he had fallen into the hands of a rival terrorist group and was released unharmed on June 3. Israelis were warned not to travel any more to Kashmir.

On December 23, an explosive device was detonated on a Budapest road frequented by Jews on their way from the former Soviet Union to Israel. Two Hungarian policemen were seriously injured in the attack.

OTHER SECURITY-RELATED MATTERS

In January, as part of the general package of assistance to Israel in the wake of the Gulf War, Germany announced that it would fund and build two submarines for the Israel Navy, at a cost of $600 million.

The U.S. Congress approved a "drawdown" of surplus American military equipment from U.S forces in Europe to the Israeli army, up to a total of $700 million, as well as the "prepositioning" of $200-million worth of equipment for emergency use by American forces.

The second trial launch of the Israeli-designed and American-funded antimissile missile, the Arrow, on March 25, achieved only partial success after the missile computer failed to convey data to its ground control. On May 31, Israel and the United States agreed in principle on the second stage of development of the project, and on June 8, they signed a memorandum of understanding to that effect. The third trial launch, on October 30, achieved no more success; the Arrow failed to intercept incoming ballistic missiles. On December 18, Israeli Arrow project manager Dov Raviv was removed from his post, after allegations of improprieties were raised against him. The entire project was temporarily suspended in order to pinpoint the reasons for the failed launchings. On August 17, Israel carried out a successful test launch of the Barak seaborne antimissile missile.

Air Force Brig. Gen. Rami Dotan, accused of widespread fraud and bribe-taking in connection with arms purchases from the United States, was convicted, on March 16, on the basis of his own confession and sentenced to 13 years' imprisonment and dishonorable discharge from the army. (See AJYB 1992, p. 435.) The court described Dotan's actions as "corruption without any precedent in the IDF." Nine other air force officers were deposed in connection with the case. On August 15, the U.S. Justice Department charged the General Electric Corporation with defrauding the American government of $33 million in connection with the Dotan affair.

Deputy Chief of Staff Maj. Gen. Ehud Barak was appointed chief of staff and promoted to the rank of lieutenant general, on March 31. Barak, the 14th IDF chief of staff, replaced Lt. Gen. Dan Shomron. The 49-year-old Barak served as commander of the elite Matkal infantry unit, was a brigade and division commander in the armored corps, head of Israeli intelligence, O/C Central Command, and deputy chief of staff. He was succeeded by Maj. Gen. Amnon Shahak.

Four Israelis were arrested on April 24 in Nicosia, Cyprus, on suspicion that they had tried to plant microphones in the Iranian embassy in Cyprus. The four were subsequently released.

Outgoing air force commander Maj. Gen. Avihu Bin Nun, in a parting interview with the air force periodical published on December 24, severely criticized the decision-making process in Israel, claiming "the country is suffering from a lack of proper governmental order." He was reprimanded by the chief of staff.

DIPLOMATIC DEVELOPMENTS

The Peace Process

From the outset, Prime Minister Yitzhak Shamir's government regarded the Gulf crisis with mixed feelings. On the one hand, Israel was relieved that the United States, along with its international coalition, was tackling Iraq, the country which arguably posed the most serious threat to Israel's security. On the other hand, there was constant apprehension that Israel would ultimately be asked to foot the diplomatic bill for the resolution of the crisis. In the days before the war, the concern was that Washington would reach a diplomatic arrangement with Baghdad that would entail pledges, unacceptable to Israel, concerning future attempts to solve the Palestinian problem. Once the war started, the apprehension focused on the "price" that Washington would pay in exchange for the support it received from Arab states, most notably Saudi Arabia and Syria. On January 7, in the wake of a Security Council resolution, passed with American support, that criticized Israel's policies in the territories, Shamir gave public vent to his fears: Israel should prepare itself for stepped-up American pressure after the Gulf crisis was resolved.

While the war was still in progress, the United States made clear on several occasions that its aftermath would include a serious diplomatic effort to initiate negotiations between Israel and the Arabs. This plan was reiterated, formally, in the joint statement issued in Washington on January 30 by Secretary of State James Baker and Foreign Minister Alexander Bessmertnykh of the USSR. Israel was concerned that the Americans would bow to Syrian pressure, backed by the Soviets, to convene a full-fledged international conference, a concept that was vehemently opposed by Shamir and his Likud government.

Indeed, the participation of Syria in the American-led coalition against Iraq had introduced a new factor into the longtime search for a mechanism by which Israel and the Arabs could start negotiating. Since the signing of the Israeli-Egyptian peace treaty in 1979, all Israeli and American initiatives had been directed at the Palestinians and, to a lesser extent, at Jordan (with the exception of the failed "peace treaty" signed in the wake of the 1982 war between Israel and Lebanon). Israelis remained skeptical of Syrian intentions and doubted whether President Hafez al-Assad would now abandon his decades of belligerency; at the same time, Jerusalem was aware that the American-Syrian alliance, even if it was ad hoc, had changed the basic equation of Middle East diplomacy.

First warnings of the change came in meetings held in February between Baker and Israeli ambassador to Washington Zalman Shoval. Baker questioned Shoval at length about the Israeli attitude toward the Golan Heights and explored, on a hypothetical basis, the possible Israeli reaction to various arrangements in the Golan, such as demilitarization or the stationing of American troops in the area. The publication of Baker's queries raised concern in Israel's political community, especially in the sizeable lobby opposed to any and all concessions in the Golan. On February 13, German foreign minister Hans Dietrich Genscher stated, after visiting Damascus, that Assad would be willing to recognize Israel's right to exist, within the framework of a general peace agreement.

That same day, New York congressman Stephen Solarz, a Democrat with close ties to the Republican foreign policy apparatus, met in Jerusalem with Shamir and Foreign Minister David Levy. Solarz presented the general blueprint of the administration's plans to promote peace after the war. The process, he said, would include both direct bilateral talks between Israel and its Arab neighbors and regional multilateral talks. The latter would include Arab states that do not have a shared border with Israel, as well as countries from other areas in the world. The initial Israeli reaction to the plan was decidedly cool. Shamir, who had agreed in 1987 to then Secretary of State George Shultz's proposal for American-Soviet cosponsorship of the process, had by now cooled to the idea, because, he said, of the instability of the current Soviet regime. "It's unclear what the Soviet policy will be," he told visiting American congressmen.

Shamir's foreboding about the upcoming peace process was reiterated in a February 25 meeting with his own Likud caucus. After the war, he said, a political process will commence with the aim of "taking from Israel, by diplomatic means, what they have been unsuccessful in seizing by force." Shamir did not elaborate who was included in the term "they."

WASHINGTON TAKES THE INITIATIVE

On February 28, with the war officially ended, President Bush announced his grand vision of a "new world order." State Department spokeswoman Margaret Tutwiler spelled out what the phrase meant in terms of the Middle East. The basic components, she said, included regional security arrangements, control of proliferation of weapons in the area, economic cooperation—and a settlement of the Arab-Israeli conflict.

Secretary Baker, Bush announced, would embark on a Middle East tour aimed at exploring ways to start implementing the American vision. Baker said that he had no specific plans in mind, and that the United States had no intention of imposing a solution on the sides. Both elements of this statement were greeted with skepticism in Israel. Jerusalem, for its part, said that it would not be proposing new ideas during Baker's visit; however, it grumbled over reports from Washington that the administration intended to abandon the linchpin of Israel's peace plan: the election of Palestinian representatives who would negotiate the details of an interim arrangement in accordance with the 1978 Camp David accords. Shamir reiterated that the government's 1989 peace plan, which first offered the idea of elections, would be the only basis for discussions with Baker. A few days later, however, Shamir corrected his statement, saying that Israel would be willing to talk to Palestinians even without elections, as long as the other principles of its 1989 initiative were preserved.

On March 6, in a celebratory address to a joint session of Congress, Bush said that the time had come to put an end to the Arab-Israeli conflict. He said that Middle East peace would be one of his administration's "top priorities," adding that a peace accord would be based on Security Council Resolutions 242 and 338, "including the principle of territory for peace." With these words, the president renewed the debate, both between Jerusalem and Washington and within Israel itself, about the meaning of that concept. Government officials said that, although Israel had accepted the resolutions and was not reneging on its acceptance, the current government believed that Israel had fulfilled its part of the "peace for territories" bargain by relinquishing the Sinai in exchange for peace with Egypt. Since the Sinai constituted 90 percent of all the areas captured in the 1967 war, Israel was under no obligation to give up any more territories; now it was up to the Arab states to make peace.

On March 8, while visiting Saudi Arabia, America's premier Gulf crisis partner, Baker secured a vague Saudi promise to "contribute" to the resolution of the Arab-Israeli conflict. Shamir, meanwhile, meeting in Jerusalem with Canada's visiting secretary of external affairs, Joe Clark, on March 9, called on both Syria and Saudi Arabia to come to the negotiating table. Indeed, Israel was eager for Saudi Arabia to join the negotiations, not least because, it was reported, Israel and Saudi Arabia had no territorial dispute, and the Likud government wanted to prove that peace could be achieved without giving back any territories.

Visiting Israel on March 10–12, Baker achieved his first breakthrough when Palestinian leaders, including Faisal Husseini, agreed to meet with him at the residence of the American consul-general in Jerusalem, thereby ending the eight-month-old Palestinian boycott of the United States that was imposed after the administration cut off its dialogue with the PLO. The meeting reflected the weakening of the PLO's position because of its ill-advised support for Iraq, and because of the U.S. position, reiterated by Baker in Cairo on his way to Jerusalem, that there was no role in the process for the PLO. As a result, PLO headquarters in Tunis found itself compelled to accede to the demand of the local leadership in the territories to allow it to meet with Baker and not to pass up another opportunity to advance the Palestinian cause. The Palestinians did submit to Baker an 11-point plan, which included a demand that the United States recognize the PLO as the sole legitimate representative of the Palestinian people. It was clear, however, that the demand was not a take-it-or-leave-it proposition.

In his meeting with Israeli leaders, on March 12, Baker outlined the American plan to convene a "regional conference," which would be cosponsored by the United States and the Soviet Union. He had already secured the agreement of Egypt, Saudi Arabia, and the Gulf states, Baker told Shamir and Levy. Following the meeting, Tutwiler told reporters that Baker was "encouraged" that Shamir had not rejected the proposal out of hand. The prime minister had, however, stipulated that any Soviet role in the peace process include a prior resumption of full diplomatic ties between Jerusalem and Moscow.

In a press conference, Baker said that, ultimately, the Middle East settlement would have to be based on the "peace for territories" principle. "If the sides want peace—they will achieve it," he said, "and if they don't—they won't." Soviet president Mikhail Gorbachev, who met with Baker in Moscow immediately following the secretary's talks in the area, said that, while the Soviet Union continued its traditional support for a full international conference, it was also willing to contemplate direct talks between the sides. It was clear that in the new array of international forces, the declining Soviet Union, which was begging the United States for financial assistance, was in no position to argue with American designs, and that public statements to the contrary were simply a way of saving face.

On March 17, Shamir told the cabinet that, in the talks with Baker, the Americans had also brought up the issue of the Israeli-controlled security zone in south Lebanon. Washington, Shamir said, was demanding that Israel withdraw from the security zone, in exchange for "adequate" security arrangements.

On March 18, Shamir said that he opposed negotiations with the group of ten Palestinians who had met with Baker, remarking that "Faisal Husseini was no less dangerous than Yasir Arafat." News reports from Washington indicated that Baker did not take kindly to Shamir's remarks.

That same day, in Washington, one of Shamir's trusted ministers, Ehud Olmert, created a political storm when he announced before the annual meeting of AIPAC, the pro-Israel lobby, that Israel would be willing to negotiate with Syria on anything, "including all their territorial demands." Shamir dissociated himself, in vague terms, from Olmert's statement, but Member of Knesset Yossi Sarid voiced the concern—or hopes—of many when he asserted that Olmert's statement had in fact been planned in advance by the Prime Minister's Office in Jerusalem. The anxiety among Jewish settlers in the Golan Heights grew considerably.

On March 21, in an interview with the NBC television network, King Hussein of Jordan announced that he would be willing to be part of a joint delegation with the Palestinians to the peace conference. Hussein's statement, which in effect canceled his July 1988 "disconnection" from the territories, was seen as an effort by the Hashemite king to regain favor lost in Washington as a result of his support for Saddam Hussein by offering a possible solution to the issue that had dogged the Middle East peacemaking efforts for over a decade—the matter of Palestinian representation.

Another sign of the changing mood occurred ten days later, on April 1, when Syrian president Assad and Egyptian president Hosni Mubarak, meeting in Alexandria, called for the convening of an international conference on the basis of UN Resolutions 242 and 338.

BAKER'S TRIPS TO THE REGION

On April 8, Baker arrived in Israel once again to continue his discussions. By now, the positive signals from the Arab world were having a definite chilling effect in Jerusalem. On the eve of Baker's visit, "senior sources" in the Likud said that if the United States pressured Israel to make unwanted concessions, Shamir would have no choice but to call for early elections, thus disrupting the process and, hopefully, gaining a mandate from the public for continued resistance to the American designs. During the visit, however, a certain reversal of roles took place. Baker was quoted as expressing pessimism about whether any Arab country would agree to come to a regional conference on Israel's terms. Israel, and especially Foreign Minister David Levy, emphasized, in glowing terms, the wide-ranging understanding that now existed between Jerusalem and Washington.

On April 11, Levy spelled out the terms of this understanding, in a statement that would, ironically, be the source of many a misunderstanding both inside the Israeli government and between Jerusalem and Washington. According to Levy, the two sides had agreed on the "two-track" system of both bilateral and multilateral talks and also on the other terms: that the process would not end up with the establishment of an independent Palestinian state; that Palestinian representatives would come "only from the territories" (i.e., not from Jerusalem); that Israel was not being asked to conduct a dialogue with the PLO; that there were several possible interpretations of Resolution 242; that negotiations with the Palestinians would be based on the government's 1989 initiative; that the Soviet Union would upgrade its relations with Israel prior to the start of the process; that the Soviets agreed with the principles of the process as presented by the United States and agreed to by Israel; and finally, that none of these understandings would be altered by the United States without Israel's prior consent. Israel agreed, Levy said, that the process would be launched by a regional conference, cosponsored by the two superpowers, on condition that the conference would be ceremonial in nature, that it would be a one-time occurrence, and that it would have no authority to intervene in the negotiations or to impose anything on any side.

A few days later, the misunderstandings began to emerge. Senior Israeli diplomats claimed that Baker had "reneged" on two of the understandings: he was no longer committed to excluding East Jerusalemites from the process, and he would no longer guarantee a one-session conference. State Department sources countered that Levy's account of the so-called understandings was "superficial" from the outset. The points elaborated by Levy were not "understandings" at all, the sources said, but rather Israeli positions which Baker had promised to do his best to "sell" to the Arab side.

Baker's third visit, on April 20, was thus marked by a sense of growing mistrust between him and the Israelis. Baker asked Shamir to reconsider his opposition to a periodic reconvening of the conference, as well as his objection to the participation of representatives of the United Nations and of the European Community. Baker tried to find a way around Israel's opposition to the inclusion of East Jerusalemites in the Palestinian delegation by proposing that they be allowed to participate in the opening "ceremony" but not in the ensuing direct talks. Shamir was not agreeable to any of the proposals.

Baker's mission suffered a more serious blow when it emerged from his talks in Riyadh that Saudi Arabia would not participate in the conference after all. The Saudi position was seen in Israel as further proof of the disingenuousness of the American tactics, since Baker had said repeatedly that the Saudis would be an "active partner" in the quest for peace. The Saudis were also subjected to the wrath of the U.S. Congress: 50 senators wrote to King Fahd and demanded that he reconsider.

A frustrated Baker returned to Jerusalem on April 26, but not before making his first visit to Amman, thus signaling both the administration's willingness to "forgive" Hussein's misconceived support for Saddam and the Jordanian king's wish to be included as a full participant in the peace process.

Baker's talks in Jerusalem were described as "tough," and sources in the Prime Minister's Office said that a full-blown crisis was looming over U.S.-Israeli relations. At one point, Baker got up from the negotiating table and said, in frustration, "Well, in that case we shall have to go to the Security Council." A dismayed Shamir responded by saying, "We are dealing with serious issues here. I don't have to accept everything you say." Baker's visit was cut short by the news of his mother's death, but it was clear that the respite, if any, would be brief.

The first days of May saw Israel trying to assign blame for the deadlock on the Arabs, while the United States was making clear that it was frustrated by the Israeli positions. The Prime Minister's Office announced that the process was stuck because the Arabs had reneged on earlier understandings. The State Department let out word that the obstacles posed by both Israel and Syria necessitated a reassessment of the entire process.

In Jerusalem, Shamir's aides were blaming Levy's "amateurishness" for the impasse, while Levy's people spoke derisively of Shamir's "intransigence." At the same time, ironically, Shamir was coming under increasing pressure within his own coalition, the right-wing parties threatening to bolt if it emerged, as reports indicated, that the conference would not be a one-time-only ceremonial affair. As had happened on previous occasions, the right wing exhibited the most realistic sense of things to come, realizing that the United States could ill afford to fail on such an ambitious diplomatic venture.

On May 11, Baker and Bessmertnykh met in Cairo, spelling out the principles that would govern the proposed conference. The conference, they agreed, would be ongoing and not a one-time-only affair—but its reconvening would require the consent of all participants. The cosponsors would issue the invitations, the European Community would be allowed to participate, and the United Nations could send a "silent observer" to the conference. The problem of the participation of East Jerusalemites remained unresolved.

Saudi Arabia and the Gulf countries, which owed their very freedom to the American resolve against Iraq, finally came through, agreeing to participate in the multilateral talks devoted to regional issues. The response in Israel, as usual, depended on the eye of the beholder: Foreign Minister Levy expressed satisfaction, but Shamir's tough aide, Yossi (Yosef) Ben-Aharon, said that the Saudi move did not constitute a positive development in the peace process.

On May 14, Baker arrived for his fourth visit, stating that it would be his last. American sources said that if Shamir refused Baker's final offer, the secretary would have no choice but to pin the blame publicly on Israel for the breakdown of his peace efforts, and on Syria, which was also rejecting some of Baker's proposals. Teams of officials from both countries sat in Jerusalem around the clock in an effort to formulate written agreements between the two countries. At the end of the visit, Shamir continued to oppose two central elements of the proposed format for the conference: the participation of the UN and the continuity of the conference. Israel did agree, for the first time, that the meeting that would launch the direct talks could be called a "peace conference."

On May 19, Jordan announced that it would not attend the conference without Syria. The Syrians, however, were showing new signs of flexibility. Foreign Minister Farouk al-Sharaa told his Belgian counterpart, on May 26, that Syria was no longer demanding UN sponsorship of the peace conference, nor was it insisting on a prior Israeli commitment to withdraw from the territories. The issue of the Golan Heights, al-Sharaa said, would be discussed at the conference in accordance with the "peace for territories" formula. A few days later, King Hussein, in an interview with the French *Le Point* magazine, said that face-to-face meetings with Israelis were still premature but would come in the very near future. "This taboo must disappear," he said.

But while the Arabs were making noises of moderation, the dialogue between Israel and the U.S. administration continued to deteriorate. Meeting with American diplomats in Washington, Ben-Aharon appeared to be reneging on understandings which the Americans believed had been reached between Baker and Shamir. According to numerous news reports, when asked to explain, Ben-Aharon responded, "Shamir does not always pay attention to details."

On June 1, President Bush dispatched letters to Shamir and to Arab leaders with questions on their final positions, and with a final plea not to let matters of procedure get in the way of potentially historic breakthroughs. Bush's intervention was described as a "make or break" move: either the responses to the letter would allow the cosponsors to issue invitations, or the process would be dead.

On June 5, Levy met with representatives of the European Community and agreed on the conditions for European participation in the conference. Levy returned from his trip much more optimistic than the Americans: while they were spreading reports of dismal prospects, Levy said he had no doubt that the conference would ultimately convene.

The next day, Shamir sent his response to Bush, and it was in no way positive.

According to reports in the Israeli press, Shamir told Bush that the United States had pressured Israel to agree to a one-time convening of the conference, and now it was asking it to agree to a continuous conference, which would allow the Arabs to emerge from the process "without direct negotiations and without peace." Shamir also explained his opposition to UN participation, saying that even a "silent observer" would be able to report to the Security Council, and that body, which Israel viewed with disfavor, could use the reports as a pretext for discussion and action on the peace process. Despite rampant pessimism in the press, Washington preferred to view Shamir's letter as a basis for further negotiations, and Levy went to Washington to continue the discussions.

Levy's mission was at least partially successful. He told the Israeli press, after meeting with Baker on June 13, that he had succeeded in diverting American displeasure and the possibility that Israel would be blamed for the breakdown of the process. Baker gave Levy a guarantee that the United States and the Soviet Union would both veto any motion to discuss the peace process in the Security Council, a pledge that ultimately persuaded Shamir to remove his objections to the participation of a UN "silent observer."

Syrian foreign minister al-Sharaa said, on June 23, that Bush's letter to Assad, which had been sent concurrently with the letter to Shamir and other Arab leaders, was "balanced and fair." The Syrian sounds of moderation, however, did not seem to be striking a positive chord in Jerusalem. Shamir and the usually moderate Levy both stepped up their verbal attacks on Damascus. Shamir said that "the United States was exaggerating in its efforts to bring Syria to the conference table, since the rejectionist positions of Damascus are well known." Even the usually upbeat Levy said, on June 25, that "Syria is arming itself for confrontation." On July 11, he said that "the peace process can be advanced even without Syria." But three days later, on July 14, Damascus upset Israel's view and threw a historic bombshell: it agreed to the terms of the conference as outlined in Bush's letter of June 1. The administration rejected allegations in Israel that it had made any secret pledges to Syria. Al-Sharaa claimed subsequently that the Americans had pledged that "Israel will have to withdraw in all the fronts in which it occupied lands," but the administration denied the claim vehemently. In late July, in an interview with *Newsweek* magazine, Syrian president Assad confirmed that the United States had not given Syria any secret assurances.

Now Israel was alone in rejecting the American proposals. This was exactly the position that Shamir, with all his toughness, had been seeking to avoid.

The administration called on Israel to reconsider its position, and Baker, despite earlier statements, announced plans for a fifth shuttle mission to the Middle East. In Damascus, he announced that Assad had agreed to an "inactive" UN observer. In Riyadh, it was revealed that Israel had rejected a Saudi offer to revoke the Arab boycott in exchange for a settlement freeze. On the eve of Baker's arrival in Jerusalem, the overall assessment, based on his past record, was that Shamir would reject the American proposals even at the risk of an unprecedented confrontation with the

United States, which might entail the irrevocable rejection of Israel's request for much-needed loan guarantees. Just hours before Baker's plane touched down, on July 21, Defense Minister Arens hinted that the expectations of a showdown might be misguided. Israel, he said, would consider modifying its positions.

AGREEMENT IN SIGHT

Indeed, the meeting between Baker and Shamir that day was probably the best the two had ever had. Shamir was reported to be very satisfied with the Syrian response, which, Baker assured him, carried no hidden strings. Shamir gave Baker his agreement in principle to the proposed format of the conference, but there was still one major problem left. Israel would attend the conference, Shamir said, provided that a mutually acceptable Palestinian delegation was formed. Since countless diplomatic efforts in the past had failed to produce such a delegation, Shamir's caveat was no small matter.

Ironically, on the day after Baker's departure, the Knesset was to debate a motion of no-confidence submitted by the left-wing parties, accusing the government of derailing the peace process. But Shamir's surprising acceptance of the Baker formulae left the critics with no ammunition, and most of the members of the chief opposition party, Labor, did not take part in the vote, which the government won comfortably, 54–27. The criticism was now being directed at the government from the right, which originally had planned to defend Shamir's refusal to go along with Baker's "dictates."

Police Minister Ronnie Milo, representing the government, was ebullient in describing the recent developments. Syria, he said, had undertaken a "revolutionary step," which was a "clear victory for Israel's policies." Housing Minister Ariel Sharon took a dim view of Milo's enthusiasm. The day before yesterday, he said, Assad had been the twin brother of Iraqi president Saddam; today, he was the favorite brother of Egyptian president Mubarak.

The stage was now set for the final act in the effort to convene a conference: the participation of East Jerusalemites in the Palestinian delegation. Indeed, it was this very question that had brought down the previous national unity government in 1990, and it was clear that on this matter Shamir would not budge. Faisal Husseini, the prominent East Jerusalem Palestinian leader, for his part, was showing no more flexibility. The participation of East Jerusalemites, he said, was the "bottom line," as far as the Palestinians were concerned.

At the end of July, Bush traveled to Moscow for a summit with President Gorbachev. The United States was eager for the superpower summit to serve as the setting for the official pronouncement on the convening of the conference. But Israel refused to give the final okay, for there were still matters to conclude. Among other things, Israel sought guarantees that the proposed peace conference would last only 24–36 hours, that the different bilateral talks would be held without any linkage between them, and that the United States would reaffirm, in writing, all past commitments to Israel.

Following what were described as very sharp exchanges between the U.S. president's party in Moscow and the Prime Minister's Office in Jerusalem, Shamir finally informed President Bush that Israel would indeed attend the conference—provided that the United States and Israel formulated, in advance, a mutually acceptable memorandum of understanding concerning the two countries' positions in the upcoming peace talks. Shamir did not insist anymore, however, that the memorandum precede the announcement on the conference.

Thus, on July 31, Bush announced in Moscow that the Middle East peace conference would convene in October. The venue had not been set, and for the next two months the international and Israeli press was rife with rumors about possible sites for the historic meeting.

On August 1, Baker arrived in Jerusalem from Moscow to start deliberations on the memorandum of understanding sought by Shamir. Although the details of the memorandum were still in dispute, Shamir did not renege on his pledge to Bush, and Baker finally had the chance to make a positive statement concerning Israel's willingness to attend the American-brokered peace conference.

On August 1, the cabinet convened to approve Shamir's agreement. Sharon said that Israel was committing "a historic mistake." Nonetheless, the cabinet approved Shamir's proposal to reply affirmatively to the United States by a vote of 16–3. Foreign Minister Levy said that it was not Israel that had said "yes" to Baker but rather Baker who had said "yes" to Israel. Shamir said that Israel had agreed to the conference, but added an important proviso, namely, that the agreement was "subject to a satisfactory solution to the issue of Palestinian Arab representation."

The U.S-Israeli honeymoon, if it existed at all, was very brief. Despite the arrival in Israel on August 7 of a team of State Department officials, it emerged that Israel and the United States were far apart on the formulation of the memorandum. Israel was also concerned, as always, that despite its pledges, the administration was injecting the PLO into the peace process, in an attempt to sway the last holdouts, the Palestinians. Shamir, on August 8, summed up his skeptical view of the process: "We are entering the new diplomatic process with open eyes and without exaggerated expectations."

On September 16, Baker arrived on his seventh visit to Israel, against the backdrop of a serious crisis between Jerusalem and Washington arising from President Bush's extraordinary September 12 speech on the loan guarantees in which he criticized the American Jewish lobby. (See below; also "Intergroup Relations" and "The United States, Israel, and the Middle East," elsewhere in this volume.) In Israel, Baker left a copy of a proposed "statement of principles" for the peace process, which now replaced the proposed memorandum of understanding, which was judged to be unachievable. Baker also showed Shamir a draft of the invitation that the United States and the Soviet Union planned to issue for the conference, but, much to the chagrin of his Israeli hosts, he refused to leave a copy behind. The glance afforded Shamir, however, was enough to worry the Israelis: Resolution 242, which Israel never liked, was mentioned no less than four times in the proposed invitation.

Baker also met with the Palestinians during this visit and offered them a "statement of principles" as well. The United States wished to solve the East Jerusalem quandary by guaranteeing the Palestinians that representatives of the city would participate in talks on the permanent settlement, which would follow an agreement on the interim solution. The United States also stated that the exclusion of East Jerusalemites would not prejudge the final negotiations on the status of the city. The PLO was not happy with the contents of the statement; nonetheless, on September 28, the organization's parliament, the Palestine National Council (PNC), approved Palestinian participation in the talks. The decision was reached after two prominent Palestinian leaders, Faisal Husseini and Hanan Ashrawi, traveled to the PNC meeting in Tunis, in direct contravention of the Israeli law prohibiting contacts with the PLO. The PLO, for its part, continued to claim that East Jerusalemites as well as representatives of the Palestinian "diaspora" would be represented at the talks from the outset.

On September 24, Levy met with Baker in New York, while both were attending the UN General Assembly. Israel continued to raise demands for written commitments from Washington, which the administration was either unable or unwilling to provide. Among other things, Israel demanded a joint statement in which both countries acknowledged the pre-1967 borders as being indefensible, as well as an American commitment to support Israel if it decided to abandon the proposed conference because of contacts between the Palestinian delegation and the PLO.

On October 13, Baker came to the Middle East for the final talks before the conference, which was now set to convene on October 29 in the Spanish capital, Madrid. The Palestinians had yet to give their final approval to the American formulas, and Baker, growing increasingly impatient, warned them, from Amman, "The bus will not pass by here again."

On October 16, Baker came to Jerusalem, bringing with him the final American proposal for the "statement of principles," as well as the final draft of the invitation. Soviet foreign minister Boris Pankin, who had replaced Bessmertnykh after the failed August coup, was also in town. On October 19, Pankin restored full diplomatic relations between the Soviet Union and Israel, as demanded by Israel in exchange for its agreement to allow Moscow to cosponsor the peace talks. A few hours later, in a joint press conference at the King David Hotel, Baker and Pankin announced that the invitations had been presented.

Shamir said that he would recommend to his cabinet that Israel accept the invitation because, as he said, "there was no other alternative." The next day, the cabinet approved Shamir's recommendation, by a vote of 16–3, with one abstention. By this time, Israel already knew that Haidar Abdel-Shafi, 71, from Gaza, would head the Palestinian delegation. Abdel-Shafi had been one of the founding members of the PLO in 1964. It was a measure of how far Israel had traveled from its original positions that none of the ministers objected to the Palestinian choice.

On October 23, Shamir announced that he would head the Israeli delegation to the conference, despite the fact that it had been called at the foreign-ministerial level and that no Arab head of state had chosen to come. Various interpretations were given to Shamir's move, including the fact that he wished to stress the importance of the talks to Israel. It was also clearly a rebuke of his own foreign minister and resulted in a serious political crisis at home, instigated by Foreign Minister Levy, who felt badly slighted. (See below, "Political Developments.") Israel, reluctant at best, was thus going to attend the Madrid conference while its government was torn by internal strife.

THE MADRID CONFERENCE

The Madrid conference, the first-ever face-to-face meeting between Israel and a group of its Arab neighbors, took place in the royal palace of the Spanish capital, with hundreds of diplomats from around the globe and close to 10,000 journalists in attendance. President Bush opened the conference on October 30, in a speech that was well received by Israelis and Arabs alike. "Peace in the Middle East need not be a dream," he said. "We seek peace, real peace. And by real peace I mean treaties. Security. Diplomatic relations. Economic relations. Trade Investment. Cultural exchanges. Even tourism." He reiterated that Resolutions 242 and 338 would serve as the basis of the various settlements and spoke of "territorial compromise," a term that allowed the Israelis to quip that the president might have been referring to "compromise" on the part of the Arabs. The United States, Bush said, would not impose its will on the sides, but would serve as a "catalyst" for progress in the talks.

Soviet president Mikhail Gorbachev, whose own position in the Soviet Union was dubious at best and whose participation in the Madrid proceedings was described as only ceremonial by many analysts, said: "Today we have a unique opportunity, and it would be unforgivable to miss this opportunity. The conference can only succeed if no one seeks any victory for one side over the other, but all seek a shared victory over a cruel past."

The other two speeches of the opening day were a disappointment to the Israeli delegation. Dutch foreign minister Hans van den Broek, representing the European Community, spoke of the need for the conference to achieve self-determination for the Palestinians and for the "essential contribution" of stopping all settlements in the territories. Egyptian foreign minister Amre Moussa described the settlements as "illegal" and said that a prerequisite to peace was a "complete withdrawal" by Israel from the occupied territories. Although he lauded Egypt's trailblazing role in forging peace with Israel, he did not mention the architect of that role, the late president Anwar Sadat.

The parties to the conflict spoke on the second day of the conference, their words demonstrating the depth of animosity still dividing them.

Prime Minister Yitzhak Shamir was the first to speak; he described the "eternal bond" between the Jewish people and the land of Israel, and the long and bloody history of Arab hostility to the Jewish presence in the Holy Land. He called on Arab leaders to "show us and the world that you can accept Israel's existence. Demonstrate your readiness to accept Israel as a permanent entity in the region. Let the people in our region hear you speak in the language of reconciliation, coexistence and peace with Israel." "The issue," Shamir said, "is not territory, but our very existence."

Palestinian delegate Haidar Abdel-Shafi spoke after Shamir, in an emotional speech marking the first-ever meeting of Israeli and Palestinian negotiators as "equals." Abdel-Shafi had to walk a fine line between his own allegiance to the PLO and Israel's threat to walk out of the conference if he specifically mentioned the Palestinian delegation's subservience to the organization in Tunis. He described the Palestine National Council, the PLO's governing body, as "our parliament" and quoted "Chairman Yasir Arafat." Shamir, though displeased, did not walk out. "We are willing to live side by side on the land," Abdel-Shafi said, but settlement in the territories "must stop now." For too long, he added, "the Palestinian people have gone unheeded, silenced and denied."

Abdel-Shafi was followed by Syrian foreign minister Farouk al-Sharaa, who sparked a series of bitter accusations and counteraccusations by making what was widely described later as a "hateful anti-Semitic speech." Al-Sharaa attacked the very essence of Zionism, described Syria's "liberal policies" toward its own Jews, and said that Israel must "give up every inch of occupied Arab lands." The subsequent speeches of the Jordanian foreign minister, Kamel Abu-Jaber, and the Lebanese foreign minister, Faris Bouez, though anti-Israel, paled in comparison to al-Sharaa's tirade.

The third and closing day of the conference was marked by further escalation in the Israeli-Syrian face-off, and by grumblings, both in the Arab and the American delegations, about the fact that Shamir was going home early, "in honor of the Sabbath." In his short reply, Shamir lambasted the Syrians, saying that their claims of leniency toward the Jews "stretch incredulity to infinite proportions." Shamir also said of the Palestinians that "twisting history and perversion of fact will not earn the sympathy they strive to acquire."

Al-Sharaa struck once again, this time producing a prestate photograph of Yitzhak Shamir (then Yezernitsky), on a "wanted" poster produced by the British Mandate authorities, who were seeking to apprehend the then leader of the Lehi underground movement. "By his own admission, he was a terrorist," al-Sharaa said.

Following summations by Baker and Soviet foreign minister Pankin, the conference disbanded, with the sides preparing for the first face-to-face encounter two days later. The bitter diatribe at the conference dismayed many, who had expected it to serve as an arena for declarations of mutual goodwill and historic reconciliation. Shamir himself, however, told reporters back in Israel that he was "not surprised."

DIRECT TALKS

On November 3, Israel held its first direct, bilateral talks with delegations from Syria and Lebanon, as well as the joint Jordanian-Palestinian delegation.

It was touch-and-go until the last minute. The Syrian delegation had balked at first at attending the direct talks, demanding that representatives of the two cosponsors be present, and that Israel undertake in advance to continue the talks in Madrid. Indeed, the Syrians failed to show up for their first scheduled meeting with the Israelis. Combined American and Saudi pressures finally convinced them to come, along with the Lebanese delegation, which was under Syrian control. The discussions with the Syrians, which lasted for three hours, were harsh and tense, hardly surprising in light of the tough stance taken by Foreign Minister al-Sharaa at the conference itself. Still, this was one of the rare instances in which a diplomatic cliché was truly meaningful: the importance of the meeting was in the very fact that it was held.

The meeting with the Jordanians and Palestinians was much more promising: Israel agreed that the joint delegation could split on occasion to discuss matters that were exclusively Palestinian or Jordanian. The decision was announced after the meeting, in another first: a joint statement, issued by delegation chairmen Haidar Abdel-Shafi and Elyakim Rubinstein. The delegations failed, however, to reach any agreement on the timing and venue of their next meeting. Israel wanted the talks to be held in the Middle East, but the Arabs were opposed. To break the deadlock, the American administration would have to step in once again.

PEACE MOVES AFTER THE CONFERENCE

In the hiatus, the Israeli Knesset reaffirmed the country's commitment to its sovereignty on the Golan Heights and pledged never to return it to the Syrians. The Syrian government condemned the decision, but Prime Minister Shamir said it did not have any bearing on the peace process, for, in his opinion, peace could be achieved with Syria even without giving back any territories.

Secretary of State James Baker gave the sides two weeks to reach agreement on their own on the venue for the talks. The Arabs, however, refused to have any direct contacts with Israel outside the formal framework of the talks; thus, direct agreement was impossible. On November 23, and notwithstanding the Israeli position, Baker summoned the sides for talks in Washington, which were to start on December 4. Israel was not happy with the invitation, which was issued without prior consultation, but decided to attend the talks on the understanding that they would be devoted only to finding an appropriate venue for the future. (See below, "Relations with the United States.") However, to underscore its dissatisfaction, as well as to protest the administration's unilateral move, Israel announced that it would show up for the talks on December 9, five days later than the proposed date. The cabinet statement indicated that its acquiescence was a result of "appreciation for the United States and in apprecation of its efforts." Ambassador Shoval told the State Department that the Israelis' tardy arrival was a result of its need for "logistical preparations" and in order to emphasize to the Arabs that they would have to negotiate directly with Israel, and not try to achieve their aims through the United States. On December 4, the State Department halls designated for the talks were opened, and the Arab delegations appeared. Israel, however, was absent. It was widely reported in the press that this absence damaged Israel's standing in public opinion.

The talks finally convened on December 10, after another day's delay caused by the Arab insistence on marking the anniversary of the *intifada*. Israel and the Jordanian-Palestinian delegation, however, did not enter the room earmarked for them, because of procedural arguments stemming from Israel's view that it was negotiating with a combined delegation and the Palestinian insistence that its delegation was an independent entity. The heads of the delegations thus met in the corridor of the State Department in an effort to resolve the problem. Israel did meet, as planned, with the Syrian and Lebanese delegations, but little progress was reported. Concurrently with the talks, the sides were waging a propaganda battle in the American media. The two main actors in the contest were, on the Israeli side, Deputy Foreign Minister Benjamin Netanyahu, and, on the Palestinian side, Hanan Ashrawi. The assessment given by Israeli journalists was that, ultimately, Ashrawi was more successful, largely because the Madrid conference had given the Palestinians' their first opportunity for worldwide exposure, while Israel's case, as well as Netanyahu himself, were already well known to Western audiences.

On December 14, the head of the Jordanian delegation, Abdel Salim a-Majali, summoned Israeli journalists and gave them their first-ever interview with a senior Jordanian official. Jordan, he said, was seeking a full peace, just like the one between Israel and Egypt.

The talks closed on December 18, and the assessments after the fact reflected the wide gulf between the sides. The Israelis, who viewed the very convening of the talks as a historic achievement, said that "real progress" had been achieved. The Arabs, who were seeking an Israeli pledge to withdraw from the territories, said that they had been "deeply disappointed." The State Department offered what was apparently the most realistic view, saying that "the talks had not been a failure." President Bush, however, said that he was disappointed that the talks had not progressed to substantive matters.

The delegations dispersed, setting January 7, 1992, as the date for the next round. Israel still insistently opposed the continuation of the discussions in Washington. On December 23 it was announced that the other arena of the peace process, the multilateral talks, would convene in Moscow at the end of January.

Relations with the United States

The outbreak of the Gulf crisis in mid-summer 1990 came in the nick of time, as far as Israel's relations with the United States are concerned. Washington's shift of focus from the Middle East peace process in general, and Israeli settlement in the occupied territories in particular, coupled with the U.S. confrontation with one of Israel's worst enemies, Iraq, all combined to avert an unprecedented clash between the two countries, which had been looming ever since the collapse of the national unity government in March 1990 and the scuttling of the efforts to arrange an Israeli-Palestinian dialogue in Cairo.

Throughout the months leading up to the war, the attitude of the Israeli government and public toward Washington was a complex mix of conflicting emotions and apprehensions. The government was relieved that America seemed intent on crushing Iraq but was constantly on guard against a last-minute "deal" for which Israel would be asked to pay the price. And while the government was relieved that the Bush administration had set the peace process aside for the time being, it was also concerned that, in the aftermath of the confrontation in the Gulf, Washington would redouble its efforts to launch talks between Israelis and Arabs.

Likewise, Israel viewed with mixed feelings the rapprochement between the United States and Syria. On the one hand, greater American influence in Damascus might mean greater moderation by the Assad regime; on the other hand, greater Syrian influence in Washington might also entail a steady American drift away from Israel. And constantly looming in the background was President Bush's adamant opposition to settlements in the territories, which clashed head on with the Likud government's commitment to greatly enhance the Jewish population of Judea, Samaria, and Gaza.

The government's mixed attitudes were somewhat at variance with the views of the public at large. For a large majority of the Israeli population, the war with Iraq was reason enough for an unprecedented surge in American popularity; with the arrival in Israel of American soldiers to operate the Patriot missile batteries, which were touted as the answer to the Iraqi missile attacks, U.S. popularity was probably at an all-time high.

At the same time, the months of January and February provided a brief respite in the usually tense personal relations between President Bush and Prime Minister Shamir. The two, who had previously maintained little direct contact, spoke frequently on the phone. Shamir expressed his admiration for Bush's resolve, and the president returned in kind by praising Shamir's leadership.

The damage caused by the Iraqi attacks on Israel, coupled with a seldom-mentioned sentiment that America "owed" Israel some compensation for its self-imposed restraint, created the background for the Israeli requests for financial assistance, which were discussed as early as January 22, just six days after the start of the war. In October 1990, the administration had approved an Israeli request for $400 million in loan guarantees for immigrant absorption, although the guarantees had yet to be given in practice. Now, however, the stakes were apparently going to be much higher. When Deputy Secretary of State Lawrence Eagleburger visited Israel during the first week of the war, he asked Finance Minister Yitzhak Modai what Israel's needs were. Israel, Modai replied, now wished to receive loan guarantees 25 times as high as the ones already approved—$10 billion, spread out over a period of five years. "I have no doubt that the United States will accede to our request," Modai said. "There is no reason why the Americans should give massive aid to Egypt, Syria, and Turkey, and deny us only because technically we are not members of the international coalition against Iraq."

There were other versions of the meeting published in the press at the time, most notably that Modai had requested $13 billion in direct aid. In any case, the size of the Israeli request astounded even some of its allies in Washington, and especially did not go down well with members of the administration, who felt that Israel was trying to exploit the situation in the Gulf for financial gain. When Defense Minister Arens, in Washington on February 12, told Secretary of State Baker that Israel expected to be compensated for its passive role in the Gulf, Baker retorted that at that very moment, while Arens was in Washington talking about money, American boys were risking their lives at the front in the fight against Israel's enemies.

The American reluctance to compensate Israel directly, as well as the administration's incessant bickering with Jerusalem over the exact terms under which the previously approved $400-million guarantees would be approved, led Israeli ambassador Zalman Shoval, in an unusual and undiplomatic move, to complain publicly in an interview with the Reuters News Agency on February 14. The ambassador said that Israel was being "given the run-around" on the loan guarantees. Shoval's remarks infuriated Bush, who described them as "outrageous" and, in a letter to Shamir, threatened to declare the ambassador "persona non grata." The Americans claimed that the approval for the $400 million was on Baker's desk when Shoval made his untimely remarks—even as the secretary read, in the *Washington Post*, that, contrary to assurances given the State Department by Shamir's aides, Israel was planning to construct another 12,000 apartments in the territories in the upcoming year.

The incident was defused when Shamir, in a letter to Bush, apologized for Shoval's remarks, and after Vice-President Dan Quayle, in a February 19 meeting with Shoval in Miami, declared the affair closed. Quayle said that the loan guarantees would be approved "within days." Indeed, two days later, on February 20, Baker approved the guarantees, despite the fact that Israel had not supplied the State Department with a comprehensive report about its expenditures in the territories. Baker's chief assistant, Dennis Ross, told Shoval that the guarantees were given, among other things, on the basis of Shamir's pledge that there were no plans to build 12,000 housing units, as reported by the *Washington Post*.

On February 25, Israel submitted a formal request for compensation for the various kinds of damage caused by the Gulf War—directly to Israeli homes and businesses in Tel Aviv, to the Israeli economy, which underwent six weeks of almost total shutdown, and as a result of the added expenditures for maintaining the military in a state of preparedness. The Israeli request was for a grant of one billion dollars. On March 2, Baker told Shoval that the administration viewed the Israeli request with favor, but the two agreed, on the spot, to reduce Israel's request to $910 million.

A few days later, the administration approved the granting of $650 million in emergency aid to Israel. In exchange, Israel agreed to postpone the submission of its second request for loan guarantees until September. Israel's acceptance of this demand, which was criticized both in Israel and among pro-Israel lobbyists in Washington, was apparently a reaction to the adverse response it had received to its aid request. In any case, it was clear that the Americans, for their part, wished to exploit the loan-guarantee issue in order to promote future American diplomatic efforts.

GROWING TENSION

In March, only a few weeks after the guns in the Gulf were silenced and the threat of Iraqi missile attacks removed—the underlying animosity between Jerusalem and Washington in general, and between Bush and Shamir in particular, returned to the surface. The *Wall Street Journal* reported on April 1 that relations between the two leaders had cooled; Bush, the newspaper said, was angered by the Israeli decision to deport four Fatah leaders, despite the American request not to do so. (The Israeli government issued the deportation orders on March 24; after losing their appeals, the four were deported to Lebanon on May 18. The Security Council condemned Israel for the action on May 24.) Housing Minister Ariel Sharon's constant public statements about the scope and scale of Israel's settlement efforts in the territories also annoyed the Americans. In Israel, the U.S. government was coming in for increasing criticism for a wide range of things, including its perceived abandonment of the Iraqi Kurdish population.

Israel's reports to the administration concerning the settlements were being eyed with ever-increasing skepticism. While the Prime Minister's Office told the State Department that only 1,000–2,000 apartments were being built, other sources, including the government's own publications, mentioned much higher numbers. On March 20, the State Department reported to Congress that over 200,000 Jews were living in 200 settlements in the occupied territories and that, contrary to the Israeli pledges, immigrants from the Soviet Union were indeed being directed there. Shamir, on April 9, told Baker that Sharon's plans for building in the territories had not received cabinet approval; but Sharon, a few days later, in an interview with the *Washington Post*, explained that his plans did not require cabinet approval in the first place. Shamir, he said, was a full partner in the plans which he had announced and which had so angered the Americans.

On April 10, Baker told Shamir that the issue of settlements was a constant thorn in the side of relations between the two countries and might ultimately damage them irreparably. The response of some Israelis—not always sanctioned by Shamir—only helped to fan the flames: on three separate occasions, Jewish settlers chose the day of Baker's arrival in Israel to set up yet another outpost in the territories.

By late April, relations were close to the boiling point. At Baker's insistence, Housing Secretary Jack Kemp canceled a planned meeting with Sharon, who was visiting Washington at the time. Margaret Tutwiler explained the move by saying that Sharon "publicly opposed American policies" in the Middle East. If Baker's move had been intended to isolate Sharon in Israel, it achieved the opposite effect; even his most severe critics were forced to join in condemning what was viewed in Israel as offensive behavior by the administration. Several months later, in an interview with the German *Der Spiegel*, Sharon showed that he had still not recovered from the insult. American "mistakes" in the Middle East, he said, had cost the lives of "tens of thousands of people."

On May 22, in testimony to the House appropriations subcommittee, Baker made plain just how seriously the Americans viewed the issue of settlements and angered many Israel supporters in the process. "There is no bigger impediment to peace," he said, "than the Israeli settlements." The statement led several prominent members of Congress to suggest openly that some sort of linkage had to be established between Israel's aid requests and its habit of ignoring American sensibilities by constantly expanding its settlement drive in the territories. Israel was outraged, as were the major American Jewish organizations. President Bush stood by his secretary of state, saying, the next day: "I'm backing the man, I'm stating the policy of the U.S.A., and so was the secretary."

Even as the atmosphere between the two countries was deteriorating, there were reminders of the mutuality that still existed. At the same time that Israel and the United States were at loggerheads over the issue of settlements, for example, the Bush administration played a pivotal role in securing the release of 15,000 Ethiopian Jews in what came to be known as "Operation Solomon" (see below). On May 23, Shamir wrote to Bush thanking him for his efforts. Several months later, in the midst of another difficult U.S.-Israeli crisis, the Americans led the campaign in the United Nations to repeal the 1975 "Zionism Is Racism" resolution.

At the end of May, Secretary of Defense Dick Cheney came to Israel for a visit. Unlike Baker and Bush, Cheney was much admired in Israel both for his leading role in the Gulf crisis and because he was perceived as a strong backer of Israel. However, even this goodwill visit was marred by yet another incident between Shamir and Bush. On May 29, Bush unveiled an ambitious and far-reaching program aimed at curtailing the proliferation of nonconventional weapons in the Middle East. A few days earlier, Shamir had asked Bush to postpone the public presentation of his program so that Israel could have a chance to submit its views on it to Cheney. Bush refused, and most of Cheney's visit was devoted to the Israelis' complaints about the Bush proposals. During Cheney's visit, Israel and the United States agreed on the development of the second stage of the Arrow missile, 72 percent of which would be funded by the U.S. government.

On June 19, as the groundwork was being laid for the presentation of the Israeli request for loan guarantees in September—in accordance with the above-mentioned agreement with the administration—Israeli ambassador Zalman Shoval, in a sober diplomatic assessment, told Jerusalem that Israel would ultimately have to choose between loan guarantees and continued settlement in the territories. Shoval's words angered Shamir and the government, which had been telling the Israeli people exactly the opposite. Shamir reprimanded Shoval, and, for the first time, openly indicated that the government planned to go "over the administration's head" in order to secure the guarantees. The American people, Shamir said, will no doubt reject the linkage between the guarantees and settlements. Somewhat reassuringly, the Israel embassy in Washington informed Jerusalem on June 29 that a stable majority in Congress supported Israel's request for guarantees.

On July 1, Bush told a press conference that the "best thing that Israel could do was to live up to the commitment it made at one point not to build any more settlements." Bush was referring to a promise which he believed Shamir had made during the first meeting between the two in 1989. Since then, Shamir had on several occasions denied making any such commitment; Bush apparently chose to disregard the denials. On July 22, National Security Adviser Brent Scowcroft admitted for the first time in public that there would indeed be some linkage between the peace process and the Israeli request for aid.

In late August, relations grew even more strained. Israel and the United States were divided over the procedures that would govern the proposed peace conference and were conducting an acrimonious dialogue on the formulation of a memorandum of understanding on the peace process, a dialogue that sank to new depths as "Israeli sources" complained about the anti-Israel sentiments of some of Baker's Jewish assistants. At the same time, Israel was gearing up to submit its request for loan guarantees, while Arab countries were telling the administration that approval of the guarantees would put U.S. diplomatic efforts in serious peril.

On September 5, Shamir refused a specific request from Bush and Baker to postpone the submission of the request for loan guarantees. Apparently, the prime minister was influenced by the rosy reports from his Washington embassy about the massive support for the guarantees in Congress and believed that the Israeli position was strong enough to overcome even outright opposition by the administration. Israel was so confident, in fact, that the 1992 budget, which was submitted to the cabinet for a first reading in early September, already included income of $2 billion to be raised on the basis of the loan guarantees.

FORMAL LOAN-GUARANTEE REQUEST

On September 6, Shoval formally submitted the loan-guarantee request. Bush, in return, formally requested that Congress not deal with the matter for a period of 120 days, so as not to hamper the peacemaking process, which had reached a critical stage. The Israeli steamroller, buttressed by AIPAC, continued to advance, however, unfazed by the president's strenuous opposition. Thus, the stage was set for Bush's unprecedented speech of September 12, a negative milestone in both U.S. relations with Israel and the relations between the American government and its own Jewish citizens. Bush said that he had "worn out the telephone" in trying to persuade senators and representatives to delay the loan-guarantee issue, but he was "up against some powerful political forces." The president depicted himself as the lone struggler against a thousand powerful lobbyists.

Israel, taken aback by the ferocity of Bush's onslaught, reacted moderately. Foreign Minister Levy said that the last thing Jerusalem wanted was a confrontation with the administration. Outside the government, however, reactions were fierce. Agriculture Minister Rafael Eitan said Israel should take back its request for guarantees; Minister Rehavam Ze'evi, the most right-wing of the cabinet ministers, went so far as to say that Bush was an "anti-Semite" who was leading Israel to a "second Holocaust." From an emotional and psychological point of view, relations between the two governments had probably never been worse. A few weeks later, Shamir himself exposed the depth of his resentment of Bush's attitudes, saying that the president had "hurt the very essence of Zionism."

In any case, it was now clear that Shamir's hopes that Israel might be rescued by the "American people" were misplaced. In an ABC poll released on September 18, no less than 86 percent supported Bush's view that discussion of the matter should be postponed. A few days later, in a *Wall Street Journal* poll, close to half of the respondents said that they opposed more aid to Israel altogether. Shamir, however, was yet to be convinced. The next day he said that "ultimately, the Americans will return to themselves. All of this will pass like a bad dream." He was also unrepentant: on September 24, at the ground-breaking ceremony for a new settlement, Shamir said that Israel would continue to settle Jews "till the edge of the horizon."

By late September, it was clear that Israel would not be able to override the president's request for a postponement. "We've waited 2,000 years, so we'll wait another four months," said Levy. The government was convinced that the setback was tactical and temporary and that ultimately the guarantees would be approved with acceptable conditions.

At the same time, a seemingly uncoordinated offensive against Jerusalem's bid for aid was being opened up on another front: the economic one. A September report to Congress noted that Israel might have difficulties repaying the debts incurred on the basis of the guarantees. And on October 3, the Export-Import Bank published a negative assessment of the resilience of the Israeli economy. In Jerusalem, most policymakers were convinced that the administration was behind these publications, and an effort was launched to refute them.

An unrelated incident in early October revealed how far the discord over the guarantees had gone. The United States joined in condemning Israel for an intelligence overflight carried out by the Israel Air Force in Iraq, and warned Israel not to repeat such missions. Security sources, stung by the unexpected American rebuke, said that Washington now was willing to criticize Israel for practically anything, even a defensive move against America's own enemy, Iraq. There were other signs of American discontent. An October 27 report in the *Washington Post* recounted Israeli efforts to assist the South African ballistic-missile program. Once again, Israelis were sure that the administration was behind the leak; its aim was not only to discredit Israel in the eyes of the public, but to weaken the still formidable support for Israel in Congress.

Israel's agreement to participate in the Madrid conference, which convened on October 30, diverted attention for a brief while. After the conference, the Americans worked on finding a site agreeable to all sides for the direct bilateral talks that were scheduled to follow. Israel wanted the talks to be held in the Middle East or somewhere in its vicinity; the Arabs objected. On November 22, Shamir came to Washington in the hope of dissuading the administration from inviting the sides for talks in Washington.

Shamir had scheduled meetings with both Baker and Bush and had notified the administration in advance that the venue of the proposed talks was one of his main concerns. Shamir emerged from his meeting with Baker and said that "progress" had been achieved on this matter and that he hoped the issue would be finalized in his meeting with the president. But before the meeting with Bush even took place, the American ambassador to Israel went to the Foreign Ministry in Jerusalem and submitted the formal American invitation for talks in Washington. Not only had the administration humiliated Shamir with this move, this time there could be no doubt that it had done so on purpose.

Shamir's ensuing meeting with Bush was held in a strained atmosphere, in complete accordance with the true state of relations between the two. After the meeting, American sources were quoted by *Ha'aretz* as saying that "the era of a special relationship between the United States and Israel is over." At the end of the year, that indeed appeared to be the case.

Other Foreign Relations

Apart from its troubles with the United States, 1991 was a watershed year for Israel's foreign relations and international standing. The collapse of the Iron Curtain and the Soviet bloc not only brought renewed recognition from those countries that had been under the direct influence of Moscow, but also freed Third World countries to establish independent links with Jerusalem. Israel's restraint during the Gulf crisis earned accolades throughout the world, and in the immediate aftermath of the war the country was inundated with foreign dignitaries who hitherto had made a point of staying away. Israel's agreement, in October, to participate in the peace process sealed what can probably be described as the most successful year for Israeli diplomacy since the establishment of the state.

THE SOVIET UNION

At the beginning of the year, Israel and the Soviet Union maintained relations at a consular level, with an independent Israeli consulate operating in Moscow, dealing, in the main, with the tens of thousands of Jews who wished to immigrate to Israel. Soviet leaders repeatedly pledged that the resumption of full ties, broken off in the wake of the 1967 Six Day War, was only "a matter of time."

On January 9, Soviet president Mikhail Gorbachev invited Israeli prime minister Yitzhak Shamir to come to Moscow. Also in January, the Soviets approached Israel directly with a proposal to establish a Middle East headquarters, located in Cyprus, that would be staffed by liaison officers from the countries of the region, as well as U.S. and other representatives, and would have sophisticated communications and surveillance equipment—with the aim of defusing tensions and avoiding misunderstandings. Israel responded favorably to the idea and proposed that "experts" from the two countries meet to discuss details and implementation.

The Soviets showed great appreciation for Israel's policy of restraint in the face of the Iraqi missile attacks; on January 31, while the war was still in progress, Soviet foreign minister Alexander Bessmertnykh wrote his counterpart, David Levy, to commend Israel's behavior.

In March, the Patriarch of the Russian Orthodox Church, Alexei II, made his first visit to Israel, where he discussed the properties owned by the church in the Holy Land and professed his wish to "open a new page" in the relations between the church and the Jewish people.

April and May saw a series of "firsts" in Soviet-Israeli relations. Prime Minister Shamir, in London, met with Soviet prime minister Vladimir Pavlov during an international summit on the establishment of the European Bank for Reconstruction and Development, in what was described as an especially cordial meeting. The next month saw the first Soviet foreign minister in Jerusalem: Bessmertnykh, touring the Middle East in conjunction with Secretary of State James Baker, arrived in Jerusalem on May 6 for a brief 24-hour stopover, during which he urged the government to agree to the American proposals on the peace process. By this time, details of the American blueprint for peace had already emerged, especially the proposal that the United States and the Soviet Union serve as cosponsors for the projected negotiations. Bessmertnykh's visit produced a flurry of speculation that the time for the resumption of full ties had arrived, but the visitor disappointed his hosts and declared only that the two countries were "on the verge" of reestablishing links at the highest level.

In September, following the aborted August revolution in Moscow, a Russian parliamentary delegation visited Israel. The same month, Foreign Minister Levy met with Bessmertnykh's successor, Boris Pankin, at the UN General Assembly in New York. The two announced that relations between the two countries would be resumed "within days."

Three weeks later, on October 18, Pankin was in Jerusalem with Baker to issue the formal invitations to the Madrid Peace Conference. Just hours before the two announced that the invitations had been sent, Pankin and Levy signed the protocol reestablishing full diplomatic ties, at the ambassadorial level, between Moscow and Jerusalem. While the timing of the move was directly linked to Israel's insistence that the Soviets could not take a leading role in the peace process without establishing full ties, Pankin described it as "a natural and logical step which is a natural outcome of the new international realities."

On October 24, Israeli ambassador Arye Levin hoisted the Israeli flag over the reestablished embassy in Moscow, which was housed in the same building the embassy had occupied up to 1967. A week later, on October 30, Shamir met with Gorbachev, hours before the start of the Madrid conference.

FORMER SOVIET REPUBLICS

On September 4, Israel recognized the breakaway Baltic republics of Latvia, Lithuania, and Estonia. At the end of the year, with the collapse of the Soviet empire and its breakup into individual republics, vast new diplomatic frontiers and challenges awaited Israel's foreign policymakers. On December 25, Israel recognized the independence of each of the separate republics, including the five Muslim republics, which mostly expressed interest in setting up independent ties with Israel. It was revealed that, in addition to its embassy in Moscow, the Foreign Ministry planned to open new embassies in one of the three Baltic countries, in Ukraine, and in two or three of the Muslim republics.

EASTERN EUROPE

All the former Eastern Bloc countries, with the exception of Albania and the splintering union of Yugoslavia, had reestablished diplomatic ties with Israel during 1989 and 1990 (Romania never severed its links). In 1991 there was a rapid deepening of the ties between Israel and these countries, especially in the economic sphere, and several high-level visits were exchanged. In most cases, these visits evoked a renewed Israeli awareness of the disappearance of the Jewish communities in these countries during the Holocaust and were seen as an opportunity to settle the historical account with the inheritors of the wartime regimes and the people who cooperated with the Nazi extermination plan.

There were no less than three high-level visits by Eastern European leaders during two weeks in May. On May 5, Czechoslovak prime minister Marian Calfa visited Israel for the annual meeting of the World Jewish Congress. His Hungarian counterpart, Antal Goncz, came a few days later. The most widely reported and sensitive visit was that of Polish president Lech Walesa, who came to Israel on May 19. In a dramatic speech to the Knesset the next day, Walesa said: "Here, at the cradle of your civilization and your rebirth, I have come to beg forgiveness." Walesa's visit was marked by a wide national debate on the degree of Polish collaboration with the Nazis during World War II and the existence of virulent Polish anti-Semitism, both then and now. Both of his main hosts—Prime Minister Yitzhak Shamir and opposition leader Shimon Peres—are Polish-born, and both escaped the impending destruction of their families and communities.

A month later, President Chaim Herzog visited Hungary and Bulgaria. In Budapest, he rededicated the main Jewish synagogue in the presence of teary-eyed representatives of the largest Jewish community remaining in Eastern Europe. The Bulgarian foreign minister made a first-ever visit to Israel on July 22. Prime Minister Yitzhak Shamir made an official visit to Sofia in August, along with his wife, Shulamit, who revisited the sights and sounds of her childhood there. In September, Romanian president Ion Iliescu came for a first visit to Israel. In October, President Herzog visited Czechoslovakia, where he participated in a ceremony unveiling a monument to the Jews who died at the Theresienstadt concentration camp. In October the official Yugoslav news agency announced Belgrade's willingness to reestablish ties with Israel, but the republic collapsed before the proposal was realized.

The last holdout, the previously remote Albania, announced on July 21 that it planned to set up ties with Jerusalem, for the first time since the establishment of the two countries. Visiting Israel on August 19, Albanian foreign minister Muhammad Kaplani signed the protocol establishing ties between Tirana and Jerusalem.

CHINA

In 1990 China and Israel had set up their first formal ties, in the form of an Israeli scientific delegation in Beijing and a Chinese tourist representative in Tel Aviv. It was clear that China was on the road to establishing formal diplomatic links with Israel, but that it wished to do so at its own pace, taking care not to alienate its Arab allies, especially the PLO, in the process.

On March 12, it was revealed that the director-general of Israel's Foreign Ministry, Reuven Merhav, the architect of Chinese-Israeli ties, was on a secret mission in Beijing. He was the highest Israeli official ever to visit that country. A significant breakthrough occurred when, on March 21, the Chinese Foreign Ministry issued an official statement acknowledging Merhav's visit. In June an official delegation of Chinese scientists came to Israel; on June 4, an agreement of cooperation was signed between the academies of sciences of the two countries.

On November 20, the *Washington Post* revealed that Defense Minister Moshe Arens had made a secret visit to Beijing, holding four days of military talks with his Chinese counterparts. The *Post* report fueled several days of speculation in the foreign press about the much-reported "clandestine" military links between the two countries. Concurrently with Arens's secret visit, the first Israeli economic delegation visited Beijing and discussed possible economic links. The head of Israel's Chamber of Commerce, Danny Gillerman, said that his Chinese hosts had assured him that relations would be established in the very near future.

In December practical preparations began for the establishment of full diplomatic ties. A senior Israeli Foreign Ministry official held talks in Beijing, and, in the last week of the year, a Chinese deputy foreign minister visited Jerusalem. PLO chairman Yasir Arafat, in a December 21 visit to Beijing, made a last-ditch effort to persuade the Chinese authorities to cancel or at least postpone their plans, but his pleas were rejected. Just like the Soviet Union, China wished to get involved in the developing peace process, and just as with Moscow, Israel insisted that any role be accompanied by full diplomatic ties. Beijing announced that it wished to participate in the multilateral peace conference, scheduled to convene in Moscow on January 28, 1992. At the end of the year it was clear that the world's most populous country would establish full ties with Israel before that date.

OTHER ASIAN COUNTRIES

Mongolia and Israel established full diplomatic ties, for the first time, on October 2. The protocol was signed by the two countries' foreign ministers in New York, where they were participating in the UN General Assembly.

A senior Japanese official came to Israel on February 23 to discuss closer ties with Jerusalem. Japan was particularly pleased with Israel's conduct during the Gulf War, and was thus inclined to go beyond its previous relationship. Manifestations of the shift were soon apparent. On April 11, the *New York Times* reported that the biggest Japanese car manufacturer, Toyota, had decided to break with its long-held policy of adherence to the Arab boycott and to start marketing cars in Israel. On May 29, Foreign Minister Taro Nakayama visited Israel, the first visit by a Japanese foreign minister.

On August 12, a senior Indian official told the Reuters News Agency that New Delhi would be setting up ties with Israel within a year. India, it was reported, was also seeking a role in the multilateral peace talks.

In November the king of the Pacific island of Tonga visited Israel on a Christian pilgrimage.

WESTERN EUROPE

Nowhere were Israel's restraint in the Gulf and its subsequent acquiescence to the American peace process more appreciated than in Western Europe. The Iraqi missile attacks on Israeli population centers elicited waves of sympathy unseen since the heady days of the 1967 war. Moreover, the PLO's support for Saddam weakened traditional Palestinian diplomatic strongholds in Western European capitals.

An exception to the rule was France, with whom relations at the beginning of 1991 reached a low point. France was seen in Israel as leading the pack of European countries interested in "appeasing" Iraqi president Saddam Hussein, even at the expense of Israel's security. There was also widespread resentment in Israel following reports that French industry had helped Saddam improve his ballistic-missile capabilities. The formal French reaction to the missile attacks was also viewed in Israel as lukewarm in comparison to that of its European Community partners.

On January 20, President Chaim Herzog wrote President François Mitterrand, protesting French policy toward Iraq. "The attempts to appease a cruel dictator," he wrote, "evoke bitter memories among us." As the missile attacks continued, Israeli criticism of the French reached a peak. Mitterrand, according to press reports, was even said to be considering a recall of his ambassador in Israel. The ambassador, Alain Pierret, made headlines himself by stating, in a February 4 interview, that some Israelis sometimes expressed themselves "like hooligans." Later in the year, Israel refused to host Foreign Minister Roland Dumas, frustrating French attempts to play a more active role in the peace process.

Germany was also heavily involved in the building of the Iraqi military machine and was thus subjected to harsh criticism in Israel, especially in the context of possible gas attacks against the Israeli civilian population. Unlike the French, however, the Germans took several steps to placate the Israeli government and its public. On January 23, just a week after the start of the war, the Bonn government announced that it would extend 250 million marks of emergency aid to Israel. Four days later, the Germans proposed the transfer of a Patriot missile battery to Israel. Although the offer was declined, on January 31 a Boeing of the Luftwaffe landed at Ben-Gurion Airport, bringing medical supplies and special gas-detection equipment. German soldiers accompanied the shipment and provided user instruction to their Israeli counterparts.

Following the war, Israel approached Germany both for loan guarantees for new immigrants and in an attempt to recover the Holocaust reparations which Israel claimed were owed by the now defunct East German regime. Bonn denied any obligation for East Germany's war reparations debts, and in June it became clear that it was following Washington's footsteps by linking any assistance for immigrant absorption to the cessation of Israeli settlement activities in the territories. On July 3, Foreign Minister Levy protested the "linkage" created by Bonn. In December, German president Richard von Weizsäcker visited Israel to participate in a concert given by the Dresden Philharmonic Orchestra.

The Netherlands supplied Israel with a Patriot missile battery, complete with Dutch military operators, in February. Portugal announced, in March, that it would appoint a resident ambassador to Israel. Spanish prime minister Felipe González made a first-ever visit to Israel by a Spanish leader, on November 30. On December 22, Turkey, seeking a role in the multilateral talks, announced that it was upgrading its relations with Israel to ambassadorial level.

The European Community, sympathetic to Israel's ordeals at the hands of Saddam and angered by the Palestinian support for him, announced on January 26 that it was canceling the limited sanctions it had imposed in protest over Israeli policies in the occupied territories. The next week, the EC decided to give Israel $170 million in emergency aid. On February 11, Foreign Minister Levy told the Knesset, in what eventually turned out to be wishful thinking, that the EC had decided to sever its links with the PLO.

Relations with the EC soured again in the summer when it emerged that Prime Minister Shamir opposed giving Europe any role in the American-brokered peace process. Foreign Minister Levy, however, was more agreeable to European participation and was thus accorded warm welcomes on his trips to European capitals. Levy, along with Secretary of State James Baker, eventually persuaded Shamir to drop his opposition, and the EC sent Dutch foreign minister Hans van den Broek to Madrid. His speech to the conference, on October 30, was regarded in Israel as disappointing, if not downright hostile.

EGYPT

The Egyptian government, a major partner in the Arab component of the international coalition against Iraq, was especially apprehensive about Israeli involvement in the war. Diplomats in Cairo were fearful that an Israeli attack on Iraq would considerably weaken the already much-maligned Egyptian decision to side with Washington against Saddam. Thus, the first two months of the year witnessed rare Egyptian commendation for Israeli policies. Nobel Prize-winning Egyptian author Naguib Mahfouz said, on February 6, that Israel's restraint showed "supreme wisdom."

The honeymoon, however, was short-lived. Israel's settlement policies in the territories rekindled Egyptian animosity and, in the summer, Israeli officials were voicing true anxiety. Israel's continued haggling with the United States over the terms of the proposed peace conference was eliciting anger and condemnation in Cairo, and President Hosni Mubarak, in a June interview with the *Financial Times*, blasted Israeli policy in harsh terms. Unconfirmed news reports, eventually repudiated, even said that Mubarak planned to recall his ambassador to Tel Aviv and was reconsidering the entire framework of Egyptian-Israeli relations.

Foreign Minister Levy went to Cairo at the end of July, meeting twice with Mubarak and thrice with his Egyptian counterpart, Amre Moussa. Levy discussed possibilities for solving the obstacles then facing the peace process, and also tried to convince Mubarak to end his boycott of Shamir and to agree to a summit between the two leaders. Mubarak, while not refusing Levy's requests outright, said that "the time was not ripe."

In October tensions flared again in the wake of Egyptian opposition to American attempts to revoke the "Zionism Is Racism" resolution in the United Nations.

OTHER AFRICAN STATES

On July 13, Israel eased previously imposed sanctions against South Africa, after that country implemented political reforms, following similar action taken by the United States just a few days earlier. In November, as a direct consequence of the lifting of the sanctions, South African president Frederik Willem de Klerk paid an official visit to Israel, where he signed a formal memorandum of understanding on cooperation between the two countries in a wide array of civilian spheres.

In August the Nigerian foreign minister came to Israel for a first visit since the Six Day War, announcing that Nigeria would soon resume full diplomatic ties. Later that month, on August 22, Congo resumed full ties with Israel. Zambia followed on December 25. In November an official Israeli economic delegation visited Angola.

THE UNITED NATIONS

Relations between Israel and the United Nations started off this year in their traditional state: bad. On January 4, the Security Council unanimously approved a resolution "deploring" the Israeli treatment of the Palestinians in the territories. Visiting the occupied territories at the beginning of the year, General Assembly president Guido de Marco, the foreign minister of Malta, said that the situation there "could not continue" and that an international conference—known to be anathema to Israeli policymakers—must be convened at once. Later in the year, de Marco angered Israelis even more by claiming that the international body "owes a responsibility not only toward the descendants of those who suffered in the concentration camps, but toward the children of the *intifada* as well."

Nonetheless, the image of the UN in Israeli eyes underwent significant transformation during the course of the year. The end of the cold-war confrontation in that body, and especially the resolute action taken by the Security Council against Iraq, convinced most Israelis that a reassessment of the UN was necessary. There were those in Israel who welcomed the change, while others feared that a Security Council that could reach unanimity on Iraq might also be able to do so in the future concerning Israel, to the detriment of the country's better interests.

However, the UN's attitude toward Israel itself was also undergoing a change. In October an Israeli was elected to the executive of the UN's environmental group, after many years in which Israeli officials were barred from such posts.

As the General Assembly convened, it became clear that the automatic "anti-Israel majority" in the United Nations was no longer as solid as it used to be. Eastern European countries, for example, opposed a November 16 resolution calling for inspection of Israel's nuclear facilities. A November 19 condemnation of Israeli policies in the territories was supported by a majority of 93–20, smaller than in the previous year. The new reality in the UN was capped and epitomized by the December 16 decision, brokered by the United States, to repeal the infamous "Zionism Is Racism" resolution of 1975. A total of 111 countries voted to nullify the decision; only 25, mainly Arab countries, opposed the motion.

On November 23, Egyptian diplomat Boutrous Boutrous-Ghali was selected to succeed Javier Pérez de Cuéllar as secretary-general of the United Nations. Israel opposed Ghali's election at first, fearing that he would not conduct an objective Middle East policy; ultimately, however, Israel joined the majority that voted for him.

DOMESTIC AFFAIRS

Political Developments

While 1990 had been one of the most turbulent in the history of Israeli politics, 1991 was relatively uneventful and peaceful. This was undoubtedly linked to the fact that the Gulf War, at the beginning, and the peace conference, at the end, were major focuses of attention throughout the year.

At the beginning of the year, Prime Minister Yitzhak Shamir's narrow coalition enjoyed the support of 64 members of the Knesset, making it beholden to the demands of most of its lesser partners. Shamir's only avenue for expanding his coalition was both narrow and controversial, but in January he decided to travel it.

The only remaining party that was a candidate to join the coalition was Moledet, led by former army general Rehavam Ze'evi. Moledet had hitherto been considered outside the consensus of Zionist parties, because of its advocacy of the "transfer" option, by which the Israeli-Palestinian conflict would be solved via the transfer— voluntary or other—of the Palestinian inhabitants of the West Bank and Gaza to other Arab lands. Shamir had held talks with Ze'evi when he was setting up his coalition in summer 1990, but these talks failed, mainly because Shamir refused to accede to Ze'evi's demand for either the defense or the police portfolio. Shamir had not persisted, especially in light of the widespread expected opposition to Ze'evi's inclusion in the cabinet.

On January 31, while the Gulf War was raging, Shamir and Ze'evi reached an agreement by which Ze'evi would become the cabinet's 20th minister, and his two votes in the Knesset would henceforth support the coalition. Ze'evi refused Shamir's offer to be the environment minister, and since he no longer insisted on other portfolios, it was agreed that he would serve as a minister-without-portfolio. Ze'evi was also to become a member of the so-called inner cabinet, where the crucial military and political decisions were made.

It was widely assumed that Shamir chose to make this move during the Gulf War, while the international community was preoccupied with other matters, so as to minimize criticism of his action. Nonetheless, many of his closest allies in the Likud objected to the move and made last-minute attempts to dissuade Shamir from bringing his agreement with Ze'evi for approval. The Left, of course, was much more outspoken, condemning Shamir for introducing Moledet's "racist" policies to the government and for thus legitimizing its views in the eyes of the public. Member of Knesset Yossi Sarid said that Shamir was forcing the government to live with the "rotten apple," referring to Ze'evi.

Shamir was not affected, however, and on February 3, his cabinet approved the addition of Moledet to the government. The vote was 14–3, with two abstentions. A few days later, the Knesset also approved the coalition agreement, by a vote of 61–54. MK Zeev Binyamin Begin, Shamir's colleague in the Likud and one of

Ze'evi's sharpest critics, refused to bow to party discipline and described Moledet's joining the government as "moral contamination." The turbulent Knesset debate was also marked by the unprecedented action of two members of the Communist party, Tamar Gozanski and Muhammad Nafa, who waved yellow stars of David, like those that Jews were forced to wear in World War II Europe. They were promptly ejected from the Knesset floor by Speaker Dov Shilansky.

The main focus of political activity during the year was inside the Likud itself, where the top ministers continued their incessant feuding. Shamir found himself at continuous odds with Housing Minister Ariel Sharon, who bitterly criticized the government from the right, and Foreign Minister David Levy, who espoused more moderate policies than Shamir and was repeatedly involved in personal clashes with Shamir and his most prominent political ally, Defense Minister Moshe Arens.

The bickering with Levy invariably involved larger diplomatic issues of the day. In early February, Arens made a quick trip to the United States to discuss Israeli reactions to the Iraqi missile attacks. Levy had planned to go to Washington several days later. While in Washington, Arens met with President Bush and Secretary of State Baker. Levy was incensed, not only because his own trip had now become superfluous, but mainly because he had not been told in advance that Arens would be meeting with Bush and Baker. Piqued, Levy canceled his visit.

In the immediate aftermath of the war, as Baker's diplomatic initiative developed, Levy was constantly attacked both by the right-wing parties and by the Likud itself for making too many "concessions" to the Americans. In several instances, Shamir warned Levy not to stray from the original blueprint of the Israeli peace plan. Relations between Levy and Shamir were also strained because of the friction between Levy and his own deputy, Benjamin Netanyahu, who was seen as being closer to the prime minister.

Relations between Levy and Shamir reached a crisis state in late October, following Shamir's decision that he would head the Israeli delegation to the Madrid Peace Conference, despite the fact that other delegations would be represented by their foreign ministers. Among other reasons for Shamir's decision, sources close to the prime minister cited Levy's decision not to take Netanyahu to Madrid, despite the latter's proven success with the foreign media. Levy's supporters in the Likud were in an uproar, interpreting Shamir's move as an injurious slight to their leader's dignity. Levy himself was reported, on October 23, to be considering his resignation. MK Arye Gamliel, from the Sephardi Shas party, labeled Shamir's decision "pure racism."

During the Madrid conference, Levy "retaliated" against Shamir by ordering Foreign Ministry personnel who were members of the Israeli delegation to the conference to come back to Israel before the conference was over. The dispute was finally resolved in a mid-November meeting between Shamir and Levy, in which it was also decided that Netanyahu would leave his post as deputy foreign minister and move to the Prime Minister's Office, where he would be in charge of Israeli public relations connected with the peace process. Levy scored yet another point against Shamir when, in mid-December, he accepted an invitation to meet with President Bush. This meeting antagonized the prime minister, whose own relations with the American president were at an all-time low.

Sharon, for his part, maintained a constant and fierce barrage of criticism against Shamir throughout the year. At the beginning of the year, he was the most vocal critic of the government's policy of restraint in the Gulf War, calling it a "crybaby" reaction. Later, when the war was over and the peace process had begun, Sharon lambasted Shamir for his acquiescence to American moves. Despite Shamir's wish to maintain a low profile on the government's settlement activities in the occupied territories, Sharon repeatedly issued public statements about the number of housing units being built, which were significantly higher than the figures submitted by Shamir's office to the public—and to the U.S. State Department. Shamir, in an August 4 cabinet meeting in which the government accepted in principle the proposal to attend a peace conference, accused Sharon of an "unbridled lust" for power. A few days before the conference itself, Sharon called for Shamir's resignation, in light of his "capitulation" to the Americans and to the Arabs.

On October 15, Binyamin Begin made a surprise announcement that he would seek the post of leader of the Likud, following Shamir.

Shamir's continued engagement in the American-brokered peace process created unrest not only in his own party but also among the seven right-wing members of the Knesset from Tzomet, Tehiya, and Moledet, who were members of his coalition as well. From May onward, these three parties, alone or in conjunction, sent repeated warnings to Shamir that his "collaboration" with the Americans would ultimately topple the government. In late July and early August, as it was becoming increasingly clear that the peace conference would become a reality, it emerged that the Tehiya party was the one in which rank-and-file dissatisfaction with the government was the most serious. On August 7, party leader Yuval Ne'eman, who opposed a Tehiya split from the government, barely succeeded in persuading party institutions from such a decision, persuading them that "we have more influence inside than outside."

The pressures on the three parties increased, however, as the date of the peace conference grew nearer. On October 19, the leaders of the three parties—Tzomet's Rafael Eitan, Tehiya's Yuval Ne'eman, and Moledet's Rehavam Ze'evi—decided on a coordinated policy. It was clear that the three were reluctant to leave their posts just because of a peace conference, which might, after all, change nothing. They therefore decided that their seven members of Knesset would bolt the coalition only when "practical negotiations" over the future of Judea, Samaria, and Gaza had begun. The three declined to offer a definition of the term "practical negotiations."

But the decision was short-lived, as far as Ne'eman and Tehiya were concerned. The next day, October 20, Tehiya's central committee decided by a vote of 34–32 to leave the government. Ne'eman resigned in protest from the leadership of the party, but, in compliance with its decisions, also submitted his resignation from the cabinet. The government's majority had now shrunk from 66–54 to 63–57.

Throughout the year, the Knesset had under consideration a constitutional change that would allow for direct elections for the prime ministership. The extended political deadlock and spate of back-room deals had produced overwhelming popular support for such a change. Prime Minister Shamir, however, had voiced only token support for the change, which would have the effect of severing the prime minister's dependence on coalition politics.

In June and July, it became increasingly clear that Shamir's lackluster support was turning into outright opposition. His office released studies by learned political science professors claiming that the change could lead to a dictatorship. Shamir, it was said, was also concerned about the possible influence that Arab voters would have on the election of the prime minister, and was not too sure of his own chances of success in a one-on-one contest with a Labor candidate. Shamir persuaded his own Likud party to support his position, and in December the Likud central committee decided to impose party discipline on its members when the matter came to a vote in the Knesset. Several Likud members, most notably Netanyahu, said they would vote for the reform anyway.

The Likud decision to impose party discipline ran contrary to an explicit pledge not to do so given to Tzomet when it joined the coalition. In response, Tzomet announced, on December 24, that it would leave the government because of the breach of the promise given in Shamir's own handwriting. As the year closed, it appeared that Shamir's coalition was about to shrink to the bare minimum of 61, with the two votes of Moledet holding the balance.

THE OPPOSITION

The Labor party, at the beginning of the year, was still recuperating from its failed effort in mid-1990 to set up an alternative government. Morale in the chief opposition party sank to a new low, first as a result of Shamir's soaring popularity during the Gulf crisis, and later as a result of the success of the American efforts to arrange a peace conference. A poll released on April 30 confirmed the justification of Labor's despondency: 55 percent said they preferred the Likud's candidates for the prime ministership. An overwhelming majority also said that they wanted the Likud to handle any future peace negotiations, rather than Labor.

There was continuous unrest on the left-wing flank of the party. It was repeatedly reported, though never confirmed, that a sizeable portion of the party's dovish element, led by Haim Ramon and Yossi Beilin, was plotting to bolt the party and join a united leftist front comprising the three left-wing parties in the Knesset: Mapam, Shinui, and the Citizens Rights Movement (*Ratz*). The rumors were enhanced when a joint delegation of leftist members of the Knesset made a controversial trip to the United States in May, where, their detractors said, they intended to "inform" on the government and on its settlement activities in the territories. The three leftist parties conducted negotiations all year on the formation of a united party, and even agreed on the order of precedence in the list of candidates for the Knesset of the yet-to-be-formed party.

Toward the summer, Labor completed its first membership drive in over a decade, with a surprisingly large number, 140,000, joining the party. The drive was a prerequisite for the implementation of the party's historic move toward partywide primaries, which would replace back-room deals as the method for choosing the party leader and candidate for prime minister, as well as its list for the Knesset. The primaries were tentatively scheduled to be held in February or March of 1992.

On the day following the completion of the registration drive, July 2, former prime minister and defense minister Yitzhak Rabin announced that he would compete against party leader Shimon Peres for the leadership of the party. Rabin's announcement produced a flurry of activity, as supporters flocked to both camps and reignited the never-quite-dormant rivalry between Labor's two top leaders.

For the first time, however, the two were not to be alone in their quest for the top. They were soon joined by a host of other Labor hopefuls who believed that the time was ripe for a "changing of the guard" in Labor and that the party had to get rid of both its perennial candidates if it hoped to regain power. Histadrut secretary-general Yisrael Kessar, former ministers Moshe Shahal and Gad Yaakobi, as well as MK Ora Namir, chairwoman of the Labor and Social Affairs Committee, all challenged Peres and Rabin for the helm. The party, meanwhile, was undergoing further institutional reform. On July 7, it approved, for the first time, the registration of party members who were not members of the Histadrut trade-union movement. On July 18, the party changed its official name from "the Alignment" (*Ma'arakh*), which was coined during the now defunct alliance with Mapam, back to "Labor" (*Mifleget Ha'avodah*). On September 2, the party decided to guarantee women one in every five party positions, including its list for the Knesset. Later that month, the party platform was amended so that, for the first time, Labor was no longer committed to opposing either a Palestinian state or negotiations with the PLO.

In a November 18 meeting of the party's largest body, the convention, it became clear that some habits die hard. Bowing to the demands of more than 500 delegates, party leaders agreed to place the socialist "red" flag on the podium, as had been the practice heretofore. Perhaps as a countermeasure, the convention adopted one of its most revolutionary and controversial decisions ever: support for the total separation of religion and state. The decision created an uproar both among the party leadership, which regarded it as self-destructive, and in religious circles, which vowed never to set up a government with Labor again. Labor's radicalism, however, was short-lived: on December 26, another meeting of the convention acceded to Peres's pleas and revoked its earlier decision.

Immigration

The tensions of the Gulf War, significant absorption problems faced by new immigrants, and the American refusal to grant Israel loan guarantees all combined to arrest the spiraling immigration from the Soviet Union. Contrary to widespread expectations that immigration would continue to rise in 1991, the number of immigrants actually dropped considerably: 147,292 came, compared to 184,602 the previous year. Another 5,000 arrived from the rest of Europe, 1,500 from the United States, and 2,500 from Australia, South America, and Asia. The most significant jump in immigration, which indeed made the shortfall from the previous year much less dramatic, was from Ethiopia: 20,010 came, compared to just over 4,000 the previous year.

Throughout the year, the government continued to wrestle with the dilemma that had dogged it since the start of the massive wave of *aliyah*, in 1989: housing or employment. The government had originally decided that housing was the first priority, and, as a direct result, there was increasing unemployment among new immigrants, a fact that was quickly relayed to potential immigrants waiting in the Soviet Union. By May, it was found that over half of the immigrants who had arrived a year earlier were still unemployed.

But the ambitious housing projects also ran into snags. On the one hand, many of the immigrants were housed in prefabricated "caravans," or mobile homes, which did not provide adequate living conditions. On the other hand, it was becoming apparent that the ambitious plans for permanent housing had been based on the optimistic scenario of over a quarter of a million immigrants in 1991. Now, the government was starting to realize, instead of a housing shortage it would be facing a housing surplus, and the government had pledged to buy from the contractors all the apartments that could not be sold on the open market.

On March 10, Housing Minister Ariel Sharon, who had been placed in charge of the "*aliyah* cabinet," which coordinated all the government's absorption activities, resigned. Sharon said that a Finance Ministry decision—subsequently revoked—to cut the "absorption basket" of benefits granted to new immigrants, as well as "failure of the government's employment policies," made his task impossible. A few days later Sharon retracted his resignation, but it was now clear to all that the government's absorption efforts were floundering.

In June, there was concern that the new immigration law about to be put into effect by the Soviet authorities would have a negative effect on Jewish immigration, but Jewish Agency representatives reached agreement with the authorities that would relieve the problem. (The law would include Jews in the overall Soviet emigration apparatus, which would slow down processing and perhaps encourage more Jews to try for immigration to the West.) At the end of the month, nonetheless, there was a burst of immigration as Jews left before the new law came into effect. In October, the first direct flight of immigrants from the USSR was inaugurated; it brought 150 Jews from Kishinev. Another direct flight arrived in November, from Moscow.

In July it was revealed that the incidence of suicides among new immigrants was 20 percent higher than among veteran Israelis. In a poll, most Soviet newcomers revealed that they were advising their relatives to delay coming to Israel until the economic situation improved. The August revolution rekindled hopes that immigration would pick up once again. However, the victory of the prodemocracy forces put that hope to rest, and indeed there were signs that some of the Jews who had already decided to come were now willing to give the new regime a chance to prove that life inside Russia could improve. The breakup of the Soviet Union in December sparked similar hopes.

In the meantime, however, the month of December provided news that created worry and even anger among Israelis: 9,000 new immigrants from the Soviet Union, it was revealed, had applied for immigrant visas to South Africa.

OPERATION SOLOMON

In March of this year, immigration of Jews from Ethiopia was once again abruptly stopped by the Marxist government of Col. Mengistu Haile-Mariam. According to reports in the Israeli press, Mengistu was disappointed that Israel had "failed to live up to its promises" to assist his regime. The Ethiopians denied the charge. One of the Ethiopian leader's chief assistants, Kasa Kabede, told Israel Army Radio on March 23 that the allegation that Ethiopia was holding the Jews as ransom for aid was in itself "extortion." The immigration had been stopped, he said, because of "widespread fraud" by the Jewish Agency officials in the Ethiopian capital, Addis Ababa.

Although Mengistu had cut off emigration after the 1984 "Operation Moses," the secret airlift from Sudan that brought more than 10,000 Jews to Israel, in late 1989 relations between Israel and Ethiopia were reinstated, and Jews were once again allowed to leave, at a slow pace but a steady one.

As the situation of the Mengistu regime grew steadily worse, with rebel forces starting to converge on the capital, Addis Ababa, there was growing concern in Israel that the Jews, most of whom had been brought to Addis Ababa to prepare for emigration, would be caught in the crossfire of the internal revolution. Israel appealed to the United States for help, and Washington began to exert steady pressure on Mengistu to rescind his prohibition on the exit of the Jews. On April 24, President Bush dispatched former senator Rudy Boschwitz as a special emissary to negotiate with the Ethiopian regime on the matter. On April 29, it was reported in Israel that the Jewish Agency was preparing for the "possible arrival of thousands of Jews from Ethiopia."

Mengistu's regime collapsed on May 22, and he himself fled the country to Zimbabwe. A few days later, on May 24–25, Israel carried out one of the most ambitious and dramatic operations in the history of Zionism: a 48-hour airlift, dubbed "Operation Solomon," during which close to 15,000 Jews were spirited out of Addis Ababa just hours before the arrival of the rebel forces. Thirty-six air force and El Al planes, as well one Ethiopian Airlines aircraft, flew in and out of Addis Ababa airport around the clock, bringing out the Jews who had been brought to the site by Jewish Agency personnel and ferrying them, packed in tightly and carrying almost no belongings, to Israel.

The complex details of the operation depended on close cooperation between Ethiopia, Israel, and the United States. The Israeli cabinet had decided on the operation in April, but the IDF insisted that it must be carried out with the explicit agreement of the Ethiopian authorities; otherwise the risk both to the Israeli aircraft and to the Jews themselves would be too great. The negotiations on the Israeli side were carried out by Uri Lubrani, a senior Israeli official, special negotiator, and coordinator of government activities in Lebanon. The United States secured the rebels' agreement not to enter the capital until the operation was finished.

Israel agreed to pay the Ethiopians $35 million, ostensibly to cover the "cost of the operation," which, on paper, was carried out by the Ethiopians. The United States had pledged to try and help the Mengistu regime reach a diplomatic settlement with the rebels. When this failed, Israel also allowed two of Mengistu's top officers to flee the country and seek asylum through Israel. In exchange, the Ethiopians released most of the Jewish population. Some 2,500 remained behind, mostly in remote villages.

The operation galvanized and inspired the Israeli public. In an unprecedented outpouring of sympathy for the newcomers, thousands of Israelis turned up at the makeshift absorption sites where the Ethiopians were placed, carrying bags of clothes and food. Even the normally reticent Prime Minister Shamir was inspired to rhetorical heights by the event: It is not every day, he said, that one is privileged to witness, in reality, a stage in the historic process of the return to Zion. Indeed, Shamir said, in the words of the Psalmist, "we were like dreamers."

In the aftermath of the operation, it emerged that Israel's problems with Ethiopia were far from over. Both the veteran Ethiopian community in Israel and the newcomers were now clamoring for the government to bring over their relatives who had converted to Christianity, known as the "Falash Mora." The Ethiopians said that there were only 6,000–8,000 of these; Jewish Agency specialists said that the numbers were much higher and that most would leap at a chance to leave war- and drought-ridden Ethiopia. The government set up a committee to study the problem.

The arrival of the newcomers sparked yet another round in Israel's perennial *kulturkampf* between the religious and the secular. On June 13, Absorption Minister Yitzhak Peretz, of the ultra-Orthodox Shas party, lashed out against the absorption of Ethiopian immigrants in the kibbutzim. There, he said, the newcomers were "coerced into apostasy." The country's jails, Peretz said, were full of Sephardim who had received their education in kibbutz. Peretz was roundly condemned by secular and kibbutz leaders, who labeled him "a relic of the Middle Ages."

On August 17, the Foreign Ministry in Jerusalem announced that it had reached an agreement with the new regime in Addis Ababa on the exit of the remaining Jews; it was agreed that first the 500–600 unquestioned Jews remaining in Addis Ababa would be released, and then the other 2,000 Jews in the remote villages. The next day the Ethiopians denied the report of an agreement, and Jewish Agency sources criticized the Foreign Ministry for making it public. The Foreign Ministry, Agency officials charged, had jeopardized the safety of the Jews only because it felt it had not gotten its fair share of the glory for Operation Solomon.

However, on September 16, a group of 60 Jews from Ethiopia arrived in Israel, and it was clear that the new Ethiopian government would allow the Jews to leave on condition that their exit not be accompanied by too much publicity and fanfare. By October, 400 Jews had arrived.

IMMIGRATION FROM OTHER COUNTRIES

On April 10, it was revealed that the government and the Jewish Agency had been conducting a secret mission to bring to Israel the last remnants of the tiny Albanian Jewish community. The liberalization in Albania, the last holdout of Marxist Europe, had allowed the authorities to bring 300 Jews to Israel. Another 350 remained behind.

The Jewish community of Bulgaria also appeared to be nearing its end: nearly a fifth of the country's 5,000 Jews came to Israel during 1991. A Jewish Agency mission to Sofia reported, in May, that most of the Bulgarian Jewish community would eventually come to Israel.

The arrival of the Ethiopians spurred the Syrian Jewish community to launch a public campaign aimed at convincing the government to push for the release of 4,000 Jews believed to be living in Syria. On September 11, in Paris, Prime Minister Shamir announced that the "day of the liberation of Syrian Jews is at hand."

On June 20, the government of Yemen denied numerous reports in the foreign press that it was allowing its remaining Jewish community of 1,500 to leave the country.

In November a Jewish Agency emissary to North America reported that American Jews were taking more interest in the possibilities for *aliyah*, because of the recession in the American economy. His report was greeted with skepticism by the authorities. In 1991, 1,360 Jews came from the United States to live in Israel, compared to 1,258 the previous year.

The Economy

The year 1991 was the second in a row marked by a massive influx of immigration and the second straight year of significant increase in investments and other economic activity. Profits and productivity were up, as was the number of jobs. The success, however, was only partial: most of the growth occurred in industries connected to housing; and unemployment continued to soar, going from 9.6 percent to 10.6 percent at the end of the year.

The government's policy was to give direct financial support to the new immigrants for a period of one year, but to let market forces control their absorption as employees. This required incentives for the business sector, such as reduction in taxes, as well as massive government investment in infrastructure. On the other hand, the government decided against managing the housing of the new immigrants through the market but rather by massive direct involvement. The result was that most government funds were diverted to housing, and the construction industry was one that expanded significantly. According to the Bank of Israel, the government did not do enough to fulfill its own policy of spurring economic growth, and by the end of the year, the economy was showing distinct signs of a slowdown.

External developments were also not fortuitous: the Gulf crisis, which began in 1990, damaged exports and created an atmosphere of uncertainty that diminished the will to invest. The Israeli economy itself came to a virtual standstill for a period of over a month, as the population cowered at home in anticipation of the Iraqi missile attacks, and Palestinian workers from the territories were barred from crossing over the Green Line. The worldwide economic recession and the ensuing slowdown in the growth of world trade had a commensurate negative effect on Israeli exports. Israel's trade deficit, for goods and services, was $7,213,000, the result of $18,739,000 in exports compared to $25,952,000 in imports. Israel's total foreign debt grew slightly, from $32 billion to $33 billion; the government share of the debt was $17 billion. On the other hand, Israel had $18 billion in foreign-currency assets, of which $6.3 billion was foreign reserves held by the Bank of Israel.

Europe was Israel's biggest trading partner, with $10 billion in imports and $5 billion in exports. The biggest European trading partner was Germany, with $2 billion in exports to Israel and $1.8 from Israel. The United States was Israel's biggest single trading partner, with $3.3 billion in exports to Israel and $3.6 billion in imports from Israel.

Business production increased by a respectable 7 percent, but this was almost exclusively the result of the government outlays for housing. The housing needs brought about a drastic jump in imports—17 percent—while exports actually decreased by slightly over 2 percent.

The expansion of the work force caused an unusual drop in real wages—4 percent—but this, once again, was mainly the result of the building industry's expansion. In other sectors, the wage level remained stable.

The number of employed Israelis was 1,583,100; the unemployment rate was 10.6 percent—8.6 percent among men and 13.4 percent among women. Some 503,000 married women were included in the work force, an increase of 10 percent over the previous year. Unemployment actually went down among veteran Israelis, but was especially high among new immigrants—between 40 and 50 percent. The high rate of unemployment was thought to be one of the main reasons for the slowdown in the rate of immigration, which, in turn, upset the short-term projections for an even faster growth of the economy.

Inflation ran at 19 percent, the normal level for the Israeli economy since the successful stabilization program of 1985. More than 3 percent of the inflation rate was created by the housing industry alone.

The state budget for 1992, submitted to the cabinet for early perusal in September, totaled $34 billion, and included a 6-percent increase in defense spending, coupled with a 3-percent across-the-board cut in other ministries. The deficit was set at 6.3 percent of the Gross Domestic Product.

KEY ECONOMIC EVENTS

On January 1, the Value Added Tax imposed on all goods was raised from 16 to 18 percent. In addition, to assist in immigrant absorption, a special "absorption levy" was imposed, at a rate of 5 percent of the annual income-tax rate.

On April 1, the basic coin of one *agora* was abolished, and the prices adjusted to the nearest 5 *agorot*, when payments are made in cash.

On May 7, responding to pressures from the public and against the wishes of the government, the Knesset decided on massive reform of mortgages. The highest mortgage, for eligibles, was doubled, from 80,000 NIS to 160,000 NIS for 25–30 year mortgages, at a maximum interest rate of 4 percent. On July 14, the government announced a series of measures aimed at alleviating the debts of those who took out mortgages during the hyperinflation years of 1980–1985.

On May 12, 45-year-old Yaakov Frankel, top economic adviser of the International Monetary Fund, was appointed governor of the Bank of Israel.

On September 1, the government announced a series of measures aimed at exposing protected local industries to competition from abroad.

On November 28, the government announced a series of measures aimed at further liberalization of the foreign currency regulations: Israeli residents could henceforth exchange one foreign currency deposit for another; the ceiling for imports using credit cards was raised from $500 annually to $1,500; the ceiling for interest rates on bank deposits held by foreigners was abolished.

On March 10, the shekel was devalued by 6 percent. On December 16, the government adjusted its foreign-exchange rate system, fixing a daily devaluation of 0.0236 percent, or 9 percent annually.

Vital Statistics

The population of Israel passed the five-million mark during the course of 1991, reaching 5,058,800 at the end of the year. The number of Jews was 4,144,600, or 81.9 percent; 701,400 Muslims, or 13.9 percent; 128,000 Christians, or 2.5 percent; and 84,800 Druze and others, or 1.7 percent. The Arab population of the West Bank was 1,005,000; of the Gaza Strip, 676,100.

The ratio of males to females continued to drop, from 990 males for every 1,000 females in 1990, to 986 in 1991. Among Jews, the ratio was 979 per thousand; among Christians, 944 per thousand; among Muslims, 1,030 per thousand. There were 105,725 births, 31,246 deaths, 24,263 marriages, and 5,662 divorces. Of 712,700 households, 67,200 were single-parent households, of which 36,600 were headed by divorcees or widows and 24,500 by never-married persons.

The Jewish population comprised 32 percent of all world Jewry, a jump of 2 percent over the previous year. It grew by 4.9 percent during the year, mainly due to the 178,200 immigrants who arrived. The Muslim population of Israel grew by 3.5 percent, just slightly above the previous year's growth rate. The Christian population grew by a dramatic 11.6 percent, due to the nearly 10,000 Christian dependents of Jewish immigrants.

Jerusalem continued to be the country's most populous city, the number of its inhabitants increasing by 20,000, to 544,200. There were 353,000 inhabitants in Tel Aviv, and 251,000 in Haifa. The population of the greater Tel Aviv metropolitan area grew by over 60,000, reaching 1,843,700 at the end of the year.

The immigration from Russia effected slight changes in the internal composition of the population: the proportion of Asian- and African-born Jews decreased by 1.4 percent, reaching 37.9 percent at the end of year; the proportion of European- or American-born Jews increased, reaching 39.7 percent. The proportion of Israeli-born Jews remained steady at 22.4 percent.

There was a sharp drop in tourism, mainly because of the Gulf War. The 943,300 tourists who came represented a drop of over 10 percent from 1990, which was itself a weak year for tourism. The continental breakdown of tourists was 8 percent from Asia, 3 percent from Africa, 56 percent from Europe, and 27 percent from North America. By individual countries, the United States continued to be the largest source of tourists, followed, at a distance, by France, the United Kingdom, and Germany.

Israel had a total of 848,000 private cars, a jump of over 40,000 over the previous year. Accidents continued to climb at an alarming rate: 19,417 in 1991, compared to 17,496 the previous year; 444 people were killed and 31,541 injured in these accidents, compared to 427 and 27,668, respectively, the previous year.

The median education of Israelis in 1991 was 11.7 years of schooling, up one-tenth of a percent from the previous year. In 1961, the median education was eight years of schooling. Among all Israelis, 11.6 percent had a postgraduate education, another 14.5 percent had a university degree, and a further 35.6 percent had finished high school; 5.6 percent of those 15 and over had no schooling at all. A total of 1,571,119 students were enrolled in educational institutions of one kind or another, up 60,000 from the previous year, most likely due to the wave of immigration. Of these, 293,000 were in kindergartens and 120,000 were enrolled in universities and other postsecondary schools. Tel Aviv University was the country's biggest institution of higher learning, with an enrollment of 21,530, followed by the Hebrew University of Jerusalem with 18,610, Bar-Ilan University with 11,930, the Technion in Haifa with 10,280, Haifa University with 8,120 students, Ben-Gurion University of the Negev with 7,490 students, and the Weizmann Institute of Science, with 680. Of the undergraduate degrees bestowed, 25 percent were in the humanities; 28 percent in the social sciences; and 16 percent in engineering and architecture.

Other Noteworthy Events

The Supreme Court appeal of John Demjanjuk, suspected of being "Ivan the Terrible" of the Treblinka death camp during World War II, continued throughout the year. On March 6, the court denied a petition by Demjanjuk's lawyer for his client's immediate release, and postponed the rendering of its judgment in order to allow the sides to gather new evidence uncovered in hitherto-secret files in the Soviet Union. On December 23, the court convened again. Demjanjuk's attorney, Yoram Sheftel, said that the Demjanjuk case was a latter-day Dreyfus affair. By the end of the year, the court had yet to make its judgment on the appeal.

The long-awaited trial of Israel's leading bankers began on July 10. The heads of eight major banks were charged with having rigged the sales of bank shares on the Israeli stock market for several years, a practice that ultimately led to the collapse of the shares and a government bailout that cost billions of taxpayer shekels. When the scandal erupted in 1983, the heads of the banks were all replaced.

On November 13, the Knesset stripped MK Yair Levy of his parliamentary immunity so that he could be prosecuted on charges of fraud, forgery, and mishandling of funds. The prosecution of Levy, a member of the ultra-Orthodox Shas party, was an offshoot of an ongoing police investigation of the party's leader, Interior Minister Arye Deri. The investigation of Deri on suspicion of misuse of government funds for both institutional and private gain continued throughout the year.

On January 2, State Comptroller Miriam Ben Porat published a scathing condemnation of the country's water conservation efforts, noting that negligent management had brought Israel's water reserves to the point of depletion.

The Israel Philharmonic Orchestra, conducted by Daniel Barenboim, played two compositions of German composer Richard Wagner, on December 29. It was the first time that the Israeli orchestra had performed anything by the German composer, whose music and philosophy had been adopted by the Nazi regime and who was widely judged to be anti-Semitic. Bowing to public protests, the orchestra performed the pieces during an open rehearsal and not in a formal concert.

British press magnate Robert Maxwell, who drowned early in November off the Canary Islands in mysterious circumstances, was laid to rest in the Mount of Olives Cemetery on November 10. He was eulogized by President Chaim Herzog. "He scaled the heights of human endeavor," said Herzog. "Kings and princes waited on him. Many admired him. Many disliked him. But none was indifferent to him." Prime Minister Yitzhak Shamir said that Maxwell had been an "enthusiastic friend of Israel."

Personalia

U.S. ambassador to Israel William Brown was replaced in August by William Harrop, a 62-year-old career diplomat.

Prof. Yoram Dinstein, 52, noted expert in international law, was appointed president of Tel Aviv University, on May 13.

Ovadia Sofer, Israeli ambassador to France, returned home after more than ten years at his post, in November. Sofer was the longest-serving Israeli diplomat abroad, and his continued stay in Paris aroused much criticism in the Israeli press.

Eliahu Matza, 56, was appointed the 11th Supreme Court judge, in March, and Mishael Cheshin, 56, the 12th, in December.

Among prominent Israelis who died this year were Herzl Rosenblum, Revisionist activist, signer of the Declaration of Independence, and editor of the daily *Yediot Aharonot* (1949–1983), in February, aged 87; Mordechai Ish-Shalom, mayor of Jerusalem (1959–1965), in February, aged 90; Miriam Bernstein-Cohen, a pioneer of the Hebrew stage in Israel, in April, aged 96; Prof. Haim Hanani, first rector of Ben-Gurion University of the Negev, in April, aged 78; Yosef Tekoah, veteran diplomat, Israeli ambassador to the United Nations, and chancellor of Ben-Gurion University, in April, aged 65; Sir Isaac Wolfson, businessman, philanthropist, and leader of British Jewry, in his home in Rehovot, in June, aged 93; Prof. Ephraim Urbach, leading scholar of Jewish law, recipient of the Israel Prize, and past president of the Israel Academy of Sciences, in July, aged 79; Prof. Yaakov Haim Polotzki, founder of the Linguistics and Egyptology faculty at the Hebrew University of Jerusalem, in August, aged 86; Yeroham Cohen, one of the founders of the Israel intelligence services and Palmach commander, in August, aged 75; Prof. Zvi Adar, first teacher of education at the Hebrew University, in August, aged 74; Prof. Mikhail Agursky, Soviet-born scientist and Sovietologist, in Moscow, while covering the August revolution for an Israeli newspaper, aged 58; Prof. Moshe Goshen-Gottstein, noted Hebrew, Semitics, and Bible scholar, in September, aged 66; Maj. Gen. (ret.) Shmuel Gonen (Gorodish), armored corps hero of the Six Day War and commander of the southern front during the 1973 war, who was subsequently removed from his post by the Agranat Commission of Inquiry, in September, aged 61; Prof. Dan Horwitz, prominent sociologist and political scientist, in September, aged 63; Avraham Tohami, founder of the prestate Irgun Zvai Leumi underground movement, in October, aged 88; Yosef Almogi, Labor party leader, government minister, mayor of Haifa, and chairman of the Jewish Agency, in November, aged 81; Mordechai Zarfati ("Mentesch"), Israel's "godfather," with prominent links to both business and criminal circles, in November, aged 76; Avraham Schweitzer, economics editor of *Ha'aretz* and leading publicist, in December, aged 68; Moshe Kastel, one of the first Israeli artists to gain international recognition, in December, aged 85; Eitan Livni, operations officer of the prestate Irgun Zvai Leumi and Herut member in three Knessets, in December, aged 72.

MENACHEM SHALEV

Israeli Culture

The Performing Arts

THE CULTURAL FOMENT AND VITALITY of the 1980s continued into the early 1990s. The direction of cultural activity, though, was inevitably influenced by two crucial social-political developments that took place during 1990 and 1991: the mass immigration of Jews from the former Soviet Union and the Gulf War.

During the Gulf War (January and February, 1991), all public performances were canceled for six weeks by order of the Civil Defense Authority of the Israel Defense Forces, and even afterward it took Israelis some time to get back into the spirit of attending concerts, plays, and dance performances. Consequently, the overall statistics of the Center for Cultural Information and Research for 1990–1991 show declines in the number of performances and attendance at cultural events.

There was some speculation that the trauma experienced by Tel Avivians during the Gulf War would leave its mark on Israel's cultural life. Tel Aviv is the center of the arts in Israel. The local Tel Aviv newspapers are arbiters of cultural fashion. Moreover, a self-consciously "yuppie" Tel Aviv cultural image developed during the 1980s, with Tel Avivians who consider themselves cosmopolitan cultivating an intense interest in Western film, theater, rock music, and the like. Many social commentators felt that Tel Avivian confidence was shaken by the war. Scuds falling in the Greater Tel Aviv area and the subsequent exile in the provinces brought many Tel Avivians to question themselves, their doubts often expressed through fiction, comedy revues, and popular music. In certain cases, artists discovered more authentic life values outside the big city. It remained to be seen whether this self-examination would continue, perhaps finding deeper expression in a Tel Aviv culture that was less alienated from the rest of the country.

The effect of the Russian *aliyah* on the cultural life of Israel became evident very quickly. The 10,000 Russian artists who immigrated to Israel during 1990 and 1991 created a "critical mass," their very number affecting the expansion of theater, musical life, and education. Despite some criticism that the Russians, although technically proficient, lacked Western approaches and interpretive skills, this serious, highly skilled cadre of immigrant artists noticeably raised the level of the various arts. In terms of cultural consumerism, surveys showed that the percentage of Russian immigrants attending cultural events was greater than that of veteran Israelis. This portended well for the future of Israeli culture.

Some general long-range trends relating to public appreciation of the arts were not as positive. A study by the Israel Institute of Applied Research comparing the use of leisure time in 1970 and 1990 indicated that, although there was an increase in the percentage of Israelis going to college, there was a decrease in participation in certain cultural activities. The numbers of people who read books, attended concerts, and visited museums remained stable, but there was a decrease in movie- and theater-going and attendance at lectures. Instead, Israelis were spending more leisure time listening to records, taking trips abroad, and sitting in nightclubs, cafes, and pubs. The degree of participation in high culture was lower among Israelis with 13+ years of education in 1990 than it was among those with 11 or more years of education in 1970. In the case of the performing arts, particularly theater, this might be attributed to a decline in the presale of tickets through organized frameworks such as schools and workers' committees, a once thriving paternalistic system of subsidized ticket distribution.

An important development in Israeli culture was the mushrooming of festivals for dance, drama, classical music, rock, and jazz. These events, held throughout the country, combined tourism with culture and created new forms of local support for the performing arts.

Theater

Israeli theater was becoming less political and more family-oriented, with both its audiences and the leading characters in plays showing signs of aging. The themes and topics of plays focused on more personal subjects, family, and parent-child relationships than on the Arab-Israeli conflict or the army and war issues that were prominent in the 1980s.

During the 1970s and 1980s, a number of native Israeli playwrights were nurtured at Haifa Theater, the hothouse of experimental, socially conscious theater of the time. *Ha'aretz* critic Michael Handelsatz has traced the two major dramatic ap- proaches that emerged: Yehoshua Sobol's socio-political theater and Hanoch Levin's more universal theater of the absurd. Sobol used social documentary and historical sources to create plays that grapple with issues of Jewish identity and the Arab-Israeli conflict. Most of the young playwrights followed his direction, and socio-political concerns dominated the theater of the '80s. Even when presenting classics, political interpretation was primary. In a production of *Waiting for Godot*, for example, the two main characters were depicted as Arab construction workers.

The other direction with which Israeli theater experimented was the absurd drama of Hanoch Levin, with tight, poetic dialogue and a grotesque, obsessively anal, misogynist vision of humanity. Although he could be bitterly satirical about Israeli social issues, as in *Queen of the Bathtub* (*Malchat Ha'ambatya*), Levin wrote out of a more universal context. However, this did not become the dominant stream. The need for political relevance was too great.

Eventually, audiences wearied of being confronted with the Arab-Israeli conflict. The *intifada* was ubiquitous in the media. Israelis did not want to see it on the stage as well. In addition, officials of the Likud government fought the use of public funds for theater which, they claimed, undermined national morale. This led to a collision course with engaged playwrights who went on to write even more vituperative plays. Ironically, the attempt to close down some of these plays and the attendant furor brought an end in 1990 to official censorship. (The censorship law, based on the British law of 1911, had been incorporated into the Israeli legal system along with other British statutes at the time of the establishment of the State of Israel.)

In the early 1990s, leading figures in Israeli theater, such as the artistic director of Jerusalem's Khan Theater, Erann Baniel, called for a different kind of esthetic, one that was less journalistic and scandal-involved and more concerned with the larger human condition. In addition to new plays on more personal themes, the movement away from political theater also led to more light, escapist theater, such as the 1991 Haifa Theater production of *Guys and Dolls* with a star-studded Israeli cast, and performances of Neil Simon comedies.

RECENT PLAYS

In spite of the general decline of socio-political theater, two of the best plays of 1990 and 1991 had themes relating to the current Israeli situation. Yehoshua Sobol's Habimah production of *Solo*, a historical drama about 18th-century philosopher Baruch Spinoza, with contemporary anticlerical, church-state implications, was one of the theatrical highlights of 1991. Spinoza is portrayed as a truth-seeker, not reluctant to embarrass the Jewish community "in the eyes of the non-Jews," something Sobol himself was accused of doing with his Holocaust play *Ghetto*. Although Sobol scrupulously presents Spinoza's theories of an abstract God, indifferent to the world, who claims that there is "no end or goal, good or bad, order or hierarchy in Nature," he also translates Spinoza's ideas into a simplistic hedonism graphically displayed on the stage, making Spinoza more of an unheroic contemporary Everyman than most critics felt was legitimate.

The Arab-Jewish conflict found expression in Ilan Hatzor's fine *intifada*-based play *Re'ulim* (The Masked), first appearing at the Acre Fringe Theater Festival and then at the Cameri Theater. It is the story of three Palestinian brothers meeting in Italy. Two of the brothers belong to the Palestinian shock forces that assassinate those thought to be informers, while the third is himself suspected of being an informer for Israeli intelligence. In the background is the painful memory of a fourth brother who was shot by Israeli soldiers. Although the play clearly relates to political issues, it is a poignant work about family relationships and loyalties under stress.

Romantic love relationships are exposed for their grotesque sexuality in the Hanoch Levin plays of this period. *Can't Choose (Ha'mitlabeit)* is the story of an unattractive bachelor seeking to get married, and the three equally unattractive options before him, while in *Hops and Hopla*, a mama's boy attempts to woo a childhood sweetheart by trying to get her to diaper him. *The Beloved (Ha'ne'ehavim)*, by Hillel Mittelpunkt, an important playwright associated with the Beersheba Theater, portrays the near-incestuous relationships of a Tennessee Williams-type family.

A moving original work at the Haifa Theater was *Vienna-on-the-Sea* (*Vina al Ha'yam*) by Edna Mazya, portraying a group of Viennese Jews at their seashore resort on the eve of the 1938 Anschluss. The most innovative dramatic work of the past two years was a five-and-a-half-hour "happening," *Arbeit Macht Frei*, which has the Holocaust as its theme but is different from anything done heretofore. Designed by Dudu Maayan of the Acre Theater Company, the work won first prize in the Acre Fringe Theater Festival during Sukkot of 1991, again indicating the importance of this festival in encouraging experimental works. *Arbeit Macht Frei*, which accommodates an audience of only 15 participants at a time, breaks down all boundaries between art and life. It begins with a tour of the Holocaust Museum of Kibbutz Lochamei Hagetaot and moves its participants from experience to experience, showing how the Israeli sensibility has been formed by Holocaust-consciousness and suggesting that the paranoia it engendered has not always been to the advantage of the Arabs. But its message is never unequivocal, as it attempts to elicit from participants their own deeply felt responses.

At a time when Israeli theater was witnessing the end of the Sobol-Levin generation and seeking new directions, awaiting the emergence of new young playwrights, the experimental group-theory approach of the Acre Theater, the innovative puppet-and-object drama of Jerusalem's Visual Theater, and the Khan Theater's community-oriented drama—subsidized by the Jerusalem Foundation—all offered vital new options. At the same time, it was possible that rejuvenation would come from the conservative but highly professional Russian immigrants who were now working on the Israeli stage, imbuing it with the "high seriousness" of classical European culture. The Russian-language Gesher Theater presented a much-acclaimed production of Tom Stoppard's *Rosencrantz and Guildenstern Are Dead*, which Israeli spectators could enjoy through earphones with simultaneous translation. Gesher saw itself as eventually performing in Hebrew as well as Russian, as the immigrants to whom it was directed became absorbed in Israeli society.

Film

Israeli film also turned away from political themes in 1990 and 1991 to personal relationships. Particularly noteworthy were *Shuru* by Sabi Gavison and *Tel Aviv Stories* by Ayelet Menachemi and Nirit Yaron. The former is about a Tel Aviv self-fulfillment cult, while the latter is a slick feminist comedy.

Although the Israeli film industry produced only 19 films in 1990 and 5 works in 1991—because of the war—there were signs of continuing expansion. The Beit Zvi Film School closed, giving way to the Jerusalem Film School, which boasted state-of-the-art equipment and offered competition to the Tel Aviv University Film School, which had dominated the education of Israel's future filmmakers. The movement to cable TV and the establishment of TV Channel Two promised new opportunities for the cultivation of film and TV in Israel. The opening of the sophisticated Golan-Globus film production complex in the Jerusalem hills raised the hope of attracting foreign filmmakers as well as encouraging a new wave of Israeli filmmakers to create works of international interest.

Dance

Israel had six professional dance companies—Batsheva, the Israel Ballet, Bat Dor, Sound and Silence, Kibbutz, and Inbal—and a number of smaller ensembles. Many of them had undergone recent transformations, as leadership was transferred from the giants who created Israeli dance to a new generation of artistic directors and choreographers.

At Inbal, Rina Sharett succeeded the pioneering Sara Levi-Tannai, who was responsible for creating a language of movement based on traditional Middle Eastern, and particularly Yemenite, ethnic dance, which emphasizes movement in a restricted area, height and depth rather than breadth. Sharett's work brings a broader range of ethnic dance languages to bear, as reflected in her "Bring My Fortune," based on North African premarital customs.

The most significant event of the last few years was the return of the internationally renowned choreographer Ohad Naharin to Israel as artistic director of the Batsheva Dance Company. Israeli-born Naharin began his dance training at Batsheva but was invited to become a member of Martha Graham's company in the United States. He later left it to explore other dance forms and started his own company based in New York.

Batsheva was founded by Martha Graham in 1964 under the auspices of Baroness Batsheva de Rothschild. Graham was its first artistic director, and Batsheva became the only foreign company in the world permitted to perform her works. Recognized for its energy and vitality, the company was constantly searching for new directions and seeking to crystallize a unique identity.

The strong, sculptured character of Ohad Naharin's approach to dance quickly became evident in such new works as "Kyr" (Wall) and "Axiom." "Kyr" was interpreted as depicting the struggles of a country under constant threat. Between the outbursts of war and violence—expressed by Naharin through fierce, almost chaotic, explosions of movement, wild jumps, and twitching bodies, accompanied by the rock music of the "Tractor's Revenge" group—are sober, modest moments of utter control, the inner strength that is the supporting wall of the country. "Axiom" shows dancers marching in a regimented line until one person breaks out to do a solo, shattering the old order by this anarchistic impulse and creating a new, less regimented one. Dance critic Heski Leskli found "an unbearable beauty of anger and despair in Naharin's works."

Music

The most important new developments on the Israeli music scene were a consequence of the influx of immigrant musicians from the former Soviet Union. It is estimated that 7,000 immigrant musicians/music teachers arrived by the end of 1991, transforming music life and music education in Israel.

All of Israel's established orchestras gained from the Russian influx, and new orchestras have flourished. The Rishon Lezion Symphony Orchestra, under the direction of Noam Sheriff, with more than half of its players new Russian immigrants, has been hailed as the country's second most important orchestra, trailing only behind the Israel Philharmonic. The last few years witnessed the creation of the New Israel Opera, in which many Russian singers appeared. New orchestras involving Russian immigrants were created in Tel Aviv, Raanana, Ramat Gan, and the Galilee. Community orchestras also thrived as a consequence of the Russian immigrants. The Hebrew University-B'nai B'rith Hillel Orchestra, under Anita Kamien, consisted primarily of Russians and played increasingly challenging works. In addition, hundreds of chamber concerts and recitals were sponsored by museums and various public and private groups seeking to give Russian immigrants the opportunity to perform. It even became popular for Israelis to invite Russian musicians to play at private parties and festive family occasions.

Although the whole country was enlisted to help absorb the immigrant Russian musicians, their disproportionate numbers and varying levels of accomplishment made it impossible for all of them to find work in their field. Viktor Fischer, artistic director of the Russian Cultural Center in Jerusalem, claimed that almost all of the musicians who were active performing artists in Russia found jobs, while those who worked previously as music teachers had considerable difficulty finding work. To help provide jobs for Russian music teachers, publicly subsidized music education was being expanded in community centers and schools.

The percentage of Israeli compositions performed in 1990 was higher than in 1989. According to composer Menachem Tzur, chairman of the Israel Composers' League, one reason was that the large number of performers created more opportunities for original Israeli works to be played. Tzur maintained, too, that Israeli composers, seeking better ways to communicate with their audiences, "are bringing lyricism back into their compositions."

One legitimate means of doing this was to integrate folk material into compositions. The Russian-born Mark Kopytman and Hungarian-born Andre Hajdu were representatives of this approach. In addition, Odeon Partos, Mordechai Seter, and Zvi Avni used Jewish and Middle Eastern materials, while Tzippy Fleischer used Arab melodies. The integration of folk themes characterized the "Mediterranean" music created by the late Paul Ben-Haim and Alexander Boscovitch in the early days of the state, which later came to be seen as too self-conscious and heavy-handed. Recent works using folklore dialectically fused it with a more sophisticated, Western musical language. The much-respected Zvi Avni, for example, returned to folk elements after having imbibed contemporary European music. He confessed that his present compositions exhibited "a very different orientalism from that found in my earlier work."

Andre Hajdu, who had written compositions based on Jewish sources—Mishnah, Psalms, Jonah, Eastern European folklorism—saw his works as postmodernist parody and eclecticism. It is this ironic stance, a distancing from the folk materials at the same time that they are used, that differentiates Hajdu and composers like him from the earlier nationalistic ones. Other composers, like Joseph Tal, continued to emphasize the European cultural tradition and the connection to Schoenberg. Menachem Tzur explained that there was a contemporary trend to look to classical composers of the recent past for inspiration, and he himself integrated them into his compositions *Letter to Schoenberg* and *Letter to Stravinsky*.

Altogether, a pluralism of musical styles had gained legitimacy. Josef Marchaim and Ron Verdberg used pop and jazz elements in their works. Some Russian immigrant composers remained conservative, imitating older composers, while others, overwhelmed by the new freedom, became super avant-garde, and still others turned to jazz for its free, improvisational style. In general, jazz had become increasingly popular in Israel. Yahud, a Tel Aviv suburb, had become a jazz center, and a jazz festival took place there each year.

Literature: Fiction

Israeli fiction flourished in 1990 and 1991, extending the rich literary pluralism that had developed in the preceding decade. The symbolic-psychological modes of "native generation" writers like Amos Oz and A.B. Yehoshua, whose narratives were often allegorical constructs of the larger monolithic Israeli experience, no longer dominated Israeli literature. With the decline in the 1980s of the secular, Ashkenazic, Labor Zionist establishment and those expressing their concerns, works of those who had until then been viewed as peripheral—Sephardim, Israeli Arabs, religious, and most of all women—moved to the center of Israeli fiction. Personal narrative without a national, public subtext became legitimate. Childhood, coming of age, and family relationships were central themes in novels of the early '90s, expressed through a variety of literary styles—magic realism, surrealism, and postmodernism. Israeli literature underwent a process of democratization that resulted in an explosion of talent.

In publishing circles there was a headiness over these new voices. A battle of editors was waged in 1990 and 1991 as to who could "discover" the brightest, most innovative novelists. Some contend that the young writers were so encouraged because translations of foreign works became increasingly expensive. But even when the new fruit was unripe, as some inevitably was, there was exhilaration in literary circles over the signs of cultural vitality.

Still, fine works by veteran writers continued to be published. In Amos Oz's *Third Condition* (*Hamatzav Hashlishi*), the fumbling impotence of the middle-aged antihero Fima Nissan can be perceived as reflecting the impotence of the Israeli intellectual in the face of the *intifada*. Nissan's refuge in sleep—escape—also characterizes the protagonist in *The Railway (Mesilat Barzel)*, the attenuated existential novel by Aharon Appelfeld about a nameless Holocaust survivor who obsessively rides the trains through Romania and Czechoslovakia. In this spare, symbolic work, Appelfeld implies that the train—with its allusion to the satanic machinery that carried millions of Jews to their destruction—is the very environment in which post-Holocaust Jewry continues to exist.

The suppressed violence, underground sexuality, and self-destruction in Appelfeld and Oz also permeate A.B. Yehoshua's masterpiece *Mr. Mani (Mar Mani)*, hailed as the most important Israeli novel of the last two years, "breaking new structural ground," according to Hebrew literature scholar Gershon Shaked. Perhaps it was a reflection of the new literary atmosphere that Yehoshua, who stems from an old Sephardic family that came to Israel at the beginning of the 19th century, had only recently begun to write about his Sephardic background. *Mr. Mani* (subsequently translated into English by Hillel Halkin) is a haunting saga of a Sephardic Jewish family, presented in reverse chronology, with the first chapter taking place in 1982 after the Lebanon War, while the last part occurs in Athens in 1848. Here the reader is introduced to the Mani family through the conversation of Avraham Mani, the progenitor of this strange clan.

The unique structure of the book consists of five conversations about the family, where only one speaker's voice is heard, and the reaction of the listener must be interpolated by the reader. Each of the speakers has been involved with a member of the Mani family, and their recollections of the Manis also mirror their own life situations. As in his previous novels, in which family relationships symbolize larger national, societal patterns, the epic of the Mani family depicts the sweep of Jewish history for more than a century, the drive for Jewish survival and, at the same time, the countermovements to assimilation and destruction. In each generation, the Mani family is caught between the two opposing tendencies. Central to the work is the assimilative yearning of Israelis to cancel out their Galut Jewish origins and return to some mythical time when Arab and Jew were one. Yehoshua ultimately rejects this fantasy and affirms Jewish existence in Israel, albeit in a casual, nonheroic, "normal" manner. But not before he has grappled with contemporary Jewish experience in all its subtle variations.

MAGIC REALISM, GROTESQUE REALISM, SURREALISM

The need to keep in touch with present Israeli reality, at the same time using it as a springboard for flights of fancy that defy that reality, might explain the emergence of many fine "coming of age" works that border on the fantastic and surrealistic. The Israeli family is the continued leitmotif in many of these works.

Meir Shalev's first novel, the best-seller *Blue Mountain (Roman Russie)*, uses the fantastical mode of magic realism to trace the amazing feats of an Israeli pioneering family. His new novel, *Esau*, is another family saga, this one interweaving elements of biblical tales into a crazy-quilt Jerusalem myth. Although Shalev is abundant in symbolic suggestiveness, he does not attempt to create, as do Yehoshua and Oz, a sustained allegorical pattern.

In *The Book of Internal Grammar* (*Sefer Hadikduk Ha'pnimi*), David Grossman exhibits the same uncanny ability to enter into a child's mind that he did in *See Under: Love* (*R'eh Erekh Ahavah*). The sexually overwrought events of his family are perceived by the child protagonist, whose own growth seems stunted. The larger-than-life scenes of his mother cooking magnificent meals for his corpulent father, the love-sick neighbor who thrills to watch the father break down wall after wall of her house with a wrecker's hammer, are all counterpointed by the adolescent protagonist's anxieties about his own sexuality and his prayers for his thyroid to grow.

Albert Swissa's *Bound Up* (*Akud*) describes a Sephardic "coming of age" in a Jerusalem slum. Written with metaphorical sweep, it combines the sordid with the sublime, the realistic with the phantasmagorical. Israelis who hoped that this would be the literary masterpiece encapsulating the experience of the Jews who came from Arab countries in the 1950s were disappointed. Although Swissa's talent was clear, some critics felt the work was overwritten. One called it "gutter theology," and *Ha'aretz* critic Ariel Hirshfeld said the young writer should have taken more time to create a more controlled work. He saw it as an example of editors allowing unripe fiction to be published.

Fifty-five-year-old Yehoshua Knaz is a "native generation" writer whose works only recently began to receive the attention they deserve. His increasing popularity reflected new appreciation of older novelists who were overlooked because of their more personal themes and nonsymbolic modes of writing. In *The Way to the Cats* (*Derekh L'hatulim*), Knaz portrays, with grotesque realism, the marginal lives of the aged. The story of Yolanda Moscovitch, ravaged and powerless in an old-age home, entangled in the familylike power struggle among its inhabitants and the cynical exploitation of the staff, was hailed a masterpiece by fellow novelist Amos Oz. "In sharp, brutal detail Knaz describes the torment, madness, absurdity, and decay that wait for all of us at the end," writes Oz.

POSTMODERNIST NOVELS

The last few years saw the publication of many postmodernist novels in which values and points of view break down. There is little or no authorial direction, and readers must impose their own personal narrative on the work to make sense of it. "With this new wave of postmodernist works," says Yigal Schwartz, "Israel is in synchrony with the literary trends of the Western world. The previous generation asserted the individual in a relativistic, humanistic approach. But for this generation reality is unreadable. There is no point of view one can rely on." This is most evident in Itamar Levy's *Letters of the Sun, Letters of the Moon* (*Otiot Hashemesh, Otiot*

Hayereh). At the simplest level, Levy's story is a narrative told from the perspective of a 12-year-old Palestinian boy during the *intifada*. But the tale becomes more than the story of a Palestinian childhood under occupation. Rather, it is a collage of storytelling, folklore, and Arab pop songs, magically fused with realistic political events. Slowly, the reader comes to realize that he can't trust any point of view.

Yoel Hoffman's much acclaimed *Christ of the Fishes* (*Christus shel Dagim*) is also not the story it seems to be—that of a German immigrant family facing one death after another—but rather a work on how one looks at this reality. By flattening perspective, introducing doubts into the narrative, and breaking down distinctions between what is important and what is peripheral in his sharply detailed, Zenlike parables, Hoffman points up the unreliability of the realistic narrative.

Orly Castel-Bloom's controversial work *Where Am I?* (*Heikhan ani nimtzet?*) can be seen as another type of postmodernist novel. It is a picaresque tale of a madcap woman who surrenders one identity after another—wife, student, professional. Angry and alienated, never remaining the same person, she gives herself to unbounded fantasies. In Yigal Schwartz's view, Castel-Bloom's contempt for convention and feeling of isolation are reminiscent of punk culture, "the common recognition of the need for, or realization of, violent social and cultural protest." Perhaps more than a social revolutionary, Orly Castel-Bloom can be seen as bringing to the surface the repressed anger and violence that have existed in the works of Israeli women writers from Devorah Baron to Amalia Kahan-Carmon and Yehudit Hendel. This resentment could be discerned in many other young women writers emerging in the last few years, such as Dorit Abusch and Elana Bernstein.

THE DETECTIVE NOVEL

Until recently, Israeli literature belonged primarily to the category of "high culture," with highly stylized works devoted to serious themes. Works of "trivial literature," including detective stories, spy novels, and cheap romances, were read, but they were translations of foreign books. In the last few years, Israel became "normalized." It was not only a nation like all other nations with thieves and murderers, it now also had writers of detective novels for Israeli audiences. Batya Gur, the pioneering figure in the field, who began with *A Saturday Morning Murder: A Psychoanalytic Case* (*Retzah b'shabbat baboker*) in the late 1980s, shows the unraveling of a murder to be an intellectual challenge. In her first book, the highly cerebral detective Michael Ohayon succeeds by mastering a knowledge of the psychoanalytic method and showing its clear parallel with murder-solving. In her next, equally intellectual, work, *A Literary Murder* (*Retzah b'hug l'sifrut*), Gur provides a solution to a murder that involves esoteric understanding of literary textual analysis. Her latest work, *Communal Sleeping: Murder in the Kibbutz* (*Linah meshutefet*), is more of a social analysis than anything else. Light escapism takes a back seat to Gur's interest in penetrating the theories underlying closed elitist societies.

In Shulamit Lapid's detective novels, *Bait* (*Pitayon*) and *Local Paper* (*M'koman*), she succeeds in creating a delightful feminist protagonist, the colorful Beersheba journalist Lizi Badichi, whose trademark is her large dangling earrings. With the help of her policeman brother-in-law, the Sephardic Lizi outwits establishment figures. While Lapid may be more entertaining than Gur, she too has extra-detective concerns. Her realistic descriptions of Israeli life expose the social injustice, snobbery, and hierarchy of Israeli society, even in outlying areas like Beersheba. Lapid has a feminist agenda as well. Although proudly independent and hard-working, Badichi is also deeply sensual and family-oriented. As "high" literature becomes more esoteric, it may be that works like these provide the necessary popular mirror Israeli society needs for self-understanding.

Literature: Poetry

In contrast to earlier periods, fiction had become increasingly central in Israeli culture, while the importance of poetry waned, as it had worldwide. At the same time, Israel still ranked among the countries that publish the largest number of poetry volumes per capita.

Works by two of Israel's most distinguished poets were published in 1990–1991: the *Collected Works* of Dan Pagis (1930–1986) and *Master of Rest* (*Adon Hamenuhah*), the last work of Avot Yeshurun (1902–1992). The poetry of both men was shaped out of reaction to their past in Europe, but they expressed their pain in diametrically opposed manners. Yeshurun made it the stuff of his innovative lyricism, while Pagis attempted to suppress memory and the personal "I" in his work.

Master of Rest expresses the fundamental issue that runs through Yeshurun's poetry of the last 40 years, the inability to resign himself to the death of his family in the Holocaust. Yeshurun continues to yearn for them and for his birthplace in Poland and feels guilty for having left them to come to Palestine in the 1920s. Consequently, he can never be entirely at one with himself in Tel Aviv. "Straddling the fault line between . . . Poland and Tel Aviv, is what compels the poet to speak, to harangue his surroundings," says poet Gabriel Levin. It accounts for Yeshurun's fractured, pastichelike style blending Yiddish, Hebrew slang, and Polish and Arabic words as well as places and people in both locales. It is his brilliant, lightning connections between worlds that made him one of Israel's most innovative poets, receiving recognition only late in life when younger, avant-garde writers began to look to him for inspiration.

Dan Pagis, who spent the first part of his adolescence in a concentration camp, leaves few biographical traces in his poetry. The personal is distanced, defamiliarized, by his imagery. Literary scholar Robert Alter has written that in Pagis, "earthly existence is seen characteristically from an immense telescopic distance. Time is surrealistically accelerated, flattened, distorted to avoid dealing with the past." In the posthumous edition of Pagis's collected works, a prose piece called "Abba," published for the first time, discusses his father's abandonment of the family, his mother's death, and the family's destruction in the Holocaust. It provides a sense of the personal aspects of Pagis's life that were neutralized in his poetry. Pagis, who with Nathan Zach and Yehuda Amichai was responsible for introducing a natural, colloquial tone into Hebrew poetry, was also an authority on Hebrew literature of the Middle Ages and Renaissance. His erudition and precision of language were utilized in creating a surrealistically sharp, intellectual poetry. "It is exactly by following a clear line of logic," writes critic Ariel Hirshfeld," that the Pagis poem, as in an Escher painting, leads to loss of orientation."

A vibrant creative impulse is clearly at work in Maya Bejerano's energetic, densely written book of poems, *Whale* (*Livyatan*). Women had come to center stage in Israeli poetry as well as in prose, and Bejerano, Leah Ayalon, Hedva Harehavi, Gavriella Elisha, and Agi Mishol were considered among the most important poets of their generation. Critic Ariel Hirshfeld attributed the leap made by women poets in the 1980s to the influence of Yona Wallach, "who took the feminist revolution upon herself."

The appearance of Avner Treinin's seventh book, *The Memory of Water* (*Zikhron Ha'mayim*), highlighted the existence of a group of Israeli poet-scientists, among whom Treinin was the most prominent. In the poems under discussion, Treinin, a professor of chemistry, writes about a scientific experiment in which water is shown to "remember" the materials dissolved in it. This becomes a metaphor for human memory and the Heraclitean nature of reality.

Another group—religious poets—had also come to the fore in recent years. It included Leah Ayalon, Admiel Kusman, Yonadav Kaplun, Esther Ettinger, Ruth Blumert, and Moshe Meir. Although each had an individual style, they shared a certain intensity of tone and a natural integration of religious images and concepts in their verse.

Art

In the world of Israeli art, group exhibitions designed around a strong central concept had become at least as important and influential as the work of individual artists. The grouping of artists together in order to make a conceptual or ideological statement appealed strongly to Israelis' strong sense of collective identity. At the same time, Israeli intellectuals and artists were constantly engaged in questions of identity, such as: What does it mean to be an Israeli? Where should Israelis locate themselves along the axis of an internationally oriented, universalistic outlook and a particularistic Jewish identity? In the art world, these questions were often formulated as: Is there anything distinctive about Israeli art? Should there be? Group exhibitions are a unique opportunity to reflect upon or attempt to answer these questions. In the late 1980s, the most important Israeli attempt to offer a definition of Israeli art was the exhibition "The Want of Matter" mounted at the Tel Aviv Museum by Sarah Breitburg. In 1991 two exhibitions made waves in the Israeli art world by offering new definitions of where Israeli art stood and what it stood for.

The first of these exhibitions, "Perspective: New Esthetic Concepts in Art of the

Eighties in Israel," curated by Daliah Manor and mounted at the Tel Aviv Museum, was in some ways a direct response to "The Want of Matter." The exhibition displayed the work of nine contemporary Israeli painters and sculptors: Dita Almog, Joshua Borkovsky, Reuven Berman Kadim, Zvi Goldstein, Gideon Gechtman, Neta Ziv, Yitzchak Livneh, Meir Pichadze, and Osvaldo Romberg. "The Want of Matter" had argued that an unfinished, piecemeal quality characterized Israeli art, and that the inexpensive and often "found" materials with which and on which Israeli artists painted and sculpted was an expression of Israel's socialist-Zionist ethos. The works in "Perspective" were chosen because they represented exactly the opposite kind of art. They had in common a cool, seductive, even glamorous look, a striving for esthetic perfection using high-quality materials.

"Perspective" was thus an open rebellion against the pioneering, socialist ethos defined as the mainstream of Israeli art in the "Want of Matter" exhibition. Daliah Manor, in the catalogue accompanying the exhibition, argues that the material and stylistic richness of the "Perspective" artists represented a "turning point and renewal" in Israeli art, made possible by the rise in the standard of living in Israel, the growing dominance of urban culture, and the ubiquity of film and television, which spread Western esthetic values and relativized local concerns.

While Israeli critics applauded the high quality of the works exhibited in "Perspective," they questioned whether they were united thematically by anything besides richness of style. Were the decorativeness and the glistening surfaces in "Perspective" a straightforward paean to esthetic beauty or an ironic statement about self-delusion, narcissism, and the seductiveness of art? A minor cultural skirmish broke out when Sarah Breitburg, curator of "The Want of Matter," dismissed "Perspective" as a celebration of bourgeois sensibility, and Manor hit back by accusing Breitburg of hypocrisy for attacking the very bourgeois society that supported the museums and the art world in which Breitburg had made her career.

In late 1991, another curator, Sarit Shapira, and another museum, the Israel Museum in Jerusalem, attempted to place Israeli art in another new context, to liberate it from the burden of parochialism while still salvaging a distinctive identity and meaning. Shapira's exhibition, called "Paths of Wandering: Emigration, Travels, Passages in Israeli Art," and the sophisticated, book-length catalogue accompanying it, suggested that a nomadic nonattachment to place, a fascination with "wandering," both geographic and mental, was a central, defining theme for Israeli artists. The theme of wandering and exile had been consciously repressed by the mainstream of Israeli art since the 1930s, Shapira argued, as part of the Zionist effort to "negate the Diaspora" as well as from an emotional and artistic attachment to the old-new homeland in Palestine. The move, in the early 1950s, of the New Horizons artists—a group that dominated the art scene through the 1960s—toward universalism and abstraction was part of the effort, Shapira claimed, to deny the specific Jewish images whose context was exile. And yet, as Shapira's exhibit attempted to show, the repressed returned, and wandering and exile remained important themes for Israeli artists. In choosing paintings, photographs, and sculptures by 21 artists, stretching across five decades, that depict suitcases, maps, ships, deserts, Bedouins, and foreign landscapes, Shapira attempted to illustrate an Israeli—or Jewish—obsession with travel, constant movement, continuous exile.

Critics responded sharply to "Paths of Wandering," some of them highly praising and vigorously criticizing the exhibition within the space of a single essay. Shapira's thesis was considered provocative and articulate, but her choice of artists and works was often criticized as arbitrary and artificial.

One broadside on Shapira came from art historian Gideon Ofrat, writing in the daily *Davar*. Even while attempting to recover from Israeli art a major theme that had been repressed, Ofrat said, Shapira continued to abide by the unwritten rules of the clique that had dominated Israeli art since the 1930s. This clique, which crystallized as the New Horizons artists under the leadership of Yosef Zaretzky, was committed to using color and form to create an international esthetic language of abstract lyricism and was dead set against any artistic references to the Jewish past. Shapira, like Sarah Breitburg before her, had continued the "boycott" of artists such as Mordechai Ardon, Naftali Bezem, Shmuel Bak, and Avraham Ofek, artists whose work was relevant to her thesis.

OFEK AND ARDON

The death of Avraham Ofek in 1991 at the age of 55 and the end of Mordechai Ardon's long career after his disablement by a stroke in 1990 at the age of 95 brought to the fore once again the issue of the control of Israeli art by a ruling elite, to the detriment of artists such as Ofek and Ardon. The work of both Ardon and Ofek overtly explored Jewish themes, using symbols and ideas drawn from Midrash, Kabbalah, and modern Jewish history. Despite the high quality of their work and their appreciation (especially Ardon's) internationally, both were virtually excluded from prestigious group shows, had not been given proper retrospective exhibitions by the most important Israeli museums (the Israel Museum in Jerusalem and the Tel Aviv Museum), and in general had been pushed to the sidelines by the mainstream art world.

Mordechai Ardon, born Mordechai Tuchow in Poland in 1896, studied with Paul Klee and Vassily Kandinsky in the Bauhaus school in Germany and immigrated to Palestine in 1933. Because the Tel Aviv scene was dominated by artists influenced by French postimpressionism, the new immigrants from Germany did not receive a warm reception from the established avant-garde in Tel Aviv. Ardon moved to Jerusalem in 1936 and began to teach in the Bezalel School of Art. He became the director of Bezalel in 1940 and remained there until 1952, when he was appointed artistic adviser to the Ministry of Education and Culture, a position he held until 1963.

In the 1940s he began to develop the symbolic style that was his signature for the rest of his life. His paintings have a geometric harmony reminiscent of Kandinsky, but they are filled with allegorical and symbolic references to Kabbalah and Jewish history. Ardon was one of the first artists to paint about the Shoah, in a triptych that now hangs in London's Tate Gallery. Ardon's work adorns the President's House in Israel and fills an entire wall at the National Library in Jerusalem. Ardons can be found hanging in the Metropolitan Museum in New York and in the Steidlich in Amsterdam. An Ardon painting was sold in Japan in 1987 for nearly a million dollars—the most ever paid for the work of an Israeli artist. Despite international recognition, and despite the fact that even his opponents did not question his artistic excellence, Ardon was "not accepted as a full and equal member in the artistic community in Israel"—as one Israeli critic wrote—because of the symbolic elements and the overt Jewishness of his work.

Avraham Ofek's career offers another example of an artist who clashed with the Israeli art establishment and fought, with imagination and charisma, to create an alternative kind of Israeli art. Born in Bulgaria in 1935, Ofek immigrated to Israel in 1949, becoming a member of Kibbutz Ein Hamifratz. Ofek studied mural painting in Italy from 1958 until 1962 and was influenced by Italian social-realist artists, who combined a deep belief in the artist's responsibility to community with a love for local landscape, myths, and iconography.

After the Yom Kippur War in 1973, Ofek began to explore Judaism, studying Bible, Midrash, and Talmud intensively and incorporating biblical themes and their midrashic interpretations into his painting and sculpture. Along with two immigrant Soviet artists, Ofek formed the Leviathan group and wrote a manifesto declaring his commitment to founding a new school of Israeli art based on Jewish sources, on primitivism, and on the magical power of the letter. Although Leviathan broke up in 1979, Ofek continued studying Jewish sources, tagging his work with midrashic inscriptions, in a continuous search for an authentic Jewish form of art. He also returned to sculpture, using elements taken from the natural landscape—stone and wood—and simple materials such as pieces of cloth and grains of rice, in an effort to create a kind of art that would have a tribal, magical power. Although many Israeli artists and critics considered Ofek a major artist, neither of the large museums had ever offered a retrospective exhibition of his work.

In the last several years, Israeli artists such as Menashe Kadishman, Larry Abramson, Udi Aloni, and many others began to draw on Judaism as a source for their iconography. What Baruch Bleich, writing in *Davar*, said about Ardon applied to Ofek as well. "Although none [of the younger Israeli artists] intends to create a purely Jewish art, as Ardon wished to, the legitimization that they have given to Jewish theology as a problem within art makes them a front opposing the secular, lyrical, abstract painting that began with New Horizons. It may well happen—and this is simply a wild guess—that in the wake of the new, postmodern wave in Israeli art, there will be a rehabilitation of Mordechai Ardon."

Jewish Thought

Jewish thought in Israel in the early 1990s was concerned, above all, with history and memory, and with the way in which interpretations of the past shape the reality of the present. Nowhere was this more evident than in the debate that raged over the remembrance of the Holocaust and its meaning for contemporary Israel. For a number of years a critique had been building, particularly among Israeli intellectuals associated with the political Left, over the place of the Holocaust in Israeli consciousness. An example of this critique can be found in "The Kitsch of Israel," an essay by Avishai Margalit, a leading Israeli philosopher of language, first printed in the *New York Review of Books* (November 24, 1988), in which he argued that the memory of the Holocaust was being violated by the context and style of its remembrance in Israel's public arena.

In 1991, *The Seventh Million*, the first popular book-length account of the way in which the trauma of the Holocaust shaped modern Israel, was published, written by Tom Segev, a weekly commentator for *Ha'aretz* newspaper, who earned a doctorate in history from Boston University. According to Segev, from 1952 onward, a series of issues and incidents pushed the Holocaust into the forefront of the Israeli public's concern: the debate over whether to accept reparations from the Germans, the Kastner trial, the capture and trial of Adolf Eichmann. Another kind of voice—especially discernible in the speeches and writings of then opposition leader Menachem Begin—began to depict the Holocaust as the quintessence of the Jewish experience, as the event symbolizing and justifying the need for a Jewish state. In time, especially after the traumas of the 1967 and 1973 wars and the rise to power of Begin's Likud party in 1977, the Holocaust, according to Segev, became a central myth for Israelis. "The more it became apparent that their secular Israeli existence alone was not enough to provide them with a rooted identity," Segev writes, "many Israelis became addicted to the legacy of the Holocaust as a kind of popular ritual and at times a bizarre veneration of memory, death, and kitsch. At a certain point the Holocaust became one of the sources of [Israeli] collective memory. . . ."

Segev's writing, while rich with anecdotes and personal testimony, covers an immense amount of material, and historians of the Holocaust and of contemporary Israel sharply questioned its accuracy. More importantly, perhaps, Segev's often judgmental and sometimes almost cynical tone spurred debate about the stand that some intellectuals had taken toward the Holocaust. Yaakov Shavit, a renowned Hebrew University historian, responded to Segev's book in a long article published in three parts in *Ha'aretz*. Shavit said that Segev had his own "contemporary political purpose" in attempting to turn the legacy of the Holocaust into a "universal history lesson detached from its specific historical connection." The political Right in Israel may have "abused" the memory of the Holocaust to convince the Jewish public that Israel was still surrounded by evil, implacable foes blinded by irrational hatred (the most famous example of this "abuse" being Prime Minister Begin's comparisons, during the Lebanon War, of Arafat to Hitler and the PLO to Nazis). But the attempts of Segev and other intellectuals, argued Shavit, to "raise the memory of the Holocaust to the level of metaphysical memory" were another kind of abuse. In attempting to delegitimize the nationalistic interpretation of the Holocaust, critics like Segev imposed a meaning on the Holocaust that denied its primary context: the long history of European anti-Semitism and "the unique fate of the Jewish people."

Y.H. BRENNER AND RABBI KOOK

Founding figures still loomed large in Israel's cultural landscape, perhaps none more so than the fiercely iconoclastic writer and publicist Yosef Hayim Brenner, who was murdered by Arabs in Jaffa in 1921, and the mystical theologian and religious Zionist leader Abraham Isaac Kook, who passed away in 1935. These two men—whom Berl Katznelson, another founding figure, once called the only two truly great people living in the Land of Israel—remained particularly influential, in large part because both had come to be seen as prophets and avatars of the new kind of Jew that the return to Zion was destined to create. In 1990 and 1991, new book-length assessments of both Brenner and Rabbi Kook demonstrated the continuing fascination of the Israeli public with these men and, in a broader sense, with the internal intellectual history of Zionism.

Brenner, for many Israelis, was a symbol of the authenticity, intellectual courage, and artless, almost poisonous honesty that some considered the characteristic qualities of the modern Israeli cultural style. Brenner was born in Russia in 1881 and educated in traditional yeshivahs, but then broke with religious faith, becoming a fiery advocate of the need for Jews to take their lives, individually and collectively, into their own hands. "The main inspiration for his writings," one Israeli critic said, "was drawn from the recognition that it is possible to live in a world in which redemption is not a possibility, either for the individual or for the collective, without falling into cynicism."

Brenner moved to Jaffa during the harsh years of the Second Aliyah. He was a tireless journalist, publicist, essayist, and fiction writer, who believed passionately that the revival of the Hebrew language and literature was of seminal importance for the renewal of the Jewish people. For many people Brenner was much more than a writer, however. He was seen as a guide by many in his generation, and, according to Muki Tzur, a writer and leader of the United Kibbutz Movement, "an unending source of faith, . . . who united the [Zionist] revolution of labor with continuity of spiritual life."

Menachem Brinker—a philosopher and scholar of Hebrew literature, and himself a beloved and charismatic figure among contemporary Israeli intellectuals—wrote *Toward Tiberias Alley*, a book that reintegrates Brenner's life, thought, and literary work. Brinker challenges the widespread assumption that Brenner's writings are autobiographical, a notion fostered by the author's own teasing hints. Another important point that Brinker succeeds in clarifying is the question of Brenner's attitude toward Judaism. Brinker points out that Brenner's often stinging opposition to Jewish tradition did not emanate from a desire to replace Judaism with a more modern, Western form of culture. Rather, Brenner felt that, until the Jewish masses had been liberated from the powerlessness and decrepitude of the Eastern European ghettos, faith and traditional culture were a distracting delusion. The feeling of moral superiority which many Jews shared was also a delusion, because it had never been tested. A Jew who was proud that his people had not oppressed anyone, Brenner said, in a characteristically sarcastic formulation, was like a castrated man proud that he had never committed adultery. Brinker's clarifications here are important because they demonstrate that Brenner was not ideologically opposed to tradition as such. In the charged atmosphere of religious-secular tensions in contemporary Israel, the suggestion of a more modulated stance on Judaism on the part of one of secular Israel's foremost cultural heroes was considered of great importance.

During the same period in which Brenner was formulating his bitter condemnations of Diaspora Jewish life and penning his dipped-in-acid portrayals of the struggles of the Zionist pioneers, Rabbi Abraham Isaac Kook was integrating the Jewish return to Zion into an encompassing mystical vision of redemption. Rabbi Kook (b. 1865), who already in Europe was known as one of the most promising Torah scholars of his time, came to the land of Israel in 1904 and was appointed first Ashkenazi chief rabbi of Palestine in 1919. In contrast to the vast majority of Orthodox scholars and spiritual leaders, both in Eastern Europe and in Palestine, who saw secular Zionism as a destructive, even demonic, force aimed at seducing Jews away from their religious mission, Rabbi Kook understood secular Zionism as part of a process that would lead to the renewal of Judaism, the enlargement of its horizons, and ultimately to redemption.

Especially since the early 1970s, when Gush Emunim leaders—most of them students of Rabbi Kook's son, Zvi Yehuda—became the dominant force within Israeli religious Zionism, Rabbi Kook's legacy had been at the center of the Israeli cultural and political debate. It is thus somewhat surprising that only in 1990, with the publication of Prof. Binyamin Ish Shalom's *Abraham Isaac Kook: Between Mysticism and Rationalism*, did a full-length academic study of Kook's thought become available.

Ish Shalom's contribution is his portrayal of a multidimensional Rabbi Kook. Despite the poetic, fragmentary nature of his theological writings, and the seeming contradiction between his rootedness in the Jewish mystical tradition and his openness to Western philosophical sources, Rabbi Kook, according to Ish Shalom, had a coherent, highly developed system of thought that informed all his writings. But, says Ish Shalom, this thought system itself is given the breath of life by the dialectical tensions and apparent contradictions that are at its root. "Any attempt to put forward one aspect or another of [Rabbi Kook's] 'torah,' " wrote Shalom Razbi, summing up Ish Shalom's work, "and to ignore the other aspects, is nothing but distortion, for the dialectical character is essential to this 'torah,' and is that which gives it its uniqueness."

Dead Sea Scrolls

The normally staid and insular world of Bible scholarship came under the glare of media attention in 1991, with some dramatic developments related to the Dead Sea Scrolls—not to their contents or nature but to the politics and management of the scroll enterprise. As the main repository of the documents and the center of scroll scholarship, Israel was the focus of the hubbub, but much of the action took place in the United States. Two specific issues were at stake: the lack of general access to the scrolls and the slow pace of their publication.

Although many of the scrolls had been deciphered and published since their discovery in the late 1940s and early 1950s, there was dissatisfaction in the scholarly world with the fact that the remainder of the material—much of it in tiny fragments—was, until the late '80s, in the hands of a small group of scholars, who maintained exclusive rights to it and published very little. The scholars involved defended the slow pace of publication by pointing to the painstaking precision required to piece together hundreds of tiny fragments, like jigsaw puzzle pieces, into meaningful documents. Their critics argued that opening the field to more participants would speed up the process. The editors also claimed that restricting access was necessary to protect the rights of designated scholars who had been assigned various scrolls and to ensure a high level of scholarly interpretation. Critics suggested that this was merely a case of normal academic competition, of scholars seeking to protect their turf.

Part of the problem was political, an outgrowth of the Arab-Israeli conflict. Until 1967, the scrolls had been under Jordanian jurisdiction, and the seven-man editorial committee charged with working on the scrolls consisted solely of Christians, largely Catholics. After the Six Day War, the scrolls—housed in the Rockefeller Museum in East Jerusalem—were technically controlled by the Israel Antiquities Authority, but that body chose to maintain the existing arrangements with the editorial committee, a decision now regarded by most observers as unfortunate. In 1985, John Strugnell of Harvard University became chairman of the committee; he appointed its first Jewish member, Prof. Emanuel Tov of the Hebrew University, and later Elisha Qimron of Ben-Gurion University. In 1990, however, Strugnell was forced to resign, accused of making anti-Semitic statements in a published interview. Tov, who succeeded him, moved quickly to respond to criticism of the committee's monopoly and enlarged the group of scholars considerably. He also imposed strict deadlines for publication. Although two non-Israelis remained as co-editors with Tov (Père Emile Puech of the Ecole Biblique and Eugene Ulrich of Notre Dame University), the Israelis had now effectively taken control of the scroll enterprise.

But matters did not rest there. An American Jew, Hershel Shanks, publisher of a popular magazine, *Biblical Archeology Review*, who had been pressing the committee publicly since 1985 to speed up the pace of scroll publication, took up a new cause, making the scrolls freely available to the entire scholarly community. This issue, with its focus on "freedom of information," was widely publicized in the United States—to the displeasure of the Israeli and other scroll scholars, who felt that the necessary correctives had been made and viewed Shanks, an American and not a scholar, with some suspicion.

In the fall of '91, a rapid succession of events took place that effectively demolished the long-standing wall of exclusivity. In September, two scholars at Hebrew Union College in Cincinnati announced publication of a computer-generated reconstruction of previously unpublished scrolls, based solely on a private concordance of words in the fragments. Shanks, in fact, published the first volume of this project. Two weeks later, the scholarly world was stunned when the Huntington Library in San Marino, California, announced that it had a set of some 3,000 photographic negatives of the scrolls, which it was willing to make available to all qualified researchers. Since this was an unauthorized collection (duplicate authorized sets had been stored for years, as a safeguard in case of war or damage to the originals, at Oxford University in England, Hebrew Union College in Cincinnati, and the Ancient Biblical Manuscript Center in Claremont, Calif.), the Israelis and the scroll editors were outraged. But Prof. Lawrence Schiffman of New York University told the *New York Times* (Sept. 22, 1991): "Most will regard those who make this material available as Robin Hoods, stealing from the academically privileged to give to those hungry for the knowledge secreted in these texts."

In October, as pressure mounted, the Israeli authorities agreed to grant free access to the photographs in the United States and in Jerusalem, but continued to limit the right to publish text editions of any untranslated material to the authorized editors. This news was greeted as unsatisfactory. In November, Shanks's Biblical Archeology Society announced that it would soon publish a facsimile edition of all the unpublished scrolls, prepared by Robert Eisenman of California State University at Long Beach and James M. Robinson of the Claremont Graduate School in California, who claimed that they had received the photographs through "an anonymous benefactor." At the end of November, at a meeting of the Society of Biblical Literature in Kansas City, the last barrier to free access fell when Emanuel Tov announced that the remaining restrictions would be removed, that publication rights would no longer be prohibited. Professor Tov promised that his team would press forward with publication of scholarly editions, and that texts would be reassigned if scholars were unable to publish expeditiously.

ROCHELLE FURSTENBERG
MICHA ODENHEIMER

World Jewish Population, 1991

THIS ARTICLE PRESENTS UPDATES, for the end of 1991, of the Jewish population estimates for the various countries of the world.[1] The estimates reflect some of the results of a prolonged and ongoing effort to study scientifically the demography of contemporary world Jewry.[2] Data collection and comparative research have benefited from the collaboration of scholars and institutions in many countries, including replies to direct inquiries regarding current estimates. It should be emphasized, however, that the elaboration of a worldwide set of estimates for the Jewish populations of the various countries is beset with difficulties and uncertainties.

Since the end of the 1980s, important geopolitical changes have affected the world scene, particularly in Eastern Europe. The major event was the political breakup of the Soviet Union into 15 independent states. Similar problems now affect other countries, such as Yugoslavia and Czechoslovakia. The Jewish population has been sensitive to these changes, large-scale emigration from the former USSR being the most visible effect. Our presentation of the geographical distribution of world Jewry takes into account the current redrawing of the world's political map. Among the changes introduced for the present volume—in comparison with previous AJYB articles—is the listing of each republic of the former USSR as a separate country, located in Europe or Asia, as appropriate. The whole Jewish population of the USSR was previously assigned to Europe.

In spite of the increased fragmentation of the global system of nations, about 94 percent of world Jewry is concentrated in ten countries. The aggregate of these major Jewish population centers virtually determines the assessment of the size of total world Jewry, estimated at 12.85 million persons at the end of 1991. The country figures for 1991 were updated from those for 1990 in accordance with the known or estimated changes in the interval—migrations, vital events (births and

[1]The previous estimates, as of 1990, were published in AJYB 1992, vol. 92, pp. 484–512.

[2]Many of these activities are carried out by, or in coordination with, the Division of Jewish Demography and Statistics at the Institute of Contemporary Jewry, the Hebrew University of Jerusalem. The authors acknowledge with thanks the collaboration of the many institutions and individuals in the different countries who have supplied information for this update.

423

deaths), and identificational changes (accessions and secessions). In addition, corrections were introduced in the light of newly accrued information on Jewish populations. Corresponding corrections were also applied retrospectively to the 1990 figures, which appear below in revised summary (see table 1), so as to allow adequate comparison with the 1991 estimates.

During the year 1991 under review here, operations of data collection and analysis relevant to Jewish population estimates were in planning or already under way in several countries. National censuses were carried out in Canada and Australia; Jewish sociodemographic surveys were completed in South Africa and in Mexico. Some of this ongoing research is part of a coordinated effort to update the profile of world Jewry that began at the outset of the 1990s.[3] Two important sources recently yielded results on major Jewish populations: the official population census of the Soviet Union held in 1989, and the National Jewish Population Survey (NJPS) in the United States completed in 1990. The respective results basically confirm the estimates we reported in previous AJYB volumes and, perhaps more importantly, our interpretation of the trends now prevailing in the demography of world Jewry.[4] At the same time, these new data highlight the increasing complexity of the sociodemographic and identificational processes underlying the definition of Jewish populations—hence the estimates of their sizes. A full review of the major conceptual problems appeared in the 1992 volume of AJYB and will not be repeated here. Users of population estimates should be aware of these difficulties and of the consequent limitations of the estimates.

Presentation of Data

The detailed estimates of Jewish population distribution in each continent and country (tables 2–7 below) aim at the concept of "core" Jewish population. We define the core Jewish population as the aggregate of all those who, when asked, identify themselves as such; or, if the respondent is a different person in the same household, are identified by him/her as Jews. The core Jewish population includes all those who converted to Judaism or joined the Jewish group informally. It excludes those of Jewish descent who formally adopted another religion, as well as other Jewish individuals who did not convert out but currently disclaim being

---

[3]Following the 1987 international conference on Jewish population problems, sponsored by the major Jewish organizations worldwide, an International Scientific Advisory Committee (ISAC) was established. Cochaired by Dr. Roberto Bachi of the Hebrew University and Dr. Sidney Goldstein of Brown University, ISAC coordinates and monitors Jewish population data collection internationally. See Sergio DellaPergola and Leah Cohen, eds., *World Jewish Population: Trends and Policies* (Jerusalem, 1992).

[4]See U.O. Schmelz, "Jewish Survival: The Demographic Factors," AJYB 1981, vol. 81, pp. 61–117; U.O. Schmelz, *Aging of World Jewry* (Jerusalem, 1984); Sergio DellaPergola, "Israel and World Jewish Population: A Core-Periphery Perspective," in *Population and Social Change in Israel*, ed. C. Goldscheider (Boulder, 1992), pp. 39–63.

Jewish. The so-called extended or enlarged Jewish populations—including Jews, ex-Jews, non-Jews of Jewish parentage, and the respective non-Jewish household members—may result in significantly higher estimates (not reported below).

We provide separate figures for each country with at least 100 resident core Jews. Residual estimates of Jews living in other smaller communities supplement some of the continental totals. For each of the reported countries, the four columns in the following tables provide the United Nations estimate of midyear 1992 total population,[5] the estimated end-1991 Jewish population, the proportion of Jews per 1,000 of total population, and a rating of the accuracy of the Jewish population estimate.

There is wide variation in the quality of the Jewish population estimates for different countries. For many Diaspora countries it would be best to indicate a range (minimum-maximum) rather than a definite figure for the number of Jews. It would be confusing, however, for the reader to be confronted with a long list of ranges; this would also complicate the regional and world totals. Yet, the figures actually indicated for most of the Diaspora communities should be understood as being the central value of the plausible range of the respective core Jewish populations. The relative magnitude of this range varies inversely to the accuracy of the estimate.

ACCURACY RATING

The three main elements that affect the accuracy of each estimate are the nature and quality of the base data, the recency of the base data, and the method of updating. A simple code combining these elements is used to provide a general evaluation of the reliability of the Jewish population figures reported in the detailed tables below. The code indicates different quality levels of the reported estimates: (A) base figure derived from countrywide census or relatively reliable Jewish population survey; updated on the basis of full or partial information on Jewish population movements in the respective country during the intervening period; (B) base figure derived from less accurate but recent countrywide Jewish population investigation; partial information on population movements in the intervening period; (C) base figure derived from less recent sources, and/or unsatisfactory or partial coverage of Jewish population in the particular country; updating according to demographic information illustrative of regional demographic trends; (D) base figure essentially conjectural; no reliable updating procedure. In categories (A), (B), and (C), the years in which the base figures or important partial updates were obtained are also stated. For countries whose Jewish population estimate of 1991 was not only updated but also revised in the light of improved information, the sign "X" is appended to the accuracy rating.

---

[5]See United Nations, Department of Economic and Social Development, Population Division, *World Population 1992* (New York, 1992).

Distribution of World Jewish Population by Major Regions

Table 1 gives an overall picture of Jewish population for the end of 1991 as compared to 1990. For 1990 the originally published estimates are presented along with somewhat revised figures that take into account, retrospectively, the corrections made in 1991 in certain country estimates, in the light of improved information. These corrections resulted in a net decrease in world Jewry's 1990 estimated size by 2,500, due to a downward correction for Great Britain, and upward corrections for Mexico and the 15 component republics of the former USSR. Some explanations are given below for the countries whose estimates were revised. The geographical breakdown in table 1 is slightly different from that in previous AJYB volumes, the main change being the split of the former USSR into its European and Asian components. The 1990 data, too, are presented here according to the new format.

The size of world Jewry at the end of 1991 is assessed at 12,849,500. According to the revised figures, between 1990 and 1991 there was an estimated gain of 45,600 people, or about +0.4 percent. Despite all the imperfections in the estimates, it is clear that world Jewry has reached "zero population growth," with the natural increase in Israel barely compensating for the demographic decline in the Diaspora.

The number of Jews in Israel rose from a figure of 3,946,700 in 1990 to 4,144,600 at the end of 1991, an increase of 197,900 people, or 5.0 percent. In contrast, the estimated Jewish population in the Diaspora declined from 8,857,200 (according to the revised figures) to 8,704,900—a decrease of 152,300 people, or 1.7 percent. These changes primarily reflect the continuing Jewish emigration from the former USSR. In 1991, the Israel-Diaspora estimated net migratory balance amounted to a gain of about 151,300 Jews for Israel. Internal demographic evolution produced further growth among the Jewish population in Israel and further decline in the Diaspora. Recently, instances of accession or "return" to Judaism can be observed in connection with the emigration process from Eastern Europe and the comprehensive provisions of the Israeli Law of Return (*Hok Hashvut*). The Law of Return grants immigrant rights to all current Jews and to their Jewish or non-Jewish spouses, children, and grandchildren, as well as to the spouses of such children and grandchildren. The existence of all such previously unincluded or unidentified individuals may have contributed to a moderate slowing down in the pace of decline of the relevant Diaspora Jewish populations, and some further gains to the Jewish population in Israel.

About half of the world's Jews reside in the Americas, with over 45 percent in North America. One-third live in Asia—including the Asian republics of the former USSR (but not the Asian parts of the Russian Republic and Turkey)—most of them in Israel. Europe, including the Asian territories of the Russian Republic and Turkey, accounts for just over 15 percent of the total. Less than 2 percent of the world's Jews live in Africa and Oceania. Among the major geographical regions listed in table 1, the number of Jews in Israel—and, consequently, in total Asia—

TABLE 1. ESTIMATED JEWISH POPULATION, BY CONTINENTS AND MAJOR GEO-
GRAPHICAL REGIONS, 1990 AND 1991

Region	1990			1991		% Change 1990–1991
	Original	Revised				
	Abs. N.	Abs. N.	Percent	Abs. N.	Percent	
World	12,806,400	12,803,900	100.0	12,849,500	100.0	+0.4
Diaspora	8,859,700	8,857,200	69.2	8,704,900	67.7	−1.7
Israel	3,946,700	3,946,700	30.8	4,144,600	32.3	+5.0
America, Total	6,278,400	6,281,400	49.0	6,319,000	49.2	+0.6
North[a]	5,845,000	5,845,000	45.6	5,885,000	45.8	+0.7
Central	46,700	49,700	0.4	49,700	0.4	—
South	386,700	386,700	3.0	384,300	3.0	−0.6
Europe, Total	2,157,800	2,150,500	16.8	2,009,800	15.6	−6.5
EC	999,600	986,600	7.7	986,900	7.6	+0.0
Other West	44,000	44,000	0.3	44,000	0.3	—
Former USSR[b]	1,000,500	1,006,200	7.9	868,100	6.8	−13.7
Other East and Balkans[b]	113,700	113,700	0.9	110,800	0.9	−2.6
Asia, Total	4,128,900	4,130,700	32.3	4,298,100	33.5	+4.0
Israel	3,946,700	3,946,700	30.8	4,144,600	32.3	+5.0
Former USSR[b]	149,500	151,300	1.2	121,900	1.0	−19.4
Other[b]	32,700	32,700	0.3	31,600	0.2	−3.4
Africa, Total	148,700	148,700	1.2	129,000	1.0	−13.2
North	10,600	10,600	0.1	10,400	0.1	−1.9
Central	23,100	23,100	0.2	3,600	0.0	−84.4
South[c]	115,000	115,000	0.9	115,000	0.9	—
Oceania	92,600	92,600	0.7	93,600	0.7	+1.1

[a]U.S.A. and Canada.
[b]The Asian regions of Russia and Turkey are included in Europe.
[c]South Africa and Zimbabwe.

increased in 1991. Moderate Jewish population gains were also estimated for North America, the European Community, and Oceania. South America, Eastern Europe, Asian countries out of Israel, and Africa sustained decreases in Jewish population size. World Jewry constitutes about 2.4 per 1,000 of the world's total population. One in about 400 people in the world is a Jew.

Individual Countries

THE AMERICAS

In 1991 the total number of Jews in the American continents was estimated at 6,319,000. The overwhelming majority (93 percent) resided in the United States and Canada, less than 1 percent lived in Central America (including Mexico), and about 6 percent lived in South America—with Argentina and Brazil the largest Jewish communities (see table 2).

United States. The 1989–1990 National Jewish Population Survey (NJPS), sponsored by the Council of Jewish Federations and the North American Jewish Data Bank (NAJDB), provided new benchmark information about the size and characteristics of U.S. Jewry and the basis for subsequent updates.[6] According to the official report of the results of this important national sample study, the core Jewish population in the United States comprised 5,515,000 persons in the summer of 1990. Of these, 185,000 were converts to Judaism. An estimated 210,000 persons, not included in the previous figures, were born or raised as Jews but converted to another religion. A further 1,115,000 people—thereof 415,000 adults and 700,000 children below age 18—were of Jewish parentage but were not Jews themselves and declared a religion other than Judaism at the time of survey. All together, these various groups formed an extended Jewish population of 6,840,000. NJPS also covered 1,350,000 non-Jewish-born members of eligible (Jewish or mixed) households. The study's enlarged Jewish population thus consisted of about 8,200,000 persons. The 1990 Jewish population estimates are within the range of a sampling error of plus or minus 3.5 percent.[7] This means a range between 5.3 and 5.7 million for the core Jewish population in 1990.

During fiscal years (October 1–September 30) 1990 and 1991, respectively 39,000

---

[6]The 1989–1990 National Jewish Population Survey was conducted under the auspices of the Council of Jewish Federations with the supervision of a National Technical Advisory Committee chaired by Dr. Sidney Goldstein of Brown University. Dr. Barry Kosmin of the North American Jewish Data Bank and City University of New York Graduate Center directed the study. See Barry A. Kosmin, Sidney Goldstein, Joseph Waksberg, Nava Lerer, Ariella Keysar, and Jeffrey Scheckner, *Highlights of the CJF 1990 National Jewish Population Survey* (New York, 1991); Sidney Goldstein, "Profile of American Jewry: Insights from the 1990 National Jewish Population Survey," AJYB 1992, vol. 92, pp. 77–173.

[7]See Kosmin et al., p. 39.

and 26,761 refugees from the Soviet Union were admitted to the United States.[8] The total of assisted refugees for calendar year 1991 was 34,715. The international migration balance of U.S. Jewry should have generated an actual increase of Jewish population size. However, based on NJPS findings, the expected influence of international migration between 1971 and 1990 did not show up in the size of U.S. core Jewish population in 1990. This indicates that the balance of other factors of core population change over that whole 20-year period must have been somewhat negative. First detailed analyses of the new NJPS data actually provide evidence of a variety of contributing factors: low levels of Jewish fertility and the "effectively Jewish" birthrate, increasing aging of the Jewish population, increasing outmarriage rate, declining rate of conversion to Judaism (or "choosing" Judaism), rather low proportions of children of mixed marriages being identified as Jewish, and a growing tendency to adopt non-Jewish rituals.[9] A temporary increase in the Jewish birthrate occurred during the late 1980s, because the large cohorts born during the "baby boom" of the 1950s and early 1960s were in the main procreative ages; however, this echo effect is about to fade away, as the much smaller cohorts born since the late 1960s reach the stage of parenthood.

Taking into account this evidence, our estimate of U.S. Jewish population size at the end of 1991 starts from the NJPS benchmark core Jewish population of 5,515,-000; assumes that the current balance of demographic and identificational changes in the core Jewish population is overall close to nil; and attempts to account for Jewish immigration which arrived in the later part of 1990, after completion of NJPS, and in 1991. Assuming a total net migration gain of about 50,000–60,000 from the USSR, Israel, and other origins for the whole of 1990, we apportioned 20,000 to the later months of 1990. A further 40,000 were added to account for net immigration in 1991. We thus suggest an estimate of 5,575,000 Jews in the United States at the end of 1991. This estimate is still conditional on further detailed scrutiny and interpretation of the NJPS findings.

The research team of the North American Jewish Data Bank (NAJDB), which was responsible for the primary handling of NJPS data files, has also continued its yearly compilation of local Jewish population estimates. These are reported elsewhere in this volume.[10] NAJDB estimated the U.S. Jewish population in 1986 at 5,814,000, including "under 2 percent" non-Jewish household members. This was

---

[8]Barry R. Chiswick, "Soviet Jews in the United States: An Analysis of Their Linguistic and Economic Adjustment," *Economic Quarterly*, July 1991, no. 148, pp. 188–211 (Hebrew), and *International Migration Review*, forthcoming 1993 (English); HIAS, news release (New York, Oct. 10, 1991; Sept. 30, 1992).

[9]See Goldstein, AJYB 1992; see also U.O. Schmelz and Sergio DellaPergola, *Basic Trends in U.S. Jewish Demography* (New York, American Jewish Committee, 1988).

[10]The first in a new series of yearly compilations of local U.S. Jewish population estimates appeared in Barry A. Kosmin, Paul Ritterband, and Jeffrey Scheckner, "Jewish Population in the United States, 1986," AJYB 1987, vol. 87, pp. 164–91. The 1992 update appears elsewhere in the present volume.

very close to our own pre-NJPS estimate of 5,700,000. The NAJDB estimate was updated as follows: 1987—5,943,700; 1988—5,935,000; 1989—5,944,000; 1990—5,981,000; 1991—5,798,000. These changes do not reflect actual sudden growths or declines, but rather corrections and adaptations made in the figures for several local communities—some of them in the light of NJPS regional results. It should be realized that compilations of local estimates, even if as painstaking as in the case of the NAJDB, are subject to a great many local biases and tend to fall behind the actual pace of national trends. This is especially true in a context of vigorous internal migrations, as in the United States. In our view, the new NJPS figure, in spite of sample-survey biases, provides a more reliable national Jewish population baseline.

Canada. In Canada the 1981 census enumerated 296,425 Jews according to religion. By adding 9,950 persons who reported "Jewish" as their single reply to the census question on ethnic origin, while not reporting any non-Jewish religion (such as Catholic, Anglican, etc.), the figure rises to 306,375. There were additional persons who did not report a non-Jewish religion but mentioned Jewish as part of a multiple response to the question on ethnic origin. After due allowance for the latter group, a total core Jewish population of 310,000 was suggested for 1981. A further 5,140 Canadians, who reported being Jewish by ethnic origin but identified with another religion were not included in our estimate.

The population census held in Canada in 1986 provided data on ethnic origins but not on religious groups. A total of 245,855 persons reported being Jewish as a single reply to the question on ethnic origin, as against 264,020 in the same category in 1981. A further 97,655 mentioned a Jewish origin as part of a multiple response to the 1986 question on ethnic origin, as compared to 30,000–40,000 in 1981. Thus, a substantial increase in the number of Canadians reporting partially Jewish ancestry seemed to offset the decline in the number of those with a solely Jewish identification according to ethnicity. Besides actual demographic and identificational trends, changes in the wording of the relevant questions in the two censuses may have influenced these variations in the size of the ethnically (or, in our terminology, extended) Jewish population of Canada.[11]

In the light of available evidence on international migration, and considering the increasingly aged Jewish population structure, it is suggested that a migratory surplus may have roughly offset the probably negative balance of internal evolution since the 1981 census. Consequently, the 1981 figure of 310,000 was kept unchanged throughout 1991. The 1991 census again included questions on both religion and ethnic origin, and its results (to be released in 1993) will provide a new baseline for the estimate of Canada's Jewish population.

Central America. Official Mexican censuses have provided rather erratic and unreliable figures. A Jewish-sponsored population survey of the Jews in the Mexico

---

[11]Statistics Canada, *1981 Census of Canada: Population: Ethnic Origin; Religion* (Ottawa, 1983, 1984); Statistics Canada, *Population by Ethnic Origin, 1986 Census: Canada, Provinces and Territories and Census Metropolitan Areas* (Ottawa, 1988).

City area was completed in 1991.[12] The results point to a Jewish community definitely less affected than others in the Diaspora by the common trends of low fertility, intermarriage, and aging. Some comparatively more traditional sectors in the community still contribute a slight surplus of births over deaths, and overall, thanks also to some immigration, the Jewish population has been quite stable or moderately increasing. The new population estimate was put at 35,000 in the Mexico City area, and at 38,000 nationally. This amounts to an upward revision of 3,000 in comparison with our previous estimate. Panama's Jewish population—the second largest in Central America—is estimated at about 5,000.

South America.[13] The Jewish population of Argentina, the largest in that geographical region, is marked by a negative balance of internal evolution. A number of local surveys conducted at the initiative of the Asociacion Mutual Israelita Argentina—AMIA, the central Jewish community organization—consistently point to growing aging.[14] Since the 1960s, while the pace of emigration and return migration was significantly affected by the nature of economic and political trends in the country, the balance of external migrations was generally negative. Accordingly, the estimate for Argentinian Jewry was reduced from 215,000 in 1990 to 213,000 in 1991.

In Brazil, the official population census of 1980 showed a figure of 91,795 Jews. Since it is possible that some otherwise identifying Jews failed to declare themselves as such in the census, a corrected estimate of 100,000 was adopted for 1980 and has been kept unchanged through 1991, assuming that the overall balance of Jewish vital events and external migrations was close to zero. The national figure of approximately 100,000 fits the admittedly rough estimates that are available for the size of local Jewish communities in Brazil.

On the strength of fragmentary information available, the estimates for Uruguay and Peru were slightly reduced, while those for Venezuela, Chile, and Colombia were not changed.

---

[12]The project, directed by Dr. Susan Lerner of the Center for Demographic and Urban Development Studies, Colegio de Mexico, and Dr. Sergio DellaPergola of the Institute of Contemporary Jewry, The Hebrew University, was sponsored by the Asociacion Mexicana de Amigos de la Universidad de Jerusalén.

[13]For a more detailed discussion of the region's Jewish population trends, see U.O. Schmelz and Sergio DellaPergola, "The Demography of Latin American Jewry," AJYB 1985, vol. 85, pp. 51–102; Sergio DellaPergola, "Demographic Trends of Latin American Jewry," in J. Laikin Elkin and G.W. Merks, eds., *The Jewish Presence in Latin America* (Boston, 1987), pp. 85–133.

[14]Rosa N. Geldstein, *Censo de la Poblacion Judia de la ciudad de Salta, 1986; Informe final* (Buenos Aires, 1988); Yacov Rubel, *Los Judios de Villa Crespo y Almagro: Perfil Sociodemografico* (Buenos Aires, 1989); Yacov Rubel, *Censo de la Poblacion Judia de Rosario, 1990* (Buenos Aires, 1992).

TABLE 2. ESTIMATED JEWISH POPULATION DISTRIBUTION IN THE AMERICAS, END 1991

Country	Total Population	Jewish Population	Jews per 1,000 Population	Accuracy Rating
Canada	27,367,000	310,000	11.3	C 1981–86
United States	255,159,000	5,575,000	21.8	A 1990
Total North America	282,651,000a	5,885,000	20.8	
Bahamas	264,000	300	1.1	C 1973
Costa Rica	3,192,000	2,000	0.6	C 1986
Cuba	10,811,000	700	0.1	C 1990
Dominican Republic	7,471,000	100	0.0	D
Guatemala	9,745,000	800	0.1	C 1983
Jamaica	2,469,000	300	0.1	B 1988
Mexico	88,153,000	38,000	0.4	A 1991 X
Netherlands Antilles	175,000	400	2.3	D
Panama	2,515,000	5,000	2.0	C 1990
Puerto Rico	3,594,000	1,500	0.4	C 1990
Virgin Islands	107,000	300	2.8	C 1986
Other	24,710,000	300	0.0	D
Total Central America	153,206,000	49,700	0.3	
Argentina	33,100,000	213,000	6.4	C 1990
Bolivia	7,524,000	700	0.1	B 1990
Brazil	154,113,000	100,000	0.6	C 1980
Chile	13,600,000	15,000	1.1	C 1988
Colombia	33,424,000	6,500	0.2	C 1986
Ecuador	11,055,000	900	0.1	C 1985
Paraguay	4,519,000	900	0.2	B 1990
Peru	22,451,000	3,100	0.1	B 1988
Suriname	438,000	200	0.5	B 1986
Uruguay	3,130,000	24,000	7.7	C 1990
Venezuela	20,186,000	20,000	1.0	C 1989
Total South America	304,454,000a	384,300	1.3	
Total	740,311,000	6,319,000	8.5	

aIncluding countries not listed separately.

EUROPE

Of the estimated over two million Jews in Europe at the end of 1991, 51 percent lived in Western Europe and 49 percent in Eastern Europe and the Balkan countries—including the Asian territories of the Russian Republic and Turkey (see table 3). In 1991 Europe lost 6.5 percent of its estimated Jewish population, mainly through the continuing emigration from the former USSR. As a consequence, for the first time, literally, in many centuries, there were more Jews in Western than in Eastern Europe.

European Community. The 12 countries forming the European Community (EC) together had an estimated Jewish population of about one million. Virtually no change was recorded as against the 1990 estimate, although different trends affected the Jewish populations in each member country. (See separate article on this subject, elsewhere in this volume.)

The estimated size of French Jewry has been assessed for several years at 530,000. Since the breakup of the USSR, France has had the third largest Jewish population in the world, after the United States and Israel. Monitoring the plausible trends of both the internal evolution and external migrations of Jews in France suggests little net change in Jewish population size since the major survey that was taken in the 1970s.[15] A study conducted in 1988 at the initiative of the Fonds Social Juif Unifié (FSJU) confirmed the basic demographic stability of French Jewry.[16]

Periodic reestimations of the size of British Jewry are carried out by the Community Research Unit (CRU) of the Board of Deputies. Based on an analysis of Jewish deaths during 1975–1979, the population baseline for 1977 was set at 336,000 with a margin of error of plus or minus 34,000.[17] The vital statistical records regularly compiled by the CRU show an excess of deaths over births in the range of about 1,500 a year. Allowing for emigration and some assimilatory losses, the update for 1984, as elaborated by the CRU, came to 330,000. Continuation of the same trends suggested an estimate of 315,000 for 1990. A study of Jewish synagogue membership indicated a decline of over 7 percent between 1983 and 1990.[18] A new national estimate, mainly based on an evaluation of Jewish death records, was being completed by the CRU at the time of this writing.[19] The preliminary results pointed to a further, substantial Jewish population decline. Pending final publication of the

---

[15]Doris Bensimon and Sergio DellaPergola, *La population juive de France: socio-démographie et identité* (Jerusalem and Paris, 1984).

[16]Erik H. Cohen, *L'Etude et l'éducation juive en France ou l'avenir d'une communauté* (Paris, 1991).

[17]Steven Haberman, Barry A. Kosmin, and Caren Levy, "Mortality Patterns of British Jews 1975–79: Insights and Applications for the Size and Structure of British Jewry," *Journal of the Royal Statistical Society*, ser. A, 146, pt. 3, 1983, pp. 294–310.

[18]Marlena Schmool and Frances Cohen, *British Synagogue Membership in 1990* (London, 1991).

[19]Steven Haberman, Marlena Schmool, *Estimates of British Jewish Population 1984–88* (London, forthcoming).

study, we adopted a provisional revised estimate of 300,000 for 1991.

In 1990, Germany was politically reunited. In the former (West) German Federal Republic, the 1987 population census reported 32,319 Jews. Jewish community records reported about 28,500 affiliated Jews at the end of 1990—an increase over previous years. Immigration compensated for the surplus of deaths over births in this aging Jewish population. Estimates for the small Jewish population in the former (East) German Democratic Republic ranged between 500 and 2,000. Our 1989 estimate for unified Germany was 35,000. In 1990, an estimated 5,000 Jewish migrants from the USSR were admitted to settle in Germany, bringing the estimate to 40,000. In 1991 immigration from the east continued, bringing to 33,692 the total number of Jews affiliated with the Jewish community. Pending clarification of the permanent impact of current immigration, we increased the figure to a conservative estimate of 42,500 at the end of 1991. Belgium, Italy, and the Netherlands each have Jewish populations ranging around 30,000. There is a tendency toward internal shrinkage of all these Jewries, but in some instances this is offset by immigration. In Belgium, the size of Jewish population is probably quite stable, owing to the comparatively strong Orthodox section in that community. In Italy, until 1984, Jews were legally bound to affiliate with the local Jewish communities, but then membership in these communities became voluntary. Although most Jews reaffiliated, the new looser legal framework may facilitate the ongoing attrition of the Jewish population.

Other EC member countries have smaller and, overall, slowly declining Jewish populations. An exception may be Spain, whose Jewish population is very tentatively estimated at 12,000.

Other Western Europe. Countries which are not EC members together account for a Jewish population of 44,000. Switzerland's Jews are estimated at below 20,000. Austria's permanent Jewish population is estimated at 7,000. While there is evidence of a negative balance of births and deaths, connected with great aging and frequent outmarriage, immigration may have offset the internal losses. The Jewish populations in Scandinavian countries are, on the whole, numerically rather stable.

Former USSR (European parts). The demographic situation of East European Jewry is rapidly changing as a consequence of the deep geopolitical changes in the region. The major event was the economic and political crisis that culminated in the disintegration of the Soviet Union as a state in 1991. Closely related to the same fateful complex of factors was the upsurge in Jewish emigration in 1990, which continued, slightly attenuated, in 1991. While mass emigration is an obvious factor of population decrease, the demography of East European Jewry has been characterized for years by very low levels of "effectively Jewish" fertility, frequent outmarriage, and heavy aging. Therefore the shrinking of the Jewish populations there must be comparatively rapid.

Data on nationalities (ethnic groups) from the Soviet Union's last official popula-

TABLE 3. ESTIMATED JEWISH POPULATION DISTRIBUTION IN EUROPE, END
1991

Country	Total Population	Jewish Population	Jews per 1,000 Population	Accuracy Rating
Belgium	9,998,000	31,800	3.2	C 1987
Denmark	5,205,000	6,400	1.2	C 1990
France	57,182,000	530,000	9.3	C 1990
Germany	80,253,000	42,500	0.5	C 1990
Great Britain	57,908,000	300,000	5.2	B 1991 X
Greece	10,182,000	4,800	0.5	B 1990
Ireland	3,486,000	1,800	0.5	B 1990
Italy	57,782,000	31,100	0.5	B 1990
Luxembourg	378,000	600	1.6	B 1990
Netherlands	15,158,000	25,600	1.7	C 1990
Portugal	9,866,000	300	0.0	B 1986
Spain	39,092,000	12,000	0.3	D
Total European Community	346,490,000	986,900	2.8	
Austria	7,776,000	7,000	0.9	C 1990
Finland	5,008,000	1,300	0.3	A 1990
Gibraltar	31,000	600	19.4	C 1981
Norway	4,288,000	1,000	0.2	B 1987
Sweden	8,652,000	15,000	1.7	C 1990
Switzerland	6,813,000	19,000	2.8	C 1980
Other	746,000	100	0.1	D
Total other West Europe	33,314,000	44,000	1.3	
Belarus	10,295,000	58,000	5.6	B 1991 X
Estonia	1,582,000	3,500	2.2	A 1991 X
Latvia	2,679,000	15,800	5.9	B 1991 X
Lithuania	3,755,000	7,300	1.9	B 1991 X
Moldova	4,362,000	28,500	6.5	B 1991 X
Russia[a]	149,003,000	430,000	2.9	B 1991 X
Ukraine	52,158,000	325,000	6.2	B 1991 X
Total former USSR in Europe	223,834,000	868,100	3.9	

TABLE 3.—*(Continued)*

Country	Total Population	Jewish Population	Jews per 1,000 Population	Accuracy Rating
Bulgaria	8,952,000	2,200	0.2	C 1990
Czechoslovakia	15,731,000	7,700	0.5	D
Hungary	10,512,000	56,500	5.4	D
Poland	38,417,000	3,700	0.1	C 1990
Romania	23,327,000	16,800	0.7	B 1988
Turkey[a]	58,362,000	19,600	0.3	C 1990
Yugoslavia[b]	23,949,000	4,300	0.2	C 1988
Total other East Europe and Balkans	182,565,000[c]	110,800	0.6	
Total	786,203,000	2,009,800	2.6	

[a]Including Asian regions.
[b]Including Slovenia, Croatia, Bosnia, and Macedonia.
[c]Including countries not listed separately.

tion census, carried out in January 1989, revealed a total of 1,450,500 Jews.[20] The figure confirmed the declining trend already apparent since the previous three censuses: 2,267,800 Jews in 1959, 2,150,700 in 1970, and 1,810,900 in 1979.

Our reservation about USSR Jewish population figures in previous AJYB volumes bears repeating: some underreporting is not impossible, but it cannot be quantified and should not be exaggerated. One should cautiously keep in mind the possible conflicting effects on census declarations of the prolonged existence of a totalitarian regime: on the one hand, stimulating a preference for other than Jewish nationalities in the various parts of the Soviet Union, especially in connection with mixed marriages; on the other hand, preserving a formal Jewish identification by coercion, through the mandatory registration of nationality on official documents such as passports. Viewed conceptually, the census figures represent the core Jewish population in the USSR. They actually constitute a good example of a large and empirically measured core Jewish population in the Diaspora, consisting of the aggregate of self-identifying Jews. The figures of successive censuses appear to be remarkably consistent with one another and with the known patterns of emigration

---

[20]*Goskomstat SSSR*, *Vestnik Statistiki* 10 (1990), pp. 69–71.

and internal demographic evolution of the Jewish population in recent decades.[21]

A substantial amount of unpublished data was known to exist about the demographic characteristics and trends of Jews in the former USSR, but it was inaccessible. Systematic analysis of such material has now become possible and is producing important new insights into recent and current trends.[22] The new data confirm the prevalence of very low fertility and birthrates, high frequencies of outmarriage, a preference for non-Jewish nationalities among the children of outmarriages, aging, and a clear surplus of Jewish deaths over Jewish births. These trends are especially visible in the Slavic republics holding a large share of the total Jewish population.

The respective figures for the enlarged Jewish population—including all current Jews as well as any other persons of Jewish parentage and their non-Jewish household members—must be substantially higher in a societal context like that of the USSR, which has been characterized by high intermarriage rates for a considerable time. It is not yet possible to provide an actual estimate of this enlarged Jewish population for lack of appropriate data. Nor can any information about the ratio between Jews and non-Jews in an enlarged Jewish population in the USSR be derived from the statistics of immigrants to Israel. Due to the highly self-selective character of *aliyah*, non-Jews have constituted a relatively small minority of all new immigrants from the USSR.[23] It is obvious, though, that the wide provisions of Israel's Law of Return (see above) apply to virtually the maximum emigration pool of self-declared Jews and close non-Jewish relatives. Any of the large figures attributed in recent years to the size of Soviet Jewry, insofar as they are based on

---

[21]U.O. Schmelz, "New Evidence on Basic Issues in the Demography of Soviet Jews," *Jewish Journal of Sociology* 16, no. 2, 1974, pp. 209–23; Mordechai Altshuler, *Soviet Jewry Since the Second World War: Population and Social Structure* (Westport, 1987).

[22]Viacheslav Konstantinov, "Jewish Population of the USSR on the Eve of the Great Exodus," *Jews and Jewish Topics in the Soviet Union and Eastern Europe* 3 (16), 1991, pp. 5–23; Mordechai Altshuler, "Socio-demographic Profile of Moscow Jews," ibid., pp. 24–40; Mark Tolts, "The Balance of Births and Deaths Among Soviet Jewry," *Jews and Jewish Topics in the Soviet Union and Eastern Europe* 2 (18), 1992, pp. 13–26; Leonid E. Darsky, "Fertility in the USSR; Basic Trends" (Paper presented at European Population Conference, Paris, 1991); Mark Tolts, "Jewish Marriages in the USSR: A Demographic Analysis" (Moscow, 1991); Mark Tolts, "Trends in Soviet Jewish Demography Since the Second World War" (Paper presented at conference, "From Revolution to Revolution: The Soviet Jews Under the Soviet Regime," Jerusalem, 1992); Mark Kupovetsky, "From Village Settlers to Urban Integration: Jews in the Soviet Union Between the Two World Wars," ibid.

[23]Israel's Ministry of Interior records the religion-nationality of each person, including new immigrants. Such attribution is made on the basis of documentary evidence supplied by the immigrants themselves and checked by competent authorities in Israel. According to data available from the Interior Ministry's Central Population Register, 90.3 percent of all new immigrants from the USSR during the period October 1989–August 1992 were recorded as Jewish. The annual trends clearly point to a growing proportion of non-Jews among the immigrants. See Sergio DellaPergola, "The Demographic Context of the Soviet Aliya," *Jews and Jewish Topics in the Soviet Union and Eastern Europe* 3 (16), 1991, pp. 41–56.

demographic reasoning, do not relate to the core but to various measures of an enlarged Jewish population. The evidence also suggests that in the USSR core Jews constitute a smaller share of the total enlarged Jewish population than in some Western countries, such as the United States.

Just as the number of declared Jews remained consistent between censuses, the number of persons of Jewish descent who preferred not to be identified as Jews was rather consistent too, at least until 1989. However, the recent political developments, and especially the emigration urge impressively illustrated by the exodus of 1990–1991, have probably led to greater readiness to declare a Jewish self-identification by persons who did not describe themselves as such in the 1989 census. In terms of demographic accounting, these "returnees" imply an actual net increment to the core Jewish population of the USSR, as well as to world Jewry.

With regard to updating the January 1989 census figure to the end of 1991 for each of the republics of the former USSR, Jewish emigration has played the major role among the intervening changes. An estimated 71,000, thereof about 60,000 declared Jews, left in 1989, as against 19,300 in 1988, 8,100 in 1987, and only 7,000 during the whole 1982–1986 period. In 1990, according to Soviet, Israeli, American, and other sources, an estimated 229,000 Jews originating in the USSR were involved in international migrations, including the resettling of those who had been in temporary accommodations in Western Europe.[24] In 1991, 148,000 immigrants from the former USSR arrived in Israel. Another minimum estimate of 42,000 migrants arrived in other countries. We estimate that of these total 190,000 migrants, about 150,000 were Jewish. At the same time, the heavy deficit of internal population dynamics continued and even intensified due to the great aging which is known to have prevailed for many decades. The aging of the remaining population was exacerbated by the significantly younger age composition of the emigrants.[25]

On the strength of these considerations, our estimate of the core Jewish population in the USSR was reduced from the census figure of 1,450,500 at the end of 1988-beginning of 1989 to 1,370,000 at the end of 1989, and to 1,150,000 at the end of 1990. In the light of better estimates prepared in relation to the present article, the 1990 estimate was revised to 1,157,500, and updated to 990,000 at the end of

---

[24]See Sidney Heitman, "Soviet Emigration in 1990," *Berichte des Bundesinstitut für Ostwissenschaftliche und internationale Studien*, vol. 33, 1991.

[25]Age structures of the Jewish population in the Russian Federal Republic in 1970 and 1979 were reported in *Goskomstat SSSR, Itogi vsesoiuznoi perepisi naseleniia 1970 goda*, vol. 4, table 33 (Moscow, 1973); *Goskomstat SSSR, Itogi vsesoiuznoi perepisi naseleniia 1979 goda*, vol. 4, part 2, table 2 (Moscow, 1989); *Goskomstat SSSR, Itogi vsesoiuznoi perepisi naseleniia 1989 goda* (Moscow, 1991). Age structures of recent Jewish migrants from the USSR to the United States and to Israel appear, respectively, in: HIAS, *Statistical Abstract*, vol. 30, no. 4 (New York, 1990); Israel Central Bureau of Statistics, *Immigration to Israel 1990*, Special Series, no. 900 (Jerusalem, 1991); Yoel Florsheim, "Immigration to Israel from the Soviet Union in 1990," *Jews and Jewish Topics in the Soviet Union and Eastern Europe* 2 (15), 1991, pp. 5–14.

1991.[26] Of these, 868,100 lived in the European republics and 121,900 in the Asian parts of the former USSR (see below). The largest Jewish populations in the European parts are in the Russian Republic (430,000) and Ukraine (325,000). A further 58,000 Jews are estimated to live in Belarus, 28,500 in the Moldovan Republic, and a combined total of 26,600 in the three Baltic states of Estonia, Latvia, and Lithuania.

Other East Europe and Balkans. The Jewish populations in Hungary and Romania and the small remnants in Bulgaria, the Czech and Slovak republics, Poland, and the former Yugoslavia are all reputed to be very overaged and to experience frequent outmarriage. In each of these countries, the ongoing processes of political liberalization have permitted greater autonomy of the organized Jewish communities and their registered membership. Although some Jews or persons of Jewish origin have come out in the open after years of hiding their identity, the inevitable numerical decline of Jewish populations in Eastern Europe is reflected in reduced estimates for 1991.

In 1991, the entire Jewish community of Albania, amounting to some 300, emigrated to Israel. The size of Hungarian Jewry—the largest in Eastern Europe outside the former USSR—is quite insufficiently known. Our estimate of 56,500 only attempts to reflect the declining trend that prevails there, too, according to the available indicators. Jewish emigration continued to take place from Romania. The January 1992 census of Romania indicated a Jewish population of 9,100. However, based on the detailed Jewish community records available there, our estimate for the end of 1991 was 16,800. In Yugoslavia, torn apart by a devastating political, military, and economic crisis, the overall core Jewish population was estimated at 4,300 at the end of 1991. Of these, roughly 1,900 lived in Serbia, 1,200 in Croatia, 1,000 in Bosnia-Herzegovina (before the collapse of civil life there), and less than 100 each in Slovenia and Macedonia. In Czechoslovakia, another country on the verge of political breakup, the Jewish population was tentatively estimated at 4,700 in the Czech Republic and 3,000 in Slovakia.

The Jewish population of Turkey, where a surplus of deaths over births has been reported for several years, is estimated at about 20,000.

ASIA

Israel. Israel accounts for 96 percent of all the nearly 4.3 million Jews in Asia, including the Asian republics of the former USSR, but excluding the Asian territories of the Russian Republic and Turkey (see table 4). By the end of 1991, Israel Jews constituted over 32 percent of total world Jewry. Israel's Jewish population grew in 1991 by about 198,000, or 5 percent. This was slightly less than in 1990 (6.2 percent growth), and the second highest growth rate since the end of the initial wave of mass *aliyah* in 1951. About 77 percent of Jewish population growth in 1991 was

---

[26]We appreciate the collaboration of Dr. Mark Tolts, of the Institute of Contemporary Jewry at the Hebrew University, in preparing these estimates.

TABLE 4.   ESTIMATED JEWISH POPULATION DISTRIBUTION IN ASIA, END 1991[a]

Country	Total Population	Jewish Population	Jews per 1,000 Population	Accuracy Rating
Israel	5,059,000[b]	4,144,600	819.3	A 1991
Armenia	3,489,000	300	0.1	B 1991 X
Azerbaijan	7,283,000	16,000	2.2	B 1991 X
Georgia	5,471,000	20,700	3.8	B 1991 X
Kazakhstan	17,048,000	15,300	0.9	B 1991 X
Kirghizstan	4,518,000	3,900	0.9	B 1991 X
Tajikistan	5,587,000	8,200	1.5	B 1991 X
Turkmenistan	3,861,000	2,000	0.5	B 1991 X
Uzbekistan	21,453,000	55,500	2.6	B 1991 X
Total former USSR in Asia[a]	68,710,000	121,900	1.8	
Hong Kong	5,800,000	1,000	0.2	D
India	879,548,000	4,700	0.0	C 1981
Iran	61,565,000	18,000	0.3	D
Iraq	19,290,000	200	0.0	D
Japan	124,491,000	1,000	0.0	C 1988
Korea, South	44,163,000	100	0.0	D
Philippines	65,186,000	100	0.0	C 1988
Singapore	2,769,000	300	0.1	B 1990
Syria	13,276,000	4,000	0.3	C 1991
Thailand	56,129,000	200	0.0	D 1988
Yemen	12,535,000	1,700	0.1	B 1990
Other	1,884,723,000	300	0.0	D
Total other Asia	3,169,475,000	31,600	0.0	
Total	3,243,244,000	4,298,100	1.3	

[a]Not including Asian regions of Russia and Turkey.
[b]End 1991.

due to the net migration balance. The total number of Jewish immigrants (176,100) was the third highest in Israel's history. More immigrants arrived in 1949 (239,950) and in 1990 (199,500). The remaining 23 percent of Jewish population growth reflected natural increase, including some cases of immigrants from the former

USSR who were previously listed as non-Jews being reregistered as Jews.[27]

Former USSR (Asian parts). The total Jewish population in the Asian republics of the former USSR was estimated at about 122,000. The largest community was in Uzbekistan (55,500), followed by Georgia (20,700), Azerbaijan (16,000), and Kazakhstan (15,300). Growing Muslim fundamentalism and the various ethnic conflicts in these areas were causes of concern and stimulated high emigration rates. Internal identificational and demographic processes were less a factor of attrition among these Jewish populations than was the case in the European republics of the former USSR. At the end of the 1980s, minimal rates of natural increase still existed among the more traditional sections of these Jewish communities, but the conditions prevailing at the beginning of the 1990s were rapidly eroding this residual surplus.[28]

Other countries. It is difficult to estimate the Jewish population of Iran for any given date, but it continues to dwindle. The estimate for 1991 was reduced to 18,000. In other Asian countries with small veteran communities—such as India, or several Muslim countries—the Jewish population tends to decline. Very small Jewish communities, partially of a transient character, exist in several countries of Southeast Asia.

AFRICA

Less than 130,000 Jews are estimated to remain now in Africa. The Republic of South Africa accounts for 88 percent of total Jews in that continent (see table 5). The last official population census, carried out in 1991, did not provide a reliable new national figure of Jewish population size. The question on religion was not mandatory, and only about 59,000 people declared themselves as Jewish. In 1980, according to the previous official census, there were about 118,000 Jews among South Africa's white population.[29] Substantial Jewish emigration since then was compensated in good part by Jewish immigration and return migration of former emigrants. Considering a moderately negative migration balance, and an incipient negative balance of internal changes, our Jewish population estimate for 1988 was reduced to 114,000. Since then, there appears to have been further decline in Jewish population. Pending publication in 1993 of the results of a Jewish-sponsored survey of South African Jewry completed in 1991, we repeat our previous estimate for 1991.[30]

---

[27]Israel Central Bureau of Statistics, *Statistical Abstract of Israel 1992* (Jerusalem, 1992). For a comprehensive review of sociodemographic changes in Israel, see U.O. Schmelz, Sergio DellaPergola, and Uri Avner, "Ethnic Differences Among Israeli Jews: A New Look," AJYB 1990, vol. 90, pp. 3–204.

[28]Tolts, "The Balance. . . ."

[29]Sergio DellaPergola and Allie A. Dubb, "South African Jewry: A Sociodemographic Profile," AJYB 1988, vol. 88, pp. 59–140.

[30]The study was directed by Dr. Allie A. Dubb and supported by the Kaplan Centre for Judaic Studies, University of Cape Town.

In recent years, the Jewish community of Ethiopia has been at the center of an international rescue effort. In the course of 1991, the overwhelming majority of Ethiopian Jews—about 20,000 people—were brought to Israel, most of them in a dramatic one-day airlift operation. (A few of these migrants were non-Jewish members of mixed households.) In connection with these events, the size of Ethiopian Jewry can be evaluated on a more accurate basis than previously. It can be estimated that the core Jewish population was about 21,000 at the end of 1990, and 1,500 at the end of 1991. The question of the status of the Christian relatives of Ethiopian Jews and of their possible numbers is being investigated by Israeli authorities.

The remnants of Moroccan and Tunisian Jewry tend to shrink slowly through emigration. It should be pointed out, though, that some Jews have a foothold both in Morocco or Tunisia and in France and other Western countries, and their geographical attribution is uncertain.

TABLE 5. ESTIMATED JEWISH POPULATION DISTRIBUTION IN AFRICA, END 1991

Country	Total Population	Jewish Population	Jews per 1,000 Population	Accuracy Rating
Egypt	54,842,000	200	0.0	C 1988
Ethiopia	52,981,000	1,500	0.0	B 1991
Kenya	25,230,000	400	0.0	B 1990
Morocco	26,318,000	8,000	0.3	D
South Africa	39,818,000	114,000	2.9	C 1980
Tunisia	8,401,000	2,200	0.3	D
Zaire	39,882,000	400	0.0	C 1990
Zambia	8,638,000	300	0.0	C 1990
Zimbabwe	10,583,000	1,000	0.1	B 1990
Other	414,992,000	1,000	0.0	D
Total	681,685,000	129,000	0.2	

OCEANIA

The major country of Jewish residence in Oceania (Australasia) is Australia, where 95 percent of the estimated total of nearly 94,000 Jews live (see table 6). The 1986 census of Australia, where the question on religion is optional, enumerated 69,065 declared Jews but also indicated that about 25 percent of the country's whole

, population either did not specify their religion or stated explicitly that they had none.[31] This large group must be assumed to contain persons who identify in other ways as Jews. In addition, Australian Jewry has received migratory reinforcements during the last decade, especially from South Africa and the former USSR. At the same time, there are demographic patterns with negative effects on Jewish population size, such as strong aging, low or negative natural increase, and some assimilation. We raised our estimate for 1991 to a provisional figure of 89,000. The new census of 1991, as well as a Jewish survey now being planned, will hopefully provide firmer data on Jewish population size and trends in Australia. The Jewish community in New Zealand is estimated at 4,500.

TABLE 6. ESTIMATED JEWISH POPULATION DISTRIBUTION IN OCEANIA, END 1991

Country	Total Population	Jewish Population	Jews per 1,000 Population	Accuracy Rating
Australia	17,596,000	89,000	5.1	C 1986
New Zealand	3,455,000	4,500	1.3	C 1988
Other	6,479,000	100	0.0	D
Total	27,530,000	93,600	3.4	

Dispersion and Concentration

Table 7 demonstrates the magnitude of Jewish dispersion. The individual countries listed above as each having at least 100 Jews are scattered over all the continents. In 1991, more than half (46 out of 87 countries) had fewer than 5,000 Jews each. In relative terms, too, the Jews were thinly scattered nearly everywhere in the Diaspora. There is not a single Diaspora country where they amounted even to 25 per 1,000 of the total population. In most countries they constituted a far smaller fraction. Only three Diaspora countries had more than 10 Jews per 1,000 in their total population; and only thirteen countries had more than 5 Jews per 1,000 of population. The respective 13 countries were, in descending order of the proportion, but regardless of the absolute number of their Jews: United States (21.8 per 1,000), Gibraltar (19.4), Canada (11.3), France (9.3), Uruguay (7.7), Moldova (6.5), Argen-

[31]Walter M. Lippmann, *Australian Jewry 1986* (South Yarra, Victoria, 1987).

tina (6.4), Ukraine (6.2), Latvia (5.9), Belarus (5.6), Hungary (5.4), Great Britain (5.2), and Australia (5.1). The other major Diaspora Jewries, having lower proportions of Jews per 1,000 of total population, were Russia (2.9 per 1,000), South Africa (2.9), and Brazil (0.6).

TABLE 7. DISTRIBUTION OF THE WORLD'S JEWS, BY NUMBER AND PROPORTION (PER 1,000 POPULATION) IN VARIOUS COUNTRIES, 1991

Number of Jews in Country	Jews per 1,000 Population					
	Total	0.0–0.9	1.0–4.9	5.0–9.9	10.0–24.9	25.0+
	Number of Countries					
Total	87a	52	21	10	3	1
100–900	24	19	4	—	1	—
1,000–4,900	22	20	2	—	—	—
5,000–9,900	8	4	4	—	—	—
10,000–49,900	19	8	8	3	—	—
50,000–99,900	4	—	1	3	—	—
100,000–999,900	8	1	2	4	1	—
1,000,000 or more	2	—	—	—	1	1
	Jewish Population Distribution (Absolute Numbers)					
Total	12,849,500b	378,400	799,100	1,639,800	5,885,600	4,144,600
100–900	9,400	7,200	1,600	—	600	—
1,000–4,900	56,700	48,700	8,000	—	—	—
5,000–9,900	56,100	29,200	26,900	—	—	—
10,000–49,900	424,700	193,300	163,100	68,300	—	—
50,000–99,900	259,000	—	55,500	203,500	—	—
100,000–999,900	2,322,000	100,000	544,000	1,368,000	310,000	—
1,000,000 or more	9,719,600	—	—	—	5,575,000	4,144,600
	Jewish Population Distribution (Percent of World's Jews)c					
Total	100.0b	2.9	6.2	12.8	45.8	32.3
100–900	0.1	0.0	0.0	—	0.0	—
1,000–4,900	0.4	0.4	0.1	—	—	—
5,000–9,900	0.4	0.2	0.2	—	—	—
10,000–49,900	3.3	1.5	1.3	0.5	—	—
50,000–99,900	2.0	—	0.4	1.6	—	—
100,000–999,900	18.1	0.8	4.2	10.7	2.4	—
1,000,000 or more	75.6	—	—	—	43.4	32.3

aExcluding countries with fewer than 100 Jews.
bIncluding countries with fewer than 100 Jews.
cMinor discrepancies due to rounding.

In the state of Israel, by contrast, the Jewish majority amounted to 819 per 1,000 in 1991, compared to 818 per 1,000 in 1990—not including the Arab population of the administered areas.

While Jews are widely dispersed, they are also concentrated to some extent (see table 8). In 1991 nearly 94 percent of world Jewry lived in the ten countries with the largest Jewish populations; and over 75 percent lived in the two largest communities—the United States and Israel. Similarly, ten leading Diaspora countries together comprised about 92 percent of the Diaspora Jewish population; three countries (United States, France, and Russia) accounted for 75 percent, and the United States alone for over 64 percent of total Diaspora Jewry.

TABLE 8. ELEVEN COUNTRIES WITH LARGEST JEWISH POPULATIONS, END 1991

| | | | % of Total Jewish Population | | | |
| | | Jewish | In the World | | In the Diaspora | |
Rank	Country	Population	%	Cumulative %	%	Cumulative %
1	United States	5,575,000	43.4	43.4	64.0	64.0
2	Israel	4,144,600	32.3	75.7	—	—
3	France	530,000	4.1	79.8	6.1	70.1
4	Russia	430,000	3.3	83.1	4.9	75.0
5	Ukraine	325,000	2.5	85.6	3.7	78.7
6	Canada	310,000	2.4	88.0	3.6	82.3
7	Great Britain	300,000	2.3	90.3	3.4	85.7
8	Argentina	213,000	1.7	92.0	2.5	88.2
9	South Africa	114,000	0.9	92.9	1.3	89.5
10	Brazil	100,000	0.8	93.7	1.2	90.7
11	Australia	89,000	0.7	94.4	1.0	91.7

U.O. SCHMELZ
SERGIO DELLAPERGOLA

Directories
Lists
Obituaries

National Jewish Organizations[1]

UNITED STATES

Organizations are listed according to functions as follows:

COMMUNITY RELATIONS

AMERICAN COUNCIL FOR JUDAISM (1943). PO Box 9009, Alexandria, VA 22304. (703)836–2546. Pres. Alan V. Stone; Exec. Dir. Allan C. Brownfeld. Seeks to advance the universal principles of a Judaism free of nationalism, and the national, civic, cultural, and social integration into American institutions of Americans of Jewish faith. *Issues of the American Council for Judaism; Special Interest Report.*

AMERICAN JEWISH ALTERNATIVES TO ZIONISM, INC. (1968). 347 Fifth Ave., Suite 900, NYC 10016. (212)213–9125. FAX: (212)213–9142. Pres. Elmer Berger; V.-Pres. Mrs. Arthur Gutman. Applies Jewish values of justice and humanity to the Arab-Israel conflict in the Middle East; rejects nationality attachment of Jews, particularly American Jews, to the State of Israel as self-segregating, inconsistent with American constitutional concepts of individual citizenship and separation of church and state, and as being a principal obstacle to Middle East peace. *Report.*

AMERICAN JEWISH COMMITTEE (1906). Institute of Human Relations, 165 E. 56 St., NYC 10022. (212)751–4000. FAX: (212)-319–6156. Pres. Alfred H. Moses; Exec. V.-Pres. David A. Harris. Seeks to prevent infraction of civil and religious rights of Jews in any part of the world; to advance

---

[1]The information in this directory is based on replies to questionnaires circulated by the editors.

the cause of human rights for people of all races, creeds, and nationalities; to interpret the position of Israel to the American public; and to help American Jews maintain and enrich their Jewish identity and, at the same time, achieve full integration in American life. Includes Jacob and Hilda Blaustein Center for Human Relations, William E. Wiener Oral History Library, William Petschek National Jewish Family Center, Jacob Blaustein Institute for the Advancement of Human Rights, Institute on American Jewish-Israeli Relations. AMERICAN JEWISH YEAR BOOK (with Jewish Publication Society); *Commentary; AJC Journal; Capital Update. Published in Israel: Alon Yedi'ot, a monthly bulletin of the Institute on American Jewish-Israeli Relations.*

AMERICAN JEWISH CONGRESS (1918). Stephen Wise Congress House, 15 E. 84 St., NYC 10028. (212)879-4500. FAX: (212)-249-3672. Pres. Robert K. Lifton; Exec. Dir. Henry Siegman. Works to foster the creative survival of the Jewish people; to help Israel develop in peace, freedom, and security; to eliminate all forms of racial and religious bigotry; to advance civil rights, protect civil liberties, defend religious freedom, and safeguard the separation of church and state. *Congress Monthly; Judaism; Boycott Report; Inside Israel.*

ANTI-DEFAMATION LEAGUE OF B'NAI B'RITH (1913). 823 United Nations Plaza, NYC 10017. (212)490-2525. FAX: (212)-661-3844. Chmn. Melvin Salberg; Dir. Abraham H. Foxman. Seeks to combat anti-Semitism and to secure justice and fair treatment for all citizens through law, education, and community relations. *ADL on the Frontline; Law Enforcement Bulletin; Dimensions: A Journal of Holocaust Studies; Hidden Child Newsletter; International Reports; Civil Rights Reports.*

ASSOCIATION OF JEWISH COMMUNITY RELATIONS WORKERS (1950). 1522 K St., NW, Suite 920, Washington, DC 20005. (202)347-4628. Pres. Marlene Gorin. Aims to stimulate higher standards of professional practice in Jewish community relations; encourages research and training toward that end; conducts educational programs and seminars; aims to encourage cooperation between community relations workers and those working in other areas of Jewish communal service.

CENTER FOR JEWISH COMMUNITY STUDIES (1970). Temple University, Center City Campus, 1616 Walnut St., Suite 513, Philadelphia, PA 19103. (215)787-1459. FAX: (215)787-7784. Jerusalem office: Jerusalem Center for Public Affairs. Pres. Daniel J. Elazar. Worldwide policy-studies institute devoted to the study of Jewish community organization, political thought, and public affairs, past and present, in Israel and throughout the world. Publishes original articles, essays, and monographs; maintains library, archives, and reprint series. *Jerusalem Letter/Viewpoints; Survey of Arab Affairs; Jewish Political Studies Review.*

CENTER FOR RUSSIAN JEWRY WITH STUDENT STRUGGLE FOR SOVIET JEWRY (1964). 240 Cabrini Blvd., #5B, New York, NY 10033. (212)928-7451. FAX: (212)795-8867. Dir.-Founder Jacob Birnbaum; Acting Chmn. Dr. Ernest Bloch; Student Coord. Glenn Richter. Campaigns for the human rights of the Jews of the former USSR, with emphasis on emigration and Jewish identity; supports programs for needy Jews there and for newcomers in Israel and USA, stressing employment and Jewish education. As the originator of the grassroots movement for Soviet Jewry in the early 1960s, possesses unique archives.

COMMISSION ON SOCIAL ACTION OF REFORM JUDAISM (1953, joint instrumentality of the Union of American Hebrew Congregations and the Central Conference of American Rabbis). 838 Fifth Ave., NYC 10021. (212)249-0100. 2027 Massachusetts Ave., NW, Washington, DC 20036. Chmn. Evely Laser Shlensky; Dir. Rabbi Eric Yoffie; Co-Dir. & Counsel Rabbi David Saperstein. Policy-making body that relates ethical and spiritual principles of Judaism to social-justice issues: implements resolutions through the Religious Action Center in Washington, DC, via advocacy, development of educational materials, and congregational programs. *Briefings (social action newsletter); Chai Impact (legislative update).*

CONFERENCE OF PRESIDENTS OF MAJOR AMERICAN JEWISH ORGANIZATIONS (1955). 110 E. 59 St., NYC 10022. (212)-318-6111. FAX: (212)644-4135. Chmn. Lester Pollack. Exec. V.-Chmn. Malcolm Hoenlein. Seeks to strengthen the U.S.-Israel alliance and to protect and enhance the security and dignity of Jews abroad. Toward this end, the Conference of Presidents speaks and acts on the basis of consensus of its 48 member agencies on issues of national and international Jewish concern. *Annual report.*

CONSULTATIVE COUNCIL OF JEWISH ORGANIZATIONS-CCJO (1946). 420 Lexington Ave., Suite 1733, NYC 10170. (212)808–5437. Pres.'s Ady Steg, Fred Tuckman, and Joseph Nuss; Sec.-Gen. Warren Green. A nongovernmental organization in consultative status with the UN, UNESCO, ILO, UNICEF, and the Council of Europe; cooperates and consults with, advises and renders assistance to the Economic and Social Council of the UN on all problems relating to human rights and economic, social, cultural, educational, and related matters pertaining to Jews.

COORDINATING BOARD OF JEWISH ORGANIZATIONS (1947). 1640 Rhode Island Ave., NW, Washington, DC 20036. (202)-857–6545. Pres. Kent E. Schiner; Exec. V.-Pres. Dr. Sidney Clearfield; Dir. Internatl. Affairs Daniel S. Mariaschin; Dir. Internatl. Council Warren Eisenberg; Dir. UN Off. Harris Schoenberg. Coordinates the UN activities of B'nai B'rith and the British and South African Boards of Jewish Deputies.

COUNCIL OF JEWISH ORGANIZATIONS IN CIVIL SERVICE, INC. (1948). 45 E. 33 St., Rm. 604, NYC 10016. (212)689–2015. Pres. Louis Weiser. Supports merit system; encourages recruitment of Jewish youth to government service; member of Coalition to Free Soviet Jews, NY Jewish Community Relations Council, NY Metropolitan Coordinating Council on Jewish Poverty, Jewish Labor Committee, America-Israel Friendship League. *Council Digest.*

INSTITUTE FOR PUBLIC AFFAIRS (*see* Union of Orthodox Jewish Congregations of America)

INTERNATIONAL CONFERENCE OF JEWISH COMMUNAL SERVICE (*see* World Conference of Jewish Communal Service)

INTERNATIONAL LEAGUE FOR THE REPATRIATION OF RUSSIAN JEWS, INC. (1963). 2 Fountain Lane, Suite 2J, Scarsdale, NY 10583. (800)448–1866. Pres. Morris Brafman; Chmn. James H. Rapp. Helped to bring the situation of Soviet Jews to world

attention; advocates in world forums for the right of Soviet Jews to repatriation.

JEWISH LABOR COMMITTEE (1934). Atran Center for Jewish Culture, 25 E. 21 St., NYC 10010. (212)477–0707. FAX: (212)-477–1918. Pres. Lenore Miller; Exec. Dir. Martin Lapan. Serves as liaison between the Jewish community and the trade-union movement; works with the AFL-CIO to combat anti-Semitism and engender support for the State of Israel and Soviet Jewry; strengthens support within the Jewish community for the social goals and programs of the labor movement; supports Yiddish cultural institutions. *Jewish Labor Committee Review; Alumni Newsletter.*

——, NATIONAL TRADE UNION COUNCIL FOR HUMAN RIGHTS (1956). Atran Center for Jewish Culture, 25 E. 21 St., NYC 10010. (212)477–0707. FAX: (212)477–1918. Chmn. Sol Hoffman; Exec. Sec. Michael Perry. Works with the American labor movement in advancing the struggle for social justice and equal opportunity and assists unions in every issue affecting human rights. Fights discrimination on all levels and helps to promote labor's broad social and economic goals.

JEWISH PEACE FELLOWSHIP (1941). Box 271, Nyack, NY 10960. (914)358–4601. FAX: (914)358–4924. Cochmn. Rabbi Charles Lippman and Rabbi Philip Bentley; Sec. Naomi Goodman. Unites those who believe that Jewish ideals and experience provide inspiration for a nonviolent philosophy and way of life; offers draft counseling, especially for conscientious objection based on Jewish "religious training and belief"; encourages Jewish community to become more knowledgeable, concerned, and active in regard to the war/peace problem. *Shalom/Jewish Peace Letter.*

JEWISH WAR VETERANS OF THE UNITED STATES OF AMERICA (1896). 1811 R St., NW, Washington, DC 20009. (202)265–6280. FAX: (202)234–5662. Natl. Exec. Dir. Herb Rosenbleeth; Natl. Commander Warren S. Dolny. Seeks to foster true allegiance to the United States; to combat bigotry and prevent defamation of Jews; to encourage the doctrine of universal liberty, equal rights, and full justice for all; to cooperate with and support existing educational institutions and establish new ones; to foster the education of ex-servicemen, ex-servicewomen, and members in the ideals and principles of Americanism. *Jewish Veteran.*

———, NATIONAL MUSEUM OF AMERICAN JEWISH MILITARY HISTORY (1958). 1811 R St., NW, Washington, DC 20009. (202)-265–6280. FAX: (202)462–3192. Pres. Florence G. Levine. Operates a museum, library, and archive dedicated to telling the story of the activities and service of American Jews in the armed forces of the U.S. *Quarterly newsletter, Routes to Roots.*

NATIONAL ASSOCIATION OF JEWISH LEGISLATORS (1976). 45 Thorndale Rd., Slingerlands, NY 12159. (518)455–2761. FAX: (518)455–2959. Exec. Dir. Albert J. Abrams; Pres. Assemblyman Byron Baer. Arranges visits to Israel for its members, has close ties with the Knesset; a Jewish legislative network on domestic issues; nonpartisan; issues newsletters from time to time.

NATIONAL CONFERENCE ON SOVIET JEWRY (formerly AMERICAN JEWISH CONFERENCE ON SOVIET JEWRY) (1964; reorg. 1971). 10 E. 40 St., Suite 1701, NYC 10016. (212)679–6122. FAX: (212)686–1193. Chmn. Richard Wexler. Exec. Dir. Mark B. Levin. Coordinating agency for major national Jewish organizations and local community groups in the U.S., acting on behalf of Soviet Jewry through public education and social action; stimulates all segments of the community to maintain an interest in the problems of Soviet Jews by publishing reports and special pamphlets, sponsoring special programs and projects, organizing public meetings and forums. *Newsbreak; annual report; action and program kits; Wrap-Up Leadership Report.*

———, SOVIET JEWRY RESEARCH BUREAU. Chmn. Charlotte Jacobson. Organized by NCSJ to monitor emigration trends. Primary task is the accumulation, evaluation, and processing of information regarding Soviet Jews, especially those who apply for emigration.

NATIONAL JEWISH COALITION (1980). 415 2nd St., NE, Suite 100, Washington, DC 20002. (202)547–7701. FAX: (202)544–2434. Natl. Chmn. Cheryl Halpern; Hon. Chmn. Max M. Fisher, George Klein, Richard J. Fox, and Amb. Joseph Gildenhorn; Exec. Dir. Matt Brooks. Promotes involvement in Republican politics among its members; sensitizes Republican leaders to the concerns of the American Jewish community; promotes principles of free enterprise, a strong national defense, and an internationalist foreign policy. *NJC Bulletin.*

NATIONAL JEWISH COMMISSION ON LAW AND PUBLIC AFFAIRS (COLPA) (1965). 135 W. 50 St., 6th fl., NYC 10020. (212)-641–8992. FAX: (212)641–7186. Pres. Allen L. Rothenberg; Exec. Dir. Dennis Rapps. Voluntary association of attorneys whose purpose is to represent the observant Jewish community on legal, legislative, and public-affairs matters.

NATIONAL JEWISH COMMUNITY RELATIONS ADVISORY COUNCIL (1944). 443 Park Ave. S., 11th fl., NYC 10016. (212)-684–6950. FAX: (212)686–1353. Chmn. Maynard I. Wishner; Sec. Frederick Frank; Exec. V.-Chmn. Lawrence Rubin. National coordinating body for the field of Jewish community relations, comprising 13 national and 117 local Jewish community relations agencies. Promotes understanding of Israel and the Middle East; freedom for Soviet Jews; equal status for Jews and other groups in American society. Through the NJCRAC's work, its constituent organizations seek agreement on policies, strategies, and programs for effective utilization of their resources for common ends. *Joint Program Plan for Jewish Community Relations.*

NATIONAL JEWISH DEMOCRATIC COUNCIL (1990). 711 Second St., NE, #100, Washington, DC 20002. (202)544–7636. FAX: (202)544–7645. Chmn. Mort Mandel; V.-Chmn. Stuart Eizenstat, Monte Friedkin, Steve Grossman; Treas. Sheldon Cohen. An independent organization of Jewish Democrats committed to strengthening the Democratic party through its members' participation in the grassroots political process; to making the party sensitive to the views of American Jews; and to encouraging American Jewish support for the party. *Capital Communiqué.*

SHALOM CENTER (1983). 7318 Germantown Ave., Philadelphia, PA 19119. (215)247–9700. FAX: (215)247–9703. Bd. Chmn. Viki List; Exec. Dir. Arthur Waskow. National resource and organizing center for Jewish perspectives on moving from the cold war toward "One Earth"—in dealing with nuclear and other environmental dangers. Assists local Jewish communities on environmental issues. "Eco-Shalom Corps" trains environmental organizers and places interns. Sponsors Sukkat Shalom, Eco-Kosher project, and Ira Silverman Memorial. Provides school curricula, sermon materials, legislative reports, liturgies, adult-education texts, and media for Jewish use. *Shalom Report.*

STUDENT STRUGGLE FOR SOVIET JEWRY, INC. (*see* Center for Russian Jewry)

UNION OF COUNCILS FOR SOVIET JEWS (1970). 1819 H St., NW, Suite 230, Washington, DC 20006. (202)775-9770. Natl. Pres. Pamela B. Cohen; Natl. Dir. Micah H. Naftalin. Its 38 local councils and 100,-000 members throughout the U.S. support and protect Soviet Jews by gathering and disseminating news on the condition and treatment of Soviet Jews; advocacy; publications and educational programs, including briefings and policy analyses. Five Bureaus on Human Rights and Rule of Law operating throughout the Soviet successor states monitor anti-Semitism and ethnic intolerance, advocate for refuseniks and political prisoners, seek to advance democracy and rule of law. *Monitor (weekly digest of news and analysis from the Soviet successor states); Status Reports on Anti-Semitism; Russia Inside (a publication of Moscow Bureau); Jewish News Weekly (news service providing information on Jewish and human-rights developments in former USSR).*

WORLD CONFERENCE OF JEWISH COMMUNAL SERVICE (1966). 3084 State Highway 27, Suite 9, Kendall Park, NJ 08824-1657. (908)821-0282. FAX: (908)821-5335. Pres. Arthur Rotman; Sec.-Gen. Joel Ollander. Established by worldwide Jewish communal workers to strengthen their understanding of each other's programs and to communicate with colleagues in order to enrich the quality of their work. Conducts quadrennial international conferences in Jerusalem and periodic regional meetings. *Proceedings of international conferences; newsletters.*

WORLD JEWISH CONGRESS (1936; org. in U.S. 1939). 501 Madison Ave., 17th fl., NYC 10022. (212) 755-5770. FAX: (212)-755-5883. Pres. Edgar M. Bronfman; Cochmn. N. Amer. Branch Prof. Irwin Cotler (Montreal) and Evelyn Sommer; Sec.-Gen. Israel Singer; Exec. Dir. Elan Steinberg. Seeks to intensify bonds of world Jewry

with Israel as central force in Jewish life; to strengthen solidarity among Jews everywhere and secure their rights, status, and interests as individuals and communities; to encourage development of Jewish social, religious, and cultural life throughout the world and coordinate efforts by Jewish communities and organizations to cope with any Jewish problem; to work for human rights generally. Represents its affiliated organizations—most representative bodies of Jewish communities in more than 80 countries and 35 national organizations in American section—at UN, OAS, UNESCO, Council of Europe, ILO, UNICEF, and other governmental, intergovernmental, and international authorities. Publications (including those by Institute of Jewish Affairs, London): *WJC Report; East European Jewish Affairs; Boletín Informativo OJI; Christian-Jewish Relations; Dateline: World Jewry; Patterns of Prejudice; Coloquio; Batfutsot; Gesher.*

CULTURAL

AMERICAN ACADEMY FOR JEWISH RESEARCH (1929). 3080 Broadway, NYC 10027. (212)678-8864. FAX: (212)678-8947. Pres. Arthur Hyman. Encourages Jewish learning and research; holds annual or semiannual meeting; awards grants for the publication of scholarly works. *Proceedings of the American Academy for Jewish Research; Texts and Studies; Monograph Series.*

AMERICAN BIBLICAL ENCYCLOPEDIA SOCIETY (1930). 24 W. Maple Ave., Monsey, NY 10952. (914)352-4609. Pres. Irving Fredman; Author-Ed. Rabbi M.M. Kasher. Fosters biblical-talmudical research; sponsors and publishes *Torah Shelemah* (Heb., 42 vols.), *Encyclopedia of Biblical Interpretation* (Eng., 9 vols.), *Divrei Menachem* (Heb., 4 vols.), and related publications. *Noam.*

AMERICAN GUILD OF JUDAIC ART (1991). PO Box 1794, Murray Hill Station, NYC 10156-0609. (212)481-8181. FAX: (212)-779-9015. Bd. Chmn. Laura Kruger; Pres. Michael Bercowicz. *Hiddur, a quarterly newsletter devoted to the Jewish visual arts; Guild Showcase, a marketing magazine supplement.*

AMERICAN JEWISH HISTORICAL SOCIETY (1892). 2 Thornton Rd., Waltham, MA 02154. (617)891-8110. FAX: (617)899-9208. Pres. Ronald C. Curhan; Exec. Dir.

Dr. Michael Feldberg. Collects, catalogues, publishes, and displays material on the history of the Jews in America; serves as an information center for inquiries on American Jewish history; maintains archives of original source material on American Jewish history; sponsors lectures and exhibitions; makes available historic Yiddish films and audiovisual material. *American Jewish History; Heritage.*

AMERICAN JEWISH PRESS ASSOCIATION (1943). c/o Northern California Jewish Bulletin, 88 First St., San Francisco, CA 94105. (415)957-9340. FAX: (415)957-0266. Pres. Marc S. Klein. Natl. Admin. Off.: 11312 Old Club Rd., Rockville, MD 20852-4537. (301)881-4113. Exec. Dir. L. Malcolm Rodman. Seeks the advancement of Jewish journalism and the maintenance of a strong Jewish press in the U.S. and Canada; encourages the attainment of the highest editorial and business standards; sponsors workshops, services for members. *Membership bulletin newsletter; Roster of Members.*

AMERICAN SOCIETY FOR JEWISH MUSIC (1974). 129 W. 67 St., NYC 10023. (212)-362-8060 X307. Pres. Jack Gottlieb; Co-V.-Pres. Michael Leavitt, Philip Miller. Promotes the knowledge, appreciation, and development of Jewish music, past and present, for professional and lay audiences; seeks to raise the standards of composition and performance in Jewish music, to encourage research, and to sponsor performances of new and rarely heard works. *Musica Judaica Journal.*

ASSOCIATION FOR THE SOCIAL SCIENTIFIC STUDY OF JEWRY (1971). University of Connecticut, Dept. of Sociology, Center for Judaic Studies, Storrs, CT 06269-2068. (203)486-2271. FAX: (203)486-6356. Pres. Arnold Dashefsky; V.-Pres. Sherry Israel; Sec.-Treas. Allen Glicksman; Journal Ed. J. Alan Winter. Arranges academic sessions and facilitates communication among social scientists studying Jewry through meetings, newsletter, and related materials. *Contemporary Jewry; ASSJ Newsletter.*

ASSOCIATION OF JEWISH BOOK PUBLISHERS (1962). 838 Fifth Ave., NYC 10021. (212)-249-0100. Pres. Rabbi Elliot L. Stevens; Doris B. Gold, chair, cooperative advertising and exhibits. As a nonprofit group, provides a forum for discussion of mutual problems by publishers, authors, and other individuals and institutions concerned with books of Jewish interest. Provides national and international exhibit opportunities for Jewish books.

ASSOCIATION OF JEWISH GENEALOGICAL SOCIETIES (1988). 1485 Teaneck Rd., Teaneck, NJ 07666. (201)837-2700. FAX: (201)837-8506. Pres. Gary Mokotoff. Confederation of over 45 Jewish Genealogical Societies (JGS) in the U.S. and Canada. Encourages Jews to research their family history, promotes membership in the various JGSs, acts as representative of organized Jewish genealogy, implements projects of interest to persons researching their Jewish family history. Annual conference where members learn and exchange ideas. Each local JGS publishes its own newsletter.

ASSOCIATION OF JEWISH LIBRARIES (1965). c/o National Foundation for Jewish Culture, 330 Seventh Ave., 21st fl., NYC 10001. (212)678-8092. FAX: (212)678-8998. Pres. Ralph R. Simon; V.-Pres. Zachary Baker. Seeks to promote and improve services and professional standards in Jewish libraries; disseminates Jewish library information and guidance; promotes publication of literature in the field; encourages the establishment of Jewish libraries and collections of Judaica and the choice of Judaica librarianship as a profession; cocertifies Jewish libraries (with Jewish Book Council). *AJL Newsletter; Judaica Librarianship.*

BEIT HASHOAH–MUSEUM OF TOLERANCE OF THE SIMON WIESENTHAL CENTER (1993). 9760 W. Pico Boulevard, Los Angeles, CA 90035. (310)553-9036. FAX: (310)553-8007. Dean-founder Rabbi Marvin Hier; Dir. Dr. Gerald Margolis; Assoc. Dean Rabbi Abraham Cooper. A unique experiential museum focusing on personal prejudice, group intolerance, struggle for civil rights, and 20th-century genocides, culminating in a major exhibition on the Holocaust. Archives, multimedia learning center designed for individualized research, 6,700-square-foot temporary exhibit space, 324-seat theater, 150-seat auditorium, and outdoor memorial plaza. *Museum Update.*

B'NAI B'RITH KLUTZNICK MUSEUM (1956). 1640 Rhode Island Ave., NW, Washington, DC 20036. (202)857-6583. FAX:

(202)857–0980. Dir. Ori Z. Soltes. A center of Jewish art and history in nation's capital, maintains temporary and permanent exhibition galleries, permanent collection of Jewish ceremonial and folk art, B'nai B'rith International reference archive, outdoor sculpture garden, and museum shop, as well as the American Jewish Sports Hall of Fame. Provides exhibitions, tours, educational programs, research assistance, and tourist information. *Semiannual newsletter; permanent collection catalogue; exhibition brochures.*

CENTER FOR HOLOCAUST STUDIES, DOCUMENTATION & RESEARCH (1974). Merged into A Living Memorial to the Holocaust-Museum of Jewish Heritage, Jan. 1991.

CENTRAL YIDDISH CULTURE ORGANIZATION (CYCO), INC. (1943). 25 E. 21 St., 3rd fl., NYC 10010. (212)505–8305. Mgr. Jacob Schneidman. Promotes, publishes, and distributes Yiddish books; publishes catalogues.

CONFERENCE ON JEWISH SOCIAL STUDIES, INC. (formerly CONFERENCE ON JEWISH RELATIONS, INC.) (1939). 2112 Broadway, Rm. 206, NYC 10023. (212)724–5336. Publishes scientific studies on Jews in the modern world, dealing with such aspects as anti-Semitism, demography, economic stratification, history, philosophy, and political developments. *Jewish Social Studies.*

CONGREGATION BINA (1981). 600 W. End Ave., Suite 1-C, NYC 10024. (212)873–4261. Pres. Joseph Moses; Exec. V.-Pres. Moses Samson; Hon. Pres. Samuel M. Daniel; Secy. Gen. Elijah E. Jhirad. Serves the religious, cultural, charitable, and philanthropic needs of the Children of Israel who originated in India and now reside in the U.S. Works to foster and preserve the ancient traditions, customs, liturgy, music, and folklore of Indian Jewry and to maintain needed institutions. *Kol Bina.*

CONGRESS FOR JEWISH CULTURE (1948). 25 E. 21 St., NYC 10010. (212)505–8040. Co-pres.'s Prof. Yonia Fain, Dr. Barnett Zumoff; Exec. Dir. Michael Skakun. An umbrella group comprising 16 constituent organizations; perpetuates and enhances Jewish creative expression in the U.S. and abroad; fosters all aspects of Yiddish cultural life through the publication of the journal *Zukunft*, the conferring of literary awards, commemoration of the Holocaust and the martyrdom of the Soviet Jewish writers under Stalin, and a series of topical readings, scholarly conferences, symposiums, and concerts. *Zukunft.*

ELAINE KAUFMAN CULTURAL CENTER (1952; formerly HEBREW ARTS CENTER). 129 W. 67 St., NYC 10023. (212)362–8060. FAX: (212)874–7865. Chmn. Leonard Goodman; Pres. Victor Smukler; Exec. Dir. Lydia Kontos. Offers instruction in music, dance, art, and theater to children and adults, combining Western culture with Jewish traditions. Presents frequent performances of Jewish and general music by leading artists and ensembles in its Merkin Concert Hall and Ann Goodman Recital Hall. The Birnbaum Library houses Jewish music scores and reference books. *Kaufman Cultural Center News; bimonthly concert calendars; catalogues and brochures.*

HEBREW CULTURE FOUNDATION (1955). 110 E. 59 St., NYC 10022. (212)339–6000. Chmn. Milton R. Konvitz; Sec. Herman L. Sainer. Sponsors the introduction and strengthening of Hebrew language and literature courses in institutions of higher learning in the United States.

HISTADRUTH IVRITH OF AMERICA (1916; reorg. 1922). 47 W. 34 St., Rm. 609, NYC 10001. (212)629–9443. Pres. Dr. David Sidorsky; Exec. V.-Pres. Dr. Aviva Barzel. Emphasizes the primacy of Hebrew in Jewish life, culture, and education; aims to disseminate knowledge of written and spoken Hebrew in N. America, thus building a cultural bridge between the State of Israel and Jewish communities throughout N. America. *Hadoar; Lamishpaha; Tov Lichtov.*

HOLOCAUST CENTER OF THE UNITED JEWISH FEDERATION OF GREATER PITTSBURGH (1980). 242 McKee Pl., Pittsburgh, PA 15213. (412)682–7111. Pres. Holocaust Comm. Jeffrey W. Letwin; Bd. Chmn. David Shapira; Dir. Linda F. Hurwitz. Develops programs and provides resources to further understanding of the Holocaust and its impact on civilization. Maintains a library, archive; provides speakers, educational materials; organizes community programs.

HOLOCAUST MEMORIAL RESOURCE & EDUCATION CENTER OF CENTRAL FLORIDA (1981). 851 N. Maitland Ave., Maitland, FL 32751. (407)628–0555. FAX: (407)-628–0555. Pres. Dr. William Michael

Hooks; Exec. V.-Pres. Tess Wise. An interfaith educational center devoted to teaching the lessons of the Holocaust. Houses permanent multimedia educational exhibit; maintains library of books, videotapes, films, and other visuals to serve the entire educational establishment; offers lectures, teacher training, and other activities. *Newsletter.*

INSTITUTE FOR RUSSIAN JEWRY, INC. (1990). PO Box 96, Flushing, NY 11367. (718)969–0911. Exec. Dir. Rosa Irgal; Sec. Azia Zverena. Disseminates knowledge of Judaism in Russian language, from historical and cultural perspectives; promotes knowledge of the religious and cultural heritage of Russian Jews through Russian folk and fine art exhibits, lecture series, music and dance workshops.

INTERNATIONAL JEWISH MEDIA ASSOCIATION (1987). U.S.: c/o St. Louis Jewish Light, 12 Millstone Campus Dr., St. Louis, MO 63146. (314)432–3353. FAX: (314)-432–0515. Israel: PO Box 92, Jerusalem 91920. 02–202–222. FAX: 02–513–642. Pres. Robert A. Cohn, Exec. Dir. Lisa Gann-Perkal (Israel); Staff Coord. Malcolm Rodman (Rockville, MD). A worldwide network of Jewish journalists in the Jewish and general media, which seeks to provide a forum for the exchange of materials and ideas, and to enhance the stature of Jewish media and journalists. *Presidents Bulletin; proceedings of international conferences on Jewish media.*

JCC ASSOCIATION LECTURE BUREAU (1922; formerly JWB). 15 E. 26 St., NYC 10010–1579. (212)532–4949. FAX: (212)481–4174. Dir. Sesil Lissberger. A nonprofit program service of JCC Association of N. America providing lecturers and performers from a broad range of Jewish and public life; also offers photo exhibits to stimulate Jewish programming of communal organizations. *The Jewish Arts—A Listing of Performers; Learning for Jewish Living—A Listing of Lecturers; Available Lecturers from Israel; Lecturers on the Holocaust.*

JEWISH ACADEMY OF ARTS AND SCIENCES, INC. (1926). c/o Ben Sachs, 888 Seventh Ave., Suite 403, NYC 10106. (212)757–1627. Hon. Pres. Abraham I. Katsh; Sec. Ben Sachs; Treas. Zvi Levavy. An honor society of Jews who have attained distinction in the arts, sciences, professions, and

communal endeavors. Encourages the advancement of knowledge; stimulates scholarship, with particular reference to Jewish life and thought; recognition by election to membership and/or fellowship; publishes papers delivered at annual convocations.

JEWISH BOOK COUNCIL (1943). 15 E. 26 St., NYC 10010. (212)532–4949. Pres. Leonard S. Gold; Dir. Paula Gribetz Gottlieb. Promotes knowledge of Jewish books through dissemination of book lists, program materials; sponsors Jewish Book Awards, Jewish Book Month; presents literary awards and library citations; cooperates with publishers of Jewish books. *Jewish Book Annual; Jewish Books in Review; Jewish Book World.*

JEWISH HERITAGE PROJECT (1981). 150 Franklin St., #1W, NYC 10013. (212) 925–9067. Exec. Dir. Alan Adelson. Strives to bring to the broadest possible audience authentic works of literary and historical value relating to Jewish history and culture. Distributor of the film *Lodz Ghetto,* which it developed, as well as its companion volume *Lodz Ghetto: Inside a Community Under Siege.*

JEWISH MUSEUM (1904, under auspices of Jewish Theological Seminary of America). 1109 Fifth Ave., NYC 10128. (212) 423–3200. Dir. Joan H. Rosenbaum; Bd. Chmn. H. Axel Schupf. Newly expanded museum opened in Spring 1993, featuring permanent exhibition on the Jewish experience. Repository of the largest collection of Judaica—paintings, prints, photographs, sculpture, coins, medals, antiquities, textiles, and other decorative arts—in the Western Hemisphere. Includes the National Jewish Archive of Broadcasting. Tours, lectures, film showings, and concerts; special programs for children; cafe, shop. *Special exhibition catalogues; annual report.*

JEWISH MUSIC COUNCIL (1944). 15 E. 26 St., NYC 10010. (212)532–4949. Chmn. Joseph Hurwitz; Coord. Paula Gribetz Gottlieb. Promotes Jewish music activities nationally; annually sponsors and promotes the Jewish Music season; encourages participation on a community basis.

JEWISH PUBLICATION SOCIETY (1888). 1930 Chestnut St., Philadelphia, PA 19103. (215)564–5925. FAX: (215)564–6640. Pres. Martin D. Cohn; Exec. V.-Pres. Rabbi Michael A. Monson; Editor-in-

Chief Dr. Ellen Frankel. Publishes and disseminates books of Jewish interest for adults and children; titles include TANAKH, religious studies and practices, life cycle, folklore, classics, art, history, belleslettres. AMERICAN JEWISH YEAR BOOK (with American Jewish Committee); *The Bookmark; JPS Catalogue.*

JEWISH SPORTS CONGRESS (1992). PO Box 4549, Old Village Station, Great Neck, NY 11023. (516) 482–5550. FAX: (516) 482–5583. Pres. David J. Kufeld; V.-Pres. Mike Cohen. An independent, nondenominational organization that promotes and supports athletics and physical fitness within the international Jewish community. In recognition of the influential force of sports in contemporary society, the organization also seeks to harness this power for increased Jewish pride, enhanced Jewish identity, stronger Jewish unity, and improved interracial relations. *Jewish Sports & Fitness.*

JUDAH L. MAGNES MUSEUM–JEWISH MUSEUM OF THE WEST (1962). 2911 Russell St., Berkeley, CA 94705. (510)549–6950. FAX: (510)849–3650. Pres. Howard Fine; Dir. Seymour Fromer. Collects, preserves, and makes available Jewish art, culture, history, and literature from throughout the world. Permanent collections of fine and ceremonial art, rare Judaica library, Western Jewish History Center (archives). The museum has changing exhibits, traveling exhibits, docent tours, lectures, numismatics series, poetry award, a museum shop. *Magnes News; special exhibition catalogues; scholarly books.*

JUDAICA CAPTIONED FILM CENTER, INC. (1983). PO Box 21439, Baltimore, MD 21208–0439. Voice (after 4 PM) (410)655–4750; TDD (410)655–6767. Pres. Lois Lilienfeld Weiner. Developing a comprehensive library of captioned and subtitled films and tapes on Jewish subjects; distributes them to organizations serving the hearing-impaired, including mainstream classes and senior adult groups, on a free-loan, handling/shipping-charge-only basis. *Quarterly newsletter.*

LEAGUE FOR YIDDISH, INC. (1979). 200 W. 72 St., Suite 40, NYC 10023. (212)787–6675. Pres. Dr. Sadie Turak; Exec. Dir. Dr. Mordkhe Schaechter. Encourages the development and use of Yiddish as a living language; promotes its modernization and standardization; publishes linguistic resource materials. *Afn Shvel (quarterly).*

LEO BAECK INSTITUTE, INC. (1955). 129 E. 73 St., NYC 10021. (212)744–6400. FAX: (212)988–1305. Pres. Ismar Schorsch; Exec. Dir. Robert A. Jacobs. A library, archive, and research center for the history of German-speaking Jewry. Offers lectures, exhibits, faculty seminars; publishes a series of monographs, yearbooks, and journals. *LBI Bulletin; LBI News; LBI Yearbook; LBI Memorial Lecture; LBI Library & Archives News.*

A LIVING MEMORIAL TO THE HOLOCAUST–MUSEUM OF JEWISH HERITAGE (1984). 342 Madison Ave., Suite 706, NYC 10173. (212)687–9141. FAX: (212)573–9847. Cochmn. George Klein, Hon. Robert M. Morgenthau, Peter Cohen, Sen. Manfred Ohrenstein; Museum Dir. David Altshuler. The museum will be New York's principal public memorial to the six million Jews murdered during the Holocaust. Scheduled to open in 1994, it will include permanent and temporary exhibition galleries, a computerized interactive learning center, a Memorial Hall, and education facilities. *Brochures; bimonthly newsletter.*

MAALOT–A SEMINARY FOR CANTORS AND JUDAISTS (1987). 1719 Wilmart St., Rockville, MD 20852. (301)231–9067. FAX: (301)230–2009. Pres./Exec. Off. David Shneyer. An educational program established to train individuals in Jewish music, the liturgical arts, and the use, design, and application of Jewish customs and ceremonies. Offers classes, seminars, and an independent study program.

MARTYRS MEMORIAL & MUSEUM OF THE HOLOCAUST OF THE JEWISH FEDERATION COUNCIL OF GREATER LOS ANGELES (1963; reorg. 1978). 6505 Wilshire Blvd., 12th fl., Los Angeles, CA 90048. (213)651–3175. FAX: (213)852–1494. Chmn. Dr. Sam Goetz; Dir. Dr. Michael Nutkiewicz. A photo-narrative museum and resource center dedicated to Holocaust history, issues of genocide and prejudice, and curriculum development. *Pages (quarterly newsletter).*

MEMORIAL FOUNDATION FOR JEWISH CULTURE, INC. (1964). 15 E. 26 St., NYC 10010. (212)679–4074. Pres. the Right Hon., the Lord Jakobovits; Exec. V.-Pres. Jerry Hochbaum. Through the grants that it awards, encourages Jewish scholarship and Jewish education, supports communities that are struggling to maintain their Jewish identity, makes possible the training of Jewish men and women for professional careers in communal service in Jewishly deprived communities, and stimulates the documentation, commemoration, and teaching of the Holocaust.

NATIONAL FOUNDATION FOR JEWISH CULTURE (1960). 330 Seventh Ave., 21st fl., NYC 10001. (212)629–0500. FAX: (212)-629–0508. Pres. Sandra Weiner; Exec. Dir. Richard A. Siegel. The leading Jewish organization devoted to promoting Jewish culture in the U.S. Administers the Council of American Jewish Museums, the Council of Archives and Research Libraries in Jewish Studies, and the Council of Jewish Theatres; supports Jewish scholarship through doctoral dissertation fellowships; provides funding to major Jewish cultural institutions through the Joint Cultural Appeal; organizes conferences, symposia, and festivals in the arts and humanities; initiated the Jewish Endowment for the Arts and Humanities. *Jewish Cultural News.*

NATIONAL YIDDISH BOOK CENTER (1980). 48 Woodbridge St., South Hadley, MA 01075. (413)535–1303. FAX: (413)535–1007. Pres. Aaron Lansky; Exec. Dir. Stephen Hays. Collects and disseminates Yiddish books; conducts activities contributing to the revitalization of Yiddish culture in America. *Der Pakn-treger/The Book Peddler.*

ORTHODOX JEWISH ARCHIVES (1978). 84 William St., NYC 10038. (212)797–9000, ext. 73. FAX: (212)269–2843 Dir. Rabbi Moshe Kolodny. Founded by Agudath Israel of America; houses historical documents, photographs, periodicals, and other publications relating to the growth of Orthodox Jewry in the U.S. and related communities in Europe, Israel, and elsewhere. Particularly noteworthy are its holdings relating to rescue activities organized during the Holocaust and its traveling exhibits available to schools and other institutions.

RESEARCH FOUNDATION FOR JEWISH IMMIGRATION, INC. (1971). 570 Seventh Ave., NYC 10018. (212)921–3871. Pres. Curt C. Silberman; Sec. and Coord. of Research Herbert A. Strauss; Archivist Dennis E. Rohrbaugh. Studies and records the history of the migration and acculturation of Central European German-speaking Jewish and non-Jewish Nazi persecutees in various resettlement countries worldwide, with special emphasis on the American experience. *International Biographical Dictionary of Central European Emigrés, 1933–1945; Jewish Immigrants of the Nazi Period in the USA.*

ST. LOUIS CENTER FOR HOLOCAUST STUDIES (1977). 12 Millstone Campus Dr., St. Louis, MO 63146. (314)432–0020. Chmn. Leo Wolf; Dir. Rabbi Robert Sternberg. Develops programs and provides resources and educational materials to further an understanding of the Holocaust and its impact on civilization. *Audio Visual and Curriculum Resources Guides.*

SEPHARDIC HOUSE (1978). 2112 Broadway, Suite 207, NYC 10023. (212)496–2173. FAX: (212)496–2264. Bd. Chmn. Rabbi Marc D. Angel; Exec. Dir. Janice E. Ovadiah. A cultural organization dedicated to fostering Sephardic history and culture; sponsors a wide variety of classes and public programs, including summer program in Paris for high-school students; publication program disseminates materials of Sephardic value; outreach program to communities outside of the New York area; program bureau provides program ideas, speakers, and entertainers. *Sephardic House Newsletter.*

SIMON WIESENTHAL CENTER, Los Angeles, CA (*see* Yeshiva University *and* Beit Hashoah–Museum of Tolerance)

SKIRBALL MUSEUM, HEBREW UNION COLLEGE (1913; 1972 in Calif.). 3077 University Ave., Los Angeles, CA 90007. (213)-749–3424. FAX: (213)749–1192. Dir. Nancy Berman; Curators Barbara Gilbert, Grace Cohen Grossman; Admin. Peggy Kayser. Collects, preserves, researches, and exhibits art and artifacts made by or for Jews, or otherwise associated with Jews and Judaism. Provides opportunity to faculty and students to do research in the field of Jewish art. *Catalogues of exhibits and collections.*

SOCIETY FOR THE HISTORY OF CZECHOSLOVAK JEWS, INC. (1961). 87–08 Santiago St., Holliswood, NY 11423. (718)468–6844. Pres. and Ed. Lewis Weiner; Sec. Joseph Abeles. Studies the history of Czechoslovak Jews; collects material and disseminates information through the publication of books and pamphlets. *The Jews of Czechoslovakia (3 vols.); Review I-V.*

SOCIETY OF FRIENDS OF THE TOURO SYNA-GOGUE, NATIONAL HISTORICAL SHRINE, INC. (1948). 85 Touro St., Newport, RI 02840. (401)847-4794. Pres. Jacob Temkin; Coord. Kirsten L. Mann. Helps maintain Touro Synagogue as a national historic site, opening and interpreting it for visitors; promotes public awareness of its preeminent role in the tradition of American religious liberty; annually commemorates George Washington's letter of 1790 to the Hebrew Congregation of Newport. *Society Update.*

SPERTUS MUSEUM, SPERTUS COLLEGE OF JUDAICA (1968). 618 S. Michigan Ave., Chicago, IL 60605. (312)922-9012. FAX: (312)922-6406. Pres. Spertus College, Dr. Howard A. Sulkin; Museum Dir. Dr. Morris A. Fred. The largest, most comprehensive Judaic museum in the Midwest with 12,000 square feet of exhibit space and a permanent collection of some 3,000 works spanning 3,500 years of Jewish history. Also includes the Zell Holocaust Memorial, Field Gallery of Contemporary Art, changing special exhibitions, and the Rosenbaum Children's Artifact Center, plus traveling exhibits for Jewish educators, life-cycle workshops, programs for seniors and the disabled, and community-generated art projects. *Newsletter; exhibition catalogues; educational pamphlets.*

TOURO NATIONAL HERITAGE TRUST (1984). 85 Touro St., Newport, RI 02840. (401)-847-0810. Pres. Bernard Bell; Exec. Dir. Kirsten L. Mann. Works to establish national conference center within Touro compound; sponsors Touro Fellow through John Carter Brown Library; presents seminars and other educational programs; promotes knowledge of the early Jewish experience in this country within the climate of religions which brought it about.

UNITED STATES HOLOCAUST MEMORIAL MUSEUM (1980). 100 Raoul Wallenberg Place, SW, Washington, DC 20024. (202)-653-9220. FAX: (202)653-7134. Chmn. Miles Lerman; Exec. Dir. Jeshajahu Weinberg. Federally chartered and privately built, its mission is to teach about the Nazi persecution and murder of six million Jews and millions of others from 1933 to 1945 and to inspire visitors to contemplate their moral responsibilities as citizens of a democratic nation. Opened in April 1993 near the national Mall in Washington, DC, the museum's permanent exhibition tells the story of the Holocaust through authentic artifacts, videotaped oral testimonies, documentary film and historical photographs. Offers educational programs for students and adults, an interactive computerized learning center, and special exhibitions and community programs. *United States Holocaust Memorial Museum Newsletter (monthly); Directory of Holocaust Institutions; Journal of Holocaust and Genocide Studies (quarterly); Days of Remembrance Guidebook (annual).*

YESHIVA UNIVERSITY MUSEUM (1973). 2520 Amsterdam Ave., NYC 10033. (212)-960-5390. Dir. Sylvia A. Herskowitz. Collects, preserves, and interprets Jewish life and culture through changing exhibitions of ceremonial objects, paintings, rare books and documents, synagogue architecture, textiles, decorative arts, and photographs. Oral history archive. Special events, holiday workshops, live performances, lectures, etc. for adults and children. Guided tours and workshops are offered. *Seasonal calendars; special exhibition catalogues.*

YIDDISHER KULTUR FARBAND–YKUF (1937). 1133 Broadway, Rm. 1019, NYC 10010. (212)691-0708. Pres. and Ed. Itche Goldberg. Publishes a bimonthly magazine and books by contemporary and classical Jewish writers; conducts cultural forums; exhibits works by contemporary Jewish artists and materials of Jewish historical value; organizes reading circles. *Yiddishe Kultur.*

YIVO INSTITUTE FOR JEWISH RESEARCH, INC. (1925). 1048 Fifth Ave., NYC 10028. (212)535-6700. FAX: (212)879-9763. Chmn. Bruce Slovin; Dir. Allan Nadler. Engages in social and cultural research pertaining to East European Jewish life; maintains library and archives which provide a major international, national, and New York resource used by institutions, individual scholars, and the public; trains graduate students in Yiddish, East European, and American Jewish studies; offers exhibits, conferences, public programs; publishes books. *Yidishe Shprakh; YIVO Annual; YIVO Bleter; Yedies fun Yivo; Jewish Folklore and Ethnology Review.*

———, MAX WEINREICH CENTER FOR ADVANCED JEWISH STUDIES (1968). 1048 Fifth Ave., NYC 10028. (212)535-6700. FAX: (212)734-1062. Dean Allan Nadler. Provides advanced-level training in Yiddish language and literature, ethnography, folklore, linguistics, and history; offers guidance on dissertation or independent research. *YIVO Annual; YIVO Bleter; Jewish Folklore & Ethnology Review.*

ISRAEL-RELATED

ALYN–AMERICAN SOCIETY FOR HANDICAPPED CHILDREN IN ISRAEL (1934). 19 W. 44 St., NYC 10036. (212)869–8085. FAX: (212)768–0979. Pres. Caroline W. Halpern; Chmn. Simone P. Blum; Exec. Dir. Joan R. Mendelson. Supports the work of ALYN Hospital, long-term rehabilitation center for severely orthopedically handicapped children, located in Jerusalem. It serves as home, school, and hospital for its patients, with a long-term goal for them of independent living.

AMERICA-ISRAEL CULTURAL FOUNDATION, INC. (1939). 41 E. 42 St., Suite 608, NYC 10017. (212)557–1600. FAX: (212)-557–1611. Bd. Chmn. Isaac Stern; Pres. Carl Glick. Supports and encourages the growth of cultural excellence in Israel through grants to cultural institutions; scholarships to gifted young artists and musicians. *Hadashot newsletter.*

AMERICA-ISRAEL FRIENDSHIP LEAGUE, INC. (1971). 134 E. 39 St., NYC 10016. (212)213–8630. FAX: (212)683–3475. Exec. V.-Pres. Ilana Artman. A nonsectarian, nonpartisan organization which seeks to broaden the base of support for Israel among Americans of all faiths and backgrounds. Activities include educational exchanges, tours of Israel for American leadership groups, symposia and public education activities, and the dissemination of printed information. *Newsletter.*

AMERICAN ASSOCIATES, BEN-GURION UNIVERSITY OF THE NEGEV (1973). 342 Madison Ave., NYC 10173. (212)687–7721. FAX: (212)370–0686. Pres. Harold L. Oshry; Exec. V.-Pres. Dr. Lee Katz. Bd. Chmn. Michael W. Sonnenfeldt. Serves as the university's publicity and fund-raising link to the U.S.; is committed to programs for the absorption of Soviet émigrés in the Negev, publicizing university activities and curricula, securing student scholarships, transferring contributions, and encouraging American interest in the university. *AABGU Reporter; BGU Bulletin; Negev; Overseas Study Program Catalog.*

AMERICAN COMMITTEE FOR SHAARE ZEDEK HOSPITAL IN JERUSALEM, INC. (1949). 49 W. 45 St., Suite 1100, NYC 10036. (212)354–8801. Pres. Charles H. Bendheim; Bd. Chmn. Ludwig Jesselson; Sr. Exec. V.-Pres. Morris Talansky. Raises funds for the various needs of the Shaare Zedek Medical Center, Jerusalem, such as equipment and medical supplies, nurses' training, and research; supports exchange program between Shaare Zedek Medical Center and Albert Einstein College of Medicine, NY. *Heartbeat Magazine.*

AMERICAN COMMITTEE FOR SHENKAR COLLEGE IN ISRAEL, INC. (1971). 855 Ave. of the Americas, NYC 10001. (212) 947–1597. FAX: (212)643–9887. Pres. H. Robert Miller; Exec. Dir. Charlotte Fainblatt. Raises funds for capital improvement, research and development projects, laboratory equipment, scholarships, lectureships, fellowships, and library/archives of fashion and textile design at Shenkar College in Israel, Israel's only fashion and textile technology college. Accredited by the Council of Higher Education, the college is the chief source of personnel for Israel's fashion and apparel industry. *Shenkar News.*

AMERICAN COMMITTEE FOR THE WEIZMANN INSTITUTE OF SCIENCE (1944). 51 Madison Ave., NYC 10010. (212)779–2500. FAX: (212)779–3209. Chmn. Alan A. Fischer; Pres. Sara Lee Schupf; Exec. V.-Pres. Bernard N. Samers. Through 14 regional offices in the U.S. raises funds, disseminates information, and does American purchasing for the Weizmann Institute in Rehovot, Israel, a world-renowned center of scientific research and graduate study. The institute conducts research in disease, energy, the environment, and other areas; runs an international summer science program for gifted high-school students. *Rehovot; Interface; Research, Weizmann Now; annual report.*

AMERICAN FRIENDS OF ASSAF HAROFEH MEDICAL CENTER (1975). 19 W. 44 St., Suite 1118, NYC 10036. (212)764–6130. FAX: (212)575–0408. Pres. Martin Lifland; Chmn. Kenneth Kronen; Exec. V.-Pres. Donald L. Gartner. Raises funds for the various needs of the Assaf Harofeh Medical Center in central Israel near Tel Aviv, such as equipment and medical supplies, medical training for immigrants, nurses' training, physiotherapy training, research, and construction of new facilities. *Newsletter.*

AMERICAN FRIENDS OF BAR-ILAN UNIVERSITY (1955). 91 Fifth Ave., Suite 200, NYC 10003. (212)337–1270. FAX: (212)337–1274. Chancellor Rabbi Emanuel Rackman; Chmn. Global Bd. of Trustees Aharon Meir; Pres. Amer. Bd. of Overseers Belda Lindenbaum; Exec. V.-Pres. Gen. Yehuda Halevy. Supports Bar-Ilan University, a traditionally oriented liberal arts and sciences institution, where all students must take Basic Jewish Studies courses as a requirement of graduation; located in Ramat-Gan, Israel, and chartered by the Board of Regents of the State of NY. *Update; Bar-Ilan News.*

AMERICAN FRIENDS OF BETH HATEFUTSOTH (1976). 110 E. 59 St., Suite 4099, NYC 10022. (212)339–6034. FAX: (212)-318–6176. Pres. Abraham Spiegel; V.-Pres. Sam E. Bloch; Exec. Dir. Gloria Golan. Supports the maintenance and development of Beth Hatefutsoth, the Nahum Goldmann Museum of the Jewish Diaspora in Tel Aviv, and its cultural and educational programs for youth and adults. Circulates its traveling exhibitions and provides various cultural programs to local Jewish communities. Includes the Douglas E. Goldman Jewish Genealogy Center (DOROT); the Center for Jewish Music, and the Grunstein Shamir Photodocumentation Center. *Beth Hatefutsoth quarterly newsletter.*

AMERICAN FRIENDS OF HAIFA UNIVERSITY (1972). 488 Madison Ave., 10th fl., NYC 10021. (212)838–8069. FAX: (212)838–3464. Pres. David I. Faust. Promotes, encourages, and aids higher and secondary education, research, and training in all branches of knowledge in Israel and elsewhere; aids in the maintenance and development of Haifa University; raises and allocates funds for the above purposes; provides scholarships; promotes exchanges of teachers and students. *Newsletter; Focus.*

AMERICAN FRIENDS OF TEL AVIV UNIVERSITY, INC. (1955). 360 Lexington Ave., NYC 10017. (212)687–5651. FAX: (212)-687–4085. Bd. Chmn. Melvin S. Taub; Pres. Saul B. Cohen; Exec. V.-Pres. Yair Kagan. Promotes higher education at Tel Aviv University, Israel's largest and most comprehensive institution of higher learning. Among its nine faculties are the Sack-ler School of Medicine with its fully accredited NY State English-language program, the Rubin Academy of Music, and 62 research institutes including the Moshe Dayan Center for Middle East & African Studies, the Jaffe Center for Strategic Studies, the Steinmetz Peace Studies Center, and the Brain Research Center. *Tel Aviv University News; Friends; FAX Flash.*

AMERICAN FRIENDS OF THE HEBREW UNIVERSITY (1925; inc. 1931). 11 E. 69 St., NYC 10021. (212)472–9800. FAX: (212)-744–2324. Pres. Barbara A. Mandel; Bd. Chmn. Harvey M. Krueger; Exec. V.-Pres. Robert A. Pearlman. Fosters the growth, development, and maintenance of the Hebrew University of Jerusalem; collects funds and conducts programs of information throughout the U.S., highlighting the university's achievements and its significance. *News from the Hebrew University of Jerusalem; Scopus magazine.*

AMERICAN FRIENDS OF THE ISRAEL MUSEUM (1972). 10 E. 40 St., Suite 1208, NYC 10016. (212)683–5190. FAX: (212)-683–3187. Pres. Maureen Cogan; Exec. Dir. Michele Cohn Tocci. Raises funds for special projects of the Israel Museum in Jerusalem; solicits works of art for exhibition and educational purposes. *Newsletter.*

AMERICAN FRIENDS OF THE SHALOM HARTMAN INSTITUTE (1976). 280 Grand Ave., Englewood, NJ 07631. (201)894–0566. FAX: (201)894–0377. Pres. Robert P. Kogod; Dir. Rabbi Donniel Hartman; Admin. Dorothy Minchin. Supports the Shalom Hartman Institute, Jerusalem, an institute of higher education and research center devoted to applying the teachings of classical Judaism to the issues of modern life. Founded in 1976 by David Hartman, the institute includes advanced research centers in philosophy, theology, political thought, education, ethics, and Halakhah; a Beit Midrash, teacher-training programs, Russian scholars program, an experimental high school, and programs for Diaspora lay leadership and Jewish communal professionals and educators.

AMERICAN FRIENDS OF THE TEL AVIV MUSEUM OF ART (1974). 133 E. 58 St., Suite 701, NYC 10022. (212)319–0555. FAX: (212)754–2987. Cochmn. David Genser, Hanno Mott. Exec. Dir. Brenda Wilkin. Raises funds for the Tel Aviv Museum of

Art for special projects, art acquisitions, and exhibitions; seeks contributions of art to expand the museum's collection; encourages art loans and traveling exhibitions; creates an awareness of the museum in the USA; makes available exhibition catalogs, monthly calendars, and posters published by the museum. *Newsletter.*

AMERICAN FRIENDS/SARAH HERZOG MEMORIAL HOSPITAL–JERUSALEM (EZRATH NASHIM) (1895). 40 E. 34 St., Suite 907, NYC 10016. (212)725–8175. FAX: (212)-683–3871. Pres. Irwin S. Meltzer; Exec. Dir. Jeannette Krauss. Conducts research, education, and patient care at Sarah Herzog Memorial Hospital in Jerusalem, which includes a 290-bed hospital, comprehensive outpatient clinic, drug-abuse clinic, geriatric center, and the Jacob Herzog Psychiatric Research Center; Israel's only independent, nonprofit, voluntary geriatric and psychiatric hospital; affiliated with Hadassah Hospital, Hebrew University, Bar-Ilan University, and other major medical schools and facilities. *Friend to Friend; To Open the Gates of Healing.*

AMERICAN ISRAEL PUBLIC AFFAIRS COMMITTEE (AIPAC) (1954). 440 First St., NW, Washington, DC 20001. (202)639–5200. FAX: (202)347–4921. Pres. Steven Grossman; Exec. Dir. Thomas A. Dine. Registered to lobby on behalf of legislation affecting U.S.-Israel relations; represents Americans who believe support for a secure Israel is in U.S. interest. Works for a strong U.S.-Israel relationship. *Near East Report; AIPAC Papers on U.S.-Israel Relations.*

AMERICAN-ISRAELI LIGHTHOUSE, INC. (1928; reorg. 1955). 30 E. 60 St., NYC 10022. (212)838–5322. Pres. Mrs. Leonard F. Dank; Sec. Frances Lentz. Provides education and rehabilitation for the blind and physically handicapped in Israel to effect their social and vocational integration into the seeing community; built and maintains Rehabilitation Center for the Blind (Migdal Or) in Haifa. *Tower.*

AMERICAN JEWISH LEAGUE FOR ISRAEL (1957). 130 E. 59 St., NYC 10022. (212)-371–1583. Pres. Rabbi Reuben M. Katz; Bd. Chmn. Joseph Landow. Seeks to unite all those who, notwithstanding differing philosophies of Jewish life, are committed to the historical ideals of Zionism; works, independently of class, party, or religious

affiliation, for the welfare of Israel as a whole. Not identified with any political parties in Israel. Member, World Confederation of United Zionists. *Bulletin of the American Jewish League for Israel.*

AMERICAN PHYSICIANS FELLOWSHIP FOR MEDICINE IN ISRAEL (1950). 2001 Beacon St., Brookline, MA 02146. (617)232–5382. Pres. Leonard F. Gottlieb, MD; Exec. Dir. Daniel C. Goldfarb. Helps Israel become a major world medical center; secures fellowships for selected Israeli physicians and arranges lectureships in Israel by prominent American physicians; runs medical seminars in Israel; coordinates U.S. and Canadian medical and paramedical emergency volunteers to Israel; supports research and health-care projects in Israel. *APF News.*

AMERICAN RED MAGEN DAVID FOR ISRAEL, INC. (1940). 888 Seventh Ave., Suite 403, NYC 10106. (212)757–1627. FAX: (212)757–4662. Pres. Robert L. Sadoff, MD; Natl. Chmn. Louis Cantor; Exec. V.-Pres. Benjamin Saxe. An authorized tax-exempt organization; the sole support arm in the U.S. of Magen David Adom (MDA), Israel's equivalent to a Red Cross Society; raises funds for MDA's emergency medical, ambulance, blood, and disaster services for Israel's military and civilian population. Helps to supply and equip ambulances, bloodmobiles, and cardiac rescue ambulances serving all hospitals and communities throughout Israel and 45 prehospital MDA Emergency Medical Clinics; provides medical supplies and scientific equipment for MDA blood programs; funds training of paramedics, lab technicians, and scientists. *Lifeline.*

AMERICAN SOCIETY FOR TECHNION–ISRAEL INSTITUTE OF TECHNOLOGY (1940). 810 Seventh Ave., 24th fl., NYC 10019. (212)-262–6200. FAX: (212)262–6155. Pres. Lewis M. Weston; Natl. Chmn. Leonard Sherman; Exec. V.-Pres. Melvyn H. Bloom. Supports the work of the Technion-Israel Institute of Technology in Haifa, which trains over 10,000 students in 19 faculties and a medical school, and conducts research across a broad spectrum of science and technology. *Technion USA.*

AMERICAN SOCIETY FOR YAD VASHEM (1981). 48 W. 37 St., NYC 10018. (212)-564–9606. FAX: (212)268–0529. Chmn.

Eli Zborowski; Exec. Dir. Selma Schiffer. Development arm of Yad Vashem, Jerusalem, the central international authority created by the Knesset in 1953 for the purposes of commemoration and education in connection with the Holocaust. *Martyrdom and Resistance (newsletter).*

AMERICAN ZIONIST FEDERATION (1939; reorg. 1949 and 1970). 110 E. 59 St., NYC 10022. (212)318–6100. FAX: (212)935–3578. Pres. Simon Reich; Exec. Dir. Karen Rubinstein. Coordinates the work of the Zionist constituency in the areas of education, *aliyah,* youth and young leadership and public and communal affairs. Seeks to involve the Zionist and broader Jewish community in programs and events focused on Israel and Zionism (e.g., Zionist Shabbat, Scholars-in-Residence, Yom Yerushalayim) and through these programs to develop a greater appreciation for the Zionist idea among American Jewry. Composed of 17 national Zionist organizations, 10 Zionist youth movements, and affiliated organizations. Offices in Chicago, Los Angeles, New York. Groups in Baltimore, Detroit, Philadelphia, Pittsburgh, Rochester, Washington, DC. *HaMakor.*

AMERICAN ZIONIST YOUTH FOUNDATION, INC. (1963). 110 E. 59 St., NYC 10022. (212)318–6123. Pres. Rabbi Joseph P. Sternstein; Exec. V.-Chmn. Don Adelman. Heightens Zionist awareness among Jewish youth through programs and services geared to high-school and college-age youngsters. Sponsors educational tours to Israel, study in leading institutions; sponsors field workers on campus and in summer camps; prepares and provides specialists who present and interpret the Israel experience for community centers and federations throughout the country. *Activist Newsletter; Guide to Education and Programming Material; Programs in Israel.*

AMERICANS FOR A SAFE ISRAEL (1971). 147 E. 76 St., NYC 10021. (212)628–9400. FAX: (212)988–4065. Chmn. Herbert Zweibon. Seeks to educate Americans in Congress, the media, and the public in general about Israel's role as a strategic asset for the West; through meetings with legislators and the media, in press releases and publications, promotes the notion of Jewish rights to Judea and Samaria and the concept of "peace for peace" as an alternative to "territory for peace." *Outpost.*

AMERICANS FOR PEACE NOW (1984). 27 W. 20 St., 9th fl., NYC 10011. (212)645–6262. FAX: (212)929–3459. Pres. Gail Pressberg. Conducts educational programs and raises funds to support the Israeli peace movement, Shalom Achshav (Peace Now), and coordinates U.S. advocacy efforts through APN's Washington-based Center for Israeli Peace and Security. *National Newsletter.*

AMERICANS FOR PROGRESSIVE ISRAEL (1952). 224 W. 35 St., Suite 403, NYC 10001. (212)868–0386. Pres. Naftali Landesman. A socialist Zionist organization that calls for a just and durable peace between Israel and all its Arab neighbors, including the Palestinian people; works for the liberation of all Jews; seeks the democratization of Jewish communal and organizational life; promotes dignity of labor, social justice, and a deeper understanding of Jewish culture and heritage. Affiliate of American Zionist Federation and World Union of Mapam, with fraternal ties to Hashomer Hatzair and Kibbutz Artzi Federation of Israel. *Israel Horizons.*

AMIT WOMEN (formerly AMERICAN MIZRACHI WOMEN) (1925). 817 Broadway, NYC 10003. (212)477–4720. Pres. Norma Holzer; Exec. Dir. Marvin Leff. The State of Israel's official *reshet* (network) for religious secondary technological education; conducts innovative children's homes and youth villages in Israel in an environment of traditional Judaism; promotes cultural activities for the purpose of disseminating Zionist ideals and strengthening traditional Judaism in America. *AMIT Woman.*

AMPAL–AMERICAN ISRAEL CORPORATION (1942). 10 Rockefeller Plaza, NYC 10020–1956. (212)586–3232. FAX: (212)649–1745. Pres. Lawrence Lefkowitz; Bd. Chmn. Michael Arnon. Finances and invests in industrial, agricultural, real estate, hotel, and tourist enterprises in Israel. *Annual report; quarterly reports.*

ARZA–ASSOCIATION OF REFORM ZIONISTS OF AMERICA (1977). 838 Fifth Ave., NYC 10021. (212)249–0100. FAX: (212)517–7968. Pres. Norman D. Schwartz; Exec. Dir. Rabbi Ammiel Hirsch. Individual Zionist membership organization devoted to achieving Jewish pluralism in Israel and strengthening the Israeli Reform movement. Chapter activities in the U.S. concentrate on these issues and on strengthening American public support for Israel. *ARZA Newsletter.*

BETAR ZIONIST YOUTH ORGANIZATION (1935). 218 E. 79 St., NYC 10021. (212)-650–1231. Central Shlicha Tova Vagami. Dir. Glenn Mones. Organizes youth groups across North America to teach Zionism, Jewish identity, and love of Israel; sponsors summer programs in Israel for Jewish youth ages 12–22; sponsors Tagar Zionist Student Activist Movement on college campuses.

BOYS TOWN JERUSALEM FOUNDATION OF AMERICA INC. (1948). 91 Fifth Ave., Suite 601, NYC 10003. (212)242–1118. FAX: (212)242–2190. Pres. Michael J. Scharf; Chmn. Josh S. Weston; V.-Chmn. Alexander S. Linchner; Exec. V.-Pres. Rabbi Ronald L. Gray. Raises funds for Boys Town Jerusalem, which was established in 1948 to offer a comprehensive academic, religious, and technical education to disadvantaged Israeli and immigrant boys from over 45 different countries, including Ethiopia, Russia, and Iran. Enrollment: over 1,400 students in jr. high school, academic and technical high school, and a college of applied engineering. *BTJ Newsbriefs; Your Town Magazine.*

CAMERA–COMMITTEE FOR ACCURACY IN MIDDLE EAST REPORTING IN AMERICA (1982). PO Box 428, Boston, MA 02258. (617) 789–3672. FAX: (617) 787–7853. Natl. Pres. Andrea Levin. Monitors and responds to media distortion in order to promote better understanding of Middle East events; urges members to alert the media to errors, omissions, and distortions; unites all friends of Israel regardless of politics or religion to correct unbalanced or inaccurate coverage of Middle East. *CAMERA Media Report (quarterly); CAMERA on Campus; Action Alerts.*

COUNCIL FOR A BEAUTIFUL ISRAEL ENVIRONMENTAL EDUCATION FOUNDATION (1973). 350 Fifth Ave., 19th fl., NYC 10118. (212)947–5709. Pres. Dina A. Evan; Admin. Dir. Donna Lindemann. A support group for the Israeli body, whose activities include education, town planning, lobbying for legislation to protect and enhance the environment, preservation of historical sites, the improvement and beautification of industrial and commercial areas, and renovating bomb shelters into parks and playgrounds. *Yearly newsletter.*

EMUNAH WOMEN OF AMERICA (formerly HAPOEL HAMIZRACHI WOMEN'S ORGANIZATION) (1948). 7 Penn Plaza, NYC 10001. (212)564–9045. FAX: (212)643–9731. Pres. Sondra H. Fisch; Exec. Dir. Shirley Singer. Maintains and supports 200 educational and social-welfare institutions in Israel within a religious framework, including day-care centers, kindergartens, children's residential homes, vocational schools for the underprivileged, senior-citizen centers, a college complex, and Holocaust study center. Also involved in absorption of Soviet and Ethiopian immigrants (recognized by Israeli government as an official absorption agency). *The Emunah Woman; Lest We Forget; Emunah Connection.*

FEDERATED COUNCIL OF ISRAEL INSTITUTIONS–FCII (1940). 4702 15th Ave., Brooklyn, NY 11219. (718)972–5530. Bd. Chmn. Z. Shapiro; Exec. V.-Pres. Rabbi Julius Novack. Central fund-raising organization for over 100 affiliated institutions; handles and executes estates, wills, and bequests for the traditional institutions in Israel; clearinghouse for information on budget, size, functions, etc., of traditional educational, welfare, and philanthropic institutions in Israel, working cooperatively with the Israeli government and the overseas department of the Council of Jewish Federations. *Annual financial reports and statistics on affiliates.*

FRIENDS OF LABOR ISRAEL (1987). 640 Fifth Ave., 16th fl., NYC 10019. (212)255–4227. FAX: (212)765–8097. Chmn. Rabbi Daniel Polish; Exec. Dir. Jonathan Jacoby. American organization committed to a program of education in America and Israel on behalf of institutions, organizations, and projects in Israel designed to promote democracy, pluralism, social justice, and peace. FLI is an affinity group of the Israel Labor movement and represents the concerns of like-minded American Jews in Labor circles. It is currently setting up a policy institute.

FRIENDS OF THE ISRAEL DEFENSE FORCES' SOLDIERS (1981). 21 W. 38 St., 5th fl., NYC 10018. (212)575–5030. FAX: (212)-575–7815. Chmn. Marvin Josephson; Pres. Stephen Rubin. Supports the Agudah Lema'an Hahayal, Israel's Assoc. for the Well-Being of Soldiers, founded in the early 1940s, which provides social, recreational, and educational programs for soldiers, special services for the sick and wounded, and much more. *"Frontline" Newsletter.*

FUND FOR HIGHER EDUCATION (1970). 1768 S. Wooster St., Los Angeles, CA 90035. (310)202-1879. Chmn. Amnon Barness; Chmn. Exec. Com. Max Candiotty. Raises funds and disseminates information in the interest of institutions of higher education in the U.S. and Israel. Over $18 million distributed to over 100 institutions of higher learning, including over $11 million in Israel and $6 million in the U.S. *In Response.*

GESHER FOUNDATION (1969). 421 Seventh Ave., #905, NYC 10001. (212) 564-0338. FAX: (212)967-2726. Pres. Matthew J. Maryles; Exec. V.-Pres. Hillel Wiener. Seeks to bridge the gap between Jews of various backgrounds in Israel by stressing the interdependence of all Jews. Runs encounter seminars for Israeli youth; distributes curricular materials in public schools; offers Jewish identity classes for Russian youth, and a video series in Russian and English on famous Jewish personalities.

GIVAT HAVIVA EDUCATIONAL FOUNDATION, INC. (1966). 224 W. 35 St., Suite 403, NYC 10001. (212)868-0353. FAX: (212)-868-0364. Chmn. Fred Howard; Exec. Dir. Steven Goldberg. Supports programs at the Givat Haviva Institute in Israel which promote tolerance and understanding between Jews and Arabs. Also sponsors programs in Holocaust education and weekend seminars for new Soviet immigrants. In N. America, hosts the Children's Art for Peace exhibit as well as public lectures by prominent Israeli speakers. *Givat Haviva News; special reports.*

GOLDA MEIR ASSOCIATION (1984). 33 E. 67 St., NYC 10021. (212)570-1443. FAX: (212)737-4326. Chmn. Alfred H. Moses; Pres. Robert C. Klutznick. Consultant, Robert I. Evans: 2300 Computer Ave., Bldg. G., Willow Grove, PA 19090. (215)-830-1406. FAX: (215)657-5161. North American support group for the Israeli association, whose large-scale educational programs address the issues of democracy in Israel, Sephardi-Ashkenazi integration, religious pluralism, the peace process, and relations between Israeli Jews and Arabs. Its "Project Democracy" has been adapted to help new Soviet immigrants integrate into Israeli society by providing them an education in democratic ideals and principles. *Newsletter.*

HABONIM-DROR NORTH AMERICA (1934). 27 W. 20 St., 9th fl., NYC 10011. (212)-255-1796. Sec.-Gen. Geremy Forman; Exec. Off. Aryeh Valdberg. Fosters identification with progressive, cooperative living in Israel; stimulates study of Jewish and Zionist culture, history, and contemporary society; sponsors summer and year programs in Israel, 5 summer camps in N. America, and *aliyah* frameworks. *Batnua; Bimat Hamaapilim.*

HADASSAH, THE WOMEN'S ZIONIST ORGANIZATION OF AMERICA, INC. (1912). 50 W. 58 St., NYC 10019. (212)355-7900. FAX: (212)303-8282. Pres. Deborah Kaplan; Exec. Dir. Beth Wohlgelernter. In America delivers factual information on the development and security of Israel to the American public; provides basic Jewish education as a background for intelligent and creative Jewish living; develops knowledgeable leadership for the American Jewish community; sponsors Young Judaea, largest Zionist youth movement in U.S.; operates six Zionist youth camps in this country; supports summer and all-year courses in Israel. Maintains in Israel Hadassah-Hebrew University Medical Center for healing, teaching, and research; Hadassah College of Technology; and Hadassah Career Counseling Institute. *Update; Headlines; Hadassah Magazine; Textures; Bat Kol; The American Scene; Communities; Connections; Vanguard; MedBriefs; Focus on Me.*

———, YOUNG JUDAEA (1909; reorg. 1967). 50 W. 58 St., NYC 10019. (212)355-7900. FAX: (212)247-9240 Natl. Dir. Rabbi Glen Karonsky; Coord. Hamagshimim (college level) Lisa Silverman; Pres. of Sr. Judaea (high-school level) Aaron Dworkin. Seeks to educate Jewish youth aged 9-22 toward Jewish and Zionist values, active commitment to and participation in the American and Israeli Jewish communities; maintains summer camps and year programs in Israel. *Hamagshimim Journal; Kol Hat'nua; The Young Judaean.*

HASHOMER HATZAIR, SOCIALIST ZIONIST YOUTH MOVEMENT (1923). 224 W. 35 St., Suite 403, NYC 10001. (212)868-0388. FAX: (212)868-0364. Natl. Sec. Jason Leizer; Dir. Raya Passi. Seeks to educate Jewish youth to an understanding of Zionism as the national liberation movement of the Jewish people. Promotes *aliyah* to kibbutzim. Affiliated with AZYF and Kibbutz Artzi Federation. Espouses socialist-Zionist ideals of peace, justice, democracy, and brotherhood. *Young Guard.*

INTERNS FOR PEACE (1976). 165 E. 56 St., NYC 10022. (212)319–4545. FAX: (212)-319–4549. Internatl. Dir. Rabbi Bruce M. Cohen; Education Dir. Karen Wald Cohen. An independent, nonprofit, nonpolitical organization, dedicated to fostering understanding and respect between Jewish and Arab citizens of Israel through community work.

ISRAEL CANCER RESEARCH FUND (1975). 1290 Avenue of the Americas, NYC 10104. (212) 969–9800. FAX: (212) 969–9822. Pres. Dr. Yashar Hirshaut; Chmn. S. Donald Friedman. The largest single source of private funds for cancer research in Israel. Has a three-fold mission: to encourage innovative cancer research by Israeli scientists; to harness Israel's vast intellectual and creative resources to establish a world-class center for cancer study; to broaden research opportunities within Israel to stop the exodus of talented Israeli cancer researchers. *Annual Report, Research Awards, "What/Where/Why," Glossary, Towards A Cure, Newsletter.*

ISRAEL HISTADRUT FOUNDATION (1960). 276 Fifth Ave., Suite 901, NYC 10001. (800)443–4256; (212)683–5454. FAX: (212)213–9233. Pres. Herbert Rothman; Exec. V.-Pres. Alvin Smolin. A membership corporation providing philanthropic support to Histadrut, the federated association of working men and women in Israel. Helps the Histadrut build and maintain its network of social-service agencies, which is the largest in Israel and benefits over 85 percent of Israel's population.

JEWISH INSTITUTE FOR NATIONAL SECURITY AFFAIRS (JINSA) (1976). 1717 K St., NW, Suite 300, Washington, DC 20006. (202)833–0020. FAX: (202)296–6452. Pres. Ted Dinerstein; Exec. Dir. Tom Neumann. A nonprofit, nonpartisan educational organization working within the American Jewish community to explain the link between American defense policy and the security of the State of Israel; and within the national security establishment to explain the key role Israel plays in bolstering American interests. *Security Affairs.*

JEWISH NATIONAL FUND OF AMERICA (1901). 42 E. 69 St., NYC 10021. (212)-879–9300. FAX: (212)517–3293. Pres. Ruth W. Popkin; Exec. V.-Pres. Dr. Samuel I. Cohen. Exclusive fund-raising agency of the world Zionist movement for the afforestation, reclamation, and development of the land of Israel, including construction of roads, parks, and recreational areas, preparation of land for agriculture, new communities, and industrial facilities; helps emphasize the importance of Israel in schools and synagogues throughout the U.S. *JNF Almanac; Land and Life.*

JEWISH PEACE LOBBY (1989). 8604 Second Ave., Suite 317, Silver Spring, MD 20910. (301)589–8764. FAX: (301)589–2722. Pres. Jerome M. Segal. A legally registered lobby promoting changes in U.S. policy vis-à-vis the Israeli-Palestinian conflict. Supports Israel's right to peace within secure borders; a political settlement based on mutual recognition of the right of self-determination of both peoples; a two-state solution as the most likely means to a stable peace. *Washington Action Alerts.*

KEREN OR, INC. (1956). 1133 Broadway, NYC 10010. (212)255–1180. Bd. Chmn. Dr. Edward L. Steinberg; Pres. Dr. Albert Hornblass; Exec. V.-Pres. Paul H. Goldenberg. Funds the Keren-Or Center for Multihandicapped Blind Children, at 3 Abba Hillel Silver St., Ramot, Jerusalem, housing and caring for 90 children, 1½ to 16 years of age. Provides long-term basic training, therapy, rehabilitative, and early childhood education to the optimum level of the individual; with major hospitals, is involved in research into causes of multihandicapped blind birth.

LABOR ZIONIST ALLIANCE (formerly FARBAND LABOR ZIONIST ORDER; now uniting membership and branches of POALE ZION–UNITED LABOR ZIONIST ORGANIZATION OF AMERICA and AMERICAN HABONIM ASSOCIATION) (1913). 275 Seventh Ave., NYC 10001. (212)366–1194, (212)366–1387. FAX: (212)675–7685. Pres. Henry L. Feingold. Seeks to enhance Jewish life, culture, and education in U.S.; aids in building State of Israel as a cooperative commonwealth, and its Labor movement organized in the Histadrut; supports efforts toward a more democratic society throughout the world; furthers the democratization of the Jewish community in America and the welfare of Jews everywhere; works with labor and liberal forces in America. *Jewish Frontier; Yiddisher Kempfer.*

LEAGUE FOR LABOR ISRAEL (1938; reorg. 1961). 33 E. 67 St., NYC 10021. (212)628-0042. Pres. Henry L. Feingold; V.-Pres. Ben Cohen. Conducts Labor Zionist educational and cultural activities for youth and adults in the American Jewish community. Promotes educational travel to Israel.

LIKUD USA (1925). 4 East 34 St., 4th fl., NYC 10016. (212)447-7887. FAX: (212)-447-7492. Chmn. George S. Meissner; Chmn. Young Leadership Div. Howard Barbanel. Educates the Jewish community and the American public about the views of Israel's Likud party; encourages support for a strong, secure State of Israel in all of its territory. *The Likud Newsletter.*

MEDICAL DEVELOPMENT FOR ISRAEL (1982). 130 E. 59 St., NYC 10022. (212)-759-3370. FAX: (212)759-0120. Bd. Chmn. Howard M. Squadron; Pres. Dr. Samuel C. Klagsbrun. Raises funds to help improve the quality of health care in Israel, its primary goal the construction of the Children's Medical Center of Israel, a 224-bed tertiary care facility for the entire region. *Brochures and newsletters.*

MERCAZ U.S.A. (1979). 155 Fifth Ave., NYC 10010. (212)533-7800. Pres. Rabbi Matthew H. Simon; Exec. Dir. Renah L. Rabinowitz. The U.S. Zionist organization for Conservative/Masorti Judaism; works for religious pluralism in Israel, defending and promoting Conservative/Masorti institutions and individuals; fosters Zionist education and *aliyah* and develops young leadership. *Mercaz News & Views.*

NA'AMAT USA, THE WOMEN'S LABOR ZIONIST ORGANIZATION OF AMERICA, INC. (formerly PIONEER WOMEN/NA'AMAT) (1925; reorg. 1985). 200 Madison Ave., 21st. fl., NYC 10016. (212)725-8010. FAX: (212)447-5187. Pres. Harriet Green; Exec. Dir. Deborah Siegel. Part of a world movement of working women and volunteers, NA'AMAT USA helps provide social, educational, and legal services for women, teenagers, and children in Israel. It also advocates legislation for women's rights and child welfare in the U.S., furthers Jewish education, and supports Habonim-Dror, the Labor Zionist youth movement. *NA'AMAT Woman magazine.*

NATIONAL COMMITTEE FOR LABOR ISRAEL-HISTADRUT (1923). 33 E. 67 St., NYC 10021. (212)628-1000. Pres. Jay Mazur; Exec. Dir. Jerry Goodman; Chmn. Trade Union Council Morton Bahr. Conducts educational and communal activities in Jewish community and promotes relations and understanding between U.S. trade unions and Israel, and Israel's Labor Federation-Histadrut. Brings together Jews, non-Jews, whites, blacks, and Hispanics to build support for Israel. Israel Histadrut Campaign raises funds for Histadrut educational, health, social, and cultural projects. *NCLI Notebook; occasional background papers.*

NEW ISRAEL FUND (1979). 1101 15 St., NW, Suite 304, Washington, DC 20005. (202)-223-3333. FAX: (202)659-2789. New York Office: 110 W. 40 St., Suite 2300, NYC 10018. (212) 302-0066. Pres. Dr. Mordechai Bar-On; Exec. Dir. Norman S. Rosenberg. A partnership of Israelis and North Americans dedicated to strengthening democracy and advancing social justice in Israel. The Fund strengthens Israel's democratic fabric by providing funds and technical assistance to the independent, public-interest sector; cultivating a new generation of public-interest leaders; and educating citizens—both in Israel and abroad—to create a constituency for democracy. *Quarterly newsletter; annual report.*

PEC ISRAEL ECONOMIC CORPORATION (formerly PALESTINE ECONOMIC CORPORATION) (1926). 511 Fifth Ave., NYC 10017. (212)687-2400. Chmn. R. Recanati; Pres. Joseph Ciechanover; Exec. V.-Pres. James I. Edelson; Treas. William Gold. Primarily engaged in the business of organizing, acquiring interest in, financing, and participating in the management of companies located in the State of Israel or Israel-related. *Annual and quarterly reports.*

PEF ISRAEL ENDOWMENT FUNDS, INC. (1922). 41 E. 42 St., Suite 607, NYC 10017. (212)599-1260. Chmn. Sidney A. Luria; Pres. Abraham J. Kremer; Sec. Harvey Brecher. A totally volunteer organization that makes grants to educational, scientific, social, religious, health, and other philanthropic institutions in Israel. *Annual report.*

PIONEER WOMEN/NA'AMAT (*see* NA'AMAT USA)

POALE AGUDATH ISRAEL OF AMERICA, INC. (1948). 4405 13th Ave., Brooklyn, NY 11219. (718)435–8228. Pres. Rabbi Fabian Schonfeld; Exec. V.-Pres. Dr. Yehudah Wurzel. Aims to educate American Jews to the values of Orthodoxy and *aliyah;* supports kibbutzim, trade schools, yeshivot, moshavim, kollelim, research centers, and children's homes in Israel. *PAI News; She'arim; Hamayan.*

——, WOMEN'S DIVISION OF (1948). Pres. Miriam Lubling; Presidium: Sarah Ivanisky, Tili Stark, Peppi Petzenbaum. Assists Poale Agudath Israel to build and support children's homes, kindergartens, and trade schools in Israel. *Yediot PAI.*

PROGRESSIVE ZIONIST CAUCUS (1982). 27 W. 20 St., 9th fl., NYC 10011. (212)675–1168. FAX: (212)929–3459. Dir. Noam Laden, Shaliach Aryeh Valdberg. A campus-based grassroots organization committed to a progressive Zionist agenda. Students organize local and regional educational, cultural, and political activities, such as speakers, films, *Kabbalot Shabbat,* and Arab-Jewish dialogue groups. The PZC Kvutzat Aliyah is a support framework for individuals interested in *aliyah* to a city or town. *La'Inyan; Babayit.*

PROJECT NISHMA (1988). 1225 15 St., NW, Washington, DC 20005. (202)462–4268. FAX: (202)462–3892. Cochmn. Theodore R. Mann, Edward Sanders, Henry Rosovsky; Exec. Dir. Thomas R. Smerling. Conducts educational programs on Israeli security and the peace process; arranges military briefings for Jewish leaders; publishes articles by senior Israeli defense and foreign policy experts; analyzes Israeli and U.S. Jewish opinion; and articulates pragmatic positions on peace and security. Sponsored by over 100 nationally active Jewish leaders from across the country.

RELIGIOUS ZIONISTS OF AMERICA. 25 W. 26 St., NYC 10010. (212)689–1414.

——, BNEI AKIVA OF NORTH AMERICA (1934). 25 W. 26 St., NYC 10010. (212)-889–5260. V.-Pres. Admin. Marc Haber; Natl. Dir. Noah Slomowitz. The only religious Zionist youth movement in North America, serving over 10,000 young people from grade school through graduate school in 16 active regions across the United States and Canada, six summer camps, seven established summer, winter, and year programs in Israel. Stresses communal involvement, social activism, leadership training, and substantive programming to educate young people toward a commitment to Judaism and Israel. *Akivon; Hamvaser; Pinkas Lamadrich; Daf Rayonot; Ma'Ohalai Torah; Zraim.*

——, MIZRACHI-HAPOEL HAMIZRACHI (1909; merged 1957). 25 W. 26 St., NYC 10010. (212)689–1414. FAX: (212)779–3043. Pres. Rabbi Sol Roth; Exec. V.-Pres. Israel Friedman. Disseminates ideals of religious Zionism; conducts cultural work, educational program, public relations; raises funds for religious educational institutions in Israel, including *yeshivot hesder* and Bnei Akiva. *Newsletters; Kolenu.*

——, MIZRACHI PALESTINE FUND (1928). 25 W. 26 St., NYC 10010. Chmn. Joseph Wilon; Sec. Israel Friedman. Fundraising arm of Mizrachi movement.

——, NATIONAL COUNCIL FOR TORAH EDUCATION OF MIZRACHI-HAPOEL HAMIZRACHI (1939). 25 W. 26 St., NYC 10010. Pres. Rabbi Israel Schorr; Dir. Rabbi Meyer Golombek. Organizes and supervises yeshivot and Talmud Torahs; prepares and trains teachers; publishes textbooks and educational materials; organizes summer seminars for Hebrew educators in cooperation with Torah Department of Jewish Agency; conducts ulpan. *Hazarkor; Chemed.*

——, NOAM-MIZRACHI NEW LEADERSHIP COUNCIL (formerly NOAM-HAMISHMERET HATZEIRA) (1970). 25 W. 26 St., NYC 10010. (212)684–6091. Chmn. Rabbi Marc Schneier; V.-Chmn. Sheon Karol. Develops new religious Zionist leadership in the U.S. and Canada; presents young religious people with various alternatives for settling in Israel through *garinei aliyah* (core groups); meets the religious, educational, and social needs of Jewish young adults and young couples. *Forum.*

SOCIETY OF ISRAEL PHILATELISTS (1949). 24355 Tunbridge Lane, Beachwood, OH 44122. (216)292–3843. Pres. Samuel Resnick; Journal Ed. Dr. Oscar Stadtler. Promotes interest in, and knowledge of, all phases of Israel philately through sponsorship of chapters and research groups, maintenance of a philatelic library, and support of public and private exhibitions. *The Israel Philatelist; monographs; books.*

STATE OF ISRAEL BONDS (1951). 575 Lexington Ave., NYC 10022. (212)644–2663. FAX: (212)644–3925. Bd. Chmn. & Internatl. Chmn. David B. Hermelin; Pres. & CEO Amb. Meir Rosenne. Seeks to provide Israel with large-scale investment funds, which are currently being allocated for immigrant absorption, through the sale of State of Israel securities worldwide.

THEODOR HERZL FOUNDATION (1954). 110 E. 59 St., NYC 10022. (212)339–6000. FAX: (212)826–8959. Chmn. Kalman Sultanik; Sec. Zelig Chinitz. Offers cultural activities, lectures, conferences, courses in modern Hebrew and Jewish subjects, Israel, Zionism, and Jewish history. *Midstream.*

———, HERZL PRESS. Chmn. Kalman Sultanik. Serves as "the Zionist Press of record," publishing books that are important for the light they shed on Zionist philosophy, Israeli history, contemporary Israel and the Diaspora, and the relationship between them. They are important as contributions to Zionist letters and history. *Midstream.*

THEODOR HERZL INSTITUTE. 110 E. 59 St., NYC 10022. (212)339–6000. Chmn. Jacques Torczyner; Dir. Ida Reich. Program geared to review of contemporary problems on Jewish scene here and abroad, presentation of Jewish heritage values in light of Zionist experience of the ages, study of modern Israel, and Jewish social research with particular consideration of history and impact of Zionism. Lectures, forums, Encounter with Creativity; musicales, recitals, concerts; holiday celebrations; visual art programs, Nouveau Artist Introductions. *Annual Program Preview; Herzl Institute Bulletin.*

UNITED CHARITY INSTITUTIONS OF JERUSALEM, INC. (1903). 1467–48 St., Brooklyn, NY 11219. (718)633–8469. FAX: (718)633–8478. Chmn. Rabbi Charlop; Exec. Dir. Rabbi Pollak. Raises funds for the maintenance of schools, kitchens, clinics, and dispensaries in Israel; free loan foundations in Israel.

UNITED ISRAEL APPEAL, INC. (1925). 110 E. 59 St., NYC 10022. (212)339–6900. FAX: (212)754–4293. Chmn. Norman H. Lipoff; Exec. V.-Chmn. Herman S. Markowitz. Provides funds raised by UJA/Federation campaigns in the U.S. to aid the people of Israel through the programs of the Jewish Agency for Israel, UIA's operating agent.

Serves as link between American Jewish community and Jewish Agency for Israel; assists in resettlement and absorption of refugees in Israel, and supervises flow and expenditure of funds for this purpose. *Annual report; newsletters; brochures.*

UNITED STATES COMMITTEE SPORTS FOR ISRAEL, INC. (1948). 1926 Arch St., Philadelphia, PA 19103. (215)561–6900. Pres. Robert E. Spivak; Exec. Dir. Barbara G. Lissy. Sponsors U.S. participation in, and fields and selects U.S. team for, World Maccabiah Games in Israel every four years; promotes education and sports programs in Israel; provides funds and technical and material assistance to Wingate Institute for Physical Education and Sport in Israel; sponsors coaching programs in Israel. *USCSFI Newsletter; commemorative Maccabiah Games journal; financial report.*

VOLUNTEERS FOR ISRAEL (1982). 330 W. 42 St., NYC 10036–6902. (212)643–4848. FAX: (212)643–4855. Pres. Rickey Cherner; Natl. Coord. Arthur W. Stern. Provides aid to Israel through volunteer work, building lasting relationships between Israelis and Americans. Affords persons aged 18–70 the opportunity to participate in various duties currently performed by overburdened Israelis on IDF bases and in other settings, enabling them to meet and work closely with Israelis and to gain an inside view of Israeli life and culture. *Quarterly newsletter; information documents.*

WOMEN'S LEAGUE FOR ISRAEL, INC. (1928). 160 E. 56 St., NYC 10022. (212)838–1997. FAX: (212)888–5972. Pres. Trudy Miner; Sr. V.-Pres. Annette Kay; Exec. Dir. Dorothy Leffler. Promotes the welfare of young people in Israel; built and maintains homes in Jerusalem, Haifa, Tel Aviv; Natanya Vocational Training and Rehabilitation Center; and the National Library of Social Work. Also many facilities and programs on the campuses of the Hebrew University. *WLI Bulletin.*

WORLD CONFEDERATION OF UNITED ZIONISTS (1946; reorg. 1958). 130 E. 59 St., NYC 10022. (212)371–1452. Copres. Bernice S. Tannenbaum, Kalman Sultanik, Melech Topiol. Promotes Zionist education, sponsors nonparty youth movements in the Diaspora, and strives for an Israel-oriented creative Jewish survival in the Diaspora. *Zionist Information Views.*

WORLD ZIONIST ORGANIZATION–AMERI-
CAN SECTION (1971). 110 E. 59 St., NYC
10022. (212)339–6000. FAX: (212)826–
8959. Chmn. Bernice S. Tannenbaum;
Exec. V.-Chmn. Zelig Chinitz. As the
American section of the overall Zionist
body throughout the world, it operates primarily in the field of *aliyah* from the free
countries, education in the Diaspora,
youth and Hechalutz, organization and information, cultural institutions, publications; conducts a worldwide Hebrew cultural program including special seminars
and pedagogic manuals; disperses information and assists in research projects concerning Israel; promotes, publishes, and
distributes books, periodicals, and pamphlets concerning developments in Israel,
Zionism, and Jewish history. *Midstream;
The Zionist Voice.*

———, DEPARTMENT OF EDUCATION AND
CULTURE (1948). 110 E. 59 St., NYC
10022. (212)339–6000. FAX: (212)826–
8959. Renders educational services to
boards and schools: study programs,
books, AV aids, instruction, teacher-in-
training service. Judaic and Hebrew subjects. Annual National Bible Contest; Israel summer and winter programs for
teachers and students.

———, NORTH AMERICAN ALIYAH
MOVEMENT (1968). 110 E. 59 St., NYC
10022. (212)339–6060. FAX: (212)826–
8959. Exec. Dir. Nellie Neeman. Promotes and facilitates *aliyah* and *klitah*
from the U.S. and Canada to Israel;
serves as a social framework for North
American immigrants to Israel. *Aliyon;
NAAM Newsletter; Coming Home.*

ZIONIST ORGANIZATION OF AMERICA
(1897). ZOA House, 4 E. 34 St., NYC
10016. (212)481–1500. FAX: (212)481–
1515. Pres. Jim Schiller; Exec. V.-Pres.
Paul Flacks. Seeks to safeguard the integrity and independence of Israel, assist in its
economic development, and foster the
unity of the Jewish people and the central-
ity of Israel in Jewish life in the spirit of
General Zionism. In Israel, owns and
maintains both the ZOA House in Tel
Aviv, a cultural center, and the Kfar Silver
Agricultural and Technical High School in
Ashkelon, with a full-time student enrollment of 700 students. Kfar Silver, under
the supervision of the Israel Ministry of
Education, focuses on academic studies,
vocational training, and programs for for-
eign students. *American Zionist Magazine;
Zionist Information Service Weekly News
Bulletin (ZINS); Public Affairs Action
Guidelines; Public Affairs Action Report for
ZOA Leaders.*

OVERSEAS AID

AMERICAN ASSOCIATION FOR ETHIOPIAN
JEWS (1969). 1828 Jefferson Place, NW,
Washington, DC 20036. (202)223–6838.
FAX: (202)223–2961. Pres. Nathan
Shapiro; Exec. Dir. William Recant. Aids
in the absorption of Ethiopian Jewish immigrants in Israel, through programs
focusing on housing, employment, and education. Informs and educates world Jewry
about the history, culture, and current situation of the Ethiopian Jewish community.
Release.

AMERICAN FRIENDS OF THE ALLIANCE IS-
RAÉLITE UNIVERSELLE, INC. (1946). 420
Lexington Ave., Suite 1733, NYC 10170.
(212)808–5437. FAX: (212)983–0094.
Pres. Henriette Beilis; Exec. Dir. Warren
Green. Participates in educational and
human-rights activities of the AIU and
supports the Alliance System of Jewish
schools, teachers' colleges, and remedial
programs in Israel, North Africa, the Middle East, Europe, and Canada. *Alliance
Review.*

AMERICAN JEWISH JOINT DISTRIBUTION
COMMITTEE, INC.–JDC (1914). 711
Third Ave., NYC 10017–4014. (212)687–
6200. FAX: (212)370–5467. Pres. Hon.
Milton A. Wolf; Exec. V.-Pres. Michael
Schneider. Provides assistance to Jewish
communities in Europe, Asia, Africa, and
the Mideast, including welfare programs
for Jews in need. Current concerns include
rescue of Jews from areas of distress; Israel's social needs, and absorption efforts
for Soviet and Ethiopian immigrants. Program expansions emphasize Jewish education in Eastern Europe and the former
USSR and nonsectarian development and
disaster assistance. *Annual report; JDC
Challenge (newsletter); Historical Album.*

AMERICAN JEWISH PHILANTHROPIC FUND
(1955). 386 Park Ave. S., 10th fl., NYC
10016. (212)OR9–0010. Pres. Charles J.
Tanenbaum. Provides resettlement assistance to Jewish refugees primarily through
programs administered by the International Rescue Committee at its offices in
Western Europe and the U.S.

AMERICAN ORT FEDERATION, INC.–ORGANIZATION FOR REHABILITATION THROUGH TRAINING (1924). 817 Broadway, NYC 10003. (212)677–4400. FAX: (212)979–9545. Pres. Murray Koppelman; Exec. V.-Pres. Marshall M. Jacobson. Provides vocational/technical education to more than 220,000 students in 38 countries throughout the world. The largest ORT operation is in Israel, where 96,000 students attend 140 ORT schools and training centers. Expanded programs meet the needs of emigration of Jews from the Soviet Union: in Israel, special vocational training and job placement programs; in the U.S., special programs in New York, Chicago, and Los Angeles, with courses in English as a second language, bookkeeping, computer operations, and business math. Annual cost of program is approximately $187 million. *American ORT Federation Bulletin; American ORT Federation Yearbook.*

———, AMERICAN AND EUROPEAN FRIENDS OF ORT (1941). 817 Broadway, NYC 10003. (212)677–4400. FAX: (212)-979–9545. Pres. Simon Jaglom; Hon. Chmn. Jacques Zwibak. Promotes the ORT idea among Americans of European extraction; supports the Litton ORT Auto-Mechanics School in Jerusalem and the ORT School of Engineering in Jerusalem. Promotes the work of the American ORT Federation.

———, AMERICAN LABOR ORT (1937). 817 Broadway, NYC 10003. (212)677–4400. FAX: (212)979–9545. Pres. Sam Fine. Promotes the vocational/technical training of more than 200,000 young people with the marketable skills they need to become productive members of society. Promotes the work of the American ORT Federation in 35 countries around the world.

———, BUSINESS AND PROFESSIONAL ORT (1937). 817 Broadway, NYC 10003. (212)-677–4400. FAX: (212)979–9545. Pres. Rose Seidel Kalich. Promotes work of American ORT Federation.

———, NATIONAL ORT LEAGUE (1914). 817 Broadway, NYC 10003. (212)677–4400. FAX: (212)979–9545. Pres. Judah Wattenberg; First V.-Pres. Tibor Waldman. Promotes ORT idea among Jewish fraternal *landsmanshaften* and individuals. Promotes the work of the American ORT Federation.

———, WOMEN'S AMERICAN ORT (1927). 315 Park Ave. S., NYC 10010. (212)505–7700. FAX: (212)674–3057. Pres. Sandy Isenstein; Exec. Dir. Tehila Elpern. Advances the programs and self-help ethos of ORT through membership, fund-raising, and educational activities. Supports 120 vocational schools, junior colleges, and technical training centers in Israel; helps meet the educational needs of Jewish communities in 30 countries; spearheads growing ORT-U.S. school operations in New York, Los Angeles, and Chicago, and associate programs in Miami and Atlanta. Maintains a wide-ranging domestic agenda which espouses quality public education, combats anti-Semitism, champions women's rights, and promotes a national literacy campaign. *Women's American ORT Reporter; Close-Ups; Direct Line; The Highest Step; Women's American ORT Yearbook.*

CONFERENCE ON JEWISH MATERIAL CLAIMS AGAINST GERMANY, INC. (1951). 15 E. 26 St., Rm. 1355, NYC 10010. (212)-696–4944. FAX: (212)679–2126. Pres. Dr. Israel Miller; Sec. and Exec. Dir. Saul Kagan. Monitors the implementation of restitution and indemnification programs of the German Federal Republic (FRG) arising from its agreements with West Germany and most recently with the united Germany, especially with respect to the new restitution law for property lost by Jewish Nazi victims on the territory of the former German Democratic Republic. Administers Hardship Fund, which distributes funds appropriated by FRG for Jewish Nazi victims unable to file timely claims under original indemnification laws. Also assists needy non-Jews who risked their lives to help Jewish survivors.

HIAS, INC. (HEBREW IMMIGRANT AID SOCIETY) (1880; reorg. 1954). 333 Seventh Ave., NYC 10001–5004. (212)967–4100. FAX: (212)967–4442. Pres. Martin Kesselhaut; Exec. V.-Pres. Martin A. Wenick. The international migration agency of the organized American Jewish community, assists in the rescue, protection, and movement of Jewish refugees and other Jewish migrants. HIAS also responds to the migration needs of other peoples at risk and represents and advocates on behalf of all these peoples, Jewish and other. *Annual report; HIAS Reporter (quarterly newsletter).*

INTERNATIONAL COALITION FOR THE RE-VIVAL OF THE JEWS OF YEMEN (ICROJOY) (1989). 150 Nassau St., Suite 1238, NYC 10038. (212)766–5556. Chmn. Dr. Hayim Tawil; V.-Chmn. Shlomo Grafi; Sec. Lester Smerka. Seeks to enrich and assist the Jewish community of the Republic of Yemen.

JEWISH RESTITUTION SUCCESSOR ORGANI-ZATION (1947). 15 E. 26 St., Rm. 1355, NYC 10010. (212)696–4944. FAX: (212)-679–2126. Sec. and Exec. Dir. Saul Kagan. Acts to discover, claim, receive, and assist in the recovery of Jewish heirless or un-claimed property; to utilize such assets or to provide for their utilization for the relief, rehabilitation, and resettlement of surviv-ing victims of Nazi persecution.

NORTH AMERICAN CONFERENCE ON ETHI-OPIAN JEWRY (NACOEJ) (1982). 165 E. 56 St., NYC 10022. (212)752–6340. FAX: (212)980–5294. Pres. Neil Jacobs; Exec. Dir. Barbara Ribakove Gordon. Provides assistance to Ethiopian Jews in Ethiopia and in Israel; informs American and other Jewish communities about their situation; works to increase involvement of world Jewish communities in assisting, visiting, and learning about Ethiopian Jews. *Life-line (membership newsletter).*

RE'UTH WOMEN'S SOCIAL SERVICE, INC. (1937). 130 E. 59 St., NYC 10022. (212)-836–1570. FAX: (212)836–1114. Pres. Rosa Strygler; Chmn. Ursula Merkin. Maintains in Israel subsidized housing for self-reliant elderly; old-age homes for more dependent elderly; Lichtenstadter Hospital for chronically ill and young accident vic-tims not accepted by other hospitals; subsi-dized meals; Golden Age clubs. *Annual dinner journal.*

THANKS TO SCANDINAVIA, INC. (1963). 745 Fifth Ave., Rm. 603, NYC 10151. (212)-486–8600. FAX: (212)486–5735. Natl. Chmn. Victor Borge; Pres. Richard Netter; Exec. Dir. Judith S. Goldstein. Provides scholarships and fellowships at American universities and medical centers to stu-dents and doctors from Denmark, Finland, Norway, and Sweden in appreciation of the rescue of Jews from the Holocaust. In-forms current and future generations of Americans and Scandinavians of these sin-gular examples of humanity and bravery; funds books about this chapter of history. *Annual report.*

UNITED JEWISH APPEAL, INC. (1939). 99 Park Ave., Suite 300, NYC 10016. (212)-818–9100. FAX: (212)818–9509. Natl. Chmn. Joel D. Tauber; Chmn. Bd. of Trustees Marvin Lender; Exec. V.-Pres. Rabbi Brian L. Lurie. The annual UJA/ Federation Campaign is the primary in-strument for the support of humanitarian programs and social services for Jews at home and abroad. In Israel, through the Jewish Agency, campaign funds help ab-sorb, educate, and settle new immigrants, build villages and farms in rural areas, sup-port innovative programs for troubled and disadvantaged youth, and promote the re-vitalization of distressed neighborhoods. The Operation Exodus Campaign provides funds for the settlement of Soviet and Ethi-opian Jews in Israel. UJA/Federation funds also provide for the well-being of Jews and Jewish communities in more than 40 other countries around the world through the American Jewish Joint Distri-bution Committee. Constituent depart-ments of the UJA include the Rabbinic Cabinet, University Programs Depart-ment, Women's Division, Young Leader-ship Cabinet, Women's Young Leadership Cabinet, and Business and Professional Women's Council.

RELIGIOUS AND EDUCATIONAL ORGANIZATIONS

AGUDATH ISRAEL OF AMERICA (1922). 84 William St., NYC 10038. (212)797–9000. Pres. Rabbi Moshe Sherer; Exec. V.-Pres. Rabbi Shmuel Bloom; Exec. Dir. Rabbi Boruch B. Borchardt. Mobilizes Orthodox Jews to cope with Jewish problems in the spirit of the Torah; speaks out on contem-porary issues from an Orthodox viewpoint; sponsors a broad range of projects aimed at enhancing religious living, education, chil-dren's welfare, protection of Jewish reli-gious rights, outreach to the assimilated and to Soviet Jewish arrivals, and social services. *Jewish Observer; Dos Yiddishe Vort; Coalition.*

———, AGUDAH WOMEN OF AMERICA–N'SHEI AGUDATH ISRAEL (1940). 84 Wil-liam St., NYC 10038. (212)363–8940. Presidium Aliza Grund, Rose Isbee; Exec. Dir. Rita Siff. Organizes Jewish women for philanthropic work in the U.S. and Israel and for intensive Torah education.

——, BOYS' DIVISION–PIRCHEI AGU-DATH ISRAEL (1925). 84 William St., NYC 10038 (212)797–9000. Natl. Dir. Rabbi Joshua Silbermintz; Natl. Coord. Rabbi Moshe Weinberger. Educates Orthodox Jewish children in Torah; encourages sense of communal responsibility. Branches sponsor weekly youth groups and Jewish welfare projects. National Mishnah contests, rallies, and conventions foster unity on a national level. *Leaders Guides.*

——, GIRLS' DIVISION—BNOS AGUDATH ISRAEL (1921). 84 William St., NYC 10038. (212)797–9000. Natl. Dirs. Devorah Streicher and Leah Zagelbaum. Sponsors regular weekly programs on the local level and unites girls from throughout the Torah world with extensive regional and national activities. *Newsletters.*

——, YOUNG MEN'S DIVISION–ZEIREI AGUDATH ISRAEL (1921). 84 William St., NYC 10038. (212)797–9000. Dir. Rabbi Labish Becker. Educates youth to see Torah as source of guidance for all issues facing Jews as individuals and as a people. Inculcates a spirit of activism through projects in religious, Torah-educational, and community-welfare fields. *Am Hatorah; Daf Chizuk; Ohr Hakollel.*

AGUDATH ISRAEL WORLD ORGANIZATION (1912). 84 William St., NYC 10038. (212)-797–9000. Chmn. Rabbi Moshe Sherer, Rabbi Yehudah Meir Abramowitz. Represents the interests of Orthodox Jewry on the national and international scenes. Sponsors projects to strengthen Torah life worldwide.

AMERICAN ASSOCIATION OF RABBIS (1978). 350 Fifth Ave., Suite 3304, NYC 10118. (212)244–3350. Pres. Rabbi Harold Lerner; Exec. Dir. Rabbi David L. Dunn. An organization of rabbis serving in pulpits, in areas of education, and in social work. *Quarterly bulletin; monthly newsletter; membership directory.*

ASSOCIATION FOR JEWISH STUDIES (1969). Widener Library M., Harvard University, Cambridge, MA 02138. Pres. Herbert H. Paper; Exec. Sec. Charles Berlin. Seeks to promote, maintain, and improve the teaching of Jewish studies in colleges and universities by sponsoring meetings and conferences, publishing a newsletter and other scholarly materials, aiding in the placement of teachers, coordinating research, and cooperating with other scholarly organizations. *AJS Review; Newsletter.*

ASSOCIATION OF HILLEL/JEWISH CAMPUS PROFESSIONALS (1949). c/o B'nai B'rith Hillel Foundation, U. of Rochester, Interfaith Chapel, Wilson Blvd., Rochester, NY 14627. (716) 275–5981. FAX: (716) 442–4279. Pres. Rabbi Paul Saiger. Seeks to promote professional relationships and exchanges of experience, develop personnel standards and qualifications, safeguard integrity of Hillel profession; represents and advocates before National Hillel Staff, National Hillel Commission, B'nai B'rith International, Council of Jewish Federations. *Handbook for Hillel Professionals; Guide to Hillel Personnel Practices.*

ASSOCIATION OF ORTHODOX JEWISH SCIENTISTS (1948). 3 W. 16 St., NYC 10011. (212)229–2340. FAX: (212)229–2319. Pres. Neil Maron; Bd. Chmn. Reuben Rudman; Exec. Dir. Joel Schwartz. Seeks to contribute to the development of science within the framework of Orthodox Jewish tradition; to obtain and disseminate information relating to the interaction between the Jewish traditional way of life and scientific developments—on both an ideological and practical level; to assist in the solution of problems pertaining to Orthodox Jews engaged in scientific teaching or research. Two main conventions are held each year. *Intercom; Proceedings; Halacha Bulletin; newsletter.*

B'NAI B'RITH HILLEL FOUNDATIONS, INC. (1923). 1640 Rhode Island Ave., NW, Washington, DC 20036. (202)857–6560. FAX: (202)857–6693. Chmn. B'nai B'rith Hillel Comm. David L. Bittker; Internatl. Dir. Richard M. Joel. Provides cultural, social, community-service, educational, and religious activities for Jewish college students of all backgrounds. Maintains a presence on over 450 campuses in the U.S., Canada, and overseas. Sponsors National Leaders Assembly, Charlotte and Jack J. Spitzer Forum on Public Policy, Jacob Burns Endowment in Ethics and the Campus, Sarah and Irving Pitt Institute for Student Leadership, National Jewish Law Students Network. *Campus Connection; Mekorot; Igeret; The Hillel Guide to Jewish Life on Campus: A Directory of Resources for Jewish College Students.*

B'NAI B'RITH YOUTH ORGANIZATION (1924). 1640 Rhode Island Ave., NW, Washington, DC 20036. (202)857–6633. FAX: (212)857–1099. Chmn. Youth Comm. Dennis Glick; Dir. Sam Fisher.

Helps Jewish teenagers achieve self-fulfillment and make a maximum contribution to the Jewish community and their country's culture; helps members acquire a greater knowledge and appreciation of Jewish religion and culture. *Shofar; Monday Morning; BBYO Parents' Line; Hakol; Kesher; The Connector.*

CANTORS ASSEMBLY (1947). 3080 Broadway, NYC 10027. (212)678-8834. FAX: (212)662-8989. Pres. Nathan Lam; Exec. V.-Pres. Samuel Rosenbaum. Seeks to unite all cantors who adhere to traditional Judaism and who serve as full-time cantors in bona fide congregations to conserve and promote the musical traditions of the Jews and to elevate the status of the cantorial profession. *Annual Proceedings; Journal of Synagogue Music.*

CENTRAL CONFERENCE OF AMERICAN RABBIS (1889). 192 Lexington Ave., NYC 10016. (212)684-4990. FAX: (212)689-6419. Pres. Rabbi Walter Jacob; Exec. V.-Pres. Rabbi Joseph B. Glaser. Seeks to conserve and promote Judaism and to disseminate its teachings in a liberal spirit. The CCAR Press provides liturgy and prayerbooks to the worldwide Reform Jewish community. *CCAR Journal: A Reform Jewish Quarterly; CCAR Yearbook.*

CLAL–NATIONAL JEWISH CENTER FOR LEARNING AND LEADERSHIP (1974). 99 Park Ave., Suite C-300, NYC 10016-1599. (212)867-8888. FAX: (212)867-8853. Pres. Rabbi Irving Greenberg; Exec. V.-Pres. Alan Bayer. Dedicated to preparing Jewish leaders to respond to the challenges of a new era in Jewish history; challenges which include the freedom to accept or reject one's Jewish heritage, the liberty to choose from an abundance of Jewish values and life-styles, and the exercise of Jewish power after the Holocaust and the rebirth of the State of Israel. *Newsletter; Sh'ma; annual calendar.*

COALITION FOR THE ADVANCEMENT OF JEWISH EDUCATION (CAJE) (1976). 261 W. 35 St., #12A, NYC 10001. (212)268-4210. FAX: (212)268-4214. Chmn. Rabbi Michael A. Weinberg; Exec. Dir. Dr. Eliot G. Spack. Brings together Jews from all ideologies who are involved in every facet of Jewish education and are committed to transmitting the Jewish heritage. Sponsors annual Conference on Alternatives in Jewish Education and Curriculum Bank; publishes a wide variety of publications; organizes shared-interest networks; offers mini grants for special projects. *Bikurim; Mekasher (a human resources directory); CAJE Jewish Education News.*

CONGRESS OF SECULAR JEWISH ORGANIZATIONS (1970). 1130 S. Michigan Ave., #2101, Chicago, IL 60605. (312)922-0386. FAX: (312)263-3634. Cochmn. Jack Rosenfeld, Larry Schofer; Exec. Dir. Gerry Revzin. An umbrella organization of schools and adult clubs; facilitates exchange curricula and educational programs for children and adults stressing our Jewish historical and cultural heritage and the continuity of the Jewish people. *Newsletter; Holiday Celebration Book.*

COUNCIL FOR JEWISH EDUCATION (1926). 426 W. 58 St., NYC 10019. (212)713-0290. FAX: (212)586-9579. Pres. Solomon Goldman; Consultant Philip Gorodetzer. Fellowship of Jewish education professionals—administrators and supervisors and teachers in Hebrew high schools and Jewish teachers colleges—of all ideological groupings; conducts annual national and regional conferences; represents the Jewish education profession before the Jewish community; cosponsors, with the Jewish Education Service of North America, a personnel committee and other projects; cooperates with Jewish Agency Department of Education and Culture in promoting Hebrew culture and studies; conducts lectureship at Hebrew University. *Jewish Education; Sheviley Hahinnukh.*

FEDERATION OF JEWISH MEN'S CLUBS, INC. (1929). 475 Riverside Dr., Rm. 244, NYC 10115. (212)749-8100. FAX: (212)316-4271. Internatl. Pres. J. Harold Nissen; Exec. Dir. Rabbi Charles E. Simon; Dir., Admin. & Communication Dr. Joel Sperber. Promotes principles of Conservative Judaism; develops family-education and leadership-training programs; offers the Art of Jewish Living series and Yom Hashoah Home Commemoration; sponsors Hebrew literacy adult-education program; presents awards for service to American Jewry. *Torchlight.*

INSTITUTE FOR COMPUTERS IN JEWISH LIFE (1978). 7074 N. Western Ave., Chicago, IL 60645. (312)262-9200. FAX: (312)262-9298. Pres. Thomas Klutznick; Exec. V.-Pres. Dr. Irving J. Rosenbaum. Explores, develops, and disseminates applications of computer technology to appropriate areas of Jewish life, with special emphasis on Jewish education; provides access to the Bar-Ilan University Responsa Project; creates educational software for use in Jewish schools; provides consulting service and assistance for national Jewish organizations, seminaries, and synagogues. *Monitor.*

JEWISH CHAUTAUQUA SOCIETY, INC. (sponsored by NATIONAL FEDERATION OF TEMPLE BROTHERHOODS) (1893). 838 Fifth Ave., NYC 10021. (212)570–0707 or (800)765–6200. FAX: (212)570–0960. Pres. Roger B. Jacobs; Chancellor/lst V.-Pres. Jay D. Hirsch; Exec. Dir. Lewis Eisenberg. Works to promote interfaith understanding by sponsoring accredited college courses and one-day lectures on Judaic topics, providing book grants to educational institutions, producing educational videotapes on interfaith topics, and convening interfaith institutes. Also supports extracurricular intergroup programming on college campuses in cooperation with Hillel and is a founding sponsor of the National Black/Jewish Relations Center at Dillard University. *Brotherhood.*

JEWISH EDUCATION IN MEDIA (1978). PO Box 180, Riverdale Sta., NYC 10471. (212)362–7633; (203)968–2225. Pres. Bernard Samers; Exec. Dir. Rabbi Mark S. Golub. Devoted to producing radio, television, film, video-cassette, and audio-cassette programming for a popular Jewish audience, in order to inform, entertain, and inspire a greater sense of Jewish identity and Jewish commitment. "L'Chayim," JEM's weekly half-hour program, airs on WOR Radio in New York and in radio and television syndication; it features outstanding figures in the Jewish world addressing issues and events of importance to the Jewish community.

JEWISH EDUCATION SERVICE OF NORTH AMERICA (JESNA) (1981). 730 Broadway, NYC 10003–9540. (212)529–2000. FAX: (212)529–2009. Pres. Neil Greenbaum; Exec. V.-Pres. Dr. Jonathan S. Woocher. The trans-denominational planning, coordinating, and service agency for Jewish education of the organized Jewish community in North America. Works with federations, central agencies for Jewish education, and other local, national, and international institutions, and undertakes activities in the areas of research, program

and human-resource development, information and resource dissemination, consultation, conferences and publications. *Agenda: Jewish Education; TRENDS; Information Research Bulletins; JESNA Update.*

JEWISH RECONSTRUCTIONIST FOUNDATION (1940). Church Rd. and Greenwood Ave., Wyncote, PA 19095. (215)887–1988. Exec. Dir. Rabbi Mordechai Liebling. Dedicated to the advancement of Judaism as the evolving religious civilization of the Jewish people. Coordinates the Federation of Reconstructionist Congregations and Havurot, Reconstructionist Rabbinical Association, and Reconstructionist Rabbinical College.

———, FEDERATION OF RECONSTRUCTIONIST CONGREGATIONS AND HAVUROT (1954). Church Rd. and Greenwood Ave., Wyncote, PA 19095. (215)887–1988. FAX: (215)576–6143. Pres. Valerie Kaplan; Exec. Dir. Rabbi Mordechai Liebling. Services affiliated congregations and havurot educationally and administratively; fosters the establishment of new Reconstructionist congregations and fellowship groups. Runs the Reconstructionist Press and provides programmatic materials. Maintains regional offices in New York and Los Angeles. *Reconstructionist.*

———, RECONSTRUCTIONIST RABBINICAL ASSOCIATION (1974). Church Rd. and Greenwood Ave., Wyncote, PA 19095. (215)576–5210. FAX: (215)576–6143. Pres. Rabbi Lee Friedlander; Exec. Dir. Rabbi Robert Gluck. Professional organization for graduates of the Reconstructionist Rabbinical College and other rabbis who identify with Reconstructionist Judaism; cooperates with Federation of Reconstructionist Congregations and Havurot in furthering Reconstructionism in N. America. *Raayanot; newsletter.*

———, RECONSTRUCTIONIST RABBINICAL COLLEGE (*see* p. 488)

JEWISH TEACHERS ASSOCIATION–MORIM (1931). 45 E. 33 St., Suite 604, NYC 10016. (212)684–0556. Pres. Phyllis L. Pullman; V.-Pres. Joseph Varon; Sec. Helen Parnes; Treas. Mildred Safar. Protects teachers from abuse of seniority rights; fights the encroachment of anti-Semitism in education; provides legal counsel to protect teachers from discrimination; offers scholarships to qualified students; encourages teachers to assume active roles in Jewish communal and religious affairs. *Morim JTA Newsletter.*

MACHNE ISRAEL, INC. (1940). 770 Eastern Pkwy., Brooklyn, NY 11213. (718)774–4000. FAX: (718)774–2718. Pres. Menachem M. Schneerson (Lubavitcher Rebbe); Dir., Treas. M.A. Hodakov; Sec. Nissan Mindel. The Lubavitcher movement's organ dedicated to the social, spiritual, and material welfare of Jews throughout the world.

MERKOS L'INYONEI CHINUCH, INC. (THE CENTRAL ORGANIZATION FOR JEWISH EDUCATION) (1940). 770 Eastern Pkwy., Brooklyn, NY 11213. (718)493–9250. Pres. Menachem M. Schneerson (Lubavitcher Rebbe); Dir., Treas. M.A. Hodakov; Sec. Nissan Mindel. The educational arm of the Lubavitcher movement. Seeks to promote Jewish education among Jews, regardless of their background, in the spirit of Torah-true Judaism; to establish contact with alienated Jewish youth; to stimulate concern and active interest in Jewish education on all levels; and to promote religious observance as a daily experience among all Jews. Maintains worldwide network of regional offices, schools, summer camps, and Chabad-Lubavitch Houses; publishes Jewish educational literature in numerous languages and monthly journal in five languages. *Conversaciones con la juventud; Conversations avec les jeunes; Schmuessen mit Kinder un Yugent; Sihot la-No-ar; Talks and Tales.*

NATIONAL COMMITTEE FOR FURTHER-ANCE OF JEWISH EDUCATION (1941). 824 Eastern Pkwy., Brooklyn, NY 11213. (718)735–0200. FAX: (718)735–4455. Pres. Milton E. Kramer. Chmn. Exec. Com. Rabbi Sholem Ber Hecht. Seeks to disseminate the ideals of Torah-true education among the youth of America; provides education and compassionate care for the poor, sick, and needy in U.S. and Israel; provides aid to Iranian Jewish youth; sponsors camps; Operation Survival, War on Drugs; Yeshivas Kol Yaakov Yehuda Hadar HaTorah, Machon Chana Women's College, and Mesivta Orh Torah; Ivy League Torah Study Program, seeking to win back college youth and others to Judaism; maintains schools in Brooklyn and Queens, family and vocational counseling services. *Panorama; Passover Handbook;* *Seder Guide; Cultbusters; Intermarriage; Brimstone & Fire.*

NATIONAL COUNCIL OF YOUNG ISRAEL (1924). 3 W. 16 St., NYC 10011. (212)929–1525. Pres. Chaim Kaminetzky; Exec. V.-Pres. Rabbi Ephraim H. Sturm. Maintains a program of spiritual, cultural, social, and communal activity aimed at the advancement and perpetuation of traditional, Torah-true Judaism; seeks to instill in American youth an understanding and appreciation of the ethical and spiritual values of Judaism. Sponsors kosher dining clubs and fraternity houses and an Israel program. *Viewpoint; Divrei Torah Bulletin.*

———, AMERICAN FRIENDS OF YOUNG ISRAEL IN ISRAEL–YISRAEL HATZA'IR (1926). 3 W. 16 St., NYC 10011. (212)929–1525. FAX: (212)727–9526. Pres. Meir Mishkoff; Dir. Rabbi Elias Lauer. Promotes Young Israel synagogues and youth work in Israel; works to help absorb Russian and Ethiopian immigrants.

———, ARMED FORCES BUREAU (1912). 3 W. 16 St., NYC 10011. (212)929–1525. Advises and guides the inductees into the armed forces with regard to Sabbath observance, *kashrut,* and Orthodox behavior. *Guide for the Orthodox Serviceman.*

———, MESILAH–INSTITUTE FOR JEWISH STUDIES (1947). 3 W. 16 St., NYC 10011. (212)929–1525. Pres. Chaim Kaminetzky; Exec. V.-Pres. Rabbi Ephraim H. Sturm; Dir. Rabbi Naphtali Harczstark. Introduces students to Jewish learning and knowledge; helps form adult branch schools; aids Young Israel synagogues in their adult education programs. *Bulletin.*

———, YOUNG ISRAEL COLLEGIATES AND YOUNG ADULTS (1951; reorg. 1982). 3 W. 16 St., NYC 10011. (212)929–1525. Chmn. Kenneth Block; Dir. Richard Stareshefsky. Organizes and operates kosher dining clubs on college and university campuses; provides information and counseling on *kashrut* observance at colleges; gives college-age youth understanding and appreciation of Judaism and information on issues important to Jewish community; arranges seminars and meetings, weekends and trips.

———, YOUNG ISRAEL YOUTH (reorg. 1968). 3 W. 16 St., NYC 10011. (212)929–1525. Dir. Richard Stareshefsky. Fosters a program of spiritual, cultural, social, and communal activities for the advancement and perpetuation of traditional Torah-true Judaism; strives to instill an understanding and appreciation of high ethical and spiritual values and to demonstrate compatibility of ancient faith of Israel with good Americanism. Operates Achva East Summer program for 8th graders, Achva West Summer program for 9th graders, and Achva Israel Summer program for 10th graders. *Monthly newsletter.*

NATIONAL HAVURAH COMMITTEE (1979). PO Box 2621, Bala Cynwyd, PA 19004–6621. (215)843–1470. FAX: (215)843–1470. Chmn. Dr. Herbert Levine; Dir. Rivkah Walton. A center for Jewish renewal devoted to spreading Jewish ideas, ethics, and religious practices through *havurot*, participatory and inclusive religious minicommunities. Maintains a directory of N. American *havurot* and sponsors a week-long summer institute, regional weekend retreats, a teacher's bureau, and a D'var Torah newspaper column. *Havurah! (newsletter).*

NATIONAL JEWISH CENTER FOR LEARNING AND LEADERSHIP (*see* CLAL)

NATIONAL JEWISH COMMITTEE ON SCOUTING (Boy Scouts of America) (1926). 1325 Walnut Hill La., PO Box 152079, Irving, TX 75015–2079. (214)580–2120. FAX: (214)580–2502. Chmn. Harry R. Rosen; Dir. Donald L. Townsend. Assists Jewish institutions in meeting their needs and concerns through use of the resources of scouting. Works through local Jewish committees on scouting to establish Tiger Cub groups (1st grade), Cub Scout packs, Boy Scout troops, and coed Explorer posts in synagogues, Jewish community centers, day schools, and other Jewish organizations wishing to draw Jewish youth. Support materials and resources on request. *Hatsofe* (*quarterly*); *Expressions* (*annually*).

NATIONAL JEWISH GIRL SCOUT COMMITTEE (1972). Synagogue Council of America, 327 Lexington Ave., NYC 10016. (212)686–8670. FAX: (212)686–8673. Chmn. Rabbi Herbert W. Bomzer; Field Chmn. Adele Wasko. Under the auspices of the Synagogue Council of America, serves to further Jewish education by promoting Jewish award programs, encouraging religious services, promoting cultural exchanges with the Israel Boy and Girl Scouts Federation, and extending membership in the Jewish community by assisting councils in organizing Girl Scout troops and local Jewish Girl Scout committees. *Newsletter.*

NATIONAL JEWISH HOSPITALITY COMMITTEE (1973). P.O. Box 15832, Philadelphia, PA 19103. (215)552–8599. Chmn. Dr. Paul Friedman; Exec. Dir. Steven S. Jacobs. Assists persons interested in Judaism—for conversion, intermarriage, or to respond to missionaries. *Special reports.*

NATIONAL JEWISH INFORMATION SERVICE FOR THE PROPAGATION OF JUDAISM, INC. (1960). 3761 Decade St., Las Vegas, NV 89121. (702)454–5872. Pres. Rabbi Moshe M. Maggal; V.-Pres. Lawrence J. Epstein; Sec. and P.R. Dir. Rachel D. Maggal. Seeks to convert non-Jews to Judaism and return Jews to Judaism; maintains College for Jewish Ambassadors for the training of Jewish missionaries, and the Correspondence Academy of Judaism for instruction on Judaism through the mail. *Voice of Judaism.*

OZAR HATORAH, INC. (1946). 1 E. 33 St., NYC 10016. (212)696–1212. Pres. Joseph Shalom; Sec. Sam Sutton. An international educational network which builds Sephardic communities worldwide through Jewish education.

P'EYLIM–AMERICAN YESHIVA STUDENT UNION (1951). 805 Kings Highway, Brooklyn, NY 11223. (718)382–0113. Pres. Jacob Y. Weisberg; Exec. V.-Pres. Avraham Hirsch. Aids and sponsors pioneer work by American graduate teachers and rabbis in new villages and towns in Israel; does religious, organizational, and educational work and counseling among new immigrant youth; maintains summer camps for poor immigrant youth in Israel; belongs to worldwide P'eylim movement which has groups in Argentina, Brazil, Canada, England, Belgium, the Netherlands, Switzerland, France, and Israel; engages in relief and educational work among North African immigrants in France and Canada, assisting them to relocate and reestablish a strong Jewish community life. *P'eylim Reporter; News from P'eylim; N'shei P'eylim News.*

RABBINICAL ALLIANCE OF AMERICA (IGUD HARABONIM) (1942). 3 W. 16 St., 4th fl., NYC 10011. (212)242–6420. FAX: (212)-255–8313. Pres. Rabbi Abraham B. Hecht;

Admin. Judge of Beth Din (Rabbinical Court) Rabbi Herschel Kurzrock. Seeks to promulgate the cause of Torah-true Judaism through an organized rabbinate that is consistently Orthodox; seeks to elevate the position of Orthodox rabbis nationally and to defend the welfare of Jews the world over. Also has Beth Din Rabbinical Court for Jewish divorces, litigation, marriage counseling, and family problems. *Perspective; Nahalim; Torah Message of the Week; Registry.*

RABBINICAL ASSEMBLY (1900). 3080 Broadway, NYC 10027. (212)678–8060. Pres. Rabbi Gerald Zelizer; Exec. V.-Pres. Rabbi Joel H. Meyers. Seeks to promote Conservative Judaism and to foster the spirit of fellowship and cooperation among rabbis and other Jewish scholars; cooperates with the Jewish Theological Seminary of America and the United Synagogue of Conservative Judaism. *Conservative Judaism; Proceedings of the Rabbinical Assembly; Rabbinical Assembly Newsletter.*

RABBINICAL COUNCIL OF AMERICA, INC. (1923; reorg. 1935). 275 Seventh Ave., NYC 10001. (212)807–7888. FAX: (212)-727–8452. Pres. Rabbi Moshe Gorlelik; V.-Pres. Rabbi Marc D. Angel. Promotes Orthodox Judaism in the community; supports institutions for study of Torah; stimulates creation of new traditional agencies. *Hadorom; Record; Sermon Manual; Tradition.*

RESEARCH INSTITUTE OF RELIGIOUS JEWRY, INC. (1941; reorg. 1964). 471 W. End Ave., NYC 10024. (212)222–6839. Chmn. Rabbi Oswald Besser; Sec. Max Retter. Engages in research and publishes studies concerning the situation of religious Jewry and its history in various countries.

SHOMREI ADAMAH/KEEPERS OF THE EARTH (1988). Church Rd. and Greenwood Ave., Wyncote, PA 19095. (215)-887–3106. FAX: (215)576–6143. Dir. Ellen Bernstein. A research, development, and education institute involved with nature and environmental issues from a Jewish perspective. Provides liturgical, educational, and other materials to members, including ecologically oriented services, sermons, and children's activities for school, camp, and home, as well as guides for study and action. Works with congregations and groups across North America on "greening" their communities. *Kol HaIlanot/Voice of the Trees (newspaper).*

SOCIETY FOR HUMANISTIC JUDAISM (1969). 28611 W. Twelve Mile Rd., Farmington Hills, MI 48334. (313)478–7610. FAX: (313)477–9014. Pres. Rosalyn Hill; Exec. Dir. Miriam Jerris; Asst. Dir. M. Bonnie Cousens. Serves as a voice for Jews who value their Jewish identity and who seek an alternative to conventional Judaism, who reject supernatural authority and affirm the right of individuals to be the masters of their own lives. Publishes educational and ceremonial materials; organizes congregations and groups. *Humanistic Judaism* (quarterly journal); *Humanorah* (quarterly newsletter).

SYNAGOGUE COUNCIL OF AMERICA (1926). 327 Lexington Ave., NYC 10016. (212)-686–8670. FAX: (212)686–8673. Pres. Rabbi Jerome K. Davidson; Bd. Chmn. Myron Pomerantz; Exec. V.-Pres. Rabbi Henry D. Michelman. Represents congregational and rabbinic organizations of Conservative, Orthodox, and Reform Jewry; acts as "one voice" for religious Jewry. *SCA News; special reports.*

TORAH SCHOOLS FOR ISRAEL–CHINUCH ATZMAI (1953). 40 Exchange Pl., NYC 10005. (212)248–6200. FAX: (212)248–6202. Pres. Abraham Pam; Exec. Dir. Henach Cohen. Conducts information programs for the American Jewish community on activities of the independent Torah schools educational network in Israel; coordinates role of American members of international board of governors; funds special programs of Mercaz Hachinuch Ha-Atzmai B'Eretz Yisroel. *Israel Education Reporter.*

TORAH UMESORAH–NATIONAL SOCIETY FOR HEBREW DAY SCHOOLS (1944). 160 Broadway, NYC 10038. (212)227–1000. Pres. Sheldon Beren; Bd. Chmn. David Singer; Exec. V.-Pres. Rabbi Joshua Fishman. Establishes Hebrew day schools in U.S. and Canada and provides a full gamut of services, including placement and curriculum guidance, teacher-training on campuses of major yeshivahs, an annual intensive teacher institute in July, and regional seminars and workshops. Publishes textbooks; runs Shabbatonim, extracurricular activities. National PTA groups; national and regional teacher conventions. *Olomeinu–Our World; Visions; Parshah Sheets; Torah Umesorah News.*

———, NATIONAL ASSOCIATION OF HE-
BREW DAY SCHOOL ADMINISTRATORS
(1960). 1114 Ave. J, Brooklyn, NY 11230.
(718)258–7767. Pres. David H. Schwartz.
Coordinates the work of the fiscal directors
of Hebrew day schools throughout the
country. *NAHDSA Review.*

———, NATIONAL ASSOCIATION OF HE-
BREW DAY SCHOOL PARENT-TEACHER
ASSOCIATIONS (1948). 160 Broadway,
NYC 10038. (212)227–1000. Natl. PTA
Coord. Bernice Brand. Acts as a clearinghouse and service agency to PTAs of Hebrew day schools; organizes parent education courses and sets up programs for
individual PTAs. *Fundraising with a Flair;
Monthly Sidrah Series Program; PTA with
a Purpose for the Hebrew Day School.*

———, NATIONAL CONFERENCE OF YE-
SHIVA PRINCIPALS (1956). 160 Broadway,
NYC 10038. (212)227–1000. Pres. Rabbi
Yitzchok Merkin; Bd. Chmn. Rabbi Bar-
uch Hilsenrath; Exec. V.-Pres. Rabbi A.
Moshe Possick. A professional organiza-
tion of primary and secondary yeshivah/
day-school principals providing yeshivah
day schools with school visitations, teacher
and principal conferences—including a
Mid-Winter Conference—and a National
Convention. *Directory of High Schools.*

———, NATIONAL LAY LEADERSHIP COM-
MITTEE (LLC) (1991). Chmn. Barry Ray;
Dir. Rabbi Zvi Shachtel. Provides a lay
leaders' executive report-professional journal; national lay leadership convention; national policy setting committees.

———, NATIONAL YESHIVA TEACHERS
BOARD OF LICENSE (1953). 160 Broadway, NYC 10038. (212)227–1000. Exec.
V.-Pres. & Dir. Rabbi Joshua Fishman. Issues licenses to qualified instructors for all
grades of the Hebrew day school and the
general field of Torah education.

UNION FOR TRADITIONAL JUDAISM (1984).
261 E. Lincoln Ave., Mt. Vernon, NY
10552. (914)667–1007. FAX: (914)667–
1023. Pres. Burton G. Greenblatt; Exec.
V.-Pres. Rabbi Ronald D. Price. Through
innovative outreach programs, seeks to
bring the greatest possible number of Jews
closer to an open-minded observant Jewish
life-style. Activities include the Kashrut
Initiative, Operation Pesah, the Panel of
Halakhic Inquiry, Speaker's Bureau, adult
and youth conferences, and congregational
services. Includes, since 1992, the MORA-

SHAH rabbinic fellowship. *Hagahelet
(quarterly newsletter); Cornerstone (journal); Tomeikh Kahalakhah (Jewish legal
responsa).*

UNION OF AMERICAN HEBREW CONGREGA-
TIONS (1873). 838 Fifth Ave., NYC 10021–
7064. (212)249–0100. FAX: (212)734–
2857. Pres. Rabbi Alexander M. Schindler;
Bd. Chmn. Melvin Merians; Sr. V.-Pres.
Rabbi Daniel B. Syme; V.-Pres. Rabbi Eric
H. Yoffie. Serves as the central congregational body of Reform Judaism in the
Western Hemisphere; serves its approximately 850 affiliated temples and membership with religious, educational, cultural,
and administrative programs. *Reform Judaism.*

———, AMERICAN CONFERENCE OF CAN-
TORS (1953). 170 W. 74 St., NYC 10023.
(212)874–4762. FAX: (212)874–8605.
Pres. Vicki L. Axe; Exec. V.-Pres. Howard
M. Stahl; Dir. of Placement Richard Bot-
ton; Admin. Asst. Susan Richardson.
Members receive investiture and commis-
sioning as cantors at recognized seminaries, i.e., Hebrew Union College–Jewish Institute of Religion, School of Sacred Music,
or Jewish Theological Seminary, as well as
full certification through HUC-JIR-SSM.
Through the Joint Cantorial Placement
Commission, the ACC serves Reform congregations seeking cantors and music directors. Dedicated to creative Judaism,
preserving the best of the past, and encouraging new and vital approaches to religious
ritual, music, and ceremonies. *Koleinu.*

———, COMMISSION ON JEWISH EDUCA-
TION OF THE UNION OF AMERICAN HE-
BREW CONGREGATIONS, CENTRAL CON-
FERENCE OF AMERICAN RABBIS, AND
NATIONAL ASSOCIATION OF TEMPLE
EDUCATORS (1923). 838 Fifth Ave., NYC
10021. (212)249–0100. Chmn. Rabbi Jonathan A. Stein; V.-Chmn. Dr. Judith Sherman, Robert E. Tornberg; Dir. Rabbi
Howard I. Bogot. Long-range planning
and policy development for congregational
programs of lifelong education; network
projects with affiliates and associate groups
including: special-needs education, Reform Jewish outreach, and Reform Day
Schools; activities administered by the
UAHC Department for Religious Education.

———, COMMISSION ON SOCIAL ACTION OF
REFORM JUDAISM (see p. 450)

——, COMMISSION ON SYNAGOGUE MANAGEMENT (UAHC-CCAR) (1962). 838 Fifth Ave., NYC 10021. (212)249–0100. FAX: (212)734–2857. Chmn. Paul Vanek; Dir. Joseph C. Bernstein. Assists congregations in management, finance, building maintenance, design, construction, and art aspects of synagogues; maintains the Synagogue Architectural Library.

——, NATIONAL ASSOCIATION OF TEMPLE ADMINISTRATORS (NATA) (1941). c/o Stephen S. Wise Temple, 15500 Stephen S. Wise Dr., Los Angeles, CA 90077–1598. (213)476–8561. FAX: (213)476–3587. Pres. Norman Fogel. Prepares and disseminates administrative information and procedures to member synagogues of UAHC; provides training of professional synagogue executives; formulates and establishes professional standards for the synagogue executive; provides placement services. *NATA Journal; Temple Management Manual.*

——, NATIONAL ASSOCIATION OF TEMPLE EDUCATORS (NATE) (1955). 707 Summerly Dr., Nashville, TN 37209–4253. (615)352–6800. FAX: (615)352–7800. Pres. Roberta Louis Goodman; Exec. V.-Pres. Richard M. Morin. Represents the temple educator within the general body of Reform Judaism; fosters the full-time profession of the temple educator; encourages the growth and development of Jewish religious education consistent with the aims of Reform Judaism; stimulates communal interest in and responsibility for Jewish religious education. *NATE News; Compass.*

——, NATIONAL FEDERATION OF TEMPLE BROTHERHOODS (1923). 838 Fifth Ave., NYC 10021. (212)570–0707. Pres. Roger B. Jacobs; Exec. Dir. Lewis Eisenberg. Dedicated to enhancing the world through the ideal of brotherhood, NFTB and its 300 affiliated clubs are actively involved in education, social action, youth activities, and other programs that contribute to temple and community life. Supports the Jewish Chautauqua Society, an interfaith educational project. *Brotherhood.*

——, WOMEN OF REFORM JUDAISM–NATIONAL FEDERATION OF TEMPLE SISTERHOODS (1913). 838 Fifth Ave., NYC 10021. (212)249–0100. FAX: (212)861–0831. Pres. Judith M. Hertz; Exec. Dir. Ellen Y. Rosenberg. Serves more than 600 sisterhoods of Reform Judaism; promotes interreligious understanding and social justice; awards scholarships and grants to rabbinic students; provides braille and large-type Judaic materials for Jewish blind; supports projects for Israel, Soviet Jewry, and the aging; is an affiliate of UAHC and the women's agency of Reform Judaism; works in behalf of the Hebrew Union College–Jewish Institute of Religion; cooperates with World Union for Progressive Judaism. *Notes for Now.*

——, YOUTH DIVISION AND NORTH AMERICAN FEDERATION OF TEMPLE YOUTH (1939). 838 Fifth Ave., NYC 10021. (212)249–0100. FAX: (212)517–7863. Dir. Rabbi Allan L. Smith; Pres. Brigitte Swenson. Seeks to train Reform Jewish youth in the values of the synagogue and their application to daily life through service to the community and congregation; runs department of summer camps and national leadership-training institute; arranges overseas academic tours, work-study programs, international student-exchange programs, and college-student programs in the U.S. and Israel, including accredited study programs in Israel. *Ani V'Atah; The Jewish Connection.*

UNION OF ORTHODOX JEWISH CONGREGATIONS OF AMERICA (1898). 333 Seventh Ave., NYC 10001. (212)563–4000. Pres. Sheldon Rudoff; Exec. V.-Pres. Rabbi Pinchas Stolper. Serves as the national central body of Orthodox synagogues; sponsors Institute for Public Affairs; National Conference of Synagogue Youth; LAVE—Learning and Values Experiences; Israel Center in Jerusalem; *aliyah* department; national OU *kashrut* supervision and certification service; Marriage Commission; "Taste of Torah" radio program; provides educational, religious, and organizational programs, events, and guidance to synagogues and groups; represents the Orthodox Jewish community to governmental and civic bodies and the general Jewish community. *Jewish Action magazine; OU Kosher Directory; OU Passover Directory; OU News Reporter; Synagogue Spotlight; Our Way magazine; Yachad magazine; Luach Limud Torah Diary Home Study Program.*

——, INSTITUTE FOR PUBLIC AFFAIRS (1989). 333 Seventh Ave., NYC 10001. (212)563–4000. FAX: (212)564–9058.

Pres. Sheldon Rudoff; Chmn. Mandell Ganchrow; Exec. Dir. William E. Rapfogel. Serves as the policy analysis, advocacy, mobilization, and programming department responsible for representing Orthodox/traditional American Jewry. *Orthodox Advocate (quarterly newsletter); Briefing (monthly updates).*

——, NATIONAL CONFERENCE OF SYNAGOGUE YOUTH (1954). 333 Seventh Ave., NYC 10001. (212)563–4000. Dir. Rabbi Raphael Butler. Central body for youth groups of Orthodox congregations; provides educational guidance, Torah study groups, community service, programs consultation, Torah library, Torah fund scholarships, Ben Zakkai Honor Society, Friends of NCSY; weeklong seminars, Travel America with NCSY, Israel Summer Seminar for teens and collegiates, and Camp NCSY East Teen Torah Center. Divisions include Senior NCSY in 18 regions and 465 chapters, Junior NCSY for preteens, Our Way for the Jewish deaf, Yachad for the developmentally disabled, Mesorah for Jewish collegiates, Israel Center in Jerusalem, and NCSY in Israel. *Keeping Posted with NCSY; Face the Nation-President's Newsletter; Oreich Yomeinu-Education Newsletter; Mitsvah of the Month.*

——, WOMEN'S BRANCH (1923). 156 Fifth Ave., NYC 10010. (212)929–8857. Pres. Deborah M.F. Turk. Seeks to spread the understanding and practice of Orthodox Judaism and to unite all Orthodox women and their synagogal organizations; services affiliates with educational and programming materials, leadership, and organizational guidance, and has an NGO representative at the UN. Supplies candelabra for Jewish patients in hospitals and nursing homes; supports Stern and Touro College scholarship funds and Jewish braille publications. *Hachodesh; Hakol.*

UNION OF ORTHODOX RABBIS OF THE UNITED STATES AND CANADA (1902). 235 E. Broadway, NYC 10002. (212)964–6337. Dir. Rabbi Hersh M. Ginsberg. Seeks to foster and promote Torah-true Judaism in the U.S. and Canada; assists in the establishment and maintenance of yeshivot in the U.S.; maintains committee on marriage and divorce and aids individuals with marital difficulties; disseminates knowledge of traditional Jewish rites and practices and publishes regulations on synago-

gal structure; maintains rabbinical court for resolving individual and communal conflicts. *HaPardes.*

UNION OF SEPHARDIC CONGREGATIONS, INC. (1929). 8 W. 70 St., NYC 10023. (212)873–0300. FAX: (212)724–6165. Pres. Rev. Dr. Solomon Gaon; Bd. Chmn. Victor Tarry. Promotes the religious interests of Sephardic Jews; prints and distributes Sephardic prayer books. *Annual International Directory of Sephardic Congregations.*

UNITED LUBAVITCHER YESHIVOTH (1940). 841–853 Ocean Pkwy., Brooklyn, NY 11230. (718)859–7600. Supports and organizes Jewish day schools and rabbinical seminaries in the U.S. and abroad.

UNITED SYNAGOGUE OF CONSERVATIVE JUDAISM (1913). 155 Fifth Ave., NYC 10010–6802. (212)533–7800. FAX: (212)-353–9439. Pres. Alan J. Tichnor; Exec. V.-Pres./CEO Rabbi Jerome M. Epstein. International organization of 800 Conservative congregations. Maintains 12 departments and 20 regional offices to assist its affiliates with religious, educational, youth, community, and administrative programming and guidance; aims to enhance the cause of Conservative Judaism, further religious observance, encourage establishment of Jewish religious schools, draw youth closer to Jewish tradition. Extensive Israel programs. *United Synagogue Review; Art/Engagement Calendar; Program Suggestions; Directory & Resource Guide; Book Service Catalogue of Publications.*

——, COMMISSION ON JEWISH EDUCATION (1930). 155 Fifth Ave., NYC 10010. (212)533–7800. FAX: (212)353–9439. Cochmn. Joshua Elkin, Dr. Miriam Klein Shapiro; Dir. Rabbi Robert Abramson. Develops educational policy for the United Synagogue of Conservative Judaism and sets the educational direction for Conservative congregations, their schools, and the Solomon Schechter Day Schools. Seeks to enhance the educational effectiveness of congregations through the publication of materials and in-service programs. *Tov L'Horot; Your Child; Dapim; Shiboley Schechter; Advisories.*

——, COMMITTEE ON SOCIAL ACTION AND PUBLIC POLICY (1958). 155 Fifth Ave., NYC 10010. (212)533–7800. FAX: (212)353–9439. Cochmn. Scott Kaplan, Teddy Zabb. Develops and implements positions and programs on issues of social action and public policy for the United Synagogue of Conservative Judaism; represents these positions to other Jewish and civic organizations, the media, and government; and provides guidance, both informational and programmatic, to its affiliated congregations in these areas.

——, JEWISH EDUCATORS ASSEMBLY (1951). 15 E. 26 St., Rm. 1350A, NYC 10010. (212)532–4949. FAX: (212)481–4174. Pres. Dr. Miriam Klein Shapiro; Exec. Dir. Bernard Dov Troy. Advances the development of Jewish education on all levels in consonance with the philosophy of the Conservative movement. Promotes Jewish education as a basis for the creative continuity of the Jewish people; sponsors an annual convention. Serves as a forum for the exchange of ideas, programs, and educational media. *Bulletins; V'Aleh Ha-Chadashot Newsletter.*

——, KADIMA (formerly PRE-USY; reorg. 1968). Cong. B'nai Jacob, 75 Rimmon, Woodbridge, CT 06525. (203)389–2111. FAX: (212)353–9439. Acting Exec. Dir. Jules A. Gutin. Involves Jewish preteens in a meaningful religious, educational, and social environment; fosters a sense of identity and commitment to the Jewish community and the Conservative movement; conducts synagogue-based chapter programs and regional Kadima days and weekends. *Mitzvah of the Month; Kadima Kesher; Chagim; Advisors Aid; Games;* quarterly *Kadima* magazine.

——, NATIONAL ASSOCIATION OF SYNAGOGUE ADMINISTRATORS (1948). 628 Pope's Island Rd., Milford, CT 06460. (203)389–2111. Pres. Rhoda F. Myers. Aids congregations affiliated with the United Synagogue of America to further the aims of Conservative Judaism through more effective administration (Program for Assistance by Liaisons to Synagogues—PALS); advances professional standards and promotes new methods in administration; cooperates in United Synagogue placement services and administrative surveys. *NASA Connections Newsletter; NASA Journal.*

——, UNITED SYNAGOGUE YOUTH OF (1951). 155 Fifth Ave., NYC 10010. (212)-533–7800. FAX: (212)353–9439. Pres. Joel Levenson; Acting Exec. Dir. Jules A. Gutin. Seeks to strengthen identification

with Conservative Judaism, based on the personality development, needs, and interests of the adolescent, in a mitzvah framework. *Achshav; Tikun Olam; A.J. Heschel Honor Society Newsletter; SATO Newsletter; USY Alumni Assn. Newsletter; USY Program Bank; Hamad'rich Newsletter for Advisors.*

VAAD MISHMERETH STAM (1976). 4902 16th Ave., Brooklyn, NY 11204. (718)-438–4963. FAX: (212)438–4980. Pres. Rabbi David L. Greenfeld. A nonprofit consumer-protection agency dedicated to preserving and protecting the halakhic integrity of Torah scrolls, phylacteries, and *mezuzot*. Publishes material for laymen and scholars in the field of scribal arts; makes presentations and conducts examination campaigns in schools and synagogues; created an optical software system to detect possible textual errors in *stam*. Offices in Israel, Strasbourg, Chicago, London, Manchester, Montreal, and Zurich. Publishes *Guide to Mezuzah* and *Guide to the Letters of the Aleph Beth. The Jewish Quill.*

WOMEN'S LEAGUE FOR CONSERVATIVE JUDAISM (1918). 48 E. 74 St., NYC 10021. (212)628–1600. Pres. Audrey Citak; Exec. Dir. Bernice Balter. Parent body of Conservative (Masorti) women's groups in U.S., Canada, Puerto Rico, Mexico, and Israel; provides programs and resources in Jewish education, social action, Israel affairs, American and Canadian public affairs, leadership training, community service programs for persons with disabilities, conferences on world affairs, study institutes, publicity techniques; publishes books of Jewish interest; contributes to support of Jewish Theological Seminary of America and its residence halls. *Women's League Outlook magazine; Ba'Olam newsletter.*

WORLD COUNCIL OF SYNAGOGUES (1957). 155 Fifth Ave., NYC 10010. (212)533–7693. Pres. Dr. Henry Sender; Rabbi of Council, Rabbi Benjamin Z. Kreitman; Admin. Dir. Ilana Lewin. International representative of Conservative organizations and congregations; promotes the growth and development of the Conservative movement in Israel and throughout the world; supports educational institutions overseas; holds biennial international conventions; represents the world Conservative movement on the Executive of

---

the World Zionist Organization. *World Spectrum.*

WORLD UNION FOR PROGRESSIVE JUDAISM, LTD. (1926). 838 Fifth Ave., NYC 10021. (212)249–0100. FAX: (212)517–3940. Pres. Donald Day; Exec. Dir. Rabbi Richard G. Hirsch; N. Amer. Dir. Martin Strelzer; Dir. Internatl. Relations & Development Rabbi Clifford Kulwin. International umbrella organization of Liberal Judaism; promotes and coordinates efforts of Liberal congregations throughout the world; starts new congregations, recruits rabbis and rabbinical students for all countries; organizes international conferences of Liberal Jews. *Rodnik; News Updates.*

SCHOOLS, INSTITUTIONS

ACADEMY FOR JEWISH RELIGION (1955). 15 W. 86 St., NYC 10024. (212)875–0540. FAX: (212)875–0541. Chmn. Presidential Council Rabbi Manuel Gold; Exec. Dean Rabbi Shohama Wiener. The only rabbinic and cantorial seminary in the U.S. at which students explore the full range of Jewish spiritual learning and practice. Graduates serve in Conservative, Reform, Reconstructionist, and Orthodox congregations, chaplaincies, and educational institutions. Programs include rabbinic and cantorial studies in NYC and on/off-campus nonmatriculated studies.

ANNENBERG INSTITUTE (formerly DROPSIE COLLEGE FOR HEBREW AND COGNATE LEARNING) (1907; reorg. 1986). 420 Walnut St., Philadelphia, PA 19106. (215)238–1290. FAX: (215)238–1540. Assoc. Dir. David M. Goldenberg. A center for advanced research in Judaic and Near Eastern studies at the postdoctoral level. *Jewish Quarterly Review.*

BALTIMORE HEBREW UNIVERSITY (1919). 5800 Park Heights Ave., Baltimore, MD 21215. (301)578–6900. FAX: (410)578–6940. Pres. Dr. Norma Fields Furst; Bd. Chmn. Beverly Penn. Offers PhD, MA, and BA programs in Jewish studies, biblical and Near Eastern archaeology, philosophy, literature, history, Hebrew language and literature; School of Continuing Education; Joseph Meyerhoff Library; community lectures, film series, seminars. *The Scribe (annual newsletter).*

———, BALTIMORE INSTITUTE FOR JEWISH COMMUNAL SERVICE. Coord. Judith Yalin; Dean Robert O. Freedman. Trains Jewish communal professionals; offers joint degree program: MA in Jewish studies from BHU; MSW from U. of Maryland.

———, BERNARD MANEKIN SCHOOL OF UNDERGRADUATE STUDIES. Dean Judy Meltzer. BA program; the Isaac C. Rosenthal Center for Jewish Education; on-site courses in Maryland and Jerusalem; interdisciplinary concentrations: contemporary Middle East, American Jewish culture, and the humanities.

———, PEGGY MEYERHOFF PEARLSTONE SCHOOL OF GRADUATE STUDIES. Dean Robert O. Freedman. PhD and MA programs; MA and MSW with University of Maryland School of Social Work and Community Planning in federation, community organization, center, and family services; MA and MEd in Jewish education and double MA in journalism with Towson State University; MA program in the study of Christian-Jewish relations with St. Mary's Seminary and University; MA program in community relations with University of Maryland Graduate School.

BRAMSON ORT TECHNICAL INSTITUTE (1977). 69–30 Austin St., Forest Hills, NY 11375. (718)261–5800. Dir. Dr. Seymour B. Forman; Admissions, Lois E. Shallit. A two-year Jewish technical college offering certificates and associate degrees in high technology and business fields, including computer programming, electronics technology, business management, word processing, and ophthalmic technology. Houses the Center for Computers in Jewish Education. Extension sites in Manhattan, Brooklyn, and the Bronx.

BRANDEIS-BARDIN INSTITUTE (1941). 1101 Peppertree Lane, Brandeis, CA 93064. (805)582–4450, (818)348–7201. FAX: (805)526–1398. Pres. Gary Brennglass; Exec. V.-Pres. Dr. Alvin Mars. A pluralistic, nondenominational Jewish institution providing programs for people of all ages: Brandeis Collegiate Institute (BCI), a leadership program for college-age adults; Camp Alonim, a positive Jewish experience for children 8–16; House of the Book Shabbat weekends for adults 25+, at which scholars-in-residence discuss historical, cultural, religious, and spiritual aspects of Judaism; Family Weekends and Grandparents Weekends. *Brandeis-Bardin Institute Newsletter; BCI Alumni News.*

BRANDEIS UNIVERSITY (1948). 415 South St.,Waltham, MA 02254. (617)736–2000. Bd. Chmn. Louis Perlmutter; Pres. Samuel O. Thier. Founded under Jewish sponsorship as a nonsectarian institution offering to all the highest quality undergraduate and graduate education. The Lown School is the center for all programs of teaching and research in the areas of Judaic studies, ancient Near Eastern studies, and Islamic and modern Middle Eastern studies. The school includes the Department of Near Eastern and Judaic Studies, which offers academic programs in the major areas of its concern; the Hornstein Program in Jewish Communal Service, a professional training program; the Cohen Center for Modern Jewish Studies, which conducts research and teaching in contemporary Jewish studies, primarily in the field of American Jewish studies, and the Tauber Institute for the study of European Jewry. *Various newsletters, scholarly publications.*

CLEVELAND COLLEGE OF JEWISH STUDIES (1964). 26500 Shaker Blvd., Beachwood, OH 44122. (216)464–4050. Pres. David S. Ariel; Dean Lifsa Schachter. Provides courses in all areas of Judaic and Hebrew studies to adults and college-age students; offers continuing education for Jewish educators and administrators; serves as a center for Jewish life and culture; expands the availability of courses in Judaic studies by exchanging faculty, students, and credits with neighboring academic institutions; grants bachelor's and master's degrees.

DROPSIE COLLEGE FOR HEBREW AND COGNATE LEARNING (*see* Annenberg Institute)

FEINBERG GRADUATE SCHOOL OF THE WEIZMANN INSTITUTE OF SCIENCE (1958). 51 Madison Ave., NYC 10010. (212)779–2500. FAX: (212)779–3209. Chmn. Stuart E. Eizenstat; Pres. Prof. Melvin Schwartz; Dean Prof. Benjamin Geiger; Exec. Dir. David S. Black. Situated on the Weizmann campus in Rehovot, Israel, provides the school's faculty and research facilities. Accredited by the Council for Higher Education of Israel and the NY State Board of Regents for the study of natural sciences, leading to MSc and PhD degrees.

GRATZ COLLEGE (1895). Old York Rd. and Melrose Ave., Melrose Park, PA 19126. (215)635–7300. FAX: (215)635–7320. Bd. Chmn. Steven Fisher; Pres. Dr. Gary S. Schiff. Offers a wide variety of undergraduate and graduate degrees and continuing education programs in Judaic, Hebraic, and Middle Eastern studies. Grants BA and MA in Jewish studies, MA in Jewish education, MA in Jewish music, MA in Jewish liberal studies, certificates in Jewish communal service, Jewish education, Israel studies, Jewish librarianship (joint graduate program with Drexel U.), and other credentials. Joint graduate program in Jewish communal service with the U. of Pennsylvania. High-school-level programs are offered by the affiliated Jewish Community High School of Gratz College. *Various newsletters, annual academic bulletin, and scholarly publications.*

HEBREW COLLEGE (1921). 43 Hawes St., Brookline, MA 02146. (617)232–8710. Pres. Dr. David M. Gordis; Bd. Chmn. Theodore H. Teplow. New England's only accredited college of Judaic studies offers bachelor's/master's degrees in Jewish studies and Jewish education and bachelor's in Hebrew literature. Two-year training institutes for afternoon-school directors, teachers, Jewish music professionals, and early childhood educators also available. Operates overnight Hebrew-speaking Camp Yavneh, Northwood, N.H.; Ulpan conversational language program; Prozdor High School; 100,000-volume library; continuing education courses; arts and film festivals on Jewish themes. Accredited by New England Assoc. Schools and Colleges. *Hebrew College Today.*

HEBREW THEOLOGICAL COLLEGE (1922). 7135 N. Carpenter Rd., Skokie, IL 60077. (312)267–9800. Acting Pres. Rabbi Dr. Jerold Isenberg. An institution of higher Jewish learning which includes a graduate school; school of liberal arts and sciences; division of advanced Hebrew studies; Fasman Yeshiva High School; Anne M. Blitstein Teachers Institute for Women. *Or Shmuel; Torah Journal; Likutei P'shatim; Turrets of Silver.*

HEBREW UNION COLLEGE–JEWISH INSTITUTE OF RELIGION (1875). 3101 Clifton Ave., Cincinnati, OH 45220. (513)221–1875. FAX: (513)221–2810. Pres. Alfred Gottschalk; Exec. V.-Pres. Uri D. Herscher; V.-Pres. Academic Affairs Samuel Greengus; V.-Pres. Paul M. Steinberg; V.-Pres. John S. Borden; Chmn. Bd. of Govs. Stanley P. Gold. Academic centers:

3101 Clifton Ave., Cincinnati, OH 45220 (1875), Dean Kenneth Ehrlich; 1 W. 4 St., NYC 10012 (1922), Dean Norman J. Cohen; 3077 University Ave., Los Angeles, CA 90007 (1954), Dean Lee Bycel; 13 King David St., Jerusalem, Israel 94101 (1963), Dean Michael Klein. Prepares students for Reform rabbinate, cantorate, religious-school teaching and administration, community service, academic careers; promotes Jewish studies; maintains libraries, archives, and museums; offers master's and doctoral degrees; engages in archaeological excavations; publishes scholarly works through Hebrew Union College Press. *American Jewish Archives; Bibliographica Judaica; HUC-JIR Catalogue; Hebrew Union College Annual; Studies in Bibliography and Booklore; The Chronicle.*

————, AMERICAN JEWISH ARCHIVES (1947). 3101 Clifton Ave., Cincinnati, OH 45220. (513)221–1875. FAX: (513)221–7812. Dir. Jacob R. Marcus; Admin. Dir. Abraham Peck. Promotes the study and preservation of the Western Hemisphere Jewish experience through research, publications, collection of important source materials, and a vigorous public-outreach program. *American Jewish Archives; monographs, publications, and pamphlets.*

————, AMERICAN JEWISH PERIODICAL CENTER (1957). 3101 Clifton Ave., Cincinnati, OH 45220. (513)221–1875. Dir. Jacob R. Marcus; Codir. Herbert C. Zafren. Maintains microfilms of all American Jewish periodicals 1823–1925, selected periodicals since 1925. *Jewish Periodicals and Newspapers on Microfilm (1957); First Supplement (1960); Augmented Edition (1984).*

————, EDGAR F. MAGNIN SCHOOL OF GRADUATE STUDIES (1956). 3077 University Ave., Los Angeles, CA 90007. (213)-749–3424. FAX: (213)747–6128. Dir. Stanley Chyet. Supervises programs leading to PhD (Education), DHS, DHL, and MA degrees; participates in cooperative PhD programs with the University of Southern California.

————, IRWIN DANIELS SCHOOL OF JEWISH COMMUNAL SERVICE (1968). 3077 University Ave., Los Angeles, CA 90007. (213)749–3424. FAX: (213)747–6128. Dir. H. Jack Mayer. Offers certificate and master's degree to those employed in Jewish communal services, or preparing for such

work; offers joint MA in Jewish education and communal service with Rhea Hirsch School; offers MA and MSW in conjunction with the University of Southern California School of Social Work, with the George Warren Brown School of Social Work of Washington University, and with the University of Pittsburgh School of Social Work; offers joint master's degrees in conjunction with USC in public administration or gerontology.

————, JEROME H. LOUCHHEIM SCHOOL OF JUDAIC STUDIES (1969). 3077 University Ave., Los Angeles, CA 90007. (213)749–3424. FAX: (213)747–6128. Dir. David Ellenson. Offers programs leading to MA, BS, BA, and AA degrees; offers courses as part of the undergraduate program of the University of Southern California.

————, NELSON GLUECK SCHOOL OF BIBLICAL ARCHAEOLOGY (1963). 13 King David St., Jerusalem, Israel 94101. FAX: 2–251–478. Dir. Avraham Biran. Offers graduate-level research programs in Bible and archaeology. Summer excavations are carried out by scholars and students. University credit may be earned by participants in excavations. Consortium of colleges, universities, and seminaries is affiliated with the school.

————, RHEA HIRSCH SCHOOL OF EDUCATION (1967). 3077 University Ave., Los Angeles, CA 90007. (213)749–3424. FAX: (213)747–6128. Dir. Sara Lee. Offers PhD and MA programs in Jewish and Hebrew education; conducts joint degree programs with University of Southern California; offers courses for Jewish teachers, librarians, and early educators on a nonmatriculating basis; conducts summer institutes for professional Jewish educators.

————, SCHOOL OF EDUCATION (1947). 1 W. 4 St., NYC 10012. (212)674–5300. FAX: (212)533–0129. V.-Pres. and Dean of Faculty Paul M. Steinberg; Dean Norman J. Cohen; Dir. Kerry M. Olitzky. Trains teachers and principals for Reform religious schools; offers MA degree with specialization in religious education; offers extension programs in various suburban centers.

————, SCHOOL OF GRADUATE STUDIES (1949). 3101 Clifton Ave., Cincinnati, OH 45220 (513)221–1875. FAX: (513)221–0321. Dir. Alan Cooper. Offers programs leading to MA and PhD degrees; offers program leading to DHL degree for rabbinic graduates of the college.

———, SCHOOL OF JEWISH STUDIES (1963). 13 King David St., Jerusalem, Israel, 94101. FAX: 2–251–478. Dean Michael Klein; Assoc. Dean Rabbi Shaul R. Feinberg. Offers first year of graduate rabbinic, cantorial, and Jewish education studies (required) for American students; program leading to ordination for Israeli rabbinic students; undergraduate semester in Jerusalem and one-year work/study program on a kibbutz in cooperation with Union of American Hebrew Congregations; public outreach programs (lectures, courses, concerts, exhibits).

———, SCHOOL OF SACRED MUSIC (1947). 1 W. 4 St., NYC 10012. (212)674–5300. FAX: (212)533–0129. Dir. Israel Goldstein. Trains cantors and music personnel for congregations; offers MSM degree. *Sacred Music Press.*

———, SKIRBALL MUSEUM (*see* p. 458)

HERZLIAH-JEWISH TEACHERS SEMINARY (1967). Division of Touro College. 844 Ave. of the Americas, NYC 10001. (212)-447–0700. Pres. Bernard Lander; Dir. Jacob Katzman.

———, GRADUATE SCHOOL OF JEWISH STUDIES (1981). 160 Lexington Ave., NYC 10016. (212)213–2230. Pres. Bernard Lander; Dean Michael A. Shmidman. Offers courses leading to an MA in Jewish studies, with concentrations in Jewish history or Jewish education. Students may complete part of their program in Israel, through MA courses offered by Touro faculty at Touro's Jerusalem center.

———, JEWISH PEOPLE'S UNIVERSITY OF THE AIR. (212)447–0700. Dir./Producer Jacob Katzman. The educational outreach arm of Touro College, it produces and disseminates Jewish educational and cultural programming for radio broadcast and on audio-cassettes.

INSTITUTE OF TRADITIONAL JUDAISM (1990). 261 E. Lincoln Ave., Mt. Vernon, NY 10552. (914)667–1007. FAX: (914)-667–1023. Rector (*Reish Metivta*) Rabbi David Weiss Halivni; Dean Rabbi Ronald D. Price. A nondenominational halakhic rabbinical school dedicated to genuine faith combined with intellectual honesty and the love of Israel. Graduates receive "*yoreh yoreh*" *smikhah*.

JEWISH THEOLOGICAL SEMINARY OF AMERICA (1886; reorg. 1902). 3080 Broadway, NYC 10027–4649. (212)678–8000. FAX: (212)678–8947 Chancellor Dr. Ismar Schorsch; Bd. Chmn. Gershon Kekst. Operates undergraduate and graduate programs in Judaic studies; professional schools for training Conservative rabbis and cantors; Melton Research Center for Jewish Education; the Jewish Museum; and such youth programs as the Ramah Camps and the Prozdor highschool division. Produces network television programs in cooperation with interfaith broadcasting commission. *Academic Bulletin; Masoret; The Melton Journal.*

———, ALBERT A. LIST COLLEGE OF JEWISH STUDIES (formerly SEMINARY COLLEGE OF JEWISH STUDIES-TEACHERS INSTITUTE) (1909). 3080 Broadway, NYC 10027. (212)678–8826. Dean Dr. Shuly Rubin Schwartz. Offers complete undergraduate program in Judaica leading to BA degree; conducts joint programs with Columbia University and Barnard College enabling students to receive two BA degrees.

———, CANTORS INSTITUTE AND SEMINARY COLLEGE OF JEWISH MUSIC (1952). 3080 Broadway, NYC 10027. (212)678–8038. Dean Rabbi Morton M. Leifman. Trains cantors, music teachers, and choral directors for congregations. Offers fulltime programs in sacred music leading to degrees of MSM and DSM, and diploma of *Hazzan.*

———, DEPARTMENT OF RADIO AND TELEVISION (1944). 3080 Broadway, NYC 10027. (212)678–8020. Dir. Marjorie Wyler. Produces radio and TV programs expressing the Jewish tradition in its broadest sense, including hour-long documentaries on NBC and ABC. Distributes cassettes of programs at minimum charge.

———, GRADUATE SCHOOL (formerly INSTITUTE FOR ADVANCED STUDY IN THE HUMANITIES) (1968). 3080 Broadway, NYC 10027. (212)678–8024. Dean Dr. Stephen P. Garfinkel. Programs leading to MA, MPhil, DHL, and PhD degrees in Jewish studies, Bible, Jewish education, history, literature, ancient Judaism, philosophy, rabbinics, and medieval Jewish studies; dual degree with Columbia University School of Social Work.

———, JEWISH MUSEUM (*see* p. 456)

——, LIBRARY OF THE JEWISH THEOLOG-ICAL SEMINARY. 3080 Broadway, NYC 10027. (212)678–8075. FAX: (212)678–8998. Librarian Dr. Mayer E. Rabinowitz. Contains one of the largest collections of Hebraica and Judaica in the world, including manuscripts, incunabula, rare books, and Cairo Geniza material. The 270,000-volume collection is housed in a state-of-the-art building and is open to the public. *New Acquisitions List; Friends of the Library Newsletter.*

——, LOUIS FINKELSTEIN INSTITUTE FOR RELIGIOUS AND SOCIAL STUDIES (1938). 3080 Broadway, NYC 10027. (212)678–8815. Assoc. Dir. Carlotta Damanda. A scholarly and scientific fellowship of clergy and other religious teachers who desire authoritative information regarding some of the basic issues now confronting spiritually minded individuals.

——, MELTON RESEARCH CENTER FOR JEWISH EDUCATION (1960). 3080 Broadway, NYC 10027. (212)678–8031. Dirs. Dr. Eduardo Rauch, Dr. Barry W. Holtz. Develops new curricula and materials for Jewish education; prepares educators through seminars and in-service programs; maintains consultant and supervisory relationships with a limited number of pilot schools; develops and implements research initiatives; sponsors "renewal" retreats for teachers and principals. *The Melton Journal.*

——, NATIONAL RAMAH COMMISSION (1951). 3080 Broadway, NYC 10027. (212)678–8881. FAX: (212)749–8251. Pres. Dr. Saul Shapiro; Natl. Dir. Sheldon Dorph. Sponsors 7 overnight Conservative Jewish camps in U.S. and Canada, emphasizing Jewish education, living, and culture; offers opportunities for qualified college students and older to serve as counselors, administrators, specialists, etc. Also programs for children with special needs (Tikvah program); offers special programs in U.S. and Israel, including Weinstein National Ramah Staff Training Institute, Ramah Israel Seminar, Ulpan Ramah Plus, and Tichon Ramah Yerushalayim. Family and synagogue tours to Israel and summer day camp in Israel for Americans.

——, PROZDOR (1951). 3080 Broadway, NYC 10027. (212)678–8824. Principal Dr. Aaron Singer. The high-school department of JTS, it provides a supplementary Jewish education for students who attend a secular (public or private) full-time high school. Classes in classical Jewish studies, with emphasis on Hebrew language, meet twice a week.

——, RABBINICAL SCHOOL (1886). 3080 Broadway, NYC 10027. (212)678–8816. Offers a program of graduate and professional studies leading to the degree of Master of Arts and ordination; includes one year of study in Jerusalem and an extensive field-work program.

——, SAUL LIEBERMAN INSTITUTE OF JEWISH RESEARCH (1985). 3080 Broadway, NYC 10027. (212)678–8994. Engaged in preparing for publication a series of scholarly editions of selected chapters of the Talmud. The following projects support and help disseminate the research: Talmud Text Database; Bibliography of Talmudic Literature; Catalogue of Geniza Fragments; Teachers Training and Curriculum Development in Oral Law for Secondary Schools.

——, SCHOCKEN INSTITUTE FOR JEWISH RESEARCH (1961). 6 Balfour St., Jerusalem, Israel 92102. (02)631288. Dir. Shmuel Glick; Coord. for Educ. Programs Simcha Goldsmith. Comprises the Schocken collection of rare books and manuscripts and a research institute dedicated to the exploration of Hebrew religious poetry (*piyyut*). *Schocken Institute Yearbook (P'raqim).*

——, UNIVERSITY OF JUDAISM (1947). 15600 Mulholland Dr., Los Angeles, CA 90077. (310)476–9777. FAX: (310)471–1278. Pres. Rabbi Robert D. Wexler; Dean of Academic Affairs Dr. Hanan Alexander; Dean of Student Affairs Rabbi Daniel Gordis. The undergraduate school, Lee College of Arts and Sciences, is an accredited liberal arts college offering a core curriculum of Jewish and Western studies, with majors including psychology, business, literature, political science, and Jewish studies. Accredited graduate programs in nonprofit business management, Jewish education, and Jewish studies, plus a preparatory program for the Conservative rabbinate. Two institutes for research and program development, the Wilstein Institute for Jewish Policy Studies and the Whizin Center for the Jewish Future. A broad range of continuing-education courses, cultural-arts programs, and a variety of outreach services for West Coast Jewish communities. *Direction Magazine; Focus Newsletter; Bulletin of General Information.*

MESIVTA YESHIVA RABBI CHAIM BERLIN RABBINICAL ACADEMY (1905). 1605 Coney Island Ave., Brooklyn, NY 11230. (718)377–0777. Exec. Dir. Y. Mayer Lasker. Maintains fully accredited elementary and high schools; collegiate and postgraduate school for advanced Jewish studies, both in America and Israel; Camp Morris, a summer study retreat; Prof. Nathan Isaacs Memorial Library; Gur Aryeh Publications.

NER ISRAEL RABBINICAL COLLEGE (1933). 400 Mt. Wilson Lane, Baltimore, MD 21208. (301)484–7200. FAX: (301)484–3060. Rabbi Yaakov S. Weinberg, Rosh Hayeshiva; Pres. Rabbi Herman N. Neuberger. Trains rabbis and educators for Jewish communities in America and worldwide. Offers bachelor's, master's, and doctoral degrees in talmudic law, as well as teacher's diploma. College has four divisions: Mechina High School, Rabbinical College, Teachers Training Institute, Graduate School. Maintains an active community-service division. Operates special program for Iranian Jewish students. *Ner Israel Update; Alumni Bulletin; Ohr Hanair Talmudic Journal; Iranian B'nei Torah Bulletin.*

RABBINICAL COLLEGE OF TELSHE, INC. (1941). 28400 Euclid Ave., Wickliffe, OH 44092. (216)943–5300. Pres. Rabbi Mordecai Gifter; V.-Pres. Rabbi Abba Zalka Gewirtz. College for higher Jewish learning specializing in talmudic studies and rabbinics; maintains a preparatory academy including a secular high school, postgraduate department, teacher-training school, and teachers' seminary for women. *Pri Etz Chaim; Peer Mordechai; Alumni Bulletin.*

RECONSTRUCTIONIST RABBINICAL COLLEGE (1968). Church Rd. and Greenwood Ave., Wyncote, PA 19095. (215)576–0800. FAX: (215)576–6143. Pres. David Teutsch; Bd. Chmn. Jacques G. Pomeranz; Genl. Chmn. Aaron Ziegelman. Coeducational. Trains rabbis for all areas of Jewish communal life: synagogues, academic and educational positions, Hillel centers, federation agencies; confers title of rabbi and grants degrees of Master and Doctor of Hebrew Letters. *RRC Report.*

SPERTUS COLLEGE OF JUDAICA (1924). 618 S. Michigan Ave., Chicago, IL 60605. (312)922–9012. FAX: (312)922–6406. Pres. Howard A. Sulkin; Bd. Chmn. Gary Edidin; V.-Pres. for Academic Affairs Byron L. Sherwin; Dir. Spertus Museum Morris A. Fred; Dir. Asher Library Michael Terry. An accredited institution of higher learning offering five master's degree programs in Jewish studies, Jewish education, Jewish communal service, and human-services administration, plus an extensive program of continuing education. Doctor of Jewish Studies degree starting Summer 1993. Offers classes at the main campus and a suburban center. Major resources of the college encompass Spertus Museum, the Asher Library, including the Chicago Jewish Archives, and Spertus College of Judaica Press.

———, SPERTUS MUSEUM (*see* p. 459)

TOURO COLLEGE (1970). Executive Offices: Empire State Bldg., 350 Fifth Ave., Suite 5122, NYC 10018. (212)643–0700. FAX: (212)643–0759. Pres. Bernard Lander; Bd. Chmn. Max Karl. Chartered by NY State Board of Regents as a nonprofit four-year college with business, Judaic studies, health sciences, and liberal arts programs leading to BA, BS, and MA degrees; emphasizes relevance of Jewish heritage to general culture of Western civilization. Also offers JD degree and a biomedical program leading to the MD degree from Technion–Israel Institute of Technology, Haifa.

———, BARRY Z. LEVINE SCHOOL OF HEALTH SCIENCES AND CENTER FOR BIOMEDICAL EDUCATION (1970). 135 Common Rd., Bldg. #10, Dix Hills, NY 11746. (516)673–3200. Dean Dr. Joseph Weisberg. Along with the Manhattan campus, offers 5 programs: 5-year program leading to MA from Touro and MD from Faculty of Medicine of Technion–Israel Institute of Technology, Haifa; BS/MA—physical therapy and occupational therapy programs; BS—physician assistant and health-information management programs.

———, COLLEGE OF LIBERAL ARTS AND SCIENCES. 844 Sixth Ave., NYC 10001. (212)447–0700. FAX: (212)779–2344. Exec. Dean Stanley Boylan. Offers comprehensive Jewish studies along with studies in the arts, sciences, humanities, and pre-professional studies in health sciences, law, accounting, business, computer science, education, and finance. Women's Division, 160 Lexington Ave., NYC 10016 (212)213–2230. FAX: (212)683–3281. Dean Sara E. Freifeld.

———, GRADUATE SCHOOL OF JEWISH STUDIES (1981). 160 Lexington Ave., NYC 10016. (212)213–2230. FAX: (212)-683–3281. Pres. Bernard Lander; Dean Michael A. Shmidman. Offers courses leading to an MA in Jewish studies, with concentrations in Jewish history or Jewish education. Students may complete part of their program in Israel, through MA courses offered by Touro faculty at Touro's Jerusalem center.

———, INSTITUTE OF JEWISH LAW. (516)-421–2244. Based at Fuchsberg Law Center, serves as a center and clearinghouse for study and teaching of Jewish law. Coedits *Dinei Israel* (Jewish Law Journal) with Tel Aviv University Law School.

———, JACOB D. FUCHSBERG LAW CENTER (1980). Long Island Campus, 300 Nassau Rd., Huntington, NY 11743. (516)421–2244. Dean Howard A. Glickstein. Offers studies leading to JD degree.

———, JEWISH PEOPLE'S UNIVERSITY OF THE AIR. (1979). 844 Sixth Ave., NYC 10001. (212)447–0700, Ext. 589. Producer/Dir. Jacob Katzman. Produces and disseminates courses in Jewish subject matter for radio broadcasting and on audiocassettes. Printed course outlines for all courses and discussion; leader's guides for some.

———, MOSCOW BRANCH. 5 Jablockkova St., 127254 Moscow, USSR. 210–86–69; 210–61–73. Offers BS program in business and BA program in Jewish studies.

———, SCHOOL OF GENERAL STUDIES. 240 E. 123 St., NYC 10021. (212)722–1575. Dean Stephen Adolphus. Offers educational opportunities to minority groups and older people; courses in the arts, sciences, humanities, and special programs of career studies.

———, TOURO COLLEGE FLATBUSH CENTER (1929). 1277 E. 14 St., Brooklyn, NY 11230. (718)253–7538. Dean Robert Goldschmidt. A division of the College of Liberal Arts and Sciences; options offered in accounting and business, education, mathematics, political science, psychology,

and speech. Classes are given on weeknights and during the day on Sunday.

———, TOURO COLLEGE ISRAEL CENTER. 23 Rehov Shivtei Yisrael, Jerusalem. 2–894–086/088. Assoc. Dean Carmi Horowitz; Resident Dir. Chana Sosevsky. Offers undergraduate courses in business, computer science, and education. Houses the MA degreee program in Jewish studies. The Touro Year Abroad Option for American students is coordinated from this center.

WEST COAST TALMUDICAL SEMINARY (Yeshiva Ohr Elchonon Chabad) (1953). 7215 Waring Ave., Los Angeles, CA 90046. (213)937–3763. Dean Rabbi Ezra Schochet. Provides facilities for intensive Torah education as well as Orthodox rabbinical training on the West Coast; conducts an accredited college preparatory high school combined with a full program of Torah-talmudic training and a graduate talmudical division on the college level. *Torah Quiz; Kobetz Migdal Ohr.*

YESHIVA UNIVERSITY (1886). Joel Jablonski Campus, 500 W. 185 St., NYC 10033–3201. (212)960–5400. FAX: (212)960–0055. Pres. Dr. Norman Lamm; Acting Chmn. Bd. of Trustees Hermann Merkin. The nation's oldest and largest independent university founded under Jewish auspices, with a broad range of undergraduate, graduate, and professional schools, a network of affiliates, a widespread program of research and community outreach, publications, and a museum. Curricula lead to bachelor's, master's, doctoral, and professional degrees. Undergraduate schools provide general studies curricula supplemented by courses in Jewish learning; graduate schools prepare for careers in medicine, law, social work, Jewish education, psychology, Jewish studies, and other fields. It has six undergraduate schools, seven graduate and professional schools, and three affiliates. *Alumni Review/Inside.*

Yeshiva University has four campuses in Manhattan and the Bronx: Joel Jablonski Campus, 500 W. 185 St., NYC 10033–3201; Midtown Center, 245 Lexington Ave., NYC 10016–4699; Brookdale Center, 55 Fifth Ave., NYC 10003–4391; Jack and Pearl Resnick Campus, Eastchester Rd. & Morris Pk. Ave., Bronx, NY 10461–1602. Undergraduate schools for men at Joel Jablonski Campus: Yeshiva College (Bd. Chmn. Jay Schottenstein; Dean Dr.

Norman S. Rosenfeld) provides liberal arts and sciences curricula; grants BA degree. Isaac Breuer College of Hebraic Studies (Dean Dr. Michael D. Shmidman) awards Hebrew teacher's diploma, AA, BA, and BS. James Striar School of General Jewish Studies (Assoc. Dean Dr. Michael D. Shmidman) grants AA degree. Yeshiva Program/Mazer School of Talmudic Studies (Dean Rabbi Zevulun Charlop) offers advanced course of study in talmudic texts and commentaries.

Undergraduate school for women at Midtown Center, 245 Lexington Ave., NYC 10016–4699. (212)340–7700: Stern College for Women (Bd. Chmn. David Yagoda; Dean Dr. Karen Bacon) offers liberal arts and sciences curricula supplemented by Jewish studies programs, awards BA, AA, and Hebrew teacher's diploma.

Sy Syms School of Business at Joel Jablonski Campus and Midtown Center (Bd. Chmn. Josh H. Weston; Dean Dr. Harold Nierenberg) offers undergraduate business curricula in conjunction with study at Yeshiva College or Stern College; grants BS degree.

Sponsors one high school for boys (Manhattan) and one for girls (Queens).

———, ALBERT EINSTEIN COLLEGE OF MEDICINE (1955). Eastchester Rd. & Morris Pk. Ave., Bronx, NY 10461–1602. (718)430–2000. Pres. Dr. Norman Lamm; Chmn. Bd. of Overseers Burton P. Resnick; Dean Dr. Dominick P. Purpura. Prepares physicians and conducts research in the health sciences; awards MD degree; includes Sue Golding Graduate Division of Medical Sciences (Dir. Dr. Barbara K. Birshtein), which grants PhD degree. Einstein College's clinical facilities, affiliates, and resources encompass Jack D. Weiler Hospital of Albert Einstein College of Medicine, Montefiore Medical Center, Bronx Municipal Hospital Center, and the Rose F. Kennedy Center for Research in Mental Retardation and Human Development. *Einstein; AECOM Today; Einstein Quarterly Journal of Biology and Medicine.*

———, ALUMNI OFFICE, 500 W. 185 Street, NYC 10033–3201. (212)960–5373. Dir. Toby Hilsenrad Weiss. Seeks to foster a close allegiance of alumni to their alma mater by maintaining ties with all alumni and servicing the following associations: Yeshiva College Alumni (Pres. Zev S. Ber-

man); Stern College for Women Alumnae (Pres. Jan Schechter); Sy Syms School of Business Alumni (Pres. Martin Lifshutz); Albert Einstein College of Medicine Alumni (Pres. Dr. Bernard Zazula); Ferkauf Graduate School of Psychology Alumni (Pres. Dr. Abraham Givner); Wurzweiler School of Social Work Alumni (Pres. Ilene Stein Himber); Rabbinic Alumni (Pres. Rabbi Bernard Rosensweig); Benjamin N. Cardozo School of Law Alumni (Chmn. Noah Gordon, Jay H. Ziffer). *Alumni Review/Inside; AECOM Alumni News; Jewish Social Work Forum.*

———, BELFER INSTITUTE FOR ADVANCED BIOMEDICAL STUDIES (1978). Eastchester Rd. & Morris Pk. Ave., Bronx, NY 10461–1602. (718)430–2801. Dir. Dr. Ernst R. Jaffé. Integrates and coordinates the Medical College's postdoctoral research and training-grant programs in the basic and clinical biomedical sciences. Awards certificate as Research Fellow or Research Associate on completion of training.

———, BENJAMIN N. CARDOZO SCHOOL OF LAW (1976). 55 Fifth Ave., NYC 10003. (212)790–0200. Pres. Dr. Norman Lamm; Acting Bd. Chmn. Earle I. Mack; Dean Dr. Frank J. Macchiarola. Provides innovative courses of study within a traditional legal framework; program includes judicial internships; grants Doctor of Law (JD) degree. Programs and services include institute for advanced legal studies; center for ethics in the practice of law; legal services clinic; institute of Jewish law; center on corporate governance; program in communications law; center for professional development; international law and human-rights program; international summer institutes on law, trade, and social change. *Cardozo Studies in Law and Literature; Cardozo Law Review; Arts and Entertainment Law Journal; Women's Law Journal; New Europe Law Review; Cardozo Law Forum.*

———, BERNARD REVEL GRADUATE SCHOOL (1937). 500 W. 185 St., NYC 10033–3201. (212)960–5253. Pres. Dr. Norman Lamm; Bd. Chmn. Irwin Shapiro; Acting Dean Dr. Arthur Hyman. Offers graduate programs in Bible, talmudic studies, Jewish history, and Jewish thought; confers MA and PhD degrees. Harry Fischel School for Higher Jewish Studies offers the Revel program during the summer.

——, DAVID J. AZRIELI GRADUATE IN-
STITUTE OF JEWISH EDUCATION AND AD-
MINISTRATION (1945). 245 Lexington
Ave., NYC 10016–4679. (212)340–7705.
Dir. Dr. Yitzchak S. Handel. Offers MS
degree in Jewish elementary and secondary
education; specialist's certificate and EdD
in administration and supervision of Jewish education. Block Education Program,
initiated under a grant from the Jewish
Agency's L.A. Pincus Fund for the Diaspora, provides summer course work to
complement year-round field instruction in
local communities.

——, FERKAUF GRADUATE SCHOOL OF
PSYCHOLOGY (1957). Eastchester Rd. &
Morris Pk. Ave., Bronx, NY 10461–1602.
(718)430–4201. Dean Dr. Barbara G.
Melamed. Offers MA in general psychology; PsyD in clinical and school psychology; and PhD in clinical, school, develop-
mental, and health psychology.

——, (affiliate) RABBI ISAAC ELCHANAN
THEOLOGICAL SEMINARY (1896). 2540
Amsterdam Ave., NYC 10033. (212)960–
5344. Chmn. Bd. of Trustees Judah Feiner-
man; V.-Pres. for Administration & Pro-
fessional Education Rabbi Robert S. Hirt;
Dean Rabbi Zevulun Charlop. Grants
semikhah (ordination) and the degrees of
Master of Religious Education, Master of
Hebrew Literature, Doctor of Religious
Education, and Doctor of Hebrew Litera-
ture.

Kollelim include Marcos and Adina
Katz Kollel (Institute for Advanced Re-
search in Rabbinics), Dir. Rabbi Hershel
Schachter; Kollel l'Horaah (Yadin Yadin)
and External Yadin Yadin (Dir. Rabbi J.
David Bleich); Caroline and Joseph S.
Gruss Kollel Elyon (Postgraduate Kollel
Program), Dir. Rabbi Aharon Kahn;
Caroline and Joseph S. Gruss Institute in
Jerusalem (Dir. Rabbi Aharon Lichten-
stein); Chaver Program (Dir. Rabbi J.
David Bleich).

The service arm of the seminary, Max
Stern Division of Communal Services (Dir.
Rabbi Robert S. Hirt), provides personal
and professional service to the rabbinate
and related fields, as well as educational,
consultative, organizational, and placement services to congregations, schools,
and communal organizations around the
world.

Other seminary programs are Jacob E.
Safra Institute of Sephardic Studies and the

Institute of Yemenite Studies; Maybaum
Sephardic Fellowship Program; Dr. Joseph and Rachel Ades Sephardic Community Outreach Program; Sephardic Community Program; Stone-Sapirstein Center
for Jewish Education; National Commission on Torah Education.

PHILIP AND SARAH BELZ SCHOOL OF
JEWISH MUSIC (1954). 560 W. 185 St.,
NYC 10033–3201. (212)960–5353. Dir.
Cantor Bernard Beer. Provides professional training of cantors and courses in
Jewish liturgical music; maintains a spe-
cialized library and conducts outreach;
awards associate cantor's certificate and
cantorial diploma.

——, (affiliate) YESHIVA OF LOS ANGELES
(1977). 9760 W. Pico Blvd., Los Angeles,
CA 90035–4701. (213)553–4478. Dean
Rabbi Marvin Hier; Bd. Chmn. Samuel
Belzberg; Dir. Academic Programs Rabbi
Sholom Tendler. Grants BA degree in Jew-
ish studies. Has university program and
graduate studies department. Also pro-
vides Jewish studies program for begin-
ners. Affiliates are high schools, Jewish
Studies Institute for Adult Education, and
Simon Wiesenthal Center.

SIMON WIESENTHAL CENTER (1977).
9760 W. Pico Blvd., Los Angeles, CA
90035–4701. (310)553–9036. FAX: (310)-
553–8007. Dean-Founder Rabbi Marvin
Hier; Assoc. Dean Rabbi Abraham
Cooper; Dir. Dr. Gerald Margolis; Exec.
Dir. Rabbi Meyer May. Regional offices in
New York, Chicago, Miami, Jerusalem,
Paris, Toronto. The largest institution of
its kind in N. America dedicated to the
study of the Holocaust, its contemporary
implications, and related human-rights issues through education and awareness. Incorporates the Beit Hashoah-Museum of
Tolerance, library, media, archives, "Testimony to the Truth" oral histories, educational outreach, research department, Jewish Studies Institute (in cooperation with
Yeshiva of Los Angeles), international social action, "Page One" (syndicated weekly
radio news magazine presenting contemporary Jewish issues). *Simon Wiesenthal
Center Annual; Response Magazine; Commitment Magazine.*

——, WOMEN'S ORGANIZATION (1928).
500 W. 185 St., NYC 10033–3201. (212)-
960–0855. Natl. Bd. Chmn. and Pres.
Dinah Pinczower. Supports Yeshiva University's national scholarship program for

students training in education, community service, law, medicine, and other professions, and its development program. *YUWO News Briefs.*

———, WURZWEILER SCHOOL OF SOCIAL WORK (1957). 500 W. 185 St., NYC 10033–3201. (212)960–0800. Pres. Norman Lamm; Chmn. Bd. of Govs. Herbert H. Schiff; Dean Dr. Sheldon R. Gelman. Offers graduate programs in social group work, social casework, community social work; grants MSW and DSW degrees and certificate in Jewish communal service. MSW programs are: Concurrent Plan, 2-year, full-time track, combining classroom study and supervised field instruction; Plan for Employed Persons (PEP), for people working in social agencies; Block Education Plan (Dir. Dr. Adele Weiner), which combines summer course work with regular-year field placement in local agencies; Clergy Plan, training in counseling for clergy of all denominations. *Jewish Social Work Forum.*

———, YESHIVA UNIVERSITY MUSEUM (see p. 459)

YESHIVATH TORAH VODAATH AND MESIVTA RABBINICAL SEMINARY (1918). 425 E. 9 St., Brooklyn, NY 11218. (718)-941–8000. Bd. Chmn. Chaim Leshkowitz. Offers Hebrew and secular education from elementary level through rabbinical ordination and postgraduate work; maintains a teachers institute and community-service bureau; maintains a dormitory and a non-profit camp program for boys. *Chronicle; Mesivta Vanguard; Thought of the Week; Torah Vodaath News; Ha'Mesifta.*

———, ALUMNI ASSOCIATION (1941). 425 E. 9 St., Brooklyn, NY 11218. (718)941–8000. Pres. Marcus Saffer; Bd. Chmn. George Weinberg. Promotes social and cultural ties between the alumni and the schools through fund-raising; offers vocational guidance to students; operates Camp Torah Vodaath; sponsors research fellowship program for boys. *Annual Journal; Hamesivta Torah periodical.*

SOCIAL, MUTUAL BENEFIT

ALPHA EPSILON PI FRATERNITY (1913). 8815 Wesleyan Rd., Indianapolis, IN 46268–1171. (317)876–1913. Natl. Pres. Richard H. Stein; Exec. V.-Pres. Sidney N. Dunn. International Jewish fraternity active on over 100 campuses in the U.S. and Canada; encourages Jewish students to remain loyal to their heritage and to assume leadership roles in the community; active in behalf of Soviet Jewry, the State of Israel, the United States Holocaust Memorial Museum, and other Jewish causes. *The Lion of Alpha Epsilon Pi (quarterly magazine).*

AMERICAN ASSOCIATION OF RUSSIAN JEWS (1989). 45 E. 33 St., New York, NY 10016. (212)779–0383 & (516)937–3819. FAX: (212)447–9603. Pres. Leonid Stolov; V.-Pres. Inna Arolovich. Helps Russian-speaking Jewish immigrants in adjusting to all aspects of American society, including employment, Jewish acculturation, and participation in social and civic activities; fights anti-Semitism and violations of human rights in the CIS; informs Americans about the situation of former Soviet Jews and the Russian-Jewish community in the U.S. *Anti-Semitism in the Former USSR, Chronicle of Violent Incidents; Information Bulletin (in Russian).*

AMERICAN FEDERATION OF JEWS FROM CENTRAL EUROPE, INC. (1938). 570 Seventh Ave., NYC 10018. (212)921–3871. Pres. Robert L. Lehman; Bd. Chmn. Curt C. Silberman; Exec. Asst. Katherine Rosenthal. Seeks to safeguard the rights and interests of American Jews of German-speaking Central European descent, especially in reference to restitution and indemnification; through its affiliate Research Foundation for Jewish Immigration sponsors research and publications on the history, immigration, and acculturation of Central European émigrés in the U.S. and worldwide; through its affiliate Jewish Philanthropic Fund of 1933 supports social programs for needy Nazi victims in the U.S.; undertakes cultural activities, annual conferences, publications; member, Council of Jews from Germany, London.

AMERICAN SEPHARDI FEDERATION (1973). 305 7th Ave., NYC 10001. (212)366–7223. FAX: (212)366–7263. Pres. Leon Levy; Exec. Dir. Harriet Frank. Central umbrella organization for all Sephardic congregations, organizations, and agencies. Seeks to preserve and promote Sephardi culture, education, and traditions. Disseminates resource material on all aspects of Sephardic life. Strives to bring a Sephardic agenda and perspective to American Jewish life. *Sephardic Highlights Newsletter.*

AMERICAN VETERANS OF ISRAEL (1949). 136 E. 39 St., NYC 10016. Pres. Paul Kaye; Sec. Sidney Rabinovich. Maintains contact with American and Canadian volunteers who served in Aliyah Bet and/or Israel's War of Independence; promotes Israel's welfare; holds memorial services at grave of Col. David Marcus; is affiliated with World Mahal. *Newsletter.*

ASSOCIATION OF YUGOSLAV JEWS IN THE UNITED STATES, INC. (1941). 130 E. 59 St., Suite 1202, NYC 10022. (212)371-6891. Pres. Mary Levine; Exec. Off. Emanuel Salom; Treas./V.-Pres. Mirko Goldschmidt. Assists all Jews originally from Yugoslavia; raises funds for Israeli agencies and institutions. *Bulletin.*

BNAI ZION–THE AMERICAN FRATERNAL ZIONIST ORGANIZATION (1908). 136 E. 39 St., NYC 10016. (212)725-1211. FAX: (212)684-6327. Pres. Werner Buckold; Exec. V.-Pres. Mel Parness. Fosters principles of Americanism, fraternalism, and Zionism; offers life insurance and other benefits to its members. The Bnai Zion Foundation supports various humanitarian projects in Israel and the USA, chiefly the Bnai Zion Medical Center in Haifa and homes for retarded children—Maon Bnai Zion in Rosh Ha'ayin and the Herman Z. Quittman Center in Jerusalem. In the U.S. sponsors program of awards for excellence in Hebrew for high school and college students. Chapters all over U.S. and a New Leadership division in Greater NY area. *Bnai Zion Voice; Bnai Zion Foundation Newsletter.*

BRITH ABRAHAM (1859; reorg. 1887). 136 E. 39 St., NYC 10016. (212)725-1211. Grand Master Robert Freeman. Protects Jewish rights and combats anti-Semitism; supports Soviet and Ethiopian emigration and the safety and dignity of Jews worldwide; helps to support Bnai Zion Medical Center in Haifa and other Israeli institutions; aids and supports various programs and projects in the U.S.: Hebrew Excellence Program—Gold Medal presentation in high schools and colleges; Camp Loyaltown; Brith Abraham and Bnai Zion Foundations. *Voice.*

BRITH SHOLOM (1905). 3939 Conshohocken Ave., Philadelphia, PA 19131. (215)878-5696. Pres. Jay W. Malis; Exec. Dir. Mervin L. Krimins. Fraternal organization devoted to community welfare, protection of rights of Jewish people, and activities which foster Jewish identity and provide support for Israel; sponsors Brith Sholom House for senior citizens in Philadelphia and Brith Sholom Beit Halochem in Haifa, a rehabilitation center for Israel's permanently war-wounded. *Brith Sholom Presents; monthly news bulletin.*

CENTRAL SEPHARDIC JEWISH COMMUNITY OF AMERICA WOMEN'S DIVISION (1941). 8 W. 70 St., NYC 10023. (212)787-2850. Pres. Emer. Emilie Levy; Pres. Irma Cardozo; Treas. Laura Capelluto; Sec. Esther Shear. Promotes Sephardic culture by awarding scholarships to qualified needy students in New York and Israel; raises funds for hospital and religious institutions in U.S. and Israel. *Annual journal.*

FREE SONS OF ISRAEL (1849). 250 Fifth Ave., Suite 201, NYC 10001. (212)725-3690. Grand Master Herbert Silverstein; Grand Sec. Rudolph Gordon. The oldest Jewish fraternal order in the U.S.; supports the State of Israel; fights anti-Semitism; helps Soviet Jewry. Maintains scholarship fund for members and children of members; insurance fund and credit union; social functions. *Free Sons Reporter.*

JEWISH LABOR BUND (Directed by WORLD COORDINATING COMMITTEE OF THE BUND) (1897; reorg. 1947). 25 E. 21 St., NYC 10010. (212)475-0059. Exec. Sec. Benjamin Nadel. Coordinates activities of Bund organizations throughout the world and represents them in the Socialist International; spreads the ideas of socialism as formulated by the Jewish Labor Bund; publishes books and periodicals on world problems, Jewish life, socialist theory and policy, and on the history, activities, and ideology of the Jewish Labor Bund. *Unser Tsait* (U.S.); *Lebns-Fragn* (Israel); *Unser Gedank* (Australia); *Unser Shtimme* (France).

SEPHARDIC JEWISH BROTHERHOOD OF AMERICA, INC. (1915). 97-45 Queens Blvd., Rego Park, NY 11374. (718)459-1600. Pres. Bernard Ouziel; Sec. Michael Cohen. A benevolent fraternal organization seeking to promote the industrial, social, educational, and religious welfare of its members. *Sephardic Brother.*

THE WORKMEN'S CIRCLE (1900). 45 E. 33 St., NYC 10016. (212)889-6800. FAX: (212)532-7518. Pres. Barnett Zumoff; Exec. Dir. Robert A. Kaplan. Promotes

Jewish identity through Jewish cultural and educational activities and programs. A fraternal benefit society (medical, dental, and legal services, life insurance, cemetery/funeral benefits); schools, camp, summer resort, Yiddish concerts, theater, and classes; public affairs/social action; projects in Israel, programs for Russian Jews; underwrites "Folksbiene" theater. Offices across U.S. and Canada. *The "Call"/Kultur un Leben.*

SOCIAL WELFARE

AMC CANCER RESEARCH CENTER (formerly JEWISH CONSUMPTIVES' RELIEF SOCIETY, 1904; incorporated as AMERICAN MEDICAL CENTER AT DENVER, 1954). 1600 Pierce St., Denver, CO 80214. (303)233–6501. Dir. Dr. Douglass C. Torney; Pres./CEO Bob R. Baker. A nationally recognized leader in the fight against cancer; employs a three-pronged, interdisciplinary approach that combines laboratory, clinical, and community cancer-control research to advance the prevention, early detection, diagnosis, and treatment of the disease. *Quarterly bulletin; annual report.*

AMCHA FOR TSEDAKAH (1990). 7700 Wisconsin Ave., Suite 500-A, Bethesda, MD 20814. (301) 652–7846. FAX: (301) 657–4180. Solicits and distributes contributions to Jewish charitable organizations in the U.S. and Israel; accredits organizations which demonstrate efficiency and fiscal integrity and also support pluralism and combat intolerance. Contributors are encouraged to earmark contributions for specific organizations; all contributions to General Fund are forwarded to the charitable institutions, as operating expenses are covered by a separate fund.

AMERICAN JEWISH CORRECTIONAL CHAPLAINS ASSOCIATION, INC. (formerly NATIONAL COUNCIL OF JEWISH PRISON CHAPLAINS) (1937). 10 E. 73 St., NYC 10021–4194. (212)879–8415. FAX: (212)-772–3977. (Cooperates with the New York Board of Rabbis.) Pres. Rabbi Irving Koslowe; Exec. Off. Rabbi Moses A. Birnbaum. Supports spiritual, moral, and social services for Jewish men and women in corrections; stimulates support of correctional chaplaincy; provides spiritual and professional fellowship for Jewish correctional chaplains; promotes sound standards for correctional chaplaincy; schedules workshops and research to aid chaplains in counseling and with religious services for Jewish inmates. Constituent, American Correctional Chaplains Association. *Chaplains Manual.*

AMERICAN JEWISH SOCIETY FOR SERVICE, INC. (1949). 15 E. 26 St., Rm. 1304, NYC 10010. (212)683–6178. Pres. Arthur Lifson; Exec. Dir. Elly Saltzman. Conducts voluntary work-service camps each summer to enable high-school juniors and seniors to perform humanitarian service.

AMERICAN JEWISH WORLD SERVICE (1985). 15 W. 26 St., 9th fl., NYC 10010. (212)683–1161. FAX: (212)683–5187. Chmn. Larry Buttenwieser; Exec. Dir. Andrew Griffel. Provides assistance on nonsectarian basis to relieve hunger, poverty, and suffering in Africa, Asia, and Latin America. Funds international sustainable, environmentally sound development projects and disaster relief; promotes awareness of these issues in the American Jewish community through volunteer groups located in major cities nationwide. *AJWS Report (quarterly newsletter).*

ASSOCIATION OF JEWISH CENTER PROFESSIONALS (1918). 15 East 26 St., NYC 10010–1579. (212)532–4949. FAX: (212)-481–4174. Pres. Michael Witkes; Exec. Dir. Marilyn Altman. Seeks to enhance the standards, techniques, practices, scope, and public understanding of Jewish Community Center and kindred agency work. *Kesher.*

ASSOCIATION OF JEWISH COMMUNITY ORGANIZATION PERSONNEL (AJCOP) (1969). 1750 Euclid Ave., Cleveland, OH 44115. (216)566–9200. FAX: (216)861–1230. Pres. Karl D. Zukerman; Pres.-Elect Peter Wells; Exec. Dir. Howard R. Berger. An organization of professionals engaged in areas of fund-raising, endowments, budgeting, social planning, financing, administration, and coordination of services. Objectives are to develop and enhance professional practices in Jewish communal work; to maintain and improve standards, practices, scope, and public understanding of the field of community organization, as practiced through local federations, national agencies, other organizations, settings, and private practitioners.

ASSOCIATION OF JEWISH FAMILY AND CHILDREN'S AGENCIES (1972). 3086 State Highway 27, Suite 11, PO Box 248, Ken-

dall Park, NJ 08824–0248. (800)634–7346.
FAX: (908)821–0493. Pres. George Wolly;
Exec. V.-Pres. Bert J. Goldberg. The national service organization for Jewish family and children's agencies in Canada and
the U.S. Reinforces member agencies in
their efforts to sustain and enhance the
quality of Jewish family and communal
life. Operates the Elder Support Network
for the National Jewish Community. *Bulletin (bimonthly); Directory; Professional
Opportunities Bulletin; Resettlement Bulletin (monthly).*

ASSOCIATION OF JEWISH FAMILY AND
CHILDREN'S AGENCY PROFESSIONALS
(1965). c/o NYANA, 17 Battery Pl., NYC
10004. (212)425–2900. FAX: (212)344–
1621. Pres. Mark Handelman. Brings together Jewish caseworkers and related professionals in Jewish family, children's, and
health services. Seeks to improve personnel
standards, further Jewish continuity and
identity, and strengthen Jewish family life;
provides forums for professional discussion at national conference of Jewish communal service and regional meetings; takes
action on social-policy issues. *Newsletter.*

BARON DE HIRSCH FUND (1891). 130 E. 59
St., NYC 10022. (212)836–1358. Pres. Arthur D. Sporn; Mng. Dir. Lauren Katzo-
witz. Aids Jewish immigrants and their
children in the U.S. and Israel by giving
grants to agencies active in educational and
vocational fields; has limited program for
study tours in U.S. by Israeli agriculturists.

B'NAI B'RITH (1843). 1640 Rhode Island
Ave., NW, Washington, DC 20036. (202)-
857–6600. FAX: (202)857–1099. Pres.
Kent E. Schiner; Exec. V.-Pres. Dr. Sidney
Clearfield. International Jewish organization, with affiliates in 51 countries. Offers
programs designed to ensure the preservation of Jewry and Judaism: Jewish education, community volunteer service, expansion of human rights, assistance to Israel,
housing for the elderly, leadership training,
rights of Soviet Jews and Jews of other
countries to emigrate and study their heritage. *International Jewish Monthly.*

———, ANTI-DEFAMATION LEAGUE OF
(*see* p. 450)

———, HILLEL FOUNDATIONS, INC. (*see* p.
473)

———, KLUTZNICK MUSEUM (*see* p. 454)

———, YOUTH ORGANIZATION (*see* p. 473)

B'NAI B'RITH WOMEN (1897). 1828 L St.,
NW, Suite 250, Washington, DC 20036.
(202)857–1370. FAX: (202)857–1380.
Pres. Joan Kort; Exec. Dir. Elaine K.
Binder. Supports Jewish women in their
families, in their communities, and in society. Offers programs that contribute to
preservation of Jewish life and values; supports treatment of emotionally disturbed
children in BBW Residential Treatment
Center in Israel; advocates for Israel and for
family issues. *Women's World.*

CITY OF HOPE NATIONAL MEDICAL CEN-
TER AND BECKMAN RESEARCH INSTI-
TUTE (1913). 1500 E. Duarte Rd., Duarte,
CA 91010. (818)359–8111. Pres. and Chief
Exec. Off. Dr. Sanford M. Shapero; Bd.
Chmn. Richard Ziman. Offers care to
those with cancer and major diseases, med-
ical consultation service for second opin-
ions, and pilot research programs in genet-
ics, immunology, and the basic life process.
*City News; City of Hope Cancer Center
Report.*

CONFERENCE OF JEWISH COMMUNAL SER-
VICE (*see* Jewish Communal Service Association of N. America)

COUNCIL OF JEWISH FEDERATIONS, INC.
(1932). 730 Broadway, NYC 10003. (212)-
475–5000. Pres. Charles H. Goodman;
Exec. V.-Pres. Martin Kraar. Provides national and regional services to more than
200 associated federations embracing 800
communities in the U.S. and Canada, aiding in fund-raising, community organization, health and welfare planning, personnel recruitment, and public relations.
*Directory of Jewish Federations, Welfare
Funds and Community Councils; Directory
of Jewish Health and Welfare Agencies (biennial); What's New in Federations; Newsbriefs; annual report.*

INTERNATIONAL ASSOCIATION OF JEWISH
VOCATIONAL SERVICES (formerly JEWISH
OCCUPATIONAL COUNCIL) (1939). 1845
Walnut St., 6th fl., Philadelphia, PA 19103.
(215)854–0233. FAX: (215)854–0212.
Pres. Marvin Simon; Exec. Dir. Dr. Marvin S. Kivitz; Asst. Dir. Shira E. Goldman.
Liaison and coordinating body for 29 vocational and family service agencies in the
U.S., Israel, and Canada that provide a
broad range of counseling, training, job-
placement, and rehabilitation services to
the Jewish and general community. These
services are available to the public as well
as many refugee populations.

INTERNATIONAL COUNCIL ON JEWISH SO-
CIAL AND WELFARE SERVICES (1961). c/o
American Jewish Joint Distribution Committee, 711 Third Ave., NYC 10017. (NY
liaison office with UN headquarters.)
(212)687–6200. Chmn. The Hon. L.H.L.
Cohen; Exec. Sec. Cheryl Mariner. Provides for exchange of views and information among member agencies on problems
of Jewish social and welfare services, including medical care, old age, welfare,
child care, rehabilitation, technical assistance, vocational training, agricultural and
other resettlement, economic assistance,
refugees, migration, integration and related problems, representation of views to
governments and international organizations. Members: six national and international organizations.

JEWISH BRAILLE INSTITUTE OF AMERICA,
INC. (1931). 110 E. 30 St., NYC 10016.
(212)889–2525. FAX: (212)689–3692.
Pres. Dr. Jane Evans; Exec. V.-Pres. Gerald M. Kass. Provides Judaic materials in
braille, talking books, and large print for
blind, visually impaired, and reading-dis-
abled; offers counseling for full integration
into the life of the Jewish community.
Comprehensive braille and talking-book library on Judaic topics; many titles in large
print. *Jewish Braille Review; JBI Voice.*

JEWISH COMMUNAL SERVICE ASSOCIATION
OF N. AMERICA (1899; formerly CONFER-
ENCE OF JEWISH COMMUNAL SERVICE).
3084 State Hwy. 27, Suite 9, Kendall Park,
NJ 08824–1657. (908)821–1871. FAX:
(908)821–5335. Pres. Ernest M. Kahn;
Exec. Dir. Joel Ollander. Serves as forum
for all professional philosophies in community service, for testing new experiences,
proposing new ideas, and questioning or
reaffirming old concepts; umbrella organization for seven major Jewish communal
service groups. Concerned with advancement of professional personnel practices
and standards. *Concurrents; Journal of
Jewish Communal Service.*

JEWISH COMMUNITY CENTERS ASSOCIA-
TION OF NORTH AMERICA (1917; formerly
JWB). 15 E. 26 St., NYC 10010–1579.
(212)532–4949. FAX: (212)481–4174.
Pres. Lester Pollack; Exec. V.-Pres. Arthur
Rotman. Central leadership agency for 275
Jewish community centers, YM-YWHAs,
and camps in the U.S. and Canada, serving
over one million Jews. Provides a variety of
consulting services and staff training programs to member centers, as well as informal Jewish educational and cultural experiences through Jewish Book and Music
Councils and JCC Association Lecture Bureau and many projects related to Israel.
U.S. government-accredited agency for the
religious, Jewish educational, and recreational needs of Jewish military personnel,
their families, and hospitalized VA patients through JWB Jewish Chaplains
Council. *Circle; Briefing; Zarkor; Personnel Reporter.*

———, JEWISH BOOK COUNCIL (see p. 456)

———, JEWISH MUSIC COUNCIL (see p.
456)

———, JWB JEWISH CHAPLAINS COUNCIL
(formerly COMMISSION ON JEWISH CHAP-
LAINCY) (1940). 15 E. 26 St., NYC 10010–
1579. Chmn. Rabbi Abraham Avrech; Dir.
Rabbi David Lapp. Recruits, endorses, and
serves Jewish military and Veterans Administration chaplains on behalf of the
American Jewish community and the
major rabbinic bodies; trains and assists
Jewish lay leaders where there are no chaplains, for service to Jewish military personnel, their families, and hospitalized veterans. *CHAPLINES newsletter.*

———, LECTURE BUREAU (see p. 456)

JEWISH CONCILIATION BOARD OF AMER-
ICA, INC. (A DIVISION OF THE JEWISH
BOARD OF FAMILY AND CHILDREN'S SER-
VICES) (1920). 120 W. 57 St., NYC 10019.
(212)582–9100. FAX: (212)245–2096.
Pres. Fredric W. Yerman; Exec. V.-Pres.
Dr. Alan B. Siskind. Offers dispute-resolu-
tion services to families, individuals, and
organizations. Social-work, rabbinic, and
legal expertise are available for family and
divorce mediation and arbitration. Fee—
sliding scale.

JEWISH FUND FOR JUSTICE (1984). 920
Broadway, Suite 605, NYC 10010. (212)-
677–7080. Bd. Chmn. Lawrence S. Levine;
Exec. Dir. Marlene Provizer. A national
grant-making foundation supporting efforts to combat the root causes of poverty
in the U.S. Provides diverse opportunities
for individual, family, and synagogue involvement through memorial, youth endowment, and synagogue challenge funds;
works cooperatively with other denominational funders and philanthropies promoting social and economic justice. *Annual
Report.*

JWB (*see* Jewish Community Centers Association of North America)

LEVI HOSPITAL (sponsored by B'nai B'rith) (1914). 300 Prospect Ave., Hot Springs, AR 71902. (501)624–1281. FAX: (501)-622–3500. Pres. Steven Kirsch; Admin. Patrick G. McCabe. Offers arthritis treatment, stroke rehabilitation, orthopedic rehabilitation, Levi Life Center, a hospice program, and a work capacity center. *Quarterly newsletter.*

MAZON: A JEWISH RESPONSE TO HUNGER (1985). 2940 Westwood Blvd., Suite 7, Los Angeles, CA 90064. (310)470–7769. FAX: (310)470–6736. Bd. Chmn. Lee H. Javitch; Exec. Dir. Irving Cramer. Raises funds by asking American Jews to contribute a suggested amount of 3 percent of the cost of life-cycle celebrations as well as through annual Passover and Yom Kippur appeals. Funds are granted to nonprofit organizations in the U.S. and abroad that work to alleviate hunger, malnutrition, and poverty. 1992 grants totaled $1.455 million. *Mazon Newsletter.*

NATIONAL ASSOCIATION OF JEWISH CHAPLAINS (1988). PO Box 7921, San Francisco, CA 94120. (415) 885–7786. FAX: (415) 885–7439. Pres. Rabbi Jeffrey M. Silberman. A professional organization for people functioning as Jewish chaplains in hospitals, nursing homes, geriatric, psychiatric, correctional, and military facilities. Provides collegial support, continuing education, professional certification, and resources for the Jewish community on issues of pastoral and spiritual care. *Journal of Pastoral Care* (cosponsor).

NATIONAL ASSOCIATION OF JEWISH FAMILY, CHILDREN'S AND HEALTH PROFESSIONALS (*see* Association of Jewish Family and Children's Agency Professionals)

NATIONAL CONGRESS OF JEWISH DEAF (1956; inc. 1961). c/o Dr. Barbara Boyd, Temple Beth Solomon of the Deaf, 13580 Osborne St., Arleta, CA 91331. Pres. Dr. Barbara Boyd. Congress of Jewish congregations, service organizations, and associations located throughout the U.S. and Canada, advocating religious spirit and cultural ideals and fellowship for the Jewish deaf. Affiliated with World Organization of Jewish Deaf. Publishes *Signs of Judaism,* a guide to sign language of Judaism. *NCJD Quarterly; Jewish Deaf Trivia.*

NATIONAL COUNCIL OF JEWISH PRISON CHAPLAINS, INC. (*see* American Jewish Correctional Chaplains Association, Inc.)

NATIONAL COUNCIL OF JEWISH WOMEN (1893). 53 W. 23 St., NYC 10010. (212)-645–4048. Pres. Susan Katz; Exec. Dir. Iris Gross. Furthers human welfare through program of community service, education, advocacy for children and youth, aging, women's issues, constitutional rights, Jewish life and Israel. Promotes education for the disadvantaged in Israel through the NCJW Research Institute for Innovation in Education at Hebrew University, Jerusalem. Promotes welfare of children in U.S. through Center for the Child. *NCJW Journal; Washington Newsletter.*

NATIONAL INSTITUTE FOR JEWISH HOSPICE (1985). 8723 Alden Drive, Suite 652, Los Angeles, CA 90048. (213)HOSPICE. Pres. Rabbi Maurice Lamm; Exec. Dir. Levana Lev. Serves as a national Jewish hospice resource center. Through conferences, research, publications, video training courses, referral, and counseling services offers guidance, training, and information to patients, family members, clergy of all faiths, professional caregivers, and volunteers who work with seriously ill Jews. *Jewish Hospice Times.*

NATIONAL JEWISH CENTER FOR IMMUNOLOGY AND RESPIRATORY MEDICINE (formerly NATIONAL JEWISH HOSPITAL/NATIONAL ASTHMA CENTER) (1899). 1400 Jackson St., Denver, CO 80206. (800)222-LUNG. Pres. Leonard M. Perlmutter; Bd. Chmn. Joseph Davis. Seeks to discover and disseminate knowledge that will prevent the occurrence of respiratory, allergic, and immunologic disorders and to develop improved clinical programs for those already afflicted. *New Direction (quarterly); Lung Line Letter (quarterly); Medical Scientific Update.*

NATIONAL JEWISH CHILDREN'S LEUKEMIA FOUNDATION (1990). 1310 48th St., Brooklyn, NY 11219. (718)853–0510. FAX: (718)435–0335. Pres. Tzvi Shor.

NORTH AMERICAN ASSOCIATION OF JEWISH HOMES AND HOUSING FOR THE AGING (1960). 10830 North Central Expressway, Suite 150, Dallas, TX 75231–1022. (214)696–9838. FAX: (214)360–0753. Pres. Bonnie G. Fass; Pres.-Elect Sheldon Blumenthal; Exec. V.-Pres. Dr.

Herbert Shore. Represents a community of not-for-profit charitable homes and housing for the Jewish aging; promotes excellence in performance and quality of service through fostering communication and education and encouraging advocacy for the aging; conducts annual conferences and institutes. *Perspectives (newsletter); Directory; Membership Handbook; From the Home & Housing Front (house organ).*

UNITED ORDER TRUE SISTERS, INC. (UOTS) (1846). 212 Fifth Ave., NYC 10010. (212)679–6790. Pres. Lenore Bloch; Exec. Admin. Dorothy B. Giuriceo. Charitable, community service, especially home supplies etc. for indigent cancer victims; supports camps for children with cancer. *Echo.*

PROFESSIONAL ASSOCIATIONS*

AMERICAN ASSOCIATION OF RABBIS (Religious, Educational)

AMERICAN CONFERENCE OF CANTORS, UNION OF AMERICAN HEBREW CONGREGATIONS (Religious, Educational)

AMERICAN JEWISH CORRECTIONAL CHAPLAINS ASSOCIATION, INC. (Social Welfare)

AMERICAN JEWISH PRESS ASSOCIATION (Cultural)

AMERICAN JEWISH PUBLIC RELATIONS SOCIETY (1957). 234 Fifth Ave., NYC 10001. (212)697–5895. Pres. Henry R. Hecker; Treas. Hyman Brickman. Advances professional status of workers in the public-relations field in Jewish communal service; upholds a professional code of ethics and standards; serves as a clearinghouse for employment opportunities; exchanges professional information and ideas; presents awards for excellence in professional attainments, including the "Maggid Award" for outstanding achievement that enhances Jewish life. *AJPRS Newsletter; AJPRS Directory.*

ASSOCIATION OF HILLEL/JEWISH CAMPUS PROFESSIONALS (Religious, Educational)

ASSOCIATION OF JEWISH CENTER PROFESSIONALS (Social Welfare)

ASSOCIATION OF JEWISH COMMUNITY ORGANIZATION PERSONNEL (Social Welfare)

ASSOCIATION OF JEWISH COMMUNITY RELATIONS WORKERS (Community Relations)

CANTORS ASSEMBLY (Religious, Educational)

CENTRAL CONFERENCE OF AMERICAN RABBIS (Religious, Educational)

COUNCIL OF JEWISH ORGANIZATIONS IN CIVIL SERVICE (Community Relations)

INTERNATIONAL JEWISH MEDIA ASSOCIATION (Cultural)

JEWISH CHAPLAINS COUNCIL, JWB (Social Welfare)

JEWISH COMMUNAL SERVICE ASSOCIATION OF N. AMERICA (Social Welfare)

JEWISH EDUCATORS ASSEMBLY, UNITED SYNAGOGUE OF AMERICA (Religious, Educational)

JEWISH MINISTERS CANTORS ASSOCIATION OF AMERICA, INC. (Religious, Educational)

JEWISH TEACHERS ASSOCIATION–MORIM (Religious, Educational)

NATIONAL ASSOCIATION OF HEBREW DAY SCHOOL ADMINISTRATORS, TORAH UMESORAH (Religious, Educational)

NATIONAL ASSOCIATION OF JEWISH CHAPLAINS (Social Welfare)

NATIONAL ASSOCIATION OF SYNAGOGUE ADMINISTRATORS, UNITED SYNAGOGUE OF AMERICA (Religious, Educational)

NATIONAL ASSOCIATION OF TEMPLE ADMINISTRATORS, UNION OF AMERICAN HEBREW CONGREGATIONS (Religious, Educational)

NATIONAL ASSOCIATION OF TEMPLE EDUCATORS, UNION OF AMERICAN HEBREW CONGREGATIONS (Religious, Educational)

NATIONAL CONFERENCE OF YESHIVA PRINCIPALS, TORAH UMESORAH (Religious, Educational)

RABBINICAL ASSEMBLY (Religious, Educational)

RABBINICAL COUNCIL OF AMERICA (Religious, Educational)

RECONSTRUCTIONIST RABBINICAL ASSOCIATION, JEWISH RECONSTRUCTIONIST FOUNDATION (Religious, Educational)

*For fuller listing see under categories in parentheses.

UNION OF ORTHODOX RABBIS OF THE U.S. AND CANADA (Religious, Educational)

WORLD CONFERENCE OF JEWISH COMMUNAL SERVICE (Community Relations)

WOMEN'S ORGANIZATIONS*

AMIT WOMEN (Israel-Related)

B'NAI B'RITH WOMEN (Social Welfare)

BRANDEIS UNIVERSITY NATIONAL WOMEN'S COMMITTEE (1948). PO Box 9110, Waltham, MA 02254–9110. (617)-736–4160. FAX: (617)736–4183. Pres. Marsha Stoller; Exec. Dir. Harriet J. Winer. Provides financial support for the Brandeis Libraries and works to enhance the image of Brandeis, a Jewish-sponsored, nonsectarian university. Offers its members opportunity for intellectual pursuit, continuing education, community service, social interaction, personal enrichment, and leadership development. Open to all, regardless of race, religion, nationality, or gender. *Imprint.*

HADASSAH, THE WOMEN'S ZIONIST ORGANIZATION OF AMERICA (Israel-Related)

NA'AMAT USA, THE WOMEN'S LABOR ZIONIST ORGANIZATION OF AMERICA (Israel-Related)

NATIONAL COUNCIL OF JEWISH WOMEN (Social Welfare)

NATIONAL FEDERATION OF TEMPLE SISTERHOODS, UNION OF AMERICAN HEBREW CONGREGATIONS (Religious, Educational)

UOTS (Social Welfare)

WOMEN'S AMERICAN ORT, AMERICAN ORT FEDERATION (Overseas Aid)

WOMEN'S BRANCH OF THE UNION OF ORTHODOX JEWISH CONGREGATIONS OF AMERICA (Religious, Educational)

WOMEN'S DIVISION OF POALE AGUDATH ISRAEL OF AMERICA (Israel-Related)

WOMEN'S DIVISION OF THE JEWISH LABOR COMMITTEE (Community Relations)

WOMEN'S DIVISION OF THE UNITED JEWISH APPEAL (Overseas Aid)

WOMEN'S LEAGUE FOR CONSERVATIVE JUDAISM (Religious, Educational)

WOMEN'S LEAGUE FOR ISRAEL, INC. (Israel-Related)

WOMEN'S ORGANIZATION, YESHIVA UNIVERSITY (Religious, Educational)

YOUTH AND STUDENT ORGANIZATIONS*

AGUDATH ISRAEL OF AMERICA (Religious, Educational)

AMERICAN ZIONIST YOUTH FOUNDATION (Israel-Related)

B'NAI B'RITH HILLEL FOUNDATIONS (Religious, Educational)

B'NAI B'RITH YOUTH ORGANIZATION (Religious, Educational)

BNEI AKIVA OF NORTH AMERICA, RELIGIOUS ZIONISTS OF AMERICA (Israel-Related)

HABONIM-DROR NORTH AMERICA (Israel-Related)

HASHOMER HATZAIR, SOCIALIST ZIONIST YOUTH MOVEMENT (Israel-Related)

KADIMA, UNITED SYNAGOGUE OF AMERICA (Religious, Educational)

NATIONAL CONFERENCE OF SYNAGOGUE YOUTH, UNION OF ORTHODOX JEWISH CONGREGATIONS OF AMERICA (Religious, Educational)

NATIONAL JEWISH COMMITTEE ON SCOUTING (Religious, Educational)

NATIONAL JEWISH GIRL SCOUT COMMITTEE (Religious, Educational)

NOAM-MIZRACHI NEW LEADERSHIP COUNCIL, RELIGIOUS ZIONISTS OF AMERICA (Israel-Related)

NORTH AMERICAN FEDERATION OF TEMPLE YOUTH, UNION OF AMERICAN HEBREW CONGREGATIONS (Religious, Educational)

NORTH AMERICAN JEWISH STUDENTS APPEAL (1971). 165 Pidgeon Hill Rd., Huntington Station, NY 11746–9998. (516)385–8771. FAX: (516)385–8772. Pres. Seth Kamil; Chmn. Dr. S. Hal Horwitz; Exec. Dir. Brenda Gevertz. Serves as central fund-raising mechanism for six national, independent Jewish student organizations; ensures accountability of public Jewish communal funds used by these agencies; assists Jewish students undertaking projects of concern to Jewish communities; advises and assists Jewish organizations in determining student project feasibility and

*For fuller listing see under categories in parentheses.

impact; fosters development of Jewish student leadership in the Jewish community. Beneficiaries include local and regional Jewish student projects; current constituents include Jewish Student Press Service, Student Struggle for Soviet Jewry, *Response Magazine*, Yugntruf Youth for Yiddish, Progressive Zionist Caucus, Project Orchim for outreach on campus, and the Beneficiary Grants Program.

STUDENT STRUGGLE FOR SOVIET JEWRY— *see* CENTER FOR RUSSIAN JEWRY (Community Relations)

YOUNG JUDAEA/HASHACHAR, HADASSAH (Israel-Related)

YUGNTRUF–YOUTH FOR YIDDISH (1964). 200 W. 72 St., Suite 40, NYC 10023. (212)787-6675. Cochmn. Dr. Adina Singer, Binyumen Schaechter; Editor David Braun. A worldwide, nonpolitical organization for high school and college students with a knowledge of, or interest in, Yiddish. Spreads the love and use of the Yiddish language; organizes artistic and social activities, including annual conference for young adults; sponsors Yiddish-speaking preschool for non-Orthodox children; disseminates new Yiddish teaching materials. *Yugntruf Journal.*

CANADA

B'NAI BRITH CANADA (1875). 15 Hove St., Downsview, ONT M3H 4Y8. (416)633-6224. FAX: (416)630-2159. Pres. Gabriel Nachman; Exec. V.-Pres. Frank Dimant. Canadian Jewry's senior organization; makes representations to all levels of government on matters of Jewish concern; promotes humanitarian causes and educational programs, community volunteer projects, adult Jewish education, and leadership development; dedicated to human rights. *Covenant Newspaper.*

——, INSTITUTE FOR INTERNATIONAL AFFAIRS (1987). 15 Hove St., Downsview, ONT M3H 4Y8. (416)633-6224. FAX: (416)630-2159. Pres. Gabriel Nachman; Natl. Dir. Paul Marcus. Identifies and protests the abuse of human rights throughout the world. Monitors the condition of Jewish communities worldwide and advocates on their behalf when they experience serious violations of their human rights. *Institute Report.*

——, LEAGUE FOR HUMAN RIGHTS (1970). 15 Hove St., Downsview, ONT M3H 4Y8. (416)633-6227. FAX: (416)-630-2159. Natl. Chmn. Prof. Stephen Scheinberg; Natl. Dir. Dr. Karen Mock. A national volunteer association dedicated to combatting racism and bigotry. Objectives include human rights for all Canadians, improved inter-community relations, and the elimination of racial discrimination and anti-Semitism. Conducts educational programs, engages in community action, and provides legal advice and action. Canadian distributor of ADL material. *Review of Anti-Semitism; Annual Audit of Anti-Semitic Incidents; Holocaust and Hope, Educators' Newsletter; Combatting Hate: Guidelines for Community Action.*

CANADIAN ASSOCIATION FOR LABOR ISRAEL (HISTADRUT) (1944). 7005 Kildare Rd., Suite 14, Cote St. Luc, PQ H4W 1C1. (514)484-9430. FAX: (514)487-6727. Pres. Harry J.F. Bloomfield. Conducts fund-raising and educational activities on behalf of Histadrut, Kupat Holim, and Amal schools in Israel.

CANADIAN FOUNDATION FOR JEWISH CULTURE (1965). 4600 Bathurst St., Willowdale, ONT M2R 3V2. (416)635-2883. Pres. Mira Koschitzky; Exec. Sec. Edmond Y. Lipsitz. Promotes Jewish studies at university level and encourages original research and scholarship in Jewish subjects; awards annual scholarships and grants-in-aid to scholars in Canada.

CANADIAN FRIENDS OF THE ALLIANCE ISRAÉLITE UNIVERSELLE (1958). PO Box 578, Victoria Station, Montreal, PQ H3Z 2Y6. (514)481-3552. Pres. Joseph Nuss. Supports the educational work of the Alliance.

CANADIAN FRIENDS OF THE HEBREW UNIVERSITY (1944). 3080 Yonge St., Suite 5024, Toronto, ONT M4N 3P4. (416)485-8000. FAX: (416)485-8565. Pres. J. Stephen Lipper; Exec. V.-Pres. Shimon Arbel. Represents the Hebrew University of Jerusalem in Canada; serves as fund-raising arm for the university in Canada; accepts Canadians for study at the university; sponsors educational programs. *Dateline Jerusalem.*

CANADIAN JEWISH CONGRESS (1919; reorg. 1934). 1590 Dr. Penfield Ave., Montreal, PQ H3G 1C5. (514)931-7531. FAX: (514)931-0548. Pres. Irving Abella; Exec. V.-Pres. Alan Rose. The official voice of Canadian Jewish communities at home and abroad; acts on all matters affecting the status, rights, concerns and welfare of

Canadian Jewry; internationally active on behalf of Soviet Jewry, Jews in Arab lands, Holocaust remembrance and restitution; largest Jewish archives in Canada. *National Small Communities Newsletter; Intercom; Ottawa Digest; National Soviet Jewry Newsletter; National Archives Newsletter; regional newsletters.*

CANADIAN ORT ORGANIZATION (Organization of Rehabilitation Through Training) (1942). 5165 Sherbrooke St. W., Suite 208, Montreal, PQ H4A 1T6. (514)481–2787. Pres. Bernard Gross; Exec. Dir. Mac Silver. Carries on fund-raising projects in support of the worldwide vocational-training-school network of ORT. *ORT Reporter.*

———, WOMEN'S CANADIAN ORT (1948). 3101 Bathurst St., Suite 604, Toronto, ONT M6A 2A6. (416)787–0339, Natl. Pres. Lydia London; Natl. Exec. Dir. Diane Uslaner. Chapters in 11 Canadian cities raise funds for ORT's nonprofit global network of schools, where Jewish students learn a wide range of marketable skills, including the most advanced high-tech professions. *Focus Magazine.*

CANADIAN YOUNG JUDAEA (1917). 788 Marlee Ave., Suite 205, Toronto, ONT M6B 3K1. (416)781–5156. FAX: (416)-787–3100. Eastern Region Shaliach Gadi-Anavi; Natl. Exec. Dir. Risa Epstein-Gamliel; Natl. Shaliach Shmuel Levkowitz. Strives to attract Jewish youth to Zionism, with goal of *aliyah;* educates youth about Jewish history and Zionism; prepares them to provide leadership in Young Judaea camps in Canada and Israel and to be concerned Jews. *The Judaean.*

CANADIAN ZIONIST FEDERATION (1967). 5250 Decarie Blvd., Suite 550, Montreal, PQ H3X 2H9. (514)486–9526. FAX: (514)483–6392. Pres. Kurt Rothschild. Umbrella organization of all Zionist and Israel-related groups in Canada; carries on major activities in all areas of Jewish life through its departments of education and culture, *aliyah,* youth and students, public affairs, and fund-raising, for the purpose of strengthening the State of Israel and the Canadian Jewish community. *Canadian Zionist.*

———, BUREAU OF EDUCATION AND CULTURE (1972). Pres. Kurt Rothschild. Provides counseling by pedagogic experts, in-service teacher-training courses and seminars in Canada and Israel; national

pedagogic council and research center; distributes educational material and teaching aids; conducts annual Bible contest and Hebrew-language courses for adults.

FRIENDS OF PIONEERING ISRAEL (1950s). 1111 Finch Ave. W., Suite 154, Downsview, ONT M3J 2E5. (416)736–1339. Pres. Joseph Podemsky. Acts as a voice of Socialist and Zionist points of view within the Jewish community and a focal point for progressive Zionist elements in Canada; Canadian representative of Mapam; affiliated with Hashomer-Hatzair and the Givat Haviva Education Foundation.

HADASSAH–WIZO ORGANIZATION OF CANADA (1917). 1310 Greene Ave., Suite 900, Montreal, PQ H3Z 2B8. (514)937–9431. FAX: (514)933–6483. Natl. Pres. Esther Matlow; Exec. V.-Pres. Lily Frank. Largest women's volunteer Zionist Organization in Canada; located in 43 Canadian cities; dedicated to advancing the quality of life of the women and children in Israel through financial assistance and support of its many projects, day-care centers, schools, institutions, and hospitals. In Canada, the organization promotes Canadian ideals of democracy and is a stalwart advocate of women's issues. *Orah Magazine.*

JEWISH IMMIGRANT AID SERVICES OF CANADA (JIAS) (1919). 5151 Cote Ste. Catherine Rd., Suite 220, Montreal, PQ H3W 1M6. (514)342–9351. FAX: (514)342–8452. Pres. Robert Kleinman; Exec. Dir. Joel Moss. Serves as a national agency for immigration and immigrant welfare.

JEWISH NATIONAL FUND OF CANADA (KEREN KAYEMETH LE'ISRAEL, INC.) (1901). 1980 Sherbrooke St. W., Suite 500, Montreal, PQ H3H 1E8. (514)934–0313. FAX: (514)934–0382. Pres. Alan Posluns; Exec. V.-Pres. Morris Zilka. Fund-raising organization affiliated with the World Zionist Organization; involved in afforestation, soil reclamation, and development of the land of Israel, including the construction of roads and preparation of sites for new settlements; provides educational materials and programs to Jewish schools across Canada.

LABOR ZIONIST ALLIANCE OF CANADA (1909). 7005 Kildare Rd., Suite 10, Cote St. Luc, PQ H4W 1C1. (514)484–1789. FAX: (514)487–6727. Pres. David Kofsky; Chmn. Toronto City Committee Julius Sokoloff; Chmn. Montreal City Committee Harry Froimovitch. Associated with the

World Labor Zionist movement and allied with the Israel Labor party. Provides recreational and cultural programs, mutual aid, and fraternal care to enhance the social welfare of its membership; actively promotes Zionist education, cultural projects, and forums on aspects of Jewish and Canadian concern.

MIZRACHI-HAPOEL HAMIZRACHI ORGANIZATION OF CANADA (1941). 159 Almore Ave., Downsview, ONT M3H 2H9. (416)-630-7575. Natl. Pres. Kurt Rothschild; Natl. Exec. V.-Pres. Rabbi Menachem Gopin. Promotes religious Zionism, aimed at making Israel a state based on Torah; maintains Bnei Akiva, a summer camp, adult education program, and touring department; supports Mizrachi-Hapoel Hamizrachi and other religious Zionist institutions in Israel which strengthen traditional Judaism. *Mizrachi Newsletter; Or Hamizrach Torah Quarterly.*

NATIONAL COUNCIL OF JEWISH WOMEN OF CANADA (1897). 1110 Finch Ave. W., #518, Downsview, ONT M3J 2T2. (416)-665-8251. Pres. Gloria Strom; Exec. Dir. Eleanor Appleby. Dedicated to furthering human welfare in Jewish and non-Jewish communities, locally, nationally, and internationally; provides essential services and stimulates and educates the individual and the community through an integrated program of education, service, and social action. *New Edition.*

NATIONAL JOINT COMMUNITY RELATIONS COMMITTEE OF CANADIAN JEWISH CONGRESS (1936). 4600 Bathurst St., Willowdale, ONT M2R 3V2. (416)635-2883, Ext. 186. FAX: (416)635-1408. Cochmn. Hal Joffe, Hershell Ezrin; Natl. Dir. Bernie M. Farber. Seeks to safeguard the status, rights, and welfare of Jews in Canada; to combat anti-Semitism and promote understanding and goodwill among all ethnic and religious groups.

STATE OF ISRAEL BONDS (CANADA-ISRAEL SECURITIES, LTD.) (1953). 3101 Bathurst Street, Suite 400, Toronto, ONT M6A 2A6. (416)789-3351. FAX: (416)789-9436. Pres. Alex Grossman; Bd. Chmn. and CEO Melvyn A. Dobrin. Mobilizes productive investment capital for the economic development of the State of Israel.

Jewish Federations, Welfare Funds, Community Councils

UNITED STATES

ALABAMA

BIRMINGHAM

BIRMINGHAM JEWISH FEDERATION (1936; reorg. 1971); PO Box 130219 (35213); (205)-879–0416. FAX: (205)879–0466. Pres. Steven Brickman; Exec. Dir. Richard Friedman.

MOBILE

MOBILE JEWISH WELFARE FUND, INC. (inc. 1966); One Office Park, Suite 219 (36609); (205)343–7197. Pres. Nancy Silverboard; Admin. Barbara V. Paper.

MONTGOMERY

JEWISH FEDERATION OF MONTGOMERY, INC. (1930); PO Box 20058 (36120); (205)-277–5820. Pres. Jake Mendel; Exec. Dir. Beverly Lipton.

ARIZONA

PHOENIX

JEWISH FEDERATION OF GREATER PHOENIX (1940); 32 W. Coolidge, Suite 200 (85013); (602)274–1800. FAX: (602)266–7875. Pres. Leonard Miller; Exec. Dir. Harold Morgan.

TUCSON

JEWISH FEDERATION OF SOUTHERN ARIZONA (1946); 3822 East River Rd. (85718); (602)577–9393. FAX: (602)577–0734. Pres. Harold Greenberg; Exec. V.-Pres. Richard Fruchter.

ARKANSAS

LITTLE ROCK

JEWISH FEDERATION OF ARKANSAS (1911); 4942 W. Markham, Suite 5 (72205); (501)-663–3571. Pres. Dr. George Wolff; Exec. Dir. (Mrs.) Hart Gottliebson.

CALIFORNIA

LONG BEACH

JEWISH FEDERATION OF GREATER LONG BEACH AND W. ORANGE COUNTY (1937; inc. 1946); 3801 E. Willow St. (90815); (213)-426–7601. FAX: (213)424–3915. Pres. Morton Stuhlbarg; Exec. Dir. Sandi Goldstein.

LOS ANGELES

JEWISH FEDERATION COUNCIL OF GREATER LOS ANGELES (1912; reorg. 1959); 6505 Wilshire Blvd. (90048); (213)852–1234. FAX: (213)655–4458. Pres. David Finegood; Acting Exec. V.-Pres. Merv Lemmerman.

OAKLAND

JEWISH FEDERATION OF THE GREATER EAST BAY (Alameda and Contra Costa counties) (1917); 401 Grand Ave. (94610); (415)-839–2900. FAX: (415)839–3996. Pres. Dr. Miles Adler; Exec. V.-Pres. Ami Nahshon.

ORANGE COUNTY

JEWISH FEDERATION OF ORANGE COUNTY (1964; inc. 1965); 1385 Warner Ave., Suite A, Tustin (92680–6442); (714)259–0655. FAX: (714)259–1635. Pres. William Shane; Exec. Dir. Edward Cushman.

This directory is based on information supplied by the Council of Jewish Federations.

PALM SPRINGS

JEWISH FEDERATION OF PALM SPRINGS (1971); 255 El Cielo N., Suite 430 (92262); (619)325-7281. Pres. Jim Horvitz; Exec. Dir. Irving Ginsberg.

SACRAMENTO

JEWISH FEDERATION OF SACRAMENTO (1948); PO Box 254589 (95865); (916)486-0906. FAX: (916)486-0816. Pres. Barbara Ansel; Exec. Dir. Ted Feldman.

SAN DIEGO

UNITED JEWISH FEDERATION OF SAN DIEGO COUNTY (1936); 4797 Mercury St. (92111-2102); (619)571-3444. FAX: (619)-571-0701. Pres. Murray L. Galinson; Exec. V. Pres. Stephen M. Abramson.

SAN FRANCISCO

JEWISH COMMUNITY FEDERATION OF SAN FRANCISCO, THE PENINSULA, MARIN, AND SONOMA COUNTIES (1910; reorg. 1955); 121 Steuart St. (94105); (415)777-0411. FAX: (415)495-6635. Pres. Donald Seiler; Exec. Dir. Wayne Feinstein.

SAN JOSE

JEWISH FEDERATION OF GREATER SAN JOSE (incl. Santa Clara County except Palo Alto and Los Altos) (1930; reorg. 1950); 14855 Oka Rd., Los Gatos (95030); (408)-358-3033. FAX: (408)356-0733. Pres. Bernie Kotansky; Exec. Dir. Paul Ellenbogen.

SANTA BARBARA

SANTA BARBARA JEWISH FEDERATION (1974); 104 W. Anapamu, Suite A. Mailing Address: PO Box 90110, Santa Barbara (93190); (805)963-0244. FAX: (805)569-5052. Pres. James Sheinfeld; Exec. Dir. Barbara Zonen.

COLORADO

DENVER

ALLIED JEWISH FEDERATION OF DENVER (1936); 300 S. Dahlia St. (80222); (303)321-3399. FAX: (303)322-8328. Pres. Stanton D. Rosenbaum; Exec. Dir. Sheldon Steinhauser.

CONNECTICUT

BRIDGEPORT

JEWISH FEDERATION OF GREATER BRIDGEPORT, INC. (1936; reorg. 1981); 4200 Park Ave. (06604); (203)372-6504. FAX: (203)-374-0770. Pres. Selig Danzig; Exec. Dir. Gerald A. Kleinman.

DANBURY

JEWISH FEDERATION OF GREATER DANBURY (1945); 39 Mill Plain Rd., Suite 4 (06811); (203)792-6353. Pres. Jean Wellington; Exec. Dir. Lauren Bernard.

EASTERN CONNECTICUT

JEWISH FEDERATION OF EASTERN CONNECTICUT, INC. (1950; inc. 1970); 28 Channing St., PO Box 1468, New London (06320); (203)442-8062. FAX: (203)444-0759. Pres. Reuben Levin; Exec. Dir. Jerome E. Fischer.

GREENWICH

GREENWICH JEWISH FEDERATION (1956); 600 W. Putnam Ave. (06830); (203)622-1434. FAX: (203)622-1237. Pres. Paula Lustbader; Interim Exec. Dir. Sol Margulies.

HARTFORD

GREATER HARTFORD JEWISH FEDERATION (1945); 333 Bloomfield Ave., W. Hartford (06117); (203)232-4483. FAX: (203)232-5221. Pres. Robert Siskin; Exec. Dir. Don Cooper.

NEW HAVEN

NEW HAVEN JEWISH FEDERATION (1928); 419 Whalley Ave. (06511); (203)562-2137. FAX: (203)787-3241. Pres. Stephen Saltzman; Exec. Dir. Jay Rubin.

NORWALK

(See Westport)

STAMFORD

UNITED JEWISH FEDERATION (inc. 1973); 1035 Newfield Ave., PO Box 3038 (06905); (203)321-1373. FAX: (203)322-3277. Pres. Benson Zinbarg; Exec. Dir. Sheila L. Romanowitz.

WATERBURY

JEWISH FEDERATION OF WATERBURY, INC. (1938); 359 Cooke St. (06710); (203)756-7234. FAX: (203)573-0368. Pres. Dr. Alan Stein; Exec. Dir. Robert Zwang.

WESTPORT-WESTON-WILTON-NORWALK

UNITED JEWISH APPEAL/FEDERATION OF WESTPORT-WESTON-WILTON-NORWALK (inc. 1980); 49 Richmondville Ave. (06880); (203)266-8197. FAX: (203)226-5051. Pres. Michael Stashower; Exec. Dir. Robert Kessler.

DELAWARE

WILMINGTON

JEWISH FEDERATION OF DELAWARE, INC. (1934); 101 Garden of Eden Rd. (19803);

(302)478–6200. FAX: (302)478–5374. Pres. William N. Topkis; Exec. Dir. Judy Wortman.

DISTRICT OF COLUMBIA

WASHINGTON

UNITED JEWISH APPEAL–FEDERATION OF GREATER WASHINGTON, INC. (1935); 6101 Montrose Rd., Rockville, MD 20852. (301)-230–7200. FAX: (301)230–7272. Pres. Edward Kaplan; Exec. V.-Pres. Ted B. Farber.

FLORIDA

BREVARD COUNTY

JEWISH FEDERATION OF BREVARD; 108-A Barton Ave., Rockledge (32955). (407) 636–1824. Pres. Dr. Leon Cohen.

COLLIER COUNTY

JEWISH FEDERATION OF COLLIER COUNTY(1974); 1250 Tamiami Trail North, Suite 304C, Naples (33940). Pres. Jerry Flagel.

DAYTONA BEACH

(See Volusia & Flagler Counties)

FT. LAUDERDALE

JEWISH FEDERATION OF GREATER FT. LAUDERDALE (1968); 8358 W. Oakland Park Blvd. (33351); (305)748–8400. FAX: (305)748–6332. Pres. Barbara Wiener; Exec. Dir. Kenneth B. Bierman.

JACKSONVILLE

JACKSONVILLE JEWISH FEDERATION (1935); 8505 San Jose Blvd. (32217); (904)-448–5000. FAX: (904)448–5715. Pres. Joan Levin; Exec. V.-Pres. Alan Margolies.

LEE COUNTY

JEWISH FEDERATION OF LEE COUNTY (1974); 6315 Presidential Court, Suite A, Ft. Myers (33919–3568); (813)481–4449. FAX: (813)275–9114. Pres. Dr. Harvey Tritel; Exec. Dir. Helene Kramer.

MIAMI

GREATER MIAMI JEWISH FEDERATION, INC. (1938); 4200 Biscayne Blvd. (33137); (305)576–4000. FAX: (305)573–2176. Pres. Howard R. Scharlin; Exec. V.-Pres. Myron J. Brodie.

ORLANDO

JEWISH FEDERATION OF GREATER ORLANDO (1949); 851 N. Maitland Ave., PO Box 941508, Maitland (32794–1508); (407)-645–5933. FAX: (407)645–1172. Pres. Robert Yarmuth; Exec. Dir. Howard Stone.

PALM BEACH COUNTY

JEWISH FEDERATION OF PALM BEACH COUNTY, INC. (1962); 501 S. Flagler Dr., Suite 305, W. Palm Beach (33401); (407)832–2120. FAX: (407)832–0562. Pres. Alec Engelstein; Exec. Dir. Jeffrey L. Klein.

PINELLAS COUNTY

JEWISH FEDERATION OF PINELLAS COUNTY, INC. (incl. Clearwater and St. Petersburg) (1950; reincorp. 1974); 301 S. Jupiter Ave., Clearwater (34615); (813) 446–1033. FAX: (813)461–0700. Pres. Stephen Wein; Exec. Dir. Robert F. Tropp.

SARASOTA

SARASOTA-MANATEE JEWISH FEDERATION (1959); 580 S. McIntosh Rd. (34232); (813)-371–4546. FAX: (813)378–2947. Pres. Doris Loevner; Exec. Dir. Norman Olshansky.

SOUTH BROWARD

JEWISH FEDERATION OF SOUTH BROWARD, INC. (1943); 2719 Hollywood Blvd., Hollywood (33020); (305)921–8810. FAX: (305)-921–6491. Pres. Dr. Howard Barron; Exec. Dir. Sumner G. Kaye.

SOUTH PALM BEACH COUNTY

SOUTH PALM BEACH COUNTY JEWISH FEDERATION (inc. 1979); 336 NW Spanish River Blvd., Boca Raton (33431); (407) 368–2737. FAX: (407)368–5240. Pres. Marvin Zale; Exec. Dir. Rabbi Bruce S. Warshal.

TAMPA

TAMPA JEWISH FEDERATION (1941); 2808 Horatio (33609); (813)875–1618. FAX: (813)876–7746. Pres. F. Sanford Mahr; Exec. V. Pres. Gary S. Alter.

VOLUSIA & FLAGLER COUNTIES

JEWISH FEDERATION OF VOLUSIA & FLAGLER COUNTIES, INC.; 793 South Nova Rd., Ormond Beach 32174. (904)672–0294. FAX: (904)673–8372. Pres. Gary Greenfield; Admin. Marilyn Brown.

GEORGIA

ATLANTA

ATLANTA JEWISH FEDERATION, INC. (1905; reorg. 1967); 1753 Peachtree Rd. NE (30309); (404)873–1661. FAX: (404)874–7043. Pres. Dr. S. Perry Brickman; Exec. Dir. David I. Sarnat.

AUGUSTA

AUGUSTA JEWISH FEDERATION (1937); PO Box 15443 (30909); (706)736–1818. FAX: (706)667–8081. Pres. Matt Marks; Exec. Dir. Michael Pousman.

COLUMBUS

JEWISH WELFARE FEDERATION OF COLUM-BUS, INC. (1941); PO Box 6313 (31907); (404)568–6668. Pres. Jack Hirsch; Sec. Irene Rainbow.

SAVANNAH

SAVANNAH JEWISH FEDERATION (1943); PO Box 23527 (31403); (912)355–8111. FAX: (912)355–8116. Pres. Ricky Eichholz; Exec. Dir. Jeff Feld.

HAWAII

HONOLULU

JEWISH FEDERATION OF HAWAII (1956); 677 Ala Moana, Suite 803 (96813); (808)531–4634. FAX: (808)531–4636. Pres. Michael Washofsky; Exec. Dir. Rabbi Melvin Libman.

ILLINOIS

CHAMPAIGN-URBANA

CHAMPAIGN-URBANA JEWISH FEDERA-TION (1929); 503 E. John St., Champaign (61820); (217)367–9872. Pres. Helen Levin; Exec. Dir. Janie Yairi.

CHICAGO

JEWISH FEDERATION OF METROPOLITAN CHICAGO (1900); 1 S. Franklin St. (60606–4694); (312)346–6700. FAX: (312)855–2474. Pres. Arthur W. Brown, Jr.; Exec. V.-Pres. Steven B. Nasatir.

JEWISH UNITED FUND OF METROPOLITAN CHICAGO (1900); 1 S. Franklin St. (60606–4694); (312)346–6700. FAX: (312)444–2086. Pres. Arthur W. Brown, Jr.; Exec. Dir. Steven B. Nasatir.

ELGIN

ELGIN AREA JEWISH WELFARE CHEST (1938); 330 Division St. (60120); (312)741–5656. Pres. Dr. Albert Simon; Treas. Richard Cutts.

PEORIA

JEWISH FEDERATION OF PEORIA (1933; inc. 1947); 5901 N. Prospect Rd., Suite 203, Town Hall Bldg., Junction City (61614); (309)689–0063. Pres. Dr. Irving J. Weigensberg; Exec. Dir. Eunice Galsky.

QUAD CITIES

JEWISH FEDERATION OF QUAD CITIES (incl. Rock Island, Moline, Davenport, Bettendorf) (1938; comb. 1973); 224 18 St., Suite 303, Rock Island (61201); (309)793–1300. Pres. Gordon Ney; Exec. Dir. Ida Kramer.

ROCKFORD

JEWISH FEDERATION OF GREATER ROCK-FORD (1937); 1500 Parkview Ave. (61107); (815)399–5497. Pres. Jay Kamin; Exec. Dir. Tony Toback.

SOUTHERN ILLINOIS

JEWISH FEDERATION OF SOUTHERN ILLI-NOIS, SOUTHEASTERN MISSOURI AND WEST-ERN KENTUCKY (1941); 6464 W. Main, Suite 7A, Belleville (62223); (618)398–6100. Pres. Ronald Rubin; Exec. Dir. Stan Anderman.

SPRINGFIELD

SPRINGFIELD JEWISH FEDERATION (1941); 730 E. Vine St. (62703); (217)528–3446. Pres. Robert Silverman; Exec. Dir. Gloria Schwartz.

INDIANA

EVANSVILLE

EVANSVILLE JEWISH COMMUNITY COUN-CIL, INC. (1936; inc. 1964); PO Box 5026 (47715); (812)477–7050. Pres. Jon Goldman; Exec. Sec. Maxine P. Fink.

FORT WAYNE

FORT WAYNE JEWISH FEDERATION (1921); 227 E. Washington Blvd. (46802); (219)422–8566. FAX: (219)423–3400. Pres. Carol Sandler; Exec. Dir. Vivian Lansky.

INDIANAPOLIS

JEWISH FEDERATION OF GREATER IN-DIANAPOLIS, INC. (1905); 615 N. Alabama St., Suite 412 (46204–1430); (317)637–2473. FAX: (317)637–2477. Pres. Stanley Talesnick; Exec. V.-Pres. Harry Nadler.

LAFAYETTE

FEDERATED JEWISH CHARITIES (1924); PO Box 708 (47902); (317)742–9081. FAX: (317)742–4379. Pres. Arnold Cohen; Finan. Sec. Louis Pearlman, Jr.

MICHIGAN CITY

MICHIGAN CITY UNITED JEWISH WELFARE FUND; 2800 S. Franklin St. (46360); (219)-874–4477. Pres. & Treas. Harold Leinwand.

NORTHWEST INDIANA

THE JEWISH FEDERATION, INC. (1941; reorg. 1959); 2939 Jewett St., Highland (46322); (219)972–2250. FAX: (219)972–4779. Pres. Jerome Gardberg; Exec. Dir. Marty Erann.

SOUTH BEND

JEWISH FEDERATION OF ST. JOSEPH VAL-LEY (1946); 105 Jefferson Centre, Suite 804

(46601); (219)233–1164. FAX: (219)288–4103. Pres. Dr. William Gitlin; Exec. V.-Pres. Kimball Marsh.

IOWA

DES MOINES

JEWISH FEDERATION OF GREATER DES MOINES (1914); 910 Polk Blvd. (50312); (515)277–6321. FAX: (515)277–4069. Pres. Harry Bookey; Exec. Dir. Elaine Steinger.

SIOUX CITY

JEWISH FEDERATION (1921); 525 14th St. (51105); (712)258–0618. Pres. Michael Potash; Exec. Dir. Doris Rosenthal.

KANSAS

WICHITA

MID-KANSAS JEWISH FEDERATION, INC. (1935); 400 N. Woodlawn, Suite 8 (67208); (316)686–4741. Pres. Ivonne Goldstein; Exec. Dir. Beverly Jacobson.

KENTUCKY

LEXINGTON

CENTRAL KENTUCKY JEWISH FEDERATION (1976); 333 Waller, Suite 5 (40504); (606)-252–7622. Pres. Michael Ades; Exec. Dir. Howard Ross.

LOUISVILLE

JEWISH COMMUNITY FEDERATION OF LOUISVILLE, INC. (1934); 3630 Dutchman's Lane (40205); (502)451–8840. FAX: (502)-458–0702. Pres. Ronald W. Abrams; Exec. Dir. Dr. Alan S. Engel.

LOUISIANA

ALEXANDRIA

THE JEWISH WELFARE FEDERATION AND COMMUNITY COUNCIL OF CENTRAL LOUISIANA (1938); 1227 Southhampton (71303); (318)445–4785. Pres. Alvin Mykoff; Sec.-Treas. Roeve Weill.

BATON ROUGE

JEWISH FEDERATION OF GREATER BATON ROUGE (1971); 11744 Haymarket Ave., Suite B; PO Box 80827 (70898); (504) 291–5895. Pres. Dr. Steven Cavalier; Exec. Dir. Louis Goldman.

NEW ORLEANS

JEWISH FEDERATION OF GREATER NEW ORLEANS (1913; reorg. 1977); 1539 Jackson Ave. (70130); (504)525–0673. FAX: (504)-568–9290. Pres. Alan Rosenbloom; Exec. Dir. Jane Buchsbaum.

SHREVEPORT

SHREVEPORT JEWISH FEDERATION (1941; inc. 1967); 2032 Line Ave. (71104); (318)-221–4129. Pres. William Braunig, Jr.; Exec. Dir. Monty Pomm.

MAINE

LEWISTON-AUBURN

LEWISTON-AUBURN JEWISH FEDERATION (1947); 74 Bradman St., Auburn (04210); (207)786–4201. Pres. Scott Nussinow.

PORTLAND

JEWISH FEDERATION COMMUNITY COUNCIL OF SOUTHERN MAINE (1942); 57 Ashmont St. (04103); (207)773–7254. FAX: (207)761–2406. Pres. Lisa Cohen; Exec. Dir. Meyer Bodoff.

MARYLAND

BALTIMORE

THE ASSOCIATED: JEWISH COMMUNITY FEDERATION OF BALTIMORE (1920; reorg. 1969); 101 W. Mt. Royal Ave. (21201); (301) 727–4828. FAX: (301)783–8991. Chmn. Suzanne F. Cohen; Pres. Darrell D. Friedman.

MASSACHUSETTS

BERKSHIRE COUNTY

JEWISH FEDERATION OF THE BERKSHIRES (1940); 235 East St., Pittsfield (01201); (413)-442–4360. FAX: (413)443–6070. Pres. Joel Greenberg; Exec. Dir. Richard Davis.

BOSTON

COMBINED JEWISH PHILANTHROPIES OF GREATER BOSTON, INC. (1895; inc. 1961); One Lincoln Plaza (02111); (617)330–9500. FAX: (617)330–5197. Chmn. Alan R. Goldstein; Exec. V.-Pres. Barry Shrage.

CAPE COD

JEWISH FEDERATION OF CAPE COD; 396 Main St., PO Box 2568, Hyannis (02601); (508)778–5588. Pres. Rachelle L. Spector.

FRAMINGHAM (Merged with Boston)

LEOMINSTER

LEOMINSTER JEWISH COMMUNITY COUNCIL, INC. (1939); 268 Washington St. (01453); (617)534–6121. Pres. Dr. Milton Kline; Sec.-Treas. Howard J. Rome.

MERRIMACK VALLEY

MERRIMACK VALLEY UNITED JEWISH COMMUNITIES (Serves Lowell, Lawrence, Andover, Haverhill, Newburyport, and 22 surrounding communities) (1988); 805 Turnpike St., N. Andover (01845); (508)688–0466. FAX: (508)682–3041. Pres. Larry Cowan; Exec. Dir. Howard Flagler.

NEW BEDFORD

JEWISH FEDERATION OF GREATER NEW BEDFORD, INC. (1938; inc. 1954); 467 Hawthorn St., N. Dartmouth (02747); (508)997–7471. FAX: (508)997–7730. Pres. Elliot Rosenfield; Exec. Dir. Will Herrup.

NORTH SHORE

JEWISH FEDERATION OF THE NORTH SHORE, INC. (1938); 4 Community Rd., Marblehead (01945); (617)598–1810. FAX: (617)639–1284. Pres. Linda Lerner; Exec. Dir. Bruce Yudewitz.

SPRINGFIELD

JEWISH FEDERATION OF GREATER SPRINGFIELD, INC. (1925); 1160 Dickinson St. (01108); (413)737–4313. FAX: (413)737–4348. Pres. Diane Troderman; Exec. Dir. Joel Weiss.

WORCESTER

WORCESTER JEWISH FEDERATION, INC. (1947; inc. 1957); 633 Salisbury St. (01609); (508)756–1543. FAX: (508)798- 0962. Pres. Michael Sleeper.

MICHIGAN

ANN ARBOR

JEWISH COMMUNITY ASSOCIATION/ UNITED JEWISH APPEAL (1986); 2939 Birch Hollow Dr. (48108). (313)677–0100. Pres. Dr. Owen Z. Perlman; Interim Dir. Nancy N. Margolis.

DETROIT

JEWISH WELFARE FEDERATION OF DETROIT (1899); 6735 Telegraph Rd., Suite 30, PO Box 2030, Bloomfield Hills (48303–2030); (313)642–4260. FAX: (313)642–4985 (executive offices); (313)642–4941 (all other departments). Pres. David K. Page; Exec. V.-Pres. Robert P. Aronson.

FLINT

FLINT JEWISH FEDERATION (1936); 619 Wallenberg St. (48502); (313)767–5922. FAX: (313)767–9024. Pres. Nancy Hanflik; Exec. Dir. David Nussbaum.

GRAND RAPIDS

JEWISH COMMUNITY FUND OF GRAND RAPIDS (1930); 2609 Berwyck SE (49506); (616)956–9365. Pres. Joseph N. Schwartz; Admin. Dir. Judy Joseph.

MINNESOTA

DULUTH–SUPERIOR

JEWISH FEDERATION & COMMUNITY COUNCIL (1937); 1602 E. Second St. (55812); (218)724–8857. Pres. David Blustin; Sec. Admin. Gloria Vitullo.

MINNEAPOLIS

MINNEAPOLIS FEDERATION FOR JEWISH SERVICE (1929; inc. 1930); 7600 Wayzata Blvd. (55426); (612)593–2600. FAX: (612)593–2544. Pres. Robert Barrows; Exec. Dir. Max L. Kleinman.

ST. PAUL

UNITED JEWISH FUND AND COUNCIL (1935); 790 S. Cleveland, Suite 201 (55116); (612)690–1707. FAX: (612)690–0228. Pres. Allen Freeman; Exec. Dir. Sam Asher.

MISSISSIPPI

JACKSON

JACKSON JEWISH WELFARE FUND, INC. (1945); 5315 Old Canton Rd. (39211–4625); (601)956–6215. Pres. Ruth Friedman; V. Pres. Erik Hearon.

MISSOURI

KANSAS CITY

JEWISH FEDERATION OF GREATER KANSAS CITY (1933); 5801 W. 115th St., Overland Park, KS (66211–1824); (913)469–1340. FAX: (913)451–9358. Pres. Ronald Goldsmith; Exec. Dir. A. Robert Gast.

ST. JOSEPH

UNITED JEWISH FUND OF ST. JOSEPH (1915); 509 Woodcrest Dr. (64506); (816)279–7154. Pres. Dorathea Polsky; Exec. Sec. Martha Rothstein.

ST. LOUIS

JEWISH FEDERATION OF ST. LOUIS (incl. St. Louis County) (1901); 12 Millstone Campus Dr. (63146); (314)432–0020. FAX: (314)432–1277. Pres. Alyn V. Essman; Exec. V. Pres. Ira Steinmetz.

NEBRASKA

LINCOLN

LINCOLN JEWISH WELFARE FEDERATION, INC. (1931; inc. 1961); PO Box 67218 (68506); (402)488–9562. Pres. Steven Seglin; Exec. Dir. Robert Pitlor.

OMAHA

JEWISH FEDERATION OF OMAHA (1903); 333 S. 132nd St. (68154–2198); (402)334–

8200. FAX: (402)334–1330. Pres. Jay R. Lerner; Exec. Dir. Howard Bloom.

NEVADA

LAS VEGAS

JEWISH FEDERATION OF LAS VEGAS (1973); 3909 S. Maryland Parkway, Suite 400 (89119); (702)732–0556. FAX: (702)732–3228. Pres. Dr. Marvin M. Perer; Interim Exec. Dir. Jerry Countess.

NEW HAMPSHIRE

MANCHESTER

JEWISH FEDERATION OF GREATER MANCHESTER (1974); 698 Beech St. (03104); (603)627–7679. Pres. Dr. David Stahl; Exec. Dir. Mark Silverberg.

NEW JERSEY

ATLANTIC COUNTY

FEDERATION OF JEWISH AGENCIES OF ATLANTIC COUNTY (1924); 505–507 Tilton Rd., Northfield (08225); (609)646–7077. FAX: (609)646–8053. Pres. Howard A. Goldberg; Exec. Dir. Bernard Cohen.

BERGEN COUNTY

UNITED JEWISH COMMUNITY OF BERGEN COUNTY (inc. 1978); 111 Kinderkamack Rd., PO Box 4176, N. Hackensack Station, River Edge (07661); (201)488–6800. FAX: (201)488–1507. Pres. Irwin Marks; Exec. V.-Pres. James Young.

CENTRAL NEW JERSEY

JEWISH FEDERATION OF CENTRAL NEW JERSEY (1940; merged 1973); Green Lane, Union (07083); (201)351–5060. FAX: (201)351–7060. Pres. Murray Pantirer; Exec. V. Pres. Burton Lazarow.

CLIFTON–PASSAIC

JEWISH FEDERATION OF GREATER CLIFTON-PASSAIC (1933); 199 Scoles Ave., Clifton (07012). (201)777–7031. FAX: (201)777–6701. Pres. Jon Gurkoff; Exec. Dir. Yosef Muskin.

CUMBERLAND COUNTY

JEWISH FEDERATION OF CUMBERLAND COUNTY (inc. 1971); 629 Wood St., Suite 204, Vineland (08360); (609)696–4445. Pres. Stanley Orlinsky; Exec. Dir. Daniel Lepow.

ENGLEWOOD

(Merged with Bergen County)

MERCER COUNTY

JEWISH FEDERATION OF MERCER COUNTY (1929; reorg. 1982); 999 Lower Ferry Rd., Trenton (08628); (609)883–5000. FAX: (609)883–2563. Pres. Richard Dickson; Exec. Dir. Haim Morag.

METROWEST NEW JERSEY

UNITED JEWISH FEDERATION OF METROWEST (1923); 60 Glenwood Ave., E. Orange (07017); (201)673–6800; (212)943–0570. FAX: (201)673–4387. Pres. Jerome Waldor; Exec. V.-Pres. Howard E. Charish.

MIDDLESEX COUNTY

JEWISH FEDERATION OF GREATER MIDDLESEX COUNTY (org. 1948; reorg. 1985); 100 Metroplex Dr., Suite 101, Edison (08817); (201)985–1234. FAX: (201)985–3295. Pres. James Stahl; Exec. V.-Pres. Michael Shapiro.

MONMOUTH COUNTY

JEWISH FEDERATION OF GREATER MONMOUTH COUNTY (1971); 100 Grant Ave., PO Box 210, Deal (07723–0210); (201)531–6200–1. FAX: (201)531–9518. Pres. Arnold Gelfman; Exec. V.-Pres. Marvin Relkin; Exec. Dir. Bonnie Komito.

MORRIS–SUSSEX COUNTY

(Merged with MetroWest NJ)

NORTH JERSEY

JEWISH FEDERATION OF NORTH JERSEY (1933); One Pike Dr., Wayne (07470); (201)595–0555. FAX: (201)595–1532. Pres. Joanne Sprechman; Exec. Dir. Barry Rosenberg.

NORTHERN MIDDLESEX COUNTY

(See Middlesex County)

OCEAN COUNTY

OCEAN COUNTY JEWISH FEDERATION (1977); 301 Madison Ave., Lakewood (08701); (201)363–0530. FAX: (201)363–2097. Pres. Zev Rosen; Exec. Dir. Michael Ruvel.

PRINCETON

PRINCETON AREA UJA–FEDERATION; 15 Roszel Rd., Princeton (08540); (609)243–9440. Pres. Dr. Eliot Freeman; Exec. Dir. Jerilyn Zimmerman.

RARITAN VALLEY

(See Middlesex County)

SOMERSET COUNTY

JEWISH FEDERATION OF SOMERSET, HUNTERDON & WARREN COUNTIES (1960); PO Box 6455, Bridgewater (08807); (201)725–6994. FAX: (908)725–9753. Pres. George Blank; Exec. Dir. Alan J. Nydick.

SOUTHERN NEW JERSEY

JEWISH FEDERATION OF SOUTHERN NEW JERSEY (incl. Camden, Burlington, and Gloucester counties) (1922); 2393 W. Marlton Pike, Cherry Hill (08002); (609)665-6100. FAX: (609)665-0074. Pres. Harvey N. Shapiro; Exec. V.-Pres. Stuart Alperin.

NEW MEXICO

ALBUQUERQUE

JEWISH FEDERATION OF GREATER ALBUQUERQUE, INC. (1938); 8205 Spain, NE (97109); (505)821-3214. FAX: (505)821-3355. Pres. Brian Ivener; Exec. Dir. Joel Brooks.

NEW YORK

ALBANY

(Merged with Schenectady; see Northeastern New York)

BROOME COUNTY

JEWISH FEDERATION OF BROOME COUNTY (1937; inc. 1958); 500 Clubhouse Rd., Vestal (13850); (607)724-2332. FAX: (607)724-2311. Pres. Marcelene H. Yonaty; Exec. Dir. Victoria Rouff.

BUFFALO

JEWISH FEDERATION OF GREATER BUFFALO, INC. (1903); 787 Delaware Ave. (14209); (716)886-7750. FAX: (716)886-1367. Pres. Dr. Richard Ament; Exec. Dir. Harry Kosansky.

DUTCHESS COUNTY

JEWISH FEDERATION OF DUTCHESS COUNTY; 110 S. Grand Ave., Poughkeepsie (12603); (914)471-9811. Pres. Marc Ritter; Exec. Dir. Allan Greene.

ELMIRA

ELMIRA JEWISH WELFARE FUND, INC. (1942); Grandview Rd. Ext., PO Box 3087 (14905); (607)734-8122. Pres. Arnold Rosenberg; Exec. Dir. Cy Leveen.

KINGSTON

JEWISH FEDERATION OF GREATER KINGSTON, INC. (inc. 1951); 159 Green St. (12401); (914)338-8131. Pres. Dr. Howard Rothstein.

NEW YORK

UJA–FEDERATION OF JEWISH PHILANTHROPIES OF NEW YORK, INC. (incl. Greater NY; Westchester, Nassau, and Suffolk counties) (Fed. org. 1917; UJA 1939; merged 1986); 130 E. 59th St. (10022); (212)980-1000. FAX: (212)867-1074. Pres. Alan S. Jaffe; Chmn. Irwin Hochberg; Exec. V.-Pres. Stephen D. Solender.

NIAGARA FALLS

JEWISH FEDERATION OF NIAGARA FALLS, NY, INC. (1935); Temple Beth Israel, Rm. #5, College & Madison Aves. (14305); (716)284-4575. Pres. Howard Rushner.

NORTHEASTERN NEW YORK

UNITED JEWISH FEDERATION OF NORTHEASTERN NEW YORK (1986); Latham Circle Mall, 800 New Loudon Rd., Latham (12110); (518)783-7800. FAX: (518)783-1557. Pres. Rabbi Martin Silverman; Exec. Dir. Norman J. Schimelman.

ORANGE COUNTY

JEWISH FEDERATION OF GREATER ORANGE COUNTY (1977); 360 Powell Ave., Newburgh (12550); (914)562-7860. Pres. Richard Levin; Exec. Dir. Debrah Borsky.

ROCHESTER

JEWISH COMMUNITY FEDERATION OF ROCHESTER, NY, INC. (1939); 441 East Ave. (14607); (716)461-0490. FAX: (716)461-0912. Pres. Linda Cornell Weinstein; Exec. Dir. Lawrence W. Fine.

ROCKLAND COUNTY

UNITED JEWISH COMMUNITY OF ROCKLAND COUNTY (1985); 240 W. Nyack Rd., W. Nyack (10994-1711). (914)627-3700. FAX: (914)627-7881. Pres. Mark Karsch; Acting Exec. Dir. Neal Potash.

SCHENECTADY

(Merged with Albany; see Northeastern New York)

SYRACUSE

SYRACUSE JEWISH FEDERATION, INC. (1918); 101 Smith St.; PO Box 510, DeWitt (13214-0510); (315)445-0161. FAX: (315)-445-1559. Pres. Philip Pinsky; Exec. V.-Pres. Barry Silverberg.

TROY

(Merged with Albany-Schenectady; see Northeastern New York)

UTICA

JEWISH FEDERATION OF UTICA, NY, INC. (1933; inc. 1950); 2310 Oneida St. (13501); (315)733-2343. Pres. Marsha Basloe; Exec. Dir. Meyer L. Bodoff.

NORTH CAROLINA

ASHEVILLE

WESTERN NORTH CAROLINA JEWISH FEDERATION (1935); 236 Charlotte St. (28801);

(704)253–0701. FAX: (704)251–9144. Pres. Robert J. Deutsch; Exec. Dir. Marlene Breger-Joyce.

CHARLOTTE

CHARLOTTE JEWISH FEDERATION (1938); PO Box 13369 (28211); (704)366–5007. FAX: (704)365–4507. Pres. Emily Zimmern; Exec. Dir. Daniel Lepow.

DURHAM–CHAPEL HILL

DURHAM–CHAPEL HILL JEWISH FEDERATION & COMMUNITY COUNCIL (1979); 1310 LeClair St., Chapel Hill (27514); (919)967–1945. Pres. Barry Nakell.

GREENSBORO

GREENSBORO JEWISH FEDERATION (1940); 713-A N. Greene St. (27401); (919)272–3189. FAX: (919)272–0214. Pres. Joslin LeBauer; Exec. Dir. Marilyn Chandler.

WAKE COUNTY

WAKE COUNTY JEWISH FEDERATION, INC. (1987); 3900 Merton Dr., Suite 108, Raleigh (27609); (919)781–5459. FAX: (919)787–0666. Pres. Joseph Woodland.

OHIO

AKRON

AKRON JEWISH COMMUNITY FEDERATION (1935); 750 White Pond Dr. (44320); (216)-867–7850. FAX: (216)867–8498. Pres. Dr. Steven Kutnick; Exec. Dir. Michael Wise.

CANTON

CANTON JEWISH COMMUNITY FEDERATION (1935; reorg. 1955); 2631 Harvard Ave., NW (44709); (216)452–6444. FAX: (216)-452–4487. Pres. Robert Narens.

CINCINNATI

JEWISH FEDERATION OF CINCINNATI (1896; reorg. 1967); 1811 Losantiville, Suite 320 (45237); (513) 351–3800. FAX: (513)351–3863. Pres. Stanley M. Chesley; Exec. V.Pres. Aubrey Herman.

CLEVELAND

JEWISH COMMUNITY FEDERATION OF CLEVELAND (1903); 1750 Euclid Ave. (44115); (216)566–9200. FAX: (216)861–1230. Pres. Bennett Yanowitz; Exec. Dir. Stephen H. Hoffman.

COLUMBUS

COLUMBUS JEWISH FEDERATION (1926); 1175 College Ave. (43209); (614)237–7686. FAX: (614)237–2221. Pres. Edwin M. Ellman; Exec. Dir. Alan H. Gill.

DAYTON

JEWISH FEDERATION OF GREATER DAYTON (1910); 4501 Denlinger Rd. (45426); (513)854–4150. FAX: (513)854–2850. Pres. Lawrence T. Burick; Exec. V.-Pres. Peter H. Wells.

STEUBENVILLE

JEWISH COMMUNITY COUNCIL (1938); 300 Lovers Lane (43952); (614)264–5514. Pres. Morris Denmark; Exec. Sec. Jennie Bernstein.

TOLEDO

JEWISH FEDERATION OF GREATER TOLEDO (1907; reorg. 1960); 6505 Sylvania Ave., PO Box 587, Sylvania (43560); (419)885–4461. FAX: (419)885–3207. Pres. James J. Akers; Exec. Dir. Steven J. Edelstein.

YOUNGSTOWN

YOUNGSTOWN AREA JEWISH FEDERATION (1935); PO Box 449, 505 Gypsy Lane (44501); (216)746–3251. FAX: (216)746–7926. Pres. Esther L. Marks; Exec. V.-Pres. Sam Kooperman.

OKLAHOMA

OKLAHOMA CITY

JEWISH FEDERATION OF GREATER OKLAHOMA CITY (1941); 2800 Quail Plaza Dr. (73120). (405)752–7307. FAX: (405)752–7309. Pres. Louis Price.

TULSA

JEWISH FEDERATION OF TULSA (1938); 2021 E. 71st St. (74136); (918)495–1100. FAX: (918)495–1220. Pres. Curtis S. Green; Exec. Dir. David Bernstein.

OREGON

PORTLAND

JEWISH FEDERATION OF PORTLAND (incl. state of Oregon and adjacent Washington communities) (1920; reorg. 1956); 6651 SW Capitol Highway (97219); (503)245–6219. FAX: (503)245–6603. Pres. Stanley D. Geffen; Exec. Dir. Charles Schiffman.

PENNSYLVANIA

ALLENTOWN

JEWISH FEDERATION OF THE LEHIGH VALLEY (SERVING ALLENTOWN, BETHLEHEM AND EASTON) (1948); 702 N. 22nd St. (18104); (215)821–5500. FAX: (215)821–8946. Pres. Lory L. Brenner; Exec. Dir. Ivan C. Schonfeld.

ALTOONA

FEDERATION OF JEWISH PHILANTHROPIES (1920; reorg. 1940; inc. 1944); 1308 17th St. (16601); (814)944-4072. Pres. Morley Cohn.

BUCKS COUNTY

(See Jewish Federation of Mercer County, New Jersey)

ERIE

JEWISH COMMUNITY COUNCIL OF ERIE (1946); 701 G. Daniel Baldwin Bldg., 1001 State St. (16501); (814)455-4474. Pres. Richard Levick.

HARRISBURG

UNITED JEWISH COMMUNITY OF GREATER HARRISBURG (1941); 100 Vaughn St. (17110); (717)236-9555. FAX: (717)236-8104. Pres. Jerry Zucker; Exec. Dir. Jordan Harburger.

JOHNSTOWN

UNITED JEWISH FEDERATION OF JOHNSTOWN (1938); 601 Wayne St. (15905); (814)-539-9891 (home). Pres. Isadore Suchman.

PHILADELPHIA

JEWISH FEDERATION OF GREATER PHILADELPHIA (includes Bucks, Chester, Delaware, Montgomery, and Philadelphia counties) (1901; reorg. 1956); 226 S. 16th St. (19102); (215)893-5600. FAX: (215)735-7977. Pres. Theodore Seidenberg; Exec. V. Pres. Don Cooper.

PITTSBURGH

UNITED JEWISH FEDERATION OF GREATER PITTSBURGH (1912; reorg. 1955); 234 McKee Pl. (15213); (412)681-8000. FAX: (412)681-3980. Pres. David S. Shapira; Exec. V.-Pres. Howard M. Rieger.

READING

JEWISH FEDERATION OF READING, PA., INC. (1935; reorg. 1972); 1700 City Line St. (19604); (215)921-2766. FAX: (215)929-0886. Pres. Alma Lakin; Exec. Dir. Daniel Tannenbaum.

SCRANTON

SCRANTON-LACKAWANNA JEWISH FEDERATION (incl. Lackawanna County) (1945); 601 Jefferson Ave. (18510); (717)961-2300. FAX: (717)346-6147. Pres. Irwin Schneider; Exec. Dir. Seymour Brotman.

RHODE ISLAND

PROVIDENCE

JEWISH FEDERATION OF RHODE ISLAND (1945); 130 Sessions St. (02906); (401)421-4111. FAX: (401)331-7961. Pres. David M. Hirsch; Exec. V.-Pres. Steve Rakitt.

SOUTH CAROLINA

CHARLESTON

CHARLESTON JEWISH FEDERATION (1949); 1645 Raoul Wallenberg Blvd., PO Box 31298 (29407); (803)571-6565. FAX: (803)556-6206. Pres. Jerry Zucker; Exec. Dir. Michael Abidor.

COLUMBIA

COLUMBIA JEWISH FEDERATION (1960); 4540 Trenholm Rd., PO Box 6968 (29260); (803)787-0580. FAX: (803)787-0475. Pres. Alan Kahn; Exec. Dir. Alexander Grossberg.

GREENVILLE

FEDERATED JEWISH CHARITIES OF GREENVILLE, INC.; PO Box 17615 (29606); (803)-244-1261. Pres. Dr. Steven J. Gold.

SOUTH DAKOTA

SIOUX FALLS

JEWISH WELFARE FUND (1938); National Reserve Bldg., 513 S. Main Ave. (57102); (605)336-2880. Pres. Laurence Bierman; Exec. Sec. Louis R. Hurwitz.

TENNESSEE

CHATTANOOGA

CHATTANOOGA JEWISH FEDERATION (1931); 5326 Lynnland Terrace, PO Box 8947 (37411); (615)894-1317. FAX: (615)894-1319. Pres. Pris Siskin; Exec. Dir. Louis B. Solomon.

KNOXVILLE

KNOXVILLE JEWISH FEDERATION (1939); 6800 Deane Hill Dr., PO Box 10882 (37939-0882); (615)693-5837. Pres. Barbara Bernstein; Exec. Dir. Conrad J. Koller.

MEMPHIS

MEMPHIS JEWISH FEDERATION (incl. Shelby County) (1935); 6560 Poplar Ave. (38138-3614); (901)767-7100. FAX: (901)-767-7128. Pres. Jerome Makowsky; Exec. Dir. Gary Siepser.

NASHVILLE

JEWISH FEDERATION OF NASHVILLE & MIDDLE TENNESSEE (1936); 801 Percy Warner Blvd. (37205); (615)356-3242. FAX: (615)352-0056. Pres. Carolyn Levine; Act. Exec. Dir. Ruth Tanner.

TEXAS

AUSTIN

JEWISH FEDERATION OF AUSTIN (1939; reorg. 1956); 11713 Jollyville Rd. (78759);

(512)331–1144. FAX: (512)331–7059. Pres. Rafael Pelc; Exec. Dir. Wayne Silverman.

DALLAS

JEWISH FEDERATION OF GREATER DALLAS (1911); 7800 Northaven Rd., Suite A (75230); (214)369–3313. FAX: (214)369–8943. Pres. Andrea Statman; Exec. Dir. Avrum I. Cohen.

EL PASO

JEWISH FEDERATION OF EL PASO, INC. (incl. surrounding communities) (1937); 405 Wallenberg Dr., PO Box 12097 (79913–0097); (915)584–4437. FAX: (915)584–0243. Pres. Joan Johnson; Exec. Dir. David Brown.

FORT WORTH

JEWISH FEDERATION OF FORT WORTH AND TARRANT COUNTY (1936); 6801 Dan Danciger Rd. (76133); (817)292–3081. FAX: (817)292–3214. Pres. Rowena Kimmell; Exec. Dir. Bruce Schlosberg.

GALVESTON

GALVESTON COUNTY JEWISH WELFARE ASSOCIATION (1936); PO Box 146 (77553); (409)763–5241. Pres. Harold Levine; Treas. Joe Nussenblatt.

HOUSTON

JEWISH FEDERATION OF GREATER HOUSTON (1936); 5603 S. Braeswood Blvd. (77096–3999); (713)729–7000. FAX: (713)-721–6232. Pres. Buster Feldman; Exec. Dir. Hans Mayer.

SAN ANTONIO

JEWISH FEDERATION OF SAN ANTONIO (incl. Bexar County) (1922); 8434 Ahern Dr. (78216); (210)341–8234. FAX: (210)341–2842. Pres. Sterling Neuman; Exec. Dir. Stan Ramati.

WACO

JEWISH FEDERATION OF WACO AND CENTRAL TEXAS (1949); PO Box 8031 (76714–8031); (817)776–3740. Pres. Mike Stupak; Exec. Sec. Martha Bauer.

UTAH

SALT LAKE CITY

UNITED JEWISH COUNCIL AND SALT LAKE JEWISH WELFARE FUND (1936); 2416 E. 1700 South (84108); (801)581–0098. Pres. Fred Tannenbaum; Exec. Dir. Roberta Grunauer.

VIRGINIA

NEWPORT NEWS–HAMPTON–WILLIAMSBURG

UNITED JEWISH COMMUNITY OF THE VIRGINIA PENINSULA, INC. (1942); 2700 Spring Rd., Newport News (23606); (804)930–1422. FAX: (804)872–9532. Pres. Joanne Roos; Exec. Dir. Barbara T. Gordon.

RICHMOND

JEWISH COMMUNITY FEDERATION OF RICHMOND (1935); 5403 Monument Ave., PO Box 17128 (23226); (804)288–0045. FAX: (804)282–7507. Pres. Helen P. Horwitz; Exec. Dir. Robert S. Hyman.

TIDEWATER

UNITED JEWISH FEDERATION OF TIDEWATER (incl. Norfolk, Portsmouth, and Virginia Beach) (1937); 7300 Newport Ave., PO Box 9776, Norfolk (23505); (804)489–8040. FAX: (804)489–8230. Pres. Dr. Charles J. Goldman; Exec. V.-Pres. Gary N. Rubin.

WASHINGTON

SEATTLE

JEWISH FEDERATION OF GREATER SEATTLE (incl. King County, Everett, and Bremerton) (1926); 2031 Third Ave. (98121); (206)443–5400. FAX: (206)443–0303. Pres. Herbert Pruzan; Exec. Dir. Michael Novick.

WEST VIRGINIA

CHARLESTON

FEDERATED JEWISH CHARITIES OF CHARLESTON, INC. (1937); PO Box 1613 (25326); (304)346–7500. Pres. Carl Lehman; Exec. Sec. William H. Thalheimer.

WISCONSIN

KENOSHA

KENOSHA JEWISH WELFARE FUND (1938); 8041 48th Ave. (53142); (414)694–6695. Pres. Richard Selsberg; Sec.-Treas. Steven Barasch.

MADISON

MADISON JEWISH COMMUNITY COUNCIL, INC. (1940); 310 N. Midvale Blvd., Suite 325 (53705); (608)231–3426. Pres. Judith Schreiber; Exec. Dir. Steven H. Morrison.

MILWAUKEE

MILWAUKEE JEWISH FEDERATION, INC. (1902); 1360 N. Prospect Ave. (53202); (414)-271–8338. Pres. Joseph M. Bernstein; Exec. Dir. Rick Meyer.

CANADA

ALBERTA

CALGARY

CALGARY JEWISH COMMUNITY COUNCIL (1962); 1607 90th Ave. SW (T2V 4V7); (403)-253–8600. FAX: (403)253–7915. Pres. Robert Kalef; Exec. Dir. Drew J. Staffenberg.

EDMONTON

JEWISH FEDERATION OF EDMONTON (1954; reorg. 1982); 7200 156th St. (T5R 1X3); (403)487–5120. FAX: (403)481–3463. Pres. Michael Goldstein; Exec. Dir. Sidney Indig.

BRITISH COLUMBIA

VANCOUVER

JEWISH FEDERATION OF GREATER VANCOUVER (1932; reorg. 1987); 950 W. 41st Ave. (V5Z 2N7); (604)266–7115. FAX: (604)266–8371. Pres. Ted Zacks; Exec. Dir. Drew Staffenberg.

MANITOBA

WINNIPEG

WINNIPEG JEWISH COMMUNITY COUNCIL (1938; reorg. 1973); 370 Hargrave St. (R3B 2K1); (204)943–0406. FAX: (204)956–0609. Pres. Mel Fages; Exec. Dir. Robert Freedman.

ONTARIO

HAMILTON

JEWISH FEDERATION OF HAMILTON, WENTWORTH & AREA (1932; merged 1971); PO Box 7258, 1030 Lower Lion Club Rd.,

Ancaster (L9G 3N6); (416)648–0605. FAX: (416)648–8388. Pres. Gerald Swaye Q.C.; Exec. Dir. Claire Mandel.

LONDON

LONDON JEWISH FEDERATION (1932); 536 Huron St. (N5Y 4J5); (519)673–3310. FAX: (519)673–1161. Pres. Robert Siskind; Exec. Dir. Gerald Enchin.

OTTAWA

JEWISH COMMUNITY COUNCIL OF OTTAWA (1934); 151 Chapel St. (K1N 7Y2); (613)232–7306. FAX: (613)563–4593. Pres. Dr. Eli Rabin; Exec. Dir. Gerry Koffman.

TORONTO

JEWISH FEDERATION OF GREATER TORONTO (1917); 4600 Bathurst St.; Willowdale (M2R 3V2); (416)635–2883. FAX: (416)635–1408. Pres. Charles S. Diamond; Exec. Dir. Allan Reitzes.

WINDSOR

JEWISH COMMUNITY COUNCIL (1938); 1641 Ouellette Ave. (N8X 1R9); (519)973–1772. FAX: (519)973–1774. Pres. Harriet Whiteman; Exec. Dir. Allen Juris.

QUEBEC

MONTREAL

ALLIED JEWISH COMMUNITY SERVICES (1965); 5151 Cote Ste. Catherine Rd. (H3W 1M6); (514)735–3541. FAX: (514)735–8972. Pres. Harvey Wolfe; Exec. Dir. Steven Drysdale.

Jewish Periodicals[1]

UNITED STATES

ALABAMA

SOUTHERN SHOFAR (1990). PO Box 130052, Birmingham, 35213. (205) 879–1191. Lawrence M. Brook. Monthly.

ARIZONA

ARIZONA JEWISH POST (1946). 3812 East River Road, Tucson, 85718. (602)529–1500. FAX: (602)577–0734. Sandra R. Heiman. Fortnightly. Jewish Federation of Southern Arizona.

GREATER PHOENIX JEWISH NEWS (1947). PO Box 26590, Phoenix, 85068. (602)870–9470. FAX: (602)870–0426. Flo Eckstein. Weekly.

CALIFORNIA

B'NAI B'RITH MESSENGER (1897). PO Box 35915, Los Angeles, 90035. (310)659–2952. Rabbi Yale Butler. Weekly.

HADSHOT L.A. (1988). 13535 Ventura Blvd., Suite 200, Sherman Oaks, 91423. (818)-783–3090. Meir Doron. Weekly. Hebrew.

HERITAGE-SOUTHWEST JEWISH PRESS (1914). 2130 S. Vermont Ave., Los Angeles, 90007. (213) 737–2122. Dan Brin. Weekly. (Also SAN DIEGO JEWISH HERITAGE, weekly; ORANGE COUNTY JEWISH HERITAGE, weekly; CENTRAL CALIFORNIA JEWISH HERITAGE, monthly.) Heritage Group.

JEWISH BULLETIN OF NORTHERN CALIFORNIA (1946). 88 First St., Suite 300, San Francisco, 94105. (415)957–9340. FAX: (415)957–0266. Marc S. Klein. Weekly. San Francisco Jewish Community Publications Inc.

JEWISH JOURNAL OF GREATER LOS ANGELES (1986). 3660 Wilshire Blvd., Suite 204, Los Angeles, 90010. (213)738–7778. FAX: (213)386–9501. Gene Lichtenstein. Weekly.

JEWISH NEWS & ISRAEL TODAY (1973). 11071 Ventura Blvd., Studio City, 91604. (818)786–4000. Phil Blazer. Monthly.

JEWISH SPECTATOR (1935). 4391 Park Milano, Calabasas, 91302. (818)591–7481. FAX: (818)591–7267. Robert Bleiweiss. Quarterly. American Friends of Center for Jewish Living and Values.

NORTHERN CALIFORNIA JEWISH BULLETIN See JEWISH BULLETIN OF NORTHERN CALIFORNIA

JEWISH STAR (1956). 109 Minna St., Suite 323, San Francisco, 94105–3728. (415)-243–4323. FAX: (415)243–0826. Nevon Stuckey. Bimonthly.

SAN DIEGO JEWISH TIMES (1979). 2592 Fletcher Pkwy., El Cajon, 92020. (619)-463–5515. Carol Rosenberg. Biweekly.

TIKKUN: A BIMONTHLY JEWISH CRITIQUE OF POLITICS, CULTURE & SOCIETY (1986). 5100 Leona St., Oakland, 94619. (415)-482–0805. FAX: (415)482–3379. Michael Lerner. Bimonthly. Institute for Labor & Mental Health.

WESTERN STATES JEWISH HISTORY (1968). 3111 Kelton Ave., Los Angeles, CA 90034. (310)475–1415. FAX: (310)475–2996. Prof. William M. Kramer. Quarterly. Western States Jewish History Association.

COLORADO

INTERMOUNTAIN JEWISH NEWS (1913). 1275 Sherman St., Suite 214, Denver,

---

[1]The information in this directory is based on replies to questionnaires circulated by the editors. For organization bulletins, see the directory of Jewish organizations.

80203. (303)861-2234. FAX: (303)832-6942. Exec. ed. Rabbi Hillel Goldberg; ed./pub. Miriam Goldberg. Weekly.

CONNECTICUT

CONNECTICUT JEWISH LEDGER (1929). 740 North Main St., West Hartford, 06117. (203)231-2424. FAX: (203)231-2428. Ed. Jonathan Tobin; exec. ed. Bertram J. Korn. Weekly. Jewish Media Group, Inc.

CONTEMPORARY JEWRY (1974 under the name JEWISH SOCIOLOGY AND SOCIAL RESEARCH). Connecticut College, New London. Jerry L. Winter. Annually. Association for the Social Scientific Study of Jewry.

JEWISH LEADER. 28 Channing St., PO Box 1468, New London, 06320. (203) 442-7395. FAX: (203) 442-8062. Sidney Schiller, mgr. Biweekly. Jewish Federation of Eastern Connecticut.

MITZVAH CONNECTION. PO Box 948, Avon, 06001. (203)675-7763. C. Dianne Zweig. Annually.

DELAWARE

JEWISH VOICE. 101 Garden of Eden Rd., Wilmington, 19803. (302) 478-6200. FAX: (302) 478-5374. Daniel Weintraub. Biweekly (monthly July/Aug.). Jewish Federation of Delaware.

DISTRICT OF COLUMBIA

B'NAI B'RITH INTERNATIONAL JEWISH MONTHLY (1886 under the name MENORAH). 1640 Rhode Island Ave., NW, Washington, 20036. (202)857-6645. Jeff Rubin. Bimonthly. B'nai B'rith.

JEWISH DEMOCRATIC ADVOCATE (1990). 711 Second St., NE, Suite 100, Washington, 20002. (202)544-7636. FAX: (202)-544-7645. Lewis Roth. Quarterly. National Jewish Democratic Council.

JEWISH VETERAN (1896). 1811 R St., NW, Washington, 20009. (202)265-6280. FAX: (202)234-5662. Albert Schlossberg. Five times a year. Jewish War Veterans of the U.S.A.

MOMENT (1975). 3000 Connecticut Ave., NW, Suite 300, Washington, 20008. (202)-387-8888. FAX: (202)483-3423. Hershel Shanks. Bimonthly. Jewish Educational Ventures, Inc.

MONITOR (1990). 1819 H Street, NW, Suite 230, Washington, 20006. (202)775-9770.

FAX: (202)775-9776. Kelly Anne Gallagher (Washington), Steven Sassaman (San Francisco). Weekly. Union of Councils for Soviet Jews.

NEAR EAST REPORT (1957). 440 First St., NW, Suite 607, Washington, 20001. (202)-639-5300. Dr. Raphael Danziger. Weekly. Near East Research, Inc.

SECURITY AFFAIRS (1978). 1717 K St., NW, Suite 300, Washington, 20006. (202)833-0020. FAX: (202)296-6452. Jim Colbert. Monthly. Jewish Institute for National Security Affairs.

WASHINGTON JEWISH WEEK. See under MARYLAND

FLORIDA

BROWARD JEWISH WORLD (1986). 2101 Corporate Blvd., Suite 315, Boca Raton, 33431. (407)997-9971. FAX: (407)997-2910. Wesley Goldstein. Weekly. Jewish Media Group, Inc.

THE CHRONICLE (1971). 580 S. McIntosh Rd., Sarasota, 34232. (813)371-4546. FAX: (813) 378-2947. Barry Millman. Fortnightly. Sarasota-Manatee Jewish Federation.

HERITAGE FLORIDA JEWISH NEWS. PO Box 3742, Fern Park, 32730. (407) 834-8787 or 834-8277. FAX: (407) 831-0507. Jeffrey Gaeser, pub.; Jill Hayflash, assoc. ed. Weekly.

JEWISH COMMUNITY ADVOCATE OF SOUTH BROWARD (1986). 2719 Hollywood Blvd., Hollywood, 33020. (305) 922-8603. FAX: (305) 921-6491. Amy Jacobson Boxer. Biweekly.

JEWISH JOURNAL (Palm Beach–Broward–Dade) (1977). 601 Fairway Dr., Deerfield Beach, 33441. (305)698-6397. FAX: (305)-429-1207. Andrew Polin. Weekly. South Florida Newspaper Network.

JEWISH PRESS OF PINELLAS COUNTY (Clearwater-St. Petersburg) (1985). 301 Jupiter Ave. S., Clearwater, 34615-6561. (813)-535-4400. FAX: (813)530-3039. Karen Wolfson Dawkins. Biweekly. Jewish Press Group of Tampa Bay (FL), Inc.

JEWISH PRESS OF TAMPA (1987). 2808 Horatio St., Tampa, 33609. (813)871-2332. FAX: (813)530-3039. Karen Wolfson Dawkins. Biweekly. Jewish Press Group of Tampa Bay (FL), Inc.

JEWISH WORLD (1982). 2101 Corporate Blvd., Suite 315, Boca Raton, 33431. (407)-833–8331. FAX: (407)659–5428. Wesley Goldstein. Weekly. Jewish Media Group, Inc.

MIAMI JEWISH TRIBUNE (1986). 3550 Biscayne Blvd., 3rd fl., Miami, 33137–3845. (305)576–9500. FAX: (305)573–9551. Bertram Korn, Jr. Weekly. Jewish Media Group, Inc.

NATIONAL JEWISH ADVOCATE (1924; formerly SOUTHERN JEWISH WEEKLY). 8301 Cypress Plaza Dr., Suite 124, Jacksonville, 32256. (904)281–0888. FAX: (904)281–0922. Lester N. Garripee. Semimonthly. First Coast Media Group.

GEORGIA

ATLANTA JEWISH TIMES (1925; formerly SOUTHERN ISRAELITE). 1575 Northside Dr., NW, Atlanta, 30318. (404)352–2400. FAX: (404)355–9388. Vida Goldgar. Weekly.

JEWISH CIVIC PRESS (1972). 3330 Peachtree Rd. NE, Suite 500, Atlanta, 30326. (404)-231–2194. Abner L. Tritt. Monthly.

ILLINOIS

CHICAGO JEWISH STAR (1991). PO Box 268, Skokie, 60076–0268. (708)674–7827. FAX: (708)674–0014. Douglas Wertheimer, ed.; Gila Wertheimer, assoc. ed. Fortnightly.

CHICAGO JUF NEWS (1972). One S. Franklin St., Rm. 722, Chicago, 60606. (312)-444–2853. FAX: (312)855–2474. Joseph Aaron. Monthly. Jewish United Fund/Jewish Federation of Metropolitan Chicago.

JEWISH COMMUNITY NEWS (1941). 6464 W. Main, Suite 7A, Belleville, 62223. (618)-398–6100. Steve Low. Every other month. Jewish Federation of Southern Illinois.

THE SENTINEL (1911). 150 N. Michigan Ave., Suite 3130, Chicago, 60601. (312)-407–0060. FAX: (312)407–0096. J.I. Fishbein. Weekly.

INDIANA

ILLIANA NEWS (1976). 2939 Jewett St., Highland, 46322. (219)972–2250. FAX: (219)972–4779. Monthly (except July/Aug.). Jewish Federation, Inc./Northwest Indiana.

INDIANA JEWISH POST AND OPINION (1935). PO Box 449097; 2120 N. Meridian

St., Indianapolis, 46202. (317)927–7800. FAX: (317)927–7807. Ed Stattman. Weekly.

NATIONAL JEWISH POST AND OPINION (1932). 2120 N. Meridian St., Indianapolis, 46202. (317)927–7800. FAX: (317)927–7807. Gabriel Cohen. Weekly.

KANSAS

KANSAS CITY JEWISH CHRONICLE. See under MISSOURI

KENTUCKY

COMMUNITY (1975). 3630 Dutchmans Ln., Louisville, 40205. (502) 451–8840. FAX: (502) 458–0702. Shiela Wallace. Biweekly. Jewish Community Federation of Louisville.

KENTUCKY JEWISH POST AND OPINION (1931). 1551 Bardstown Rd., Louisville, 40205. (502)459–1914. Julie D. Segal. Weekly.

LOUISIANA

COMMUNITY. See JEWISH VOICE

JEWISH CIVIC PRESS (1965). PO Box 15500, New Orleans, 70175. (504)895–8785. Abner Tritt. Monthly.

JEWISH VOICE (1989). 924 Valmont St., New Orleans, 70115. (504)895–8784. FAX: (504)895–8785. Michael Blackman, ed.; Abner Tritt, pub. Semiweekly. Jewish Federation of Greater New Orleans.

MARYLAND

BALTIMORE JEWISH TIMES (1919). 2104 N. Charles St., Baltimore, 21218. (410)752–3504. Gary Rosenblatt. Weekly.

MODERN JUDAISM (1980). Johns Hopkins University Press, 2715 N. Charles St., Baltimore, 21218–4319. (410)516–6944. FAX: (410)516–6968. (Editorial address: 92 Riverside Dr., Binghamton, NY 13905.) Steven Katz. Three times a year.

PROOFTEXTS: A JOURNAL OF JEWISH LITERARY HISTORY (1980). Johns Hopkins University Press, 2715 N. Charles St., Baltimore, 21218–4319. (410)516–6944. FAX: (410)516–6968. Edit. address (for contributors): NEJS Dept., Brandeis U., Waltham, MA 02254. Alan Mintz, David G. Roskies. Three times a year.

WASHINGTON JEWISH WEEK (1930, as the NATIONAL JEWISH LEDGER). 12300 Twinbrook Pkwy., Suite 250, Rockville,

20852. (301)230–2222. FAX: (301)881–6362. Eric Rozenman. Weekly.

MASSACHUSETTS

AMERICAN JEWISH HISTORY (1893). Two Thornton Rd., Waltham, 02154. (617)891–8110. FAX: (617)899–9208. Marc Lee Raphael. Quarterly. American Jewish Historical Society.

BOSTON JEWISH TIMES (1945). 169 Norfolk Ave., Boston, 02119. (617)442–9680. Sten Lukin. Fortnightly.

JEWISH ADVOCATE (1902). 15 School St., Boston, 02108. (617)367–9100. FAX: (617)-367–9310. Robert Israel. Weekly.

JEWISH CHRONICLE (1927). 131 Lincoln St., Worcester, 01605. (508)752–3400. FAX: (508)752–9057. Sondra Shapiro. Biweekly.

JEWISH REPORTER (1970). 76 Salem End Rd., Framingham, 01701. (508)879–3300. FAX: (508)879–5856. Marcia T. Rivin. Monthly. Combined Jewish Philanthropies of Greater Boston.

JEWISH WEEKLY NEWS (1945). PO Box 1569, Springfield, 01101. (413)739–4771. Charles F. Bennett. Weekly.

JOURNAL OF THE NORTH SHORE JEWISH COMMUNITY (1977). 324 B Essex St., Swampscott, 01907. (617)581–7110. FAX: (617)581–7630. Bette W. Keva. Biweekly. Russian section. North Shore Jewish Press Ltd.

MICHIGAN

DETROIT JEWISH NEWS (1942). 27676 Franklin Rd., Southfield, 48034. (313)354–6060. FAX: (313)354–6069. Gary Rosenblatt. Weekly.

HUMANISTIC JUDAISM (1968). 28611 W. Twelve Mile Rd., Farmington Hills, 48334. (313)478–7610. FAX: (313)477–9014. M. Bonnie Cousens, Ruth D. Feldman. Quarterly. Society for Humanistic Judaism.

MINNESOTA

AMERICAN JEWISH WORLD (1912). 4509 Minnetonka Blvd., Minneapolis, 55416. (612)920–7000. FAX: (612)920–6205. Marshall Hoffman. Weekly.

MISSOURI

KANSAS CITY JEWISH CHRONICLE (1920). 7373 W. 107 St., Suite 250, Overland Park, KS 66212. (913)648–4620. FAX: (913)381–

9889. Ruth Baum Bigus. Weekly. Sun Publications.

ST. LOUIS JEWISH LIGHT (1947). 12 Millstone Campus Dr., St. Louis, 63146. (314)-432–3353. FAX: (314)432–0515. Robert A. Cohn. Weekly. St. Louis Jewish Light, Inc.

NEBRASKA

JEWISH PRESS (1920). 333 S. 132 St., Omaha, 68154. (402)334–8200. FAX: (402)334–5422. Morris Maline. Weekly. Jewish Federation of Omaha.

NEVADA

JEWISH REPORTER (1976). 3909 S. Maryland Pkwy., Las Vegas, 89119–7520. (702)732–0556. FAX: (702)732–3228. Marla Gerecht. Monthly (except July and Aug.). Jewish Federation of Las Vegas.

LAS VEGAS ISRAELITE (1965). PO Box 14096, Las Vegas, 89114. (702)876–1255. FAX: (702)364–1009. Michael Tell. Biweekly.

NEW JERSEY

AVOTAYNU (1985). 1485 Teaneck Rd., Teaneck, 07666. (201)837–2701. FAX: (201)-837–8506. Sallyann Amdur Sack. Quarterly.

JEWISH COMMUNITY NEWS. 199 Scoles Ave., Clifton, 07012. (201) 777–8313. FAX: (201) 777–6701. Edith Sobel. Biweekly. Greater New Jersey Federation and Clifton-Passaic Federation.

JEWISH COMMUNITY VOICE (1941). 2393 W. Marlton Pike, Cherry Hill, 08002. (609)-665–6100. FAX: (609)665–0074. Harriet Kessler. Fortnightly. Jewish Federation of Southern NJ.

JEWISH HORIZON (1981). 812 Central Ave., Westfield, 07090. (908)654–0077. FAX: (908)654–4567. Fran Gold. Weekly.

JEWISH RECORD (Atlantic City area) (1939). 1525 S. Main St., Pleasantville, 08232. (609)383–0999. Martin Korik. Weekly.

JEWISH STANDARD (1931). 1086 Teaneck Rd., Teaneck, 07666. (201)837–8818. FAX: (201)833–4959. Rebecca Kaplan Boroson. Weekly.

JEWISH STAR (1975). 100 Metroplex Dr., Edison, 08817. (908)985–1234. FAX: (908)-985–3295. Marlene A. Heller. Bimonthly. Jewish Federation of Greater Middlesex County.

JEWISH VOICE (1982). 100 Grant Ave., Deal, 07723. (908)531–6200. FAX: (908)531–9518. Jo Ann Abraham. Monthly. Jewish Federation of Greater Monmouth County.

JEWISH VOICE & OPINION (1987). 73 Dana Place, Englewood, 07631. (201) 569–2845. FAX: (201)569–1739. Susan L. Rosenbluth. Monthly.

JOURNAL OF JEWISH COMMUNAL SERVICE (1899). 3084 State Hwy. 27, Suite 9, Kendall Pk, 08824–1657. (908)821–1871. FAX: (908)821–5335. Gail Naron Chalew. Quarterly. Jewish Communal Service Association of N. America.

JUDAICA NEWS (1989). PO Box 1130, Fair Lawn, 07410. (201)796–6151. FAX: (201)-796–6545. Terry Cohn. Quarterly.

METROWEST JEWISH NEWS (1947). 901 Route 10, Whippany, 07981–1157. (201)-887 3900. FAX: (201)887–4152. David Frank. Weekly. United Jewish Federation of MetroWest.

NEW MEXICO

THE LINK (1971). 8205 Spain NE, Suite 107, Albuquerque, 87109. (505)821–3214. FAX: (505)821–3351. Rebeca Zimmermann. Monthly. Jewish Federation of Greater Albuquerque.

NEW YORK

AFN SHVEL (1941). 200 W. 72 St., Suite 40, NYC, 10023. (212)787–6675. Mordkhe Schaechter. Quarterly. Yiddish. League for Yiddish, Inc.

AGENDA: JEWISH EDUCATION (1949; formerly PEDAGOGIC REPORTER). JESNA, 730 Broadway, NYC, 10003. (212)529–2000. FAX: (212)529–2009. Rabbi Arthur Vernon. Three times a year. Jewish Education Service of North America, Inc.

ALGEMEINER JOURNAL (1972). 211 63 St., Brooklyn, 11220. (718)492–6420. FAX: (718)492–6571. Gershon Jacobson. Weekly. Yiddish-English.

AMERICAN JEWISH YEAR BOOK (1899). 165 E. 56 St., NYC, 10022. (212)751–4000. FAX: (212)751–4017. David Singer, Ruth R. Seldin. Annually. American Jewish Committee and Jewish Publication Society.

AMERICAN ZIONIST (1910). 4 E. 34 St., NYC, 10016. (212)481–1500. FAX: (212)-481–1515. Paul Flacks. Quarterly. Zionist Organization of America.

AMIT WOMAN (1925). 817 Broadway, NYC, 10003. (212)477–4720. FAX: (212)353–2312. Micheline Ratzersdorfer. Five times a year. AMIT Women (formerly American Mizrachi Women).

AUFBAU (1934). 2121 Broadway, NYC, 10023. (212)873–7400. FAX: (212)496–5736. Henry Marx, ed.; Herman Pichler, assoc. ed. Fortnightly. German. New World Club, Inc.

BITZARON (1939). PO Box 623, Cooper Station, NYC, 10003. (212)293–5977. Hayim Leaf. Quarterly. Hebrew; English abstracts. Hebrew Literary Foundation and Jewish Culture Foundation of New York University.

BUFFALO JEWISH REVIEW (1918). 15 E. Mohawk St., Buffalo, 14203. (716)854–2192. FAX: (716)854–2198. Harlan C. Abbey. Weekly. Kahaal Nahalot Israel.

THE CALL (1933). 45 E. 33 St., NYC, 10016. (212)889–6800, ext. 210. FAX: (212)532–7518. Diane H. Merlin. Bimonthly. The Workmen's Circle.

CCAR JOURNAL: A REFORM JEWISH QUARTERLY (formerly JOURNAL OF REFORM JUDAISM) (1953). 192 Lexington Ave., NYC, 10016. (212)684–4990. FAX: (212)689–1649. Lawrence A. Englander. Quarterly. Central Conference of American Rabbis.

CIRCLE (1943). 15 E. 26 St., NYC, 10010–1579. (212)532–4949. FAX: (212)481–4174. Dr. Shirley Frank. Quarterly. Jewish Community Centers Association of North America (formerly JWB).

COMMENTARY (1945). 165 E. 56 St., NYC, 10022. (212)751–4000. FAX: (212)751–1174. Norman Podhoretz, Neal Kozodoy. Monthly. American Jewish Committee.

CONGRESS MONTHLY (1933). 15 E. 84 St., NYC, 10028. (212)879–4500. Maier Deshell. Seven times a year. American Jewish Congress.

CONSERVATIVE JUDAISM (1945). 3080 Broadway, NYC, 10027. (212)678–8049. FAX: (212)749–9166. Rabbi Shamai Kanter. Quarterly. Rabbinical Assembly.

ECONOMIC HORIZONS (1953). 350 Fifth Ave., Suite 1919, NYC, 10118. (212)971–0310. FAX: (212)971–0331. Ronny Bassan. Quarterly. American-Israel Chamber of Commerce and Industry, Inc.

FORVERTS (YIDDISH FORWARD) (1897). 45 E. 33 St., NYC, 10016. (212)889–8200. FAX: (212)684–3949. Mordechai Strigler. Weekly. Yiddish. Forward Association, Inc.

FORWARD (1897). 45 E. 33 St., NYC, 10016. (212)889–8200. FAX: (212)447–6406. Seth Lipsky. Weekly. Forward Publishing Company, Inc.

HADAROM (1957). 275 Seventh Ave., NYC, 10001. (212)807–7888. Rabbi Gedalia Dov Schwartz. Annually. Hebrew. Rabbinical Council of America.

HADASSAH MAGAZINE (1914). 50 W. 58 St., NYC, 10019. (212)333–5946. FAX: (212)-333–5967. Alan M. Tigay. Monthly (except for combined issues of June–July and Aug.–Sept.). Hadassah, the Women's Zionist Organization of America.

HADOAR (1921). 47 W. 34 St., Rm. 609, NYC, 10001. (212)629–9443. FAX: (212)-629–9472. Shlomo Shamir, ed.; Dr. Yael Feldman, lit. ed. Biweekly. Hebrew. Hadoar Association, Inc., Organ of the Histadruth of America.

HAMACHNE HACHAREIDI (1980). PO Box 216, Brooklyn, 11218. (718)438–1263. FAX: (718)438–1263. Rabbi Yisroel Eichler. Weekly. Khal Machzikei Hadas.

ISRAEL HORIZONS (1952). 224 W. 35 St., Rm. 403, NYC, 10001. (212)868–0386. Ralph Seliger. Quarterly. Americans for Progressive Israel.

ISRAEL QUALITY (1976). 350 Fifth Ave., Suite 1919, NYC, 10118. (212)971–0310. Beth Belkin. Quarterly. Government of Israel Trade Center and American-Israel Chamber of Commerce and Industry.

JBI VOICE (1978). 110 E. 30 St., NYC, 10016. (212)889–2525. FAX: (212)689–3692. Dr. Jacob Freid. Monthly (except May/June, July/Aug.) (audio cassettes). Jewish Braille Institute of America, Inc.

JEWISH ACTION MAGAZINE (1950). 333 Seventh Ave., 18th fl., NYC, 10008. (212)563–4000, X 147. Charlotte Friedland. Quarterly. Union of Orthodox Jewish Congregations of America.

JEWISH BOOK ANNUAL (1942). 15 E. 26 St., NYC, 10010. (212)532–4949. Jacob Kabakoff. English-Hebrew-Yiddish. Jewish Book Council.

JEWISH BOOK WORLD (1945). 15 E. 26 St., NYC, 10010. (212)532–4949. William

Wollheim. Quarterly. Jewish Book Council.

JEWISH BRAILLE REVIEW (1931). 110 E. 30 St., NYC, 10016. (212)889–2525. Jacob Freid. Monthly, except May/June, July/Aug. English braille. Jewish Braille Institute of America, Inc.

JEWISH CURRENTS (1946). 22 E. 17 St., Suite 601, NYC, 10003–3272. (212)924–5740. Morris U. Schappes. Monthly (July/Aug. combined). Association for Promotion of Jewish Secularism, Inc.

JEWISH EDUCATION (1929). 426 W. 58 St., NYC, 10019. (212)713–0290. FAX: (212)-586–9579. Dr. Alvin I. Schiff. Three times a year. Council for Jewish Education.

JEWISH FRONTIER (1934). 275 Seventh Ave., 17th fl., NYC, 10001. (212)229–2280. FAX: (212)675–7685. Nahum Guttman. Bimonthly. Labor Zionist Letters, Inc.

JEWISH JOURNAL (1969). 210 E. Sunrise Hwy., Suite 304, Valley Stream, NY 11581. (516)561–6900. FAX: (516)561–6971. Harold Singer. Weekly.

JEWISH LEDGER (1924). 2535 Brighton-Henrietta Town Line Rd., Rochester, 14623. (716)427–8521. FAX: (716)427–8521. Barbara Morgenstern. Weekly.

JEWISH OBSERVER (1963). 84 William St., NYC, 10038. (212)797–9000. Rabbi Nisson Wolpin. Monthly (except July and Aug.). Agudath Israel of America.

JEWISH OBSERVER (1978). PO Box 510, DeWitt, 13214. (315)445–0161. FAX: (315)-445–1559. Mollie Leitzes Collins. Biweekly. Syracuse Jewish Federation, Inc.

JEWISH POST OF NY (1974). 57 E. 11 St., NYC, 10003. (212)505–6959. FAX: (212)-505–1224. Henry J. Levy. Bimonthly.

JEWISH PRESS (1950). 338 Third Ave., Brooklyn, 11215. (718)330–1100. FAX: (718)935–1215. Rabbi Sholom Klass. Weekly.

JEWISH SOCIAL STUDIES (1939). 2112 Broadway, Rm. 206, NYC, 10023. (212)724–5336. Tobey B. Gitelle. Quarterly. Conference on Jewish Social Studies, Inc.

JEWISH SPORTS & FITNESS (1992). PO Box 4549, Old Village Station, Great Neck, 11023. (516)482–5550. FAX: (516)482–5583. David J. Kufeld. Quarterly. The Jewish Sports Congress.

JEWISH TELEGRAPHIC AGENCY COMMU-
NITY NEWS REPORTER (1962). 330 Sev-
enth Ave., 11th fl., NYC 10001–5010.
(212)643–1890. FAX: (212)643–8498. Mark
Joffe, Rifka Rosenwein, Mark A. Seal.
Weekly.

JEWISH TELEGRAPHIC AGENCY DAILY
NEWS BULLETIN (1917). 330 Seventh
Ave., 11th fl., NYC 10001–5010. (212)-
643–1890. FAX: (212)643–8498. Mark
Joffe, Rifka Rosenwein, Mark A. Seal.
Daily.

JEWISH TELEGRAPHIC AGENCY WEEKLY
NEWS DIGEST (1933). 330 Seventh Ave.,
11th fl., NYC 10001–5010. (212)643–1890.
FAX: (212)643–8498. Mark Joffe, Rifka
Rosenwein, Mark A. Seal. Weekly.

JEWISH WEEK (1876; reorg. 1970). 1501
Broadway, NYC, 10036–5503. (212)921–
7822. FAX: (212)921–8420. Phillip Ritzen
berg. Weekly.

JEWISH WORLD (1965). 1104 Central Ave.,
Albany, 12205. (518)459–8455. FAX:
(518)459–5289. Laurie J. Clevenson.
Weekly.

JOURNAL OF REFORM JUDAISM. See CCAR
JOURNAL

JUDAISM (1952). 15 E. 84 St., NYC, 10028.
(212)879–4500. FAX: (212)249–3672. Dr.
Ruth B. Waxman. Quarterly. American
Jewish Congress.

KOL HAT'NUA (VOICE OF THE MOVEMENT)
(1975). c/o Young Judea, 50 W. 58 St.,
NYC, 10019. (212)247–9221. FAX: (212)-
247–9240. Daniel Malino. Four times a
year. Young Judaea-Hashachar.

KULTUR UN LEBN–CULTURE AND LIFE
(1967). 45 E. 33 St., NYC, 10016. (212)-
889–6800. Joseph Mlotek. Three times a
year. Yiddish. The Workmen's Circle.

LAMISHPAHA (1963). 47 W. 34 St., Rm. 609,
NYC, 10001–3012. (212)629–9443. FAX:
(212)629–9472. Dr. Hanita Brand. Illustrated. Monthly (except July and Aug.).
Hebrew. Histadruth Ivrith of America.

LIKUTIM (1981). 110 E. 30 St., NYC, 10016.
(212)889–2525. Joanne Jahr. Two to four
times a year (audio cassettes). Hebrew.
Jewish Braille Institute of America, Inc.

LILITH—THE JEWISH WOMEN'S MAGAZINE
(1976). 250 W. 57 St., #2432, NYC,
10107. (212)757–0818. Susan Weidman
Schneider. Quarterly.

LONG ISLAND JEWISH WORLD (1971). 115
Middle Neck Rd., Great Neck, 11021. (516)-
829–4000. FAX: (516)829–4776. Jerome W.
Lippman. Weekly.

MARTYRDOM AND RESISTANCE (1974). 48
W. 37 St., 9th fl., NYC 10018–4708. (212)-
564–1865. FAX: (212)268–0529. Eli Zborowski. Bimonthly. International Society
for Yad Vashem.

MELTON JOURNAL (1982). 3080 Broadway,
NYC, 10027. (212)678–8031. Eduardo
Rauch, Barry W. Holtz. Biannually. Mel-
ton Research Center for Jewish Education.

MIDSTREAM (1954). 110 E. 59 St., NYC,
10022. (212)759–6208. FAX: (212)318–
6176. Joel Carmichael. Monthly. Theodor
Herzl Foundation, Inc.

MODERN JEWISH STUDIES ANNUAL (1977).
Queens College, NSF 350, 65 30 Kissena
Blvd., Flushing, 11367. (718)997–3622. Joseph C. Landis. Annually. American Association of Professors of Yiddish.

NA'AMAT WOMAN (1926). 200 Madison
Ave., Suite 2120, NYC, 10016. (212)725–
8010. Judith A. Sokoloff. Five times a year.
English-Yiddish-Hebrew. NA'AMAT USA,
the Women's Labor Zionist Organization
of America.

OLOMEINU—OUR WORLD (1945). 5723 18th
Ave., Brooklyn, 11204. (718)259–1223.
FAX: (718)259–1795. Rabbi Yaakov
Fruchter, Rabbi Nosson Scherman.
Monthly. English-Hebrew. Torah Umeso-
rah-National Society for Hebrew Day
Schools.

PASSOVER DIRECTORY (1923). 333 Seventh
Ave., NYC, 10001. (212)563–4000. FAX:
(212)564–9058. Shelley Scharf. Annually.
Union of Orthodox Jewish Congregations
of America.

PEDAGOGIC REPORTER. See AGENDA: JEW-
ISH EDUCATION

PROCEEDINGS OF THE AMERICAN ACAD-
EMY FOR JEWISH RESEARCH (1920). 3080
Broadway, NYC, 10027. (212)678–8864.
FAX: (212)678–8947. Dr. Nahum Sarna.
Annually. English-Hebrew-French-Arab-
ic-Persian-Greek. American Academy for
Jewish Research.

RCA RECORD (1953). 275 Seventh Ave.
NYC, 10001. (212)807–7888. FAX: (212)-
727–8452. Rabbi Mark Dratch. Quarterly.
Rabbinical Council of America.

REFORM JUDAISM (1972; formerly DIMEN-
SIONS IN AMERICAN JUDAISM). 838 Fifth
Ave., NYC, 10021. (212)249–0100. Aron
Hirt-Manheimer. Quarterly. Union of
American Hebrew Congregations.

THE REPORTER (1972). 500 Clubhouse Rd.,
Vestal, 13850. (607)724–2360. FAX: (607)-
724–2311. Marc S. Goldberg. Weekly.
Jewish Federation of Broome County, Inc.

THE REPORTER (1966; formerly WOMEN'S
AMERICAN ORT REPORTER). 315 Park
Ave. S., NYC, 10010. (212)674–7700. FAX:
(212)674–3057. Eve M. Jacobson Kessler.
Quarterly. Women's American ORT, Inc.

RESPONSE (1967). 27 W. 20 St., 9th fl., NYC,
10011–3707. (212)675–1168. FAX: (212)-
929–3459. Bennett Lovett Graff, Adam
Margolis. Quarterly. Response Magazine
Inc.

SHEVILEY HA-HINNUKH (1939). 426 W. 58
St., NYC, 10019. (212)713–0290. FAX:
(212)586–9579. Quarterly. Hebrew. Council for Jewish Education.

SH'MA (1970). c/o CLAL, 99 Park Ave.,
Suite S-300, NYC 10016. (212)867–8888.
FAX: (212)867–8853. Eugene B. Borowitz,
Irving Greenberg, Harold M. Schulweis,
sr. eds.; Nina Beth Cardin, ed. Biweekly
(except June, July, Aug.). CLAL–The Na-
tional Jewish Center for Learning and
Leadership.

SULLIVAN COUNTY JEWISH STAR (1991).
PO Box 776 (2793 Route 209 South),
Wurtsboro, 12790. (914)888–4680. FAX:
(914)888–2209. Edith Schapiro. Monthly.
Jewish Focus, Inc.

SYNAGOGUE LIGHT AND KOSHER LIFE
(1933). 47 Beekman St., NYC, 10038.
(212)227–7800. Rabbi Meyer Hager.
Quarterly. The Kosher Food Institute.

TRADITION (1958). 275 Seventh Ave., NYC,
10001. (212)807–7888. Rabbi Emanuel
Feldman. Quarterly. Rabbinical Council
America.

TRENDS (1982). 730 Broadway, NYC, 10003.
(212)529–2000. FAX: (212)529–2009.
Leora W. Isaacs. Irregularly. Jewish Education Service of North America, Inc.

UNITED SYNAGOGUE REVIEW (1943). 155
Fifth Ave., NYC, 10010. (212)533–7800.
FAX: (212)353–9439. Lois Goldrich. Bian-
nually. United Synagogue of Conservative
Judaism.

UNSER TSAIT (1941). 25 E. 21 St., 3rd fl.,
NYC, 10010. (212)475–0055. Editorial
committee. Monthly. Yiddish. Jewish
Labor Bund.

VOICE OF THE DUTCHESS JEWISH COMMU-
NITY (1990). 110 Grand Ave., Poughkeep-
sie, 12603. (914)471–9811. Dena Hirsh.
Monthly. Jewish Federation of Dutchess
County, Inc.

WOMEN'S AMERICAN ORT REPORTER. See
THE REPORTER

WOMEN'S LEAGUE OUTLOOK (1930). 48 E.
74 St., NYC, 10021. (212)628–1600. FAX:
(212)772–3507. Janis Sherman Popp.
Quarterly. Women's League for Conservative Judaism.

WORKMEN'S CIRCLE CALL. See THE CALL

YEARBOOK OF THE CENTRAL CONFERENCE
OF AMERICAN RABBIS (1890). 192 Lexing-
ton Ave., NYC, 10016. (212)684–4990.
FAX: (212)689–1649. Rabbi Elliot L. Ste-
vens. Annually. Central Conference of
American Rabbis.

YIDDISH (1973). Queens College, NSF 350,
65–30 Kissena Blvd., Flushing, 11367.
(718)997–3622. Joseph C. Landis. Quarterly. Queens College Press.

DI YIDDISHE HEIM (1958). 770 Eastern
Pkwy., Brooklyn, 11213. (718)493–9250.
Rachel Altein. Quarterly. English-Yid-
dish. Neshei Ub'nos Chabad-Lubavitch
Women's Organization.

YIDDISHE KULTUR (1938). 1133 Broadway,
Rm. 1019, NYC, 10010. (212)243–1304.
Itche Goldberg. Bimonthly. Yiddish. Yid-
disher Kultur Farband, Inc.—YKUF.

YIDDISHE SHPRAKH (1941). 1048 Fifth Ave.,
NYC, 10028. (212)231–7905. Dr.
Mordkhe Schaechter. Irregularly. Yiddish.
YIVO Institute for Jewish Research, Inc.

DOS YIDDISHE VORT (1953). 84 William St.,
NYC, 10038. (212)797–9000. Joseph Fried-
enson. Monthly. Yiddish. Agudath Israel
of America.

YIDDISHER KEMFER (1900). 275 Seventh
Ave., NYC, 10001. (212)675–7808. Mor-
dechai Strigler. Biweekly. Yiddish. Labor
Zionist Alliance.

DER YIDDISHER VEG (1981). 1274 49th St.,
Suite 1974, Brooklyn, 11219. (718)435–
9474. FAX: (718)438–1263. Meir Dov
Grosz. Weekly. Yiddish. Archives of
Chasidai Belz.

YIVO ANNUAL (1946). 1048 FIFTH AVE., NYC, 10028. (212)535–6700. FAX: (212)-879–9763. Deborah Dash Moore. Annually. YIVO Institute for Jewish Research, Inc.

YIVO BLETER (1931). 1048 Fifth Ave., NYC, 10028. (212)535–6700. David E. Fishman. Biannually. Yiddish. YIVO Institute for Jewish Research, Inc.

YOUNG ISRAEL VIEWPOINT (1952). 3 W. 16 St., NYC, 10011. (212)929–1525. FAX: (212)727–9526. Tovah Holzer. Quarterly. National Council of Young Israel.

YOUNG JUDAEAN (1910). 50 W. 58 St., NYC, 10019. (212)303–8271. Linda K. Schaffzin. Four times a year between Sept. and June. Hadassah Zionist Youth Commission.

YUGNTRUF: YIDDISH YOUTH MAGAZINE (1964). 200 W. 72 St., Suite 40, NYC, 10023. (212)787–6675. FAX: (212)769–2820. David S. Braun. Three times a year. Yiddish. Yugntruf Youth for Yiddish.

ZUKUNFT (THE FUTURE) (1892). 25 E. 21 St., NYC, 10010. (212)505–8040. Yonia Fain. Bimonthly. Yiddish. Congress for Jewish Culture.

NORTH CAROLINA

AMERICAN JEWISH TIMES OUTLOOK (1934; reorg. 1950). PO Box 33218, Charlotte, 28233. (704)372–3296. Ruth Goldberg. Monthly. The Blumenthal Foundation.

CHARLOTTE JEWISH NEWS (1978). 5007 Providence Rd., Charlotte, 28226. (704) 366–5007, ext. 268. FAX: (704) 365–4507. Rita Mond. Monthly (except July). Jewish Federation of Greater Charlotte.

OHIO

AKRON JEWISH NEWS (1929). 750 White Pond Drive, Akron, 44320. (216)869–2424. FAX: (216)867–8498. Toby Liberman. Fortnightly. Akron Jewish Community Federation.

THE AMERICAN ISRAELITE (1854). 906 Main St., Rm. 508, Cincinnati, 45202. (513)621–3145. FAX: (513)621–3744. Phyllis R. Singer. Weekly.

AMERICAN JEWISH ARCHIVES (1948). 3101 Clifton Ave., Cincinnati, 45220. (513)221–1875. Jacob R. Marcus, Abraham J. Peck. Semiannually. American Jewish Archives of Hebrew Union College–Jewish Institute of Religion.

CLEVELAND JEWISH NEWS (1964). 3645 Warrensville Center Rd., Cleveland, 44122. (216)991–8300. FAX: (216)991–9556. Cynthia Dettelbach. Weekly. Cleveland Jewish Publication Co.

DAYTON JEWISH CHRONICLE (1961). 118 Salem Ave., Dayton, 45406. (513)222–0783. Leslie Cohen Zukowsky. Weekly.

INDEX TO JEWISH PERIODICALS (1963). PO Box 18570, Cleveland Hts., 44118. (216)-381–4846. Lenore Pfeffer Koppel. Annually.

JEWISH JOURNAL (1987). PO Box 449, Youngstown, 44501. (216)744–7902. FAX: (216)746–7926. Sherry Weinblatt. Biweekly (except July/Aug.). Youngstown Area Jewish Federation.

OHIO JEWISH CHRONICLE (1922). 2862 Johnstown Rd., Columbus, 43219. (614)-337–2055. FAX: (614)337–2059. Judith Franklin. Weekly.

STARK JEWISH NEWS (1920). 2631 Harvard Ave. NW, Canton, 44709. (216)452–6444. FAX: (216)452–4487. Adele Gelb. Monthly. Canton Jewish Community Federation.

STUDIES IN BIBLIOGRAPHY AND BOOKLORE (1953). 3101 Clifton Ave., Cincinnati, 45220. (513)221–1875. FAX: (513)221–0321. Herbert C. Zafren. Irregularly. English-Hebrew-German. Library of Hebrew Union College–Jewish Institute of Religion.

TOLEDO JEWISH NEWS (1951). 6505 Sylvania Ave., Sylvania, 43560. (419)885–4461. FAX: (419)885–3207. Laurie Cohen. Monthly. Jewish Federation of Greater Toledo.

OKLAHOMA

TULSA JEWISH REVIEW (1930). 2021 E. 71 St., Tulsa, 74136. (918)495–1100. FAX: (918)495–1220. Ed Ulrich. Monthly. Jewish Federation of Tulsa.

OREGON

JEWISH REVIEW (1959). 6800 SW Beaverton-Hillsdale Hwy., Suite C, Portland, 97210. (503) 292–4913. FAX: (503)292–8965. Paul Haist. Fortnightly. Jewish Federation of Portland.

PENNSYLVANIA

COMMUNITY REVIEW (1925). 100 Vaughn St., Harrisburg, 17110. (717)236–9555. FAX: (717)236–8104. Carol L. Cohen.

Fortnightly. United Jewish Community of Greater Harrisburg.

JEWISH CHRONICLE OF PITTSBURGH (1962). 5600 Baum Blvd., Pittsburgh, 15206. (412)687-1000. FAX: (412)687-5119. Joel Roteman. Weekly. Pittsburgh Jewish Publication and Education Foundation.

JEWISH EXPONENT (1887). 226 S. 16 St., Philadelphia, 19102. (215)893-5700. FAX: (215)546-3957. Albert Erlick. Weekly. Jewish Federation of Greater Philadelphia.

JEWISH POST (1988). 301 Oxford Valley Rd., Yardley, 19067. (215)321-3443. FAX: (215)321-7245. Brenda Lesley Segal. Bimonthly.

JEWISH QUARTERLY REVIEW (1910). 420 Walnut St., Philadelphia, 19106. (215)-238-1290. FAX: (215)238-1540. Leon Nemoy, David M. Goldenberg. Quarterly. Annenberg Institute.

JEWISH TIMES (1976). 103A Tomlinson Rd., Huntingdon Valley, 19006. (215)938-1177. FAX: (215)938-0692. Matthew Schuman. Weekly. Jewish Federation of Greater Philadelphia.

NEW MENORAH (1978). 7318 Germantown Ave., Philadelphia, 19119-1793. (215)-242-4074. FAX: (215)247-9703. Arthur Waskow, Rabbi Shana Margolin. Quarterly. P'nai Or Religious Fellowship.

RECONSTRUCTIONIST (1934). Church Rd. and Greenwood Ave., Wyncote, 19095. (215)887-1988. Quarterly. Federation of Reconstructionist Congregations and Havurot.

RHODE ISLAND

JEWISH VOICE. 130 Sessions St., Providence, 02906. (401)421-4111. FAX: (401)331-7961. Jane S. Sprague. Monthly. Jewish Federation of Rhode Island.

RHODE ISLAND JEWISH HISTORICAL NOTES (1954). 130 Sessions St., Providence, 02906. (401)331-1360. Judith Weiss Cohen. Annually. Rhode Island Jewish Historical Association.

SOUTH CAROLINA

CHARLESTON JEWISH JOURNAL. 1645 Wallenberg Blvd., Charleston, 29407. (803)-571-6565. FAX: (803)556-6206. Eileen F. Chepenik. Bimonthly. Charleston Jewish Federation.

TENNESSEE

HEBREW WATCHMAN (1925). 4646 Poplar Ave., Suite 232, Memphis, 38117. (901)-763-2215. Herman I. Goldberger. Weekly.

OBSERVER (1934). 801 Percy Warner Blvd., Nashville, 37205. (615)356-3242. FAX: (615)352-0056. Judith A. Saks. Biweekly (except July). Jewish Federation of Nashville.

SHOFAR. PO Box 8947, Chattanooga, 37414. (615)894-1317. FAX: (615)894-1319. Marlene Solomon. Monthly. Chattanooga Jewish Federation.

TEXAS

JEWISH HERALD-VOICE (1908). PO Box 153, Houston, 77001-0153. (713)630-0391. FAX: (713)630-0404. Jeanne Samuels. Weekly.

JEWISH JOURNAL OF SAN ANTONIO (1973). 8434 Ahern, San Antonio, 78216. (210)-341-8234. FAX: (210)341-2842. Layney Cohen Berkus. Monthly (11 issues). Jewish Federation of San Antonio.

TEXAS JEWISH POST (1947). 3120 S. Expressway, Fort Worth, 76110. (817)927-2831. FAX: (817)429-0840. 11333 N. Central Expressway, Dallas, 75243. (214)-692-7283. FAX: (214)692-7285. Jimmy Wisch. Weekly.

VIRGINIA

RENEWAL MAGAZINE (1984). 7300 Newport Ave., Norfolk, 23505. (804)489-8040. FAX: (804)489-8230. Reba Karp. Quarterly. United Jewish Federation of Tidewater.

UJF VIRGINIA NEWS (1959). 7300 Newport Ave., Norfolk, 23505. (804)489-8040. FAX: (804) 489-8230. Reba Karp. 21 issues yearly. United Jewish Federation of Tidewater.

WASHINGTON

JEWISH TRANSCRIPT (1924). 2031 Third Ave., Suite 200, Seattle, 98121. (206)441-4553. FAX: (206)441-2736. Craig Degginger. Fortnightly. Jewish Federation of Greater Seattle.

WISCONSIN

WISCONSIN JEWISH CHRONICLE (1921). 1360 N. Prospect Ave., Milwaukee, 53202. (414)271-2992. FAX: (414)271-0487. Andrew Muchin. Weekly. Milwaukee Jewish Federation.

INDEXES

INDEX TO JEWISH PERIODICALS (1963). PO
Box 18570, Cleveland Hts., OH 44118.
(216)381–4846. Lenore Pfeffer Koppel.
Annually.

NEWS SYNDICATES

JEWISH TELEGRAPHIC AGENCY, INC.
(1917). 330 Seventh Ave., 11th fl., NYC.,
10001–5010. (212)643–1890. FAX: (212)-
643–8498. Mark Joffe, Rifka Rosenwein,
Mark A. Seal. Daily.

CANADA

CANADIAN JEWISH HERALD (1977). 17 An-
selme Lavigne, Dollard des Ormeaux, PQ
H9A 1N3. (514)684–7667. Dan Nimrod.
FAX: (514)737–7636. Irregularly. Dawn
Publishing Co., Ltd.

CANADIAN JEWISH NEWS (1971). 10 Gate-
way Blvd., #420, Don Mills, ONT M3C
3A1. (416)422–2331. FAX: (416)422–3790.
Patricia Rucker. Weekly.

CANADIAN JEWISH OUTLOOK (1963). 6184
Ash St., #3, Vancouver, BC V5Z 3G9.
(604)324–5101. FAX: (604)325–2470.
Henry M. Rosenthal. Monthly. Canadian
Jewish Outlook Society.

CANADIAN ZIONIST (1934). 5250 Decarie
Blvd., Suite 550, Montreal, PQ H3X 2H9.
(514)486–9526. FAX: (514)483–6392. Five
times a year. English-Hebrew. Canadian
Zionist Federation.

DIALOGUE (1988). 1590 Dr. Penfield Ave.,
Montreal, PQ H3G 1C5. (514)931–7531.
FAX: (514)931–3281. Rebecca Rosenberg.
Semiannually. French-English. Canadian
Jewish Congress, Quebec Region.

JEWISH POST & NEWS (1987). 117 Hutchings
St., Winnipeg, MAN R2X 2V4. (204)694–
3332. Matt Bellan. Weekly.

JEWISH STANDARD (1930). 77 Mowat Ave.,
Suite 016, Toronto, ONT M6K 3E3. (416)-
537–2696. Julius Hayman. Fortnightly.

JEWISH WESTERN BULLETIN (1930). 3268
Heather St., Vancouver, BC V5Z 3K5.
(604)879–6575. FAX: (604)879–6573. Samuel Kaplan. Weekly.

JOURNAL OF PSYCHOLOGY AND JUDAISM
(1976). 1747 Featherston Dr., Ottawa,
ONT K1H 6P4. (613)731–9119. Reuven P.
Bulka. Quarterly. Center for the Study of
Psychology and Judaism.

OTTAWA JEWISH BULLETIN & REVIEW
(1954). 151 Chapel St., Ottawa, ONT K1N
7Y2. (613)789–7306. FAX: (613)789–4593.
Myra Aronson. Biweekly. Jewish Community Council of Ottawa.

WINDSOR JEWISH FEDERATION (1942).
1641 Ouellette Ave., Windsor, ONT N9E
1T9. (519)973–1772. FAX: (519)973–1774.
Dr. Allen Juris. Quarterly. Windsor Jewish Community Council.

Louis Finkelstein (1895–1991)

THE LIFE OF LOUIS FINKELSTEIN—scholar, educational leader, and religious spokesman—coincided with the ideational and institutional maturation of American Judaism. In this development, Finkelstein, who died in New York on November 29, 1991, played a major role.

Judge Simon H. Rifkind, mourning the death of his lifelong friend, summed up Finkelstein's accomplishments in the following way:

> Dr. Finkelstein [was] essentially a scholar, a very great scholar. . . . I credit him with changing the position of Judaism in American society. . .with the transformation of the American synagogue. . .and with an enormous change of the climate of interreligious activity in America. In his role as chancellor of the [Jewish Theological] Seminary, he lifted that institution to the unquestioning premiership of Jewish scholarship with a high reputation in the intellectual communities in the United States and the rest of the world.

Finkelstein headed the Jewish Theological Seminary of America for more than three decades (1940–1972), during which time it ordained 662 rabbis. As acknowledged head of Conservative Judaism, he led the movement to become the most numerous in American Judaism, and to establish its presence in Europe, Israel, and South America. As the first American-born and American-trained Judaic scholar to attain highest academic distinction, he reintroduced Judaism to the academic world, building intellectual bridges to other faiths and scholarly disciplines. His own contribution to these endeavors is a bibliography of over 375 books, monographs, essays, and reviews, fashioned over the course of three-quarters of a century.[1]

Early Years

Louis Finkelstein was born on June 14, 1895, in Cincinnati, Ohio, to Rabbi Simon and Hannah Brager Finkelstein. The parents had come to America eight years earlier from Slobodka, a city in Lithuania famed for its great *yeshivah*, in which the young rabbi had received his education.

In a touching tribute to his parents, found in the foreword to his father's commentary on the prayer book, *Siah Yitzhak*, Finkelstein recalls that "it was my custom when still in the home of my parents to rise before dawn for study of the sacred texts." About his mother, Finkelstein observes: "Even though my father was an avid scholar, still she would urge him on to study more. It caused her great unhappiness that father had to spend so much time on congregational demands and communal

---

[1] Menahem Schmelzer, Burton Visotzky, Micha F. Oppenheim, *A Bibliography of the Writings of Louis Finkelstein* (New York, 1977); Ora Hamelsdorf, *A Supplement*. . . (1986).

needs—time he could have spent in study." Mrs. Finkelstein labored mightily to maintain the values of Slobodka as the family moved from Cincinnati to Syracuse to Brooklyn, finally settling in that borough's heavily Jewish Brownsville neighborhood.

On August 29, 1911, Finkelstein wrote to Dr. Solomon Schechter, president of the Jewish Theological Seminary of America:

> I have decided to take up the study of the ministry and desire to enter the Jewish Theological Seminary. I am the son of Rabbi S. Finkelstein of Brooklyn, and am sixteen years of age. I have just graduated from High School and would like to make arrangements in reference to Seminary work before I enter college. My studies in Hebrew have been quite extensive, having reviewed the Bible, and "Tanach" several times, and am thoroughly conversant with the same. Have also studied the following "Msechtoth" of the Talmud: Chulin, Gittin, Kiduschin, Baba Kama, Baba Metzia, and am now studying Baba Bathra; with all of which I am very well acquainted. I would like to see you in reference to this matter and greatly appreciate the favor of an appointment with you.

Finkelstein began concurrent studies at the Seminary and at the College of the City of New York in September, 1911. Amazingly, he remained at the Seminary for 80 years, first as a student (1911–1919), and then as instructor in Talmud (1920–1924), Solomon Schechter Lecturer, associate professor and professor of theology (1924–1934), assistant to the president (1934–1937), provost (1937–1940), president (1940–1951), chancellor (1951–1972), and, finally, chancellor emeritus (1972–1991).

While studying at the Seminary, Finkelstein received his BA from the College of the City of New York in 1915 and a PhD from Columbia University in 1918, with a dissertation on *The Commentary of David Kimchi on Isaiah, Edited, With His Unpublished Allegorical Commentary on Genesis, on the Basis of Manuscripts and Early Editions, Part I, Chapters 1–39*. Upon his ordination in 1919, Finkelstein became rabbi of Kehilath Israel, a prestigious acculturated but traditionalist congregation in the Bronx that had long Seminary associations. A year later Finkelstein was invited to join the Seminary faculty on a part-time basis as instructor in Talmud.

The first years of Finkelstein's career were marked by a succession of significant achievements. Among those were the appearance of his first published article, "Recent Hellenistic Literature," in the *Jewish Quarterly Review* in 1921. In 1923 Louis Ginzberg, the Seminary's professor of Talmud, granted Finkelstein a special *hattarat hora'ah* ordination attesting to his mastery of talmudic literature—the first of only two such certificates that Ginzberg granted during his long teaching career. In 1924, Finkelstein's first book, *Jewish Self Government in the Middle Ages*, was published by the Jewish Theological Seminary.

Conservative Judaism

While Finkelstein's teaching at the Seminary proved successful and his list of publications was growing, his chosen priority in the decade of the 1920s was his congregation. The synagogue grew in numbers and its facilities were expanded; added to the worship services were a Friday-evening lecture forum, a Young People's League, and youth activities. Kehilath Israel was a model "modern synagogue" with programs designed to meet the needs of every member of every family.

Of growing interest to Finkelstein during these years was the Conservative movement, and especially its organization of rabbis, the Rabbinical Assembly of America. In 1927, Finkelstein, as vice-president, delivered an address at the group's annual convention that was his first attempt to delineate a comprehensive ideology for Conservative Judaism. Among the things Finkelstein had to say were the following:

> *Our Attitude Toward the Torah*: Judaism is a developing religion, which has undergone an historical change . . . of growth, self-expression and foliation. . . . Because we regard the Torah as prophetically inspired . . . the legalism of the rabbis as the finest and highest expression of human ethics, we accept the written and oral law as binding and authoritative. . . . We are drawn to the Torah by love for its ceremonies, its commandments, its rules, and its spirit. We delight in its study, and find in it comfort and consolation, discipline and guidance.

> *Our Attitude Toward Change in Ceremonial*: As to the proposed innovations and new interpretations, there is none of us so bigoted as to refuse to cooperate with those who are attempting them, provided always that the ultimate purpose of change is to strengthen the attachment of Israel to the whole of the Torah, and that it does not defeat its own ends by striking at the fundamentals of Judaism.

> *Our Attitude Toward Palestine*: We want to see Palestine . . . rebuilt as the spiritual center of Israel. . . . We want Eretz Israel established as a Jewish community; if possible as an autonomous one.

> *Our Attitude Toward the Hebrew Language*: We are entirely sympathetic to the establishment of Hebrew as the language of conversation, Jewish literature and learning. . . . A Hebrewless Judaism we conceive to be an impossibility.

Finkelstein concluded his address with a powerful call to arms:

> We are the only group in Israel who have a modern mind and a Jewish heart, prophetic passion and western science. . . . And it is because we are alone in combining the two elements that can make a rational religion, that we may rest convinced that given due sacrifice and willingness on our part, the next generation will be saved by us. Certainly it can be saved by no other group.

Teacher, Scholar, Administrator

At the urging of Professor Ginzberg, Finkelstein was asked in 1931 to assume full-time responsibilities at the Seminary as the Solomon Schechter Professor of Theology. In 1934, Finkelstein was appointed assistant to the president and in 1937, provost. Finkelstein's freedom from congregational work allowed more time for his scholarly activities as well as greater participation in the larger academic world and in national Jewish communal life. It also enabled Cyrus Adler, the president of the Seminary, who turned 70 in 1933, to rely more and more on his "devoted colleague." Two important works that Finkelstein published during this period were *Akiba: Scholar, Saint, Martyr* (1936) and *The Pharisees* (1938). While both were works of basic academic scholarship, they also sought to overcome negative Christian stereotypes with regard to "legalism." Thus Finkelstein observes about Akiba: " . . . the contour of Western thought, generally, has been affected by his philosophy. His ideas involved those of Maimonides, Gersonides and Crescas. These men influenced a whole series of Latin writers from Thomas Aquinas to Spinoza, who in turn laid the foundation of modern thought. . . . In our generation special interest attaches to Akiba as one of the builders of civilization."

Finkelstein characterized Pharisaism as "Prophetism in action" and sought to establish a kinship between it and American Puritanism. This point was developed in an address that he delivered in 1937 as the culmination of a year of scholarly festivities celebrating the 50th anniversary of the founding of the Jewish Theological Seminary, which was a *tour de force* of polemical confrontation:

> It is not our purpose to revive the ancient, unnecessary and even unspiritual controversy regarding the relative merits of Judaism and Christianity. The Judeo-Christian tradition, properly understood, is a single system of thought, of which Judaism is the core, and Christianity the periphery. It is a tradition which recognizes the discipline of the law as essential to human behavior, and which sees in proper conduct one of the most effective methods for man to approach God. . . .

> It was a very legalistic Christianity which in the form of Puritanism laid the foundations of our own great republic. . . . The Pharisees and the Puritans who in different ages advocated almost precisely the same patterns of behavior . . . both those of ancient Jerusalem and those of modern New England have been presented to us as bigoted fanatics and narrow-minded casuists by men who rebel against the necessary discipline of life. . . . The truth is that we need Law and Discipline in life, but that this law and discipline must take cognizance of the goals they are intended to serve.

In 1938, at Finkelstein's initiative, the Institute for Religious and Social Studies was founded and became a part of the Seminary's program, with clergymen of all faiths meeting together weekly for study and discussion. This was followed in 1940 by the establishment of the Conference on Science, Philosophy and Religion, which yielded 18 volumes of symposia, coedited by Finkelstein.

As provost (1937–1940), Finkelstein became the administrative head of the Seminary. His immediate challenges were the precarious financial situation of the institution and the need to augment the faculty. Annual contributions in 1937 amounted to only $23,000, while only three members remained of Schechter's famed faculty— Louis Ginzberg, Alexander Marx, and Mordecai Kaplan. By 1945, annual contributions rose to over $500,000; added to the faculty were Boaz Cohen and Robert Gordis—both graduates of the Seminary—as well as H.L. Ginsberg, Saul Lieberman, Sholom Spiegel, and Abraham Joshua Heschel.

Study and research continued—and would continue—to be a central preoccupation for Finkelstein, even as his administrative and public responsibilities multiplied. He wrote and edited numerous books, articles, and reviews on a broad spectrum of Jewish topics, including the widely used *Jews: Their History, Culture and Religion* (1949), *American Spiritual Autobiographies* (1948), and *Social Responsibility in an Age of Revolution* (1971), all of which he edited. Discussing Finkelstein's scholarship, Judah Goldin wrote, in his *Encylopedia Judaica* article on him: "He published more than a hundred critical investigations of fundamental documents of Judaism, exploring the historical and social conditions reflected in liturgical texts . . . proving their antiquity." Goldin notes that Finkelstein's *Pharisees* "roused controversy because of his assertions that economic and social conditions influenced the formation of Pharisaic ideology. These studies lifted the discussion of historical problems from the parochial or purely doctrinal to the broad plane of social history." After retirement in 1972, he worked on a critical edition of the *Sifra*, a fourth-century commentary on the book of Leviticus.

Goldin summarizes Finkelstein's scholarship in these words: "In all his scholarly work Finkelstein exhibited a fastidious attention to detail, particularly to textual variants in manuscripts, early printed editions, and citations in geonic and post-geonic literary works, and an awareness of what is central in each period. In both his scholarly and his administrative activities, he made enormous contributions to an understanding and acceptance of the values and insights of talmudic-rabbinic Judaism."

President and Chancellor

When Cyrus Adler passed away on April 7, 1940, Finkelstein was named acting president; soon thereafter "acting" was removed.

In the aftermath of the Holocaust, American Jewry emerged as the leading Jewish community in the world. "Finkelstein envisioned the Seminary guiding American Jewry as it responded to the challenges of its new position," writes Pamela Nadell in *Conservative Judaism in America* (1988). She notes:

In a special conference held in 1946, Finkelstein publicly outlined the postwar plans he had forged in his early years as president. First, the Seminary would have to produce a large number of rabbis for American and even for world Judaism to organize and staff the hundreds of new congregations he expected to spring up in the coming years. . . . These synagogues and their schools would need 2,000 teachers. Educating large numbers means that the Seminary would have to expand its faculty, add to its Library, which had suffered during the Depression, and fund more scholarships. Furthermore, it should educate not only rabbis but also cantors, scholars and Jewish social workers. Because the New York school could not possibly do this job alone, the Conservative movement would have to establish Seminary colleges throughout North America. . . . The Seminary must reach out to Jewish laity by enriching their adult education programs, hosting summer retreats, expanding its museum, and producing radio shows. It must engage in interfaith dialogue and assert its moral leadership in ethical affairs to teach a world that had once gone mad never to do so again. What is most remarkable is not the scope of Finkelstein's vision but the fact that he accomplished so much of what he set out to do.

To accomplish his aims, Finkelstein recruited a corps of highly motivated, skilled associates. Chief among them were such Seminary-trained rabbis as Simon Greenberg, Max Arzt, Moshe Davis, and Bernard Mandelbaum. With their eye on the future, they and other colleagues established a broad program of recruitment and training of rabbis, scholars, and teachers, using as vehicles the network of Ramah camps, the Leadership Training Fellowship of High School Students, the Prozdor High School, a joint program for undergraduates with Columbia University, and a special track in the rabbinical school for promising scholars. Many of today's leading Jewish scholars in American and Israeli universities, as well as on the Seminary faculty, were drawn to their life's work through these activities.

The *Jewish Theological Seminary of America Register* for 1940–41, the year of Finkelstein's ascendancy to the presidency, listed the components of the institution: Rabbinical Department; Teachers Institute; Seminary College of Jewish Studies; Israel Friedlaendar Classes; Library; Museum of Jewish Ceremonial Objects; Seminary Institute of Jewish Affairs; and Institute of Interdenominational Studies. At the commencement exercises in 1941, the first over which the new president presided, eight men were ordained "Rabbi, Teacher and Preacher," while nine students received degrees of Bachelor of Jewish Pedagogy from the Teachers Institute, and six, Bachelor of Hebrew Literature.

The *Register* for 1970–73, Finkelstein's last years in office as chancellor, describes the Seminary as "the academic and spiritual center of the Conservative movement in Judaism" and lists the following programs and institutions:

> With five degree-granting schools at its New York campus (The Graduate Rabbinical School, The School of Judaica, The Teachers Institute-Seminary College of Jewish Studies, The Cantors Institute and the Seminary College of Jewish Music) and a sixth in Los Angeles (The University of Judaism) the Seminary has a student body exceeding 800 and a faculty of close to 100 full and part-time scholars.

In addition, there were the following "academic adjuncts": The Institute for Religious and Social Studies, the Herbert H. Lehman Institute of Talmudic Ethics, the Seminary Israel Institute, the Abbell Research Institute in Rabbinics, the American Jewish History Center, the Melton Research Center for Jewish Education, and in Israel, the Schocken Institute for Jewish Research and the American Students Center. To these need be added such outreach extensions as the Jewish Museum, Ramah Camps, and the weekly "Eternal Light" radio and "Frontiers of Faith" TV series.

Even as the Seminary was expanding, the fame of its chief officer was growing. In 1944, Finkelstein received from Columbia University the first of the dozen honorary degrees that he was awarded. The October 15, 1951, issue of *Time*, America's most popular news magazine, placed a portrait of Finkelstein on its cover and made his life and views the center of a feature article on Jews and Judaism in America. In June 1963, President John F. Kennedy appointed Finkelstein as one of his representatives to the coronation of Pope Paul VI.

Movement Tensions

Finkelstein's leadership of the Seminary and Conservative Judaism was not without controversy. There were Seminary alumni who were critical of the rapidly expanding program of the institution—institutes, conferences, radio and TV programs—because they saw these as peripheral intrusions which threatened to drain resources and energies from the central components of the Seminary—the Rabbinical School and the Teachers Institute. There were those, many of them leaders of the Rabbinical Assembly and the United Synagogue, who argued that the Seminary's staunch traditionalism was inimical to the dynamic nature of Conservative Judaism. Finally, there were those who criticized Finkelstein as being insufficiently Zionist. In the 1940s and early 1950s, Finkelstein had, in fact, been less than enthusiastic about *political* Zionism. Among other reasons, he was reluctant to give allegiance to a movement that he saw as replacing religious identity with nationalism. By the 1960s, however, the Seminary and the Conservative movement had established close ties with Israel, and the rancor was barely a memory.

During the more than three decades that he headed the Seminary, Finkelstein was the acknowledged leader of Conservative Judaism. He labored hard to maintain the primacy of the Seminary in all matters pertaining to the Conservative movement and to promote a strong traditionalist policy. Thus, in 1947, when the United Synagogue sought to accord a central role to lay leaders in a projected formulation of an ideology for Conservative Judaism, Finkelstein thwarted the attempt, arguing that only rabbis and scholars had the requisite credentials to undertake such an effort. In 1952, when the Rabbinical Assembly began to vigorously pursue a solution to the problem of the *agunah* (abandoned wife) that the traditionalists on the Seminary faculty considered a departure from strict *halakhic* process, Finkelstein insisted that the Seminary be given a role in the endeavor. The resultant Joint Law Conference succeeded in removing decision making from the Rabbinical Assembly, effectively restraining an adventurous interpretation of the law for 14 years, till 1968, when the Joint Law Conference was dissolved.

In a Conservative movement that had from its inception accepted and permitted diversity and that was committed to both tradition and change, Finkelstein's self-chosen role was that of the upholder of tradition and restraining influence on those impatient for change. This was due in large measure to Finkelstein's own traditionalist sensibility, but also to his understanding of the tripartite institutional composition of Conservative Judaism and the role that each element should play. The United Synagogue, because of its "worldly" nature, would be the advocate for change; the Seminary, as an institution of learning and conservator and transmitter of the "eternal verities," would naturally be the defender and promoter of traditionalism;

while the Rabbinical Assembly, exposed to the demands of both tradition and change, would serve as mediator. As time went on, and the United Synagogue became ever more worldly and the Rabbinical Assembly ever more drawn to change, Finkelstein labored all the harder to have the Seminary function as the champion of tradition.

It may well be that Finkelstein's greatest contribution to Conservative Judaism was to demand, with all the influence and vigor at his command, spiritual content and *halakhic* discipline of a movement growing at so rapid a pace that sociological considerations threatened to overwhelm theological imperatives. Still, some might argue that inhibiting the evolutionary expansion of *halakhic* parameters in the 1940s, 1950s, and 1960s only helped to hasten the revolutionary changes that occurred in the 1970s and 1980s.

Louis Finkelstein was a charismatic personality, a forceful leader, and a passionate advocate. To those who knew him best he was a harmonious amalgam of biblical prophet, rabbinic sage, 19th-century *rav*, and 20th-century executive. A correspondent for the *New York Times* visiting him in his 90th year (1985) found him at work on his critical edition of the *Sifra*. Asked why after being so involved in world events he had decided to return to the sacred texts, Finkelstein replied, "I never left them." He continued working on his *magnum opus* almost to the last day of his life, six years later.

ABRAHAM J. KARP

Isaac Bashevis Singer (1904–1991)

W HEN ISAAC BASHEVIS SINGER DIED in Florida on July 24, 1991, it could be accurately said that Yiddish prose fiction died with him. He was the last in a series of great Yiddish story writers and novelists that began with Mendele Mokher Seforim in the 1870s but has no successors. Although a smattering of Yiddish fiction will no doubt go on being written in years to come, it is hard to imagine a new author of Singer's stature emerging from the ultra-Orthodox ghettos of America and Israel, the last islands on earth where Yiddish is the spoken language of a community.

True, Singer himself emerged from the ultra-Orthodox community of Jewish Poland, where he was born on July 14, 1904, in the small town of Leoncin, the son of the Hassidic rabbi Pinchas Mendel Singer and of the daughter of a rabbi, Bassheva Zilberman. (It was from his mother that he took the pen name of Bashevis.) But the critical difference is that when Singer—whose family moved to Warsaw in 1908—gave up the observant life of a rabbinical student in his late teens and decided to follow in the footsteps of his older brother, Israel Joshua, and become a writer, he found waiting for him beyond the threshold of the study house a city of tremendous Jewish vitality, teeming with Yiddish newspapers, literary magazines, theaters, artistic circles, and political and cultural movements of every kind. Not only were there publishers and an audience for his stories, of which the first to see print appeared in the journal *Literatishe Bletter* in 1924, but also the bohemian Yiddish world he now entered was quickly assimilated by his literary imagination alongside the religious environment he grew up in, both functioning there henceforward as mirroring halves of a single totality.

Indeed, one of the main features of Singer's fiction is that tradition and modernity are not treated in it as thematic opposites, the way they are in most 20th-century Yiddish and Hebrew literature—the one being associated with social obligation, restriction, and repression, but also with structure, meaning, and community, and the other with alienation, anomie, and dissolution as well as with individual striving and freedom. In Singer, all of these oppositions are already located within the world of tradition itself, of which modernity seems not so much a discontinuity as a more formless replication.

This can be seen clearly in Singer's first novel, *Satan in Goray* (English translation, 1958), which was serialized and then published in book form in Warsaw in 1935. Set in 1666 in an isolated Polish shtetl modeled on his mother's native town of Bilgoray, *Satan in Goray* tells of the chiliastic fervor caused by the belief in the false messiah Sabbetai Zevi, which leads to the abandoning of all religious and social restraints in the course of a Jewish Walpurgis-year. Although Singer's Goray, which

535

is already fully populated by the imps, devils, dybbuks, and crazed and possessed individuals who were later to become his trademark, was based on the historical facts of Sabbatianism, these fully confirmed his own vision in which pious Jews too—and by extension all human beings, even at their most disciplined—harbor the demons of moral and sexual debauchery within themselves and have no need of the philosophies of secularism to find rationalizations for releasing them.

The same year, 1935, Singer emigrated from Poland to America, leaving behind a wife and small son who shortly afterward traveled to Russia and then settled in Palestine. His first years in New York were isolated and unproductive. "When I came [to America]," he later said of this period, "it seemed to me that Yiddish was finished; it was very depressing. The result was that for five or six or seven years I couldn't write a word. . . . By the age of forty many writers, including my brother, had composed great masterpieces, and I hadn't accomplished anything except for one small book—*Satan in Goray*." He was ultimately helped out of this "literary amnesia," as he called it, by his association with the *Forward*, the Yiddish newspaper that began publishing his stories in its pages and served—in some ways quite literally until his marriage to Alma Haimann in 1940—as an American home. It was there, from 1945 to 1948, that he serialized his second novel, *The Family Moskat* (English, 1950), a panoramic canvas of prewar Jewish Poland written in the mode of social realism that his brother, I.J. Singer, the author of the family novel *The Brothers Ashkenazi*, was better known for. *The Family Moskat* was followed by two more large novels in the same vein, *The Manor* (English, 1967) and *The Estate* (English, 1970), which continued the saga of Polish Jewry back into the 19th century.

But social realism—in which he was perhaps competing with his brother on grounds unfavorable to his own talents—was not Bashevis's forte, and if he was meanwhile acquiring a reputation among serious critics in America, this was more for his short stories, the first volume of which, *Gimpel the Fool*, came out in English in 1954. (Its title story had appeared the year before in *Partisan Review*, in a translation by Saul Bellow, and marked the beginning of Singer's recognition outside the severely diminished world of post-Holocaust Yiddish letters.) Here one already sees all the elements of the "Singer style," in part formed by his years of writing for the Yiddish press, that was gradually winning a growing non-Yiddish and even non-Jewish readership: the firm commitment to a clear story line at a time when serious modern fiction was increasingly moving the other way; the sharp, aggressive prose that never paused to reflect on itself or to be deflected from its narrative purpose; the concentration on idiosyncratic and socially marginal characters who often tend to be driven by some peculiar obsession or mania; and last but not least, the uninhibited mix of natural and supernatural elements in settings often less traditional than that of *Satan in Goray*.

Thus, in a typical story in *Gimpel the Fool*, "The Mirror," an imp lures a bored housewife into her bedroom mirror with promises of sexual pleasure that turn into the torments of Hell. Whether Singer did or did not believe in the existence of the supernatural creatures who people many of his tales (in the numerous interviews he liked to give he sidestepped the issue with coyly ambiguous answers), these served him as a means of demarcating various states of the human soul in a manner most compatible with his narrative methods. One can speak of an imp or of unconscious fantasies; of Hell experienced in a mirror or of the tawdry sufferings of actual adultery; the difference between folklore and psychology, as far as Singer was concerned, was that he could get to the point more quickly, dramatically, and picturesquely via the coordinates of folklore. The territory of the soul, he believed, was the same in all ages, but the ancients had mapped it more readably than the moderns.

There are significantly, however, almost no angels in Singer's fiction. Here, underneath its often mischievous surface, lies its fundamental paradox, for although virtue in it is clearly labeled as virtue and sin as sin, almost everything that is most active and passionate in its characters inclines them to the realm of sin. There is thus something contrived in Singer's attempt to preserve a semblance of traditional moral order in a universe in which energy is the undisputed domain of evil and a passive quietism the chief refuge of good. Nowhere perhaps is this dilemma better illustrated than in his novel *The Magician of Lublin* (first serialized in the *Forward* in 1958 and published in English in 1960), whose protagonist—a professional performer with Houdini-like skills—repents a life of libertinism in the book's final pages by locking himself remorsefully in an empty cell, the only confinement he has been unable to escape from in his life. Singer always claimed to be a great admirer of Spinoza, and there is indeed something Spinozistic in the withdrawal and monkish contemplation with which *The Magician of Lublin* ends.

After *The Slave* (English translation, 1962), which was serialized in the *Forward* in 1961 and in which Singer returned again to a complex moral allegory set in the world of medieval Poland, he wrote no more major novels. He did, however, continue to publish numerous short stories (many of them in the prestigious *New Yorker*), which appeared in several collections, such as *The Spinoza of Market Street* (1961), *Short Friday and Other Stories* (1964), *A Friend of Kafka* (1970), and *Passions* (1976), as well as the short novels *Enemies: A Love Story* (1972) and *Shosha* (1978). By now he was widely regarded in the United States almost as an American author; many of his stories from this period, although their first drafts were written in Yiddish, were first published and even edited in English translation, and his receipt of the National Book Award in 1970 and 1974, as well as such Broadway and Hollywood adaptations of his fiction as the stage play *Taibele and Her Demon* (1979) and *Yentl* (1983), made him a nationally known figure even before his receipt of the 1978 Nobel Prize for literature.

It would be unfair to say that Singer has been more admired by Gentiles than by Jews, and even in translation there are subtleties in his narratives that only knowledgeable Jewish readers will notice. It is true, however, that the American Jewish community reacted to him with ambivalence—part in pride at his accomplishment and part in defensiveness at his depictions of Jewish life, which often went to an opposite extreme from the pious sentimentalization of shtetl culture prevalent after the Holocaust. Certainly Singer was no historian, and his description of historical Jewish communities was literature, not fact. Yet in some ways he belonged to the same broad spectrum of Jewish revisionism, best represented in the world of scholarship by Gershom Scholem (who, like Singer, was intrigued by Sabbatianism and its offshoots), which sought to reverse apologetic 19th-century conceptions of Judaism as a religion of decorum and rationality by stressing the latter's mythic and mystical qualities and pointing to the great gap that often existed between the beliefs preached by rabbinic leadership and the folk practices of common Jews. For both Scholem and Singer, this deep rapport with the irrational elements in the human psyche was what gave Judaism its true power, but it was a power that could easily turn on those who tapped it; hence, its great fascination.

The serious critics have been of two minds about Singer. On the one hand, there are those like Robert Alter who caution us not to look for nonexistent depths in him: he should be approached, Alter has written, "not as an explorer of theological and philosophical profundities or as an 'epic' portrayer of a vanished world, but as a magical teller of tales." On the other hand, one finds commentators like David Neal Miller in his *Fear of Fiction: Narrative Strategies in the Works of Isaac Bashevis Singer* who argue that, far from being an immensely gifted but essentially unreflective storyteller, Singer was a "self-conscious modernist," much of whose work has been an experiment with "recurring narrative situations . . . of increasingly ambiguous fictional status." Irving Howe, one of the few major critics to have read Singer in Yiddish, takes an intermediate position when he observes, "If Singer's work can be grasped only on the assumption that he is crucially a 'modernist' writer, one must add that in other ways he remains profoundly subject to Jewish tradition." And Howe concludes an essay on Singer by remarking:

"What finally concerns Singer most is the possibilities for life that remain after the exhaustion of the human effort, after failure and despair have come and gone. Singer watches his stricken figures from a certain distance, with enigmatic intent and no great outpouring of sympathy, almost as if to say that before such collapse neither judgment nor sympathy matter very much. Yet in all of his fiction the Promethean effort occurs, obsessional, churning with new energy and delusion. In the knowledge that it will, that it must recur, there may also lie hidden a kind of pity, for that too we would expect, and learn to find, in the writer who created Gimpel."

HILLEL HALKIN

Obituaries: United States[1]

BACHRACH, ALICE, communal worker; b. NYC, May 24, 1902; d NYC, Oct. 23, 1991; educ.: NY School of Fine and Applied Art. V.-pres., National Girl Scouts and chwmn. its *American Girl* magazine; exec. comm. member, NY Blood Center; trustee, Parsons School of Design; bd. mem., USO, during WWII and Korean War; mem., civilian adv. com., Women's Army Corps. Mem., bd. of govs., Hebrew Union Coll.-Jewish Inst. of Religion, for over 40 years; v.-pres. for 19 years and hon. bd. mem., Natl. Jewish Welfare Bd., and organizer and chwmn. its women's div.; v.-pres. and bd. mem., YM-YWHA of NYC; bd. mem., women's div., Fed. of Jewish Philanthropies; mem., Temple Emanu-El, NYC.

BENNETT, LOUIS L., social work exec., comunal worker; b. NYC, Jan. 15, 1909; d. Miami Beach, Fla., Dec. 25, 1991. Educ.: St. John's University (LLB); Columbia U. School of Social Work. Private practice of law, 1931–71. Asst. regional dir., US Office of Community War Services, 1941–45; organizer and exec. dir., Veterans Service Center, NYC, 1944–45; regional housing expediter, Natl. Housing Agency, 1945–47; asst. exec. dir., Amer. Jewish Com., 1947–49; lst exec. dir., New York Assoc. for New Americans, 1949–52; asst. exec. v.- chmn, UJA, 1952–56; exec. dir., Jewish Child Care Assoc. of NY, 1956–60; asst. exec. dir., Community Council. of Greater NY, 1960–62; regional rep., Bureau of Family Services, 1962–65; regional rep.,

Office of Aging, Dept. of Health, Educ. and Welfare, 1962–65; deputy regional commissioner, HEW Social and Rehab. Service, 1967–70; prof., dean of students, chmn., student personnel services, Baruch Coll., 1970–72. Consultant to various state and private agencies and US Dept. of Ed.; bd. mem.: Community Council of Greater NY, NY State Welfare Conf., Child Welfare League, NY State Assoc. of Children's Insts., Council of Social Work Ed., Natl. Conf. of Social Welfare; mem.: functional planning com., Fed. of Jewish Philanthropies of NY; examining panel, NY State and NY City civil service commissions; NY Gov.'s Comm. on Aging; del., 1971 White House Conf. on Aging. Recipient: Superior Service Award, HEW.

BIRNBAUM, MAX, educator, communal worker; b. NYC, Feb. 24, 1910; d. W. Orange, NJ, June 21, 1991. Educ.: U. Wisconsin, Columbia U., Rutgers U., NYU. Highschool teacher and supervisor of social studies; dir., dept. of education and training, Amer. Jewish Com., 1951–70, and consultant thereafter; leader of intergrouprelations training courses for educators, employers, citizen groups, and govt. workers; founder and dir., Rutgers U. Workshop in Human Relations; educ. consultant, Natl. Conf. of Christians and Jews; staff mem., Boston U. Summer Laboratory in Human Relations; fellow, Natl. Training Laboratories; author, articles in various pubs.; coauthor, *Comparative Guide to American Colleges*.

---

[1]Including American Jews who died between January 1 and December 31, 1991.

BOLZ, SANFORD H., attorney; b. Albany, N.Y., May 3, 1915; d. Washington, D.C., Aug. 5, 1991. Educ.: Cornell U. (BA, LLB). Research asst., NY State Law Revision Comm., 1938–39; law firm assoc., 1939–41; appeals atty., NLRB, 1941–43; enforcement atty., OPA, 1943–44; chief counsel, transp. and shipping, Lend-Lease, 1944–46; private law practice: Washington, 1946–60, 1965–68; California, 1960–65; Washington counsel: American Jewish Cong., 1948–60; American Jewish Com., 1965–68; genl. counsel, sr. v.-pres., N.Y. State Chamber of Commerce, 1968–80; consultant, labor arbitrator, lecturer, private practice, thereafter. Dem. cand. for Cong., 12th dist., Calif., 1964. Mem. of bar: US Supreme Court, N.Y., Calif., D.C. Recipient: Man of the Year, Temple Sinai, Washington; Washington Jewish Community Council Award.

BREITEL, CHARLES D., judge, communal worker; b. NYC, Dec. 12, 1908; d. NYC, Dec. 1, 1991. Educ.: U. Michigan, Columbia U. (LLB). Law firm assoc., 1933–35; deputy asst. dist. atty., staff of Thomas E. Dewey, 1935–37; special rackets investigator, 1938–41; chief, indictment bur., 1941; assoc. of Dewey in private law practice, 1942; counsel to Gov. Dewey, 1943–50; appointed justice, N.Y. State supreme court, 1950, elected 1951; assoc. justice, appellate div., first dept., 1952–66; judge, N.Y. State court of appeals, 1967–73; chief judge, 1974–78; of counsel, Proskauer Rose Goetz & Mendelsohn, NYC, 1978–85. Adj. prof., Columbia Law School, 1963–69, and mem. its bd. of visitors; mem.: N.Y. State Postwar Public Works Planning Comm., 1943–45; Gov.'s Comm. on State Educ. Prog., 1945–47; Fed. Comm. on Internatl. Rules of Judicial Procedure, 1958–66; Pres.'s Comm. on Law Enforcement and Admin. of Justice, 1965–67; admin. tribunal, Inter-Amer. Devel. Bank, 1982–88; judicial panel, Center for Public Resources, 1982 on; bd. mem., Fund for Modern Courts. Fellow: Amer. Soc. Arts and Sciences; Amer. Bar Found. (hon.); v.-pres., NYC bar assoc.; mem.: Amer. Law Inst., Inst. Judicial Admin., N.Y. State Bar Assoc., N.Y. County Lawyers Assoc. Mem., bd. govs., Amer. Jewish Com., chmn. its domestic affairs com., mem. exec. com., N.Y. chap., and mem. publication com., *Commentary* magazine; mem. B'nai B'rith.

CHAIKIN, SOL, labor leader, communal worker; b. NYC, Jan. 9, 1918; d. NYC, Apr. 1, 1991. Educ.: City Coll. of NY, Brooklyn Law School. Served USAF, WWII. Spent his entire career in the International Ladies Garment Workers Union: organizer, Fall River, Mass.;1940–41; business agent, Boston and Lowell locals, 1941–43; mgr., Springfield local, 1946–48; mgr., W. Mass. dist. council, 1948–56; dir., lower Southwest Region, 1956–59; asst. dir., Northeast Dept., 1959–65; v.-pres of the International, 1965–73; sec.-treas., 1973–75; and pres., 1975–86. "Look for the union label" ad campaign launched under his aegis. Helped plan Javits Convention Center in NYC, serving as chmn. its operating corp. and acting pres. 1989-Dec. 1990. V.-pres. and mem. exec. council, AFL-CIO, first chmn. its Amer. Council of Ed., leader of its first official mission to S. Africa, 1983, and an early supporter of Polish Solidarity and other foreign labor movements. Chmn., Amer. Trade Union Council for Histadrut; trustee, Brandeis U. and chmn., bd. of trustees, its Heller graduate school of social welfare; trustee: Fashion Inst. of Technology; Long Island Jewish Medical Center; bd. mem.: East River Housing Corp., N.Y. Urban Coalition, Internatl. Rescue Com., American ORT Fed.; hon. trustee, Temple Emanuel of Great Neck, N.Y.

CLAYMAN, JACOB, labor leader, communal worker; b. Boston, Mass., Jan. 21, 1905; d. Silver Spring, Md., May 24, 1991. Educ.: Oberlin Coll. (working his way through as a steel worker), U. Michigan Law School. Private law practice, Ohio, 1930–43; mem. Ohio state legislature, 1941–43; genl. counsel, Ohio CIO, 1943–49 and sec.-treas., 1949–56; asst. to pres., Amalgamated Clothing Workers of Amer., 1956–58; AFL-CIO rep., Ohio state legislature, 1958–60; admin. dir., industrial union dept., AFL-CIO, 1960–73 and sec.-treas., pres., to 1979, in which position organized the 1975 Jobs Now rally in Washington; pres., Natl. Council of Senior Citizens, 1979–89. Founding pres., Consumer Fed. of Amer.; bd. mem.: Leadership Conf. on Civil Rights, UN Assoc. of USA, Greater Washington Lung Assoc., Natl. United Way Fund; v.-pres., Amer. Immigration and Citizenship Conf.; chmn., Natl. Civil Liberties Clearing House; v.-pres., Jewish Labor Com.

COHEN, GERSON D., professor, seminary chancellor; b. NYC, Aug. 26, 1924; d. NYC, Aug. 16, 1991. Educ.: City Coll. of NY, Jewish Theol. Sem. of Amer. (ord.), Columbia U. (PhD). At JTS: librarian, 1950–57; teaching fellow in Talmud, 1953–57; lect., Jewish lit. and institutions, 1957–60; visiting asst. prof., 1961–64; visiting assoc. prof., 1965–66; visiting prof., 1966–70; Jacob H. Schiff prof., hist., 1970–86; Disting. Service prof., 1986 on; chancellor, 1972–86, emer. thereafter. During his tenure as chancellor, guided the deliberations that led to the decision to ordain women as rabbis; oversaw the rebuilding and expansion of the seminary library after a major fire; and expanded the seminary's programs in Israel. At Columbia: Gustav Gottheil lect. in Semitic langs., 1950–60; assoc. prof., history, 1963–67; prof., Jewish hist., 1967–70; dir., Center for Israel and Jewish Studies, 1968–70; adj. prof. and seminar assoc., 1970 on. Mem. bd. of visitors: Harvard U. Divinity School, 1979–83; Princeton U. Chapel Adv. Council, 1981–85; mem.: President's Comm. on the Holocaust; bd. of sponsors, Legal Aid Soc.; bd. mem., Jewish Pub. Soc. and chmn. its publications com.; bd. mem.: Leo Baeck Inst., Conf. on Jewish Social Studies, Alliance Israélite Universelle. Author: *Sefer Ha-Qabbalah: The Book of Tradition*, a critical ed. and commentary on the work by Abraham Ibn Daud (1967); *The American Contribution to the Reshaping of the Jewish Past* (1974); *Studies in the Variety of Rabbinic Cultures* (1991), which includes "Story of the Four Captives" (1961), "Zion in Rabbinic Literature" (1961), "The Song of Songs and the Jewish Religious Mentality" (1966), "Messianic Postures of Ashkenazim and Sephardim" (1967), "Esau as Symbol in Early Medieval Thought" (1967), "Reconstruction of Gaonic History" (1972), "German Jewry as a Mirror of Modernity" (1975), and other studies; "The Talmudic Age," in *Great Ages and Ideas of the Jewish People* (1956); "The Jews in the Arab World" and "The Jews in Medieval Europe" in *The Columbia History of the World* (1976); "The State of the Jews: Reflections on Jewish Normality, Agony, and Glory" (1982), an address delivered at the 92nd St. Y; articles in the *Encyclopedia Britannica* and elsewhere. Recipient: Fellow, Amer. Acad. for Jewish Research; Townsend Harris Medal,

CCNY Alumni Assoc.; hon. doctorates: Princeton U., Trinity Coll., NYU, CUNY, Yale U., HUC-JIR, Brandeis U.

COMAY, SHOLOM D., corporate executive, communal leader; b. Pittsburgh, Pa., Sept. 28, 1937; d. Chautauqua, N.Y., May 18, 1991. Educ.: Brandeis U., U. Pittsburgh Law School. Partner, Kaufman & Harris law firm, Pittsburgh, 1963–75; housing court magistrate, 1967–71; v.-chmn., sec., and genl. counsel, Action Industries, Inc., a marketer of housewares and giftware promotional programs, since 1975. Chmn., Pittsburgh Found.; mem. adv. com., Forbes Fund; bd. mem.: United Way of Allegheny County, Pittsburgh Symphony, Pittsburgh Ballet Theater, Harmarville Rehab. Center, Montefiore Found; pres. and chmn., Health and Welfare Planning Assoc. of Allegheny County. Natl. pres., Amer. Jewish Com., 1989 on, having previously served as treas., mem. bd. of govs. and exec. com., chmn. domestic affairs and natl. affairs comms. and natl. housing com. and pres. Pittsburgh chap.; mem., president's council, Brandeis U.; treas. and bd. mem., United Jewish Fed. of Pittsburgh, chmn. its budget and allocation com., com. on elderly, and demographic com. Recipient: Brotherhood Award, Natl. Conf. of Christians and Jews; special citation, Allegheny County Bar Assoc.

DELAKOVA (BUDMOR), KATYA, dancer, teacher; b. Vienna, Austria, Sept. 8, 1914; d. Titusville, N.J., Apr. 10, 1991; in US since 1939. Educ.: Academy of Music and Dance (Vienna). A leading figure in the development of modern Jewish dance; in the '30s, was a teacher and choreographer in Yugoslavia and toured Europe with performances of dances on contemporary Jewish themes. In the '40s, based in New York, with fellow dancer (and first husband) Fred Berk, created the Jewish Dance Guild and the Jewish Dance Repertory Group, devoted to interpreting "Palestinian and Jewish folk dance." In addition to performing, they taught the first courses in Jewish dance at the 92nd St. Y and at the Jewish Theological Seminary and conducted popular folk-dance festivals. In the '50s (now divorced), lived in Israel, teaching, heading a dance group, and developing an interest in Eastern movement disciplines. In the '60s, in New York, extended her own studies in ballet, modern dance, and jazz; from 1966–75 headed an interdepartmental program on "The Art of Moving" at Sarah Lawrence Coll. and taught at the Walden and Hebrew Arts Schools; with second husband Moshe Budmor conducted workshops in movement, sound, and music in Europe, Israel, and the US. An active mem. of Havurah Bet in Princeton, N.J.

FORMAN, ROBERT P., communal executive; b. Pittsburgh, Pa., July 8, 1928; d. Philadelphia, Pa., Jan. 13, 1991. Educ.: U. Pittsburgh (BA, MSW). Assoc. exec. v.-pres., Greater Miami Jewish Fed.; exec. dir. for administration, management, and fiscal affairs, UJA-Fed. of Greater NY; exec. v.-pres., Jewish Federation of Greater Philadelphia, 1976–91. Chmn., Council of Jewish Feds. Large City Exec.; mem., bd. of overseers, U. Penna. School of Social Work; mem., professional adv. com., United Way; consultant: Irish-American Partnership; Jewish community of London, England.

FRIEDMAN, MAURICE H., physician, researcher; b. E. Chicago, Ind., Oct. 27, 1903; d. Sarasota, Fla., Mar. 8, 1991. Educ.: U. Chicago (BA, PhD, MD). Served US Air Force, WWII. Instr., physiology, U. Chicago, 1926–28; instr. and asst. prof., physiology, U. Penna., 1928–36; researcher in reproductive physiology, Beltsville Agric. Research Center, 1936–42; private practice, Washington, D.C., 1946–59; assoc. prof., Georgetown U. Medical School; v.-chmn. dept. of medicine, Washington Hosp. Center. Developer of the "rabbit test" for pregnancy in the '30s. Financial adv., Planned Parenthood Assoc.; bd. mem.: Natl. Symphony Orch., Community Chest.

FRYMER, BERYL, educator, communal worker; b. Tomashgrod (Sarny), Poland, May 16, 1913; d. NYC, Jan. 19, 1991; in US since 1940. Educ.: Yeshivah, Poland; U. Liège, Belgium (LLD); Ecole des Sciences Politiques, Paris. Sec.-gen., Zionist socialist movement, Belgium, 1936–37; dir., Zionist youth fed. of W. Europe, 1937–40; dir., JNF youth dept., Paris, 1937–39; emissary to the US for Polish govt. in exile, on behalf of Polish Jews in France, 1940; exec. dir., Fed. of Polish Jews, Chicago, 1940–43; exec. dir., Jewish Natl. Workers Alliance, Chicago, 1941–45; sec.-gen., Labor Zionist Org. of USA and Canada, 1945–53; educ. dir., Histad-

rut labor council of Tel Aviv-Yafo, Israel, 1953–78; special envoy to Zionist labor movement in US, 1978 on. Mem.: Zionist Action Com., Israel Labor Party Central Com., Israel Journalists Assoc.; del., Zionist Congresses. Founder, Friends of Labor Israel, 1979, and chmn., 1983–91; mem. exec. com.: Congress of Jewish Culture, Fed. of Polish Jews, World Cong. of Yiddish and Yiddish Culture, UJA labor dept., Jewish Labor Com., and others. Author of numerous articles on politics and culture in French, Yiddish, English, and Hebrew, as well as several books; syndicated Yiddish newspaper columnist ("News from the Jewish World"). Recipient: Bezalel Shahar Prize for Adult Educ., Israel; Labor Zionist Alliance Service Award; Lifetime Achievement Award, Cong. of Jewish Culture; and other honors.

GROSS, CHAIM, sculptor; b. Kolomea, Galicia, Mar. 17, 1904; d. NYC, May 4, 1991; in US since 1921. Educ.: Educational Alliance, Beaux Arts Inst. of Design, Arts Students League. Teacher, Educational Alliance Arts School, for 68 years; teacher, New School for Social Research, for more than 40 years; worked in Public Works Arts Project in the '30s; his works exhibited in 75 museums in US and Israel. An expressionist, best known for hardwood sculptures of dynamic and exuberant figures, such as mothers with children, dancers, and acrobats; also worked in stone and clay (for bronze casting); also did watercolors, many on Jewish themes, and pen-and-ink drawings that reflected darker feelings about relatives who perished in the Holocaust. Founder, Sculptors Guild, 1938, and active mem. thereafter. Recipient: many honors, incl. Silver Medal, Paris Exposition, 1937; 2nd prize, sculpture, Met. Museum of Art, 1942; Award of Merit, Amer. Acad. of Arts and Letters, 1963; inducted into Natl. Inst. of Arts and Letters, 1964; named mem. of Amer. Acad. of Arts and Letters, 1983.

GURIN, ARNOLD, professor; b. NYC, Dec. 5, 1917; d. Boston, Mass., Feb. 15, 1991. Educ.: City Coll. of NY, Columbia U. School of Social Work, U. Michigan (PhD). Dir. budget resch., Council of Jewish Feds. and Welfare Funds, 1945–53 and dir. its field service, 1953–58; lect.: N.Y. School of Social Work, 1951–53, 1956–58; Michigan State U. School of Social Work, 1958–62; assoc. prof., social administration, Brandeis U., 1962, and prof. 1966–71; dean, Heller School for Advanced Studies in Social Welfare, 1971–76; Maurice B. Hexter prof. of American philanthropy, 1971-83. Dir., community org. curriculum project, Council on Social Work Educ., 1965–68; mem., HEW training grants review panel, 1963–68; visiting prof., Hebrew U. School of Social Work, Jerusalem, 1980; chmn., internatl. com. on evaluation of Project Renewal in Israel, 1981–85. Bd. mem., Natl. Conf. Social Welfare; mem.: Natl. Assoc. Social Workers, Amer. Sociol. Soc. Coauthor: *Community Organization and Social Plannning*; author: numerous articles in professional journals.

HAMLIN, ISADORE, organization executive, communal worker; b. Cambridge, Mass., Jan. 22, 1917; d. NYC, Mar. 1, 1991. Educ.: Cornell U. Served US Army, WWII. Admin. officer, Washington, D.C. office of the Jewish Agency (later the Embassy of Israel), 1945–49; asst. dir., Jewish Agency, NYC, 1949–61; exec. dir., Jewish Agency, Amer. Section, 1961–71; exec. dir., World Zionist Org.-Amer. Section, 1971–74, and exec. v.-chmn., 1974–88. Mem., natl. exec. com., Intercollegiate Zionist Fed. of Amer., 1940–41; mem. bd. dirs. and exec. com., Jewish Telegraphic Agency; cochmn., Social Service Div., UJA of N.Y.; mem., Labor Zionist Alliance. Recipient: Bronze Star; first Natl. B'nai B'rith Fellowship Award for advanced Jewish study; hon. life fellow, World Zionist Genl. Council.

HARTSTEIN, JACOB I., professor, communal worker; b. Stary Sambor, Austria, Sept. 10, 1912; d. NYC, Nov. 19, 1991; in U.S. since 1920. Educ.: Yeshiva Coll., City Coll. of NY (MS), Columbia U. (MA), NYU (PhD). High-school teacher, social studies, English, 1932–36; supt. of schools, bd. of secular ed., United Yeshivas, 1945–48. Held acad. and admin. posts at four insts. of higher learning: Yeshiva U.—sec., Teachers Inst., 1929–37; registrar, instr., asst. prof. and prof., educ., 1935–53; dir., grad. div., 1944–48; dean, grad. schools, 1948–53. Long Island U.—lect. and asst. prof., educ. and psych., 1938–45; prof. and chmn., depts. of educ. and psych., 1945–60; dir., grad. school, 1951–53 and dean, 1953–61; dean, school of educ., 1961–64. Kingsborough Community Coll. of CUNY—founding pres., 1964–69. City Coll. of NY—prof. educ., 1969–83. Re-

search consultant to US Navy and US Office of Educ.; founder and pres., Council of Higher Educ. Insts. in NYC; mem.: Mayor's and Governor's Coms. on Scholastic Achievement, Bd. of Jewish Educ. of NY, natl. program and educ. coms., ADL; bd. mem.: Bd. of License for Personnel in Jewish Schools, Religious Zionists of Amer., Jewish Natl. Fund, Higher Educ. Div.-UJA; trustee, Bar-Ilan U.; v.-pres., Fifth Ave. Synagogue, NYC. Recipient: Fellow, Jewish Acad. of Arts and Sciences; hon. doctorate, Yeshiva U., and other honors.

HYMES, VIOLA, communal worker; b. Chicago, Ill., May 7, 1906; d. Minneapolis, Minn., Mar. 1, 1991. Educ.: U. Minn. Mem.: Minneapolis bd. of educ., 1963–69; President Kennedy's Comm. on the Status of Women, 1961–63; President Johnson's Council on the Status of Women, 1963–68; chwmn.: Minnesota Comm. on the Status of Women, 1963–67; Minn. Adv. Com. on Aging, 1973- 81. Pres., National Council of Jewish Women, 1959–63; pres., Minneapolis sect., NCJW, 1938–42; v.pres., Internatl. Council of Jewish Women, 1957–61. Recipient: AAUW Woman of the Year; Outstanding Achievement Award, U. Minn.; Hannah G. Solomon Award, NCJW, and other honors.

JANOWSKI, MAX, cantor, composer; b. Berlin, Germany, Jan. 29, 1912; d. Hyde Park, Ill., Apr. 8, 1991; in US since 1937. Educ.: Schwarenka Conservatory of Music, Berlin. Served US Navy, WWII. Head, piano dept., Mosashino Acad., Tokyo, early 1930s; music dir., K.A.M. Isaiah Israel Cong., Chicago, 1938–91. Published over 110 compositions—Jewish liturgical works for chorus, orchestral works, cantatas, and oratorios. Best-known works: "Ovinu Malkenu" and "Sim Shalom." Was also a conductor, choir director, voice teacher, pianist, and organist. Recipient: Solomon Schechter Award (twice), United Syn. of Amer.; K'vod Award, Cantors Assembly of Amer.

KATZ, MENKE, poet, teacher; b. Svintsyan, Lithuania, Apr. 12, 1906; d. Spring Glen, N.Y., Apr. 24, 1991; in US since 1920. Educ.: Columbia U., Jewish Theological Seminary, Jewish Teachers' Seminary. Editor, *Bitterroot* (internatl. poetry quarterly), 1962–91; teacher of Yiddish; teacher of poetry. Au.: 18 vols. of poetry, 9 in Yiddish, 9 in English. His 2-vol. epic poem *Brendik Shtetl* (("Burning Village"), 1938, brought him recognition, and the English version, 1972, was nominated for a Pulitzer Prize. Began publishing English poetry in 1950s, appearing in *Atlantic Monthly*, the *New York Times*, and other publications. Recipient: Stephen Vincent Benét Narrative Poetry Award, 1970, 1974.

KESTENBERG, MILTON, attorney, communal worker; b. Lodz, Poland, (?), 1912; d. NYC, Nov. 20, 1991; in US since 1939. Educ.: U. Vilna, U. Warsaw, St. John's U. (LLD). Founder and pres., Kenyon Associates, real-estate management firm in Manhattan. As a lawyer, represented Holocaust survivors, particularly those who had been children at the time, with claims for reparations and restitution of property in the German courts. Cofounder, with his wife, a psychoanalyst, of Internatl. Study of Organized Persecution of Chidren in the Holocaust (for which they collected hundreds of interviews worldwide), Child Development Research, and Assoc. of Children Survivors. Author: "Discriminatory Aspects of the German Indemnification Policy," in *Generations of the Holocaust*.

KLEIN, DONALD H., organization executive; b. NYC, 1933 (?); d. NYC, Mar. 6, 1991. Educ.: City Coll. of NY, Columbia U. School of Social Work. Dir., Jewish feds., Hollywood, Fla. and Stamford, Conn.; asst. exec. v.-chmn., Natl. United Jewish Appeal; exec. v.-pres., Amer. ORT Fed., 1980–91.

KLING, SIMCHA, rabbi, author; b. Ft. Thomas, Ky., Jan. 27, 1922; d. Louisville, Ky., Feb. 26, 1991. Educ.: Gymnasia Hertzlia, Tel Aviv; U. Cincinnati, Columbia U., Jewish Theol. Sem. of Amer. (ord., DHL). Asst. rabbi and educ. dir., Cong. B'nai Amoona, St. Louis, 1948–51; rabbi: Beth Beth David Syn., Greensboro, N.C., 1951–65; Cong. Adath Jeshurun, Louisville, Ky., 1965–88 and emer. thereafter. Lect.: U. Louisville, Bellarmine Coll. Pres., N.C. Assoc. of Rabbis and Louisville Bd. of Rabbis; pres., Louisville Hebrew Speaking Circle; founder: United Syn. Youth and MERCAZ; mem., Amer. Jewish Hist. Soc., Histadrut Ivrit, and AIPAC. Author: *Nachum Sokolow: Servant of His People*, *Menachem Ussishkin: The Mighty Warrior*, *Am ve-Artzo: The People and Its Land*, and other works on Zionism; *Em-*

bracing Judaism (on conversion), and articles, reviews, and translations in various publications. Recipient: hon. doctorates, JTS, Bellarmine Coll.

KOSINSKI, JERZY N., writer; b. Lodz, Poland, June 14, 1933; d. NYC, May 3, 1991; in US since 1957. Educ.: U. Lodz, Columbia U. Asst. prof., sociol., Polish Acad. of Sciences, Warsaw, 1955–57; grad. study, Columbia, 1958–65; Ford Found. fellow, 1958–60; Guggenheim lit. fellow, 1967; fellow, Center for Advanced Studies, Wesleyan U., 1969–70; sr. fellow, Council for the Humanities, vis. lect., Princeton U., 1969–70; vis. prof., Yale School of Drama and resident fellow, Davenport Coll., 1970–73; fellow, Timothy Dwight Coll., Yale U., 1986 on. Hon. bd. chmn., Found. for Polish-Jewish Studies; pres., founder, Jewish Presence Found.; cochmn., Found. for Ethnic Understanding; bd. chmn., Polish-Amer. Resources Corp.; exec. bd. mem. and pres., PEN, 1973–75; bd. mem.: Natl. Writers Club, Internatl. League for Human Rights; chmn. artists and writers com. and mem. natl. adv. council, ACLU; mem. Authors Guild, Century Assoc. Author: 2 colls. of essays, under pseud. Joseph Novak: *The Future Is Ours, Comrade* (1960); *No Third Path* (1962). His novel *The Painted Bird* (1965), a somewhat autobiog. account of a boy's harrowing experiences during the Holocaust, received critical acclaim. Other works incl. *Steps*, *Being There* (and its screenplay), *The Devil Tree*, *Cockpit*, *Blind Date*, *Passion Play*, *Pinball*, *The Hermit of 69th St.* Recipient: Natl. Book Award, 1968 (*Steps*); Award in Lit., Amer. Acad. Arts and Letters, 1970; Brith Sholom Humanitarian Freedom Award; Best Screenplay of Year, Writers Guild of Amer., 1979 (*Being There*); hon. doctorates: Albion Coll., Potsdam Coll., and Spertus Coll. of Judaica (to which he bequeathed his literary and artistic estate), and other honors.

KRAMARSKY, LOLA, communal worker; b. Hamburg, Germany, (?), 1896; d. NYC, Feb. 28, 1991; in US since 1940. Lived in Holland 1932–39, where she became involved in rescuing children from the Nazi threat. An active mem. of Hadassah from her arrival in the US, served as natl. treas., natl. v.-pres., chwmn. Youth Aliyah and wills and bequests; fund-raising coord.; natl. pres., 1960–64; natl. chwmn. Hadassah Medical Org., 1965–69; del. to World

Zionist Congs. Named life mem., Zionist Genl. Council of the WZO, 1978. Founder: Hadassah-Hebrew U. Medical Center, Amer. Friends of the Israel Museum; mem., Cong. Shearith Israel, NYC.

KWELLER, GOLDIE B., communal worker; b. Brooklyn, NY, Nov. 14, 1922; d. NYC, June 9, 1991. Educ.: Herzliah Hebrew HS, Hunter Coll., Pratt Inst. Sisterhood pres., Jewish Center of Kew Gardens Hills and 1st woman elected to bd. of dirs.; longtime active mem. in Women's League for Conservative Judaism, serving as natl. pres., 1978–82; pres., MERCAZ, 1989–91; mem., bd. of overseers, Jewish Theol. Sem. of Amer.; treas., v.-pres., pres., mem. bd. dirs., Met. Region, United Syn. of Amer.; v.-pres., World Council of Syns.; sec.: Natl. Assoc. Solomon Schechter Day Schools, Amer. sect.-World Jewish Cong.; del., Jewish Agency Exec.; trustee, Jewish Braille Inst.; mem. bd. of dirs.: JNF, Alfred U. Recipient: JTS Community Leadership Award; JTS Solomon Schechter Medal; Woman of the Year, Queens UJA-Fed.; Women's League for Conservative Judaism Aderet V'Emunah Award.

LAND, EDWIN H., inventor, business executive; b. Norwich, Conn., May 7, 1909; d. Cambridge, Mass., Mar. 1, 1991. Educ.: Harvard Coll. (no degree). A largely self-taught scientist who held patents for over 530 inventions, incl. the instant, one-step Polaroid photographic process which he developed in the '30s and '40s. Co-founder, Land-Wheelwright Labs., 1932; founder and chmn., Polaroid Corp., 1937–1982, pres. 1937–1975, as well as CEO and dir. research; founder, Rowland Inst. for Science, 1980. Trustee, Ford Found.; pres., Amer. Acad. Arts and Sciences. Recipient: hon. doctorates from Harvard U., Tufts U., Poly. Inst. Brooklyn, Yale U., Columbia U., Brandeis U., and other insts.; numerous honors, incl. Presidential Medal of Freedom and Natl. Medal of Science.

LICHTENSTADTER, ILSE, professor; b. Hamburg, Germany, Sept. 10, 1907; d. Boston, Mass., May 22, 1991; in US since 1938. Educ.: U. Frankfurt (PhD), Oxford U. (PhD). Judaica cataloguer, Jewish Theol. Sem., 1938–45; lect.: Arabic lit. and Islamic culture, Asia Inst., NYC, 1942–52; dept. regional studies, NYU, 1952–60; hist. dept., Rutgers U., 1959–60; Arabic, Harvard U., 1960–74. Mem. Amer. Oriental Soc., Middle East Studies Assoc. Author:

Women in the Aiyam-al-Arab, Islam and the Modern Age, Introduction to Classical Arabic Literature, and other works; ed. *Kitab al-Muhabbar*; genl. ed., *Library of Classical Arabic Literature*.

LITEWKA, JULKO, communal worker; b.(?), Poland, Mar. 14, 1912; d. NYC, Sept. 1, 1991; in US since 1941. Joined the Jewish Labor Bund at age 10 in Poland; served as youth sec. 1933–39; worked as a garment presser in NY while continuing activity in the Bund; genl. sec., 1985–91. Mem. exec. com., Jewish Labor Com.; mem.: Workmen's Circle, Cong. for Jewish Culture.

LURIA, SALVADOR E., physician, biologist; b. Turin, Italy, Aug. 13, 1912; d. Lexington, Mass., Feb. 6, 1991; in US since 1940. Educ.: U. Turin (MD). Research fellow, Curie Lab., Inst. of Radium, Paris, 1938–40; research asst., bacteriology, Columbia U., 1940–42; instr., asst. prof., assoc. prof., Indiana U., 1943–50; prof., U. Illinois, 1950–59; prof., microbiology, Mass. Inst. Technology, 1959–78, and inst. prof. emer. thereafter; founder and dir., MIT Center for Cancer Research, 1972–85; also taught world lit. course to grad. students at MIT and medical students at Harvard. His Nobel-prize-winning research (with associates) was for "discoveries concerning the replication mechanism and the genetic structure of viruses," which helped lay the foundation for modern molecular biology. A vocal critic of the war in Vietnam, lack of safeguards in nuclear-power industry, and Israel's invasion of Lebanon. Corecipient, Nobel Prize for medicine, 1969. Recipient: Natl. Book Award, 1974, for a nonacademic work, *Life: The Unfinished Experiment*; hon. doctorates: U. Chicago, U. Palermo, and many others.

NATHAN, ERNEST, business exec., communal worker; b. Augsburg, Germany, June 21, 1905; d. Providence, R.I., Nov. 2, 1991; in US since 1930. Educ.: Inst. Textile Tech., Reutlingen, Germany (chemical eng.). Pres.: Warwick Chemical Co., 1930–52; exec. v.-pres., PEC Israel Econ. Corp., 1952–54; pres., dir., Chemo Products, Inc., 1954–61; pres., Elmwick Sensors, 1961–81. Dir., PEC Israel Econ. Corp., 1948 on; mem. bd. govs., Technion-Israel Inst. Technology; pres., Temple Beth-El, Providence.

NEMEROV, HOWARD, poet, writer; b. NYC, Mar. 1, 1920; d. St. Louis, Mo., July 5, 1991. Educ.: Harvard Coll. Pilot, USAF and RAF, WWII. Instr., Hamilton Coll., 1946–48; mem. fac., Bennington Coll., 1948–66; prof.: Brandeis U., 1966–69; Washington U., St. Louis, 1969–90; poet laureate of the US, 1988–90. Author: More than two dozen works of fiction, essays, and poetry, incl. *The Collected Poems of Howard Nemerov* (1977) and *A Howard Nemerov Reader* (1991). Recipient: Award for Novel, Amer. Inst. Arts and Letters, 1961; fellow: Amer. Acad. Arts and Sciences, Amer. Acad. Poets; Pulitzer Prize and Natl. Book Award, 1978 (for *Collected Poems*); National Medal of Arts (1987), Bollingen Prize, Theodore Roethke Memorial Prize, Guggenheim fellowship; inducted into Natl. Inst. Arts and Letters, 1960; named mem. Amer. Acad. Arts and Letters, 1976; hon. doctorates from 13 colls. and univs. and many other honors.

PANITZ, DAVID H., rabbi; b. Baltimore, Md., Mar. 6, 1918; d. Paterson, N.J., Jan. 25, 1991. Educ.: Baltimore City Coll.; Johns Hopkins U., Baltimore Hebrew Coll., Jewish Theol. Sem. of Amer. Served US Army, WWII. Assoc. rabbi, B'nai Jeshurun, NYC, 1946–51; rabbi: Cong. Adas Israel, Washington, D.C., 1951–59; Temple Emanuel, Paterson, N.J., 1959–88, and emer. thereafter. Cofounder and pres., N.J. Bd. of Rabbis; chmn., interreligious affairs com., ADL, and rep. on Jewish missions to the Vatican, 1983 and 1985; cochmn., Natl. Rabbinic Cabinet, Israel Bonds; v.-pres., Jewish Conciliation Bd. of Amer.; sec., Rabbinical Assembly, and chmn. its placement comm.; fellow, Herbert Lehman Inst. of Talmudic Ethics, JTS. Mem. fac.: George Washington U., American U., Howard U., JTS. V.-pres.: N.J. Family and Children's Service; chmn., Passaic County Alcoholic and Narcotic Rehab. Bd.; chaplain, Paterson hosps., police and fire depts., and Passaic County jail. Recipient: hon. doctorate, JTS.

PAPP (PAPIROFSKY), JOSEPH, theatrical producer, director; b. Brooklyn, NY, June 22, 1921; d. NYC, Oct. 31, 1991. Served US Navy, WWII. Early career as actor, mgr., dir., Actors Laboratory Theater, Hollywood; dir., Equity Library Theater, NYC; stage mgr., CBS TV. Founded New York Shakespeare Festival, offering free performances of Shakespeare's plays, in a church basement on the Lower East Side, 1954; moved it to Central Park in 1956; inaugurated permanent Delacorte Theater

in the park, 1962; purchased landmark Astor Library in lower Manhattan (former home of HIAS) in 1966, converting it into his HQ and a six-theater complex called the New York Shakespeare Festival Public Theater. Regarded as the leading figure in noncommercial and institutional theater in the US; championed and helped the careers of many young playwrights and actors; originated two landmark Amer. musicals, *Hair* and *A Chorus Line*, which went on to achieve commercial success; three plays he produced won Pulitzer Prizes and his plays won more than 20 Tony Awards. In the last decade of his life, produced the Yiddish "Songs of Paradise" at Public Theater and assisted YIVO by arranging benefits. Recipient: numerous awards, incl. Special Tony Award for Prof. Excellence and Disting. Achievement in Theater; Gold Medal for Disting. Service to the Arts, Amer. Acad. Arts and Letters.

PERILMAN, NATHAN A., rabbi; b. Marietta, Ohio, June 2, 1905; d. Briarcliff Manor, N.Y., Feb. 27, 1991. Educ.: U. Pittsburgh, Hebrew Union Coll. Asst. rabbi, assoc. rabbi, sr. rabbi, Temple Emanu-El, NYC, 1932–1973. Pres., Assoc. Reform Rabbis of NYC; cochmn., rabbis' div., Fed. Jewish Philanthropies; bd. mem.: Educational Alliance, 92nd St. YM-YWHA, Jewish Braille Inst., Jewish Statistical Bur., Amer. Friends of Hebrew U.; mem. exec. com.: Amer. Jewish Com., N.Y. Fed. Reform Syns.; trustee, Hebrew Union Coll. School of Educ. and Sacred Music; mem. bd. govs., HUC; mem.: Gov. Dewey's Comm. for Children, US State Dept. mission to Germany. Recipient: hon. doctorates, Florida Southern Coll., Hebrew Union Coll.

PETUCHOWSKI, JAKOB J., professor, rabbi; b. Berlin, Germany, July 30, 1925; d. Cincinnati, Ohio, Nov. 12, 1991; in US since 1948. Educ.: U. London; Gateshead Yeshivah; Hebrew Union Coll. (ord. and PhD). Asst. to Rabbi Leo Baeck and youth dir., World Union for Progressive Judaism, London, 1946–48; rabbi: Welch, W. Va., 1949–55; Washington, Pa., 1955–56. Asst. prof., rabbinics, Hebrew Union Coll., 1956–59; assoc. prof. 1959–63; prof. 1963–65; prof., rabbinics and theology, 1965–74; research prof., Jewish theology and liturgy since 1974; prof., Judeo-Christian studies, since 1981; 1st dir. of Jewish studies, Jerusalem campus of HUC, 1963. Visiting prof.: Oxford, Harvard U. School of Divinity, Theological Fac. of Lucerne, Switz., U. Arizona, Antioch Coll., Tel Aviv U., and others. Author: over 600 scholarly articles and 36 books, incl. *The Theology of Haham David Nieto* (1954, 1970); *Ever Since Sinai: A Modern View of Torah* (1961); *Prayerbook Reform in Europe* (1968); *Heirs of the Pharisees* (1970, 1986); *Understanding Jewish Prayer* (1972); and *When Jews and Christians Meet* (1988). Recipient: Fellow, Amer. Acad. for Jewish Research; hon. doctorates, U. Cologne, Brown U.; Decorated Order of Merit 1st class, Fed. Republic of Germany.

PILPEL, HARRIET, attorney; b. NYC, (?) 1912; d. NYC, Apr. 23, 1991. Educ.: Vassar Coll.; Columbia U. (MA, LLB). Sr. partner, Greenbaum, Wolff & Ernst; counsel, Weil, Gotshal & Manges; genl. counsel: Planned Parenthood Fed., Amer. Civil Liberties Union, Assoc. for Voluntary Surgical Contraception; special counsel, Planned Parenthood of NYC; mem.: Kennedy and Johnson Comms. on the Status of Women; panel of experts, US Govt. Copyright Off.; 1st v.-chwmn., natl. adv. council, Amer. Civil Liberties Union; mem.: bd. visitors, Columbia U. Law School; bd. mem., Population Resource Center; cochwmn., Natl. Coalition Against Censorship; chwmn., panel on law and planned parenthood, Internatl. Planned Parenthood Fed.; trustee, NY Ethical Culture Soc.; chwmn., devel. law and policy program, Columbia U. Center for Population and Family Health; cochwmn., Natl. Coalition Against Censorship; founding mem., the Women's Forum; mem. com. on law, social action, and urban affairs, Amer. Jewish Cong.. Recipient: NY Civil Liberties Found. Award, SIECUS Award, Margaret Sanger Award, Louise Waterman Wise Laureate Award, Earl Warren Civil Liberties Award, Columbia U. Law School Medal for Excellence, and other honors.

PORTER, SYLVIA F., columnist, author; b. Patchogue, N.Y., June 18, 1913; d. Pound Ridge, N.Y., June 5, 1991. Educ.: Hunter Coll. Worked in a small investment counseling firm in Wall St.; began writing in financial journals, then a weekly column on US govt. securities in *American Banker*; columnist on economics and personal finance, *New York Post*, 1935–1978, *Daily News*, 1978 on, and syndicated internationally in 450 newspapers. Author: many

books, beginning with *How to Make Money in Government Bonds* (1939) and *If War Comes to the American Home* (1941), and incl. *Sylvia Porter's Money Book: How to Earn It, Spend It, Save It, Invest It, Borrow It and Use It to Better Your Life* (1975), which sold more than a million copies.

POSTER, HERBERT, editor; b. NYC, Mar. 7, 1913; d. NYC, May 22, 1991. Educ.: U. Michigan. Free-lance writer; co-founder, International Universities Press; writer, Amer. Jewish Com., 1948–50; asst. ed., *Congress Weekly*, 1951–65; ed., *Congress Bi-Weekly*, later *Congress Monthly*, 1966–81, published by the Amer. Jewish Congress.

RAPOPORT, LOUIS, journalist, author; b. Los Angeles, Calif., Nov. 7, 1942; d. Jerusalem, Israel, June 20, 1991. Educ.: U. Calif., Berkeley. Owner, poster business; teacher, Soledad prison; reporter, ed., *San Francisco Chronicle*; settled in Israel 1973; held various editorial positions at *Jerusalem Post*, incl. ed. internatl. edition, chief night ed., and asst. to the ed.; corresp., *Los Angeles Jewish Journal* and public radio station KCRW-FM, Los Angeles. Through his reporting and his books, credited with bringing world attention to the causes of Ethiopian and Soviet Jews. Author: *The Lost Jews: Last of the Ethiopian Falashas* (1980); *Redemption Song: The Story of Operation Moses* (1986); *Shake Heaven and Earth: Peter Bergson and the Rescue of the Jews of Europe* (1988); *Stalin's War Against the Jews: The Doctors' Plot and the Soviet Solution* (1990); co-au. and ed., *Anatoly and Avital Shcharansky: The Journey Home* (1986).

SANDERS, RONALD, writer, professor; b. Union City, N.J., July 7, 1932; d. NYC, Jan. 11, 1991. Educ.: Kenyon Coll., Columbia U. Served US Army, 1953–55. Lect., history, Queens Coll., 1958–65; assoc. ed., *Midstream* magazine, 1965–73, and ed., 1973–75. Author: *Israel: The View from Masada* (1966); *The Downtown Jews: Portrait of an Immigrant Generation* (1969); *Reflections on a Teapot* (1972); *Lost Tribes and Promised Lands* (1978); *The Days Grow Short: The Life and Music of Kurt Weill* (1980); *The High Walls of Jerusalem* (1984); *Shores of Refuge: A Hundred Years of Jewish Emigration* (1988); co-ed.: *Socialist Thought: A Documentary History* (1964). Recipient: Fulbright fellowship, 1960–61; B'nai B'rith

Book Award, 1970; NY Public Library Literary Lion Award, 1987.

SCHAFLER, SAMUEL, rabbi, educator; b. NYC, Feb. 20, 1929; d. Boston, Mass., Apr. 3, 1991. Educ.: City Coll. of NY; Jewish Theol. Sem. of Amer. (ord.; PhD). Rabbi, Knesseth Israel Syn., Gloversville, NY, 1952–55; assoc. dir., United Syn. Comm. on Jewish Educ., 1955–61; rabbi, Temple Gates of Prayer, Flushing, N.Y., 1961–76; adj. prof., Jewish history, Queens Coll., 1974–76; fellow in community planning, Bd. of Jewish Educ. of N.Y., dir., Ramah Israel community program, 1968–76; supt., Chicago Bd. of Jewish Educ., 1976–1987; pres., Hebrew Coll. of Boston, Mass., 1987 on. Ed.: *Synagogue School* and *Our Age* magazine; assoc. ed., *Pedagogic Reporter*. Author: articles in numerous magazines and journals.

SIEGMEISTER, ELIE, composer, author; b. NYC, Jan. 15, 1909; d. Manhasset, N.Y., Mar. 10, 1991. Educ.: Columbia U.; studied with Nadia Boulanger, Paris; Ecole Normale de Musique, Paris; Juilliard Grad. School of Music. Prof., music, Hofstra U., 1949–76; composer-in-residence, 1966–76; conductor Hofstra Symphony Orch., 1953–65. In 1930s, collected and notated American folk music, which he published in 1940 in *A Treasury of American Song*, with critic Olin Downs, and performed across the US with Amer. Ballad Singers, 1942–46. Composed 8 operas, 8 symphonies, and numerous songs, choral settings, concertos, orchestral works, and chamber pieces. Author: (in addition to *Treasury*): *Work and Sing*, *Invitation to Music*, *Harmony and Melody*, *The New Music Lover's Handbook*, and articles in various publications. Mem. bd. dirs., ASCAP, and cochmn. its symphony and concert com. Recipient: named member Amer. Acad. Arts and Letters, 1990.

SILVERMAN, IRA D., organization executive, communal leader; b. Rockville Centre, N.Y., Jan. 20, 1945; d. NYC, June 23, 1991. Educ.: Harvard Coll., Princeton U. (MPA). Dean of admissions, Woodrow Wilson School, Princeton U., 1968–71; dir., federal relations, Assoc. Amer. Univs., 1971–72; dir., Inst. Jewish Policy Planning and Research, Syn. Council of Amer., 1972–76; natl. program dir., Amer. Jewish Com., 1977–81; pres., Reconstructionist Rabbinical Coll., 1981–86; exec.

dir., 92nd St. YM-YWHA, 1986–1988; exec. v.-pres., Amer. Jewish Com., 1988–1990. V.-pres., Assoc. Princeton Graduate Alumni; mem. adv. bd.: Princeton U. dept. of religion, Princeton U. chapel, Brandeis U. Center for Modern Jewish Studies, Brandeis U. Program in Jewish Communal Service; bd. mem.: New Israel Fund, Mazon, Natl. Found. for Jewish Culture, Amer. Jewish World Service; ed. bd. mem., *Hadassah* magazine.

SILVERSTEIN, ELIZABETH BLUME, attorney, communal worker; b. Newark, N.J., Nov. 2, 1892; d. NYC, Feb . 3, 1991. Educ.: New Jersey (now Rutgers) Law School, 1911 (LLB at age 19, too young for admission to the bar). Clerked for two years; admitted to the bar in 1913; maintained own law office in Newark from then until mid-'80s. First woman lawyer in N.J. to practice law and first woman to try homicide cases unassisted; an expert in criminal law, admitted to US Supreme Court bar in 1922. Legal advisor to draft bd., WWI; v.-pres., Woman Lawyers Assoc.; N.J. state del., Natl. Assoc. Woman Lawyers; del., Republican natl. convention, 1932. Elected to 1st and 2nd Amer. Jewish Cong., 1917, 1923; mem. its exec. com. in 1920s, immigration com., and hon. v.-pres., 1929; del., 1st World Jewish Congress, Geneva, Switz., 1936; pres., Louis D. Brandeis Lodge, Independent Order B'rith Abraham, first woman mem. its natl. exec., chwmn. com. on Jewish rights, and asst. to Grand Master; mem. Hadassah, Zionist org., and other orgs.

SWIFT, ISAAC L., rabbi; b. Liverpool, England, Oct. 19, 1910; d. Englewood, N.J., May 24, 1991; in US since 1954. Educ.: Liverpool U., Oxford U., Yeshivat Etz Chaim, Israel (ord.). Rabbi: London, Eng., 1940s; Sydney, Aus., 1951–54; Cong. Anshe Sfard, Brooklyn, N.Y., 1954–60; Cong. Ahavath Torah, Englewood, N.J., 1960–84; emer. thereafter. Founder: Moriah Day School, Englewood, N.J., and Frisch Yeshiva High School of Northern N.J.; founder and 1st pres., Rabbinical Council of Bergen County. Fac. mem.: Herzl Inst., 92nd St. YM-YWHA; Touro Coll.; guest lect., U. N. Carolina. Mem.: Rabbinical Council of Amer., Religious Zionists of Amer. Recipient: Jewish studies chairs established in his name at U. N. Carolina and at Jewish Community Center of Teaneck, N.J.

TABAK, ISRAEL, rabbi; b. Bucovina, Romania, Dec. 7, 1904; d. Jerusalem, Israel, Apr. 16, 1991; in US since mid-1920s. Educ.: Yeshivahs in Romania and Poland, Yeshiva U. (ord.), NYU, Johns Hopkins U. (PhD). Rabbi: Union City, N.J., 1926–31; Cong. Shaarei Zion, Baltimore, Md., 1931–76. Instr., Ner Israel Coll., Baltimore; mem.: Baltimore Bd. of Jewish Educ. and bd. of Talmudical Acad.; pres., Rabbinical Council of Amer., late 1940s, as well as hon. pres., mem. exec. com., and mem. prayer book comm.; natl. chmn. and exec. bd. mem., Religious Zionists of Amer.; del., World Zionist Cong., 1933; bd. mem.: JWB, Union of Orthodox Jewish Congs.; del., Syn. Council of Amer. Author: *Treasury of Holy Day Thoughts, Judaic Lore in Heine—The Heritage of a Poet, Heine and His Heritage, Rashi and the Western World*, and other works. Recipient: hon. doctorate, Yeshiva U.

WOLF, EDWIN, II, rare-books specialist; communal worker; b. Philadelphia, Pa., Dec. 6, 1911; d. Philadelphia, Pa., Feb. 20, 1991. Educ.: private schools in England. Served counterintelligence corps, US Army, WWII. Cataloger, bibliographer, mgr., Rosenbach Co. (rare books and manuscripts), 1930–52; lect., bibliography, Bryn Mawr Coll., 1941–42; associated with the Library Co. of Phila. (founded by Benjamin Franklin, 1731) as curator, 1953–55, and librarian, 1955–84; Rosenbach fellow in bibliography, U. Pa., 1964; Lyell reader in bibliography, Oxford U., 1985–86. Pres.: Greater Phila. Cultural Alliance, 1977–78; Bibliog. Soc. of Amer; v.-pres., United Fund of Phila; mem., Mayor's Cultural Adv. Com., 1984–86; assoc. trustee, U. of Pa. Pres.: Jewish Publication Soc. of Amer., 1955–59, and chmn. its publications com.; Fed. of Jewish Charities of Greater Phila., 1959–62; Natl.

Found. for Jewish Culture, 1960–65; *Jewish Exponent*, 1966–68; mem. exec. council, Amer. Jewish Hist. Soc.; bd. mem., JWB. Coauthor: *History of the Jews of Philadelphia*; *Rosenbach: A Biography*; author: *American Songsheets, Slip Ballads, & Poetical Broadsides, 1850–1870*; *Philadelphia: A Portrait of an American City*; *At the Instance of Benjamin Franklin: A Brief History of the Library Company*; as well as exhibition catalogues, articles in magazines and journals, and other works. Recipient: Guggenheim fellowship, 1961; Athenaeum Lit. Award, Penn Club Award, Amer. Printing Hist. Assoc. Award, Disting. Pennsylvanian Award, and other honors; hon. doctorates: Coll. of Jewish Studies, Chicago; LaSalle U.; U. Pa.

WOLK, ASHER, journalist, editor; b. (?), Poland, Aug. 13, 1913; d. NYC, Nov. 16, 1991; in US since 1933. Educ.: Hebrew Sem., Vilna, Lithuania; Yeshiva U. Served US Army, WWII. Journalist since 1946; dir., Jewish press relations, World Zionist Org., 1953–89; founder, Hebrew Publications for Children, and ed.-in- chief, *Olam Hadash* magazine, 1960 on. Mem.: Bnai Zion, Farband, ZOA, Yiddish Writers Union, Histadruth Ivrith. Author: political articles for the *Jewish Forward* and *Algemeiner-Journal*.

ZALES, GLADYS D., communal worker; b. NYC, Mar. 16, 1914; d. Greenwich, Conn., Nov. 1, 1991. Natl. v.-pres., Hadassah, mem. its natl. bd., chwmn. of various coms. and two natl. conventions, and pres. Conn. region; membership chwmn. and mem. exec. com., Natl. Council of Negro Women; del., White House Conf. on Civil Rights; bd. mem., Family and Children Services of Stamford, Conn.; founder, Albert Einstein Coll. of Medicine; del. to several World Zionist Congresses.

Calendars

SUMMARY JEWISH CALENDAR, 5753–5757 (Sept. 1992–Sept. 1997)

HOLIDAY	5753			5754			5755			5756			5757		
	1992			1993			1994			1995			1996		
Rosh Ha-shanah, 1st day	M	Sept.	28	Th	Sept.	16	T	Sept.	6	M	Sept.	25	Sa	Sept.	14
Rosh Ha-shanah, 2nd day	T	Sept.	29	F	Sept.	17	W	Sept.	7	T	Sept.	26	S	Sept.	15
Fast of Gedaliah	W	Sept.	30	S	Sept.	19	Th	Sept.	8	W	Sept.	27	M	Sept.	16
Yom Kippur	W.	Oct.	7	Sa	Sept.	25	Th	Sept.	15	W	Oct.	4	M	Sept.	23
Sukkot, 1st day	M	Oct.	12	Th	Sept.	30	T	Sept.	20	M	Oct.	9	Sa	Sept.	28
Sukkot, 2nd day	T	Oct.	13	F	Oct.	1	W	Sept.	21	T	Oct.	10	S	Sept.	29
Hosha'na' Rabbah	S	Oct.	18	W	Oct.	6	M	Sept.	26	S	Oct.	15	F	Oct.	4
Shemini 'Azeret	M	Oct.	19	Th	Oct.	7	T	Sept.	27	M	Oct.	16	Sa	Oct.	5
Simhat Torah	T.	Oct.	20	F	Oct.	8	W	Sept.	28	T	Oct.	17	S	Oct.	6
New Moon, Heshwan, 1st day	T	Oct.	27	F	Oct.	15	W	Oct.	5	T	Oct.	24	S	Oct.	13
New Moon, Heshwan, 2nd day	W	Oct.	28	Sa	Oct.	16	Th	Oct.	6	W	Oct.	25	M	Oct.	14
New Moon, Kislew, 1st day	Th	Nov.	26	S	Nov.	14	F	Nov.	4	Th	Nov.	23	T	Nov.	12
New Moon, Kislew, 2nd day				M	Nov.	15				F	Nov.	24			
Hanukkah, 1st day	S	Dec.	20	Th	Dec.	9	M	Nov.	28	M	Dec.	18	F	Dec.	6
New Moon, Tevet, 1st day	F	Dec.	25	T	Dec.	14	Sa	Dec.	3	Sa	Dec.	23	W	Dec.	11
New Moon, Tevet, 2nd day				W	Dec.	15	S	Dec.	4	S	Dec. 1996	24			
Fast of 10th of Tevet	S	Jan. 1993	3	F	Dec.	24	T	Dec.	13	T	Jan. 1996	2	F	Dec.	20

	1993	1994	1995	1996	1997
New Moon, Shevat	Sa Jan. 23	Th Jan. 13	M Jan. 2	M Jan. 22	Th Jan. 9
Hamishshah-'asar bi-Shevat	Sa Feb. 6	Th Jan. 27	M Jan. 16	M Feb. 5	Th Jan. 23
New Moon, Adar I, 1st day	S Feb. 21	F Feb. 11	T Jan. 31	T Feb. 20	F Feb. 7
New Moon, Adar I, 2nd day	M Feb. 22	Sa Feb. 12	W Feb. 1	W Feb. 21	Sa Feb. 8
New Moon, Adar II, 1st day			Th Mar. 2		S Mar. 9
New Moon, Adar II, 2nd day			F Mar. 3		M Mar. 10
Fast of Esther	Th Mar. 4	Th Feb. 24	W Mar. 15	M Mar. 4	Th Mar. 20
Purim	S Mar. 7	F Feb. 25	Th Mar. 16	T Mar. 5	S Mar. 23
Shushan Purim	M Mar. 8	Sa Feb. 26	F Mar. 17	W Mar. 6	M Mar. 24
New Moon, Nisan	T Mar. 23	S Mar. 13	Sa Apr. 1	Th Mar. 21	T Apr. 8
Passover, 1st day	T Apr. 6	S Mar. 27	Sa Apr. 15	Th Apr. 4	T Apr. 22
Passover, 2nd day	W Apr. 7	M Mar. 28	S Apr. 16	F Apr. 5	W Apr. 23
Passover, 7th day	M Apr. 12	Sa Apr. 2	F Apr. 21	W Apr. 10	M Apr. 28
Passover, 8th day	T Apr. 13	S Apr. 3	Sa Apr. 22	Th Apr. 11	T Apr. 29
Holocaust Memorial Day	S Apr. 18	F Apr. 8*	Th Apr. 27	T Apr. 16	S May 4
New Moon, Iyar, 1st day	W Apr. 21	M Apr. 11	S Apr. 30	F Apr. 19	W May 7
New Moon, Iyar, 2nd day	Th Apr. 22	T Apr. 12	M May 1	Sa Apr. 20	Th May 8
Israel Independence Day	M Apr. 26	Sa Apr. 16†	F May 5*	W Apr. 24	M May 12
Lag Ba-'omer	S May 9	F Apr. 29	Th May 18	T May 7	S May 25
Jerusalem Day	W May 19	M May 9	S May 28	F May 17*	W June 4
New Moon, Siwan	F May 21	W May 11	T May 30	S May 19	F June 6
Shavu'ot, 1st day	W May 26	M May 16	S June 4	F May 24	W June 11
Shavu'ot, 2nd day	Th May 27	T May 17	M June 5	Sa May 25	Th June 12
New Moon, Tammuz, 1st day	Sa June 19	Th June 9	W June 28	M June 17	Sa July 5
New Moon, Tammuz, 2nd day	S June 20	F June 10	Th June 29	T June 18	S July 6
Fast of 17th of Tammuz	T July 6	S June 26	S July 16	Th July 4	T July 22
New Moon, Av	M July 19	Sa July 9	F July 28	W July 17	M Aug. 4
Fast of 9th of Av	T July 27	S July 17	S Aug. 6	Th July 25	T Aug. 12
New Moon, Elul, 1st day	T Aug. 17	S Aug. 7	Sa Aug. 26	Th Aug. 15	T Sept. 2
New Moon, Elul, 2nd day	W Aug. 18	M Aug. 8	S Aug. 27	F Aug. 16	W Sept. 3

*Observed Thursday, a day earlier, to avoid conflict with the Sabbath.
†Observed Thursday, two days earlier, to avoid conflict with the Sabbath.

CONDENSED MONTHLY CALENDAR
(1992-1995)

1991, Dec. 8–Jan. 5 1992]   TEVET (29 DAYS)   [5752

Civil Date	Day of the Week	Jewish Date	SABBATHS, FESTIVALS, FASTS	PENTATEUCHAL READING	PROPHETICAL READING
Dec. 8	S	Tevet 1	New Moon, second day; Hanukkah, seventh day	Num. 28:1–15 Num. 7:48–53	
9	M	2	Hanukkah, eighth day	Num. 7:54–8:4	
14	Sa	7	Wa-yiggash	Gen. 44:18–47:27	Ezekiel 37:15–28
17	T	10	Fast of 10th of Tevet	Exod. 32:11–14 Exod. 34:1–10 (morning and afternoon)	Isaiah 55:6–56:8 (afternoon only)
21	Sa	14	Wa-yehi	Gen. 47:28–50:26	I Kings 2:1–12
28	Sa	21	Shemot	Exod. 1:1–6:1	Isaiah 27:6–28:13 29:22–23 *Jeremiah 1:1–2:3*
Jan. 4	Sa	28	Wa-'era'	Exod. 6:2–9:35	Ezekiel 28:25–29:21

Italics are for
Sephardi Minhag.

1992, Jan. 6–Feb. 4]   SHEVAṬ (30 DAYS)   [5752

Civil Date	Day of the Week	Jewish Date	SABBATHS, FESTIVALS, FASTS	PENTATEUCHAL READING	PROPHETICAL READING
Jan. 6	M	Shevaṭ 1	New Moon	Num. 28:1–15	
11	Sa	6	Bo'	Exod. 10:1–13:16	Jeremiah 46:13–28
18	Sa	13	Be-shallah (Shabbat Shirah)	Exod. 13:17–17:16	Judges 4:4–5:31 *Judges 5:1–31*
20	M	15	Hamishshah 'asar bi-Shevaṭ		
25	Sa	20	Yitro	Exod. 18:1–20:23	Isaiah 6:1–7:6 9:5–6 *Isaiah 6:1–13*
Feb. 1	Sa	27	Mishpaṭim	Exod. 21:1–24:18	Jeremiah 34:8–22 33:25–26
4	T	30	New Moon, first day	Num. 28:1–15	

Italics are for Sephardi Minhag.

1992, Feb. 5–Mar. 5] ADAR I (30 DAYS) [5752

Civil Date	Day of the Week	Jewish Date	SABBATHS, FESTIVALS, FASTS	PENTATEUCHAL READING	PROPHETICAL READING
Feb. 5	W	Adar I 1	New Moon, second day	Num. 28:1–15	
8	Sa	4	Terumah	Exod. 25:1–27:19	I Kings 5:26–6:13
15	Sa	11	Tezawweh	Exod. 27:20–30:10	Ezekiel 43:10–27
22	Sa	18	Ki tissa'	Exod. 30:11–34:35	I Kings 18:1–39 *I Kings 18:20–39*
29	Sa	25	Wa-yakhel (Shabbat Shekalim)	Exod. 35:1–38:20 Exod. 30:11–16	II Kings 12:1–17 *II Kings 11:17–12:17*
Mar. 5	Th	30	New Moon, first day	Num. 28:1–15	

Italics are for Sephardi Minhag.

1992, Mar. 6–Apr. 3]   ADAR II (29 DAYS)   [5752

Civil Date	Day of the Week	Jewish Date	SABBATHS, FESTIVALS, FASTS	PENTATEUCHAL READING	PROPHETICAL READING
Mar. 6	F	Adar II 1	New Moon, second day	Num. 28:1–15	
7	Sa	2	Peḳude	Exod. 38:21–40:38	I Kings 7:51–8:21 *I Kings 7:40–50*
14	Sa	9	Wa-yikra' (Shabbat Zakhor)	Levit. 1:1–5:26 Deut. 25:17–19	I Samuel 15:2–34 *I Samuel 15:1–34*
18	W	13	Fast of Esther	Exod. 32:11–14 Exod. 34:1–10 (morning and afternoon)	Isaiah 55:6–56:8 (afternoon only)
19	Th	14	Purim	Exod. 17:8–16	Book of Esther (night before and in the morning)
20	F	15	Shushan Purim		
21	Sa	16	Ẓaw	Levit. 6:1–8:36	Jeremiah 7:21–8:3 9:22–23
28	Sa	23	Shemini (Shabbat Parah)	Levit. 9:1–11:47 Num. 19:1–22	Ezekiel 36:16–38 *Ezekiel 36:16–36*

Italics are for
Sephardi Minhag.

1992, Apr. 4–May 3]   NISAN (30 DAYS)   [5752

Civil Date	Day of the Week	Jewish Date	SABBATHS, FESTIVALS, FASTS	PENTATEUCHAL READING	PROPHETICAL READING
Apr. 4	Sa	Nisan 1	Tazria' (Shabbat Ha-hodesh); New Moon	Levit. 12:1–13:59 Exod. 12:1–20 Num. 28:9–15	Ezekiel 45:16–46:18 *Ezekiel 45:18–46:15*
11	Sa	8	Mezora' (Shabbat Ha-gadol)	Levit. 14:1–15:33	Malachi 3:4–24
17	F	14	Fast of Firstborn		
18	Sa	15	Passover, first day	Exod. 12:21–51 Num. 28:16–25	Joshua 5:2–6:1, 27
19	S	16	Passover second day	Levit. 22:26–23:44 Num. 28:16–25	II Kings 23:1–9, 21–25
20	M	17	Hol Ha-mo'ed, first day	Exod. 13:1–16 Num. 28:19–25	
21	T	18	Hol Ha-mo'ed, second day	Exod. 22:24–23:19 Num. 28:19–25	
22	W	19	Hol Ha-mo'ed, third day	Exod. 34:1–26 Num. 28:19–25	
23	Th	20	Hol Ha-mo'ed, fourth day	Num. 9:1–14 Num. 28:19–25	
24	F	21	Passover, seventh day	Exod. 13:17–15:26 Num. 28:19–25	II Samuel 22:1–51
25	Sa	22	Passover, eighth day	Deut. 15:19–16:17 Num. 28:19–25	Isaiah 10:32–12:6
30	Th	27	Holocaust Memorial Day		
May 2	Sa	29	Ahare mot	Levit. 16:1–18:30	I Samuel 20:18–42
3	S	30	New Moon, first day	Num. 28:1–15	

Italics are for Sephardi Minhag.

1992, May 4–June 1]   IYAR (29 DAYS)   [5752

Civil Date	Day of the Week	Jewish Date	SABBATHS, FESTIVALS, FASTS	PENTATEUCHAL READING	PROPHETICAL READING
May 4	M	Iyar 1	New Moon, second day	Num. 28:1–15	
8	F*	5	Israel Independence Day		
9	Sa	6	Kedoshim	Levit. 19:1–20:27	Amos 9:7–15 *Ezekiel 20:2–20*
16	Sa	13	Emor	Levit. 21:1–24:23	Ezekiel 44:15–31
21	Th	18	Lag Ba-'omer		
23	Sa	20	Be-har	Levit. 25:1–26:2	Jeremiah 32:6–27
30	Sa	27	Be-ḥukkotai	Levit. 26:3–27:34	Jeremiah 16:19–17:14
31	S	28	Jerusalem Day		

*Observed Thursday, a day earlier, to avoid conflict with the Sabbath.

Italics are for Sephardi Minhag.

1992, June 2–July 1]　　　　SIWAN (30 DAYS)　　　　[5752

Civil Date	Day of the Week	Jewish Date	SABBATHS, FESTIVALS, FASTS	PENTATEUCHAL READING	PROPHETICAL READING
June 2	T	Siwan 1	New Moon	Num. 28:1–15	
6	Sa	5	Be-midbar	Num. 1:1–4:20	Hosea 2:1–22
7	S	6	Shavu'ot, first day	Exod. 19:1–20:23 Num. 28:26–31	Ezekiel 1:1–28 3:12
8	M	7	Shavu'ot, second day	Deut. 15:19–16:17 Num. 28:26–31	Habbakuk 3:1–19 *Habbakuk 2:20–3:19*
13	Sa	12	Naso'	Num. 4:21–7:89	Judges 13:2–25
20	Sa	19	Be-ha'alotekha	Num. 8:1–12:16	Zechariah 2:14–4:7
27	Sa	26	Shelaḥ lekha	Num. 13:1–15:41	Joshua 2:1–24
July 1	W	30	New Moon, first day	Num. 28:1–15	

Italics are for Sephardi Minhag.

1992, July 2–July 30]   TAMMUZ (29 DAYS)   [5752

Civil Date	Day of the Week	Jewish Date	SABBATHS, FESTIVALS, FASTS	PENTATEUCHAL READING	PROPHETICAL READING
July 2	Th	Tammuz 1	New Moon, second day	Num. 28:1–15	
4	Sa	3	Koraḥ	Num. 16:1–18:32	I Samuel 11:14–12:22
11	Sa	10	Ḥukkat	Num. 19:1–22:1	Judges 11:1–33
18	Sa	17	Balak	Num. 22:2–25:9	Micah 5:6–6:8
19	S	18	Fast of 17th of Tammuz	Exod. 32:11–14 34:1–10 (morning and afternoon)	Isaiah 55:6–56:8 (afternoon only)
25	Sa	24	Pineḥas	Num. 25:10–30:1	I Kings 18:46–19:21

1992, July 31–Aug. 29]   AV (30 DAYS)   [5752

Civil Date	Day of the Week	Jewish Date	SABBATHS, FESTIVALS, FASTS	PENTATEUCHAL READING	PROPHETICAL READING
July 31	F	Av 1	New Moon, first day	Num. 28:1–15	
Aug. 1	Sa	2	Mattot, Mas'e	Num. 30:2–36:13	Jeremiah 2:4–28 3:4 *Jeremiah 2:4–28 4:1–2*
8	Sa	9	Devarim (Shabbat Ḥazon)	Deut. 1:1–3:22	Isaiah 1:1–27
9	S	10	Fast of 9th of Av	Morning: Deut. 4:25–40 Afternoon: Exod. 32:11–14 Exod. 34:1–10	(Lamentations is read the night before) Jeremiah 8:13–9:23 (morning) Isaiah 55:6–56:8 (afternoon)
15	Sa	16	Wa-ethannan (Shabbat Naḥamu)	Deut. 3:23–7:11	Isaiah 40:1–26
22	Sa	23	'Ekev	Deut. 7:12–11:25	Isaiah 49:14–51:3
29	Sa	30	Re'eh; New Moon, first day	Deut. 11:26–16:17 Num. 28:9–15	Isaiah 66:1–24 *Isaiah 66:1–24 I Samuel 20:18,42*

Italics are for Sephardi Minhag.

1992, Aug. 30–Sept. 27]   ELUL (29 DAYS)   [5752

Civil Date	Day of the Week	Jewish Date	SABBATHS, FESTIVALS, FASTS	PENTATEUCHAL READING	PROPHETICAL READING
Aug. 30	S	Elul 1	New Moon, second day	Num. 28:1–15	
Sept. 5	Sa	7	Shofeṭim	Deut. 16:18–21:9	Isaiah 51:12–52:12
12	Sa	14	Ki teze'	Deut. 21:10–25:19	Isaiah 54:1–10
19	Sa	21	Ki tavo'	Deut. 26:1–29:8	Isaiah 60:1–22
26	Sa	28	Niẓẓavim	Deut. 29:9–30:20	Isaiah 61:10–63:9

Civil Date	Day of the Week	Jewish Date	SABBATHS, FESTIVALS, FASTS	PENTATEUCHAL READING	PROPHETICAL READING
Sept. 28	M	Tishri 1	Rosh Ha-shanah, first day	Gen. 21:1–34 Num. 29:1–6	I Samuel 1:1–2:10
29	T	2	Rosh Ha-shanah second day	Gen. 22:1–24 Num. 29:1–6	Jeremiah 31:2–20
30	W	3	Fast of Gedaliah	Exod. 32:11–14 Exod. 34:1–10 (morning and afternoon)	Isaiah 55:6–56:8 (afternoon only)
Oct. 3	Sa	6	Wa-yelekh (Shabbat Shuvah)	Deut. 31:1–30	Hosea 14:2–10 Micah 7:18–20 Joel 2:15–27 *Hosea 14:2–10* *Micah 7:18–20*
7	W	10	Yom Kippur	Morning: Levit. 16:1–34 Num. 29:7–11 Afternoon: Levit. 18:1–30	Isaiah 57:14–58:14 Jonah 1:1–4:11 Micah 7:18–20
10	Sa	13	Ha'azinu	Deut. 32:1–52	II Samuel 22:1–51
12	M	15	Sukkot, first day	Levit. 22:26–23:44 Num. 29:12–16	Zechariah 14:1–21
13	T	16	Sukkot, second day	Levit. 22:26–23:44 Num. 29:12–16	I Kings 8:2–21
14–16	W–F	17–19	Hol Ha-mo'ed, first to third days	W Num. 29:17–25 Th Num. 29:20–28 F Num. 29:23–31	
17	Sa	20	Hol Ha-mo'ed, fourth day	Exod. 33:12–34:26 Num. 29:26–31	Ezekiel 38:18–39:16
18	S	21	Hosha'na' Rabbah	Num. 29:26–34	
19	M	22	Shemini 'Azeret	Deut. 14:22–16:17 Num. 29:35–30:1	I Kings 8:54–66
20	T	23	Simhat Torah	Deut. 33:1–34:12 Gen. 1:1–2:3 Num. 29:35–30:1	Joshua 1:1–18 *Joshua 1:1–9*
24	Sa	27	Be-re'shit	Gen. 1:1–6:8	Isaiah 42:5–43:10 *Isaiah 42:5–21*
27	T	30	New Moon, first day	Num. 28:1–15	

Italics are for
Sephardi Minhag.

1992, Oct. 28–Nov. 25]   ḤESHWAN (29 DAYS)   [5753

Civil Date	Day of the Week	Jewish Date	SABBATHS, FESTIVALS, FASTS	PENTATEUCHAL READING	PROPHETICAL READING
Oct. 28	W	Heshwan 1	New Moon, second day	Num. 28:1–15	
31	Sa	4	Noah	Gen. 6:9–11:32	Isaiah 54:1–55:5 *Isaiah 54:1–10*
Nov. 7	Sa	11	Lekh lekha	Gen. 12:1–17:27	Isaiah 40:27–41:16
14	Sa	18	Wa-yera'	Gen. 18:1–22:24	II Kings 4:1–37 *II Kings 4:1–23*
21	Sa	25	Ḥayye Sarah	Gen. 23:1–25:18	I Kings 1:1–31

Italics are for
Sephardi Minhag.

1992, Nov. 26–Dec. 24]   KISLEW (29 DAYS)   [5753

Civil Date	Day of the Week	Jewish Date	SABBATHS, FESTIVALS, FASTS	PENTATEUCHAL READING	PROPHETICAL READING
Nov. 26	Th	Kislew 1	New Moon	Num. 28:1–15	
28	Sa	3	Toledot	Gen. 25:19–28:9	Malachi 1:1–2:7
Dec. 5	Sa	10	Wa-yeze'	Gen. 28:10–32:3	Hosea 12:13–14:10 *Hosea 11:7–12:12*
12	Sa	17	Wa-yishlah	Gen. 32:4–36:43	Hosea 11:7–12:12 *Obadiah 1:1–21*
19	Sa	24	Wa-yeshev	Gen. 37:1–40:23	Amos 2:6–3:8
20–24	S-Th	25–29	Hanukkah, first to fifth days	S Num. 7:1–17 M Num. 7:18–29 T Num. 7:24–35 W Num. 7:30–41 Th Num. 7:36–47	

Italics are for Sephardi Minhag.

1992, Dec. 25–Jan. 22, 1993] ṬEVET (29 DAYS)   [5753

Civil Date	Day of the Week	Jewish Date	SABBATHS, FESTIVALS, FASTS	PENTATEUCHAL READING	PROPHETICAL READING
Dec. 25	F	Ṭevet 1	New Moon; Ḥanukkah, sixth day	Num. 28:1–15 Num. 7:42–47	
26	Sa	2	Mi-ḳeẓ; Ḥanukkah, seventh day	Gen. 41:1–44:17 Num. 7:48–53	Zechariah 2:14–4:7
27	S	3	Ḥanukkah, eighth day	Num. 7:54–8:4	
Jan. 2	Sa	9	Wa-yiggash	Gen. 44:18–47:27	Ezekiel 37:15–28
3	S	10	Fast of 10th of Ṭevet	Exod. 32:11–14 Exod. 34:1–10 (morning and afternoon)	Isaiah 55:6–56:8 (afternoon only)
9	Sa	16	Wa-yeḥi	Gen. 47:28–50:26	I Kings 2:1–12
16	Sa	23	Shemot	Exod. 1:1–6:1	Isaiah 27:6–28:13 29:22–23 Jeremiah 1:1–2:3

Italics are for Sephardi Minhag.

1993, Jan. 23–Feb. 21]   SHEVAṬ (30 DAYS)   [5753

Civil Date	Day of the Week	Jewish Date	SABBATHS, FESTIVALS, FASTS	PENTATEUCHAL READING	PROPHETICAL READING
Jan. 23	Sa	Shevaṭ 1	Wa-'era'; New Moon	Exod. 6:2–9:35 Num. 28:9–15	Isaiah 66:1–24
30	Sa	8	Bo'	Exod. 10:1–13:16	Jeremiah 46:13–28
Feb. 6	Sa	15	Be-shallah (Shabbat Shirah); Hamishshah-'asar bi-Shevaṭ	Exod. 13:17–17:16	Judges 4:4–5:31 *Judges 5:1–31*
13	Sa	22	Yitro	Exod. 18:1–20:23	Isaiah 6:1–7:6 9:5–6 *Isaiah 6:1–13*
20	Sa	29	Mishpaṭim (Shabbat Sheḳalim)	Exod. 21:1–24:18 Exod. 30:11–16	II Kings 12:1–17 *II Kings 11:17–12:17 I Sam. 20:18, 42*
21	S	30	New Moon, first day	Num. 28:1–15	

Italics are for Sephardi Minhag.

1993, Feb. 22–Mar. 22]   ADAR (29 DAYS)   [5753

Civil Date	Day of the Week	Jewish Date	SABBATHS, FESTIVALS, FASTS	PENTATEUCHAL READING	PROPHETICAL READING
Feb. 22	M	Adar 1	New Moon, second day	Num. 28:1–15	
27	Sa	6	Terumah	Exod. 25:1–27:19	I Kings 5:26–6:13
Mar. 4	Th	11	Fast of Esther	Exod. 32:11–14 Exod. 34:1–10 (morning and afternoon)	Isaiah 55:6–56:8 (afternoon only)
6	Sa	13	Tezawweh (Shabbat Zakhor)	Exod. 27:20–30:10 Deut. 25:17–19	I Samuel 15:2–34 *I Samuel 15:1–34*
7	S	14	Purim	Exod. 17:8–16	Book of Esther (night before and in the morning)
8	M	15	Shushan Purim		
13	Sa	20	Ki tissa' (Shabbat Parah)	Exod. 30:11–34:35 Num. 19:1–22	Ezekiel 36:16–38 *Ezekiel 36:16–36*
20	Sa	27	Wa-yakhel, Pekude (Shabbat Ha-hodesh)	Exod. 35:1–40:38 Exod. 12:1–20	Ezekiel 45:16–46:18 *Ezekiel 45:18–46:15*

Italics are for Sephardi Minhag.

1993, Mar. 23–Apr. 21]   NISAN (30 DAYS)   [5753

Civil Date	Day of the Week	Jewish Date	SABBATHS, FESTIVALS, FASTS	PENTATEUCHAL READING	PROPHETICAL READING
Mar. 23	T	Nisan 1	New Moon	Num. 28:1–15	
27	Sa	5	Wa-yikra'	Levit. 1:1–5:26	Isaiah 43:21–44:24
Apr. 3	Sa	12	Zaw (Shabbat Ha-gadol)	Levit. 6:1–8:36	Malachi 3:4–24
5	M	14	Fast of Firstborn		
6	T	15	Passover, first day	Exod. 12:21–51 Num. 28:16–25	Joshua 5:2–6:1, 27
7	W	16	Passover, second day	Levit. 22:26–23:44 Num. 28:16–25	II Kings 23:1–9, 21–25
8	Th	17	Hol Ha-mo'ed, first day	Exod. 13:1–16 Num. 28:19–25	
9	F	18	Hol Ha-mo'ed, second day	Exod. 22:24–23:19 Num. 28:19–25	
10	Sa	19	Hol Ha-mo'ed, third day	Exod. 33:12–34:26 Num. 28:19–25	Ezekiel 37:1–14
11	S	20	Hol Ha-mo'ed, fourth day	Num. 9:1–14 Num. 28:19–25	
12	M	21	Passover, seventh day	Exod. 13:17–15:26 Num. 28:19–25	II Samuel 22:1–51
13	T	22	Passover, eighth day	Deut. 15:19–16:17 Num. 28:19–25	Isaiah 10:32–12:6
17	Sa	26	Shemini	Levit. 9:1–11:47	II Samuel 6:1–7:17 *II Samuel 6:1–19*
18	S	27	Holocaust Memorial Day		
21	W	30	New Moon, first day	Num. 28:1–15	

Italics are for Sephardi Minhag.

1993, Apr. 22–May 20]   IYAR (29 DAYS)   [5753

Civil Date	Day of the Week	Jewish Date	SABBATHS, FESTIVALS, FASTS	PENTATEUCHAL READING	PROPHETICAL READING
Apr. 22	Th	Iyar 1	New Moon, second day	Num. 28:1–15	
24	Sa	3	Tazria', Meẓora'	Levit. 12:1–15:33	II Kings 7:3–20
26	M	5	Israel Independence Day		
May 1	Sa	10	Aḥare mot, Ḳedoshim	Levit. 16:1–20:27	Amos 9:7–15 *Ezekiel 20:2–20*
8	Sa	17	Emor	Levit. 21:1–24:23	Ezekiel 44:15–31
9	S	18	Lag Ba-'omer		
15	Sa	24	Be-har, Be-ḥuḳḳotai	Levit. 25:1–27:34	Jeremiah 16:19–17:14
19	W	28	Jerusalem Day		

Italics are for Sephardi Minhag.

1993, May 21–June 19]   SIWAN (30 DAYS)   [5753

Civil Date	Day of the Week	Jewish Date	SABBATHS, FESTIVALS, FASTS	PENTATEUCHAL READING	PROPHETICAL READING
May 21	F	Siwan 1	New Moon	Num. 28:1–15	
22	Sa	2	Be-midbar	Num. 1:1–4:20	Hosea 2:1–22
26	W	6	Shavu'ot, first day	Exod. 19:1–20:23 Num. 28:26–31	Ezekiel 1:1–28 3:12
27	Th	7	Shavu'ot, second day	Deut. 15:19–16:17 Num. 28:26–31	Habbakuk 3:1–19 *Habbakuk 2:20–3:19*
29	Sa	9	Naso'	Num. 4:21–7:89	Judges 13:2–25
June 5	Sa	16	Be-ha'alotekha	Num. 8:1–12:16	Zechariah 2:14–4:7
12	Sa	23	Shelaḥ lekha	Num. 13:1–15:41	Joshua 2:1–24
19	Sa	30	Korah; New Moon, first day	Num. 16:1–18:32 Num. 28:9–15	Isaiah 66:1–24 *Isaiah 66:1–24* *I Samuel 20:18, 42*

Italics are for
Sephardi Minhag.

1993, June 20–July 18]   TAMMUZ (29 DAYS)   [5753

Civil Date	Day of the Week	Jewish Date	SABBATHS, FESTIVALS, FASTS	PENTATEUCHAL READING	PROPHETICAL READING
June 20	S	Tammuz 1	New Moon, second day	Num. 28:1–15	
26	Sa	7	Ḥukkat	Num. 19:1–22:1	Judges 11:1–33
July 3	Sa	14	Balak	Num. 22:2–25:9	Micah 5:6–6:8
6	T	17	Fast of 17th of Tammuz	Exod. 32:11–14 Exod. 34:1–10 (morning and afternoon)	Isaiah 55:6–56:8 (afternoon only)
10	Sa	21	Pineḥas	Num. 25:10–30:1	I Kings 18:46–19:21
17	Sa	28	Maṭṭot, Masʿe	Num. 30:2–36:13	Jeremiah 2:4–28 3:4 *Jeremiah 2:4–28 4:1–2*

Italics are for Sephardi Minhag.

1993, July 19–Aug. 17]   AV (30 DAYS)   [5753

Civil Date	Day of the Week	Jewish Date	SABBATHS, FESTIVALS, FASTS	PENTATEUCHAL READING	PROPHETICAL READING
July 19	M	Av 1	New Moon	Num. 28:1–15	
24	Sa	6	Devarim (Shabbat Ḥazon)	Deut. 1:1–3:22	Isaiah 1:1–27
27	T	9	Fast of 9th of Av	Morning: Deut. 4:25–40 Afternoon: Exod. 32:11–14 Exod. 34:1–10	(Lamentations is read the night before) Jeremiah 8:13–9:23 (morning) Isaiah 55:6–56:8 (afternoon)
31	Sa	13	Wa-ethannan (Shabbat Naḥamu)	Deut. 3:23–7:11	Isaiah 40:1–26
Aug. 7	Sa	20	'Eḳev	Deut. 7:12–11:25	Isaiah 49:14–51:3
14	Sa	27	Re'eh	Deut. 11:26–16:17	Isaiah 54:11–55:5
17	T	30	New Moon, first day	Num. 28:1–15	

1993, Aug. 18–Sept. 15]   ELUL (29 DAYS)   [5753

Civil Date	Day of the Week	Jewish Date	SABBATHS, FESTIVALS, FASTS	PENTATEUCHAL READING	PROPHETICAL READING
Aug. 18	W	Elul 1	New Moon, second day	Num. 28:1–15	
21	Sa	4	Shofeṭim	Deut. 16:18–21:9	Isaiah 51:12–52:12
28	Sa	11	Ki teze'	Deut. 21:10–25:19	Isaiah 54:1–10
Sept. 4	Sa	18	Ki tavo'	Deut. 26:1–29:8	Isaiah 60:1–22
11	Sa	25	Niẓẓavim, Wa-yelekh	Deut. 29:9–31:30	Isaiah 61:10–63:9

Civil Date	Day of the Week	Jewish Date	SABBATHS, FESTIVALS, FASTS	PENTATEUCHAL READING	PROPHETICAL READING
Sep. 16	Th	Tishri 1	Rosh Ha-shanah, first day	Gen. 21:1–34 Num. 29:1–6	1 Samuel 1:1–2:10
17	F	2	Rosh Ha-shanah, second day	Gen. 22:1–24 Num. 29:1–6	Jeremiah 31:2–20
18	Sa	3	Ha'azinu (Shabbat Shuvah)	Deut. 32:1–52	Hosea 14:2–10 Micah 7:18–20 Joel 2:15–27 *Hosea 14:2–10* *Micah 7:18–20*
19	S	4	Fast of Gedaliah	Exod. 32:11–14 Exod. 34:1–10 (morning and afternoon)	Isaiah 55:6–56:8 (afternoon only)
25	Sa	10	Yom Kippur	Morning: Levit. 16:1–34 Num. 29:7–11 Afternoon: Levit. 18:1–30	Isaiah 57:14–58:14 Jonah 1:1–4:11 Micah 7:18–20
30	Th	15	Sukkot, first day	Levit. 22:26–23:44 Num. 29:12–16	Zechariah 14:1–21
Oct. 1	F	16	Sukkot, second day	Levit. 22:26–23:44 Num. 29:12–16	I Kings 8:2–21
2	Sa	17	Hol Ha-mo'ed, first day	Exod. 33:12–34:26 Num. 29:17–22	Ezekiel 38:18–39:16
3–5	S–T	18–20	Hol Ha-mo'ed, second to fourth days	S Num. 29:20–28 M Num. 29:23–31 T Num. 29:26–34	
6	W	21	Hosha'na' Rabbah	Num. 29:26–34	
7	Th	22	Shemini 'Azeret	Deut. 14:22–16:17 Num. 29:35–30:1	I Kings 8:54–66
8	F	23	Simhat Torah	Deut. 33:1–34:12 Gen. 1:1–2:3 Num. 29:35–30:1	Joshua 1:1–18 *Joshua 1:1–9*
9	Sa	24	Be-re'shit	Gen. 1:1–6:8	Isaiah 42:5–43:10 *Isaiah 42:5–21*
15	F	30	New Moon, first day	Num. 28:1–15	

Italics are for Sephardi Minhag.

1993, Oct. 16–Nov. 14]   HESHWAN (30 DAYS)   [5754

Civil Date	Day of the Week	Jewish Date	SABBATHS, FESTIVALS, FASTS	PENTATEUCHAL READING	PROPHETICAL READING
Oct. 16	Sa	Heshwan 1	Noah; New Moon, second day	Gen. 6:9–11:32 Num. 28:9–15	Isaiah 66:1–24
23	Sa	8	Lekh lekha	Gen. 12:1–17:27	Isaiah 40:27–41:16
30	Sa	15	Wa-yera'	Gen. 18:1–22:24	II Kings 4:1–37 *II Kings 4:1–23*
Nov. 6	Sa	22	Hayye Sarah	Gen. 23:1–25:18	I Kings 1:1–31
13	Sa	29	Toledot	Gen. 25:19–28:9	I Samuel 20:18–42
14	S	30	New Moon, first day	Num. 28:1–15	

Italics are for
Sephardi Minhag.

1993, Nov. 15–Dec. 14]   KISLEW (30 DAYS)   [5754

Civil Date	Day of the Week	Jewish Date	SABBATHS, FESTIVALS, FASTS	PENTATEUCHAL READING	PROPHETICAL READING
Nov. 15	M	Kislew 1	New Moon, second day	Num. 28:1–15	
20	Sa	6	Wa-yeze'	Gen. 28:10–32:3	Hosea 12:13–14:10 *Hosea 11:7–12:12*
27	Sa	13	Wa-yishlah	Gen. 32:4–36:43	Hosea 11:7–12:12 *Obadiah 1:1–21*
Dec. 4	Sa	20	Wa-yeshev	Gen. 37:1–40:23	Amos 2:6–3:8
9–10	Th–F	25–26	Hanukkah, first, second days	Th Num. 7:1–17 F Num. 7:18–29	
11	Sa	27	Mi-kez; Hanukkah, third day	Gen. 41:1–44:17 Num. 7:24–29	Zechariah 2:14–4:7
12–13	S–M	28–29	Hanukkah, fourth, fifth days	S Num. 7:30–41 M Num. 7:36–47	
14	T	30	New Moon, first day; Hanukkah, sixth day	Num. 7:42–47 Num. 28:1–15	

Italics are for Sephardi Minhag.

1993, Dec. 15–Jan. 12, 1994] ṬEVET (29 DAYS)   [5754

Civil Date	Day of the Week	Jewish Date	SABBATHS, FESTIVALS, FASTS	PENTATEUCHAL READING	PROPHETICAL READING
Dec. 15	W	Ṭevet 1	New Moon, second day; Hanukkah, seventh day	Num. 28:1–15 Num. 7:48–53	
16	Th	2	Hanukkah, eighth day	Num. 7:54–8:4	
18	Sa	4	Wa-yiggash	Gen. 44:18–47:27	Ezekiel 37:15–28
24	F	10	Fast of 10th of Ṭevet	Exod. 32:11–14 Exod. 34:1–10 (morning and afternoon)	Isaiah 55:6–56:8 (afternoon only)
25	Sa	11	Wa-yeḥi	Gen. 47:28–50:26	I Kings 2:1–12
Jan. 1	Sa	18	Shemot	Exod. 1:1–6:1	Isaiah 27:6–28:13 29:22–23 *Jeremiah 1:1–2:3*
8	Sa	25	Wa-'era'	Exod. 6:2–9:35	Ezekiel 28:25–29:21

Italics are for Sephardi Minhag.

1994, Jan. 13–Feb. 11]   SHEVAṬ (30 DAYS)   [5754

Civil Date	Day of the Week	Jewish Date	SABBATHS, FESTIVALS, FASTS	PENTATEUCHAL READING	PROPHETICAL READING
Jan. 13	Th	Shevaṭ 1	New Moon	Num. 28:1–15	
15	Sa	3	Bo'	Exod. 10:1–13:16	Jeremiah 46:13–28
22	Sa	10	Be-shallaḥ (Shabbat Shirah)	Exod. 13:17–17:16	Judges 4:4–5:31 *Judges 5:1–31*
27	Th	15	Hamishshah-'asar bi-Shevaṭ		
29	Sa	17	Yitro	Exod. 18:1–20:23	Isaiah 6:1–7:6 9:5–6 *Isaiah 6:1–13*
Feb. 5	Sa	24	Mishpaṭim	Exod. 21:1–24:18	Jeremiah 34:8–22 33:25–26
11	F	30	New Moon, first day	Num. 28:1–15	

Italics are for Sephardi Minhag.

1994, Feb. 12–Mar. 12]   ADAR (29 DAYS)   [5754

Civil Date	Day of the Week	Jewish Date	SABBATHS, FESTIVALS, FASTS	PENTATEUCHAL READING	PROPHETICAL READING
Feb. 12	Sa	Adar 1	Terumah; New Moon, second day (Shabbat Shekalim)	Exod. 25:1–27:19 Num. 28:9–15 Exod. 30:11–16	II Kings 12:1–17 *II Kings 11:17–12:17*
19	Sa	8	Tezawweh (Shabbat Zakhor)	Exod. 27:20–30:10 Deut. 25:17–19	I Samuel 15:2–34 *I Samuel 15:1–34*
24	Th	13	Fast of Esther	Exod. 32:11–14 34:1–10 (morning and afternoon)	Isaiah 55:6–56:8 (afternoon only)
25	F	14	Purim	Exod. 17:8–16	Book of Esther (night before and in the morning)
26	Sa	15	Ki tissa'; Shushan Purim	Exod. 30:11–34:35	I Kings 18:1–39 *I Kings 18:20–39*
Mar. 5	Sa	22	Wa-yakhel (Shabbat Parah)	Exod. 35:1–38:20 Num. 19:1–22	Ezekiel 36:16–38 *Ezekiel 36:16–36*
12	Sa	29	Pekude (Shabbat Ha-hodesh)	Exod. 38:21–40:38 Exod. 12:1–20	Ezekiel 45:16–46:18 *Ezekiel 45:18–46:15* *I Samuel 20:18, 42*

Italics are for Sephardi Minhag.

Civil Date	Day of the Week	Jewish Date	SABBATHS, FESTIVALS, FASTS	PENTATEUCHAL READING	PROPHETICAL READING
Mar. 13	S	Nisan 1	New Moon	Num. 28:1–15	
19	Sa	7	Wa-yiḵra'	Levit. 1:1–5:26	Isaiah 43:21–44:24
24	Th	12	Fast of Firstborn		
26	Sa	14	Zaw (Shabbat Ha-gadol)	Levit. 6:1–8:36	Malachi 3:4–24
27	S	15	Passover, first day	Exod. 12:21–51 Num. 28:16–25	Joshua 5:2–6:1, 27
28	M	16	Passover, second day	Levit. 22:26–23:44 Num. 28:16–25	II Kings 23:1–9, 21–25
29	T	17	Ḥol Ha-mo'ed, first day	Exod. 13:1–16 Num. 28:19–25	
30	W	18	Ḥol Ha-mo'ed, second day	Exod. 22:24–23:19 Num. 28:19–25	
31	Th	19	Ḥol Ha-mo'ed, third day	Exod. 34:1–26 Num. 28:19–25	
Apr. 1	F	20	Ḥol Ha-mo'ed, fourth day	Num. 9:1–14 28:19–25	
2	Sa	21	Passover, seventh day	Exod. 13:17–15:26 Num. 28:19–25	II Samuel 22:1–51
3	S	22	Passover, eighth day	Deut. 15:19–16:17 Num. 28:19–25	Isaiah 10:32–12:6
8	F	27	Holocaust Memorial Day*		
9	Sa	28	Shemini	Levit. 9:1–11:47	II Samuel 6:1–7:17 *II Samuel 6:1–19*
11	M	30	New Moon, first day	Num. 28:1–15	

*Observed Apr. 7, to avoid conflict with the Sabbath.

Italics are for Sephardi Minhag.

1994, Apr. 12–May 10] IYAR (29 DAYS) [5754

Civil Date	Day of the Week	Jewish Date	SABBATHS, FESTIVALS, FASTS	PENTATEUCHAL READING	PROPHETICAL READING
Apr. 12	T	Iyar 1	New Moon, second day	Num. 28:1–15	
16	Sa	5	Tazria', Mezora'; Israel Independence Day*	Levit. 12:1–15:33	II Kings 7:3–20
23	Sa	12	Ahare mot, Kedoshim	Levit. 16:1–20:27	Amos 9:7–15 *Ezekiel 20:2–20*
29	F	18	Lag Ba-o'mer		
30	Sa	19	Emor	Levit. 21:1–24:23	Ezekiel 44:15–31
May 7	Sa	26	Be-har, Be-hukkotai	Levit. 25:1–27:34	Jeremiah 16:19–17:14
9	M	28	Jerusalem Day		

*Observed Apr. 14, to avoid conflict with the Sabbath.

Italics are for Sephardi Minhag.

1994, May 11–June 9]   SIWAN (30 DAYS)   [5754

Civil Date	Day of the Week	Jewish Date	SABBATHS, FESTIVALS, FASTS	PENTATEUCHAL READING	PROPHETICAL READING
May 11	W	Siwan 1	New Moon	Num. 28:1–15	
14	Sa	4	Be-midbar	Num. 1:1–4:20	Hosea 2:1–22
16	M	6	Shavu'ot, first day	Exod. 19:1–20:23 Num. 28:26–31	Ezekiel 1:1–28 3:12
17	T	7	Shavu'ot, second day	Deut. 15:19–16:17 Num. 28:26–31	Habbakuk 3:1–19 *Habbakuk 2:20–3:19*
21	Sa	11	Naso'	Num. 4:21–7:89	Judges 13:2–25
28	Sa	18	Be-ha'alotekha	Num. 8:1–12:16	Zechariah 2:14–4:7
June 4	Sa	25	Shelaḥ lekha	Num. 13:1–15:41	Joshua 2:1–24
9	Th	30	New Moon, first day	Num. 28:1–15	

*Italics are for
Sephardi Minhag.*

1994, June 10–July 8] TAMMUZ (29 DAYS) [5754

Civil Date	Day of the Week	Jewish Date	SABBATHS, FESTIVALS, FASTS	PENTATEUCHAL READING	PROPHETICAL READING
June 10	F	Tammuz 1	New Moon, second day	Num. 28:1–15	
11	Sa	2	Koraḥ	Num. 16:1–18:32	I Samuel 11:14–12:22
18	Sa	9	Ḥukkat	Num. 19:1–22:1	Judges 11:1–33
25	Sa	16	Balak	Num. 22:2–25:9	Micah 5:6–6:8
26	S	17	Fast of 17th of Tammuz	Exod. 32:11–14 34:1–10 (morning and afternoon)	Isaiah 55:6–56:8 (afternoon only)
July 2	Sa	23	Pineḥas	Num. 25:10–30:1	I Kings 18:46–19:21

Italics are for Sephardi Minhag.

1994, July 9–Aug. 7]   AV (30 DAYS)   [5754

Civil Date	Day of the Week	Jewish Date	SABBATHS, FESTIVALS, FASTS	PENTATEUCHAL READING	PROPHETICAL READING
July 9	Sa	Av 1	Maṭṭot, Mas'e; New Moon	Num. 30:2–36:13 Num. 28:9–15	Jeremiah 2:4–28 3:4 *Jeremiah 2:4–28* *4:1–2* *Isaiah 66:1, 23*
16	Sa	8	Devarim (Shabbat Ḥazon)	Deut. 1:1–3:22	Isaiah 1:1–27
17	S	9	Fast of 9th of Av	Morning: Deut. 4:25–40 Afternoon: Exod. 32:11–14 34:1–10	(Lamentations is read the night before) Jeremiah 8:13–9:23 (morning) Isaiah 55:6:56–8 (afternoon)
23	Sa	15	Wa-etḥannan (Shabbat Naḥamu)	Deut. 3:23–7:11	Isaiah 40:1–26
30	Sa	22	'Eḳev	Deut. 7:12–11:25	Isaiah 49:14–51:3
Aug. 6	Sa	29	Re'eh	Deut. 11:26–16:17	Isaiah 54:11–55:5 *Isaiah 54:11–55:5* *I Samuel 20:18, 42*
7	S	30	New Moon, first day	Num. 28:1–15	

Italics are for Sephardi Minhag.

1994, Aug. 8–Sept. 5]   ELUL (29 DAYS)   [5754

Civil Date	Day of the Week	Jewish Date	SABBATHS, FESTIVALS, FASTS	PENTATEUCHAL READING	PROPHETICAL READING
Aug. 8	M	Elul 1	New Moon, second day	Num. 28:1–15	
13	Sa	6	Shofeṭim	Deut. 16:18–21:9	Isaiah 51:12–52:12
20	Sa	13	Ki teẓe'	Deut. 21:10–25:19	Isaiah 54:1–10
27	Sa	20	Ki tavo'	Deut. 26:1–29:8	Isaiah 60:1–22
Sept. 3	Sa	27	Niẓẓavim	Deut. 29:9–30:20	Isaiah 61:10–63:9

Civil Date	Day of the Week	Jewish Date	SABBATHS, FESTIVALS, FASTS	PENTATEUCHAL READING	PROPHETICAL READING
Sept. 6	T	Tishri 1	Rosh Ha-shanah, first day	Gen. 21:1–34 Num. 29:1–6	I Samuel 1:1–2:10
7	W	2	Rosh Ha-shana, second day	Gen. 22:1–24 Num. 29:1–6	Jeremiah 31:2–20
8	Th	3	Fast of Gedaliah	Exod. 32:11–14 34:1–10 (morning and afternoon)	Isaiah 55:6–56:8 (afternoon only)
10	Sa	5	Wa-yelekh (Shabbat Shuvah)	Deut. 31:1–30	Hosea 14:2–10 Micah 7:18–20 Joel 2:15–27 *Hosea 14:2–10* *Micah 7:18–20*
15	Th	10	Yom Kippur	Morning: Levit. 16:1–34 Num. 29:7–11 Afternoon: Levit. 18:1–30	Isaiah 57:14–58:14 Jonah 1:1–4:11 Micah 7:18–20
17	Sa	12	Ha'azinu	Deut. 32:1–52	II Samuel 22:1–51
20	T	15	Sukkot, first day	Levit. 22:26–23:44 Num. 29:12–16	Zechariah 14:1–21
21	W	16	Sukkot, second day	Levit. 22:26–23:44 Num. 29:12–16	I Kings 8:2–21
22–25	Th–S	17–20	Ḥol Ha-mo'ed	Th Num. 29:17–25 F Num. 29:20–28 Sa Exod. 33:12–34:26 Num. 29:23–28 S Num. 29:26–34	Ezekiel 38:18–39:16
26	M	21	Hosha'na' Rabbah	Num. 29:26–34	
27	T	22	Shemini 'Azeret	Deut. 14:22–16:17 Num. 29:35–30:1	I Kings 8:54–66
28	W	23	Simḥat Torah	Deut. 33:1–34:12 Gen. 1:1–2:3 Num. 29:35–30:1	Joshua 1:1–18 *Joshua 1:1–9*
Oct. 1	Sa	26	Be-re'shit	Gen. 1:1–6:8	Isaiah 42:5–43:10 *Isaiah 42:5–21*
5	W	30	New Moon, first day	Num. 28:1–15	

Italics are for
Sephardi Minhag.

1994, Oct. 6–Nov. 3]   ḤESHWAN (29 DAYS)   [5755

Civil Date	Day of the Week	Jewish Date	SABBATHS, FESTIVALS, FASTS	PENTATEUCHAL READING	PROPHETICAL READING
Oct. 6	Th	Ḥeshwan 1	New Moon, second day	Num. 28:1–15	
8	Sa	3	Noah	Gen. 6:9–11:32	Isaiah 54:1–55:5 *Isaiah 54:1–10*
15	Sa	10	Lekh lekha	Gen. 12:1–17:27	Isaiah 40:27–41:16
22	Sa	17	Wa-yera'	Gen. 18:1–22:24	II Kings 4:1–37 *II Kings 4:1–23*
29	Sa	24	Ḥayye Sarah	Gen. 23:1–25:18	I Kings 1:1–31

Italics are for Sephardi Minhag.

1994, Nov. 4–Dec. 3]   KISLEW (30 DAYS)   [5755

Civil Date	Day of the Week	Jewish Date	SABBATHS, FESTIVALS, FASTS	PENTATEUCHAL READING	PROPHETICAL READING
Nov. 4	F	Kislew 1	New Moon	Num. 28:1–15	
5	Sa	2	Toledot	Gen. 25:19–28:9	Malachi 1:1–2:7
12	Sa	9	Wa-yeze'	Gen. 28:10–32:3	Hosea 12:13–14:10 *Hosea 11:7–12:12*
19	Sa	16	Wa-yishlah	Gen. 32:4–36:43	Hosea 11:7–12:12 *Obadiah 1:1–21*
26	Sa	23	Wa-yeshev	Gen. 37:1–40:23	Amos 2:6–3:8
Nov. 28– Dec. 2	M–F	25–29	Hanukkah, first to fifth days	M Num. 7:1–17 T Num. 7:18–29 W Num. 7:24–35 Th Num. 7:30–41 F Num. 7:36–47	
3	Sa	30	Mi-kez; New Moon, first day; Hanukkah, sixth day	Gen. 41:1–44:17 Num. 28:9–15 Num. 7:42–47	Zechariah 2:14–4:7

Italics are for
Sephardi Minhag.

1994, Dec. 4–Jan. 1, 1995]   ṬEVET (29 DAYS)   [5755

Civil Date	Day of the Week	Jewish Date	SABBATHS, FESTIVALS, FASTS	PENTATEUCHAL READING	PROPHETICAL READING
Dec. 4	S	Tevet 1	New Moon, second day; Hanukkah, seventh day	Num. 28:1–15 Num. 7:48–53	
5	M	2	Hanukkah, eighth day	Num. 7:54–8:4	
10	Sa	7	Wa-yiggash	Gen. 44:18–47:27	Ezekiel 37:15–28
13	T	10	Fast of 10th of Ṭevet	Exod. 32:11–14 Exod. 34:1–10 (morning and afternoon)	Isaiah 55:6–56:8 (afternoon only)
17	Sa	14	Wa-yeḥi	Gen. 47:28–50:26	I Kings 2:1–12
24	Sa	21	Shemot	Exod. 1:1–6:1	Isaiah 27:6–28:13 29:22–23 *Jeremiah 1:1–2:3*
31	Sa	28	Wa-'era'	Exod. 6:2–9:35	Ezekiel 28:25–29:21

Italics are for Sephardi Minhag.

SELECTED ARTICLES OF INTEREST IN RECENT VOLUMES
OF THE AMERICAN JEWISH YEAR BOOK

OBITUARIES

Leo Baeck	By Max Gruenewald 59:478–82
Salo W. Baron	By Lloyd P. Gartner 91:544–554
Jacob Blaustein	By John Slawson 72:547–57
Martin Buber	By Seymour Siegel 67:37–43
Abraham Cahan	By Mendel Osherowitch 53:527–29
Albert Einstein	By Jacob Bronowski 58:480–85
Felix Frankfurter	By Paul A. Freund 67:31–36
Louis Ginzberg	By Louis Finkelstein 56:573–79
Jacob Glatstein	By Shmuel Lapin 73:611–17
Sidney Goldmann	By Milton R. Konvitz 85:401–03
Hayim Greenberg	By Marie Syrkin 56:589–94
Abraham Joshua Heschel	By Fritz A. Rothschild 74:533–44
Horace Meyer Kallen	By Milton R. Konvitz 75:55–80
Mordecai Kaplan	By Ludwig Nadelmann 85:404–11
Herbert H. Lehman	By Louis Finkelstein 66:3–20
Judah L. Magnes	By James Marshall 51:512–15
Alexander Marx	By Abraham S. Halkin 56:580–88
Reinhold Niebuhr	By Seymour Siegel 73:605–10
Joseph Proskauer	By David Sher 73:618–28
Maurice Samuel	By Milton H. Hindus 74:545–53
John Slawson	By Murray Friedman 91:555–558
Leo Strauss	By Ralph Lerner 76:91–97
Max Weinreich	By Lucy S. Dawidowicz 70:59–68
Chaim Weizmann	By Harry Sacher 55:462–69
Stephen S. Wise	By Philip S. Bernstein 51:515–18
Harry Austryn Wolfson	By Isadore Twersky 76:99–111

Index

Aaron, Rafi, 229
Abbey, Maurice, 247
Abdel-Meguid, Ahmad Esmat, 137, 150
Abdel-Shafi, Haidar, 153, 370, 372, 373
Abessera, Michel, 224
Abo Shandi, Mahmood, 219
Abramowitz, Moe, 231
Abramowitz, Stanley, 57*n*
Abramson, Larry, 417
Abu Ayash, Radwan, 249
Abu Iyad, 349, 350
Abu-Jaber, Kamel, 372
Abu Musa, 355
Abu Nidal, 349, 350
Abu Odeih, Adnan, 136
Abusch, Dorit, 412
Abu Sharif, Bassam, 148
Academy for Jewish Religion, 483
Achilli, Michele, 274
Achimeir, Yossi, 145
Adam, A., 46*n*
Adar, Zvi, 402
Adenauer, Konrad, 10
Adler, Cyrus, 530, 531
Afn Shvel, 519
African National Congress, 103
Agenda: Jewish Education, 519
Agha, Zakaria al-, 148, 151
Agudah Women of America, 472
Agudath Israel of America, 97, 109, 111, 114, 116, 176, 472
Agudath Israel World Organization, 473
Aguilar v. Felton, 112
Agursky, Mikhail, 402
Ahmad, Zia, 327
Aichinger, Ilse, 299
AIPAC, 98, 100, 161, 462
Akoka, Jacky, 62*n*

Akron Jewish News, 523
Albania, 384, 397
Albert Einstein College of Medicine, 490
Alderman, Geoffrey, 8*n*, 62*n*
Alexander, Hanan, 324
Alexei II, Patriarch, 382
Alfred, Alex, 246
Algemeiner Journal, 519
Alispur, Rosa, 351
Allaf, Muwaffaz al-, 157
Allen, Michelle, 228
Allfrey, Anthony, 245
Allied Jewish Community Services, 216
Almog, Dita, 415
Almogi, Yosef, 402
Aloni, Jenny, 299
Aloni, Udi, 417
Alpar, Gitta, 299
Alpert, Rebecca, 191
Alpha Epsilon Pi Fraternity, 492
Alsheikh, Rahamin, 357, 358
Altaras, Adriana, 295
Altaras, Thea, 298
Alter, Robert, 413, 538
Altissimo, Renato, 273
Altman, Natan, 308
Altshul, Bill, 326
Altshuler, Mordechai, 437*n*
ALYN-American Society for Handicapped Children in Israel, 460
A-Majali, Abdel Salim, 374
AMC Cancer Research Center, 494
Amcha for Tsedakah, 494
America-Israel Cultural Foundation, 460
America-Israel Friendship League, 460
American Academy for Jewish Research, 453

595

Levinson, Nathan Peter, 299
Levitas, Ilya, 306
Levitsky, Bela, 351
Levitt, Gloria, 231
Levitte, Georges, 27n
Lévy, Bernard-Henri, 255
Levy, Caren, 36n, 51n, 53n, 80n, 433n
Levy, David, 126, 132–135, 137–140,
143, 144, 149, 150, 151, 153, 160,
161, 166, 168, 217, 274, 341, 342,
345, 361, 362, 364–367, 369, 370,
371, 380, 382, 383, 386, 387, 390
Levy, Itamar, 411
Levy, Michael, 241
Levy, Nat, 246
Levy, Yair, 401
Lewin, Nathan, 99
Lewis, Chaim, 245
Lezov, Sergei, 13n
Liberles Adina Weiss, 27n, 28n
Liberty Lobby, 89
Library of the Jewish Theological Semi-
nary, 487
Lichtenstadter, Ilse, 545
Lichtenstein, Heiner, 13n
Lieberman, Joseph, 86, 170
Lieberman, Saul, 530
Liebermann, Dov, 39n, 45n, 52n
Lieff, Abraham, 230
Lifsh, Yosef, 92
Lifton, Robert Jay, 245
Likud USA, 467
Likutim, 521
Lilith, 521
Lindwer, Willy, 266
Link, 519
Lipman, S.L., 28n
Lipman, V.D., 28n
Lipper, J. Stephen, 231
Lippman, Walter M., 443n
Lipski, Jan Josef, 18
Lipson, Henry, 246
Litewka, Julko, 545
Littman, Sol, 221
Litvinoff, Barnet, 245
A Living Memorial to the Holocaust–
Museum of Jewish Heritage, 457
Livneh, Yitzchak, 415

Livni, Eitan, 402
Lixl-Purcell, A., 298
Lockshin, Martin, 230
Loebl, Euegen, 4n
Long Island Jewish World, 521
Lorch, Steven, 326
Los Angeles Hillel Council, 96
Los Angeles Jewish Community Rela-
tions Council, 96
Louis Finkelstein Institute for Religious
and Social Studies, 487
Lowensohn, Shmuel, 244
Löwenthal, Richard, 300
Lowey, Nita, 86
Lubavitch Organization, 113
Lubavitcher Yeshivoth, United, 481
Lubbers, Rudolf, 260
Lubbers, Willem, 261
Lubliner, Manfred, 299, 300
Lubrani, Uri, 357, 396
Luckmann, T., 55n
Luitjens, Jacob, 220
Lukacs, Yehuda, 245
Luria, Salvador, 281, 545
Lurvink, Peter, 269
Luzzati, Michele, 280
Lyons, Rudolph, 246

Maalot-A Seminary for Cantors and
Judaists, 457
Maayan, Dudu, 406
Maccise, Camilo, 105
Machne Israel, 476
Madar, Rafi, 352
Madonna, 97
Magonet, Jonathan, 245
Mahfouz, Naguib, 387
Maida, Adam, 104
Maitre, Jacques, 56n
Major, John, 232, 233, 234, 235, 240
Makarov, Vladimir, 353
Malone, James W., 106
Mandel, Arnold, 28n
Mandela, Nelson, 103
Mandelbaum, Bernard, 532
Mankowitz, Wolf, 244
Mann, Theodore, 171, 172, 247
Mannheimer, Renato, 45n, 51n, 80n